ENTREPRENEURSHIP AS ORGANIZING

We see potential
As the sky as our limit.
Hopes are intended dreams.

Ellison Cielo Gartner

Wherever possible, the articles in these volumes have been reproduced as originally published using facsimile reproduction, inclusive of footnotes and pagination to facilitate ease of reference.

For a list of all Edward Elgar published titles visit our website at
www.e-elgar.com

Entrepreneurship as Organizing

Selected Papers of William B. Gartner

William B. Gartner

Professor of Entrepreneurship and the Art of Innovation, Copenhagen Business School, Denmark and Professor of Entrepreneurship, California Lutheran University, USA

EE Edward Elgar
PUBLISHING

Cheltenham, UK • Northampton, MA, USA

Published by
Edward Elgar Publishing Limited
The Lypiatts
15 Lansdown Road
Cheltenham
Glos GL50 2JA
UK

Edward Elgar Publishing, Inc.
William Pratt House
9 Dewey Court
Northampton
Massachusetts 01060
USA

A catalogue record for this book
is available from the British Library

Library of Congress Control Number: 2015914076

This book is available electronically in the **Elgar**online
Business subject collection
DOI 10.4337/9781783476947

MIX
Paper from
responsible sources
FSC
www.fsc.org   FSC® C013056

ISBN 978 1 78347 114 0 (cased)
ISBN 978 1 78347 694 7 (eBook)

Printed and bound in Great Britain by TJ International Ltd, Padstow

Contents

Acknowledgements

The editor and publishers wish to thank the authors and the following publishers who have kindly given permission for the use of copyright material.

Academy of Management for articles: William B. Gartner (1985), 'A Conceptual Framework for Describing the Phenomenon of New Venture Creation', *Academy of Management Review*, **10** (4), October, 696–706; Jerome Katz and William B. Gartner (1988), 'Properties of Emerging Organizations', *Academy of Management Review*, **13** (3), July, 429–41.

Blackwell Publishing Ltd for articles: William B. Gartner (1988), '"Who Is an Entrepreneur?" Is the Wrong Question', *American Journal of Small Business*, **12** (4), Spring, 11–32; William B. Gartner, Barbara J. Bird and Jennifer A. Starr (1992), 'Acting as If: Differentiating Entrepreneurial from Organizational Behavior', *Entrepreneurship Theory and Practice*, **16** (3), Spring, 13–31; William B. Gartner, Kelly G. Shaver and Jianwen (Jon) Liao (2008), 'Opportunities as Attributions: Categorizing Strategic Issues from an Attributional Perspective', *Strategic Entrepreneurship Journal*, **2** (4), December, 301–15.

Elsevier for articles: William B. Gartner, Terence R. Mitchell and Karl H. Vesper (1989), 'A Taxonomy of New Business Ventures', *Journal of Business Venturing*, **4** (3), May, 169–86; William B. Gartner (1990), 'What Are We Talking About When We Talk About Entrepreneurship?', *Journal of Business Venturing*, **5** (1), January, 15–28; Donald A. Duchesneau and William B. Gartner (1990), 'A Profile of New Venture Success and Failure in an Emerging Industry', *Journal of Business Venturing*, **5** (5), September, 297–312; William B. Gartner (1993), 'Words Lead to Deeds: Towards an Organizational Emergence Vocabulary', *Journal of Business Venturing*, **8** (3), May, 231–9; Elizabeth J. Gatewood, Kelly G. Shaver and William B. Gartner (1995), 'A Longitudinal Study of Cognitive Factors Influencing Start-Up Behaviors and Success at Venture Creation', *Journal of Business Venturing*, **10** (5), September, 371–91; Nancy M. Carter, William B. Gartner and Paul D. Reynolds (1996), 'Exploring Start-Up Event Sequences', *Journal of Business Venturing*, **11** (3), May, 151–66; William B. Gartner, Jennifer A. Starr and Subodh Bhat (1999), 'Predicting New Venture Survival: An Analysis of "Anatomy of a Start-Up." Cases from *Inc*. Magazine', *Journal of Business Venturing*, **14** (2), March, 215–32; Nancy M. Carter, William B. Gartner, Kelly G. Shaver and Elizabeth J. Gatewood (2003), 'The Career Reasons of Nascent Entrepreneurs', *Journal of Business Venturing*, **18** (1), January, 13–39; William B. Gartner (2007), 'Entrepreneurial Narrative and a Science of the Imagination', *Journal of Business Venturing*, Special Issue: Entrepreneurial Narrative: Greif Symposium on Emerging Organizations, **22** (5), September, 613–27.

Greenwood Publishing Group, Inc. via the Copyright Clearance Center's RightsLink service for excerpt: William B. Gartner and Candida G. Brush (2007), 'Entrepreneurship as Organizing:

Emergence, Newness, and Transformation', in Mark P. Rice and Timothy G. Habbershon (eds), *Entrepreneurship: The Engine of Growth, Volume 2*, Chapter 1, 1–20.

Now Publishers for article: W.B. Gartner (2006), 'A "Critical Mess" Approach to Entrepreneurship Scholarship', in Anders Lundström and Sune Halvarsson (eds), *Entrepreneurship Research: Past Perspectives and Future Prospects*, Chapter 10, in the *Foundations and Trends in Entrepreneurship* journal, **2** (3), 213–22, references.

SAGE Publications Ltd for article: William B. Gartner (2010), 'A New Path to the Waterfall: A Narrative on a Use of Entrepreneurial Narrative', *International Small Business Journal*, **28** (1), February, 6–19.

Springer Science and Business Media B.V. for article: Jianwen Liao and William B. Gartner (2006), 'The Effects of Pre-venture Plan Timing and Perceived Environmental Uncertainty on the Persistence of Emerging Firms', *Small Business Economics*, **27** (1), August, 23–40.

Wilson Learning Corporation for articles: William B. Gartner (1985), 'Did River City Really Need a Boys' Band?', *New Management*, **3** (1), Summer, 29–34; William B. Gartner (1986), 'The Oz in Organization', *New Management*, **4** (1), Summer, 15–21.

Introduction

William B. Gartner

[W]hat you pride yourself on, the things that you think are your insight and contribution ... no one ever even *notices* them. It's as though they're just for you. What you say in passing or what you expound because you know it too well, because it really bores you, but you feel you have to get through this in order to make your grand point, *that's* what people pick up on. *That's* what they underline. *That's* what they quote. *That's* what they attack, or cite favorably. *That's* what they can use. What you really think you're doing may or may not be what you're doing, but it certainly isn't communicated to others. I've talked about this to other critics, to other writers; they haven't had quite my extensive sense of this, but it strikes an answering chord in them. One's grand ideas are indeed one's grand ideas, but there are none that seem to be useful or even recognizable to anyone else. It's a very strange phenomenon. It must have something to do with our capacity for not knowing ourselves. (Bloom, 1991: 232)

The quote from Harold Bloom has been the in the back of my mind since I agreed to Alan Sturmer's generous suggestion that Edward Elgar Publishing would publish selected portions of my work. (Thank you Howard for the initial book in this series [Aldrich, 2011] and its success. It paved the way for this effort.) The format of the book (as you see in the Table of Contents) involves an introduction that provides an overview of the selected works, the articles selected for publication, and a conclusion: an exciting opportunity, but also humbling in its own way.

So, this Introduction is an attempt to identify what I think matters in the research and writing that my colleagues[1] and I have generated over the past 30 years. But, it is tinged with some apprehension. I have found myself in this place of retrospection before (Gartner, 2004a, 2008b, Chapter 21, this volume): offering interpretations of what I thought I was doing and why I thought what I was doing made sense and had value for other scholars in the entrepreneurship field. But, when I look back and see how other scholars have used my/our work, and how they have cited an article in a way that sometimes makes sense to me and sometimes not, I have this feeling, much as what Bloom has expressed, that the insights I had (or have now) about what a particular article is about and why it was written is simply out of my control. The ideas, insights and facts in these articles take on lives of their own. New ideas and different ideas sprout from the ground of our/my early work. And, I realize that, in this retrospective effort, I view our/my prior work differently as well, as I read how others have used this work and how my own experience as an entrepreneurship scholar has evolved.

So, this Introduction is not an attempt to 'set the record straight' on the 'true' meanings and intentions of our/my prior research. Rather, I consider this Introduction as a reflection at a particular moment in time (Fall 2013 and Spring 2014) where I attempted to consider our/my entire research experience (as expressed in the articles selected for publication). My plan is to offer a retrospective reflexive tour of our/my research: describe how and why I remember particular research articles were developed (both in terms of the context of ideas at that time, but also in how particular collaborative efforts emerged) and offer some thoughts about why I think these articles might matter, overall, as a contribution to the foundation for what, I believe, entrepreneurship is and how and why it works as it does.

The articles in the book are listed sequentially, by time, rather than by topic. I think particular articles were created in the context of prior work, so, by listing them by time, their relationship to one another, as both an evolution of certain ideas over time, but also as an expansion on certain themes, may become more apparent. I also believe that publishing these articles chronologically may prevent specific articles from being categorized as dealing, mainly, with specific ideas or themes. As I hope to address in this Introduction, some articles were written with different intentions than what might be assumed at face value when reading them without the context of their prior history. What might be a glaring problem with the introduction is that I didn't attempt to put a substantial amount of effort into connecting my research to current research in the entrepreneurship field. As I've indicated recently (Gartner, 2014b) staying current in the entrepreneurship field, particularly as my research cuts across so many topics, is difficult. As the Bloom quote aptly expresses, how my research is used or connected to other research, is not really mine to suggest, in the end, anyway.

The book spans 25 years of published work (1985–2010). So, for the sake of having some way to divide up the book, I've divided the material, loosely, by decade: 1980s, 1990s, and 2000s in the Table of Contents. But, ironically, I don't think that this work can be so easily divided by decade as the only way to categorize them. While I suggest that the work be read sequentially, as a way to see how, broadly, certain ideas evolve over time, this Introduction will be better served by headings that emphasize certain touchstones in the chronology. So, there is a chronology, and there are themes.

I have also decided to write a haiku for each article. Why? The poetic enables one to see differently that which already is (Gartner, 2008a, 2009; Weick, 2011). Or, maybe it is more obtusely expressed in this aphorism from Gary Snyder: 'Poetry is how language experiences itself'. And, each poem is another way of 'telling back' the story (Bruner, 1986). This Introduction will end with a few brief thoughts about the nature of entrepreneurship.

As this Introduction is essentially an autobiographical account, I would assume that there will be no mystery that (turning Charles Dickens' words around in *David Copperfield*): 'I shall be the hero of my own life and that station will be not be held by anybody else' (Dickens, 2004: 13). Yet, in the back of mind is the quote from Bloom that begins this chapter. What matters in my work is really left to others to decide and to understand. I have some insights, but the work is what it is, with or without me. So, I am well aware that an autobiographical overview might be viewed as hubris. I hope this chapter reflects the munificence of the friendships I have enjoyed, and, I apologize to my colleagues if this account is not as inclusive or appreciative of your efforts and thoughts.

Reflection stares back.
I see. Who is this? Old man.
Where did the years go?[2]

A tale of two Karls

I begin with a retelling (see Gartner, 2004a, 2008b) of the genesis of the development of my scholarship in entrepreneurship. Rather than repeat those stories, I will approach the creation of the foundation of my initial insights into entrepreneurship as a recognition of the primacy of the two 'Karls' in my life: Vesper and Weick. I believe that my approach to entrepreneurship might be considered a blend of their views on new venture creation (Vesper, 1980) and organizing (Weick, 1979). For me, both books support a perspective that begins with variation. In Karl Vesper's (1980) book, there is an explicit recognition of different: backgrounds of entrepreneurs; reasons that entrepreneurs get into business; ways that entrepreneurs go about starting businesses; kinds of businesses that are started; and entry strategies that these emerging and new businesses utilize. While there are different intellectual facets to the ideas that comprise Karl Weick's (1979) book, a substantial portion of the text is based on Campbell's (1965, 1974) sociocultural evolutionary perspective that begins with variation (as further elaborated in Weick, 1979: 147) as beginning with the flows of experience 'ecological change' that is 'enacted' (for example, through such activities as 'saying, doing, spinning webs of significance, adapting and producing variations'). Both descriptions, here, of Karl Vesper's and Karl Weick's scholarship are a bit simplistic, yet the gist of their more elaborate explorations is, from my view, that the process of organization creation begins with variation. When we look at new venture creation, we see that there are different kinds of: people who start organizations; types of organizations that are started; environments; and ways of starting organizations.

The article 'A Conceptual Framework for Describing the Phenomenon of New Venture Creation' (Chapter 1, this volume), which originated as a part of my dissertation (Gartner, 1982), is both a recognition of variation as a key aspect of new venture creation, as well as a framework for making sense of how scholars might identify and describe this variation in their studies. As a precursor to later articles on entrepreneurs themselves, what should be noted is that the framework article does not deny that there are characteristics of entrepreneurs that matter (such as: background, experience, and attitudes) rather, it suggests that certain characteristics of entrepreneurs will matter, more or less, depending on the other three factors: type of firm started, type of environment, and type of startup process. One cannot study the characteristics of entrepreneurs without accounting for their context (firm, environment, and process). In re-reading the framework article, I'm struck with how prescient it is in identifying topics that later occupied entrepreneurship scholars such as opportunity (p.699), partners/teams (p.701), and women (p.703). Yet, if one does a close historical inspection of research prior to Gartner (Chapter 1, this volume), these topics (that is, opportunity, partners/teams, and women) have always been primary focal points of entrepreneurship scholarship. Be that as it may, the framework article best summarizes itself:

> the paper provides a means of making a fundamental shift in the perspective on entrepreneurship: away from viewing entrepreneurs and their ventures as an unvarying, homogeneous population, and towards a recognition and appreciation of the complexity and variation that abounds in the phenomenon of new venture creation. (Chapter 1, this volume: 704)

Differences among entrepreneurs, the way they start new ventures, the ventures 'themselves' and the context of the startup process, all matter: it is not one aspect of the phenomenon of entrepreneurship that is important to account for, it is all four.

The Fundamental
Attribution Error is THE
Entrepreneur. Yet?

Running parallel to the framework article was an empirical exploration (Gartner, Mitchell, and Vesper, Chapter 6, this volume) 'A Taxonomy of New Business Ventures', a way to understand the variation I found in the sample of new ventures that I studied for my dissertation. The sense-making struggle of the empirical exploration of my dissertation is described at length in Gartner (2008b) so here I will only highlight that the 'taxonomy' article tried to find some mid-range way of talking about entrepreneurs that would be a happy medium between 'all entrepreneurship is the same' versus 'all entrepreneurship is different'. The general idea of coming up with a way to categorize the variation across new ventures into similar groups is based on Bill McKelvey's work (see 1978, 1982) on organizational systematics. My understanding of the systematic approach to studying organizations focuses on this question: What characteristics of organizations can be used to determine whether they are similar or different from one-another? For example, we tend to think of a type of firm, such as a 'high technology business', but high technology can be comprised of computer manufacturers, software developers, biological science companies, telecommunications – the list could go on and on with various subcategories of high-technology firms. And, within those categories, such as software developers for example, are these firms really that similar, or are they different? Is a developer of a computer operating system similar to the developer of computer games, or mobile phone apps? Having some way to determine whether a group of firms is really similar to each other is important, if we want to say anything about their characteristics as a group. If I begin with a view that entrepreneurships (entrepreneurs, firms, environments, processes) are likely to be different from one another, then, my challenge becomes: Are there any ways to find similarities among these different new ventures? The taxonomy article is one approach, based on ideas taken from Miller and Friesen (1978) (and for further elaborations of their work see Miller, 1987; Miller, Friesen and Mintzberg, 1984) for finding similarities among what appear to be a disparate group of organizations.

If one looks at the dates of publication for these two articles that came out of the dissertation, the frameworks article appeared in 1985, and, the taxonomy article appeared in 1989. (Three years and seven years, respectively, after the dissertation. 'Getting published', at least for me, had/has significant time lags.) The reasons for the publication lag for the taxonomy article were due to issues of inter-rater reliability (there was none), and, the taxonomic methods themselves that led to questions about the reliability of the data as well as the ability to replicate the taxonomic groups by other scholars. The article met with years of rejection from many of the management and entrepreneurship journals. One journal editor noted, in a rejection of the article, that taxonomies were a fad that had passed. Yet, Ian C. MacMillan, founder, and at the time editor, of the *Journal of Business Venturing*, with mixed responses from his reviewers, allowed the manuscript to be published. Thank you Ian!

My own view of the taxonomy article is that while the methods for generating the data (entrepreneur-submitted quantitative questionnaires and researcher-created in-depth case studies based on telephone interviews) may lack the sophisticated genius of Miller and Friesen's work for generating inter-rater reliability, and that quantitative taxonomic methods have a bit of art in their construction, the article does provide a way to celebrate a mid-range approach to both recognizing differences and similarities among entrepreneurs, their firms, environments and startup processes. The article sticks to the perspective of the framework article:

There is no 'average' in entrepreneurship. Exploring opportunities is more often doing things differently, rather than following the typical. By recognizing many different types of new business ventures, we are more likely to see and appreciate the diversity inherent in entrepreneurship. (Chapter 6, this volume: 184)

> Snowflakes fall to the
> Ground. A blanket of white. Can
> I pull them apart?

One way to talk about the process of entrepreneurship

As part of the struggle of finding some mid-range between 'all entrepreneurs are alike' or 'all entrepreneurs are different', I wrote mini-cases (very short one-page stories) about each of the 106 entrepreneurships in my study (Gartner, 1982). These mini-cases served to highlight critical aspects of each new venture creation across all four of the dimensions (individual, firm, environment, process). The act of writing so many cases that were, as one aspect of their composition, an attempt to describe the sequence of events that occurred, seemed to guide me towards an appreciation of how stories (even very short stories) might illustrate the complex interaction among intentions, actions, interactions, and reactions over time. I don't believe that entrepreneurial stories necessarily unfold into an illustration that provides a clear or perfectly accurate picture of what occurred; rather, stories can highlight critical incidents of creation over time.

It is a tricky business to critically evaluate the nature of what a story is (see the final article in this volume, Chapter 21). And, in the middle of the 1980s I had neither the skills nor competencies to explore stories in a sophisticated way. Yet, there were stories that I felt could provide important insights into the process of entrepreneurship that might be appreciated in a way that an amateur (from the French, 'lover of' and generally defined as a person who does something for the pleasure of it) might find stories worthwhile. So, in parallel to attempts to generate research that would appear in traditional academic forms (that is, journal articles), I began a series of 'meditations' on stories that intrigued me as illustrations of how the process of entrepreneurship actually occurs. These writings can be pejoratively labeled as 'just-so stories'. I have included two such writings in this collection: 'Did River City Really Need a Boys' Band?' (Chapter 2, this volume) and 'The Oz in Organization' (Chapter 3, this volume). And there are others in much the same genre (Gartner, 1987, 1990, 1993).

My recollection of my intentions surrounding the creation of these articles centers on James Hillman's work on archetypal psychology (see Hillman, 1972, 1975a, 1975b) and his interest in imagination and the image in 'seeing psychologically'. I was/am very caught up in this idea of how images are inherent in imagination, and that images evoke significant power in one's thoughts and actions. I tried to use both of these stories as ways for us to see, through images, how entrepreneurship occurs.

Chapter 2 is based on Meredith Willson's *Music Man*. He wrote the lyrics, songs and book for the *Music Man*, which premiered on Broadway in 1957 and was adapted for film in 1962. Having grown up in Iowa (where the action of the story occurs), and having played in John Philip Sousa's band, Meredith Willson combined his love and nostalgia of both experiences (after working on the play for eight years and thirty revisions) into a delightful story of a kind of entrepreneur ('flim-flam man'): selling the idea of 'boys' bands' to wayward country towns, pocketing deposits for band instruments and uniforms, and then skipping town before these boys' bands actually emerge. The musical shows how Harold Hill, the protagonist of the story, sells the idea of the boys' band to skeptical townsfolk using captivating images of how the boys' lives will be ruined without a band, and rallies them around images of how transformational a boys' band will look. I use the story to mull over aspects of how Harold Hill's activities in creating the boys' band are analogous to some aspects of the process of corporate entrepreneurship. There are two issues about the article that I want to emphasize, one expressed in the article, the other not. The first issue centers on how focusing on entrepreneurs seems to evoke the world of dreams and creativity (see for example, the article by Cornelissen, 2013). I will circle back again and again throughout articles I've written to a touchstone quote from Collins and Moores' (1964) study of post World War II manufacturers in Michigan:

> In this period of fear and doubt, however, these men found creativity. At the time when it became necessary for them to reorganize their lives and to reestablish their futures, they had the capacity not only to dream but to transmute their dreams to action. They create the business of which they were dreaming. Between the idea and the act falls the shadow. This shadow, which these men had to explore, and out of which they had to hammer reality, lay immediately ahead. They had now to organize the universe around them in such a way that they could progress in establishing their new business. The first act of this direction is what we will call the act of creation. (p. 164)

This quote is such a poetic sense of the nature of entrepreneurship yet it comes through observing such a dry topic as manufacturing entrepreneurs. There is something magical about the entrepreneurial process that is evoked in their description. And, in the *Music Man* story, we see how a future vision is evoked and nurtured until it becomes, initially, a sorry state of reality. A boys' band is indeed created, but the boys play pathetically, given that their learning has been through the 'think method'. Yet, this is enough of a start that the town can re-imagine the boys' band into something significant and wonderful, as the musical ends with a 'real' marching band and the finale – '76 Trombones'.

Second, there is one aspect of the show/movie that I didn't point out in the article, the often 'irrationality' of our motivations and actions that frequently serve as the basis for what actually occurs: in this instance, through the love that develops between Harold Hill and Marian the Librarian. There is, at the basis of the story, a dynamic between Harold Hill's original intentions of flim-flamming the town and moving on with the townsfolk's money before an actual band is produced *and* his emerging love for Marion the Librarian, who draws him into staying and seeing through the creation of a very meager band of boys. For those with some musical interest, the dynamic is captured in the two key songs of the musical: '76 Trombones', and 'Good Night My Someone'. They are inverted melodies of the other. In terms of lyrics, one offers an expansive vision of a band that you can see in your imagination: 76 trombones, 110 coronets, 1000 reeds springing up like weeds, horse platoons, big bassoons, and so on. And, the other, a hope in a future love, unfulfilled, unknown, unseen, yet expected. Two visions, one seen, the other not, collide. And love unfolds. I find that the logical positivist or neo-rationalistic perspective tends to point one towards rational explanations of behaviors and motivations, yet, at the basis of many stories that entrepreneurs tell, it is something else (that is, love, beauty, altruism, hope). I'll come back to this later on in this chapter.

Finally, James O'Toole, who was at that point the editor of *New Management* saw something in this article and published it, as well as awarding the article 'Best Article' for 1985. Thank you, Jim, for publishing this article and the two others (Chapters 2 and 3, this volume; Gartner, 1987).

Take the money and

Run. What has love got to do

With it? Everything.

'The Oz in Organization' (Chapter 3, this volume) offers some thoughts about the relationship between 'doing' and 'being'. The article focuses on the film *The Wizard of Oz* (LeRoy and Fleming, 1939) that is loosely based on L. Frank Baum's book, *The Wizard of Oz* (Baum, 1900). For those few unfamiliar with the film, a quick synopsis is (another 'telling back' the story [Bruner, 1986]): Dorothy, a girl growing up on a farm in Kansas, while running away from home (with her little dog Toto) is swept up in a tornado that carries her off to the Land of Oz. Upon landing in Oz, the house that she rode out the tornado in has fallen on and killed one of the two wicked witches who rule parts of Oz. The remaining wicked witch promises revenge. In Dorothy's odyssey to return to Kansas (on the Yellow Brick Road), she meets up with three characters – the Scarecrow, the Tin Man, and the Lion – who, through various challenges, assist Dorothy in destroying the second wicked witch, while they also gain for themselves a heart (Tin Man), a brain (Scarecrow), and courage (Lion). And, Dorothy is told by one of the good witches that her ruby slippers (gained as a result of killing the first wicked witch) could have taken her back to Kansas all along (which Dorothy subsequently does). The film ends with Dorothy back in Kansas saying: 'there is no place like home'.

As will be discussed in more detail in the next section regarding the 'Who Is an Entrepreneur?' (Chapter 4, this volume) article, I believe that actions can lead to character or more strongly stated: actions are character. If we consider a person who is generous, I contend that the characteristic of generosity comes about through actions of giving. By giving, generosity becomes an aspect of that person's character. What we do changes who we are. We become our actions, rather than our actions manifesting 'who we are'.

In the film, *The Wizard of Oz*, we see that the Scarecrow has a brain because he thinks, the Tin Man has a heart because he loves, and the Lion has courage because he acts (through his heart and mind). Certainly, each of these 'characters' in the story already had a brain, a heart, and courage, yet these characteristics could only become manifest through their actions during their journey in the land of Oz. Can you have a brain without thinking, a heart without loving, or courage without acting? If a person doesn't give, can this person be considered 'generous'? This perspective might be plausible within issues involved with process and content views of situations: organizing versus organization (Weick, 1979). I think this is a dilemma in the study of entrepreneurship: whether actions are the outcomes of intentions (or characteristics) or whether actions embed themselves in intentions and become characteristics. I believe that 'what we do' essentially comprises 'who we are'; that is, for example, a painter paints, and it is the act of painting that makes the painter. I think it would be difficult for someone to claim the characteristic or identity of painter without engaging in painting. So, a focus on actions is critical for an understanding of the development of identity and character.

> How can we know the
> Dancer from the dance? Action
> Manifests Being.

Another way to talk about the process of entrepreneurship

I strongly believe that the most fruitful way to understand the nature of entrepreneurship is through a behavioral approach (see Bird, 1989). The article 'Who Is an Entrepreneur? Is the Wrong Question' (Chapter 4, this volume) was an initial step at outlining what a behavioral approach to entrepreneurship is, and how it might be carried out. While I've provided some commentaries on aspects of the genesis of this article and its intellectual motivation (see Gartner, 2004a, 2008b), I will focus my comments here on my surprise and regret that the article tends to be read as an attack on the value of exploring the characteristics of entrepreneurs, rather than a forceful argument to direct entrepreneurship scholarship towards entrepreneurial behaviors. I hope that, earlier in this chapter, I have shown that I have championed a view of entrepreneurship that involves diversity among kinds of individuals, firms, environments, and processes. There is no one type of entrepreneur, no one type of startup, no one type of entrepreneurial environment, and no one way that organizations come into existence. In the 'Who' article, my initial discussion of the trait view was an attempt to dissuade scholars from seeking to look for a particular set of traits and characteristics that could identify 'the entrepreneur'. In Murray Davis' (1971) way of talking about what is interesting, my intention was not to set up an 'A' versus 'not A' debate, that is, a debate about the value of exploring entrepreneurial traits and characteristics as the 'A' versus 'not A'. Rather, my intention was to point out that looking for a set of characteristics that would typify 'the entrepreneur' would not be successful once one realized the diversity among entrepreneurial: individuals, firms, environments, and processes. If this assumption is correct: that there is a diversity of entrepreneurships, then I think the question becomes 'what would be the more fruitful way to explore and understand this diversity'?

I think focusing on traits tends to devolve into assuming that there are entrepreneurial characteristics that are applicable across all entrepreneurs. This just doesn't make sense to me, or, I believe, to be backed up with sufficient empirical evidence. But, looking at behaviors can, I believe, be framed in a way to provide a logic for kinds of activities that, in a broad way, nearly all entrepreneurs engage in when organizing, yet also account for diversity in their activities in specific contexts. And, one of the significant reasons for focusing on behaviors is that the function of the entrepreneur becomes a process, rather than a state of being. Individuals act entrepreneurially at times, and, at other times, they don't. A behavioral view seeks to explore and understand what occurs when individuals do act entrepreneurially. A behavior view, then, does not treat entrepreneurship as a state of being: it is an activity that one can engage in at various times or not.

Rather than hammer this point over and over again, as I'll have ample opportunities to do so in subsequent articles that explore entrepreneurial behaviors, I'll emphasize two other points about this article. First, the article tries to grapple with the ontological nature of entrepreneurship: What is entrepreneurship? How do we define it? How do we know it when we see it? The 'Who' article provides seven pages of empirical and normative definitions of entrepreneurship (Chapter 4, this volume, pp. 13–20) to challenge readers to consciously identify what they believe the phenomenon of entrepreneurship is actually about. I sense that we often have implicit assumptions about the phenomenon of entrepreneurship that we often don't consciously articulate, and my intuition is that conflicts among findings and views of entrepreneurship are often about ontological issues rather than about methods or the evidence, itself. So, when we study or look at entrepreneurship, are we studying or looking at the same phenomenon? This issue of definitions, and their value in entrepreneurship scholarship will come up, again and again, in later work.

Second, the article provides a pathway for how scholarship in entrepreneurial behavior might occur. I think the questions Mintzberg (1973) asks about the nature of managerial work continue to apply to the nature of entrepreneurial work. Here, I am going to substitute 'entrepreneur, entrepreneurial, and entrepreneurship' for 'manager, managerial, and management':

> We must be able to answer a number of specific questions before we can expect [entrepreneurial] training and [entrepreneurial] science to have any real impact on practice:
> What kinds of activities does the [entrepreneur] perform? What kinds of information does he process? With who must he work? Where? How frequently?
> What are the distinguishing characteristics of [entrepreneurial] work? What is of interest about the media that [entrepreneurs] use, the activities he prefers to engage in, the flow of these activities during the workday, his use of time, the pressures of the job?
> What basic roles can be inferred from the study of the [entrepreneur's] activities? What roles does the [entrepreneur] perform in moving information, in making decisions, in dealing with people?
> What variations exist among [entrepreneurial] jobs? To what extent can basic differences be attributed to the situation, the incumbent, the job, the organization, the environment?
> To what extent is [entrepreneurship] a science? To what extent is the [entrepreneur's] work programmed that is, repetitive, systematic, predictable)? To what extent is it programmable? To what extent can the [entrepreneurship] scientist 'reprogram' [entrepreneurial] work? (Mintzberg, 1973: 3)

These two broad themes – (1) What is the nature of entrepreneurship? and (2) How does entrepreneurship occur behaviorally? – will be, in various forms, the predominant issues addressed in many of the articles in this book.

There are times in life
When a person rushes to
Pursue hopefulness.[3]

What is entrepreneurship?

If one is going to study entrepreneurship as the creation of organizations, then, what does organization creation entail? There are four articles which I believe provide various attempts to offer theory and insights into the nature of entrepreneurship as a phenomenon: 'Properties ...' (Chapter 5, this volume); 'Acting As If ...' (Chapter 9, this volume); 'What Are We Talking About ...' (Chapter 8, this volume); and '... Emergence Vocabulary' (Chapter 10, this volume). Chapter 5 bases itself in organization theory and tries to generate a framework for understanding what an emerging organization is vis-à-vis what established organizations are. Chapter 9 offers a way to relate the idea of entrepreneurial behavior to ideas in the organizational behavior field. Chapter 8 offers insights into what scholars already think and assume about the nature of entrepreneurship. Chapter 10 provides suggestions for how scholars might think about the nature of entrepreneurship.

The genesis of Chapter 5 begins with a recollection of my first experiences of Jerry Katz. He is a virtual encyclopedia of facts and insights into a world of organization theory and entrepreneurship that my brain did not have the capacity to contain. Being around his command of ideas and facts about entrepreneurship and organization theory was like discovering a treasure chest of rare gold and silver coins and jewels and being overwhelmed with this limitless abundance. And, it is not just his command of the facts and ideas that impressed me, it is his ability to make the connections between them. I often think of two quotes from Charles Eames: (1) 'Eventually everything connects – people, ideas, objects. The quality of the connections is the key to quality per se' and (2) 'The details are details. They make the product. *The connections, the connections, the connections*. It will in the end be these details that give the product life.' (I will attribute both quotes to being somewhere in Caplan, 1976.) My interpretation of the Charles Eames' remarks on connections is that: how and why certain details (facts and ideas) get put together, that is, assembled (or connected), is where there is tremendous value. There are plenty of facts and ideas out there. It is the relationships between these facts and ideas that is critical. I believe the value of Chapter 5 is in how the various details of what emerging organizations are, are actually connected together. The chapter, then, reflects Jerry's genius.

If, from my view, entrepreneurship is fundamentally about the process of organizing, and particularly about organization creation, then what are entrepreneurs actually creating when they create an organization? Chapter 5 attempts to answer that question. Creating an organization involves assembling four different aspects of what organizations are: intentionality, resources, boundaries, and exchange. Identifying these four properties as fundamental to the process of organization creation, and, suggesting ways in which these properties might be made visible and studied is the gist of the chapter.

I don't think it is by coincidence that Barbara Bird's (1988) article on intentions appeared in the same issue of the *Academy of Management Review* as Chapter 5. I think we are in agreement that, typically, the genesis of the organizing process begins with intention (for example, 'purposefulness, goals') on the part of an individual or individuals (Reynolds, 2007: 67). There are reasons why organizations come into existence that are either provided by the entrepreneur(s) or are externally co-created through interactions among the entrepreneur(s) and their situations (Chapter 5, this volume: 431). Organizational goals, or a meaning for why the organization exists, which is separate from the entrepreneur(s)' own goals and intentions, will eventually emerge over time, if the organization is to come into existence. What I am emphasizing here is that organization emergence begins with actions among individuals that will result in 'organization' which involves an entity that is separate from the organizers, themselves. It is critical to realize this. While an entrepreneur may begin the organizing effort with particular goals and purposes in mind, as the organization emerges, the organization takes on its own life and meanings: the organizational imperative (Gartner and Bellamy, 2009: 20–21; Hart and Scott, 1975; Scott and Hart, 1989). Organizations that emerge from entrepreneur(s)' efforts are not the entrepreneurs; just as children are not their parents, even though children come from the same mix of DNA as their parents. Or, for example, an Eames chair is not Charles and Ray Eames. The chair is a manifestation of some aspects of the Eames' creative process, but, once the chair is made, it exists and has a 'life' of its own, irrespective of what the Eames intended the chair to be, or be used for. So, creations are not their creators. So, while individual intentions are likely to be critical aspects of the formation of an organization, the organization, as it emerges, will assume its own purposes and direction. Organizations are not their organizers. I realize there is a lot of research on the importance of the entrepreneurs' skills and knowledge to the direction of the emerging venture (for example, Shane, 2000), yet I suggest, at some point, the organization is likely to have its own imperatives and values. Whether my belief is accurate should be empirically explored and verified.

One of the cruxes, then, of the process of organization creation is that an organization must become an entity that is not the entrepreneur, per se (even though, we point out, it is possible to have an organization of one person). The idea of 'boundary' as a characteristic of the emerging organization implies that organizations evolve into something separate and distinct, and, that organizations have their own 'identity' (Chapter 5, this volume: 432) which reveals itself through such markers as: legal status, tax identification, mailing address, business name, phone number, and so on.

Within the boundary that emerges to identify what is or is not the emerging organization, are resources (for example, human and financial capital, organizational routines, and processes) that provide the energy and impetus to provide value (for example, goods and services) to others through the process of exchange. Since the idea of resources plays such a significant role in entrepreneurship scholarship (see Alvarez and Barney, 2002; Alvarez and Busenitz, 2001) and in chapters in this book, I will not address it here. I will elaborate on the idea and meanings of resources later on in this Introduction.

In order for an organization to survive over time, there needs to be exchanges that occur so that the emerging organization receives the resources necessary to continue operations. While the tendency is to think of exchanges as sales transactions, where an organization exchanges something of value to someone else for a profit, it should also be noted that exchanges such as investments or loans to the emerging organization are other types of transactions where value is exchanged.

All four properties, then, are inter-related to each other, and, as a whole, would characterize the emergence of an organization. What we noted in the article was that scholars tend to use one of the operalizations (that is, markers) of a particular property to indicate the existence of a new organization. We suggest that scholars be careful in their selection of specific markers for signaling the creation of an organization (that is, Aldrich et al., 1989). As I tend to focus on a level of analysis that is at the level of behavior, the ability to specifically identify when, exactly, an emerging organization is indeed an organization, is a bit tricky, as is the phenomenon itself.

Chrysalis. Pupa.
Ugly names for the forming
Of the butterfly.

In looking back at the article in Chapter 9 in this volume, I admire our attempt to comprehensively address the nature of entrepreneurial behavior. Even before the publication of her book *Entrepreneurial Behavior* (Bird, 1989), Barbara and I had engaged in many conversations about how to move research efforts forward on the behavioral aspects of entrepreneurship. I had met Jennifer Starr while I was 'slumming' off-and-on at Wharton with infrequent day trips up from Georgetown University in Washington DC to see what Ian and Venkat were up to with their growing herd of doctoral students. Jennifer and I had begun a series of collaborations on the nature of entrepreneurial work (see Gartner and Starr, 1993). So, when Lanny Herron, Harry Sapienza, and Deborah Smith-Cook provided an invitation to participate in a series of special issues in *Entrepreneurship Theory and Practice* on different disciplinary perspectives on entrepreneurship, it seemed an opportune time to combine our efforts and interests in entrepreneurial behavior.

Here are some quick points that I see as highlights of the article: (1) entrepreneurial behavior is an aspect of the process of organizational emergence; (2) just as ideas about the nature of behaviors in organizational behavior are muddled, so are perspectives on entrepreneurial behavior; (3) recognizing variation as inherent in the process of organizational emergence will require a recognition of variation in relevant entrepreneurial behaviors; (4) the study of entrepreneurial behavior requires a significant willingness to be open to a broad range of methods and perspectives in order to appreciate the variation and nuances in these activities; (5) more data collection rather than more theorizing is needed; and (6) entrepreneurial behavior is inherently imaginative and future oriented as characterized in the words 'as if'.

> Emerging organizations are thoroughly equivocal realities (Weick, 1979) that *tend* towards non-equivocality through entrepreneurial action. In emerging organizations entrepreneurs offer plausible explanations of current and future equivocal events as non-equivocal interpretations. Entrepreneurs talk and act 'as if' equivocal events were non-equivocal. Emerging organizations are elaborate fictions of proposed possible future states of existence. In the context of the emerging organization, action is taken in expectation of a non-equivocal event occurring in the future. (Chapter 9, this volume: 17)

In hindsight, we missed a significant opportunity to connect this 'as if' perspective to the philosophical ideas in Vaihinger's (1924) *The Philosophy of 'As If'*. My simplistic reading of Vaihinger's work suggests that individuals must create a belief system and act 'as if' this belief system were true in order to live. Living life 'as if', therefore, is imaginative: we consciously or unconsciously create a fiction of the world. I suggest that living life requires a certain form of entrepreneurial thought and activity for all individuals. In living 'as if' we construct our reality, and live it whether this 'fiction' is true or not. Truth, then, is less important than plausibility, particularly when having plausible beliefs might spur actions that bring views of a future reality into existence (Weick, 1984). I am drawn to the idea of 'as if' as an aspect of entrepreneurship because the creation of organizations does require entrepreneurs to offer plausible stories of the future that others may join (as customers, suppliers, employees, investors, and so on) or not. I think these plausible future stories become real to others when entrepreneurs are able to live them out. There is a performance aspect to entrepreneurship that needs to be captured in the study of entrepreneurial behavior. Whether the performance of entrepreneurship can be 'scripted' (which might be thought of as planned), or considered as improvisational (which might be labeled as effectual [Sarasvathy, 2008] or bricolaged [Baker and Nelson, 2005]), the future of an organization comes into existence through action. Understanding entrepreneurial behavior is therefore critical to understanding the process of organization creation. Finally, it should be noted that Sarasvathy (2008) brings up important insights into Vaihinger's logic of 'as if' as it applies to entrepreneurship, and while she suggests that 'as if assumptions are an appropriate way of generating useful hypotheses' (p. 193), she proposes an effectual perspective based on 'even if'. I am ambivalent about her use of 'even if' as a more encompassing idea of the 'as if' perspective, but I do appreciate her genius in recognizing that entrepreneurs see constraints in the emergence process, and 'even if' those constraints exist, are willing to act imaginatively in new ways that bring about new worlds.

Act 'as if' and it
Maybe. Possibility
Sees itself through me.

My initial experiences with the academic journal review process involved submitting manuscripts for review which then began a dialogue among the author, editor(s), and reviewers about a variety of ontological (what is the phenomenon) and epistemological (given a particular definition of the phenomenon, what, then, is known about it) issues. What am I doing research on, and, what do we know about it? In the first decade of my research, many of the concerns about the articles I submitted for review stemmed from, what I believed to be, unconscious beliefs about what entrepreneurship is. I would get back comments from reviewers such as: 'That is not entrepreneurship' and 'The kinds of firms you are studying are not entrepreneurial firms'. Rarely did reviewers offer insights into what their own beliefs and views about entrepreneurship might be, except to indicate that my definition of entrepreneurship was not theirs nor did the kind of phenomenon I was studying represent their view of the entrepreneurship phenomenon. And, rejections resulted. This led me to explore this question: 'What is entrepreneurship?' And, more specifically: 'What do academics mean when they talk about what entrepreneurship is?'

The article 'What Are We Talking About When We Talk About Entrepreneurship?' (Chapter 8, this volume) was a systematic attempt to surface the unconscious views that various academics held about their beliefs about entrepreneurship. Without belaboring the methods used to engage academics in the process of uncovering definitions of entrepreneurship, the results of this effort identified eight broad themes, or issues, that would characterize aspects of entrepreneurship as a phenomenon: the entrepreneur, innovation, organization creation, creating value, profit or non-profit, growth, uniqueness, and the owner/manager. The gist of this article tends to be misread, as far as I can tell, by many scholars. These eight themes are points of *disagreement* among academics regarding their views of what entrepreneurship is. For example, some scholars believe that entrepreneurship must involve innovation, while other scholars do not. Some scholars believe that entrepreneurship must involve organization creation, while others do not. Some scholars believe that entrepreneurship involves creating value, is for profit only, must grow, be unique, and involve ownership, while other scholars do not. Is there an agreed upon definition of entrepreneurship? No. Are there issues where there is significant disagreement about the nature of entrepreneurship? Yes. The eight themes merely outline the parameters for delineating the boundaries for discussing what might differentiate entrepreneurship from other types of phenomenon. Conversations about entrepreneurship circle around these eight themes, rather than around other kinds of words and ideas. Entrepreneurship scholars typically don't talk about 'plastics' or 'crop rotation' or the 'weather' when they talk about entrepreneurship. I'm not sure whether this point is obvious or not. The article does not come up with a definition of entrepreneurship, per se. It comes up with a way to identify whether a scholar is having a discussion about entrepreneurship, or not. These eight themes are broadly the points of discussion that entrepreneurship scholars will have, among themselves. I suggest that the findings of this article posit that the field of entrepreneurship centers around these eight themes as descriptors of what the phenomenon of what entrepreneurship might entail, or not. And, it should be noted that when this research was conducted in the late 1980s, the word 'opportunity' was used only once in the 44 definitions provided. I believe that if a survey exploring definitions of entrepreneurship were to be conducted today (Fall 2013), the points of discussion among entrepreneurship scholars have shifted. Be that as it may, the language we use to talk about entrepreneurship matters.

> How do I know what
> I think until I see what
> I say? Organize.[4]

Ivan Bull was very kind to invite me to participate in a conference on entrepreneurship theory that he hosted at the University of Illinois at Urbana-Champaign in October 1991. I hoped to use this conference as a way to actualize certain fantasies I had about a vision of the nature of entrepreneurship. I had wanted to conduct a multi-media event that combined clips of films and some photos into a presentation on ways to see aspects of the phenomenon of entrepreneurship: 'Aspects of Organizational Emergence'. If you can think, historically, about the state of the art in computers and presentation equipment in 1991, then this fantasy was a difficult task to accomplish. Showing something on a screen typically required the use of overhead projectors with acetate (plastic) sheets. Showing a film clip required either a film projector or a videotape machine. I remember my presentation as a fiasco of shuffling between various machines to project still and moving images, and having nothing work according to plan. What I wanted the audience to see never occurred.

The article 'Words Lead to Deeds: Towards an Organizational Emergence Vocabulary' (Chapter 10, this volume) is a significant reworking of my original intentions to provide a visual experience that could evoke new ways to talk about the phenomenon of entrepreneurship. So, when you read this article, behind the words are images from Robert Irwin installations (Irwin, 1985) and clips from the films 'Powers of Ten' (Eames and Eames, 1968/1977) and 'Tops' (Eames and Eames, 1969). To see the image in imagination was the goal never achieved. For 'Words Lead to Deeds' I was left with the challenge of developing a vocabulary of words that described the phenomenon of entrepreneurship that I could see, but not show.

This is my favorite article in the entire collection. This is partially to do with memories of my original vision, and partially to do with how playful and ironic the article is for evoking a sense of entrepreneurship. The article is 'light' (Kundera, 1984). The framework of the article is loosely based on Wallace Stevens's poem 'Notes towards a Supreme Fiction' (Stevens, 1954/1990: 380–411). The definitions of the words about organizational emergence (Chapter 10, this volume: 232), and my commentary on them offer some very powerful insights into some of the paradoxes and conundrums of entrepreneurship and the challenge of studying it. I hope readers will appreciate the double entendre in founder (that is, one that establishes; as well as, to become disabled, to give way, to come to grief, fail). To found is to establish and give way – come to grief (Shepherd, 2003). And, the play on words with emerge (to become manifest), emergence (the act of emerging) and emergency (an unforeseen combination of circumstances that calls for immediate action). This could be another way to talk about the entrepreneurial aspects of 'Knightian uncertainty' (Knight, 1921). Entrepreneurships are those unforeseen combinations of circumstances where entrepreneurs act. The use of Max Apple's short story 'Peace' (Apple, 1989) is a beautiful depiction of these ironies in entrepreneurship: Jay Wilson founds and founders, the entrepreneurship emerges through emergency.

Much of the story of 'Peace' revolves around exploiting an opportunity to purchase 600,000 *Star Wars* plastic swords (originally retailing for $7.95) for 10 cents each. Jay's original business partner's advice: 'Buy them, then stab yourself 600,000 times'. Jay moves forward with the purchase, and soon comes to realize that the swords appear to be unsellable at any price. I find the dialogue Jay has with Abraham, the individual who originally sold him the swords as a profound commentary on entrepreneurship.

Jay seeks out Abraham, furious:

> '... you set me up. You knew how much cash I had. You led me straight to those swords and set the price just at the top of my budget. Do you get the whole sixty?'
> 'No,' Huang said, 'only half.'
> 'You bastard.'
> 'Not bastard. Straight business.'
> 'You knew nobody wanted them. You offered them all over town.'
> 'All over the world,' Haung said. 'Dime. Very cheap price. Required very big risk ...'
> 'You just took my money,' Jay said. 'You knew I'd never be able to sell.'
> 'No. I knew Abraham Huang could not sell. Maybe Jay Wilson sell. This is business.' (Apple, 1989: 60)

'Maybe Jay Wilson sell' – each individual makes decisions about their future circumstances. We can't really predict, exactly, what will occur, either for ourselves, or for others. There is room for the imagination and for situations to evolve in non-predictable ways. And, so it is with Jay Wilson's experiences in 'Peace'. The story has a happy ending. Through what appears to be a sense of hopelessness at not selling any of the swords, Jay is desperately running home when he sees a procession of priests and ministers that leads him toward an experience that presents him with an idea for a way he can sell the swords at a profit. And it comes to pass. All 600,000 swords are purchased for 2 dollars each for use in a peace event – Turn *Star Wars* into ploughshares. Through what appear to be random circumstances (being exactly at the right place at exactly the right time) with an active imagination of how the *Star Wars* swords might become something else, the emergency emerges and becomes an entrepreneurship. Not all entrepreneurship stories are so dramatic.

Said before (but worth repeating again and again): The language of entrepreneurship matters.

> Words are windows for seeing what was earlier hidden or missing. The variety of words we use to talk about organizational emergence will provide us with the requisite variety to see and understand the variation in this phenomenon. (Chapter 10, this volume: 238)

Opportunity:
From Porta – Doorway; Passage
Through. Fortune opens.

And ... another way to talk about the process of entrepreneurship: empirical evidence on entrepreneurial behavior

I view much of the effort I spent during the decade of the 1990s as focused on generating evidence and insights into the process of how entrepreneurs create organizations. All of the papers in this section involve collaborative efforts among very good friends of mine. There are so many special moments that are embedded in and around all of this work. The stories that are conveyed for each of these articles are merely a patina on the depth of the joy and delight I have had over the years in conversations, dinners, and adventures. Reader and Watkins (2006) hint at the importance of friendships in both collaborative research and in the generation of citation patterns (which reflect what articles a scholar tends to pay attention to). I believe that so much of what could be written about the development of particular scholarly articles and lines of research could be based on the nuances of the relationships among the co-authors. I will try to keep my stories to a minimum here.

The Duchesneau and Gartner article (Chapter 7, this volume) is an exploration and replication of the methods and ideas in Van de Ven, Hudson, and Schroeder's (1984) study that compared six low-performing and six high-performing educational software ventures. We closely followed their multi-level framework (entrepreneurial, organizational, and ecological factors) in a study of the Fresh Juice Distribution business. Don Duchesneau had called me one day to ask whether I would supervise his dissertation. He was living in Florida. I told him that he would need to meet me and talk, face-to-face, before I could make a decision. He responded 'Are you available if I can fly up tomorrow?' I was and he did. How different it is to be working on a dissertation with an entrepreneur who has resources. Don had started a number of Fresh Juice Distribution (FJD) businesses, and his wide-ranging contacts in the industry were the foundation for his dissertation: a broad exploration of the history of many of the FJD firms that subsequently succeeded (13 firms) or failed (13 firms). We had twice as many firms that were the basis for the Van de Ven, Hudson, and Schroeder (1984) study. This article is carved from Don's dissertation efforts.

While the paper covers a range of individual, behavioral, and strategic factors that play a role in new venture success or failure, the factors I want to emphasize here are the behavioral ones. We identified eight types of behaviors that could differentiate between the successful and unsuccessful firms: clarity of the business idea (clear); breadth of vision (broad); number of startup behaviors undertaken (many and varied); time spent in planning (lengthy); the breadth of the planning process (very broad); engaging in market research (some versus none); using professional advisors (yes); and whether the firm was purchased as a way to gain entry into the FJD business (no). Of these behaviors that led to success, one behavior will tend to consistently surface in later research as both a primary factor in success at getting into business, but also as a factor in succeeding in business: planning. I want to make sure that readers understand that the process of planning is not the same as writing a business plan. And that, even in writing a business plan, there is both the process of planning and the process of writing the document itself. While there seems to be a growing concern about the value of business plans, the evidence here, and in subsequent research presented later, suggests that the process of business planning (for example, gathering evidence, talking to customers, analyzing competition, identifying a viable business model) is a necessary component of both success at starting a business and success at staying in business. This article makes a strong case that business planning (the process) matters. What confounds the issue of whether business plans matter is in fathoming the evidence scholars collect about business plans: whether the entrepreneurs actually undertook the process of business planning, or whether their efforts were entirely devoted to writing a document without gathering evidence gained from a business planning process. Business plans that represent business planning efforts tend to be significantly correlated with success.

There are two other findings that I think are interesting. First, is the observation that individuals who tended to purchase firms were less likely to do the significant 'due diligence' required in the purchase process: purchasers tended to rely solely on the past performance of these firms for sale, and rarely undertook efforts to understand the changing competitive dynamics of the industry. Sellers were offering firms that were on a trajectory to fail while buyers were making assumptions (based on past performance) that these firms would continue to have potential. This is additional evidence in support of the many findings about Akerlof's (1970) ideas about the 'market for lemons': the information asymmetries in buying and selling under uncertainty. The second point is that industries evolve over time (nothing new here, but still worth saying) and that behavior that worked at one moment in the industry's life cycle may not work at later times. Context matters.

> Success beckons. Those
> Who come later must follow
> A different path.

Always, the first image that comes to mind when thinking about Kelly Shaver and Betsy Gatewood is spending an afternoon at Monet's house in Giverny, those indelible images: the bright pinkness of the house facade, thousands of multi-colored roses, and the cool placidness of the water lily ponds. One of many wonderful adventures we have had together. My resume bears so many marks of their involvement in my life. And, my life bears more profound signs of their constant and supportive friendship and camaraderie.

'A Longitudinal Study of Cognitive Factors Influencing Start-Up Behaviors and Success at Venture Creation' (Chapter 11, this volume) is deeply embedded in Betsy and Kelly's skills and competencies. The article does so many different things well. It is one of the first longitudinal studies that measures the relationship between an entrepreneur's initial cognitive perspectives and subsequent success at starting an ongoing firm. It provides a comprehensive framework of identifiable and measurable behaviors for studying the entrepreneurial process. And, it offers important insights into the relationship between cognitions, behaviors, and success at getting into business.

I will briefly point out the paper's insights on the cognitive side. The paper is grounded theoretically, in attribution theory, and, as such, links it to a foundation of theory and empirical evidence that extends beyond entrepreneurship scholarship, per se. It is a social psychology article, first. Indeed, I believe 'A Longitudinal Study ...' is perhaps one of the best psychologically-based entrepreneurship articles of the 1990s. The article lays out a way to think about entrepreneurship in an attributional way. It provides a method for identifying attributional perspectives in an entrepreneur's statements. And, it shows how those statements influence subsequent persistence in starting new ventures. The article also demonstrates how the construct of 'locus of control' can be thoughtfully applied in a rigorous way to the study of entrepreneurs. The major finding worth pointing out is that females who offered internal/ stable attributions (for example, 'I have always wanted to be my own boss') and males who offered external/stable attributions (for example, 'I have identified a market need') were significantly more likely to succeed at getting into business than those individuals who offered other types of attributions.

The summary of reasons for getting into business found in Table 2 (Chapter 11, this volume: 377), paints in broad brush stokes a picture that individuals engage in entrepreneurial activity for a variety of reasons: identified a market need, desire of autonomy, to make more money, utilize skills and experience, and the desire to accomplish something (plus many others). Different types of reasons for different types of people can matter differentially. That insight may seem obvious, but its implications are more far reaching if one has a perspective that variation in entrepreneurship is fundamental to the phenomenon.

The list of new venture creation behaviors described on pages 389 and 390 of the article (ibid.) is, from my point of view, one of the more comprehensive and detailed lists of entrepreneurial behaviors that exist in the entrepreneurship literature. While the behavioral aspects of the article were not the primary focus of the article, the generation of this list of behaviors and how they were utilized could benefit scholars interested in developing more evidence for the value of a behavioral view of entrepreneurship. The list is based on a thorough exploration of prior theoretical and empirical research on entrepreneurial behavior as well as a rigorous field test using Small Business Development Center counselors/advisors to evaluate the validity and reliability of the behaviors as measures of entrepreneurial activity. The 29 behaviors that resulted from this effort are divided into five major categories of activities: gathering marketing information, estimating potential profits, finishing the groundwork for the product/service, developing the structure of the company, and setting up business operations. I wish this list of activities had become the list of behavioral activities in subsequent longitudinal data collection efforts on nascent entrepreneurs (for example, Gartner, Carter, and Reynolds, 2004; Gartner et al., 2004; Reynolds, 2007; Reynolds and Curtin, 2008). These 29 behaviors are able to grasp, in a much more comprehensive and detailed way *how* the process of venture creation might actually be seen, in context, and measured. It recognizes that some broad behaviors, such as 'marketing to customers' involves a variety of activities: (1) gathering information on who would be my customers; (2) making sales/revenue projections; (3) marketing the product or service itself; (4) supporting customers with installation and adjustment; and (5) supporting customers with training. And, therefore, implicitly recognizes that these marketing behaviors span many of the five categories of activities. Certainly, there are a number of other behaviors that could be identified as involved with 'marketing to customers' (for example, I would have added 'selling to customers' as separate and in addition to [3] marketing the product or service). Be that as it may, this list of 29 behaviors is where I would begin in building a set of identifiable activities that would appear to capture the essence of what individuals are doing when they engage in the process of starting new businesses.

The finding that nascent entrepreneurs who start businesses were more likely to devote substantially more hours to activities involved with 'setting up business operations', that is, engaging in the tangible activities of operating a business (for example, purchasing inputs, organizing these inputs, and selling the outputs) is a precursor to later work (Chapter 12, this volume) that generated a similar insight: visible actions that signal concrete business operations increase chances for the development of on-going businesses. (Visible) actions matter.

Giverny. Paris.
Red Rock. Sonoma. US. I
Miss the Adventure.

I can, even now, in my head, so clearly hear Nancy Carter's voice on the phone as she said: 'We have the data that can explore your ideas about entrepreneurial behavior. Do you want to join up?' My involvement with the development of the Panel Study of Entrepreneurial Dynamics began with Nancy Carter's reaching out to include me in the work she and Paul Reynolds were doing on the study of nascent entrepreneurs over time. As has been described in other venues (Gartner et al., 2004; Reynolds, 2000), the article 'Exploring Start-Up Event Sequences' (Chapter 12, this volume) was (at least for me) the genesis for the intention to develop a sufficiently large generalizable sample of individuals who were identified early in the process of starting ventures who could be followed for a number of years until their efforts resulted in business startups or not. I had suggested earlier (Gartner, 1989) that entrepreneurship research needed generalizable longitudinal data on the entrepreneurial process, so that we could determine what kinds of characteristics, skills, attitudes and behaviors might actually have some influence on success at getting into business. Being able to measure 'change over time' is critical. And, Nancy and Paul had this kind of data: individuals contacted during their initial efforts at startup, and then, six to 18 months later. While it was a very small random sample – 71 cases – this was large enough to glean some important insights into the process of venture creation.

The highlight of the article that I think is most intriguing is Figure 1 (Chapter 12, this volume: 160) and the analyses of this graph. As context, one finding from many of the various longitudinal studies on nascent entrepreneurs is that there is a significant portion of individuals who begin the startup process that seem to be continually 'still trying'. I sense this proportion of individuals hovers around 30 percent of all people who say they are engaged in the process of business startup. The 'still trying' appear to be 'always trying', but never quitting or getting into business. Figure 1 shows vividly that the 'still trying' group appears to engage in significantly fewer activities that would either propel them into business, or provide insights that their business concepts would not work. Many of the 'still trying' are therefore, actually 'not trying'. They are talkers not doers: saying they are trying, but not. While some kinds of businesses will take a very long time to come into existence, on average, sustained activity (working more than 30 hours a week at the startup process) will result in an entrepreneur either getting into business, or quitting the startup process within about two years. Supporting the finding described earlier in Gatewood, Shaver, and Gartner (Chapter 11, this volume), individuals who took actions that made the venture real (that is, formed legal entity, asked others for money, hired employees, purchased facilities and equipment) were more likely to get into business. I continue to support the speculation we offered that those individuals who 'gave up' were doing so because they found that their business idea proved to not work. Not all opportunities that are pursued will necessarily work out. And, only through investing time and resources into developing those ideas can entrepreneurs find out whether they will work. Also, then, if one looks at the numbers (not just in this study, but, in other studies of the startup process), it should be pointed out that most venture creation efforts are not successful. (In general, about 70 percent of the individuals who begin the process of business startup either quit or are 'still trying'.) Entrepreneurship is primarily about pursuing ideas that don't work.

Since this article has a lot of visibility given its use as a foundation piece for the Panel Study of Entrepreneurial Dynamics, I'm not sure I can add much more to the ongoing discussion of its insights and value.

> Give yourself to the
> Process until it works or
> Not. Effort Matters.

If I recollect this correctly, Karl Vesper once told me that he felt that one of the primary drivers of the rise of the entrepreneurial economy in the United States beginning in the 1980s was the influence of *Inc. Magazine*. Whether *Inc. Magazine* caused more entrepreneurial activity (which I believe it did because it provided an awareness of the phenomenon in an engaging way), the magazine did have its pulse on entrepreneurship, particularly in capturing aspects of emerging high growth businesses (for example, the *Inc. 500*, and the *Inc. 100*).[5] For me, the magazine reflected the vast creativity and diversity in entrepreneurial activity. *Inc. Magazine* profiled companies and ideas that seemed to go beyond what one what thought is possible. Much of the fun of reading the magazine was in learning about how such seemingly bizarre ideas could develop into viable businesses (for example, Animalens, Inc. – rose colored contact lenses for chickens).

For a number of years the magazine ran in-depth profiles of emerging companies that also included evaluations and recommendations from experts (venture capitalists, industry experts, industry competitors, and entrepreneurs). These evaluations piqued my curiosity about the ability to predict whether an emerging entrepreneurial venture would succeed or not. Much of what academics in entrepreneurship appear to do is develop predictive models of entrepreneurial success, so, I wondered whether my colleagues and I could develop a model that might predict the success or failure of emerging ventures better than other types of experts. The *Inc. Magazine* articles gave us this occasion. 'Predicting New Venture Survival: An Analysis of "Anatomy of a Start-up." Cases from *Inc.* Magazine' (Chapter 13, this volume) used 27 magazine articles in the *Inc. Magazine* series 'Anatomy of a Start-up' as the data, and we cobbled together an 85-item questionnaire to code every possible aspect of the entrepreneurial situation that might influence whether the startup would succeed, or not. While there are many methodological issues that can be pointed out as concerns in how the research was conducted, the results, I think, offer some insights that are valid and plausible, as well as point in the direction of later ideas in the narrative arena. Successful startups required entrepreneurs to change over time (in skills, abilities, and actions) that are easy to talk about in the stories portrayed in the magazine articles, but difficult to account for in the quantitative methods used. Entrepreneurs were interacting with various stakeholders (suppliers, customers, funders) over time to, as we now would currently label, 'co-create' (Fletcher, 2006, 2007; Sarasvathy, 2008) their startups. The interactions are easy to talk about in a story, difficult to account for in a quantitative model. The discussion reflected this concern about the interactive changes of entrepreneurs over time in the insights we offered about the differences in predictions among the investors and the entrepreneurs. The comments that investors offered in making their evaluations about the possible success of a startup rarely offered a sense of future contingencies that the entrepreneur might surmount, so, these evaluations tended to be more pessimistic about the possibility of success. I ascribe this pessimism to the sense that when an investor provides resources to a startup, the investor loses a certain amount of control over the entrepreneur, and, ultimately, the success of the venture will depend on the capabilities and skills of the entrepreneurs (though there is much debate in the entrepreneurship literature about this). So, an investor makes a bet on the current situation with the trend line moving out based on the given fact pattern. Investors seemed to believe there was less of a chance that entrepreneurs would change. The expert entrepreneurs tended to suggest ways that entrepreneurs in these startups might come up with new ways to adjust the current fact pattern, and often believed that the entrepreneurs in the startup stories might creatively come up with fixes to current or future problems. I link this view to the issues discussed earlier in the short story 'Peace'. Random things occur that are impossible to predict, but those situations can be taken advantage of in ways that move a startup forward in positive ways. Entrepreneurs count on these occurrences. The stories in the magazine articles reflect that, as well. Again, quantitatively modeling random occurrences, and new behaviors and insights from entrepreneurs: difficult. Narrative methods seem to have more space to recognize what actually happens.

Finally, I was so very pleased that the editor and chief of *Inc. Magazine*, George Gendron, thought that the article was insightful enough to write a column in the magazine about it 'The seven habits of highly effective start-ups' (Gendron, 1999: 11).

> We live and act now.
> The day before tomorrow.
> Our dreams are not there.

One of the joys and frustrations of working with the Panel Study of Entrepreneurial Dynamics (Gartner et al., 2004) is that the dataset is so 'vast'. The number of questions about the startup process is really overwhelming as there are so many different facets of the startup phenomenon that are accounted for. Yet, this 'vastness' of items in the PSED is also a joy for providing a researcher with a way to tinker with various ideas and issues that might come up about the nature of entrepreneurship. 'The Career Reasons of Nascent Entrepreneurs' (Chapter 14, this volume) was one of the articles that emerged from a number of different efforts among my colleagues and I.

Kelly Shaver, Betsy Gatewood, and I had taken a strong interest in exploring the reasons nascent entrepreneurs offer for starting new ventures in the PSED dataset, Question 104: Why do you want to start this business? This is an open-ended question that we felt would offer both variety and a depth of insights into the motivations that nascent entrepreneurs ascribe to their efforts. Our first major effort at exploring these open-ended responses (Shaver et al., 2001) was actually begun in 1999, and the coding process for analyzing the open-ended responses was tedious and time-consuming, though ultimately rich in insights (see Chapter 20, this volume). I recall that our feeling was, during the coding process, that there had to be other fixed response questions in the PSED dataset that might be similar to the kinds of responses we were getting in the open-ended analyses. These fixed-response questions might be more 'analyzable'. There were such questions. The paper 'Doing it for yourself' (Gartner, Shaver, and Gatewood, 2000), which won the National Federation of Independent Businesses Award at the 2000 Babson Entrepreneurship Research Conference, was the result. Once these results became visible, in conversations with Nancy Carter we realized that she had been the person who had originally championed these questions in the PSED dataset, and, that she had additional literature on the logic of these questions that would be valuable to furthering this line of inquiry (see Carter, Gartner, and Shaver, 2004). It was at this point that we joined forces for the paper 'The Career Reasons of Nascent Entrepreneurs' (Chapter 14, this volume).

As I've pointed out earlier (Chapter 4, this volume), one of the fundamental issues that continually crops up in exploring the nature of entrepreneurship is the question of whether entrepreneurs are different from other kinds of individuals, and, more specifically, whether entrepreneurs have different reasons for why they are motivated to start businesses that are different than the kinds of reasons that other individuals offer for getting jobs. I sense that it has crossed most people's minds that they would assume that entrepreneurs would start businesses for different reasons than people who look for employment. The urtext on this discussion is Shaver and Scott (1991), who lay out a model for how and why the reasons that individuals have in their minds might influence their behaviors (to start a business). Exploring career reasons, then, is important for discerning whether reasons matter as a basis for taking entrepreneurial action. (And, I hope one might see the connections between 'reasons' and Barbara Bird's ideas [1988] about intentions.)

We explored six different categories of reasons that people give for getting into business (self realization, financial success, roles, innovation, recognition, and independence). There were no differences between entrepreneurs on self-realization, financial success, innovation and independence, which were the four major reasons that both groups gave for making career choices. These would typically be, one would assume, the categories that entrepreneurs would be different on. Rather, there were small differences on the two lesser categories of roles and recognition. We speculated that these results suggested that entrepreneurs cared less about what others thought about the career choices they made and felt there was less of a need to worry about following family role models in deciding on their entrepreneurial activities. While differences on these categories were significantly different between the two groups, their priority among all respondents was significantly smaller (that is, all respondents cared less about roles and recognition than about financial success or self-realization). Our primary conclusion was that differences between entrepreneurs and others on these career reasons was qualitatively minor, and, essentially, there aren't differences in the reasons that entrepreneurs and others give for choosing careers. Given that the PSED sample involves asking entrepreneurs during the process of startup about their reasons for getting into business, I would weight this finding heavily against any beliefs that entrepreneurs pursue new venture creation for reasons any different than those who look to pursue other career paths.

> Score from one to five
> Why you are here in this world?
> Only six dreams matter?

I believe that no prospective activity, particularly that of entrepreneurship, could ever occur without some glimmer of intention and thought (Bird, 1988; Katz and Gartner, Chapter 5, this volume). Therefore, if one believes that there would be intention inherent in entrepreneurship, there would be, by necessity, some aspect of 'planning'. Business planning is a method for recognizing and solving problems that an entrepreneur faces during the emergence of a new venture. As such, it is a complicated set of activities and awarenesses that we tend to dump into the jumble of the label of 'business plan'. Yet, it doesn't take much imagination to realize that the process of business planning could (or not) involve a myriad of activities and decisions: finding customers, determining customer needs, selling products/services to customers based on assumed determined needs, getting feedback from customers, identifying and acquiring resources to develop and operate the venture, setting up the venture, finding employees and suppliers, and so on. Research on business planning, therefore, often seems like a confusion of contradictory findings and conclusions because our concepts of what people are doing when they engage in 'business planning' is as varied as our beliefs about who entrepreneurs are.

My career has tried to tackle the issue of the value of business planning in a variety of ways. Besides my original dissertation work, which tried to account for the activity of business planning as one aspect of the startup process (Chapter 6, this volume), I've tried to parse out various insights into how business planning is part of the process of solving problems that entrepreneurs face as they create new ventures (see Gartner, 1984, 1985, 1986, 1988; Gartner and Thomas, 1993). Business planning is a series of activities that entrepreneurs undertake to purposefully move their venture ideas into the context of an ongoing venture. As this is a process, business planning is not only an activity that occurs at one point in time, but, also, across time (for most entrepreneurs engaged in that activity). With that perspective in mind...

The genesis of the work on the value of business planning as it is explored through the Panel Study of Entrepreneurial Dynamics came about because of layover at Heathrow for a flight back to Chicago after the Babson Entrepreneurship Research Conference in Glasgow in 2004. Jon Liao was waiting for the same flight back, and we struck up a conversation about issues involved in the PSED, particularly issues involved with the behavior variables, and one idea led to another, and we began a collaboration on a series of projects involved with the value of business plans for venture success (Gartner and Liao, 2005, 2007; Liao and Gartner, Chapter 16, this volume, 2008). As both Gartner and Liao (2007) and Liao and Gartner (2008) offer comprehensive reviews of the business planning literature as it relates to entrepreneurship, I'll summarize those overviews by suggesting that while the results about the value of business planning appear to be mixed (as to its efficacy), the results do tend to lean towards a conclusion that engaging in the business planning process (for example, indicating 'yes' to the question: Did you do a business plan?) improves the likelihood of developing an ongoing venture. The results from Chapter 16 in this volume bear this conclusion out: entrepreneurs who engaged in any form of business planning were 2.6 times more likely to have either started a business or still be in the process of starting a business than those individuals who quit the process.

What I find interesting about the paper are the interactive effects between when planning activities occur and perceptions of environmental uncertainty. We found that when entrepreneurs perceived uncertain environments, they were more likely to continue to persist in venture creation if they engaged in planning, while if environments are perceived as certain, then they were more likely to persist in venture creation if they engaged in planning late in the venture creation process. In one sense this result is obvious: planning helps reduce perceived uncertainty that can then help entrepreneurs take action in a particular direction. Planning clears the fog so that a path is revealed. Yet, what is more interesting is that planning can be a way to make sense of what one already knows and has accomplished. I believe, inherently, that individuals need at points to make sense of what is happening to them before they can, again, move forward. I think this reflects the dual nature of planning: it enables one to make sense of the past and helps guide one's future. Both are needed. At some points retrospection is helpful, and at other points, prospection is helpful. It all depends on context (Gartner, Chapter 1, this volume).

What I conclude from my forays into the data of the PSED is that action matters more than the reasons that people might offer for why they take action. As later articles will reflect, I lean towards thinking of our situations as socially constructed. And, I emphasize the word 'construct'. It is the act of assembly, of putting together. It is what entrepreneurship is: organizing. And, that involves action.

The trail ceases at
A bramble or horizon.
Either way: Forward.

Opportunity vocabulary

Did the Shane and Venkataraman (2000) article on the importance of opportunity to the phenomenon of entrepreneurship fundamentally change the way we think about the nature of entrepreneurship, or not (Arend, 2014)? I believe: it did and it didn't. I believe that they were able to legitimize the entrepreneurship field in a way that helped bring it significant scholarly attention and effort. I believe that the entrepreneurship field needed such a platform to launch many substantial theoretical and empirical research projects (Gartner, 2001). We are better for their article because the field is larger and populated with more enthusiastic and skilled scholars. What didn't happen from the article immediately, was – or what didn't occur in many subsequent theoretical and empirical research efforts were – efforts to address the conundrum of opportunity, itself: what is an opportunity? Now, there is much more interest and thought about 'what opportunities are' (see Dimo Dimov's work: 2007a, 2007b, 2011), so, I've included two articles in this volume that are, essentially, commentaries on the nature of opportunity. I believe that the focus on opportunity has many of the same ontological problems that a focus on the nature of entrepreneurship has previously undertaken. Rather than: What do we talk about when we talk about entrepreneurship? (Chapter 8, this volume), the question is: What do we talk about when we talk about opportunity?

'The Language of Opportunity' (Chapter 15, this volume) came out of the first 'Movements' conference organized by Chris Steyaert and Daniel Hjorth with the generous support of funds from Magnus Aronsson at ESBRI in Stockholm, Sweden. The original intention of this paper was to 'tweak' Scott Shane, who I hoped would be at the conference, as a response to the article he had written in *Organization Science*: 'Prior Knowledge and the Discovery of Entrepreneurial Opportunities' (Shane, 2000). As I've written elsewhere (Gartner, 2012), I've had a long love–hate relationship with this article. I think it is brilliant, yet I've always been unsatisfied with 'what is missing' from the article as Scott offers compelling insights into the process of opportunity discovery. What is missing for me was evidence that entrepreneurs actually thought and talked in the same ways that they were depicted in the case studies. As the article only offered selected excerpts of interviews, I felt there were other stories and insights that simply weren't being told. What this means is this: if I ask an entrepreneur the question 'how did you discover your opportunity?' I will get an answer, of some sort, where the entrepreneur tries to provide me with what I want: a story about discovery. If I tell the entrepreneur to respond to this: 'Tell me the story of how you got into business', the entrepreneur tries to provide me with what I want, as well: a business startup story. If I ask an entrepreneur to respond to this: 'Tell me about the last five years of your life'. I might get a story that has very little to do with the startup of a business. I can say, very emphatically, that entrepreneurs will tell very different stories in response to those three questions. If we ask about the discovery of an opportunity, entrepreneurs respond with a story about discovery. If we ask about the creation of their businesses, then, they respond with business creation stories (that rarely talk about the word 'opportunity' per se). So, if we ask about discovery, we find it. If we ask about creation we find it.

> In other words, if scholars talk about opportunity in certain ways, it is likely that our language will constrain our ability to consider other possible meanings that might be used by others, particularly those individuals who engage in the phenomenon of opportunity: entrepreneurs. (Chapter 15, this volume: 104)

The entrepreneurs I have talked with simply didn't think or talk in the manner of the evidence presented in Scott's 'Prior Knowledge' article when the questions are about the creation of businesses, rather than the discovery (or creation) of opportunities. The focus of 'The Language of Opportunity' was to present evidence that suggested that entrepreneurs don't think or talk about opportunities, at all. The idea of 'opportunity' is our language, the language of scholars studying entrepreneurship. We create meanings that then become the meanings that we seek to find entrepreneurs using as well. I'm more interested in the meanings that the entrepreneurs, themselves, use for making sense of their own experiences.

A few issues in this book chapter are worth noting. We offer two perspectives on the nature of how opportunities emerge: discovery and enactment. We suggest this dichotomy in 2003, a few years before Alvarez and Barney's (2007) article on the discovery versus creation dichotomy was offered. The enactment perspective is built on links to a literature on how opportunities are perceived that stems from the sense making (Weick, 1979) and strategic identity literatures (see Daft and Weick, 1984; Dutton and Jackson, 1987; Jackson and Dutton, 1988). What has always baffled me in discussions of the nature of opportunity in the entrepreneurship field is that the strategic identity literature on perceptions of opportunities and threats has been, for the most part, ignored. Why is that? In the strategic identity literature, opportunities are not only given a theoretical framework for how and why they are perceived as opportunities, the concept, itself, is defined, measured and tested in a variety of settings. Why has the entrepreneurship field failed to recognize these previous contributions and sought, instead, a path to 'reinvent the wheel'?

My conjecture is this: to recognize the prior research contributions from the strategy, organizational behavior and organization theory fields to the study of opportunities might call into question whether the study of opportunities is really the distinctive domain of entrepreneurship scholarship. If opportunities have been thoughtfully explored by other disciplines, then, there is less of a case to be made that the study of opportunities is a unique attribute of entrepreneurship scholarship. Be that as it may, there does seem to be an a-historical sensibility in the entrepreneurship field that tends to ignore what has been done before.

As Chapter 15 is about the language used by entrepreneurs when they talk about opportunity (or not), we first explore the meanings behind what a language would be like if they were to use a 'discovery' vocabulary:

In terms of the language that would depict the opportunity discovery perspective, obviously, the word 'discovery' suggests that information can be found, noticed, made visible, exposed, or seen ... Opportunity discovery, therefore, involves seeing in its many forms, the objective characteristics of circumstances ... We would initially, at this point, suggest that if entrepreneurs do in fact, discover opportunities, we would expect that their language would reflect the use of such 'discovery' words as: see, notice, find, look. (Chapter 15, this volume: 108)

The language for enactment involves, in its own way, a sort of intellectual sophistry, in that enactment, and language about the experience of enactment, has an inherent retrospective view of past and current actions.

If an entrepreneur recognizes an opportunity, as such, it would be only as an aspect of the retrospective sense making that follows action ... What the idea of retrospective sense making implies is that the 'discovery' of an opportunity would merely be a realization, and, therefore, a labeling of an ongoing set of entrepreneurial activities, one of which would be, 'the recognition of an opportunity.' In the opportunity enactment perspective, 'discovery' is a bracketing of a cacophony of experiences and activities that entrepreneurs are engaged in. (ibid.: 109–10)

Enactment, therefore, is different than creation.

Chapter 15, in a crude way, attempts to analyze 443 written responses from nascent entrepreneurs in the PSED1 dataset (Gartner et al., 2004) in response to this question: 'Briefly, how did the original idea for starting a business develop?' We used a word count program to analyze the frequency of words (across all 443 statements) that described their experiences. What we found was that discovery language (for example, words like: saw, find, found, look, notice) were in only 38 of the 443 statements (about 9 percent). The word discovery was never used. We suggest, based on the frequency of certain words that were used, that entrepreneurs tended to talk about the development of their businesses in words that described their own desires and abilities: 'I' 'want' 'my' 'own' 'business'. And, for those entrepreneurs who used discovery language, their statements tended to be framed retrospectively.

The second issue that Chapter 15 focuses on is the role of action as a precursor to realization. While I've indicated earlier in this Introduction that intention is usually inherent in taking action, there is evidence from the PSED data that a significant percentage of nascent entrepreneurs (45 percent) engage in startup actions without intentional conscious interest in starting a business. As would be evident from an enactment perspective, many nascent entrepreneurs are involved in various activities, that, retrospectively, they realize are on a path towards business creation. Using ideas in Friedel (2001) about the process of discovery among Nobel scientists, we play with the word 'serendipity' (loosely defined as accidental discovery) to suggest that discovery is, in the end, 'noticing' something of value within the process of 'doing science'. The basic idea of Shane's article (2000) is correct, prior knowledge bounds the ability of individuals to notice opportunities. But, prior knowledge is based on actions and activities which are within the realm of each individual's choices and interests. Isn't Pasteur's statement: 'in observation, chance favors the prepared mind' another way of stating the prior knowledge argument? Yet, when one looks at the process of science, it is based on a myriad of mundane activities that doing science involves. The surprise of discovery is merely a marker along the way of science-as-practice. By analogy, then, doing entrepreneurship would be denoted, at times, by 'discovery' realizations. I ask then, why should these realizations of discovery be a more important focus compared to the realizations of other events or activities in the entrepreneurial process?

> What is the nature
> Of experience without
> Words to describe it?

'Opportunities as Attributions: Categorizing Strategic Issues from an Attributional Perspective' (Chapter 20, this volume) offers prior theory and measures of various opportunity constructs from the strategic issue identification literature (see Daft and Weick, 1984; Dutton and Jackson, 1987; Jackson and Dutton, 1988), and grounds this research in the larger literature of attribution theory (Heider, 1958; Kelley, 1973; Weiner, 1985). The article opens the door to the depth and breadth of prior scholarship on opportunity and identifies a number of ways that the opportunity construct has been operationalized. Prior scholarship on opportunity from the strategic issue identification literature is significant. It really is a wonder that it has been ignored, as it does provide a comprehensive foundation for any research efforts on opportunity that are currently undertaken. To ignore this literature, I believe, is a great mistake for the entrepreneurship field.

Opportunities, broadly, are situations that are perceived to be positive, controllable, and involve personal gain. Seen from an attributional perspective, opportunities tend to be internal/variable (I can take effort to solve the problem) and internal/stable (I have the ability to solve the problem). Opportunities, then, are positive situations (desirable) that individuals perceive as feasible (they have the abilities and can undertake effort to achieve their desires).

We explore the attributions that nascent entrepreneurs offer in response to these open ended questions: 'Briefly, how did the original idea for starting a business develop?' And, 'what major problems have you had in starting this business?' We found that nascent entrepreneurs tended to describe opportunities as internal (stable and variable) and problems as variable (internal and external). Opportunities, from an attributional perspective, come from within the individual: Ability (internal/stable) is something that entrepreneurs already have, and effort (internal/variable) is something that entrepreneurs can do. Problems are seen as either something that can be solved with effort (internal/variable) or outside of one's control – bad luck (external/variable). Obviously, there is an overlap in perceptions where opportunities can also be perceived as problem (internal/variable) situations and the difference being that opportunities are perceived as positive situations whereas problems are perceived as negative situations, yet both will require effort to solve. The article ends at the same place as 'The Language of Opportunity' article does:

> We wonder whether asking entrepreneurs whether they discovered or created their opportunities forces them to conceptualize their past experiences to account for discovery or creation having occurred, even if they did not. If some other process has taken place, a question about discovery or creation is unlikely to uncover it. There is an opportunity, then, to devote more attention to the language used to talk about the nature of opportunity. If we seek a science of the imagination (Gartner, 2007 [Chapter 18, this volume]; Schendel and Hitt, 2007), approaches to understanding the phenomenon of opportunity may depend on ideas, methods and observations that are not within the repertory of our current scholarly norms. (Chapter 20, this volume: 312–13)

And this, then, leads us to the final set of articles that attempts to take on that task.

Begin where you are.
Go to where you hope to be.
Feasibility.

Other paths to understanding entrepreneurship
Chapters 17, 18, 19 and 21 in the book offer a sense of the kinds of struggles I currently confront as an entrepreneurship scholar and some ideas about ways I'm trying to move forward towards understanding what entrepreneurship is (yet, also cognizant of David Hume's aphorism: 'No ought from is'). The order in which these articles will be discussed will begin with a framework for thinking about the nature of entrepreneurship 'Entrepreneurship as Organizing: Emergence, Newness, and Transformation' (Chapter 19, this volume), segue into a plea for a broader and more cacophonific use of theories and methods in entrepreneurship scholarship 'A "Critical Mess" Approach to Entrepreneurship Scholarship' (Chapter 17, this volume), and end with two meditations on the value of narrative methods and ideas in the entrepreneurship field: 'Entrepreneurial Narrative and a Science of the Imagination' (Chapter 18, this volume) and 'A New Path to the Waterfall: A Narrative on a Use of Entrepreneurial Narrative' (Chapter 21, this volume).

Chapter 19, 'Entrepreneurship as Organizing', is loosely based on evolutionary ideas in organization studies (see Aldrich and Ruef, 2006). What Candy Brush and I tried to emphasize in this chapter was a more nuanced sense of how the process of organization emergence actually happens. In simplistic terms, the evolutionary perspective tends to place a great deal of emphasis on selection and retention mechanisms, and, particularly, on the power of selection to shape the outcomes of the venture formation process. There is often an inherent assumption that the selection process occurs in situations where selections are made among 'blind variations' that have been generated: entrepreneurs generate various differences (in behaviors, processes, organizations, markets, products, and so on) and the environment selects out certain of these efforts as survivors. My sense of 'blind variation' is the assumption that entrepreneurs don't know which variations will be successful: they are blind in knowing the outcomes of their intended actions. In our model of organizing, we hint at a more active role for entrepreneurs in the venture formation process. Our belief is that entrepreneurs have some capability to 'select' their own selection mechanisms, that is, entrepreneurs can choose certain kinds of environmental factors that will impact their prospective venture's changes of future success. Entrepreneurs, then, are 'less blind' and have some forbearance in determining their own futures. How might this work? If we assume that all emerging ventures will need some set of resources (Chapter 5, this volume) as an aspect of their creation, then, entrepreneurs have options for choosing the kinds of resources and the ways in which those resources might be acquired. Studies of venture capital often look at the kinds of firms that are selected for investment, but what is rarely considered are all of the entrepreneurs who decided against venture capital investment as a way to enable their firms to emerge and develop. Some entrepreneurs might decide to grow through internally generated cash flows, while others might find ways to get customers or suppliers to finance critical resources (that is, having customers pay up-front for a consulting contract or for the cost of work in process). The environment, then, is not 'fixed' as a set of constraints on the entrepreneur; rather the entrepreneur's imagination and creativity play a role in determining the context in which a purposefully selected environment impacts the emerging firm. So, rather than a straight-line march from enactment to selection to retention, we see cycles of entrepreneurial activity between enactment, selection, and retention. These cycles of emergence, newness, and transformation, then, are the primary avenues for entrepreneurial activity. Entrepreneurship, then, operates in the in-between, of the three major processes involved in organizational evolutionary theory. Emergence is between enactment and selection, newness is between selection and retention, and transformation is between retention and enactment. So, for example, in our model, then, in the process of emergence entrepreneurs learn from their activities about what works or not, and make choices about how the emerging firm might be more able to survive in different situations versus others. Obviously, these choices are bets made on ambiguous future states. Certain bets will pay off, and others won't. The point worth emphasizing is that entrepreneurs are likely to play a larger role in their fates than most evolutionary models recognize. This is not to say that such activities will lead to success, in fact, in most cases, these emerging efforts will fail. Firms are, indeed, selected out to survive. Yet, it is not about whether the majority of efforts fail, it is that some efforts succeed. It is the idea in Wallace Steven's poem, 'The Well Dressed Man with a Beard': sometimes it all depends on something so slight as a cricket's horn that makes all of the difference. Such small nuances are hard to pick up in the ways we do research, but it is in these very small, very subtle choices and actions that organizations actually emerge, survive, and are transformed. So, evolutionary processes in organizations, then, are less deterministic, more interactive, more conscious, and more amenable to entrepreneurial effort than what our results often suggest. We see the outcomes of selection and retention, but we don't see the processes: the false starts, the surmises, guesses, attempts, hypotheses, and so on that play out along the way. (So, that thought should provide a glimmer of why I've drifted into narrative approaches: stories provide ways to allow recognition of those issues.)

The second aspect of the paper worth noting is the reanalysis of the articles used in Busenitz et al. (2003) to offer another way to look at past trends and future directions in the entrepreneurship field. In the Busenitz et al. article, 97 entrepreneurship articles published between 1985 and 1999 that were selected from leading management journals are categorized into four broad categories and the intersections among those four categories: modes of organizing, opportunities, individuals and teams and environments. We use those same articles, then, and segment them across type of organizing (emergence, newness, and transformation) by level of analysis (individual, firm, environment) to show that 75 percent of these articles are firm level studies and that 53 percent of these studies focus on newness. And, that only 22 percent of the entrepreneurship identified looked at the process of organization emergence (at any level of analysis). Most of mainstream entrepreneurship research appears to be focused on existing firms struggling with liability of newness issues, rather than on either emergence or transformation. Certainly, given that the articles used in the study were from 1985 to 1999, the focus of research may have significantly changed. Given that the PSED and GEM efforts were becoming more widely used after this time period, we may see a shift towards a larger percentage of research at both the individual and environmental levels, as well as a larger focus on emergence and transformation in these years after 1999.

> Between here and there
> Hermes guide of souls, giver
> Of luck, plies his trade.

Are you familiar with Kabuki Theatre? It is a very stylized form of Japanese theatre that involves intricate sets, elaborate costumes and make-up on the actors, and a unique choreography of movement and speech, as ways to tell stories about the human condition. Now, think about all of the other ways that people have staged dramas and performances. Kabuki Theatre is just a small portion of how the human condition can be portrayed and (en) acted. I believe that many of the traditional forms of academic scholarship in the entrepreneurship area have similar characteristics to Kabuki Theatre. Journal articles have a stylized form that limits what can be said (and known) about entrepreneurship. The research methods that entrepreneurship scholars use, while elegant and rigorous (in certain ways), have often taken on a form of orthodoxy similar to the limitations of Kabuki. I feel the entrepreneurship field seems to be caught up in ways of knowing and ways of writing about what we know that have serious limitations. We are doing Kabuki Theatre in our scholarship while there are many other ways in which we might know and talk about entrepreneurship.

The 'Critical Mess Approach' (Chapter 17, this volume) is one of a series of efforts (Gartner, 2004b, 2006) to ponder the challenge of trying to engage in the phenomenon of entrepreneurship from a variety of perspectives, methods, and venues. The genesis of the idea is imbedded in the logic offered for a special issue on qualitative methods that Sue Birley graciously asked me to be involved in. In our introduction to that special issue (Gartner and Birley, 2002), we offered the story of a bibliophile, Michael Zinman, and his strategy for collecting books:

> You don't start off with a theory about what you're trying to do. You don't begin by saying 'I'm trying to prove x.' You build a big pile. Once you get a big enough pile together – the critical mess – you're able to draw conclusions about it. You see patterns. (Singer, 2001: 66)

My intention in this article is not to denigrate the need for a focus on particular topics and issues in entrepreneurship with specific methods. Rather, I ask that scholars be more omnivorous in their interests in entrepreneurship as a phenomenon. I believe our sense of what appropriate data is for engaging in entrepreneurship scholarship is somewhat limited, and, as a field, we need to collect more sources of information and collect this information in ways that we have not traditionally used. If an inherent aspect of the entrepreneurial phenomenon is 'variation', then, we are more likely to find variation by being open to a wider variety of methods, data sources, and perspectives. This belief is based on Weick's (1979: 193) dictum 'Complicate Yourself', complicated problems and situations need complicated people. Studying entrepreneurship requires that.

Classification
Begins with collection. Then
A thoughtful sorting.

Finally, two articles in this collection (that is, 'Entrepreneurial Narrative', Chapter 18, and 'A New Path ...', Chapter 21) suggest an approach to studying entrepreneurship that involves narrative methods and an openness to using a variety of narrative sources for 'data'. In some respects, we come full circle back to those articles presented earlier in the collection (that is, 'River City', Chapter 2, and 'Oz in Organization', Chapter 3) where story becomes the focus of scholarly inquiry for exploring the nature of entrepreneurship. 'Entrepreneurial Narrative' and 'A New Path ...' describe an epiphany of sorts in the progression of my career in entrepreneurship scholarship. I want to be clear that my interest in narrative and narrative methods in entrepreneurship scholarship is not an abandonment of traditional methods. I still do Kabuki theatre. And, I still believe in the value of many of the traditional methods and approaches to entrepreneurship scholarship as valid and insightful ways to understand the entrepreneurial phenomenon. So, my plea, now, is not either/or, it is 'and'. I am not taking sides between narrative approaches and traditional approaches. Narrative methods and narrative data help 'complicate yourself'.

The article 'Entrepreneurial Narrative' (Chapter 18, this volume) is an introduction to a special issue devoted to various analyses of the same story: the creation of a toy store (Allen, 2007). I believe the special issue offers a profound introduction into the power of narrative and narrative methods for exploring entrepreneurship. For me, the experience of seeing how narrative approaches could see so many different aspects of entrepreneurship within a single story was like the experience of watching Dorothy go from her black and white Kansas world to the Technicolor wonders of the Land of Oz. I won't review all of the articles in the special issue here, so I encourage you to locate the special issue and read it. The articles are breathtaking in their scope and insights. The experience was a turning point in my development as a scholar in the entrepreneurship field.

What I believe is worth reemphasizing now, in Chapter 18, is the attempt to champion narrative perspectives and methods as being 'ontologically complete'. Narrative methods have their own rules: their own ways of knowing and understanding, and particularly, skills in discerning, that are different than traditional logio-scientific methods and practices. What must be understood is that both methods (logio-scientific practices and narrative practices) do not end up in the same place. They are two different forms of knowing and understanding. They are two different paths that do not have the same destination. To study entrepreneurship through narrative methods and ideas does not provide the same kinds of insights that traditional logio-scientific methods will offer. Both approaches offer insights, and, these insights will be different.

<blockquote>
A new path to the
Waterfall will take you to
A different place.
</blockquote>

The last article in the collection 'A New Path ...' (Chapter 21, this volume) begins with an allusion to T.S. Eliot's poem *Four Quartets* (Eliot, 1943), but the title of the article 'A New Path to the Waterfall' is taken from the title of a book by Raymond Carver (1989) and a line from one of the poems in the book: 'Looking for Work' (Carver, 1989: 19). Raymond Carver is primarily known for his short stories that often describe revelatory moments in the mundane experiences of everyday life. (And, I suggest you find his perfect story 'A Small, Good Thing' as a way of seeing another way that entrepreneurship is and becomes.) The poem 'Looking for Work' describes the sensibility of aspiration within the reality of the commonplace. I wanted the tenor of the article to reflect that.

A significant portion of the 'A New Path ...' article is essentially a much shorter autobiographical reprise of many of the ideas I have discussed in this Introduction. There are some nuances and some differences in the issues discussed, but I believe the general ideas are essentially the same: the struggle to grasp the complexities, variation, and subtleties of entrepreneurship as a phenomenon. What should be reemphasized here, are two points. First, the kinds of quantitative scholarship published in most academic journals need to be more transparent in making visible the details of the data used. I suggest that scholars who publish articles in academic journals make their data available to others immediately upon publication of the article. I believe that one of the values of secondary datasets such at the Panel Study of Entrepreneurial Dynamics is that scholars can reexamine the findings of any of the studies using that data. We need more opportunities for others to closely examine our work. I believe that having multiple perspectives that use the same data, as well as replications of previous studies, helps us as a community of scholars to better learn from each other. The critical mess of scholarship requires not only the addition of more findings about the phenomenon, it requires adding to the pile the data upon which those findings are based. I do recognize the difficulties and costs of sharing data among our colleagues, but I believe there are creative ways that collaborative efforts among scholars could be enhanced if more efforts to share data and information were undertaken. I also make the same suggestion for qualitative research efforts. Interview data and field notes need to be made more visible to other scholars. In my own research efforts in the narrative area, I've tried to use readily available texts (that is, books) and published interviews that can be found on the Internet.

The second point to make is: the need for different paths for the dissemination and discussion of scholarly work in entrepreneurship. I fear the increasing hegemony of such lists as the *Financial Times* Top 45 (a selected list 45 academic journals that the *Financial Times* uses to evaluate a business school's research rank) as a primary indicator of knowledge dissemination. I find it ironic that while the phenomenon we study involves the creation of new markets, new forms of production and new products and services, we would then be willing to submit to institutional frameworks where we would limit ourselves to publishing in a limited number of outlets. How sad. I believe one of the strengths and reasons for the growth of the entrepreneurship field has been the creativeness of the scholars within this field to develop new journals, handbooks, and other kinds of publications as valid and respected sources of knowledge in our field (Katz, 2003). I hope this continues and that the entrepreneurship field be open to embracing radical methods and outlets (that is, not just using the Internet as ways to disseminate information, rather to pursue such venues as visual art, performance, plays, novels, short stories, poems, and 'events'). While I have some fear that the development of new scholarly forms and outlets might fail to build a scholarly community (Gartner, 2013), I am more fearful that our community will fail to innovate and be open to the many different ways we might share and express our insights into the entrepreneurial phenomenon.

Do I have answers? No. Am I lost? Yes: 'In the dark wood … in the middle way … risking enchantment' (Eliot, 1943). But, isn't that what scholarship is about? Not having the answers and being willing to find them (or to have them find you)?

> When you are lost the
> Forest knows where you are. You
> Must let it find you.[6]

Conclusion

As this Introduction is, for the most part, a summary and some sense making of the articles in the book, this conclusion is, therefore, a summary of the summary.

I realize I have been very fortunate to grow up in the entrepreneurship field as it, itself, grew up. So, I have been lucky to have enjoyed so many opportunities to publish my ideas in a variety of journals and books using such a wide range of methods, 'data sources' and genres. Certainly, I'm a product of my times. Soon: a historical artifact. (I have many instances of being at some academic conference and a young scholar will come up to me and say with a beaming smile: 'I thought you were dead!' Soon, yes, as we all, eventually, will be history.) So, ever aware of Bloom's dictum that begins this Introduction: if I were to hope that there were any ideas and thoughts from my work that might 'stick' (Heath and Heath, 2007), and realizing the futility of this hope, here are a few ideas that I still hope will stick with you, anyway.

Entrepreneurship as organizing

I believe that the phenomenon of entrepreneurship is, essentially, an 'organizing' process (Gartner, 1985; Schumpeter, 1934; Weick, 1979). So, what essentially differentiates entrepreneurship from other kinds of creative acts (such as art or innovation) involves the Schumpeterian–Weickian sensibility of 'combining', that is, organizing something: individuals, firms, environments, groups, products, markets, and so on. Entrepreneurship as organizing should always evoke this view of putting things together (broadly defined). The sensibility, then, is behavioral (Schumpeter) and cognitive (Weick), as a social process. Entrepreneurship is not something that one does alone: it must always involve others (Chapter 5, this volume).

I've used such words as 'emergence' to hint at how this combining/organizing process occurs. I believe the articles in this book, as a whole, then, are efforts to come to some understanding of the various aspects of what 'entrepreneurship as organizing' means, both theoretically and empirically. It has been 30 years since Gartner's 1985 article (Chapter 1, this volume): has the idea of 'entrepreneurship as organizing' reached a better sense of clarity? Does the idea resonate as some true insight into the phenomenon?

Variation and taxonomy

As entrepreneurs are in the process of generating new combinations (organizing their world), they intrinsically generate 'difference'. I realize that there is a discussion in the academic literature on differences between 'replicators' (those that repeat what others have done before) and 'innovators' (those that are doing something entirely new). I think that replicators and innovators are on a continuum, with no entrepreneurial effort being a pure form of one or the other. Once we consider the variable of time in the entrepreneurial process, we must see that starting a similar business will be different because the original business was started in the past. Things change. So, starting a fast food restaurant (that is, McDonalds) today, is still different than the same fast food restaurant started in the past. They are different because the world has changed. Maybe not in blatantly overt ways, but there have been changes in the environment that make any startup different from all those that have preceded it. I've used the dictum: 'there is no average in entrepreneurship' as a way to get at this sensibility. Entrepreneurship always involves some process of creating difference (because of changes in time, location or the specific resources utilized, customers change as well as their preferences and desires). So, there will always be differences among every entrepreneurial effort.

What this implies for entrepreneurship scholarship is the requirement to recognize the many, many different ways that entrepreneurship occurs. I suggest, at this point, that we err on the side of discovering diversity in entrepreneurial efforts. It might seem that we would then devote much of our scholarship to looking at what appear to be unique events, yet, I think that it is in these unique events that we will make our most important discoveries about how variation in entrepreneurship actually occurs and, by implication, how chances for the creation of unique value is created. I believe the entrepreneurship field has focused too much on 'selection' and the winners that we see after selection processes have taken their toll. We would be better served by looking at how many different ways that emerging entrepreneurial efforts were undertaken. I believe there is significant value in understanding how and why these differences in entrepreneurial efforts manifest themselves. And, frankly, in order for selection mechanisms to work, the mechanisms that will eventually pick the 'winners' from the 'losers', the selection process needs something to select. I believe the more diversity in entrepreneurial efforts, in general, will increase the chances for providing better outcomes. Difference matters. Variation matters. And, while most new entrepreneurial efforts do not work out in specific instances, there is some evidence that others learn from these various attempts. So, failing matters. And, even if there isn't any learning, the generation of different ways to do things, even when those efforts don't work, still provide a repertoire of possibilities (Gartner, 2014a). Trying matters. The stuff of success is built on the many attempts that didn't work. Has the entrepreneurship field comprehensively covered all of the different ways that entrepreneurial efforts fail? Are we recognizing all of the anomalies and outliers? Do we have methods to see where the differences among entrepreneurial efforts actually differ?

Recognizing difference, then, leads to appreciating the value of taxonomy. If we start with the idea that, inherently, all entrepreneurial efforts are different from each other, then, with some sense of humility, we should seek to then understand where the commonalities are among these efforts. I believe the field, as a whole, has too easily embraced categorization schemes that may not offer nuanced insights. While I have often used industry classification codes as a way to identify similar kinds of entrepreneurial efforts, I continue to wonder how much insight was lost in these groupings. And, in many of these studies 'outliers' have been eliminated, as they tend to skew averages and standard deviations within these groups. Maybe the interesting insights are in these outliers?

If we are concerned about differences, we should be careful when we group cases together. Taxonomic methods are sensitive to differences and commonalities. So, I would like to see more systematic efforts to both identify the diversity in entrepreneurial efforts as well as thoughtful ways the see the commonalities among these efforts. I don't have a solution to these issues. I do know that taxonomic practices are critical for helping the entrepreneurship field to move forward.

Uncertainty, prediction, and the imagination
What intrigues me about the world of organizing is seeing that these processes are loosely coupled (Weick, 1976). That is, the connections between events are less deterministic than one might imagine. There is significant room for situations to be unpredictable: weird things happen. No one seems to behave as we thought. Yet, one of the values of science involves the world of 'if then': If these circumstances occur, then we would predict this outcome (with some sense of statistical confidence). As scholars we ascertain those factors that influence

situations and then assume that events will unfold accordingly. Often things do not. Maybe we ascribe it to the 'error term' in our equations. Or the sense that our predictive models are probabilistic: chances are events can play out in different ways from what we predict (but, still, even with the differences, we assume the rightness of our predictive model to predict). Yet, I believe that things turn out differently for a different reason.

I believe that one reason for the unpredictableness of entrepreneurship involves the role of the imagination in entrepreneurial action. Human beings have the capacity to think about their futures in ways that are not necessarily connected to their current situations. And, they can act on their beliefs about whether they can set into action the reality that they see in their minds. Imagination changes everything. Prediction often depends on ascertaining the factors that comprise the past and present, while imagination evokes a belief in factors of the future (that are yet to be made real, but have the possibility of being so: Gartner, 2014a).

Entrepreneurship, as a creative act, involves ways that individuals are able to involve others in their future dreams (Chapter 9, this volume). I'm not sure how to explore this idea using my current research skills. I drift towards narrative because I sense that narrative methods and perspectives are more sensitive to how people imagine and articulate the future in what they say and do. Accounting for imagination is, by far, the most critical issue for scholars to truly understand the nature of entrepreneurship.

Behavior matters

I will define behavior as the words and actions that individuals undertake: speaking (and writing) and doing. Entrepreneurial behavior involves words and actions undertaken by individuals in the process of organizing. I like Chris Steyaert's idea of 'entrepreneuring' (2007) because it captures the sense that entrepreneurship is inherently a process. It involves activities: the behaviors of individuals, solely and among others. People are doing stuff. Entrepreneurship is not a noun in the same way that organization is not a noun (Weick, 1979). The phenomenon of entrepreneurship is not static. It evolves over time. While many of the articles in this book identify a number of the behaviors that individuals involved in the process of entrepreneurship undertake, the goal in the back of my mind has always been to notate these actions in ways that they could, in some respects, be replicated. Ideally, I imagine something similar to Labanotation in dance (this is before video recordings of dance could be used as documentation). What really happened when a particular organizing effort emerged? To be able to accurately depict the choreography of the words and actions and interactions among all of the individuals involved would be my ideal. This is the kind of information I would like to work with and the kind of information we need if we are to get a sense of how behaviors matter in the process of organization emergence. I am hoping for important strides in both theorizing and empirical research on entrepreneurial behavior. As the imagination works through action, depicting action is crucial.

Other ways of knowing

As I have mentioned earlier in this chapter, much of academic scholarship in entrepreneurship takes the form of journal articles or book chapters that use very specific forms (formats, structures, language) of conveying information and insights. Are these forms the only ways we can talk about the phenomenon? I don't believe this to be so. I have been turning, ever so slowly, towards a path that explores entrepreneurship with the kinds of methods and insights used in the humanities: creative writing (fiction and other forms), rhetoric, philosophy, aesthetics, history, performance, and the arts. I believe that pursuing a path using the humanities and the arts will offer new ways to know about entrepreneurship as well as new ways of talking about the phenomenon (see Steyaert and Hjorth, 2002).

My experiences with entrepreneurs lead me to believe that these individuals are often linguistic innovators in their own right. In order for them to imagine and construct the future they often invent their own language to help others see what is in store for them. Scholars often do not appreciate or celebrate that the practice of entrepreneurship by entrepreneurs involves the creation of concepts, metaphors and ideas. Entrepreneurs are scholars of their own situations. They offer hypotheses about the future, they have theories about their situations, and they have a literature of beliefs and experiences that provide a foundation for their actions. We need to pay attention to them in ways that can 'let them speak' rather than imposing our world-view.

The questions we ask entrepreneurs reflect our agendas and beliefs about the nature of entrepreneurship. I find that entrepreneurs work diligently to fit their sensibilities and ideas into our constructs. We get what we ask for rather than finding out what they might really believe and think. And, then we talk about what we find in ways that are only graspable by other scholars who have an ability to read in the stilted forms we write in. Ugh. So, there needs to be more space in academic scholarship for ways to let entrepreneurs speak for themselves.

As an example of the power of paying attention to entrepreneurs, I would point to the most significant theoretical development to happen in entrepreneurship over the past 20 years: Sarasvathy's (2001, 2008) theory of effectuation. This theory is based on close observation and conversations with entrepreneurs. She provided a context for entrepreneurs to share their own insights and perceptions in a way that let them speak for themselves. This, I believe, is the power of using methods that recognize entrepreneurs as the theorists and scientists that they are.

And, I would love to see, and for the scholarly community to appreciate, a wider array of forms for talking about entrepreneurship. Currently I am spending a lot of time with the film *The Social Network* (Fincher, 2010), and its portrayal of the founding of Facebook. As the film is a fictionalization of *The Accidental Billionaires* (Mezrich, 2009), a biography of the founding of Facebook, one can toggle between the two works to compare and contrast how both works come to some sense of the organizing process, as well as their views of what constitutes a significant event in Facebook's emergence. What intrigues me with the film and book is in parsing out what there is to learn. I think the film and book have a theory about the entrepreneurial process, and these works present evidence to support that theory. They offer a sequence of events about how entrepreneurship occurs. They present a model of factors that influence the organizing process. As millions of individuals have seen this film (probably fewer have read the book), I wonder what kinds of insights they gain from these experiences? Is *The Social Network* one of the primary ways that individuals in our society learn about entrepreneurial processes?

I believe the film, then, is a different way to understand entrepreneurship. And this method of conveying insights is a valid form of knowing (Bruner, 1986). So, while the theory and sights in *The Social Network* don't appear as a series of bullet points on PowerPoint slides, or as a framework in a journal article, I believe there is just as much insight in this fiction. But it's conveyed in a different way, as part of the critical mess of various ways we grasp what it is, and what it means to live our lives in an ambiguous world where we are always walking through the doorway from the present into the future. I'm intrigued by how others imagine how the imagination works. So, it may take imagination (and the forms that imagination often takes, for example, fiction) in order to grasp what imagination is and how it works.

I believe the entrepreneurship field will be more vibrant, insightful, persuasive, and relevant to entrepreneurial practice if we are open to more ways of understanding (Gartner, 2014b). I am looking forward to seeing how this will manifest itself.

Finally, this chapter was likely an exercise in not knowing myself: of probably missing what was truly important, of seeing the wrong things, and of being interested in issues that no one else found as important as I, but …

I did the best I

Could with what I had. What more

Can be said for now?[7]

Notes

1. I believe it is particularly important to point out that my research efforts take place within the context of supportive friends and colleagues. I don't think of my writing as being a singular affair. I write with and for others and they write with and for me. So, ideas and interests blend in these efforts. I'm a product of their generosity.
2. Or, as Zhang Ruitu wrote long ago: 'As you have passed many years writing books behind closed doors, the pines long ago have all grown scales like old dragons'.
3. The poem is a play on the words in this quote – 'You know', Giono said to me, 'There are also times in life when a person has to rush off in pursuit of hopefulness' (Giono, 1985: 51).
4. Weick (1979: 133).
5. I think the *Inc. 500* has a lot of insights that scholars should take more advantage of. For example, Gideon Markman and I did an article (Markman and Gartner, 2002) that tapped just a bit of the information *Inc. Magazine* has collected on high growth firms in the United States to look at the relationship of growth rates with profitability.
6. The haiku is based on the poem 'Lost' by David Wagoner (1976).
7. A play on this quote from Joe Louis: 'I made the most of my ability and I did my best with my title'.

References

Akerlof, George A. (1970), 'The market for "lemons": Quality uncertainty and the market mechanism', *Quarterly Journal of Economics*, **84** (3), 488–500.

Aldrich, H.E. (2011), *An Evolutionary Approach to Entrepreneurship*, Cheltenham, UK and Northampton, MA, USA: Edward Elgar Publishing.

Aldrich, H.E., A. Kalleberg, P. Marsden and J. Cassell (1989), 'In pursuit of evidence: Five sampling procedures for locating new businesses', *Journal of Business Venturing*, **4** (6), 367–86.

Aldrich, H.E. and M. Ruef (2006), *Organizations Evolving*, 2nd edn, London, UK: SAGE Publications.

Allen, T. (2007), 'A toy store(y)', *Journal of Business Venturing*, **22** (5), 628–36.

Alvarez, S.A. and J.B. Barney (2002), 'Resource-based theory and the entrepreneurial firm', in M.A. Hitt, R.D. Ireland, M.S. Camp and D. Sexton (eds), *Strategic Entrepreneurship: Creating a New Mindset*, Oxford, UK: Wiley-Blackwell, pp. 89–105.

Alvarez, S.A. and J.B. Barney (2007), 'Discovery and creation: Alternative theories of entrepreneurial action', *Strategic Entrepreneurship Journal*, **1** (1–2), 11–26.

Alvarez, S.A. and L.W. Busenitz (2001), 'The entrepreneurship of resource-based theory', *Journal of Management*, **27** (6), 755–75.

Apple, M. (1989), 'Peace', *Harpers Magazine*, **278** (February), 56–61.

Arend, R.J. (2014), 'Promises, premises … An alternative view on the effects of the Shane and Venkataraman 2000 AMR Note', *Journal of Management Inquiry*, **23** (1), 38–50.

Baker, T. and R.E. Nelson (2005), 'Creating something from nothing: Resource construction through entrepreneurial bricolage', *Administrative Science Quarterly*, **50** (3), 329–66.

Baum, L.F. (1900), *The Wizard of Oz*, Chicago, IL, USA: George M. Hill Company.

Bird, B.J. (1988), 'Implementing entrepreneurial ideas: The case for intention', *Academy of Management Review*, **13** (3), 442–53.

Bird, B.J. (1989), *Entrepreneurial Behavior*, Glenview, IL, USA: Scott, Foresman.

Bloom, H. (1991), 'The art of criticism: Interview by Antonio Weiss', *Paris Review*, **33** (Spring), 178–232.

Bruner, J. (1986), *Actual Minds, Possible Worlds*, Cambridge, MA, USA: Harvard University Press.

Busenitz, L.W., G.P. West III, D. Shepherd, T. Nelson, G.N. Chandler and Z. Zacharakis (2003), 'Entrepreneurship research in emergence: Past trends and future directions', *Journal of Management*, **29** (3), 285–308.

Campbell, D.T. (1965), 'Variation and selective retention in socio-cultural evolution', in H.R. Barringer, G.I. Blansten and R. Mack (eds), *Social Change in Developing Areas*, Cambridge, MA, USA: Schenkman, pp. 19–49.

Campbell, D.T. (1974), 'Evolutionary epistemology', in P.A. Schilpp (ed.), *The Philosophy of Karl R. Popper* (Vol. 14, Part I), LaSalle, IL, USA: Open Court, pp. 413–63.

Caplan, R. (1976), *Connections: The Work of Charles and Ray Eames*, Los Angeles, CA, USA: Frederick S. Wright Art Gallery, University of California.

Carter, N.M., W.B. Gartner and K.G. Shaver (2004), 'Career reasons', in W.B. Gartner, K.G. Shaver, N.M. Carter and P.D. Reynolds (eds), *Handbook of Entrepreneurial Dynamics: The Process of Business Creation*, Thousand Oaks, CA, USA: SAGE Publications, pp. 142–52.

Carver, R. (1989), *A New Path to the Waterfall*, New York, USA: Atlantic Monthly Press.

Collins, O.F. and D.G. Moore (1964), *The Enterprising Man*, East Lansing, MI, USA: Michigan State University Press.

Cornelissen, J.P. (2013), 'Portrait of an entrepreneur: Vincent van Gogh, Steve Jobs, and the entrepreneurial imagination', *Academy of Management Review*, **38** (4), 700–709.

Daft, R.L. and K.E. Weick (1984), 'Toward a model of organizations as interpretation systems', *Academy of Management Review*, **9** (2), 284–95.

Davis, M.S. (1971), 'That's interesting', *Philosophy of the Social Sciences*, **1** (2), 309–44.

Dickens, C. (2004), *David Copperfield*, London, UK: Penguin.

Dimov, D. (2007a), 'From opportunity insight to opportunity intention: The importance of person–situation learning match', *Entrepreneurship Theory and Practice*, **31** (4), 561–83.

Dimov, D. (2007b), 'Beyond the single-person, single-insight attribution in understanding entrepreneurial opportunities', *Entrepreneurship Theory and Practice*, **31** (5), 713–31.

Dimov, D. (2011), 'Grappling with the unbearable elusiveness of entrepreneurial opportunities', *Entrepreneurship Theory and Practice*, **35** (1), 57–81.

Dutton, J.E. and S.E. Jackson (1987), 'Categorizing strategic issues: Links to organizational action', *Academy of Management Review*, **12** (1), 76–90.

Eames, C. and R. Eames (1968/1977), *Powers of Ten* (Film), New York, USA: IBM.

Eames, C. and R. Eames (1969), *Tops* (Film), Venice, CA, USA: Office of Charles and Ray Eames.

Eliot, T.S. (1943), *Four Quartets*, New York, USA: Harcourt Brace & Company.

Fincher, D. (2010), *The Social Network* (Film), Los Angeles, USA: Columbia Pictures.

Fletcher, D.E. (2006), 'Entrepreneurial processes and the social construction of opportunity', *Entrepreneurship and Regional Development*, **18**, 421–40.

Fletcher, D.E. (2007), 'Toy story: The narrative world of entrepreneurship and the creation of interpretive communities', *Journal of Business Venturing*, **22**, 649–72.

Friedel, R. (2001), 'Serendipity is no accident', *Kenyon Review*, **23** (2), 36–47.

Gartner, W.B. (1982), An empirical model of the business startup, and eight entrepreneurial archetypes. Unpublished doctoral dissertation. Seattle, WA, USA: University of Washington.

Gartner, W.B. (1984), 'Problems in business startup: The relationships among entrepreneurial skills and problem identification for different types of new ventures', in J.A. Hornaday, F. Tarpley, Jr., J.A. Timmons and K.H. Vesper (eds), *Frontiers of Entrepreneurship Research*, Wellesley, MA, USA: Babson College, pp. 496–512.

Gartner, William B. (1985), The loss of intentionality: The failure of the Work Activity School to explain why managers behave as they do. Paper presented at the Academy of Management National Meeting (August), San Diego, CA, USA.

Gartner, W.B. (1986), Entrepreneurial work. Paper presented at the Multidisciplinary Perspectives on Entrepreneurship Conference (April), Montreal, Canada.

Gartner, W.B. (1987), 'A pilgrim's progress', *New Management*, **4** (4), 4–7.

Gartner, W.B. (1988), Finding intention in activity: A new approach for entrepreneurial research. Paper presented at the Academy of Management National Meeting (August), Anaheim, CA, USA.

Gartner, W.B. (1989), 'Some suggestions for research on entrepreneurial traits and characteristics', *Entrepreneurship Theory and Practice*, **14** (1), 27–38.

Gartner, W.B. (1990), 'To live: The obligation of individuality. A review of the film *Ikiru*, directed by Akira Kurosawa', *Organizational Behavior Teaching Review*, **14** (2), 138–43.

Gartner, W.B. (1993), 'Can't see the trees for the forest. A review of the film *The Man Who Planted Trees*, directed by Frederick Back', *Journal of Management Education*, **17** (2), 269–74.

Gartner, W.B. (2001), 'Is there an elephant in entrepreneurship? Blind assumptions in theory development',

Entrepreneurship Theory and Practice, **25** (4), 27–39.

Gartner, W.B. (2004a), 'The edge defines the (w)hole: Saying what entrepreneurship is (not)', in C. Steyaert and D. Hjorth (eds), *Narrative and Discursive Approaches in Entrepreneurship*, Cheltenham, UK and Northampton, MA, USA: Edward Elgar Publishing, pp. 245–54.

Gartner, W.B. (2004b), 'Achieving "Critical Mess" in entrepreneurship scholarship', in J.A. Katz and D. Shepherd (eds), *Advances in Entrepreneurship, Firm Emergence, and Growth* (Vol. 7), Greenwich, CT, USA: JAI Press, pp. 199–216.

Gartner, W.B. (2006), 'Entrepreneurship, psychology and the "Critical Mess"', in J.R. Baum, M. Frese and R.A. Baron (eds), *The Psychology of Entrepreneurship*, Mahwah, NJ, USA: Lawrence Erlbaum Associates Inc., pp. 325–34.

Gartner, W.B. (2008a), 'Entrepreneurship – Hop', *Entrepreneurship Theory and Practice*, **32** (2), 361–8.

Gartner, W.B. (2008b), 'Variations in entrepreneurship', *Small Business Economics*, **31**, 351–61.

Gartner, W.B. (2009), 'Thirteen ways of looking at entrepreneurship', in D. Hjorth and C. Steyaert (eds), *The Politics and Aesthetics of Entrepreneurship*, Cheltenham, UK and Northampton, MA, USA: Edward Elgar Publishing, pp. 10, 30, 54, 71, 91, 112, 128, 147, 161, 179, 201, 220 and 229.

Gartner, W.B. (2012), 'Entrepreneurship as organization creation', in D. Hjorth (ed.), *Handbook of Organizational Entrepreneurship*, Cheltenham, UK and Northampton, MA, USA: Edward Elgar Publishing, pp. 21–30.

Gartner, W.B. (2013), 'Creating a community of difference in entrepreneurship scholarship', *Entrepreneurship and Regional Development*, **25** (1–2), 5–15.

Gartner, W.B. (2014a), 'Notes towards a theory of entrepreneurial possibility', in E. Chell and M. Karatas-Ozkan (eds), *Handbook of Research in Small Business and Entrepreneurship*, Cheltenham, UK and Northampton, MA, USA: Edward Elgar Publishing, pp. 25–37.

Gartner, W.B. (2014b), 'Organizing entrepreneurship research', in A. Fayolle (ed.), *Handbook of Research in Entrepreneurship*, Cheltenham, UK and Northampton, MA, USA: Edward Elgar Publishing, pp. 13–22.

Gartner, W.B. and M.B. Bellamy (2009), *Enterprise*, Cincinnati, OH, USA: Cengage/South-Western Publishing.

Gartner, W.B. and S. Birley (2002), 'Introduction to the special issue on qualitative methods in entrepreneurship research', *Journal of Business Venturing*, **17** (5), 387–95.

Gartner, W.B., N.M. Carter and P.D. Reynolds (2004), 'Business startup activities', in W.B. Gartner, K.G. Shaver, N.M. Carter and P.D. Reynolds (eds), *Handbook of Entrepreneurial Dynamics: The Process of Business Creation*, Thousand Oaks, CA, USA: SAGE Publications, pp. 285–98.

Gartner, W.B. and J. Liao (2005), Making sense and cents making in pre-venture business planning: Evidence from the Panel Study of Entrepreneurial Dynamics. Paper presented at the Babson College Kauffman Foundation Entrepreneurship Research Conference (June), Wellesley, MA, USA.

Gartner, W.B. and J. Liao (2007), 'Pre-venture planning', in C. Moutray (ed.), *The Small Business Economy for Data Year 2006: Report to the President*, Washington, DC, USA: US Small Business Administration Office of Advocacy, pp. 212–64.

Gartner, W.B., K.G. Shaver, N.M. Carter and P.D. Reynolds (2004), *Handbook of Entrepreneurial Dynamics: The Process of Business Creation*, Thousand Oaks, CA, USA: SAGE Publications.

Gartner, W.B., K.G. Shaver and E.J. Gatewood (2000), 'Doing it for yourself: Career attributions of nascent entrepreneurs', in P.D. Reynolds, E. Autio, C.G. Brush, W.D. Bygrave, S. Manigart, H.J. Sapienza and K.G. Shaver (eds), *Frontiers of Entrepreneurship Research 2000*, Wellesley, MA, USA: Babson College, pp. 13–24.

Gartner, W.B. and J.A. Starr (1993), 'The nature of entrepreneurial work', in S. Birley and I.C. MacMillan (eds), *Entrepreneurship Research: Global Perspectives*, Amsterdam: North-Holland, pp. 35–67.

Gartner, W.B. and R.J. Thomas (1993), 'Factors affecting new product forecasting accuracy in new firms', *Journal of Product Innovation Management*, **10** (1), 35–52.

Gendron, G. (1999), 'The seven habits of highly effective start-ups', *Inc. Magazine*, **23** (3), 11.

Giono, J. (1985), *The Man Who Planted Trees*, Chelsea, VT, USA: Chelsea Green.

Hart, D.K. and W.G. Scott (1975), 'The organizational imperative', *Administration & Society*, **7** (3), 259–85.

Heath, C. and D. Heath (2007), *Made to Stick: Why Some Ideas Survive and Others Die*, New York, USA: Random House.

Heider, F. (1958), *The Psychology of Interpersonal Relations*, New York, USA: Wiley.

Hillman, J. (1972), *The Myth of Analysis: Three Essays in Archetypal Psychology*, Evanston, IL, USA: Northwestern University Press.

Hillman, J. (1975a), *Loose Ends: Primary Papers in Archetypal Psychology*, Dallas, TX, USA: Spring Publications.

Hillman, J. (1975b), *Re-visioning Psychology*, New York, USA: Harper & Row.

Irwin, R. (1985), *Being and Circumstance: Notes Toward a Conditional Art*, New York, USA: Lapis Press/Pace Gallery.

Jackson, S.E. and J.E. Dutton (1988), 'Discerning threats and opportunities', *Administrative Science Quarterly*, **33**, 370–387.

Katz, J.A. (2003), 'The chronology and intellectual trajectory of American entrepreneurship education: 1876–1999', *Journal of Business Venturing*, **18** (2), 283–300.

Kelley, H.H. (1973), 'The processes of causal attribution', *American Psychologist*, **28**, 107–28.

Knight, F.H. (1921), *Risk, Uncertainty and Profit*, Boston, MA, USA: Houghton Mifflin.

Kundera, M. (1984), *The Unbearable Lightness of Being*, New York, USA: Harper & Row.

LeRoy, M. (Producer) and V. Fleming (Director) (1939), *The Wizard of Oz* (Film), USA: Metro-Goldwyn-Mayer (MGM).

Liao, J. and W.B. Gartner (2008), Are planners doers? Pre-venture planning and the startup behaviors of entrepreneurs in the PSED. Paper presented at the Babson Entrepreneurship Research Conference (June), Chapel Hill, NC, USA.

Markman, G.D. and W.B. Gartner (2002), 'Is extraordinary growth profitable? A study of *Inc. 500* fast growth companies, *Entrepreneurship Theory and Practice*, **27** (1), 65–75.

McKelvey, B. (1978), 'Organizational systematics: Taxonomic lessons from biology', *Management Science*, **24** (13), 1428–40.

McKelvey, B. (1982), *Organizational Systematics: Taxonomy, Evolution, Classification*, Oakland, CA, USA: University of California Press.

Mezrich, B. (2009), *The Accidental Billionaires*, New York, USA: DoubleDay.

Miller, D. (1987), 'The genesis of configuration', *Academy of Management Review*, **12** (4), 686–701.

Miller, D. and P.H. Friesen (1978), 'Archetypes of strategy formulation', *Management Science*, **24** (9), 921–33.

Miller, D., P.H. Friesen and H. Mintzberg (1984), *Organizations: A Quantum View*, Englewood Cliffs, NJ, USA: Prentice-Hall.

Mintzberg, H. (1973), *The Nature of Managerial Work*, New York, USA: Harper & Row.

Reader, D. and D. Watkins (2006), 'The social and collaborative nature of entrepreneurship scholarship: A co-citation and perceptual analysis', *Entrepreneurship Theory and Practice*, **30** (3), 417–41.

Reynolds, P. (2007), 'New firm creation in the United States: A PSED I overview', *Foundations and Trends in Entrepreneurship*, **3** (1), 1–150.

Reynolds, P. and R. Curtin (2008), 'Business creation in the United States: Panel study of entrepreneurial dynamics. II initial assessment', *Foundations and Trends in Entrepreneurship*, **4** (3), 155–307.

Reynolds, P.D. (2000), 'National study of U.S. business start-ups: Background and methodology', in J.A. Katz (ed.), *Advances In Entrepreneurship, Firm Emergence and Growth* (Vol. 4), Stamford, CT, USA: JAI Press, pp. 153–228.

Sarasvathy, S.D. (2001), 'Causation and effectuation: Toward a theoretical shift from economic inevitability to entrepreneurial contingency', *Academy of Management Review*, **26** (2), 243–63.

Sarasvathy, S.D. (2008), *Effectuation*, Cheltenham, UK and Northampton, MA, USA: Edward Elgar Publishing.

Schendel, D. and M.A. Hitt (2007), 'Comments from the editors: Introduction to Value 1', *Strategic Entrepreneurship Journal*, **1** (1–2), 1–6.

Schumpeter, J.A. (1934), *The Theory of Economic Development: An Inquiry into Profits, Capital, Credit, Interest, and the Business Cycle* (Vol. 55), New York, USA: Transaction Publishers.

Scott, W.G. and D.K. Hart (1989), *Organizational Values in America*, New York, USA: Transaction Books.

Shane, S. (2000), 'Prior knowledge and the discovery of entrepreneurial opportunities', *Organization Science*, **11** (4), 448–69.

Shane, S. and S. Venkataraman (2000), 'The promise of entrepreneurship as a field of research', *Academy of Management Review*, **25** (1), 217–26.

Shaver, K.G., W.B. Gartner, E. Crosby, K. Bakalarova and E.J. Gatewood (2001), 'Attributions about entrepreneurship: A framework and process for analyzing reasons for starting a business', *Entrepreneurship Theory and Practice*, **26** (2), 5–32.

Shaver, K.G. and L.R. Scott (1991), 'Person, process, choice: The psychology of new venture creation', *Entrepreneurship Theory and Practice*, **16** (2), 23–45.

Shepherd, D.A. (2003), 'Learning from business failure: Propositions of grief recovery for the self-employed', *Academy of Management Review*, **28** (2), 318–28.

Singer, M. (2001), 'The book eater', *The New Yorker*, **LXXVI** (5 February), 62–71.

Stevens, W. (1954/1990), *The Collected Poems of Wallace Stevens*, New York, USA: Vintage.

Steyaert, C. (2007), '"Entrepreneuring" as a conceptual attractor? A review of process theories in 20 years of entrepreneurship studies', *Entrepreneurship and Regional Development*, **19** (6), 453–77.

Steyaert, C. and D. Hjorth (2002), '"Thou Art a Scholar, Speak to it ..." – on spaces of speech: A script', *Human Relations*, **55** (7), 767–97.

Vaihinger, H. (1924), *The Philosophy of 'As If'*, Translated by C.K. Ogden, New York, USA: Harcourt Brace.

Van de Ven, A.H., R. Hudson and D.M. Schroeder (1984), 'Designing new business startups: Entrepreneurial, organizational, and ecological considerations', *Journal of Management*, **10** (1), 87–108.

Vesper, K.H. (1980), *New Venture Strategies*, Englewood Cliffs, NJ, USA: Prentice-Hall.

Wagoner, D. (1976), *Collected Poems 1956–1976*, Bloomington, IN, USA: Indiana University Press.

Weick, K.E. (1976), 'Educational organizations as loosely coupled systems', *Administrative Science Quarterly*, **21** (1), 1–19.

Weick, K.E. (1979), *The Social Psychology of Organizing*, New York, USA: McGraw-Hill.

Weick, K.E. (1984), 'Small wins: Redefining the scale of social problems', *American Psychologist*, **39** (1), 40–49.
Weick, K.E. (2011), 'Reflections: Change agents as change poets – on reconnecting flux and hunches', *Journal of Change Management*, **11** (1), 7–20.
Weiner, B. (1985), 'An attributional theory of achievement motivation and emotion', *Psychological Review*, **92**, 548–73.

Academy of Management Review, 1985, Vol. 10, No. 4, 696-706.

A Conceptual Framework for Describing the Phenomenon of New Venture Creation

WILLIAM B. GARTNER
Georgetown University

A review of the entrepreneurship literature suggests that differences among entrepreneurs and among their ventures are as great as the variation between entrepreneurs and nonentrepreneurs and between new firms and established firms. A framework for describing new venture creation integrates four major perspectives in entrepreneurship: characteristics of the individual(s) who start the venture, the organization which they create, the environment surrounding the new venture, and the process by which the new venture is started.

The major thrust of most entrepreneurship research has been to prove that entrepreneurs are different from nonentrepreneurs (Brockhaus, 1980a, 1980b; Carland, Hoy, Boulton, & Carland, 1984; Collins & Moore, 1964; DeCarlo & Lyons, 1979; Hornaday & Aboud, 1971; Howell, 1972; Komives, 1972; Litzinger, 1965; McClelland, 1961; McClelland & Winter, 1969; Palmer, 1971; Schrier, 1975; Shapero, 1975) and that entrepreneurial firms are different from nonentrepreneurial firms (Collins & Moore, 1970; Cooper, 1979; Smith, 1967; Thorne & Ball, 1981). The basic assumption underlying this research is that all entrepreneurs and their new ventures are much the same. The present paper suggests that the differences among entrepreneurs and among their ventures are much greater than one might expect; in fact, the diversity may be larger than the differences between entrepreneurs and nonentrepreneurs and between entrepreneurial firms and nonentrepreneurial firms. Once the diversity among entrepreneurs and their ventures is recognized, the necessity for finding a way to classify them becomes apparent. Groups sharing

similar characteristics must exist within the universe of entrepreneurs and their ventures. How are these groups revealed? Many different characteristics have been employed in past research to describe entrepreneurs and their ventures. Do the characteristics themselves fall into groups? In other words, does one subset of characteristics describe a single aspect of new venture creation, such as the environment surrounding the new venture, or the features of the organization that results?

This paper attempts to organize the many variables that have been used in past research to describe entrepreneurs and their ventures into a comprehensive framework. Far from being reductive, this new view of the entrepreneurship literature should provide valuable insights into the process of new venture creation by showing it to be a complex and multidimensional phenomenon. Once a clear retrospective analysis of the literature is provided, future research can proceed on more solid footing. Instead of many different researchers palpating different parts of the elephant and reaching reductive conclusions, at least all will know the name, if not the nature, of the beast with which they are dealing.

Much past research has been unidimensional, focusing on a single aspect of new venture creation, and its main purpose has been to show how entrepreneurs or their firms differ from nonentrepreneurs or nonentrepreneurial firms. (In fact, it might be said that unidimensional research goes

The research leading to this paper was supported in part by a grant from the National Science Foundation and is based on the author's doctoral dissertation. Additional support was provided by the Center for Entrepreneurial Studies, University of Virginia.

Requests for reprints should be sent to William B. Gartner, Center for Entrepreneurship Studies, School of Business Administration, Georgetown University, Washington, D.C. 20057.

hand in hand with the attitude that all entrepreneurs and their firms are alike, the task of the unidimensional research being to prove how all things entrepreneurial differ from all things nonentrepreneurial.) It has been consistently pointed out, however, in reviews of literature on entrepreneurs, for example, (Brockhaus, 1982; Glueck & Mescon, 1980; McCain & Smith, 1981) that variables that are assumed to differentiate entrepreneurs from nonentrepreneurs (managers, for instance) frequently do not bear up under close scrutiny. Yet the search for these elusive variables continues, and entrepreneurs and prospective entrepreneurs are subjected to batteries of psychological tests in attempts to isolate the single spring that makes them tick differently from others. As with other aspects of new venture creation, attempts are made to isolate key variables that separate entrepreneurial situations from nonentrepreneurial ones. Pennings (1980, 1982a, 1982b) has explored environments that support new venture creation; Van de Ven (1980) and Kimberly (1979) have focused on the process of venture creation.

This search for key variables is a motivation for research only if the task of entrepreneurial research is taken to be the distinction of entrepreneurs and things entrepreneurial from nonentrepreneurs and nonentrepreneurial situations. If a much different perspective is taken, the perspective that there are many different kinds of entrepreneur and many ways to be one and that the firms they create vary enormously as do the environments they create them in, then the burden shifts. How is each new venture creation different from another? Researchers need to think in terms of a combination of variables that make up each new venture creation (Van de Ven, Hudson, & Schroeder, 1984). The creation of a new venture is a multidimensional phenomenon; each variable describes only a single dimension of the phenomenon and cannot be taken alone. There is a growing awareness that the process of starting a business is not a single well-worn route marched along again and again by identical entrepreneurs (Hartman, 1983). New venture creation is a complex phenomenon: entrepreneurs and their firms vary widely; the actions they take or do not take and the environments they operate in and respond to are equally diverse — and all these

elements form complex and unique combinations in the creation of each new venture. It is not enough for researchers to seek out and focus on some concept of the "average" entrepreneur and the "typical" venture creation. New organizational forms evolve through variation, and this variation in new venture creation needs to be studied (Aldrich, 1979; Hannan & Freeman, 1977; Pfeffer & Salancik, 1978; Weick, 1979). This insistence on variation can be seen, for example, in Vesper (1979), who posits 11 different kinds of entrepreneur, and in a recent study by Cooper and Dunkelberg (1981), which reveals that entrepreneurs in certain industries can be very different from those in other industries.

Once the variation and complexity in new venture creation is recognized, it then is necessary to find a framework for systematically discovering and evaluating the similarities and differences among new ventures (McKelvey, 1982). Once it is no longer assumed that all entrepreneurs and their ventures present a homogeneous population, then other homogeneous subsets within the entrepreneurial universe must be sought out in order that entrepreneurial research can produce meaningful results. A primary value of the framework for describing new venture creation presented here is that it provides a systematic means of comparing and contrasting complex ventures; it provides a way to conceptualize variation and complexity.

A Framework for Describing New Venture Creation

Definitions of key words such as entrepreneur are often various and always a problem in the study of entrepreneurship (Brockhaus, 1980b; Komives, 1969; Long, 1983). Because the entrepreneur is only one dimension of this framework, it seems more important in this paper to define the term "new venture creation." Such a definition can be outlined here with less trepidation, if only because there is less precedent.

New venture creation is the organizing (in the Weickian sense) *of new organizations.* "To organize is to assemble ongoing interdependent actions into sensible sequences that generate sensible outcomes" (Weick, 1979, p. 3). The definition of new venture creation is synonymous with the definition of the new organization developed by the Strategic Planning Institute (1978, p. 1-2):

a new business venture launched as one of the following:

1. an independent entity
2. a new profit center within a company which has other established businesses, or
3. a joint venture which satisfies the following criteria:

   1. Its founders must acquire expertise in products, process, market and/or technology.
   2. Results are expected beyond the year in which the investment is made.
   3. It is considered a new market entrant by its competitors.
   4. It is regarded as a new source of supply by its potential customers.

The importance of this definition should not be overlooked, because it recognizes the multidimensional aspects of new venture creation. First, it emphasizes that individuals with expertise are a key element of the new venture. At the same time that it recognizes the new venture as an organizational entity, it stresses that the new venture is not instantaneously produced, but evolves over time (beyond a year). The new venture is seen further within the context of its environment: it is forced to seek out resources, and it competes in the market place. All these aspects of the new venture must be kept in mind if it is to be adequately described and classified.

Figure 1 presents a framework for describing the creation of a new venture across four dimensions: (a) individual(s)—the person(s) involved in starting a new organization; (b) organization—the kind of firm that is started; (c) environment—the situation surrounding and influencing the new organization; and (d) new venture process—the actions undertaken by the individual(s) to start the venture.

Any new venture is a gestalt (Miller, 1981) of variables from the four dimensions. No new venture creation can be comprehensively described, nor can its complexity be adequately accounted for, unless all of its four dimensions are investigated and an attempt is made to discover how variables from each dimension interact with variables from other dimensions.

This framework is the first to combine the four dimensions of venture creation, though other researchers have sought to combine two or more of the dimensions. This "thinking across dimensions" is especially apparent in the work of those theorists and researchers who have developed entrepreneurial classification schemes. Classifications of entrepreneurs themselves are often based on two dimensions: individual characteristics plus new venture process considerations — the word often used is "style." Danhoff (1949) based his scheme on the entrepreneur's openness to innovation; Cole (1959) on the sophistication of the entrepreneur's decision making tools; and Dailey (1971) according to bureaucratic or entrepreneurial style. Smith (1967) divided entrepreneurs by a stylistic orientation — craftsman or opportunistic. Filley and Aldag (1980) used management orientation. Vesper (1979, 1980) in two similar classifications differentiated among entrepreneurs by the activities involved in business formation and operation, and in another scheme (1980) by competitive strategy. In Cooper (1979) entrepreneurs are linked to particular environments, and, as cited previously, Cooper and Dunkelberg's (1981) study matches different entrepreneurs and their characteristics to the types of firms they are likely to start. In Vesper's (1979) classification the entrepreneur's type of firm is also a factor, as it is in several other classification studies (Braden, 1977; Filley & Aldag, 1980; Smith, 1967). Recently, Van de Ven et al.'s (1984) empirical study examined educational software firms on the basis of three dimen-

Figure 1. A framework for describing new venture creation.

698

sions: entrepreneurial—background characteristics and psychological attributes of the founding entrepreneurs; organizational—planning and organizational activities undertaken before and after company startup; and ecological—support and resources made available to influence the development of the industry. These classification schemes and frameworks are ways of stepping back to get an overall picture, a process like model-building, which involves integration and synthesis.

Individual(s)

Whether an entrepreneur is viewed as a "captain of industry," a hard-headed risk bearer (Mill, 1848), risk taker (Palmer, 1971) or a "rapacious risk avoider" (Webster, 1976); whether he merely metamorphoses into an entrepreneur at certain moments and is something else the rest of the time (Danhoff, 1949), or whether his need for achievement (McClelland, 1961) and capacity for innovation (Schumpeter, 1934) are always ticking away; whether he is a "displaced person" (Shapero, 1975), something close to a juvenile delinquent (Gould, 1969), or a "man apart" (Liles, 1974) with an absolutely clear-headed (veridical) perception of reality (Schrage, 1965), an aberrant "artist" with an "innate sense of impending change" (Hill, 1982); or whether he is, indeed, that completely political animal, a community builder (Schell & Davig, 1981), the entrepreneur is overwhelmingly perceived to be different in important ways from the nonentrepreneur, and many researchers have believed these differences to lie in the background and personality of the entrepreneur.

One often pursued avenue has been the attempt to develop a psychological profile of the entrepreneur and to measure such psychological characteristics as need for achievement (DeCarlo & Lyons, 1979; Hornaday & Aboud, 1971; McClelland, 1961; McClelland & Winter, 1969; Schwartz, 1976). However, other researchers have not found need for achievement useful in describing entrepreneurs (Brockhaus, 1980b; Litzinger, 1965; Schrage, 1965); still others have questioned the value and validity of using psychological characteristics of any kind to describe entrepreneurs (Brockhaus, 1982; Glueck & Mescon, 1980; Jenks, 1965; Kilby, 1971; McCain & Smith,

1981; Van de Ven, 1980). However, the following psychological characteristics have been used in many studies and may have some validity in differentiating among types of entrepreneurs (Brockhaus, 1982):

1. Need for achievement
2. Locus of control
3. Risk taking propensity

Some researchers have found it fruitful to look at the entrepreneur's background, experience, and attitudes. Some individual characteristics that may be of value in describing entrepreneurs are:

1. Job satisfaction (Collins & Moore, 1970; Komives, 1972)
2. Previous work experience (Cooper, 1970; Lamont, 1972; Susbauer, 1972)
3. Entrepreneurial parents (Collins & Moore, 1970; Roberts & Wainer, 1968; Schrier, 1975; Secrest, 1975; Shapero, 1972; Susbauer, 1972)
4. Age (Komives, 1972; Liles, 1974; Roberts & Wainer, 1968; Secrest, 1975; Thorne & Ball, 1981)
5. Education (Brockhaus & Nord, 1979; Collins & Moore, 1964; Howell, 1972; Roberts, 1969; Susbauer, 1969)

Process

In 1949 Danhoff wrote, "Entrepreneurship is an activity or function and not a specific individual or occupation . . . the specific personal entrepreneur is an unrealistic abstraction" (p. 21). Other theorists have pursued this idea of function and have tried to differentiate the entrepreneurial function from other more routine functions such as the managerial function (Baumol, 1968; Cole, 1965; Hartmann, 1959; Leibenstein, 1968; Schumpeter, 1934). This "dynamic" aspect of the entrepreneur has been acknowledged in the work of eight researchers who have enumerated certain actions that an entrepreneur performs in order to create a new venture. Except for Peterson and Berger (1971), who described the entrepreneurial activities of record producers, these studies were theoretical, that is, based on general observation rather than systematic research. The similarities in their views are summarized here; six common behaviors are listed (the order does not imply a sequence of actions):

1. The entrepreneur locates a business opportunity (Cole, 1965; Kilby, 1971; Maidique, 1980; Schumpeter, 1934; Vesper, 1980).
2. The entrepreneur accumulates resources (Cole, 1965; Kilby, 1971; Leibenstein, 1968; Peterson & Berger, 1971; Schumpeter, 1934; Vesper, 1980).

3. The entrepreneur markets products and services (Cole, 1965; Kilby, 1971; Leibenstein, 1968; Maidique, 1980; Peterson & Berger, 1971; Schumpeter, 1934; Vesper, 1980).
4. The entrepreneur produces the product (Kilby, 1971; Maidique, 1980; Peterson & Berger, 1971; Schumpeter, 1934; Vesper, 1980).
5. The entrepreneur builds an organization (Cole, 1965; Kilby, 1971; Leibenstein, 1968; Schumpeter, 1934).
6. The entrepreneur responds to government and society (Cole, 1965; Kilby, 1971).

Environment

Much of the current concern (Peters & Waterman, 1982) over how to design organizations that keep and encourage innovative individuals is an indirect acknowledgment that entrepreneurs do not operate in vacuums — they respond to their environments. The existence of highly supportive regional entrepreneurial environments (Cooper, 1970; Draheim, 1972; Pennings, 1982b; Susbauer, 1972) — including "incubator organizations" — can, from one perspective, be said actually to *create* entrepreneurs. The idea of "pushes" and "pulls" from the environment has found its way into many studies of entrepreneurship (Shapero & Sokol, 1982).

In organization theory literature, two different views of the environment have been developed. One perspective, environmental determinism, sees the environment as an outside set of conditions to which the organization must adapt (Aldrich, 1979; Aldrich & Pfeffer, 1976; Hannan & Freeman, 1977). The other perspective, strategic choice, sees the environment as a "reality" that organizations create via the selectivity of their own perceptions (Child, 1972; Starbuck, 1976; Weick, 1979). In the entrepreneurship literature, both perspectives on the environment have been taken. In the present paper those characteristics that are viewed as relatively fixed conditions imposed on the new venture from without are called environmental variables. Variables over which the organization has more control (strategic choice variables) are more readily viewed as characteristics of the organization itself and are treated as such.

In an overview of 17 research papers on environmental variables that influenced new venture creation, Bruno and Tyebjee (1982) found 12 factors that they judged stimulated entrepreneurship:

1. Venture capital availability
2. Presence of experienced entrepreneurs
3. Technically skilled labor force
4. Accessibility of suppliers
5. Accessibility of customers or new markets
6. Governmental influences
7. Proximity of universities
8. Availability of land or facilities
9. Accessiblity of transportation
10. Attitude of the area population
11. Availability of supporting services
12. Living conditions

Another study of environmental influences on new venture creation was Pennings' studies of organization birth frequencies (1980, 1982a, 1982b). Pennings found that organization birth rates were high in areas with: high occupational and industrial differentiation; high percentages of recent immigrants in the population; a large industrial base; larger size urban areas; and availability of financial resources.

Another field of research has taken the deterministic perspective regarding the environment and new ventures: industrial economics. Oliver Williamson (1975) explored the process by which the failure of markets to coordinate efficiently the production and distribution of goods and services often resulted in the start-up of organizations to coordinate the production function through administration. Porter (1980) focused on the competitive environment that confronts firms in a particular industry. Porter's work provides five environmental influences on organizations: barriers to entry, rivalry among existing competitors, pressure from substitute products, bargaining power of buyers, and bargaining power of suppliers.

Organization

Despite a bold early attempt by Stauss (1944) to direct the focus away from the entrepreneur and toward his created organization (by claiming, somewhat tortuously, that the firm is the entrepreneur), most subsequent studies of new venture creation have neglected to comment on or even communicate certain characteristics of the organizations on which they focused. The assumption behind this seems to derive from two other assumptions: (a) if all entrepreneurs are virtually alike and (b) they all go through the same process to create their ventures, then (c) the organizations they create must, like widgets, not be of any interest in themselves.

Many research samples in entrepreneurship studies are selected, for example, without regard to type of firm (i.e., manufacturing, service, retail, wholesale). Of the studies that have indicated the type of firm, Smith (1967), Cooper (1970), Collins and Moore (1970), Susbauer (1972), and Braden (1977) studied manufacturing firms, and most focused on high technology manufacturing firms. Litzinger (1965) studied motel firms, and Mescon and Montanari (1981) studied real estate firms. However, researchers in these studies made no attempts to compare the type of firm studied to other types of firm to determine what difference type of firm might make in the process of new venture creation. Cooper and Dunkelberg (1981), Gartner (1982), and Van de Ven et al. (1984) have begun to link type of firm across other dimensions, such as entrepreneurial background and response to environment.

The presence of partners is another firm characteristic suggested by Timmons, Smollen, and Dingee (1977) as a vital factor in starting certain types of firm, and some research has mentioned partners as a characteristic of the firms studied (Cooper, 1970; DeCarlo & Lyons, 1979).

Strategic choice variables are treated here as characteristics of the organization. Porter (1980) identified three generic competitive strategies that firms may "choose": (a) overall cost leadership, (b) differentiation, and (c) focus. Vesper (1980) identified 14 competitive entry wedges: the new product or service, parallel competition, franchise entry, geographical transfer, supply shortage, tapping unutilized resources, customer contract, becoming a second source, joint ventures, licensing, market relinquishment, sell off of division, favored purchasing by government, and governmental rule changes.

Conclusion

Listing each variable of new venture creation under the appropriate dimension of the framework illustrates the potential for a high degree of complexity in the interaction of these variables within the multidimensional phenomenon of venture creation (Figure 2).

The four dimensional conceptual framework can be seen as a kaleidoscope, as an instrument through which to view the enormously varying patterns of new venture creation. Past attempts to differentiate the typical entrepreneur and his/her typical creation from all nonentrepreneurs and all nonnew ventures have, whether intentionally or not, advanced the notion that all entrepreneurs are alike and all new venture creation is the same. However, there clearly is a wide variation in the kinds of new ventures that are started. For example, are there similarities between the creation of a waterbed store by a 20-year old college student and the creation of a personal computer company by three engineers? Are the differences between them more important than the similarities? What is the value of comparing the creation of a pet store by two unemployed physical therapists to the creation of a 5,000-acre business park by four real estate developers? The goal is not to smooth over any differences that might exist among these new ventures or to throw these very different individuals into the same pot in order to extract the typical qualities of the typical entrepreneur. The goal is to identify the specific variables that describe how each new venture was created, in order that meaningful contrasts and comparisons among new ventures can be made.

First must come careful description with an eye to variation. The search for key variables, for general principles, for universally applicable laws of entrepreneurship that has characterized much of the entrepreneurship literature betrays an impatience with the slow methodical process of description. Attention to careful observation and description is the basis of good scientific research (McKelvey, 1982). In what does all this careful description of new ventures result? A collection of uniquely described ventures, each different from all the others? Once good description is achieved, then good comparisons and contrasts can be made, and subsets of similar ventures can be established. These homogeneous populations are needed before any general rules or theories of new venture creation can be postulated. The lack of such homogeneous samples in the past has led to conflicts in the results of research studies.

The conceptual framework presented here provides a way of analyzing past research studies. Each study can be broken down into the types of individuals, organizations, environments, and processes that were investigated. One way in which the framework can be useful is in identify-

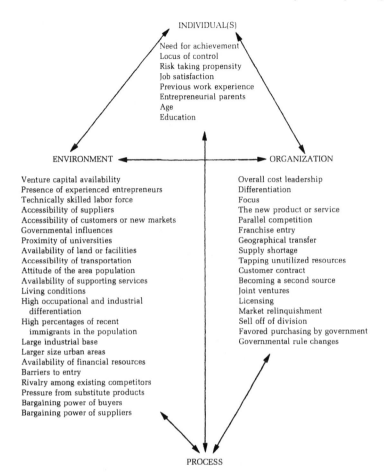

INDIVIDUAL(S)

Need for achievement
Locus of control
Risk taking propensity
Job satisfaction
Previous work experience
Entrepreneurial parents
Age
Education

ENVIRONMENT

Venture capital availability
Presence of experienced entrepreneurs
Technically skilled labor force
Accessibility of suppliers
Accessibility of customers or new markets
Governmental influences
Proximity of universities
Availability of land or facilities
Accessibility of transportation
Attitude of the area population
Availability of supporting services
Living conditions
High occupational and industrial
  differentiation
High percentages of recent
  immigrants in the population
Large industrial base
Larger size urban areas
Availability of financial resources
Barriers to entry
Rivalry among existing competitors
Pressure from substitute products
Bargaining power of buyers
Bargaining power of suppliers

ORGANIZATION

Overall cost leadership
Differentiation
Focus
The new product or service
Parallel competition
Franchise entry
Geographical transfer
Supply shortage
Tapping unutilized resources
Customer contract
Becoming a second source
Joint ventures
Licensing
Market relinquishment
Sell off of division
Favored purchasing by government
Governmental rule changes

PROCESS

The entrepreneur locates a business opportunity
The entrepreneur accumulates resources
The entrepreneur markets products and services
The entrepreneur produces the product
The entrepreneur builds an organization
The entrepreneur responds to government and society

Figure 2. Variables in new venture creation.

702

ing those aspects of new venture creation neglected by a particular study. New research may
then be designed to account for these lacunae.
For example, Brockhaus defines his sample of
entrepreneurs as:

> Individuals who within three months prior to the
> study had ceased working for their employers and
> at the time of the study owned as well as managed
> business ventures. . . . The businesses whose own-
> ers served as participants were selected from the
> listing of businesses licensed by St. Louis County,
> Missouri during the months of August and Sep-
> tember, 1975 (1980a, p. 39).

Although Brockhaus, unlike other researchers,
attempts to close in on the actual entrepreneurial
function by interviewing his entrepreneurs
within a few months of the creation of their
ventures, useful and necessary distinctions
among the individuals and their new ventures
are not made. One is not sure what types of firms
were studied (retail, service, manufacturing, etc.)
or whether the St. Louis environment was likely
to influence certain types of individuals to create
certain types of firms. Is the process of starting a
venture in St. Louis different, or is the process
different for certain types of businesses or certain kinds of individuals? Accounting for type of
firm, environment, and process in this study
would enhance comparison among the individuals in the study and individuals in other studies.

In analyzing results of research studies, a focus
on differences in one of the four dimensions
might explain conflicting results. For example,
studies such as Collins and Moore (1970) suggest
that individuals who start firms are social misfits
who do not fit into most organizations. Yet other
studies such as Cooper (1970) suggest that individuals who start successful firms are good team
players. On closer examination it is seen that
Collins and Moore studied manufacturing firms
that were more like job shops in the 1950s, and
Cooper studied high technology firms in the
1960s. High technology industries might require
more skills than one individual would be likely
to have, necessitating that individuals combine
their abilities in teams in order to start an organization successfully.

In addition to providing a means by which past
research can be analyzed, the framework outlines
a format for future research methodologies and
for reporting such research. More careful atten-

tion must be paid to the research sample. For
example, women entrepreneurs are a popular
research topic. If similarities are discovered
among women who start firms, are these similarities a result of similar environments? Can differences be attributed solely to psychological or
background characteristics? What is the value of
research results that are based on such unex-
amined and possibly heterogeneous sample populations?

Even in a narrowly selected research sample,
the framework might be useful in drawing the
researcher's attention to considerations inherent
in each of the four dimensions, in order that conclusions regarding the virtual sameness of all the
members of the sample may not be made too
hastily. For example, in a sample of new organizations in the micro-computer industry, a number of considerations might be made. What is the
variation among the entrepreneurs in their work
backgrounds, education, age? How do competitive strategies used by these new organizations
vary? Are there regional or other subenvironments
in the industry that cause variations in firms and
strategies? What is the variation in the venture
creation process: do all individuals devote equal
time to financing the organization, hiring personnel, marketing? What differences exist between "new" and "old" firms in this industry?

The brief review of the literature provided earlier is only a running start at a comprehensive
analysis and evaluation of the entrepreneurship
literature. For example, in a study of individuals
who start firms, who are the individuals? Are the
individuals in McClelland's samples (McCelland,
1961; McCelland & Winter, 1969) similar to those
in Brockhaus (1980a) or Schrage (1965)? More
about the similarities and differences within and
among past research samples needs to be known.
There are many dimensions and variables across
which these samples may be compared.

The framework also points up the importance
of interactions of variables among dimensions in
understanding new venture creation. How does
an individual's background influence the type of
activities undertaken to start an organization?
Does the marketing individual devote his time to
marketing instead of manufacturing, and are there
some environments or firms that require more
marketing? Is the process of starting a retail store

similar to that of starting a steel mill? Are entry strategies used by new organizations in the robotics industry similar to those used in the brewery industry?

The framework for describing new venture creation provides the possibility of describing subsets within the unwieldy set of all entrepreneurs and all new ventures. Newly created ventures that display meaningful similarities across the four dimensions could be described and classified together (Gartner, 1982). Significant generalizations regarding some or all new venture creations might emerge, generalizations that do not, however, attempt to mask the variation in new venture creation.

This paper does not purport to answer specific

questions about how new ventures are started or provide specific developmental models for new venture creation. No claim is made that the framework or the list of variables is comprehensive; the claim is only that the description of new ventures needs to be more comprehensive than it is at present. A great many more questions are asked here than are answered. However, the paper provides a means of making a fundamental shift in the perspective on entrepreneurship: away from viewing entrepreneurs and their ventures as an unvarying, homogeneous population, and towards a recognition and appreciation of the complexity and variation that abounds in the phenomenon of new venture creation.

References

Aldrich, H. E. (1979) *Organizations and environments*. Englewood Cliffs, NJ: Prentice-Hall.

Aldrich, H. E., & Pfeffer, J. (1976) Environments of organizations. *Annual Review of Sociology*, 76-105.

Baumol, W. J. (1968) Entrepreneurship in economic theory. *American Economic Review*, 58(2), 64-71.

Braden, P. (1977) *Technological entrepreneurship* (Michigan Business Reports, No. 62). Ann Arbor: University of Michigan.

Brockhaus, R. H. (1980a) The effect of job dissatisfaction on the decision to start a business. *Journal of Small Business Management*, 18(1), 37-43.

Brockhaus, R. H. (1980b) Risk taking propensity of entrepreneurs. *Academy of Management Journal*, 23, 509-520.

Brockhaus, R. H. (1982) The psychology of the entrepreneur. In C. A. Kent, D. L. Sexton, & K. H. Vesper (Eds.), *Encyclopedia of entrepreneurship* (pp. 39-56). Englewood Cliffs NJ: Prentice-Hall.

Brockhaus, R. H., & Nord, W. R. (1979) An exploration of factors affecting the entrepreneurial decision: Personal characteristics vs. environmental conditions. *Proceedings of the National Academy of Management*, 364-368.

Bruno, A. V., & Tyebjee, T. T. (1982) The environment for entrepreneurship. In C. A. Kent, D. L. Sexton, & K. H. Vesper (Eds.), *Encylopedia of entrepreneurship* (pp. 288-307). Englewood Cliffs, NJ: Prentice-Hall.

Carland, J. W., Hoy, F., Boulton, W. R., & Carland, J.A.C. (1984) Differentiating entrepreneurs from small business owners: A conceptualization. *Academy of Management Review*, 9, 354-359.

Child, J. (1972) Organizational structure, environment and performance: The role of strategic choice. *Sociology*, 6, 1-22.

Cole, A. H. (1959) *Business enterprise in its social setting*. Cambridge, MA: Harvard University Press.

Cole, A. H. (1965) An approach to the study of entrepreneurship: A tribute to Edwin F. Gay. In H.G.J. Aitken (Ed.), *Explorations in enterprise* (pp. 30-44). Cambridge, MA: Harvard University Press.

Collins, O. F., & Moore, D. G. (1964) *The enterprising man*. East Lansing: Michigan State University.

Collins, O. F., & Moore, D. G. (1970) *The organization makers*. New York: Appleton-Century-Crofts.

Cooper, A. C. (1970) The Palo Alto experience. *Industrial Research*, 12(5), 58-61.

Cooper, A. C. (1979) Strategic management: New ventures and small business. In D. E. Schendel & C. W. Hofer (Eds.), *Strategic management* (pp. 316-327). Boston: Little, Brown.

Cooper, A. C., & Dunkelberg, W. C. (1981) A new look at business entry: Experiences of 1,805 entrepreneurs. In K. H. Vesper (Ed.), *Frontiers of entrepreneurship research* (pp. 1-20). Wellesley, MA: Babson College.

Daily, C. A. (1971) *Entrepreneurial management: Going all out for results*. New York: McGraw-Hill.

Danhoff, C. H. (1949) Observations on entrepreneurship in agriculture. In A. H. Cole (Ed.), *Change and the entrepreneur* (pp. 20-24). Cambridge, MA: Harvard University Press.

DeCarlo, J. F., & Lyons, P. R. (1979) A comparison of selected personal characteristics of minority and non-minority female entrepreneurs. *Journal of Small Business Management*, 17(4), 22-29.

Draheim, K. P. (1972) Factors influencing the rate of formation of technical companies. In A. C. Cooper & J. L. Komives (Eds.), *Technical entrepreneurship: A symposium* (pp. 3-27). Milwaukee, WI: Center for Venture Management.

Filley, A. C., & Aldag, R. J. (1980) Organizational growth and types: Lessons from small institutions. In B. Staw & L. Cummings (Eds.), *Research in organizational behavior* (Vol. 2, pp. 279-320). Greenwich, CT: JAI Press.

Gartner, W. B. (1982) *An empirical model of the business startup, and eight entrepreneurial archetypes.* Unpublished doctoral dissertation, University of Washington, Seattle.

Glueck, W., & Mescon, T. (1980) *Entrepreneurship: A literature analysis of concepts.* Paper presented at the annual meeting of the Academy of Management, Detroit, MI.

Gould, L. C. (1969) Juvenile entrepreneurs. *American Journal of Sociology,* 74, 710-719.

Hannan, M. T., & Freeman, J. (1977) The population ecology model of organizations. *American Journal of Sociology,* 82, 929-964.

Hartman, C. (1983) Who's running America's fastest growing companies? *Inc.,* 5(8), 41-47.

Hartmann, H. (1959) Managers and entrepreneurs: A useful distinction? *Administrative Science Quarterly,* 3, 429-457.

Hill, R. (1982) The entrepreneur: An artist masquerading as a businessman? *International Management,* 37(2), 21-22, 26.

Hornaday, J., & Aboud, J. (1971) Characteristics of successful entrepreneurs. *Personnel Psychology,* 24(2), 141-153.

Howell, R. P. (1972) Comparative profiles—Entrepreneurs versus the hired executive: San Francisco Peninsula semiconductor industry. In A. C. Cooper & J. L. Komives (Eds.), *Technical entrepreneurship: A symposium* (pp. 47-62). Milwaukee, WI: Center for Venture Management.

Jenks, L. (1965) Approaches to entrepreneurial personality. In H. G. J. Aitken (Ed.), *Explorations in enterprise* (pp. 80-92). Cambridge, MA: Harvard University Press.

Kilby, P. (1971) Hunting the heffalump. In P. Kilby (Ed.), *Entrepreneurship and economic development* (pp. 1-40). New York: Free Press.

Kimberly, J. R. (1979) Issues in the creation of organizations: Initiation, innovation, and institutionalization. *Academy of Management Journal,* 22, 437-457.

Komives, J. L. (Ed.). (1969) *Karl A. Bostrum seminar in the study of enterprise.* Milwaukee, WI: Center for Venture Management.

Komives, J. L. (1972) A preliminary study of the personal values of high technology entrepreneurs. In A. C. Cooper & J. L. Komives (Eds.), *Technical entrepreneurship: A symposium* (pp. 231-242). Milwaukee, WI: Center for Venture Management.

Lamont, L. M. (1972) The role of marketing in technical entrepreneurship. In A. C. Cooper & J. L. Komives (Eds.), *Technical entrepreneurship: A symposium* (pp. 150-164). Milwaukee, WI: Center for Venture Management.

Leibenstein, H. (1968) Entrepreneurship and development. *American Economic Review,* 58(2), 72-83.

Liles, P. R. (1974) *New business ventures and the entrepreneur.* Homewood, IL: Irwin.

Litzinger, W. D. (1965) The motel entrepreneur and the motel manager. *Academy of Management Journal,* 8, 268-281.

Long, W. (1983) The meaning of entrepreneurship. *American Journal of Small Business,* 8(2), 47-59.

Maidique, M. A. (1980) Entrepreneurs, champions and technological innovation. *Sloan Management Review,* 21(2), 59-76.

McCain G., & Smith, N. (1981, Summer) A contemporary model of entrepreneurial style. *Small Business Institute Review,* 40-45.

McClelland, D. (1961) *The achieving society.* Princeton, NJ: Van Nostrand.

McClelland, D., & Winter, D. G. (1969) *Motivating economic achievement.* New York: Free Press.

McKelvey, B. (1982) *Organizational systematics—Taxonomy, evolution, classification.* Berkeley: University of California Press.

Mescon, T., & Montanari, J. (1981) The personalities of independent and franchise entrepreneurs: An empirical analysis of concepts. *Journal of Enterprise Management,* 3(2), 149-159.

Mill, J. S. (1848) *Principles of political economy with some of their applications to social philosophy.* London: J. W. Parker.

Miller, D. (1981) Toward a new contingency approach: The search for organization gestalts. *Journal of Management Studies,* 18, 1-26.

Palmer, M. (1971) The application of psychological testing to entrepreneurial potential. *California Management Review,* 13(3), 32-39.

Pennings, J. M. (1980) Environmental influences on the creation process. In J. R. Kimberly & R. Miles (Eds.), *The organization life cycle* (pp. 135-160). San Francisco: Jossey Bass.

Pennings, J. M. (1982a) Organizational birth frequencies. *Administrative Science Quarterly,* 27, 120-144.

Pennings, J. M. (1982b) The urban quality of life and entrepreneurship. *Academy of Management Journal,* 25, 63-79.

Peters T. J., & Waterman, R. H. (1982) *In search of excellence.* New York: Harper & Row.

Peterson, R. A., & Berger, D. G. (1971) Entrepreneurship in organizations: Evidence from the popular music industry. *Administrative Science Quarterly,* 16, 97-107.

Pfeffer, J., & Salancik, G. R. (1978) *The external control of organizations.* New York: Harper & Row.

Porter, M. E. (1980) *Competitive strategy: Techniques for analyzing industries and competitors.* New York: Fress Press.

Roberts, E. B. (1969) Entrepreneurship and technology. In W. Gruber & D. Marquis (Eds.), *Factors in the transfer of technology* (pp. 219-237). Cambridge, MA: M.I.T. Press.

Roberts, E. B., & Wainer, H. A. (1968) New enterprise on Rte. 128. *Science Journal,* 4(12), 78-83.

Schell, D. W., & Davig, W. (1981) The community infrastructure of entrepreneurship. In K. H. Vesper (Ed.), *Frontiers of entrepreneurship research* (pp. 563-590). Wellesley. MA: Babson College.

Schrage, H. (1965) The R & D entrepreneur: Profile of success. *Harvard Business Review,* 43(6), 56-69.

Schrier, J. W. (1975) Entrepreneurial characteristics of women. In J. W. Schrier & J. Susbauer (Eds.), *Entrepreneurship and enterprise development: A worldwide perspective* (pp. 66-70). Milwaukee, WI: Center for Venture Management.

Schumpeter, J. A. (1934) *The theory of economic development* (R. Opie, Trans.). Cambridge, MA: Harvard University Press.

Schwartz, E. B. (1976) Entrepreneurship: A new female frontier. *Journal of Contemporary Business.* 5, 47-76.

Secrest, L. (1975) Texas entrepreneurship. In J. W. Schrier & J. Susbauer (Eds.), *Entrepreneurship and enterprise development: A worldwide perspective* (pp. 51-65). Milwaukee, WI: Center for Venture Management.

Shapero, A. (1972) The process of technical company formation in a local area. In A. C. Cooper & J. L. Komives (Eds.), *Technical entrepreneurship: A symposium* (pp. 63-95). Milwaukee, WI: Center for Venture Management.

Shapero, A. (1975) The displaced, uncomfortable entrepreneur. *Psychology Today,* 9(6), 83-88.

Shapero, A., & Sokol, L. (1982) The social dimensions of entrepreneurship. In C. A. Kent, D. L. Sexton, & K. H. Vesper (Eds.), *Encylclopedia of entrepreneurship* (pp. 72-90). Englewood Cliffs, NJ: Prentice-Hall.

Smith, N. (1967) *The entrepreneur and his firm: The relationship between type of man and type of company.* East Lansing: Michigan State University.

Starbuck, W. H. (1976) Organizations and their environments. In M. Dunnette (Ed.), *Handbook of industrial and organizational psychology* (pp. 1069-1123). Chicago: Rand McNally.

Stauss, J. H. (1944) The entrepreneur: The firm. *Journal of Political Economy,* 52(2), 112-127.

Strategic Planning Institute. (1978) *The startup data manual.* Unpublished manuscript. Cambridge, MA: Strategic Planning Institute.

Susbauer, J. C. (1969) *The technical company formation process: A particular aspect of entrepreneurship.* Unpublished doctoral dissertation, University of Texas, Austin.

Susbauer, J. C. (1972) The technical entrepreneurship process in Austin, Texas. In A. C. Cooper & J. L. Komives (Eds.),

Technical entrepreneurship: A symposium (pp. 28-46). Milwaukee, WI: Center for Venture Management.

Thorne, J. R., & Ball, J. G. (1981) Entrepreneurs and their companies: Smaller industrial firms. In K. H. Vesper (Ed.), *Frontiers of entrepreneurship research* (pp. 65-83). Wellesley, MA: Babson College.

Timmons, J. A., Smollen, E, & Dingee, A. L. M. (1977) *New venture creation.* Homewood, IL: Irwin.

Van de Ven, A. H. (1980) Early planning, implementation and performance of new organizations. In J. R. Kimberly & R. Miles (Eds.), *The organization life cycle* (pp. 83-134). San Francisco: Jossey Bass.

Van de Ven, A. H., Hudson, R., & Schroeder, D. M. (1984) Designing new business startups: Entrepreneurial, organizational, and ecological considerations. *Journal of Management,* 10(1), 87-107.

Vesper, K. H. (1979) Commentary. In D. E. Schendel & C. W. Hofer (Eds.), *Strategic management* (pp. 332-338). Boston: Little, Brown.

Vesper, K. H. (1980) *New venture strategies.* Englewood Cliffs, NJ: Prentice-Hall.

Vesper, K. H. (1981) Scanning the frontier of entrepreneurship research. In K. H. Vesper (Ed.), *Frontiers of entrepreneurship research* (pp. vii-xiv). Wellesley, MA: Babson College.

Vesper, K. H. (1982a) Expanding entrepreneurship research. In K. H. Vesper (Ed.), *Frontiers of entrepreneurship research* (pp. vii-xx). Wellesley, MA: Babson College.

Vesper, K. H. (1982b) Introduction and summary of entrepreneurship research. In C. A. Kent, D. L. Sexton, & K. H. Vesper (Eds.), *Encyclopedia of entrepreneurship* (pp. xxxi-xxxviii).

Webster, F. A. (1976) A model for new venture initiation: A disclosure on rapacity and the independent entrepreneur. *Academy of Management Review,* 1(1), 26-37.

Weick, K. E. (1979) *The social psychology of organizing* (2nd ed.). Reading, MA: Addison-Wesley.

Williamson, O. E. (1975) *Markets and hierarchies, analysis and antitrust implications.* New York: Free Press.

William B. Gartner is Assistant Professor of Business and Director of the Center for Entrepreneurship Studies in the School of Business Administration, Georgetown University.

706

[2]

DID RIVER CITY REALLY NEED A BOYS' BAND?

William B. Gartner

orporate intrapreneuring— encouraging entrepreneurs to work within the organization, rather than to strike out on their own with their innovative ideas—has become as faddish as aerobic exercise among executives who are falling all over one another in their zeal to establish skunk works and other kinds of homes for organizational mavericks. But has anyone really examined the consequences of having entrepreneurs among the more conforming crowd? Entrepreneurs do, indeed, bring change wherever they go. The change, however, is neither planned nor controllable; moreover, entrepreneurs are frequently gifted con artists, who know that they won't be able to quite pull off their grand schemes. Anyone who has ever been in the presence of these entrepreneurs knows that it is almost impossible to escape their spell. And, thanks to them, good things *do* happen. But the good things may not be the ones the corporation was looking for.

Executives enamored with the idea that entrepreneurs are the cure for their organizational problems would do well to recall Broadway's *The Music Man*; they might find that the cure could be more serious than the disease! Focusing on Meredith Willson's 1957 musical will not give us a formula or recipe for transforming real-world organizations, but it may provide a perspective that our "real-world" orientation prevents us from seeing.

"Professor" Harold Hill, a traveling salesman, is our entrepreneur, and he embodies all the stereotypes that make one suspicious of the breed. Harold Hill isn't even his real name; he's had to change it because of a brush with the law. He keeps one step ahead of his past, which is shady (he once sold steam automobiles, he confesses, but he had to get out of that line fast because "*somebody actually invented one*"). So negative is his influence that, after Hill visits a town, the townsfolk tar and feather the next poor salesman who shows up. Hill's latest successful *modus operandi* is to convince the citizens of a small town that they need a boys' marching band. Then he sells the townspeople not just instruments, music, and uniforms, but music lessons as well.

The catch is that Harold Hill can't read or play a note of music. "*He can't tell a bass drum from a pipe organ,*" we are told by a fellow salesman. Hill stays in each town long enough for the instruments and uniforms to be delivered, but as soon as he collects payment from the hopeful mothers and fathers, he skips town on the night train. For our purposes, we can say that entrepreneur Hill is in the business of selling one organization—the boys' band— to another, larger organization—the town.

River City, Iowa, the fictitious locale of the play, is a town where stubborness has been raised to an art form. When we first meet the townspeople, they sing an entire song about why their chip-on-the-shoulder, drop-dead attitude toward newcomers makes them proud. Of course, this stubborness merely sweetens the challenge for Hill, and he easily penetrates their defenses and sells them the band. In the process, both Harold Hill and River City are irrevocably changed—and this change looks very much like the change that intrapreneurs cause in a corporation.

■ How Does Hill Do It?

On the day Hill arrives in River City, he sees workmen moving a pool table into the billiard parlor where before there was only an innocent billiards table. (Billiards is a sport, while pool is a vice, as everyone knows.) It is the Fourth of July, and the citizenry is out on the street in a festive mood. In just a few minutes Hill convinces the townspeople that the pool table will mean acute moral, mental, and physical degradation for the youth of River City. He says it will usher in beer drinking, horse racing, time frittering, shameless dancing music, dime store novels, cigarette smoking, and the memorizing of shocking jokes from *Captain Billy's Whiz Bag*! And what is the only way to save River City's youth? Hill has the solution: a boys' band!

Note that the establishment of River City doesn't make their decision because it would be nice to have a boys' band, or even because every other town has one: Instead, they perceive a real threat to the "corporation's" existence. In effect, the town's decision is defensive, reactive, rather than being classically innovative or creative. The lesson here is that corporate entrepreneurship differs from corporate innovation or corporate creativity, though it can include these two elements. While

William B. Gartner is assistant professor and director of the Center for Entrepreneurial Studies at Georgetown University. He is also chairman of the Entrepreneurship Interest Group of the Academy of Management.

29 **NEW**MANAGEMENT

innovation and entrepreneurship are often spoken of in the same breath, in fact, entrepreneurs see solutions in terms of forming new organizations, which may not necessarily be innovation. Hill sees the solution to the pool table problem in terms of a new organization, the boys' band. But there *are* other nonentrepreneurial solutions: eliminate the pool table, impose curfews on the young boys, divert their attention with gifts of bicycles, horses, or ice cream.

Paradoxically, the organization's resistance to change—change of the pool table kind—becomes one of Hill's major weapons. But it is not that easy: In place of the poisonous pool table vision, Hill has to present another, desirable vision of change: the band. It is Hill's *vision* that is our central concern, because it is not really the instruments and uniforms that he sells, but his vision of the boys' band. And his vision is *how* he sells what he sells (his medium is his message, as it were). Hill's vision is so clear and powerful that he believes it himself—at least while he's singing about it. Seventy-six golden trombones shining in the sun, on the march down the street! "*A hundred and ten cornets right behind!*" "*A thousand reeds springing up like weeds,*" thundering tympani in horse platoons, big fat bassoons, cannons firing, thundering all the way! And all those kids marching! He even tells the eager boys that they will have red stripes down the outsides of their trouser legs. Who couldn't visualize this? Who wouldn't want this? The people line up to order their instruments.

Return to corporate reality for a moment. It can be seen that one function of the entrepreneur may be to articulate an exciting vision in a clear and understandable way, to convince people that they are "*closing [their] eyes to a situation [they] do not wish to acknowledge,*" and then to open their eyes to a new vision. If entrepreneurs are people who do this well, who can rouse people to share their vision, then it seems

Publisher's note: Image removed due to copyright restrictions.

30

small wonder that in many corporations these Harold Hills are often segregated from the rest of the corporate citizens in "venture groups" or separate divisions. In an organization where control is essential, these individuals could easily get things out of control.

I am the last person to want to romanticize the entrepreneur and create a hero where none exists. Most of my research has been in the direction of stripping away the so-called special personality traits of the entrepreneur and countering the notion that entrepreneurs are born, not made. However, in spending time around entrepreneurs, I have often noted their seemingly magical ability to inspire others with their vision, to seem a bit larger than life. Even the soberest researchers seem to have encountered this aspect of the entrepreneurs they study. Orvis Collins and David Moore, in the middle of their book *The Enterprising Man*, an empirical, traditional, dry piece of research about post-World War II Michigan manufacturers (certainly an unromanticizable lot if there ever was one), engaged in the following flight of inspired prose, making the entrepreneur an almost mythic figure hammering the universe (!) into shape around him:

In this period of fear and doubt, however, these men found creativity. At a time when it became necessary for them to reorganize their lives and to reestablish their futures, they had the capacity not only to dream but to transmute their dreams to action. They created the business of which they were dreaming. Between the idea and the act falls the shadow. This shadow, which these men had to explore, and out of which they had to hammer reality, lay immediately ahead. They had now to organize the universe around them in such a way that they could progress in establishing their new business. The first act in this direction is what we will call the act of creation.

It seems that it is difficult to talk about entrepreneurs without discussing dreams and vision, and getting oneself caught up in both.

Meanwhile back in the corporation of River City, there are some people who think that Harold Hill is nothing but a con man, a shyster, a rip-off artist. Mayor Shinn is one of them. Mayor Shinn is a forward-looking man, a fine citizen, who wants the town to change and grow, but only according to his plan, which includes the pool table (since he is the owner of the town's pool parlor). The mayor wants to see Hill's professorial credentials, so he sends the town's school board to Hill's hotel. Their voices, unbeknownst to them all these years, form a perfect quartet: bass, baritone, tenor, and high tenor. Hill gives them some words to sing, and they discover that they have been a barbershop quartet all along, but weren't aware of it. More converts for Hill, the nonprofessor who can't read a note.

In a similar vein, the town's bad boy, Tommy, is about to be sent to reform school, but Hill gets him thinking about the problem of how a marching piccolo player can hold his music and play at the same time. Tommy gets to work on a piccolo music-holder R&D project and stays out of trouble. The mothers and matrons of the town, a gossipy bunch whose idea of an invitation to a picnic is *"you can eat your fill of all the food you bring yourself,"* are organized by Hill into a dance committee. Even the level-headed Marian the Librarian comes under Harold's spell: When she finally has proof that "Professor" Hill is a fraud and a cheat, she withholds this information from the mayor, and tells Harold, *"There were bells on the hill, but I never heard them ringing . . . till there was you."*

Hill seems to have an uncanny power to see hidden talents and abilities in others; he opens people's eyes to what is there, to untold possibilities, to things they haven't seen before.

Publisher's note:
Image removed
due to copyright
restrictions.

■ **The Downside**

But maybe we should beware of falling under Hill's spell ourselves. Maybe the mayor is right, and Hill is a rip-off artist. Hill's intentions are certainly unequivocal—he's going to wait just until the instruments and uniforms arrive, then collect his money and get out of town. Not exactly a noble vision. And it is an inordinate amount of money with which the professor plans to abscond, and most of it comes from townspeople who can barely afford it. Meanwhile, the town's business is going undone. The school board quartet, as the mayor angrily points out, "*is singing up street and down alley instead of tending to city matters*"; Tommy's piccolo music-holder cuts off the circulation to the player's fingers (a "*minor flaw*"); when the matron ladies give their Rustle of Spring dance performance, concluding with a pose in which they think they resemble "*two Grecian urns and a fountain*," they are clumsy and ludicrous; and Marian is on the way to having her heart broken by this traveling salesman/seducer, the play's "hero." So the mayor is clearly right, the town has been completely taken in by a fast-talking spinner of unfulfillable dreams. And for us to praise the entrepreneurial skills of Harold Hill must mean that we have been taken in by him, too.

When the boys' instruments arrive, they all want to start on their lessons. But Hill says they must wait until the uniforms are delivered before their lessons begin. In the meantime, anxious to maintain his music professor role, he gives the boys a few words of instruction in his own patented "think system" of musical practice, "*where you don't bother with notes*" or even touch the instrument. The boys are directed to think hard about the "Minuet in G" until they get their uniforms. On the evening that the uniforms arrive and Harold collects his money, Charlie (another traveling salesman) blows into town unexpectedly and interrupts the Ice Cream Sociable where the townspeople are gathered. He tells them the truth about Hill: "*There isn't any band, there never has been any band and there never will be any band!*" The people are outraged and want their money back; they rush off through the town to hunt Hill down "*like a mad dog!*"

Meanwhile, Hill has fallen in love with Marian and, for the first time in his despicable career, can't bring himself to catch the night train. Before the rest of the people catch up with him, Hill is found by Winthrop, Marian's acutely disappointed little brother, who asks Hill if he really is a "*big liar*" and a "*dirty rotten crook.*" Hill admits that he is, but he tells the boy, "*You're a wonderful kid, I thought so from the first. That's why I wanted you in the band.*" "*What band?*" asks the boy sarcastically. "*I always think there's a band, kid.*" (Apparently Hill subscribes to his own "think system.") The townspeople rush in, and Hill is led back to the assembly hall in handcuffs, while someone goes off to warm up the tar and collect the feathers. The mayor asks if there is anyone present in the room who doesn't think Hill

32

Publisher's note:
Image removed
due to copyright
restrictions.

should be tarred and feathered. One by
one the formerly stubborn, gossipy, and
glum people whose lives Hill has changed
stand up. The mayor screams at them:
*"Have you forgotten the clear
understanding and warranty that your
children would be taught to play in a
band? Well, where's the band? Where's
the band?"*

On cue, the boys shuffle into the
assembly hall; some of their uniforms are
too big and drag on the floor. They try to
line themselves up in an acceptable
formation and hold their instruments in
what they hope are the proper playing
positions. They all look to Harold, their
bandleader. Harold looks around
desperately for a place to hide, but there is
none. *"Think, men, think!"* he pleads as
he raises a broken stick to "conduct"
them. They play the "Minuet in G," as it
has never been played before, just barely
recognizable, and River City's citizens
think it's the greatest thing they've ever
heard. The mothers and fathers in the
audience beam with pride. The people
cheer. Harold and Marian embrace.
Curtain.

■   Questions, Questions, Questions
Have the townspeople received a good
return on their investment? Is there a
band or isn't there? Hasn't Harold Hill
been vastly overpaid for the sorry band
he's managed to put together? Even if he
had the skills to teach the boys, could Hill
ever have delivered on his "Seventy-Six
Trombones" vision? Is that pre-change
vision the yardstick against which the

results must be measured? Would there
have been any band at all unless such a
vision was presented, and the townspeople
taken advantage of? After their experience
with Hill, will the townspeople still be as
fearful that the controlled and pleasant
corporate life of their town could be
ripped apart by the evils of pool (or any
other threatening vision of the future)?
Couldn't the townspeople have changed
for the better, into more open-minded and
modern people, without having to go
through this Harold Hill band fracas?
Couldn't the townspeople have changed
themselves by an effort of will, by a more
disciplined version of the Hill "think
system?" Couldn't they have "planned
and implemented" this change
themselves? Why is it so easy for us to
answer these questions in regard to the
fiction of River City and its relation to
Harold Hill and not in regard to the
corporation and its relation to the
entrepreneur and new venture creation?

■   Lessons for Corporations
Executives considering intrapreneurial
solutions to problems in their
organizations should be aware of the
following issues: First, entrepreneurs are
going to turn up in their organizations
whether they want them or not. Like Hill
coming to town, an organization will
inevitably hire someone who has
entrepreneurial characteristics, someone
bent on stirring up "trouble" in the
organization, complaining about the "pool
hall" and the other pet projects generated
by the "city fathers." Most organizations

will act like most Iowa towns and tar and feather the entrepreneur before the company can get any further stirred up. Yet the Hills are the "troublemakers" an organization needs for renewal. After all, getting stirred up was not such a bad thing for River City. Hence, executives need to consider what they will do when some individual in their organization inevitably cries, *"We have trouble in River City!"*

Second, change seems rarely to come about unless members of the organization can really *see* that the organization is in trouble. We are, for the most part, creatures of habit, and only when those habits are shown to put us in jeopardy do we ever consider behaving in a different manner. "Trouble" needs to be a concrete identifiable situation. Hill could specifically describe what "trouble" was to River City—beer drinking, horse racing, time frittering, shameless dancing music, dime store novels, cigarette smoking. What images do most organizations use that can stir their members to recognition of a serious threat to their way of life? For River City the vision of their boys being corrupted was the source of particular images that stirred them to action. Every organization, too, has a particular set of values, a belief system about who and what it is, and what poses a threat. The threatening images must be found within each organization's culture.

Third, organization members have to *see* what they are changing to. The primary function of the entrepreneur appears to be one of imagination—that is, creating images of some future state that others can see in their mind's eye, believe in, and act on. Such images need to be concrete. Hill's image of the boy's band had specific descriptions of shining instruments, striped pants, and the sights and sounds of a band marching down Main Street. Entrepreneurs can create and articulate similarly concrete images that give other organization members something else to hold on to besides the worn images of their present situation or

the threatening images of the future. The imagination is a powerful source of human energy.

Fourth, the specific outputs of an entrepreneurial endeavor (profits, sales, and so forth) are probably not as important as the changes that will occur in the rest of the organization, although the temptation is to measure the changes in market-transaction terms. The boys' band is a rather sorry output, but the town itself has been dramatically renewed. Organizations often put their hopes in the "boys' band" and seek to measure the performance of this small component of the overall organization, yet fail to account for all the subtle changes that occur in other units that were influenced by being near the entrepreneurial endeavor. Hence, executives might want to reconsider whether separating entrepreneurs from the rest of the organization by hiding them in venture groups or new venture subsidiaries deprives the rest of the organization of opportunities for renewal.

Finally, executives should realize that the outcomes of organizational change can rarely be planned or controlled. The River City fathers thought they were going to establish a pool hall and, because of some entrepreneur, ended up with a boys' band. For many weeks, River City was out of the control of the town fathers. Townspeople were taken over by a new and exciting vision of what their town could be. Entrepreneurs in an organization will do this. Once change begins, it can sweep aside what was thought to be planned and permanent.

I wonder what happened to Harold Hill. Did he remain the leader of the boys' band? Did he become mayor of River City? Or, like a corporate intrapreneur, was he blamed by the organization the first time things started to go wrong?

[3]

THE OZ IN ORGANIZATION

William B. Gartner

All management is the management of change. All management is about making or allowing change in organizational structure and strategy and in the behaviors and attitudes of the organization's members. Yet change is such a fundamental aspect of our thoughts about management that we often lose sight of what change actually is about.

An underlying premise is that organizations change for the better, that they "grow," that they "mature." Even though we may be all grown-ups in pin-striped suits carrying designer attaches, we often live in organizations that behave childishly. This organizational immaturity is frequently found in newer, entrepreneurial organizations, yet many established businesses have not grown up, either. Organizational immaturity is not having a sense of oneself, not knowing who one is or what one is about. It is not knowing how to be, how to act. To grow up, to become mature, is to undergo those changes that define our *person*ality, that reveal our intrinsic nature. But what are the characteristics of a mature organization?

Our initial image of organizational maturity comes from a poster by Edward Sorel (it was commissioned by New York's New School for Social Research). The poster, in light watercolors and pen and ink, depicts the Scarecrow, Tin Man, and Lion from *The Wizard of Oz* flying over Manhattan in a balloon. The top of the poster reads, "For a heart, courage, and a brain." The more I mull over this line—and imagine those three characters floating above the bustle of the city—the more I believe this whimsical drawing captures what change is about, particularly what change toward maturity is about. There it is, three intertwined parts of ourselves represented by the Scarecrow, Tin Man, and Lion, held up by slender threads to a balloon that is controlled only by the breeze. Indeed, the process of change sometimes seems to be like that—so elusive and random, so beyond our control. Yet, suddenly, we find

ourselves "there" instead of "here." We are changed. We grew up. We are not in Kansas anymore. How did it happen?

■ The Story

The Wizard of Oz is the story of Dorothy, a girl in Kansas, who decides to run away from home. Shortly thereafter, she regrets her decision and turns back, only to be swept up by a tornado before she can reach the safety of her storm cellar. She is swept away to the land of Oz. There, the Munchkins suggest that the only way back to Kansas is to follow the yellow brick road to the Emerald City, where the Wizard of Oz might help her. In her journey she meets the Scarecrow, Tin Man, and Lion. Each character in the story has a wish: Dorothy wants to go home, the Scarecrow wants a brain, the Tin Man wants a heart, and the Lion wants courage. In the Emerald City, the Wizard demands that they perform a task before he will grant their wishes. The task is to bring back the broom of the Wicked Witch of the West. In the process of completing this task, misfortunes befall them—the Scarecrow is shredded to pieces, and Dorothy is captured by the Wicked Witch and slated to be executed. But the Tin Man, the Lion, and the Scarecrow (restuffed) sneak into the Wicked Witch's castle and save Dorothy. They get the broom (accidentally) by melting the Wicked Witch with a pail of water meant to stop a fire on the Scarecrow. Upon presenting the broom to the Wizard of Oz, the foursome then realize that the Wizard is a mere human being without magical powers. Yet, they all learn that, in the accomplishment of the task, they have been granted their wishes. That is, they discovered that they possessed their desired traits all along.

This is a wonderful story about how individuals mature. It provides many lessons about how change happens, what kinds of changes there are, and what kinds of mechanisms are valuable for creating the types of change that make organizations better. Let us amplify the images in the story in order to re-imagine the meaning of change.

William B. Gartner is an assistant professor and director of the Center for Entrepreneurship Studies at the Georgetown business school. He was the 1983 Heizer award winner for research on new ventures. His current research and teaching focuses on organization creation and on developing "post-modernist" ways of thinking about the practice of management.

■ Kansas As Stuckness

The film begins on Henry and Emmalina Gale's farm—drab little buildings surrounded by a vast expanse of Kansas prairie. Everything is not merely in black and white, *it's all gray*. The farm works by a clumsy kind of competence. The Gale's farmhands, Hunk, Hickory, and Zeke, would make good cases for a study titled "In Search of Mediocrity: Lessons from Poor Performers." Hickory is in charge of the machinery; when he is not working on the wagon, he is fiddling with a wind machine that always breaks down when the wind comes up. Hunk has all kinds of ideas for Dorothy about how to improve her life. The ideas all make sense (if Toto, the dog, chases Miss Gulch's cat, then don't let Toto near Miss Gulch's house), but they are the kind of ideas that are useful when you don't have problems in the first place. Zeke, known for his "boldness," is reduced to a bundle of terrified jello when Dorothy falls into a pigpen. The farmhands seem competent enough, the farm runs, but we are glad that they work for the Gales and not for us.

The grayness, the flatness, the institutionalized incompetence, give a sense of being stuck on the Gale's farm. We know the familiar signs of "stuckness" in organizations: nothing seems to work; bureaucratic infighting; that feeling of directionlessness; more complaints than accolades; anyone coming into the office means another problem; and stupid memos that breed more stupid memos in response. Employees are quitting, coming in late, and acting like zombies, going through empty motions. Stuckness for the manager is that dread of coming into the office each day—compounded by a fear of never being able to leave. Stuckness is the feeling of helplessness that comes of seeing that one's choices and actions appear to make no difference; in fact, they seem to make the situation worse. It's a feeling of doom, hopelessness, or terror that, in the future, things will stay the same or, more

likely, they will get worse. It's no new products; it's the barren prairie of dwindling profits and spiralling costs. Stuckness is dead center, the point of total inertia.

Stuckness is the desperation that leads to calling in high-powered consultants, to shuffling off to seminars, to looking somewhere else for the answers: What book was that on the best seller list last week? Get fifty copies and pass them out to everyone in the office. Stuckness is knowing one is grasping at straws, but feeling there is nothing else to hold on to.

Stuckness is seeing one's mistakes blow up into one's worst fears. Dorothy's dog, Toto, has bitten the crabbiest person in the county, Almira Gulch. Stuckness is knowing that Almira Gulch will come to take your dog, and you can't seem to get anyone to do anything about it. Is it any wonder that Dorothy sings "Somewhere Over the Rainbow?" But the song ends with Miss Gulch taking Toto away . . . and Dorothy is stuck.

A point here is that change begins when things go wrong. We don't change when things are going our way. Dorothy would not have changed if Toto had not bitten Miss Gulch. One of the saving graces for most organizations is that in competitive environments there are always crises, things are always going wrong. One of the ways to respond to a crisis is to run away. After Toto escapes from Miss Gulch's basket, Dorothy and Toto run away from home to avoid any further misfortunes with Miss Gulch. This is the beginning of unstuckness. Once Dorothy has run away, then some real change can occur in her situation.

■ Getting Unstuck

How does one start the change process in organizations? Get out of the office. Get out of the place where one is stuck. There is something about moving physically that helps one move psychologically as well. That is the reason why we have "retreats" that take us physically away from the

"A point here is that change begins when things go wrong. We don't change when things are going our way."

organization. It is why Hewlett and Packard practiced "management by walking around."

But what happens when Dorothy runs away? Not far from home she meets Professor Marvel. He is able to read the past, present, and future in his crystal ball. He makes a big deal about seeing the obvious and states, "You are running away from home. . . . They don't understand you. They don't appreciate you . . . " Does he sound like the consultant you have recently hired? Professor Marvel looks into the crystal and "sees" that Auntie Em is heartbroken over Dorothy's leaving. Dorothy realizes that she must get back and rushes home. But now the weather has taken a drastic turn for the worse. Dorothy barely makes it back before the tornado descends upon the farm house and carries her off.

This is what happens in "management by walking around." To get unstuck physically is to invite a tornado. Leave the security of the office, and you will find a whirlwind chasing you! Leave your turf, and you will get swept away by what is outside. But only by leaving "home" can change begin.

Change is never planned, as much as we would like to think so. "Planned change" is an oxymoron. Change is the whirlwind that comes and sweeps you up into it. (James Hillman, an archetypal psychologist, says that a tornado, being a sort of vacuum, empty at the center, represents the unlived part of yourself. It sucks you in because that's where you need to go!) The only thing that one has control over is to get out of the office— what happens then depends on the whirlwind. This is frightening. We expect that we can go out and look around, try to find some new direction, but we get swept away. We cannot get back into our own office. Is Dorothy really better off? Shouldn't she have just stayed at home and taken her punishment? Were things really that bad?

Photographs from *The Wizard of Oz* reprinted by permission from MGM

■ In the Land of Oz

Where does the whirlwind go? Dorothy's whirlwind takes her to a Technicolor dream world, the land of Oz. Our memories of the movie are, perhaps, a poor guide to what Oz is all about. We think of those sweet little Munchkins, the Emerald City (a pleasant kind of place), the yellow brick road, singing, and dancing and fun. But the land of Oz is not all sugarplums. On landing in Oz, Dorothy makes an enemy: Her house unintentionally crushes the Wicked Witch of the East, whose sister witch then vows revenge on Dorothy. Dorothy despairs of ever getting home. Oz is not familiar ground, everything is strange, one doesn't know how to behave. There are serious threats to one's welfare. (At least Dorothy knows her enemy. However much it might help some organizations, rarely do one's real life enemies shriek, "I'll get you my little pretty," and fly off in a cloud of smoke and fire.)

Dorothy is no explorer, no junior anthropologist; she's not much of an adventurer at heart. All she wants is to get back home. But, since Dorothy's house is transported to Oz, there is that sickly sense that "home" will never be the same again. She certainly cannot rely on another tornado to get her back. To get back home one needs to go by a new route. The trip down the yellow brick road is

"At least Dorothy knows her enemy. However much it might help some organizations, rarely do one's real life enemies shriek, 'I'll get you my little pretty,' and fly off in a cloud of smoke and fire."

17 **NEW**MANAGEMENT

really the path of self-discovery, and going home is to find out who you are. It's a trip that both organizations and individuals take. The irony is that you find yourself by going outside, looking around, and then trying to make a mad dash back home . . . only to find that you can't get back in. What happens now? If you are not on the familiar ground of Kansas, how do things work here in Oz?

Once Dorothy starts out for the Emerald City she hooks up with the Scarecrow, Tin Man, and Lion. This threesome is an excellent symbol of the three aspects of our lives (and of organizations) that undergo change when the road out of stuckness is taken—brain, heart, and courage.

"Little time is spent in most organizational change programs on understanding what people do and teaching them how to do it better."

Publisher's note:
Image removed
due to copyright
restrictions.

■ If I Only Had a Brain

The Scarecrow is stuck. He is a bag of clothes stuffed with straw hanging from a pole in a cornfield. His dangling arms point this way and that, giving conflicting directions to Dorothy as she stands at a fork in the yellow brick road. The Scarecrow is stuck because he lacks a brain. Why does an organization need a brain? Brain skills are the "how to" or "know how" skills. In Peter Drucker's words, they lead to "doing things right." Surprisingly, the brain skills are often the most neglected in organizational change. The how-to skills are the techniques of the job: knowing how the semiconductors are made; knowing how the forms are filled out; knowing how the windshield on the car gets fitted. Brain skills are not only manual or technical skills, they also involve knowing the inner, unwritten workings of the organization: knowing the ropes in organizational politics; knowing who makes what happen and who can put up road blocks. The brain knows how to navigate the organization's political landscape.

When we want people to be better workers, we often try to change their attitudes and their motivation. Yet, frequently, improving their performance is more a matter of thoroughly teaching them the skills to get the job done. If one doesn't know how to type correctly, if one doesn't have the proper skills to install the windshield, if one doesn't know that Ms. Johnson is the real decision maker on new products, then being the most motivated person in the world isn't going to get the job done. Brain skills are so fundamental that we forget how important they are. Little time is spent in most organizational change programs on understanding what people do and teaching them how to do it better. Workers often get sent to training ("orientation" for us white-collar workers) when they are first hired, but what then? Does your organization continually teach you to do the job that you are in? And what if the territory changes, what if

18

Kansas becomes Oz, then how do you go about relearning the job? If training in your organization stops after the managerial training program—or after apprenticeship, or the ninety-day grace period—then your organization is not recognizing the importance of brain skills in getting work done. Education in organizations needs to be continual, especially when we recognize that most organizations spend much more time in Oz than they care to admit.

■ If I Only Had a Heart

The Tin Man is found rusted into immobility, poised with an ax raised above his head, stuck. While his rust is easily fixed with squirts of oil, he still feels hollow. He wants a heart. What is having a heart? It is knowing who one is and knowing what to do. It's Peter Drucker's "Knowing the right thing to do." Corporate executives are often portrayed as ruthless creatures without feelings (feelings being signs of weakness and vulnerability). In our culture, "thinking with the heart" is often differentiated from "thinking with the head." Today, "thinking with the heart" is an attempt to redeem "feeling" from the context of ineffectuality and sentimentality to which the culture has relegated it. It is an attempt to give "feeling" a good name and to restore its original meaning: To have a "feeling" for something is to know whether it's good or bad, right or wrong, beautiful or ugly. Feeling is tied to our faculty for valuation, for judgement. If we think of feeling in this way, then heart becomes something other than the sticky verses on Hallmark cards. So, when the Tin Man wants a heart, he wants character. To have a heart is to have a sense of oneself, to "Know thyself." A heart is the stuff of humanity.

To focus on heart, on ourselves, on "who we are," is not to focus on so-called excellence. Excellence is an exterior label for what are intrinsic qualities. An organization that is searching for excellence often ends up doing what everyone else is doing, and not what it should be doing. The problem with holding up "excellent" companies as models for behavior is that many people take the examples literally, and seek to become like the examples through imitation. We rush out to copy the superficial aspects of "excellent" companies and ignore the painstaking effort most of these companies went through to find themselves, to find their niches, to find their competencies. Only IBM can be IBM. IBM's success is because IBM knows who it is. IBM knows what it is about. IBM has its own heart. (Hearts can also be lost.) Heart is not some new wardrobe purchased from the latest consultant's boutique. Heart can only be bought through constant confrontation with ourselves.

■ If I Only Had Courage

To see ourselves is truly a frightening thing. Our inadequacies are always there. The Cowardly Lion has a heart and a brain, but they are not enough. He knows he's a lion, and he has his pouncing and roaring skills down pat, but between the knowledge and the act is a chasm. The day-to-day "living out" of who we are and how to do it (doing the right thing and doing things right) is what courage is about. It's the exercising of the heart and brain. Without action we have heads of straw and are rusty and hollow inside. With knowledge of self, with knowledge of how to get the job done, comes a corresponding responsibility to act. That takes courage.

Courage is an obvious manifestation of maturity. Those who know they have a heart and brain do the courageous thing: they grow up. They make the hard choices, they act, and they face the consequences. It is not easy. In almost every scene the Cowardly Lion says three words, "I am afraid." With hearts and brains we can see the consequences of our actions, and often the consequences have punishing effects. Therefore, we *should* be afraid when we introduce new products, lay off employees,

"Those who know they have a heart and brain do the courageous thing: they grow up."

close down plants, say "no" to the boss, invest in new plant and equipment. Doing anything new *should* have an aura of fearfulness. Who knows what is in the future? Only the foolish would think that around every corner is easy street. Our choices may not always be right, we may never know whether other choices would have worked better, and even the clearly right choices may still be difficult to accomplish.

■ Facing Ourselves

Oz is not a land of navel-gazing. We don't get to know ourselves in a vacuum. We know ourselves through our actions, and our fondest ideas about ourselves are sometimes roundly contradicted by a single act, or non-act. Dorothy and her friends do not get their wishes fulfilled by sitting around the Wizard's castle (creating a facade like the Wizard's) but by setting out to capture the witch's broom. In the process they discover, as the Wizard later tells them, that they have possessed heart, courage, and a brain all along. They did not get these things consumer-fashion from outside themselves. When the Wizard gives the Scarecrow a diploma, the Tin Man a testimonial, and the Lion a medal, these

Publisher's note: Image removed due to copyright restrictions.

are simply tokens for achievements that cannot be viewed from the outside. And, all along, Dorothy's ruby slippers could have magically taken her home, but she has to win this knowledge via her difficult adventure. In the doing comes the being. Self-knowledge comes through activity, through undergoing change with our eyes open, not closed in wishful thinking.

■ Managerial Lessons

Here is what a trip to Oz teaches us about seeing where and who we are in organizations:

Change Requires Problems. Change only seems to happen when things get bad, or when things go from bad to worse. If you say, "Well, things around here aren't *that* bad. I've seen worse in other organizations," there won't be change. "Not that bad," leaves us in Kansas, and we will never get off the farm. Change comes when one says, "Things are bad around here. It's not working." There is a lot to be said for being unhappy with one's situation and admitting it, although unhappiness is not the American land-of-smiles way. America is the place where you "have a good day," every day. But what kind of adventure would we have had if Dorothy had stayed on the farm? What if she had said, "Well, Miss Gulch has taken Toto, but things aren't *that* bad. It could be worse."

You Cannot Know Where Change Will Take You. Change is a whirlwind. It picks one up and sets one down in the strangest of places. Thus, for individuals and organizations, the issue is not trying to control change (which is impossible), but making sense of the situation once the change has occurred. Being caught up in the whirlwind is the frenzied state that occurs when something important is happening. In Kurt Lewin's terms, the whirlwind is "unfreezing." During this unfreezing stage, everything is turbulent, the solid slips away, and there is nothing to hold on to. Let the whirlwind go where it may, let the old slip away. If you think

Publisher's note:
Image removed
due to copyright
restrictions.

"In the transition from entrepreneur to manager, what
often gets lost is the entrepreneur's vision."

you can control it, you will be torn to
pieces by its force.

Seeing What We Are Doing.
Productivity in organizations is getting the
job done. Accomplishment requires the
right skills. If employees don't have the
proper skills and abilities to do the job
right, motivation doesn't do it. Training
programs thus should insure that all
members of the organization have the
right skills. Managers have to ask: What
are you doing? What specific activities
does the job entail? What kinds of skills
are required to do the job? Do the skills
match the job? What might be changed in
the job to enable the individual to work
more effectively? At the organizational
level, we have to ask ourselves: What are
we doing here? What are the tasks of the
organization? Are we providing resources
and effort to accomplish the tasks of the
organization? If we see that our time is
spent paper shuffling in a battle of
strategic memo warfare, then we have to
admit that we have a problem.

Doing What We Are Seeing. The task
of the leader is to see. In the transition
from entrepreneur to manager, what often
gets lost is the entrepreneur's vision. What
the initial founder "sees" never gets
transferred. So entrepreneurial companies
flounder because either the entrepreneur
stays and has to "see" for everyone (but is
unable to see enough to get everyone's job
done), or the hired managers lack the
entrepreneur's vision. Leaders in an
organization must enable *others* to have a
vision; leaders must paint a picture of our
hearts and brains in action. This vision
gives a purposefulness to our actions,
because then we will have thought about
why we are acting the way we are. Good
leaders always talk about what they are
seeing, their vision of (and for) the
organization. Good leaders are able to
articulate for us what it's like over the
rainbow. They see the Oz in organization.

21 **NEW**MANAGEMENT

0363-9428/88/124$1.50
Copyright 1988 by the
University of Baltimore
Educational Foundation

"Who Is an Entrepreneur?" Is the Wrong Question

William B. Gartner

Entrepreneurship is the creation of organizations. What differentiates entrepreneurs from non-entrepreneurs is that entrepreneurs create organizations, while non-entrepreneurs do not. In behavioral approaches to the study of entrepreneurship an entrepreneur is seen as a set of activities involved in organization creation, while in trait approaches an entrepreneur is a set of personality traits and characteristics. This paper argues that trait approaches have been unfruitful and that behavioral approaches will be a more productive perspective for future research in entrepreneurship.

> My own personal experience was that for ten years we ran a research center in entrepreneurial history, for ten years we tried to define the entrepreneur. We never succeeded. Each of us had some notion of it—what he thought was, for his purposes, a useful definition. And I don't think you're going to get farther than that. (Cole, 1969, p. 17)

> How can we know the dancer from the dance? (Yeats, 1956)

Arthur Cole's words have taken on the deeper tones of prophecy. Recent reviews of the entrepreneurship literature have found few changes in this dilemma in the sixteen years since Cole's statement. Brockhuas and Horwitz's (1985) review of the psychology of the entrepreneur concluded that "The literature appears to support the argument that there is no generic definition of the entrepreneur, or if there is we do not have the psychological instruments to discover it at this time. Most of the attempts to distinguish between entrepreneurs and small business owners or managers have discovered no significant differentiating features." (pp. 42-43) Other scholars have concurred that a common definition of the entrepreneur remains elusive (Carsrud, Olm and Edy, 1985; Sexton and Smilor, 1985; Wortman, 1985).

Cole's early doubts about whether the entrepreneur could be defined have not stopped researchers from attempting to do so. Much research in the entrepreneurship field has focused on the person of the entrepreneur, asking the question, Why do certain individuals start firms when others, under similar conditions, do not? Asking *why* has led us to answering with *who:* Why did X start a venture? Because X has a certain inner quality or qualities. This focus can be identified in any research which seeks to identify traits that differentiate entrepreneurs from non-entrepreneurs: need for achievement (Komives, 1972; McClelland, 1961; McClelland and Winter, 1969), locus of control (Brockhaus, 1980a; Brockhaus and Nord, 1979; Hull, Bosley, and Udell, 1982; Liles, 1974), risk taking (Brockhaus, 1980b; Hull, Bosley, and Udell, 1982; Liles, 1974; Mancuso, 1975; Palmer, 1971), values (DeCarlo and Lyons, 1979; Hornaday and Aboud, 1971; Hull, Bosley, and Udell, 1980; Komives, 1972), age (Cooper, 1973; Howell, 1972; Mayer and Goldstein, 1961) are but a few examples. X starts a venture because of qualities that made X who (s)he is. Entrepreneurship research has long asked, "Who is an entrepreneur?"

I believe the attempt to answer the question "Who is an entrepreneur?," which focusses on the traits and personality characteristics of entrepreneurs, will neither lead us to a definition of the entrepreneur nor help us to understand the phenomenon of entrepreneurship. This search for characteristics and traits of the entrepreneur is labeled in this article as the trait approach. In this approach the entrepreneur is the basic unit of analysis and the entrepreneur's traits and characteristics are the key to explaining entrepreneurship as a phenomenon, since the entrepreneur "causes" entrepreneurship. The purpose of the first part of this article is to look at research based on the trait view of entrepreneurship and to show that this view alone is inadequate to explain the phenomenon of entrepreneurship. Another approach is needed to help us refocus our thoughts on entrepreneurship. That approach—the behavioral approach—will be presented and the two approaches will be compared and contrasted.

THE TRAIT APPROACH

In the trait approach the entrepreneur is assumed to be a particular personality type, a fixed state of existence, a describable species that one might find a picture of in a field guide, and the point of much entrepreneurship research has been to enumerate a set of characteristics describing this entity known as the entrepreneur. One indication of the tenacity of this point of view—i.e., once an entrepreneur, always an entrepreneur, since an entrepreneur is a personality type, a state of being that doesn't go away—can be seen in the selection of samples of "entrepreneurs" in many well-regarded research studies (Table 1). In many studies "entrepreneurs" are sampled many years after having started their firms. Hor "entrepreneurs" are sampled many years after having started their firms. Hornaday and Aboud (1971), for example, chose to study individuals who headed neurs" were interviewed anywhere from two to sixteen years after startup. Is the owner/manager of an ongoing firm two or ten or even fifteen years after startup an entrepreneur? If this individual is included in a sample of entrepreneurs, what does that imply about the researcher's definition of the entrepreneur, and what will the resulting data reflect?

Table 1 is an attempt to organize concisely much of the major literature on the entrepreneur and entrepreneurship. It represents a succumbing to the grand temptation that haunts many writers and researchers in the entrepreneurship field: if we could just systematically go back and extract, categorize, and organize what has already been discovered about the entrepreneur, we will return with the pieces of a puzzle which we can then fit together into the big picture, and the entrepreneur will appear defined on the page. Table 1 is most emphatically not the big picture. Instead Table 1 shows:

(1) that many (and often vague) definitions of the entrepreneur have been used (in many studies the entrepreneur is never defined);

Table 1

Definitions, Samples, and Characteristics of Entrepreneurs

Author(s)	Type[1]	Definition	Sample	Characteristics
Brockhaus (1980)	E	. . . an entrepreneur is defined as a major owner and manager of a business venture not employed elsewhere. (p. 510)	31 individuals who, within the three months prior to the study, had ceased working for their employers and at the time of the study owned as well as managed business ventures. These businesses (type unspecified) were licensed by St. Louis County Missouri during the months of August and September 1975.	Risk taking propensity
Cole (1959)	N	. . . the purposeful activity (including an integrated sequence of decision) of an individual or group of individuals, undertaken to initiate, maintain, or aggrandize a profit-oriented business unit for the production or distribution of economic goods and services. (p. 7)		
Collins and Moore (1970)	E	We distinguish between organization builders who create new and independent firms and those who perform entrepreneurial functions within already established organizations. Perhaps we are, after all, thinking of the entrepreneur in the way Schumpeter viewed him: "everyone is an entrepreneur only when he actually 'carries out new combinations,' and loses that character as soon as he has built up his business. (p. 10)	Owners of 110 Michigan manufacturing firms established between 1945 and 1958 with 20 or more employees. Interviews were from 2 to 16 years after startup.	Parents' occupation, education, previous job satisfaction, social attitudes

(continued overleaf)

Table 1 (cont'd)

Author(s)	Type[1]	Definition	Sample	Characteristics
Cooper and Dunkelberg (1981)	E	This paper reports upon what we believe to be the largest and most varied sample of entrepreneurs studied to date. The findings are from a survey of 1805 owner-managers.	1805 members of National Federation of Independent Business, all types of industries/businesses started pre-1941 to 1979	Parents, immigrants, education, number of previous jobs, age
Davids (1963)	E	Founders of new businesses (p. 3)	521 owners of firms in Georgia and Texas. Firms were 1 to 10 years old, in manufacturing, retail, wholesale, construction and service.	Education, # of children, religious, sports and club affiliations
DeCarlo and Lyons (1979)	E	None given	Random selection of 122 individuals from a pooled listing of female entrepreneurs drawn from the business and manufacturing directories of several Mid Atlantic states, from directories of women business owners, and from directories of minority-owned firms.	Age, marriage rate, education, previous entrepreneurial effort, regimentation, means of starting, achievement, autonomy, aggression, independence, leadership, support, conformity
Draheim (1972)	E	Entrepreneurship—the act of founding a new company where none existed before. Entrepreneur is the person and entrepreneurs are the small group of persons who are new company founders. The term is also used to indicate that the founders have some significant ownership stake in the business (they are not only employees) and that their intention is for the business to grow and prosper beyond the self-employment stage. (p. 1)	Survey of other studies on technical companies from Buffalo (42), Palo Alto (265) and Twin Cities (90).	Credibility, fear of losing job, prior work experience, "track record," degree of "state of the art technology"
Durand, (1975)	E	None given		

Ely and Hess (1937)	N	The person or group of persons who assume the task and responsibility of combining the factors of production into a business organization and keeping this organization in operation . . . he commands the industrial forces, and upon him rests the responsibility for their success of failure. (p. 113)	27 male and 8 female participants from the black community of a large Midwestern metropolitan area. All 35 were either owners or operators of businesses (type and age unspecified) or were seriously considering entering business at the conclusion of the course (p. 79)	Achievement motivation, locus of control, training
Gomolka (1977)	E	None given	A nationwide mail questionnaire completed by the owners of minority business organizations. 644 sampled, 220 usable responses. All types of industries/businesses. Mean age of business was 16.1 years.	Sex, age, ethnicity, education, parents' work and social background
Gould (1969)	E	None given	119 boys attending high school in Seattle, Washington who had juvenile court records (p. 712)	Deliquent associations, perception of opportunity, social class, achievement motivation
Hartman (1959)	N	A distinction between manager and entrepreneur in terms of their relationship to formal authority in the industrial organization . . . . The entrepreneur may justify his formal authority independently or he may describe it as delegated from others, notably from the stockholders. But within the organization he alone is the source of all formal authority. Management is defined residually as "not being the source of all authority." The borderline between the entrepreneur and the manager is thus relatively precise. (p. 450-451)		

(continued overleaf)

Table 1 (cont'd)

Author(s)	Type[1]	Definition	Sample	Characteristics
Hisrich and O'Brien (1981)	E	None given	21 female entrepreneurs in greater Boston area in service and construction businesses	Self discipline and perseverance, desire to succeed, action orientation, goal orientation, energy level
Hornaday and Aboud (1971)	E	The "successful entrepreneur" was defined as a man or woman who started a business where there was none before, who had at least 8 employees and who had been established for at least 5 years.	60 entrepreneurs from East Coast in manufacturing, sales, and services businesses. No industry specified.	Need for achievement, autonomy, aggression, recognition, independence leadership, regimentation, family background, power, innovative tendencies
Hornaday and Bunker (1970)	E	. . . the "successful" entrepreneur was an individual who had started a business, building it where no previous business had been functioning, and continuing for a period of at least 5 years to the present profit-making structure . . . with 15 or more employees. (p. 50)	20 individuals from Boston area. Manufacturing and service businesses at least five years old.	Need for achievement, intelligence, creativity, energy level, taking initiative, self-reliance, leadership, desire for money, recognition desire, accomplishment drive, power, affiliation, tolerance of uncertainty
Howell (1972)	E	Entrepreneurship—the act of founding a new company where none existed before. Entrepreneur is the person and entrepreneurs are the small group of persons who are new company founders. The term is also used to indicate that the founders have some significant ownership stake in the business (they are not only employees) and that their intention is for the business to grow and prosper beyond the self-employment stage. (p. 1)	12 founders of semi-conductor companies in Palo Alto area. Average age of companies was 5 years.	Age, marital status, outside activities, educational level, number of previous jobs, previous job pushes, influences

Hull, Bosley, and Udell, (1980)	E	A person who organizes and manages a business undertaking assuming the risk for the sake of profit. For present purposes, this standard definition will be extended to include those individuals who purchase or inherit an existing business with the intention of (and effort toward) expanding it. (p. 11)	57 owners or partial owners of business (type and age unspecified). 31 of the 57 had helped create the business or had been involved with the creating of a business in the past.	Interest in "money or fame," social desirability, task preferences, locus of control, risk propensity, creativity, achievement
Lachman (1980)	E	The entrepreneur is perceived as a person who uses a new combination of production factors to produce the first brand in an industry.	29 males who started at least one new enterprise in Israel which was the first in the industry. (Type and age not specified)	Age, years in Israel, education, father's occupation, achievement motivation, achievement orientation
Lavington (1922)	N	In modern times the entrepreneur assumes many forms. He may be a private business man, a partnership, a joint stock company, a cooperative society, a municipality or similar body. (p. 19)		
Leibenstein (1968)	N	By routine entrepreneurship we mean the activities involved in coordinating and carrying on a well-established, going concern in which the parts of the production function in use (and likely alternatives to current use) are well known and which operates in well established and clearly defined markets. By N-entrepreneurship we mean the activities necessary to create or carry on an enterprise where not all the markets are well established or clearly defined and/or in which the relevant parts of the production function are not completely known. (p. 73)		

(continued overleaf)

Table 1 (cont'd)

Author(s)	Type[1]	Definition	Sample	Characteristics
Liles (1974)	N	We have examined the entrepreneur who is involved in substantial ventures and have considered what we found in light of traditional thinking that he is a special type of individual—somehow an unusual and uncommon man—a man apart. It probably is true that very successful entrepreneurs *become* men apart. But, at the beginning, when they make the decision to start an entrepreneurial career, they are in most respects very much like many other ambitious, striving individuals. (p. 14)		
Litzinger (1965)	E	The distinction is drawn between "entrepreneurs" who are goal and action oriented as contrasted to "managers" who carry out policies and procedures in achieving the goals . . . Owners of mom and pop motels appear as the entrepreneurial type who have invested their own capital and operate a business (p. 268)	15 mom and pop owner-operators of motels (age unspecified) in Northern Arizona along Highway 66.	Risk preference, independence, leadership, recognition, support, conformity, benevolence, structure, consideration
McClelland (1961)	E	. . . someone who exercises some control over the means of production and produces more than he can consume in order to sell (or exchange) it for individual (or household) income . . . In practice such people turned out to be traders, independent artisans and firm operators (p. 65)	Middle level managers from Harvard and MIT Executive programs, General Electric unit managers, managers from Turkey, Italy, Poland, Indian mechanics	Achievement, optimism, affiliation, power, conscientiousness, optimism, asceticism, belief in achieved status, market morality

Author		Definition	Sample	Traits/Characteristics
Mescon and Montanari (1981)	E	Entrepreneurs are, by definition, founders of new businesses.	31 real estate brokers who owned and operated their own firms in north central region of the United States. Age of firm not specified	Achievement, autonomy, dominance, endurance, order, locus of control
Palmer (1971)	N	... the entrepreneurial function involves primarily risk measurement and risk taking within a business organization. Furthermore, the successful entrepreneur is that individual who can correctly interpret the risk situation and then determine policies which will minimize the risk involved ... Thus, the individual who can correctly measure the risk situation, but is unable to minimize the risk, would not be defined as an entrepreneur. (p. 38)		
Say (1816)	N	The agent who unites all means of production and who finds in the value of the products ... the re-establishment of the entire capital he employs, and the value of the wages, the interest and the rent which he pays, as well as the profits belonging to himself. (p. 28-29)		
Schrage (1965)	E	None given	22 R&D companies, less than 10 years old, in service, consulting, and manufacturing.	Veridical perception, achievement motivation, power motivation, awareness of impaired performance under tension
Schumpeter (1934)	N	... entrepreneurship, as defined, essentially, consists in doing things that are not generally done in the ordinary course of business routine, it is essentially a phenomenon that comes under the wider aspect of leadership. (p. 254)		
Stauss (1944)	N	This paper is an argument to advance the proposition that the *firm* is the *entrepreneur*.		

(*continued overleaf*)

Table 1 (cont'd)

Author(s)	Type[1]	Definition	Sample	Characteristics
Thorne and Ball (1981)	E	None given	51 founders of smaller manufacturing firms and firms servicing these companies. Average age of business was 11 years.	Age, number of previous ventures, education, family background
Wainer and Rubin (1969)	E	The entrepreneur in McClelland's scheme is "the man who organizes the firm (the business unit) and/or increases its productive capacity." (p. 178)	51 technically based service and manufacturing companies that were spin offs from MIT, 4-10 years old	Achievement, power, affiliation
Welsch and Young (1982)	E	None given	53 owners of small businesses. Average size of 10 full time employees and 4 part time employees. All types of industries and businesses. (No age given.)	Locus of control, Machiavellianism, self-esteem, risk taking, openness to innovation, rigidity, government regulation, economic optimism

[1] (N) Normative, (E) Empirical

(2) there are few studies that employ the same definition;

(3) that lack of basic agreement as to "who an entrepreneur is" has led to the selection of samples of "entrepreneurs" that are hardly homogeneous. This lack of homogeneity occurs not only among the various samples listed, but actually *within* single samples. For many of the samples it could be said that variation *within* the sample is more significant, i.e., it could tell us more than variation between the sample and the general population.

(4) that a startling number of traits and characteristics have been attributed to the entrepreneur, and a "psychological profile" of the entrepreneur assembled from these studies would portray someone larger than life, full of contradictions, and, conversely, someone so full of traits that (s)he would have to be a sort of generic "Everyman."

BEHAVIORAL AND TRAIT APPROACHES TO ENTREPRENEURSHIP

I think the study of the entrepreneur is actually one step removed from the primary phenomenon of entrepreneurship—the creation of organizations, the process by which new organizations come into existence (Vesper, 1982). This behavioral approach views the creation of an organization as a contextual event, the outcome of many influences. The entrepreneur is part of the complex process of new venture creation. This approach to the study of entrepreneurship treats the organization as the primary level of analysis and the individual is viewed in terms of activities undertaken to enable the organization to come into existence (Gartner, 1985). The personality characteristics of the entrepreneur are ancillary to the entrepreneur's behaviors. Research on the entrepreneur should focus on what the entrepreneur does and not who the entrepreneur is.

This behavioral view of entrepreneurship is not new. Many authors have asked as their primary question, "How does an organization come into existence?" (Herbert & Link, 1982; Shapero & Sokol, 1982). Arthur Cole, for example, taking a behavioral viewpoint, quoted Say (1816) and defined the entrepreneur as an economic agent who:

> unites all means of production—the labor of the one, the capital or the land of the others—and who finds in the value of the products which result from their employment the reconstitution of the entire capital that he utilizes, and the value of the wages, the interest, and the rent which he pays, as well as the profits belonging to himself. (Cole, 1946, p. 3)

This view places the entrepreneur within the process of new venture creation, performing a series of actions that result in the creation of an organization. However, after setting out admirably to define the entrepreneur according to a behavioral orientation, Cole immediately falls back to the "who is an entrepreneur" approach, and we are once more with traits and characteristics:

> This person, this entrepreneur, *must have special personal qualities:* . . . (from Say) judgement, perseverance, and a knowledge of the world as well as of business. (p. 3, emphasis added)

Although the behavioral view of entrepreneurship is not new, it seems that it has always been a difficult view to maintain (Peterson, 1981). As we have seen, the entrepreneur has long seemed to many researchers to be a special person whose qualities need to be investigated. In 1980 Van de Ven issued a warning to entrepreneurship researchers not to be tempted into studies of traits and characteristics:

> Researchers wedded to the conception of entrepreneurship for studying the creation of organizations can learn much from the history of research on leadership. Like the studies of entrepreneurship, this research began by investigating the traits and personality characteristics of leaders. However, no empirical evidence was found to support the expectation that there are a finite number of characteristics or traits of leaders and that these traits differentiate successful from unsuccessful leaders. More recently, research into leadership has apparently made some progress by focusing on the behavior of leaders (that is, on what they do instead of what they are) and by determining what situational factors or conditions moderate the effects of their behavior and performance. (p. 86)

Jenks (1950) and Kilby (1971) have also strongly criticized research which seeks to develop personality profiles of the entrepreneur; both have encouraged researchers to study the behaviors and activities of entrepreneurs. In empirical research (Brockhaus, 1980; Brockhaus & Nord, 1979; Sexton & Kent, 1981) have found that when certain psychological traits are carefully evaluated, it is not possible to differentiate entrepreneurs from managers or from the general population based on the entrepreneur's supposed possession of such traits.

The trait approach to entrepreneurship research is understandably persistent. Entrepreneurs often *do* seem like special people who achieve things that most of us do not achieve. These achievements, we think, must be based on some special inner quality. It is difficult *not* to think this way. But let us try to step outside this way of thinking. We can illustrate this point with a story. What if the United States suddenly found itself unable to field a team of baseball players that could win in world competition? One response to such a problem might be to do research on baseball players to learn "Who is a baseball player?," so that individuals with baseball playing propensity could be selected from the population. Such studies might determine that, on average, baseball players weigh 185 pounds, are six feet tall, and most of them can bench press over 250 pounds. We could probably develop a very good personality profile of the baseball player. Based on upbringing and experience we could document a baseball player's locus of control, need for achievement, tolerance of ambiguity, and other characteristics that we thought must make for good baseball playing. We could then recruit individuals with this set of characteristics and feel confident once again in our competitive edge. Yet, this type of research simply ignores the obvious— that is, the baseball player, in fact, plays baseball. Baseball involves a set of behaviors—running, pitching, throwing, catching, hitting, sliding, etc.—that baseball players exhibit. To be a baseball player means that an individual is behaving as a baseball player. A baseball player is not something one is, it is something one does, and the definition of a baseball player cannot stray far from this obvious fact without getting into difficulty.

This might be said about any occupation—manager, welder, doctor, butcher. How can we know the baseball player from the game? How can we know the entrepreneur from starting an organization?

While this baseball metaphor might help to make the difference between behavioral and trait viewpoints very clear and keep it clear, this clarity is not so easily achieved in real life empirical research, and researchers' viewpoints become cloudy and out of focus. Behavioral and trait issues merge and conclusions are vague and don't really tell us anything.

AN EXAMPLE OF THE TRAIT VIEWPOINT

An article by Carland, Hoy, Boulton and Carland (1984), "Differentiating Entrepreneurs from Small Business Owners: A Conceptualization" is, I believe, a good recent example of research which continues in the long tradition of "if-we-can-just-find-out-who-the-entrepreneur-is-then-we'll-know-what-entrepreneurship-is." By singling out this article I do not mean to imply that it is any better or worse than the myriad of other entrepreneurship articles that take the trait approach. I have chosen it because it is the first review article on entrepreneurship to appear in a major journal since 1977, and after such a long hiatus, my reaction was to focus hard on the offering.

As noted above, the central issue in trait approach research is to distinguish entrepreneurs from other populations of individuals. And, indeed, the Carland, et al. article begins by rearticulating the perpetual dilemma of entrepreneurship researchers:

> If entrepreneurs exist as entities distinct from small and large organizations and if entrepreneurial activity is a fundamental contributor to economic development, *on what bases may entrepreneurs be separated from nonentrepreneurial managers in order for the phenomenon of entrepreneurship to be studied and understood?* (p. 355—emphasis added)

Carland, et al. do recognize that the owner/manager of the ten or fifteen-year-old firm is not necessarily engaged in entrepreneurship, and therefore these "small business owners," as Carland et al. calls them, should not be included in a sample of entrepreneurs. However, when it comes to distinguishing between the entrepreneur and the small business owner, it can be shown that Carland et al. are hindered by trait views, by focusing on the entrepreneur and who (s)he is as the primary level of analysis. After a selective review of the literature, the paper concludes with some definitions which attempt to distinguish the entrepreneur from the small business owner:

> Entrepreneur: An entrepreneur is an individual who establishes and manages a business for the principal purposes of profit and growth. The entrepreneur is characterized principally by innovative behavior and will employ strategic management practices in the business.

> Small business owner: A small business owner is an individual who establishes and manages a business for the principal purpose of furthering personal goals. The business must be the primary source of income and will consume the majority of one's time and resources. The owner perceives the business

as an extension of his or her personality, intricately bound with family needs and desires. (p. 358)

From the previous discussion, focusing on the intentionality of the individual in order to determine whether that individual is an entrepreneur is just another variation on the trait theme, and requires us to investigate the psychology of the entrepreneur and establish a psychological profile of the entrepreneurial entity. Furthermore, even if we take the definitions at face value, we are immediately aware that the definitions raise more questions than they answer. If by definition a small business owner establishes a business to further personal goals and an entrepreneur establishes a business for profit and growth, then what do we do with the individual whose personal goal is to establish a business for profit and growth? (Are the goals of profit and growth to be considered impersonal goals?) How do we distinguish personal goals from goals of profit and growth? Are we not, then, embroiled in another dilemma of distinguishing? When you define small business owners as having a business which is their primary source of income and will consume the majority of their time, do you not thereby imply that entrepreneurs start organizations that will *not* be their primary source of income, and will *not* occupy the majority of their time and resources? (Are we to assume that the entrepreneurs are off spending the majority of their time pursuing personal goals, which, by definition, cannot be related to their organizations?) If small business owners perceive the business as an extension of their personalities, intricately bound with family needs and desires, as opposed to entrepreneurs who do not perceive their firms in this way, then isn't this definition of small business likely to include such family run organizations as Marriott, Best, and Nordstrom, leaders of their industries in both profits and growth? To suggest that entrepreneurial startups are not intricately bound up with the personality of the founders is to suggest that organizations such as Apple, Hewlett-Packard, Lotus, and Microsoft are not entrepreneurial.

The last part of the Carland et al. entrepreneurial definition ties the state of being an entrepreneur to innovative behavior and strategic management practices. Carland et al. use a Schumpeterian definition of innovative behavior (p. 357) which identifies five innovative strategic postures: (1) introduction of new goods, (2) introduction of new methods of production, (3) opening of new markets (4) opening of new sources of supply, and (5) industrial reorganization. Correlating entrepreneurship with innovation, although it is intuitively appealing, and seems to take more of a behavioral viewpoint, leads to the problem of identifying which firms in an industry are the innovative ones. Would the first entrant in an industry be considered the entrepreneurial firm, while all subsequent entrants would be small businesses? How are we to determine the degree of difference between one product and another similar product which constitutes innovation? Do new methods of manufacturing/marketing/distributing the product count as innovative, and, again, what is the degree of difference between the truly innovative and the not so innovative? Among the fifty or so personal computer manufacturing companies, e.g., Compaq, Columbia, Leading Edge, Intertec, ACT Ltd., Polo Microsystems, Tava, Stearns Computer, Wyse Technology, Microcraft, Electro Design, STM Electronics, MAD Computer, Seequa Computer, GRiD Systems, Bytec-Comterm, Seattle Computer, Durango Systems, Otrona Advance Systems, which are the innovators; which are the small businesses?

Correlating innovation with entrepreneurship implies that almost all firms in an industry which sell to similar customer groups would be considered small businesses. The Carland et al. definitions, while intending to achieve greater precision, actually increase the ambiguity in what is already a definitional dilemma. Operationalizing these definitions—pinpointing who is an entrepreneur—becomes more and more difficult as Van de Ven (1980) warned.

Carland et al. discuss some past research studies in order to identify and list many characteristics that have been attributed to entrepreneurs. As I mentioned earlier, this is the grand temptation. Entrepreneurship research has reached such a point of accumulation of data that the Carland et al. attempt to sort out past research according to characteristics studied and to list these characteristics in a table (Table 1: Characteristics of Entrepreneurs, p. 356) certainly might seem like the most effective way to proceed in attempting to reach a definition of who is an entrepreneur (although it is hoped that my own Table 1 has shown that such a mega-table is not the answer). On setting up the table, however, it becomes immediately clear, as Carland et al. admit, that the studies which investigated these characteristics and attributed them to entrepreneurs were not all empirical, and more importantly, as Carland et al. point out, the research samples were by no means homogeneous. As discussed earlier, the authors of these past studies usually did not provide important information regarding their samples; e.g., what type of industry or type of firm was studied. The past studies usually made broad generalizations in defining an entrepreneur, and the samples, therefore, included executives, managers, salespersons, and small business persons. Once Carland et al. set up the table and recognize difficulties with it, we are left wondering about the relevance of including Table 1 in a paper whose main purpose is to distinguish entrepreneurs from small business owners.[1] Carland et al. end the discussion of Table 1 with this question:

> Are the characteristics listed in Table 1 those of entrepreneurs, of small business owners, or of some mixture that may or may not be capable of demonstrating the entrepreneurial function of economic development?

By ending the discussion in this way they view Table 1 as worthless. In the Carland et al. attempt to distinguish the entrepreneur from the small business owner do we come any closer to a definition of the entrepreneur or to an understanding of entrepreneurship? I hope I have shown the Carland et al. article is a

---

[1]Carland et al. attempt to make sense of the wide range of characteristics attributed to entrepreneurs in their Table 1 by stating that Vesper's view (1980) (that several types of entrepreneurs exist) may be an appropriate view, and by implying that different entrepreneurs may possess different characteristics, thus accounting for the wide range of them in their table. However, Carland et al. quickly undercut Vesper's notion of entrepreneurial types by calling Vesper's typology ''a continuum along which several 'types' of entrepreneurs exist,'' and then insisting that the entrepreneurs along the continuum differ, not merely by possesing different characteristics, but by displaying different *degrees of intensity* of the set of characteristics which makes a person an entrepreneur. We are back to making fine distinctions and measuring imponderables. Vesper's notion of entrepreneurial types is reduced by Carland et al. to a caste system, with the most entrepreneurial entrepreneurs (the purest types) at the furthest end of the continuum. This is another illustration of the extremes to which the trait view may take us: the entrepreneur is an entity like an accordian file who can be more full or less full of entrepreneurial ''stuff.''

good example of where we end up when, with every good intention, we ask the wrong question. Who is an entrepreneur? is the wrong question.

ENTREPRENEURSHIP IS THE CREATION OF ORGANIZATIONS

Organization creation (Vesper, 1982), I believe, separates entrepreneurship from other disciplines. Studies of psychological characteristics of entrepreneurs, sociological explanations of entrepreneurial cultures, economic and demographic explanations of entrepreneurial locations, etc., all such investigations in the entrepreneurship field actually begin with the creation of new organizations. *Entrepreneurship is the creation of new organizations*. The purpose of this paper is not to substitute one highly specific entrepreneurial definition for another. "Entrepreneurship is the creation of new organizations" is not offered as a definition, but rather it is an attempt to change a long held and tenacious viewpoint in the entrepreneurship field. If we are to understand the phenomenon of entrepreneurship in order to encourage its growth, then we need to focus on the process by which new organizations are created. This may seem like a simple refinement of focus (i.e., look at what the entrepreneur does, not who the entrepreneur is), but it is actually a rather thoroughgoing change in our orientation. From this perspective, other issues in the field might be seen with new clarity.

An example of such an issue: if entrepreneurship is behavioral, then it can be seen that these behaviors cease once organization creation is over. One of the problems in the entrepreneurship field is deciding when entrepreneurship ends (Vesper, 1980). (Actually, the Carland et al. attempt to distinguish entrepreneurs from small business owners might be approached more fruitfully if looked at from the behavioral perspective of entrepreneurship ending.) The organization can live on past its creation stage to such possible stages as growth, maturity, or decline (Greiner, 1972; Steinmetz, 1969). From the process viewpoint, the individual who creates the organization as the entrepreneur takes on other roles at each stage—innovator, manager, small business owner, division vice-president, etc. Entrepreneurs, like baseball players, are identified by a set of behaviors which link them to organization creation. Managers, small business owners, etc., are also identified by their behaviors. As long as we adhere to the behavioral approach and view entrepreneurship as something one does and not who one is, then we can more effectively avoid the Carland et al.-type definitional dilemmas. But once we are tempted to view the entrepreneur, the manager, the small business owner, etc., as states of being, we become embroiled in trying to pin down their inner qualities and intentions. This approach may not completely resolve the question of when entrepreneurship ends, but it makes us look at the organization, rather than the person, for our answer. Entrepreneurship ends when the creation stage of the organization ends.

IMPLICATIONS FOR RESEARCH ON THE ENTREPRENEUR

Reorientation toward a behavioral approach to entrepreneurship begins by asking the primary question, "How do organizations come into existence?" We should think of entrepreneurs in regard to the role they play in enabling organizations to come into existence (Jenks, 1950; Kilby, 1971; Peterson, 1981; Van de

Ven, 1980). The focus will be on research questions that ask (among other things) what individuals do to enable organizations to come into existence, rather than on the traits and characteristics of these individuals.

Entrepreneurship research should follow the path of research taken in managerial behaviors (Mintzberg, 1973). The issues that Mintzberg articulated regarding managers are the issues which also confront entrepreneurship. Substitute the word entrepreneur for manager, and entrepreneurial for managerial in Mintzberg's statement of the purpose of his study:

> We must be able to answer a number of specific questions before we can expect managerial training and management science to have any real impact on practice:
>
> What kinds of activities does the manager perform? What kinds of information does he process? With who must he work? Where? How frequently?
>
> What are the distinguishing characteristics of managerial work? What is of interest about the media the manager uses, the activities he prefers to engage in, the flow of these activities during the workday, his use of time, the pressures of the job?
>
> What basic roles can be inferred from the study of the manager's activities? What roles does the manager perform in moving information, in making decisions, in dealing with people?
>
> What variations exist among managerial jobs? To what extent can basic differences be attributed to the situation, the incumbent, the job, the organization, and the environment?
>
> To what extent is management a science? To what extent is the manager's work programmed (that is, repetitive, systematic and predictable)? To what extent is it programmable? To what extent can the management scientist "reprogram" managerial work? (Mintzberg, 1973: 3)

I believe that research on entrepreneurial behaviors must be based on field work similar to Mintzberg's study of managerial work. Researchers must observe entrepreneurs in the process of creating organizations. This work must be described in detail and the activities systematized and classified. Knowledge of entrepreneurial behaviors is dependent on field work.

The results of this field work should also be able to answer additional questions. What are the specific organization creation skills that an entrepreneur needs to know? (Palmer, 1971) If we've given up the perspective that tells us that an entrepreneur is born with these skills and abilities, then we must ask how are these skills acquired? Some research suggests that entrepreneurial skills are "learn-as-you-go" (Collins & Moore, 1970; Gartner, 1984). Entrepreneurs who have started one organization seem to be more successful and more efficient in the startup of their second and third organizations (Vesper, 1980). If this is usually true, then what expertise, what special knowledge do these entrepreneurs gain from doing their first startup? One skill they might learn is how to identify and evaluate problems. A new organization is confronted by many problems, and some problems are more important than others. It would seem that the more successful entrepreneurs develop expertise in judging which problems need immediate attention (Hoad & Rosko, 1964; Lamont, 1972).

The process of team formation needs to be studied (Timmons, 1979). How and why do individuals enter a new venture? How do they claim ownership of a new idea, organization, etc.? How is *esprit de corps* generated? How do individuals convince themselves that entering a new organization will benefit them (Kidder, 1981)?

All new ventures need some type of support, e.g., financial, legal, marketing, technological. This assistance can be obtained in many ways. In internal startups the entrepreneur has to convince senior management to provide support (Scholl-hammer, 1982). What is the political process—the strategies—that the entrepreneur undertakes to gain internal assistance? Is this any different than the process undertaken by independent entrepreneurs to persuade venture capitalists to invest in their ventures? In either case, we need to make this process more efficient and successful because it appears that few new venture plans gain support. The importance of business plans to the process of obtaining venture capital and support needs to be studied (Roberts, 1983). What are the features of successful business plans?

CONCLUSION

How do we know the dancer from the dance? When we view entrepreneurship from a behavioral perspective we do not artifically separate dancer from dance, we do not attempt to fashion a reassuring simplicity. The behavioral approach challenges us to develop research questions, methodologies and techniques that will do justice to the complexity of entrepreneurship (Gartner, 1985). The creation of an organization is a very complicated and intricate process, influenced by many factors and influencing us even as we look at it. The entrepreneur is not a fixed state of existence, rather entrepreneurship is a role that individuals undertake to create organizations.

REFERENCES

Brockhaus, R. H. (1980). Risk taking propensity of entrepreneurs. *Academy of Management Journal, 23*(3), 509-520.

Brockhaus, R. H. & Horwitz, P. S. (1985). The psychology of the entrepreneur. In D. L. Sexton & R. W. Smilor (Ed.) *The Art and Science of Entrepreneurship.* Cambridge, MA: Ballinger.

Brockhaus, R. H. & Nord, W. R. (1979). An exploration of factors affecting the entrepreneurial decision: Personal characteristics vs. environmental conditions. *Proceedings of the Annual Meeting of the Academy of Management.*

Carland, J. W., Hoy, F., Boulton, W. R., & Carland, J. C. (1984). Differentiating entrepreneurs from small business owners: A conceptualization. *Academy of Management Review, 9*(2), 354-359.

Carsrud, A. L., K. W. Olm & Eddy, G. G. (1985). Entrepreneurship: Research in quest of a paradigm. In D. L. Sexton & R. W. Smilor (Ed.) *The Art and Science of Entrepreneurship.* Cambridge, MA: Ballinger.

Cole, A. H. (1942, December). Entrepreneurship as an area of research. *The Tasks of Economic History* (Supplement to the *Journal of Economic History*). 118-126.

Cole, A. H. (1944). A report on research in economic history. *The Journal of Economic History,* 6(1), 49-72.

Cole, A. H. (1946). An approach to the study of entrepreneurship: A tribute to Edwin F. Gay. *The Tasks of Economic History* (Supplement VI of the *Journal of Economic History*), 1-15.

Cole, A. H. (1959). *Business enterprise in its social setting*. Cambridge: Harvard University Press.

Cole, A. H. (1969). Definition of entrepreneurship. In J. L. Komives (Ed.), *Karl A. Bostrom Seminar in the Study of Enterprise*. Milwaukee: Center for Venture Management, 10-22.

Collins, O. F. & Moore, D. G. (1970). *The organization makers*. New York: Appleton-Century-Crofts.

Cooper, A. C. & Dunkelberg, W. C. (1981). A new look at business entry: Experiences of 1805 entrepreneurs. In K. H. Vesper (Ed.), *Frontiers of Entrepreneurship Research: The Proceedings of the Babson conference on Entrepreneurship Research*. Wellesley, Mass.: Babson College. 1-20.

Davids, L. E. (1963). *Characteristics of Small Business Founders in Texas and Georgia*. Washington, D.C.: Small Business Administration.

DeCarlo, J. F. & Lyons, P. R. (1979). A comparison of selected personal characteristics of minority and non-minority female entrepreneurs. *Journal of Small Business Management, 17*, 22-29.

Draheim, K. P. (1972). Factors influencing the rate of formation of technical companies. In A. C. Cooper & J. L. Komives (Eds.), *Technical entrepreneurship: A Symposium*. Milwaukee: Center for Venture Management, 3-27.

Durand, D. E. (1975). Effects of achievement motivation and skill training on the entrepreneurial behavior of black businessmen. *Organizational Behavior and Human Performance, 14*(1), 76-90.

Ely, R. T. & Hess, R. H. (1937). *Outlines of economics* (L Med.). New York: MacMillan.

Gartner, W. B. (1984). Problems in business startup: The relationships among entrepreneurial skills and problem identification for different types of new ventures. In Hornaday, J. A., Tarpley, F., Timmons, J. A. & Vesper, K. H. (Eds.) *Frontiers of Entrepreneurship Research: The Proceedings of the Babson Conference on Entrepreneurship Research*. Wellesley, Mass.: Babson College, 496-512.

Gartner, W. B. (1985). A framework for describing the phenomenon of new venture creation. *Academy of Management Review, 10*, 696-706.

Gomolka, E. (1977). Characteristics of minority entrepreneurs and small business enterprises. *American Journal of Small Business, 11*, 12-22.

Gould, L. C. (1969). Juvenile entrepreneurs. *American Journal of Sociology, 74*(6), 710-719.

Greiner, L. E. (1972). Evolution and revolution as organizations grow. *Harvard Business Review*, (July-August), 37-46.

Hartman, H. (1959). Managers and entrepreneurs: A useful distinction? *Administrative Science Quarterly, 3*, 429-457.

Herbert, R. F. & Link, A. N. (1982). *The Entrepreneur: Mainstream Views and Radical Critiques*. New York: Praeger.

Hisrich, R. D. & O'Brien, M. (1981). The woman entrepreneur from a business and sociological perspective: Their problems and needs. In K. H. Vesper (Ed.), *Frontiers of Entrepreneurship Research: The Proceedings of the Babson Conference on Entrepreneurship Research*. Wellesley, Mass.: Babson College, 21-39.

Hoad, W. M. & Rosko, P. (1964). *Management factors contributing to the success and failure of new small manufacturers*. Ann Arbor: University of Michigan.

Hornaday, J. & Aboud, J. (1971). Characteristics of successful entrepreneurs. *Personnel Psychology, 24,* 141-153.

Hornaday, J. & Bunker, C. (1970). The nature of the entrepreneur. *Personnel Psychology, 23,* 47-54.

Howell, R. P. (1972). Comparative profiles: Entrepreneurs versus the hired executive: San Francisco peninsula semiconductor industry. In A. C. Cooper & J. L. Komives (Eds.), *Technical entrepreneurship: A Symposium.* Milwaukee: Center for Venture Management, 47-62.

Hoy, F. & Vaught, B. (1980). The rural entrepreneur: A study in frustration. *Journal of Small Business Management, 18,* 19-24.

Hull, D. L., Bosley, J. J. & Udell, G. G. (1980). Reviewing the heffalump: Identifying potential entrepreneurs by personality characteristics. *Journal of Small Business Management, 18,* 11-18.

Jenks, L. H. (1950). Approaches to entrepreneurial personality. *Explorations in Entrepreneurial History, 2,* 91-99.

Kidder, T. (1981). *The soul of a new machine.* Boston: Little, Brown & Company.

Kilby, P. (1971). Hunting the heffalump. In P. Kilby (Ed.), *Entrepreneurship and economic development.* New York: Free Press, 1-40.

Komives, J. L. (1972). A preliminary study of the personal values of high technology entrepreneurs. In A. C. Cooper & J. L. Komives (Eds.), *Technical entrepreneurship: A Symposium.* Milwaukee: Center for Venture Management, 231-242.

Lachman, R. (1980). Toward measurement of entrepreneurial tendencies. *Management International Review, 20*(2), 108-116.

Lamont, L. M. (1972). What entrepreneurs learn from experience. *Journal of Small Business Management, 10*(3), 36-41.

Lavington, F. (1922). *Trade cycle: An account of the causes producing rhythmical changes in the activity of business* (Vol. 3). London: P. S. King.

Leibenstein, H. (1968). Entrepreneurship and development. *American Economic Review, 58,* 72-83.

Liles, P. (1974). Who are the entrepreneurs? *MSU Business Topics, 22,* 5-14.

Litzinger, W. D. (1965). The motel entrepreneur and the motel manager. *Academy of Management Journal, 8,* 268-281.

McClelland, D. (1961). *The achieving society.* Princeton, NJ: Van Nostrand.

McClelland, D. & Winter, D. G. (1969). *Motivating economic achievement.* New York: Free Press.

Mescon, T. & Montanari, J. (1981). The personalities of independent and franchise entrepreneurs: An empirical analysis of concepts. *Journal of Enterprise Management, 3*(2), 149-159.

Mill, J. S. (1948). *Principles of political economy with some of their applications to social philosophy.* London: J. W. Parker.

Palmer, M. (1971). The application of psychological testing to entrepreneurial potential. *California Management Review, 13*(3), 32-39.

Peterson, R. A. (1981). Entrepreneurship and organization. In P. C. Nystron & W. H. Starbuck (Eds.), *Handbook of Organization Design*, (Vol. 1). Oxford: Oxford University Press, 65-83.

Roberts, E. B. (1983). Business planning in the startup high-technology enterprise. In J. A. Hornaday, J. A. Timmons & K. H. Vesper (Eds.), *Frontiers of Entrepreneurship Research: Proceedings of the 1983 Conference on Entrepreneurship Research*. Wellesley, Mass.: Babson College, 107-117.

Ronstadt, R. (1984). *Entrepreneurship*. Dover, Mass.: Lord Publishing.

Say, J. A. (1816). *A Treatise on Political Economy*. London: Sherwood, Neeley and Jones.

Schollhammer, H. (1982). Internal corporate entrepreneurship. In C. A. Kent, D. L. Sexton, & K. H. Vesper (Eds.), *Encyclopedia of entrepreneurship*. Englewood Cliffs: Prentice-Hall, 209-223.

Schrage, H. (1965). The R & D entrepreneur: Profile of success. *Harvard Business Review, 43*, 56-69.

Schumpeter, J. A. (1934). *The theory of economic development*. Translated by R. Opie. Cambridge: Harvard University Press.

Sexton, D. L. & Kent, C. A. (1981). Female executives versus female entrepreneurs. In K. H. Vesper (Ed.) *Frontiers of Entrepreneurship Research: The Proceeding of the 1981 Babson Conference on Entrepreneurship Research*. Wellesley, Mass.: Babson College, 40-45.

Sexton, D. L. & Smilor, R. W. (1986). Introduction. In D. L. Sexton & R. W. Smilor (Ed.) *The Art and Science of Entrepreneurship*. Cambridge, MA: Ballinger.

Shapero, A. & Sokol, L. (1987). Social dimensions of entrepreneurship. In C. A. Kent, D. L. Sexton, & K. H. Vesper (Eds.), *Encyclopedia of entrepreneurship*. Englewood Cliffs: Prentice-Hall, 72-90.

Stauss, J. H. (1944). The entrepreneur: The firm. *Journal of Political Economy, 52*(2), 112-127.

Steinmetz, L. L. (1969). Critical stages of small business growth: When they occur and how to survive them. *Business Horizons*, 29-36.

Thorne, J. R. & Ball, J. G. (1981). Entrepreneurs and their companies. In K. H. Vesper (Ed.), *Frontiers of Entrepreneurship Research: The Proceedings of the Babson Conference on Entrepreneurship Research*. Wellesley, Mass.: Babson College, 65-83.

Timmons, J. (1979). Careful self-analysis and team assessment can aid entrepreneurs. *Harvard Business Review*, 198-206.

Van de Ven, A. H. (1980). Early planning, implementation and performance of new organizations. In J. R. Kimberly & R. Miles (Eds.), *The organization life cycle*. San Francisco: Jossey Bass, 83-134.

Vesper, K. H. (1980). *New Venture Strategies*. Englewood Cliffs, NJ: Prentice Hall.

Vesper, K. H. (1982). Introduction and summary of entrepreneurship research. In C. A. Kent, D. L. Sexton, K. H. Vesper (Eds.), *Encyclopedia of entrepreneurship*. Englewood Cliffs: Prentice-Hall, xxxi-xxxviii.

Wainer, H. A. & Rubin, I. M. (1969). Motivation of R&D entrepreneurs: Determinants of company success. *Journal of Applied Psychology, 53*(3), 178-84.

Welsch, H. P. & Young, E. C. (1982). The information source selection decision: The role of entrepreneurial personality characteristics. *Journal of Small Business Management, 20,* 49-57.

Wortman, M. S. (1985). A unified framework, research typologies, and research prospectuses for the interface between entrepreneurship and small business. In D. L. Sexton & R. W. Smilor (Ed.) *The Art and Science of Entrepreneurship.* Cambridge, MA: Ballinger.

Yeats, W. B. (1956). Among school children. In *The collected poems of W. B. Yeats.* New York: Macmillan.

William B. Gartner is an Assistant Professor in the School of Business Administration, Georgetown University.

[5]

© Academy of Management Review, 1988, Vol. 13, No. 3, 429–441.

Properties of Emerging Organizations

JEROME KATZ
Saint Louis University
WILLIAM B. GARTNER
Georgetown University

This article explores the characteristics of emerging organizations and suggests that emerging organizations can be identified by four properties: intentionality, resources, boundary, and exchange. These properties are defined and discussed. Suggestions are made for selecting samples for research on emerging organizations. Implications for research and theory on new and emerging organizations are discussed.

Two important concerns regarding research on new organizations have not been adequately addressed: how and why samples of new organizations are identified and selected. Studies of new organizations confront the researcher with the difficult problem of identifying the essential properties by which organizations make themselves known. The irony is that when we turn to the literature for guidance on how to identify new organizations, our theories and definitions about organizations assume that they already exist; that is, the starting point for our theories begins at the place where the emerging organization ends. Our goal is to probe the interaction between entrepreneurship and organization theory to generate an understanding of the properties of emerging organizations and to offer possible avenues for further research.

The challenge of research on new organizations is to move toward studying organizations-in-creation, not just retrospectively studying organizations that exist (Aldrich, Rosen, & Woodward, 1986, 1987). Identifying the properties of emerging organizations gives researchers a framework for distinguishing the different ways in which the organization creation process might occur as well as a way of organizing the search for organizations-in-creation.

The focus on properties of emerging organizations permits us to study emerging organizations as a natural extension, linked by common variables, to studies of existing organizations. Through such efforts, we hope that research on entrepreneurship can be better linked to organization theory, particularly work on new organizations, organizational stages, and innovation.

This article seeks to answer the questions: What is an organization and what properties does it possess as it comes into existence? Emerging organizations are organizations-in-creation, that is, organizations at the stage in which all properties necessary to be an organization come together. Studying the emerging organization, therefore, explores the territory between the preorganization and the new organization.

Samples of convenience are used for most research on new organizations. This may be due to the difficulty of finding new organizations, but it also may reflect a lack of theory to guide researchers to a starting point for developing sampling frames. It is questionable whether these samples of convenience (which often include spin-offs of divisions from existing organizations, mergers and consolidations, and organizations that move to new locations) can be defined as representative of the population of new organizations. For example, samples based on new incorporations are unlikely to be representative of the population of new organizations because these include organizations founded as sole proprietorships and partnerships many years before incorporation (Birch & MacCracken, 1981). We contend that population ecology- and entrepreneurship-based studies of new organizations could be dramatically altered if sampling frames were developed that identified "newer" new organizations. Because we recognize the inextricable link between theory and method (Kuhn, 1970), the remainder of this article provides theory about emerging organizations as well as strategies for identifying them.

Properties of Emerging Organizations

Definitions of organizations pose serious problems for researchers who attempt to identify the characteristics of emerging organizations. Many theories include complex properties that occur only after organizations achieve some particular size (Etzioni, 1964; March & Simon, 1958; Miles, 1980; Scott, 1964; Udy, 1958). Definitions based on bureaucracy (such as Blau, Heydebrand, & Stauffer's [1966] small bureaucracies, Mintzberg's [1979] simple structure, and Jaques' [1976] stratum-2 and stratum-3 bureaucracies) include organizations with more than one person, levels of hierarchy, and a division of labor. Similarly, definitions based on social organizations (Barnard, 1938; Blau & Scott, 1962; Bonjean, 1966; Nelson, 1968) include organizations with two or more people, thereby excluding smaller entities such as one-person or psuedo-organizations (Star, 1979).

Definitions of organizations tend to focus on the characteristics of organizations from either a structural or a process viewpoint (Hall, 1977). Structuralists, such as Weber (1947) and Blau et al. (1966), focus on the structural attributes (span of control, hierarchy, etc.) of the organization, whereas process theorists, such as Weick (1979), Sarason (1972), and Aldefer (1977), focus on the processes (often cognitive) used by individuals or groups to define the existence of the

organization. Also, there are other viewpoints that combine both structural and process ideas (Brittain & Freeman, 1980; Carroll & Mayer, 1985; Georgopoulus, 1972; Hall, 1977; Hunt, 1972; Katz & Kahn, 1978; Kimberly, 1980; March & Simon, 1958; McKelvey, 1980; Miller, 1978; Mintzberg, 1979; Thompson, 1967; Van de Ven, 1980a).

Most traditional researchers of entrepreneurship (Collins & Moore, 1964; Cooper & Dunkelburg, 1981; Mayer & Goldstein, 1961; McCelland & Winter, 1969; Vesper, 1980) do not define organizations in organization theory terms. Instead, these researchers are likely to identify *types* of organizations, such as manufacturing, retailing, and so forth.

We contend that midrange definitions that encompass both process and structural viewpoints are the most useful for identifying the characteristics of emerging organizations. In particular, we find McKelvey's definition very useful for identifying emerging organization properties: An organization is a "myopically purposeful [boundary-maintaining] activity system containing one or more conditionally autonomous myopically purposeful subsystems having input-output resource ratios fostering survival in environments imposing particular constraints" (1980, p. 115).

This definition was chosen for a number of reasons. First, it is well grounded in theory: McKelvey elegantly assimilates both process and structural characteristics from many previous theories. Second, this definition considers the dynamism of organizations as an essential focus of study. Third, the ecological perspective on which this definition is based has led to significant research on new organizations (Delacroix & Carroll, 1983; Hannan & Freeman, 1987; Singh, Tucker, & House, 1986). Finally, McKelvey's focus on organizational form (particularly variation in organizational forms) and his search for taxonomic characteristics of organizations fits our interest in identifying the properties of emerging organizations.

Organizations emerge from the interaction of agents (individuals, partners, groups, parent organizations, etc.) and the environment. This particular type of interaction is unusual because it reflects a synergy (Lewin, 1936; Maier, 1963) of agent and environmental connections. In more recent form, the outcome of the synergy has been called emergent properties by Katz and Kahn (1978). This concept inspired the identification of properties of emerging organizations outlined below.

McKelvey's definition illustrates four major properties of organizations (including those organizations in the process of creation): intentionality, resources, boundaries, and exchange. These properties, which have both structural (resources and boundaries) and process (intentionality and exchange) characteristics, are the minimum necessary for identifying the existence of an organization. Also, these properties are reflected across organization theories, especially across systems-oriented theories. The following sections relate each of these properties to corresponding ideas in the entrepreneurship and organization theory literature and offer suggestions for how these properties might be studied further.

Intentionality

In the organization theory literature, the word *intention* is derived from the works of process and cognitively oriented theorists (Aldefer, 1977; Sarason, 1972; Shapero, 1975; Weick, 1979) who focus on intentional factors, such as sense making, organizing, and enacting realities. Their ideas are the least restrictive examples of intention because they use post hoc intention as well as prior intention and focus on goals directly related to individual or group cognitive homeostasis, rather than higher order and more externalized goals.

We see *organizational intentionality* as a label describing an agent's seeking information that can be applied toward achieving the goal of creating a new organization; McKelvey said it another way: organizations are "myopically purposeful" (1980, p. 115). Organizational intentionality at the time of creation reflects the goals of the agents or founding entrepreneurs (e.g., Dooley, 1972; Van de Ven, 1980a) and the goals

of the various environmental sectors, for example, capital and industrial (Maidique, 1980; Yip, 1982), technological (Cole, 1965), government-legal (Vesper, 1983), and community (Bease, 1981; Birley, 1985; Pennings, 1982). At the very beginning of the organization, intentionality may be no more than these cross-level goals, but as the organization continues to exist as a separate entity, it will possess goals that are increasingly distinct from those of the agents and the environment. This separate intentionality can be indirectly evidenced through common belief structures regarding the goals, purposes, history, traditions, and methods that emerge within the organization, such as studies of organizational culture (Deal & Kennedy, 1982; Martin & Powers, 1983; Sarason, 1972), studies of the symbolic aspects of organizations (Salancik & Pfeffer, 1977), studies of family business (Beckhard & Dyer, 1983; Savage, 1979), and studies of innovative organizations (Hackman, 1984; Kanter, 1984).

Resources

The importance of resources has seen its most recent emergence in the works of the resource dependence theorists (Pfeffer, 1978; Salancik & Pfeffer, 1977), the strategic planners (MacMillan, 1983; Yip, 1982), and the ecological theorists (Aldrich, 1979; Hannan & Freeman, 1978; McKelvey, 1980).

In organization creation, resources refer to the physical components (versus informational or ideational components inherent in intention) that combine to form an organization. Human and financial capital, property (real estate, equipment, raw materials), and credit form the building blocks of most organizations (Cole, 1965; Kilby, 1971; Vesper, 1980). As the organization and strategic theorists cited in the preceding paragraph indicate, the ease of obtaining these resources determines the strategic direction and geographic distribution of new organizations (Hannan & Freeman, 1978; Liebenstein, 1968).

Boundary

In organization theory, boundary plays an important but underemphasized role; often it is described in terms no more detailed than semipermeable boundary (Katz & Kahn, 1978; Tannenbaum, 1968) or boundary-maintaining activity systems (McKelvey, 1980), or it is used as the precursor for describing other interests, such as boundary-spanning activities (Adams, 1976). In organization creation, however, boundary is of major importance.

Boundary is defined as barrier conditions between the organization and its environment (Katz & Kahn, 1978). That is, the organization itself exerts control over some of the resources in its environment (Schumpeter, 1934), namely, those within the boundary, and establishes the physical and legal basis for exchange across its boundary (Cole, 1965; Kilby, 1971). In establishing a boundary, the entrepreneur, parent organization, or environment establishes the organization's identity beyond that of the creating agent. The creation of a boundary as one of the properties of the organization also implies the establishment of subsystems of maintenance (Cole, 1965; Georgopoulus, 1972; Katz & Kahn, 1978). Before committing to establishing an organizational boundary, the agent can easily stop collecting resources and cease stating entrepreneurial intentions. With the boundary in place, and with the environment reacting to the bounded organization as well as to the agent of its creation, the creating agent is required to attend to organizational maintenance and must moderate some activities through the new entity.

At a practical level, the establishment of boundaries, such as incorporations, tax number requests, and phone listings, offers the first concrete and somewhat cleanly defined sampling frames for observing organizations early in their creation.

Boundary also distinguishes the individual-as-organization from the individual-as-worker. Researchers as disparate as system theorists (Katz & Kahn, 1978) and dramaturgial sociologists (Goffman, 1959) have used the idea of individuals conducting particular types of activity, such as role behavior within a boundary, as a way of defining the presence of an organization. Given an individual's intention to start an organization and the resources earmarked for it, boundary serves to isolate these elements from the other aspects of the individual's life. This is readily seen when an individual establishes organizational boundary-identifying conditions such as obtaining identifying symbols (organization name, mailing address, post office box, telephone number, and tax identification or tax-exemption number) that distinguish work done as an organization member (i.e., inside the boundary conditions) from work done as an individual (i.e., work done outside the boundary conditions).

Exchange

Exchange in organization theory and entrepreneurial theory refers to cycles of transactions. These transactions can be across the borders of subsystems (Georgopoulus, 1972; Katz & Kahn, 1978; Miller, 1978), within an organization, as in the example of managing human relations (Kilby, 1971), or across the organizational boundary with individuals, the environment, or other organizations (Singh, Tucker, & House, 1986).

Common to most of these theories are two notions: the repetitiveness or cyclic nature of the exchange process and the need for the exchange to benefit the organization. Once established, exchange cannot stop without the organization facing eventual dissolution. Unlike boundary, there is an implicit normative element in exchange, making it easier to say that one exchange is more efficient or effective than another.

This poses a particular problem in newly created organizations, especially autonomous ones. Over a given period of time, the exchanges in these organizations may be inefficient, such as selling products below cost in order to establish a market share. Because of this, exchange is viewed as the most dynamic and volatile of the four properties. Also, researchers who focus solely on studying profitable exchanges may unduly restrict the identification and selection of newly created organizations in their early stages. Unlike McKelvey (1980), whose concern was for effective organizations in the long run, we are concerned with the existence of any exchange process, not merely those that are advantageous to the organization.

Because extraorganizational exchanges take place in an established environment, identifying firms engaged in exchange is relatively easy. The other three properties must be in place for exchange to occur in an ongoing manner. The environment's demands for records indicating exchange in the legal, financial, and organizational sectors offer additional evidence of the firm's existence (i.e., financial reports, credit ratings, transaction records, such as sales slips, etc.).

These four properties of emerging organizations are necessary for an organization to exist. Unfortunately, because the properties do not become visible simultaneously, the opportunity to find newly created organizations, especially organizations that die during creation, is differentially affected by the choice of any of the four properties as a sampling variable.

Identifying the Emerging Organization

Ironically, despite our attempts to define what an organization is and what its creation looks like, we still must be prepared to conceptually define and deal with the organization-in-creation. The four properties characterize a complete organization. Yet we need to know more about the process by which an organization evolves from nothing to something; that is, we need to explore that period of time in which the preorganization becomes the new organization. In effect, to study organization creation, we must use one, two, or three properties as sampling frames to probe when preorganizations might eventually become organizations.

The entrepreneurship literature is filled with examples of different agents: new ventures (MacMillan, 1983; Timmons, 1973), new units (Perkins, Nieva, & Lawler, 1978; Van de Ven, 1980a; Walton, 1980), corporate entrepreneurship programs (Kanter, 1984; Kimberly & Quinn, 1984; Schon, 1967), ecological perspectives (Aldrich,

1979; Hannan & Freeman, 1978), and government policies (Vesper, 1983). The problem with most research on organization creation is that the researcher studies the organization only after it has come into existence, although there are exceptions, such as the study of the founding of People Express (Hackman, 1984) or studies of the formation of new units in existing firms (Kimberly, 1979; Kimberly & Quinn, 1984; Sarason, 1972; Van de Ven, 1980).

Identifying the types of firms used in studies of new organizations takes on particular importance because of three influences. First, interpretation disputes arising from the use of standardized databases by Birch and MacCracken (1981), Reynolds, West, and Finch (1985), and Armington and Olde (1982) produced a new wave of concern for what is being measured when claims are made that an organization has come into existence. Similarly, Birley (1984) showed that significant differences in the identification of new firms result from the selection of the database. Second, Star (1979) and Katz (1981) sought to account for nascent or precursor states of conventional organizations by describing the characteristics of one-person firms. Third, McKelvey (1980) sought to develop taxonomies of organizational characteristics for use in the analysis of organizational life datasets. Taken together, these events suggest a new approach to defining the organization, one based on describing existing entities, rather than one based on theoretical models. Such description has a tradition in biology, largely in taxonomic work, and reflects what McKelvey calls an asymptotic model.

For all three types of studies, using a particular database was dependent largely on practical reasons (e.g., Which database has the largest number of entries? Which database can I obtain access to?), rather than theoretical reasons (e.g., Does the database cover the population I am interested in?). The selection and assessment of the database was not guided by organization theory. However, definitions do make a difference in identifying the type of organization and its stage of creation.

For example, Birley's (1985) idea of the emerging organization assumes that an entrepreneur goes through the sequence of generating an idea, setting up the firm, hiring employees, and trading products. Identifying organizations as they seek to trade products catches firms at a later stage than identifying them when they are hiring employees. For this reason, Birley used unemployment insurance and Dun and Bradstreet databases in order to sample firms at an earlier stage.

By using the four properties of emerging organizations described, researchers can build a framework for analyzing potential sources of new organizations in a way that permits the identification of organizations early in their creation process. Sources of new organizations used by a variety of researchers are categorized in Table 1.

Although the four properties define an organization, they may not appear simultaneously. This preorganizational period (called gestation by Van de Ven, 1980a, and prehistory by Perkins, Nieva, & Lawler, 1978) in the organization's life is vital because many fundamental decisions about industry, location, size, market, and administrative intensity may be made during this time. As a result, it is worth considering the usefulness of the four properties as sampling frames for discovering emerging organizations at the earliest possible moment.

Because the issues of identifying firms using boundary and exchange processes have been considered in great detail by Birley (1985), Reynolds, West, and Finch (1985), Birch and Mac-Cracken (1981), and Armington and Olde (1982), we will focus on the properties of intention and resources as alternative means of identifying new organizations.

Using Intention to Identify Emerging Organizations

If intention is described as individuals indicating their interest in organization creation, several sources of information may be of value for identifying emerging organizations.

Table 1
Studies Using the Four Properties of Emerging Organizations

Properties	Example (Source)
Intention	Newspaper ads for potential restauranteurs (Katz, 1984)
	Networks for aspiring and active entrepreneurs (Alrich, Rosen, & Woodward, 1986)
Resources	Informal investor networks (Neiswander, 1985)
	Venture capitalists' files (Sandberg & Hofer, 1986)
	Bank files (Churchill & Lewis, 1985)
Boundary	Tax numbers (Mayer & Goldstein, 1961)
	Licenses/permits (Hannan & Freeman, 1978; Katz, 1983)
Exchange	Directories (phone, Chamber of Commerce, etc.) (Birley, 1984)
	Unemployment insurance forms (Birley, 1985)
	Credit reports (Birch & MacCracken, 1981; Reynolds, West, & Finch, 1985)

1. Subscription lists to entrepreneurial magazines such as *Entrepreneur, In Business, Venture,* and *Inc.* (especially the first two), which are oriented toward individuals who are interested in starting their own businesses;

2. Membership lists of entrepreneurial organizations, such as Women Working at Home. This approach was used by Aldrich, Rosen, and Woodward (1986);

3. Directories of students or recent graduates, or directories of members of professional societies for professions or occupations that tend to have a high percentage of self-employed individuals. Star's (1979) list of occupations is helpful for identifying those occupations of individuals who are more likely to be involved in organization creation;

4. Client lists of specialized organizations (e.g., the Small Business Development Centers) and entrepreneurial training companies, which help individuals develop business plans;

5. Participant lists from corporate entrepreneurship and redesign programs to identify firms considering new ventures;

6. Participant lists from conferences on entrepreneurship, such as the Association of Collegiate Entrepreneurs conference, university entrepreneurship conferences, new business fairs, franchise fairs, and inventors and innovation fairs;

7. Participant lists from conferences on new society-wide problems, such as conferences on AIDS, day care, home health care, and public-private partnerships, that would identify individuals who might start both profit and nonprofit organizations to deal with these issues.

These are examples of places where a researcher might locate potential entrepreneurs who are seeking information about aspects of organization creation. By seeking information, individuals may indicate an intention to start an organization. Identifying categories of information demanders, such as self-employed professions, comes in part from a model of self-employed career choice developed by Katz (1981). As mentioned earlier, the selection of any of these lists will influence the types of emerging organization one is likely to study.

Using Resources to Identify Emerging Organizations

Previous conventions for categorizing resources (money, plant, equipment, employees, etc.) are adequate as a starting point. If information is considered a resource, the previous list of sources also could be included here.

1. Applications for loans from banks, savings and loans, finance companies, and the Small Business Administration;

2. Applications for grants from corporate and private foundations, umbrella fund-raising organizations such as the United Way, and political fund-raising organizations;

3. Notices of employment opportunities in newspapers and trade journals;

4. Lists of new purchasers or renters of commercial equipment;

5. Directories of new occupants in office buildings and commercial centers;

6. Lists of self-employed individuals, found through the Dun and Bradstreet files, to identify people who have loaned money to emerging firms;

7. Omnibus marketing surveys to identify individuals who have loaned money to or worked for family or friends starting a firm;

8. Surveys of real estate agents to identify individuals inquiring about sites for firms.

Implications

Using four properties of intentionality, resources, boundary, and exchange as guidelines for identifying and selecting emerging organizations has implications for both methods and theory in organization theory and entrepreneurship. For example, life cycle models of organizations, such as those described by Van de Ven (1980a) in organization theory and Timmons, Smollen, and Dingee (1977) in entrepreneurship, would benefit from an expanded description of the variables characterizing organizational birth.

We find that traditional organization theory models (e.g., Greiner, 1972), strategy models (Porter, 1980) of organizational stages, or even the traditional entrepreneurship models of organizational stage (Timmons, Smollen, & Dingee, 1977) are less important to understanding the creation process than we originally thought. We find that most theories of organizational stages have a macro perspective (organizational changes in structure or process are studied over long periods of time, from birth to maturity), whereas our perspective is micro (organizational changes in structure or process are studied primarily at the gestation, prebirth, and birth stages) encompassed by the establishment of intention, boundary, resources, and exchange. Consequently, organization creation models, like Katz and Kahn's (1978) initial stages and Van de Ven's (1980b) three-stage model, are more useful in describing these micro interests. Researchers might benefit from increasing the degree of detail in traditional theories of organizational stages to include important within-state events, or, perhaps, by combining micro and macro stage theories.

Finally, the ability to identify and select organizations-in-creation by using the four properties provides an opportunity to explore how the study of emerging organizations might have an impact on some theoretical issues in organization theory and entrepreneurship.

Emerging Organizations and the Population Ecology Perspective

Population ecology's original question "Why are there so many kinds of organizations?" (Hannan & Freeman, 1977) places particular emphasis on variation due to newly created organizational forms as a major source of change in organizational populations (Aldrich, 1979; Hannan & Freeman, 1984; McKelvey, 1980). Recent critiques of the population ecology perspective have questioned the validity of the claim of organizational diversity, and as a result, researchers have asked, "Why are organizations so similar?" (DiMaggio & Powell, 1983). This view posits that new organizations pattern themselves after existing organizations; therefore, there will be little diversity in organizational forms among the population of existing organizations. We suggest that there is a high degree of diversity in organizational populations, but this has not been recognized because the samples of new organizations that have been used are too old. The effects of selection or institutionalization of the population of new organizations (depending on your point of view) have already occurred by the time most samples are identified and studied. For example, liability of newness arguments (Carroll, 1983; Singh, Tucker, & House, 1986; Stinchcomb, 1965) could be much stronger if based on samples of organizations identified at earlier ages. Singh, Tucker, and House (1986) found only a modest degree of liability of newness in their population of new organizations. This, we believe, was due to their basing their sample of organizations on one property—boundary (incorporation data).

Because most sampling frames focus on one type of property (intention, resources, exchange, boundary), there may be some advantage to selecting sampling frames that reflect properties more likely to occur (or more likely to be recorded) earlier in the process of emergence. In the Singh et al. (1986) example, it is plausible that some of the organizations they studied may have emerged (demonstrated all four properties) long before formal incorporation was sought. Incorporated organizations may represent *old* new organizations, that is, organizations late in their process of emergence. If the Singh et al. (1986) sample had been an intention-based study (which captures organizations at an earlier age), a larger diversity of organizational forms would have existed, and it is likely that the liability of newness among these organizations would have been much higher.

Diversity in organizational forms is likely to be greatest when organizations are being organized, that is, when organizations are emerging, not after they have become established organizations. We view the organization-in-creation as very transitory. Because an emerging organization lacks structural inertia, agents may try and abandon many organizational forms until either some type of organizational fit (both internal and external) is made or failure occurs as resources are expended in the organizing process. This is because the costs of changing various goals, structures, and so forth are so much lower for the emerging versus established organization. The opportunity to identify organizations-in-creation through the four properties enhances a researcher's abilities both to observe this variation and to study how it is generated.

In addition, selection pressures of emerging organizations are likely to be greatest when the organization is forming rather than when the organization already exists because emerging organizations are likely to have few reserves (Galbraith, 1973) to buffer shocks from environmental pressures. So while new combinations of organization forms are being attempted in these emerging organizations, selection pressures are simultaneously eliminating most of them. The emerging organization is therefore a unique situation in which both the organization's abilities to adapt and environmental selection pressures are high. By using the four properties as a framework for selecting samples of emerging organizations, we are likely to find a larger population of diverse organizational forms to observe the effects of variation, adaptation, institutionalization, and selection.

Emerging Organizations and the Entrepreneurship Perspective

A continuing challenge to entrepreneurship researchers has been to focus on the process by which organizations are created (Vesper, 1980). Schumpeter's view (1934) that entrepreneurship involves creating new technologies, ideas, products, markets, and organizational forms is similar to the previous discussion on variation. It is likely that doing something new will involve creating variations of existing forms. Yet entrepreneurship researchers have been reluctant to focus on emerging organizations and have frequently settled for retrospective work on smaller existing organizations (Wortman, 1985). The effect of studying organization creation after the fact has been to muddy the waters further in differentiating new entrepreneurial organizations from existing small businesses (Carland, Hoy, Boultan, & Carland, 1984). The use of the four properties as a framework for selecting samples of emerging organizations is clearly appropriate for enabling entrepreneurship researchers to study organizations-in-creation. The ability to identify organizations early in the creation process should be valuable for determining the success and failure of different strategies for organizing. Vesper (1983) suggested that most entrepreneurial activities end in near-misses—organizations that die while emerging. Studies of newly incorporated organizations, for ex-

ample, are likely to be conducted too late to observe these near-misses. It is therefore possible that because researchers have not observed emerging organizations and new organizations early on, they have not recognized most entrepreneurial activity.

Conclusion

The four properties of emerging organizations provide a framework for identifying and selecting new organizations. The four properties also provide commonalities between entrepreneurship and organization theory as well as links between studies of emerging organizations and existing organizations. Yet these properties also have value for identifying organizations-before-creation, that is, preorganizations. Prior to the existence and interaction of the four properties, there is something more than randomness but less than an organization. These preorganizations vary according to which properties are used, what order the properties appear in, and how long the properties last. By focusing on organizations-in-creation, that is, the transition from preorganization to new organization, we are likely to acquire a better understanding of the nature of the concept of emergence and the answer to the question "How do organizations come into existence?"

Research on emerging organizations is fraught with inherent ambiguity. Emerging organizations are likely to be small, fragile, and volatile. The process of organizational emergence may be analogous to the types of interactions that take place at the atomic and subatomic levels in physics. In order for us to identify, analyze, and understand the organization-in-creation we must change our perceptions and methodologies. Heisenberg's ideas on indeterminancy and complementarity (1958, 1971) may provide insights into the limits of our quest.

References

Adams, J. S. (1976) The structure and dynamics of behavior in organizational boundary roles. In M. D. Dunnette (Ed.), *Handbook of industrial and organizational psychology* (pp. 1175–1200). Chicago: Rand McNally.

Alderfer, C. P. (1977) Group and intergroup relations. In J. R. Hackman & J. L. Suttle (Eds.), *Improving life at work: Behavioral science approaches to organizational change* (pp. 227–296). Santa Monica, CA: Goodyear.

Aldrich, H. E. (1979) *Organizations and environments.* Englewood Cliffs, NJ: Prentice-Hall.

Aldrich, H. E., Rosen, B., & Woodward, W. (1986) *Social behavior and entrepreneurial networks.* Paper presented at the Babson Conference on Entrepreneurship Research, Boston.

Aldrich, H. E., Rosen, B., & Woodward, W. (1987) *The impact of social networks on business founding and profit: A longitudinal study.* Paper presented at the Babson Conference on Entrepreneurship Research, Malibu, CA.

Armington, C., & Olde, M. (1982) Small business, how many jobs? *The Brookings Review,* 12(2), 14–17.

Barnard, C. I. (1938) *The functions of the executive.* Cambridge, MA: Harvard University Press.

Bease, S. J. (1981) *A study of entrepreneurship by region and SMSA size.* Philadelphia: Public/Private Ventures.

Beckhard, R., & Dyer, W. G., Jr. (1983) Managing continuity in the family owned business. *Organizational Dynamics,* 12(2), 5–12.

Birch, D. L., & MacCracken, S. (1981) *Corporate evolution: A micro-based analysis.* Cambridge, MA: Massachusetts Institute of Technology, Program for Neighborhood and Regional Change.

Birley, S. J. (1984) Finding the new firm. *Academy of Management Proceedings,* 64–68.

Birley, S. (1985) The role of networks in the entrepreneurial process. In J. Hornaday, J. Timmons, & K. Vesper (Eds.), *Frontiers of entrepreneurship research* (pp. 325–337). Wellesley, MA: Babson College.

Blau, P. M., Heydebrand, W. V., & Stauffer, R. E. (1966) The structure of small bureaucracies. *American Sociological Review,* 31, 179–191.

Blau, P. M., & Scott, W. R. (1962) *Formal organizations.* San Francisco: Chandler.

Bonjean, C. M. (1966) Mass, class and the industrial community: A comparative analysis of managers, businessmen, and workers. *American Journal of Sociology,* 72(2), 149–162.

Brittain, J. W., & Freeman, J. H. (1980) Organizational proliferation and density dependent selection. In J. R. Kimberly & R. H. Miles (Eds.), *The organizational life cycle* (pp. 291–338). San Francisco: Jossey-Bass.

Carland, J. W., Hoy, F., Boulton, W. R., & Carland, J. C. (1984) Differentiating entrepreneurs from small business owners: A conceptualization. *Academy of Management Review,* 9, 354–359.

Carroll, G. R. (1983) A stochastic model of organizational mortality: Review and reanalysis. *Social Science Research,* 12, 303–329.

Carroll, G. R., & Mayer, K. U. (1985) Job shift patterns in the Federal Republic of Germany: The effect of social class, industrial sector and organizational size. Working Paper OBIR-4, University of California, Berkeley.

Churchill, N. C., & Lewis, V. L. (1985) Bank lending to new and growing enterprises. In J. Hornaday, J. Timmons, & K. Vesper (Eds.), *Frontiers of entrepreneurship research* (pp. 338–357). Wellesley, MA: Babson College.

Cole, A. (1965) An approach to the study of entrepreneurship: A tribute to Edwin F. Gay. In H. G. J. Aitken (Ed.), *Explorations in enterprise* (pp. 30–44). Cambridge, MA: Harvard University Press.

Collins, O. F., & Moore, D. G. (1964) *The enterprising man.* East Lansing, MI: Michigan State University, Bureau of Business and Economic Research.

Cooper, A. C., & Dunkelberg, W. C. (1981) A new look at business entry: Experiences of 1,805 entrepreneurs. In K. H. Vesper (Ed.), *Frontiers of entrepreneurship research* (pp. 1–20). Wellesley, MA: Babson College.

Deal, T. E., & Kennedy, A. A. (1982) *Corporate cultures.* Reading, MA: Addison-Wesley.

Delacroix, J., & Carroll, G. R. (1983) Organizational founding: An ecological study of the newspaper industries of Argentina and Ireland. *Administrative Science Quarterly,* 28, 274–291.

DiMaggio, P. J., & Powell, W. W. (1983) The iron cage revisited: Institutional isomorphism and collective rationality in organizational fields. *American Sociological Review,* 48, 147–160.

Dooley, A. R. (1972) Graduate student views on entrepreneurship and courses in entrepreneurship. In A. C. Cooper & K. H. Vesper (Eds.), *Technical entrepreneurship: A symposium* (pp. 210–230). Milwaukee: Center for Venture Management.

Etzioni, A. (1964) *Modern organizations.* Englewood Cliffs, NJ: Prentice-Hall.

Galbraith, J. R. (1973) *Designing complex organizations.* Reading, MA: Addison-Wesley.

Georgopoulus, B. S. (1972) The hospital as an organization and problem solving system. In B. S. Georgopoulus (Ed.),

Organization research on health institutions (pp. 9–48). Ann Arbor, MI: ISR.

Goffman, E. (1959) *The presentation of self in everyday life.* Garden City, NY: Doubleday.

Greiner, L. E. (1972) Evolution and revolution as organizations grow. *Harvard Business Review.* 50(4), 37–46.

Hackman, J. R. (1984) The transition that hasn't happened. In J. R. Kimberly & R. E. Quinn (Eds.), *Managing organizational transitions* (pp. 22–59). Homewood, IL: Irwin.

Hall, R. H. (1977) *Organizations: Structure and process.* Englewood Cliffs, NJ: Prentice-Hall.

Hannan, M. T., & Freeman, J. H. (1977) The population ecology of organizations. *American Journal of Sociology,* 82, 929–964.

Hannan, M. T., & Freeman, J. H. (1984) Structural inertia and organizational change. *American Sociological Review,* 49, 149–164.

Hannan, M. T., & Freeman, J. H. (1987) The ecology of organizational founding: American labor unions, 1836–1985. *American Journal of Sociology,* 92, 910–943.

Heisenberg, W. K. (1958) *Physics and philosophy.* New York: Harper & Row.

Heisenberg, W. K. (1971) *Physics and beyond.* New York: Harper & Row.

Hunt, J. W. (1972) *The restless organization.* Sydney, Australia: Wiley.

Jaques, E. (1976) *A general theory of bureaucracy.* New York: Halsted.

Kanter, R. M. (1983) *The change masters.* New York: Simon & Schuster.

Kanter, R. M. (1984) Managing transition in organization culture: The case of participative management at Honeywell. In J. R. Kimberly & R. E. Quinn (Eds.), *Managing organizational transitions* (pp. 195–217). Homewood, IL: Irwin.

Katz, D., & Kahn, R. L. (1978) *The social psychology of organizations.* New York: Wiley.

Katz, J. A. (1981) *A psychosocial cognitive model of employment status choice.* Unpublished doctoral dissertation, University of Michigan, Ann Arbor.

Katz, J. A. (1984) One person organizations as a resource for researchers and practitioners. *American Journal of Small Business,* 8(3), 24–30.

Kilby, P. (1971) Hunting the heffalump. In P. Kilby (Ed.), *Entrepreneurship and economic development* (pp. 1–40). New York: Free Press.

Kimberly, J. R. (1979) Issues in the creation of organizations: Initiation, innovation and institutionalization. *Academy of Management Journal,* 22, 437–457.

Kimberly, J. R. (1980) Initiation, innovation and institutionalization in the creation process. In J. R. Kimberly & R. H. Miles (Eds.), *The organizational life cycle* (pp. 18–43). San Francisco: Jossey-Bass.

Kimberly, J. R., & Miles, R. H. (1980) *The organizational life cycle.* San Francisco: Jossey-Bass.

Kimberly, J. R., & Quinn, R. E. (1984) *Managing organizational transitions.* Homewood, IL: Irwin.

Kuhn, T. S. (1970) *The structure of scientific revolutions.* Chicago: University of Chicago Press.

Lawler, E. E. (1978) The new plant revolution. *Organizational Dynamics,* 6(3), 3–12.

Lewin, K. (1936) *Principles of typological psychology.* New York: McGraw-Hill.

Liebenstein, H. (1968, May) Entrepreneurship and development. *American Economic Review,* 58, 72–83.

MacMillan, I. C. (1983) The politics of new venture management. *Harvard Business Review,* 61(6), 8–10, 12, 16.

Maidique, M. A. (1980) Entrepreneurs, champions and technological innovation. *Sloan Management Review,* 21(4), 59–76.

Maier, N. R. F. (1963) *Problem solving discussions and conferences.* New York: McGraw-Hill.

March, J. G., & Simon, H. A. (1958) *Organizations.* New York: Wiley.

Martin, J., & Powers, M. E. (1983) Organizational stories: More vivid and persuasive than quantitative data. In B. M. Staw (Ed.), *Psychological foundations of organizational behavior* (2nd ed., pp. 161–169). Glenview, IL: Scott, Foresman.

Mayer, K. B., & Goldstein, S. (1961) *The first two years: Problems of small firm growth and survival.* Washington, DC: Small Business Administration.

McClelland, D. C., & Winter, D. G. (1969) *Motivating economic achievement.* New York: Free Press.

McKelvey, B. (1980) *Organizational systematics.* Berkeley: University of California Press.

Miles, R. H. (1980) *Organizational behavior.* Glenview, IL: Scott, Foresman.

Miller, J. G. (1978) *Living systems.* New York: McGraw-Hill.

Mintzberg, H. (1979) *The structuring of organizations.* Englewood Cliffs, NJ: Prentice-Hall.

Neiswander, D. K. (1985) Informal seed state investors. In J. A. Hornaday, J. Timmons, & K. H. Vesper (Eds.), *Frontiers* of entrepreneurship research (pp. 142–154). Wellesley, MA: Babson College.

Nelson, J. I. (1968) Participation and integration: The case of the small businessman. *American Sociological Review*, 33, 427–438.

Pennings, J. M. (1980) Environmental influences on the creation process. In J. R. Kimberly & R. H. Miles (Eds.), *The organizational life cycle* (pp. 134–163). San Francisco: Jossey-Bass.

Pennings, J. M. (1982) The urban quality of life and entrepreneurship. *Academy of Management Journal* 25, 63–79.

Perkins, D. N. T., Nieva, V. F., & Lawler, E. E. (1978) *Causal forces in the creation of a new organization*. Ann Arbor, MI: ISR.

Pfeffer, J. (1978) *Organizational design*. Arlington Heights, IL: AHM.

Pfeffer, J., & Salancik, G. R. (1978) *The external control of organizations*. New York: Harper & Row.

Porter, M. E. (1980) *Competitive strategy*. New York: Free Press.

Reynolds, P. D., West, S., & Finch, M. D. (1985) Estimating new firms and new jobs: Consideration using the Dun and Bradstreet Files. In J. A. Hornaday, J. Timmons, & K. H. Vesper (Eds.), *Frontiers of entrepreneurship research* (pp. 383–398). Wellesley, MA: Babson College.

Salancik, G. R., & Pfeffer, J. (1977) Who gets power and how they hold on to it: A strategic contingency model of power. *Organizational Dynamics*, 5(4), 2–22.

Sandberg, W. R., & Hofer, C. W. (1986) The effects of strategy and industry structure on new venture performance. In R. Ronstadt, J. A. Hornaday, R. Peterson, & K. H. Vesper (Eds.), *Frontiers of entrepreneurship research* (pp. 244–266). Wellesley, MA: Babson College.

Sarason, S. B. (1972) *The creation of settings and future societies*. San Francisco: Jossey-Bass.

Savage, D. (1979) *Founders, heirs and managers*. Beverly Hills, CA: Sage.

Schon, D. (1967) *Technology and change*. New York: Delacorte.

Schumpeter, J. A. (1934) *The theory of economic development* (R. Opie, Trans.). Cambridge, MA: Harvard University Press.

Scott, W. R. (1964) Theory of organizations. In R. E. L. Faris (Ed.), *Handbook of modern sociology* (pp. 485–529). Chicago: Rand McNally.

Shapero, A. (1975) The displaced, uncomfortable entrepreneur. *Psychology Today*, 9(6), 83–88.

Singh, J. V., Tucker, D. J., & House, R. J. (1986) Organizational legitimacy and the liability of newness. *Administrative Science Quarterly*, 31, 171–193.

Star, A. D. (1979) Estimates of the number of quasi and small businesses, 1948 to 1972. *American Journal of Small Business*, 4(2), 44–52.

Stinchcombe, A. L. (1965) Social structure and organizations. In J. G. March (Ed.), *Handbook of organizations* (pp. 153–193). Chicago: Rand McNally.

Tannenbaum, A. S. (1968) *Control in organizations*. New York: McGraw-Hill.

Thompson, J. D. (1967) *Organizations in action*. New York: McGraw-Hill.

Timmons, J. A. (1973) Motivating economic achievement: A five year appraisal. *Proceedings of the American Institute of Decision Sciences*.

Timmons, J. A., Smollen, L. E., & Dingee, A. L. (1977) *New venture creation*. Homewood, IL: Irwin.

Udy, S. H. (1958) Bureaucratic elements in organizations. *American Sociological Review*, 23, 415–418.

Van de Ven, A. H. (1980a) Early planning, implementation, and performance of new organizations. In J. R. Kimberly & R. H. Miles (Eds.), *The organization life cycle* (pp. 83–134). San Francisco: Jossey-Bass.

Van de Ven, A. H. (1980b) Problem solving, planning and innovation, Part I: Test of the program planning model. *Human Relations*, 33, 711–740.

Vesper, K. H. (1980) *New venture strategies*. Englewood Cliffs, NJ: Prentice-Hall.

Vesper, K. H. (1983) *Entrepreneurship and national policy*. Chicago: Heller Institute.

Walton, R. E. (1980) Establishing and maintaining high commitment work systems. In J. R. Kimberly & R. H. Miles (Eds.), *The organization life cycle* (pp. 208–290). San Francisco: Jossey-Bass.

Weber, M. (1947) *The theory of social and economic organization* (A. M. Henderson & T. Parsons, Trans.). New York: Free Press.

Weick, K. E. (1979) *The social psychology of organizing* (2nd ed.). Reading, MA: Addison-Wesley.

Wortman, M. S. (1985) A unified framework, research typologies, and research prospectuses for the interface between entrepreneurship and small business. In D. L. Sexton & R. W. Smilor (Eds.), *The art and science of entrepreneurship* (pp. 273–332). Cambridge, MA: Ballinger.

Yip, G. S. (1982) *Barriers to entry*. Lexington, MA: Lexington.

Jerome A. Katz (Ph.D., University of Michigan) is Assistant Professor of Management and Decision Sciences, School of Business and Administration, Saint Louis University. Please address all correspondence to him at: Institute of Entrepreneurial Studies, Saint Louis University, 3674 Lindell Boulevard, St. Louis, MO 63108.

William B. Gartner (Ph.D., University of Washington) is an Assistant Professor in the School of Business Administration, Georgetown University.

The authors thank participants in the 1986 Academy of Management symposium on organizational founding—Jack Brittain, Robert Brockhaus, Glen Carroll, Arnold Cooper, John Freeman, and Andrew Van de Ven—for their critiques of the ideas expressed in this paper.

[6]

A TAXONOMY

OF NEW

BUSINESS

VENTURES

WILLIAM B. GARTNER
Georgetown University

TERENCE R. MITCHELL AND KARL H. VESPER
University of Washington, Seattle

EXECUTIVE SUMMARY

In this study we develop and validate an empirically grounded taxonomy of new business ventures (NBVs) using qualitative and quantitative data generated from interviews of and questionnaire responses from 106 entrepreneurs. The taxonomy describes eight different types (gestalts) of NBVs. These eight types are profiled across four dimensions:

Individual: What kinds of background characteristics, abilities, skills, and motivations do these entrepreneurs have?

Organizational: What kinds of competitive strategies and organization structures are used by NBVs?

Environmental: What kinds of competitive environments are NBVs created in?

Process: What kinds of activities are pursued, and how much effort is devoted to the activities that entrepreneurs undertake to create their NBVs?

An NBV gestalt is an ideal type generated through cluster analysis. It is a composite summary of the case descriptions of the NBVs that fell into each particular cluster. Although each NBV gestalt is a complex combination of many different characteristics, a simplistic description of each NBV gestalt is outlined to provide an overall view of the taxonomy.

Type 1: Escaping to Something New: Individuals who start these firms seek to escape from their previous jobs—jobs that from their perspective offer few rewards in terms of salary, challenging work, and promotion opportunities. The new venture is in a different industry and is a different type of work than the entrepreneur's previous job. This firm enters an established highly competitive market and offers goods/services similar to its competitors.

Type 2: Putting the Deal Together: The concern of the entrepreneurs in this group is to assemble the different aspects of the business (suppliers, wholesale and retail channels, customers) into a "deal" in which each participant in the deal can be assured of winning. Contacts are a crucial factor.

Address correspondence to William B. Gartner, School of Business Administration, Old North Building, Georgetown University, Washington, D.C. 20057.

Journal of Business Venturing **4**, 169–186
© 1989 Elsevier Science Publishing Co., Inc., 655 Avenue of Americas, New York, NY 10010

0883-9026/89/$3.50

Type 3: Roll Over Skills/Contacts: Before the start-up the entrepreneur worked in a position using technical skills and expertise similar to those required in the new venture. He or she spends little time selling, marketing, or advertising because customer contacts from a previous position are used. This firm provides goods or services that are based on the owner's professional expertise and are usually generic services (e.g., auditing, advertising). The firm competes by offering better service than competitors.

Type 4: Purchasing a Firm: Since this is a purchase, a great deal of time is spent acquiring capital for the acquisition. The venture is viewed as a turn-around situation from the previous owners. Upon acquisition a great amount of time is spent evaluating the firm's products and services. The firm competes by adapting to the changing needs of customers.

Type 5: Leveraging Expertise: This entrepreneur is among the best in his or her technical field. The firm starts with the help of partners. The firm enters an established market and competes through flexibility in adapting to customer needs since the entrepreneur is keenly aware of changes in the environment. A great deal of time is devoted to sales. The environment is characterized by high technical change and complexity.

Type 6: Aggressive Service: The firm is a very aggressive service-oriented firm, usually a consulting firm in a very specialized area. The environment requires that the entrepreneur have professional or technical expertise of some kind. Knowing the right people in this industry is very important for making sales or for gaining access to those who influence which firms have the opportunity to make sales.

Type 7: Pursuing the Unique Idea: The firm is created because of a new idea for a product or service that is not being offered. The products or services are not technically sophisticated or difficult to manufacture. Since this is the first firm in the marketplace to offer such products/services, there is some uncertainty as to whether customers can be found.

Type 8: Methodical Organizing: The methodical aspect of the start-up is reflected in the entrepreneur's use of planning both in acquiring the skills and performing the tasks required for the new venture. The firm's products or services are similar to those of other firms, but the firm has some new twist, either a slightly different way to manufacture the product or provide the service or by selling to a slightly different customer.

The NBV taxonomy outlines a situation-based framework that may be useful for helping potential entrepreneurs match their skills, abilities, and interests to possible new venture types.

INTRODUCTION

Research that compares the "average" entrepreneur or new venture to the "average" nonentrepreneur or established business usually overlooks the diversity that exists within the entrepreneurial phenomenon itself. That is, a wide range of entrepreneurs, new business ventures (NBVs), start-up processes, and new business environments exist (Gartner 1985). No "average" or "typical" entrepreneur can represent all entrepreneurs. No "average" or "typical" NBV can represent all NBVs. We believe that there is a significant degree of variation within the population of entrepreneurs and NBVs and that the study of this diversity will lead us to a better understanding of entrepreneurship. To look for the "average" in entrepreneurship is to overlook variation. For example, to regard differences among entrepreneurs as mere deviations from some entrepreneurial mean is, in effect, to discourage inquiry. This perspective on the diversity of NBVs is similar to the population ecology approach, which indicates that the study of new organizations is essentially the study of variation (Aldrich 1979; Hannan and Freeman 1977; McKelvey 1982).

Furthermore, the creation of NBVs is a complex multidimensional phenomenon shaped by the interaction of many variables (Gartner 1985). Questions such as—What kind of NBV does the entrepreneur seek to create and what are some of the demands inherent in the creation of that particular kind of business? What is the environment (real or perceived) surrounding the NBV's creation and how will that shape the creation process? What are the different activities various entrepreneurs undertake to bring their NBVs into existence?—suggest a whole array of interactions. The environment influences the way an entrepreneur acts, the entrepreneur's actions shape the environment, and the structure and function of the specific NBV created may lead and control the whole creation process. Research on NBVs cannot explain this phenomenon solely by focusing on the entrepreneur.

In this study we apply a taxonomic approach which recognizes both variation and complexity in NBVs to identify some commonly occurring NBV types. Taxonomic approaches are an important methodology for uncovering relationships in complex phenomena, and many organization researchers suggest that the development of taxonomies is an essential part of the research process (Miller 1981; Miller and Mintzberg 1983; McKelvey 1975; 1982; Woo et al. 1988). Taxonomic approaches are valuable for the development of both descriptive parsimony (taxonomies identify frequently occurring combinations) and theory (taxonomies specify critical characteristics for differentiating among NBV types, enable generalizations to be made about members in a particular category, and facilitate in the emergence of integrative profiles of different NBVs) (Woo et al. 1988). We used gestalts (Miller 1981) as a way of describing similarities among NBVs. That is, in developing the taxonomy, we looked for common patterns among the NBVs, and when we found a pattern we tried to give it a rich description across many variables (gestalt) rather than a unidimensional "definition."

MULTIDIMENSIONAL CHARACTERISTICS OF NEW BUSINESS VENTURES

In a comprehensive review of the entrepreneurship literature, Gartner (1985) suggested that NBV creation is a multidimensional phenomenon which can be described across four major dimensions: *individual* (who is the entrepreneur?), *organizational* (what do new organizations look like?), *environmental* (what surrounds the new organization?), and *process* (what do entrepreneurs do?)

One perspective on NBVs has been to focus on the entrepreneur as the primary "cause" of organization creation. This "individual perspective" seeks to discover those personality traits, psychological characteristics, and background experiences that may differentiate individuals who start organizations from those who do not (Brockhaus 1982; Brockhaus and Horwitz 1985; Carsrud et al. 1985; Hornaday and Aboud 1971; McClelland 1961; Palmer 1971; Wortman 1985).

Another perspective in entrepreneurship research is the organizational perspective, which examines the structure (i.e., size, span of control; Van de Ven et al. 1984) and competitive strategy (Miller and Camp 1985; Porter 1980; Vesper 1980) of the NBV.

A third perspective in entrepreneurship research that focuses on the environment has most often used the population ecology model, which views organizations in the context of environmental influences and the creation of organizations as determined by factors in the environment (Aldrich 1979; Bruno and Tyebjee 1982; Pennings 1980, 1982a, 1982b; Pfeffer and Salancik 1978). Other environmental approaches have looked at environmental "pushes and pulls" (Shapero and Sokal 1982), sociocultural influences (Hagen 1980; Kilby 1971; McClelland 1961), and industrial economics (Porter 1980; Williamson 1975) as ways of explaining the formation of new organizations.

The process perspective has examined the activities entrepreneurs undertake to create the NBV (Cole 1965; Kilby 1971; Leibenstein 1968; Maidique 1980; Peterson and Berger 1971; Schumpeter 1934; Van de Ven 1980; Vesper 1980).

Van de Ven, Hudson and Schroeder (1984) organized past entrepreneurship research around three of these perspectives (individual, organizational, environmental) and called upon entrepreneurship researchers to explore the phenomenon of organization creation from many viewpoints. However, a problem for researchers is how to maintain many viewpoints and, at the same time, describe the phenomenon in a coherent way, preserving its perceived complexity yet rendering it understandable. One way to maintain a nonreductive view of a complex situation is the gestalt approach (Miller 1981; Miller and Friesen 1978, 1984).

METHODOLOGY[1]

In brief, there were three phases in the research process. In the first phase a literature review helped to uncover key variables that have been attributed to the NBV creation process, and open-ended interviews were then conducted with a sample of entrepreneurs to uncover variables which they perceived to be important influences on the NBV creation process. There were seven in-person interviews lasting from two to four hours, and 133 telephone interviews lasting from ten minutes to one hour. After each interview a brief case describing the history of the NBV was written up.

To obtain the sample, we identified, through the help of professors teaching entrepreneurship courses, 211 individuals who had recently started businesses in the United States or Canada. Of these, 69 individuals could not be located, 2 individuals were too busy to participate, 140 individuals participated in the unstructured interviews, and 106 of those interviewed completed the subsequent mailed questionnaire. All quantitative analyses used to describe the sample are based on the 106 returned questionnaires.

It was thought that this sample of entrepreneurs and their organizations might have been obviously different from the general population of entrepreneurs and NBVs. We compared our sample to other entrepreneurship research samples that provided comparable statistics (Collins and Moore 1964; Komives 1972; Liles 1974; Roberts and Wainer 1968; Thorne and Ball 1982) and to demographic statistics based on studies of the United States population (Bureau of the Census 1980). Comparisons with these studies suggest that the entrepreneurs and firms used in this study had many representative qualities that might approximate the characteristics of the population of all new firms. Given the incomplete descriptions of these other samples of new firms, it could not be proven that the entrepreneurs and firms in this research were generalizable to individuals and firms in the general population of all new firms.

In the second phase of the research, a questionnaire was developed and administered in which variables from each of the four dimensions were measured. Fifty-five separate variables were measured by the questionnaire (14 individual characteristic questions, 20 process characteristic questions, 11 firm characteristic questions, and 10 environmental characteristic questions). Each question addressed a specific variable, and most questions were answered according to a Likert-type scale. The questionnaire was distributed to the

---

[1]Because the methodological description for this research is complex and lengthy, the authors have made available a detailed description of the methodology entitled, "A Methodology Appendix for A Taxonomy of New Business Ventures." This appendix includes a thorough description of the research sample, copies of the questionnaires used in the study, factor scores and loadings, a correlation matrix, and a discussion of the reliability and validity tests of the cluster analysis. This appendix may be obtained by writing to: Dr. William B. Gartner, School of Business Administration, Old North Building, Georgetown University, Washington, D.C. 20057.

140 entrepreneurs who were interviewed; 106 entrepreneurs (75.7%) completed and returned the questionnaire.

To eliminate redundancy in the variables, a variable reduction strategy was used based on a method suggested by Daling and Tamura (1970). The SPSS subprogram FACTOR: PA1 (Nie et al. 1975) used principal component analysis to reduce the 55 variables to a smaller set of 19 orthogonal components or factors, which accounted for 72.1% of the variance in the data. Factors with eigen values greater than 1.0 were selected. These factors were then used as a reference frame to identify a near orthogonal subset of 19 variables. The variable with the greatest loading for each factor was selected. While the failure to use the factors in subsequent analyses is unorthodox, the authors felt the primary purpose of the factor analysis was to reduce the 55 variables to a less redundant number. The legitimacy of the factors as useful constructs was questioned since only 55 variables were used to generate 19 factors. The 19 variables rather than the 19 factors were used because they allowed for more straightforward comparisons of the new organizations. A score on each variable (a whole number on a scale of 1 to 5) facilitated clearer interpretation than a factor score (a + or − decimal number with no set scale). Other research studies in the social sciences that have sought to comprehensively describe and compare organizations using cluster analysis, which were models for this research, have also used single variables rather than factors (Goronzy 1970; Miller and Friesen 1978; 1980; Pinto and Pinder 1972; Pugh et al. 1969; Samuel and Mannheim 1970). The 19 variables are listed in Table 1. The outcome of the factor analysis is a set of 19 nearly orthogonal variables which provide a comprehensive quantitative representation of an organization creation across all four dimensions.

TABLE 1   Variable Questions and New Business Venture Gestalt Mean Scores

Variable Questions	Types									
	1	2	3	4	5	6	7	8	$\bar{X}$	F
Individual Characteristics										
In your previous work experiences the opportunities for advancement were (1—Great, 5—None)	3.24	2.56	2.67	2.22	2.42	2.30	1.50	1.63	2.32	2.647[b]
How similar were your previous work experiences to the work in your new venture? (1—Same, 5—Unrelated)	4.18	2.11	2.83	3.00	2.71	2.70	4.00	3.63	3.15	3.681[c]
What was your interest in starting a company prior to starting your business? (1—Always Interested, 5—Never Interested)	2.06	2.56	2.42	2.11	3.86	1.50	1.88	2.38	2.35	2.283[b]
At the beginning of this venture, what chance did you see that the business might fail? (1—0%, 5—95%)	2.06	1.56	2.25	1.56	1.29	2.10	2.13	3.88	2.10	8.75[c]
Organizational Characteristics										
At the start of your business did you have any partners who were involved in the day to day operation of the firm? (1–yes, 0–No)	0.76	0.11	0.33	0.33	1.00	0.20	0.63	0.75	0.51	4.843[c]

TABLE 1   Continued

Variable Questions	1	2	3	4	5	6	7	8	$\overline{X}$	F
When did your firm begin to offer its products/services in relation to its competitors? (1—First, 5—After Others)	4.53	3.67	3.91	2.67	4.00	3.10	1.38	4.63	3.49	5.547c
How is the quality of your firm's products/services compared to its competitors? (1—Low, 5—High)	3.65	2.89	3.92	3.67	4.29	4.30	4.50	4.25	3.43	6.649c
How similar are your firm's products/services to competitors'? (1—Different, 5—Same)	3.12	2.22	3.08	3.44	2.29	2.50	2.00	2.88	2.69	3.094c
How flexible is your firm in adapting products/services to customer need compared to competitors? (1—Much Lower, 5—Much Higher)	4.00	3.56	3.58	4.33	5.00	4.40	4.00	3.63	4.06	4.475c
Environmental Characteristics										
How complex is the technology and skills required to manufacture products or deliver services in this industry? (1—Simple, 5—Complex)	2.52	2.89	4.17	3.00	4.14	4.10	2.38	3.38	3.32	7.799c
How important are contacts with suppliers in this industry? (1—Important, 5—Not Important)	2.11	1.78	3.83	2.67	3.14	1.70	2.75	2.63	2.58	3.985c
How much expertise do most customers have in purchasing the types of products/services in your industry? (1—High, 5—None)	3.71	3.89	3.33	3.44	2.71	2.30	2.88	2.25	3.06	3.112c
Process Characteristics										
How much time did you spend: (1—A lot, 5—None)										
Convincing customers to buy your firm's products/services	3.00	3.11	3.83	2.33	1.71	1.40	4.13	1.25	2.59	7.802c
Seeking advice from lawyers, consultants, bankers, friends?	3.41	3.67	3.75	3.11	3.29	2.40	2.63	1.88	3.02	2.580b
Seeking resources to start your venture? (loans, equity, supplies, etc.)	3.18	3.00	4.00	2.78	3.57	3.20	2.50	2.00	3.03	1.932a
Advertising, issuing press releases, sending out brochures?	3.35	3.22	3.08	3.33	3.29	3.00	4.00	2.38	3.21	0.876
Manufacturing the product or delivering the service?	3.47	2.78	2.50	2.11	2.14	2.20	2.13	1.50	2.35	2.785b
Did you purchase a firm or start this venture? (1—Yes, 0—No)	0.06	0	0	0.89	0	0	0	0	0.11	34.607c
At the beginning of the start-up how much time did you commit to this venture? (1—Full Time, 5—Part Time)	2.35	3.89	1.50	2.22	2.86	1.10	3.00	2.50	2.43	3.109c
Percentage of the 80 NBVs in each type	21.25	11.25	15.0	11.25	8.75	12.5	10.0	10.0		

[a] $p \leq 0.10$.
[b] $p \leq 0.05$.
[c] $p \leq 0.01$.

The third phase of the research used cluster analysis to compare and classify the NBVs. In cluster analysis NBVs were compared with one another in order to discover whether a limited number of natural groups underlie the data (Anderberg 1973; Sneath and Sokal 1973; Lorr 1983), in this case, to discover whether certain NBV patterns occur. The cluster analysis followed a five-step procedure suggested by Anderberg (1973) and Sneath and Sokal (1973).

From the 106 NBVs, a random sample of 26 was held out, reducing the population used for cluster construction to 80. The hold-out sample was for subsequent use as a verification test. The method to cluster the data was Ward's hierarchical clustering method (Ward 1963). The Ward method is suggested for use in exploratory analysis such as this, when at the outset little or nothing is known about the possible composition of the clusters (Anderberg 1973). To arrive at a set of viable clusters, subjective evaluation was aided by information in the brief case descriptions and the distinctive 19-point plotted score pattern for each case. Eight clusters appeared to emerge from this exercise. The case descriptions falling into each cluster were condensed to an "ideal type" verbal case description, or gestalt, for each cluster.

Most taxonomies are not evaluated for their reliability and validity (McKelvey 1975; Miller and Friesen 1978; 1984). We sought to enhance the generalizability of our findings by testing the taxonomy using five independent methods suggested by Infometrix (1981), and Miller and Friesen (1978; 1984). Two tests for reliability (Infometrix 1981) indicated that the eight NBV gestalts possessed a high degree of internal consistency; that is, the NBVs within each cluster were very similar and each cluster was very different from the other clusters. Therefore, the NBV gestalts appeared to be highly reliable. The three tests for external validity, while statistically verified ($p < 0.01$ for all three tests), suggest a weak classification scheme. Using a validity test suggested by Miller and Friesen (1978), 14 (53.8%) of the 26 NBVs in the holdout sample fell into the space occupied by the eight NBV gestalts. A reclustering of the 80 NBVs and the 26 members of the holdout sample together resulted in 58% of the 80 members remaining in their original groups. In a second questionnaire in which the entrepreneurs were asked to identify which NBV gestalt they belonged to, 40% of those responding identified themselves with the same NBV gestalt as assigned by the cluster analysis. Since some of the NBV gestalts decomposed with the addition of the hold-out sample, the taxonomy generated should not be considered the final word for classifying new organizations.

RESULTS

An NBV gestalt is an ideal type. It is a composite summary of the case descriptions of the NBVs that fell into a particular cluster. Therefore, no individual NBV is an exact representation of its gestalt. Each NBV gestalt, in its most raw form, is a pattern of mean scores on the 19 variables constructed from the variable scores of the NBVs falling into a cluster. Table 1 lists the mean scores on the 19 variables for the eight NBV gestalts. An F score in the far right column indicates a significant difference among the mean scores on each variable. As Table 1 shows, certain NBV gestalts have similar scores on some of the variables. An NBV gestalt is differentiated from other gestalts because of its distinct *pattern* of scores, not because of individual differences on every variable. As a guide for comparing the NBV gestalts, Table 2 was constructed to identify significant differences along each of the 19 variables. In addition, detailed qualitative descriptions of each NBV are offered to round out the description of each NBV gestalt.

TABLE 2 Profiles of New Business Ventures

	Type							
	1 Escaping to Something New	2 Putting the Deal Together	3 Rollover Skills/ Contacts	4 Purchasing a Firm	5 Leveraging Expertise	6 Aggressive Service	7 Pursuing the Unique Idea	8 Methodical Organizing
Individual Characteristics								
Opportunities for advancement in previous work	Low	NS	NS	NS	NS	NS	High	High
Similarity of previous work to work in new venture	Low	High	High	NS	High	High	Low	Low
Previous interest in starting a company	NS	NS	NS	NS	High	High	High	NS
Perception of risk of new venture failure	NS	Low	NS	Low	Low	High	NS	High
Organizational Characteristics								
Active partners involved in operations	Likely	No	No	No	Yes	No	Likely	Likely
Product/service pioneer	NS	NS	NS	NS	NS	NS	Yes	NS

(continued overleaf)

(continued)

Relative quality of products/services	NS	NS	NS	NS	High	High	High	High
Relative similarity of products/services	NS	Unique	Similar	Similar	Unique	NS	Unique	NS
Relative flexibility to adapt to customer's needs	NS	NS	NS	High	High	High	NS	NS
Environmental Characteristics								
Technology	Simple	NS	Complex	NS	Complex	Complex	Simple	NS
Importance of contacts	NS	High	NS	NS	NS	High	NS	NS
Customer expertise in product purchasing	Low	Low	Low	Low	High	High	High	High
Process Characteristics (How much did you spend?)								
Selling	NS	NS	Low	NS	High	High	Low	High
Seeking advice	NS	Low	Low	NS	NS	High	High	High
Seeking resources	NS	NS	Low	High	NS	NS	High	High
Advertising	NS	NS	NS	NS	NS	NS	NS	NS
Manufacturing/delivery service	NS	NS	NS	High	High	NS	High	High
Purchase firm	NS	NS	NS	Yes	NS	NS	NS	NS
Time commitment at start-up	NS	Part-time	Full-time	NS	NS	Full-time	Part-time	NS

NS, not a significant differentiating variable for this gestalt.

Type 1: Escaping to Something New

Individuals who start these firms seek to escape from their previous jobs—jobs that from their perspective offer few rewards in terms of salary, challenging work, and promotion opportunities. The new venture is in a different industry and is a different type of work than the entrepreneur's previous job. The entrepreneur begins the business part-time and eventually works up to a full-time commitment. Capital requirements are met through savings and easily obtained loans from family and friends. The majority of the entrepreneur's time is devoted to finding a location for the business and in making sales. This is a business oriented toward the general or "average" consumer. This firm enters an established market and offers goods or services similar to its competitors. The goods are not technically complex (e.g., pets, furniture, clothes, musical instruments), yet the environment is very competitive because of the many other firms offering similar products and services.

An example of Type 1 was Ms. 44 who started a pet store. She had no background in the pet business. Ms. 44 was formerly a secretary. Her partner was her sister who had been a speech therapist. Both women had become dissatisfied with their jobs. After spending a couple of months talking about owning a business, they convinced themselves that they could do it. Their first step was to take classes at the university on how to start a business and from the Small Business Administration on how to establish a business in their town. After these classes it took them about three months to establish their business. They did a market location study and found a building in a good area. They signed a lease and began redoing the interior by themselves. The business was financed with their own money. During this time they went to other pet stores in the area and asked for advice. One owner allowed them to look at the books and acquainted them with the right suppliers. They ran this person's shop for a couple of days. Why are they still in business? First, they believe in the products they sell and enjoy the pet business. Their customers know that they like what they're doing. Second, they have established a good reputation around town based on their knowledge of pets and the business. Third, they provide good service. Their customers could purchase most of the goods they sell for cheaper prices at other places, but people shop at their store because of the advice they get.

Type 2: Putting the Deal Together

The concern of the entrepreneurs in this group is to assemble the different aspects of the business (suppliers, wholesale and retail channels, customers) into a "deal" in which each participant in the deal can be assured of winning. There are two types of firms in this group. The first is the real estate developer. This entrepreneur has experience working for other firms putting deals together. This experience is the basis for the entrepreneur's business start-up. The other type of firm is the "novelty" firm. The entrepreneur comes up with a very good idea for a product, finds a manufacturer to make the product, makes sales calls to wholesalers and retailers, and generates primary demand for the product. A firm is created that coordinates the different functions of the idea package. For both types of firm it is important to know the right people. The real estate developer needs to know the land owners, the builders, and the investors for the project. The novelty entrepreneur has to make sales to purchasing agents in key stores. Contacts are a crucial aspect of putting deals together.

An example of the real estate developer in Type 2 was Mr. 42. His previous work was very similar, working for the state housing authority developing housing for the elderly. His real estate business was created to assist other companies in getting contracts from the state to build housing for the elderly. His firm essentially put deals together: getting money from the state to build the housing, getting a designer for the units, a builder willing to construct them for a given price, and a person to provide the land. His start-up actions were to incorporate and then to put some of his own money into the corporation. The jobs that he was able to get were from people he already knew.

Type 3: Roll Over Skills/Contacts

Before the start-up the entrepreneur worked in a position using technical skills and expertise similar to those required in the new venture. He or she does not have a long-term desire to start a firm, and only considers doing so after job advancement and career and salary growth are blocked in a previous job. This entrepreneur views the new firm as a risky venture. Little time is spent in searching for capital beyond the savings of the entrepreneur. Since he or she is very familiar with the industry, little time is spent studying the industry or learning the technical requirements of the job. The entrepreneur spends little time selling, marketing, or advertising because customer contacts from a previous position are used. The individual makes a full-time commitment to the new venture by quitting the previous job at the outset. This firm provides goods or services based on the owner's professional expertise, such as CPAs and consultants. Firms in this gestalt offer generic services (e.g., auditing, personnel agencies, advertising). The firm competes by offering better service than competitors.

An example of Type 3 was Mr. 6 who started a firm providing consulting services in the area of management compensation. He had been doing exactly the same work for another company for the previous six years, but he felt he could do just as well on his own. To start his business he contacted a lawyer to incorporate. Mr. 6 contacted some of his previous clients for work. Developing a reputation for good work was very important because most of his clients (corporations) knew one another. Mr. 6 also wrote articles in trade journals in order to build a strong reputation in his industry.

Type 4: Purchasing a Firm

The entrepreneur's work background is similar to the venture acquired. His or her previous job provided opportunities for advancement and growth, but this individual has had a long-term interest in owning a business and perceives this venture as low risk. Since this is a purchase, a great deal of time is spent acquiring capital for the acquisition. Much time is devoted to financial planning. Upon purchase there is a full-time commitment. The venture is viewed as a turn-around situation from the previous owners. Upon acquisition a great amount of time is spent evaluating the firm's products and services. The entrepreneur feels he or she must get to know all the different aspects of the business on intimate terms as owner/manager. There are two types of firms in this group: the purchased firm and the firm that is family owned or started with family assistance. Both types offer products and services of the same type and quality as their competitors. The firms compete by adapting to the changing needs of customers. The types of goods and services offered are not complex.

An example of Type 4 was Mr. 4, who purchased a bike shop. He described himself as a bike person. It had been his childhood dream to own a bike shop. After retirement from the military he decided to go to school. While in school he found a bike shop and bought out the owner. The reason he decided to buy instead of starting his own shop was that he saw that the town could only afford to have one bike shop. Since he bought the firm its sales have quadrupled. What makes this business successful? (1) His enthusiasm for biking. (2) Good service—better than any other place in the area. (3) He went to school to learn how to operate a business, using such things as inventory control and marketing, in which he did a study of bike purchasing patterns for his area. (4) He has no competition in terms of other bike shops. Some of the department stores sell bikes. No other store in the area services bikes. He has 99% of the repair market.

Type 5: Leveraging Expertise

This entrepreneur is an expert, and is among the best in his or her technical field. Past work experiences provided a great deal of opportunity for growth, and the individual has had little interest in starting a venture. But an opportunity presents itself (usually an idea for a new product or for the modification of an old product that his or her present employer declines to pursue) and there seems little risk of failure. The firm starts with the help of partners. The firm enters an established market and competes by offering products/services that are different in many respects from competitors'. The firm is highly flexible in adapting to customer needs since the entrepreneur's expertise makes him or her keenly aware of changes in the environment. A great deal of time is devoted to sales. The environment is characterized by high technical change and complexity. Customers are purchasing agents or committees who analyze the products/services before purchase. Other firms pose a low competitive threat since this firm's products/services have special features that attract customers and the products/services are of higher quality.

An example of Type 5 was Mr. 60 who owned a business with partners that supplied a particular type of software for a particular application on minicomputers. His previous work was in writing software for the same type of applications but for larger computers. When minicomputers were introduced, he and his four partners saw an opportunity to start a business that catered to the small computer, so they quit their jobs and started this firm. The firm is nationally known as the best supplier of the particular software packages and systems they design. Most of their clients are Fortune 500 corporations.

Type 6: Aggressive Service

The firm is a very aggressive service-oriented firm, usually a consulting firm in a very specialized area such as technology transfer or executive recruiting. The entrepreneur's involvement level is very high; a great deal of time is spent selling and identifying customers, advertising, and scanning for new opportunities. Little time is spent searching for resources since start-up costs are low or since the entrepreneur knows people who will contribute the resources. This individual always wanted to start a business. The work is similar to his or her previous work or educational training. The environment requires that the entrepreneur have professional or technical expertise of some kind. The products/services are offered to a very narrow range of customers who have specific needs. Knowing the right people in this industry is very important for making sales or for gaining access to those who influence which firms have the opportunity to make sales. The firms enters a marketplace which is relatively new. The firm's products and services are somewhat better and different than those of other firms.

An example of Type 6 was Mr. 85 who owned an investment banking company. His previous work experience was as an investment banker for three firms on Wall Street. A very aggressive and outgoing person, he was always meeting new people and making contacts. Out of his contact base grew opportunities to make deals as an investment banker.

To start his company he took the following actions: (1) he filed papers of incorporation ; (2) he got an office; (3) he talked with many people in the investment banking business; (4) he expanded his contacts, using present contacts to make others. He also developed an innovative way to provide investment banking services which he marketed to his clients. He sought out new markets. He found that certain areas of the United States lacked the services he provided and he marketed in those areas.

Type 7: Pursuing the Unique Idea

The firm is created because of a new idea for a product or service that is not being offered. The products/services are not technically sophisticated or difficult to manufacture. The firm is flexible in changing its products to meet customer needs. Products are of high quality. Since this is the first firm in the marketplace to offer such products/services, there is some uncertainty as to whether customers can be found. The work in the new venture is different from the entrepreneur's work in previous job. The entrepreneur is uncertain whether enough resources can be acquired to begin the venture and whether the products/services can be delivered with the high quality envisioned. For all of these reasons, start-up seems risky. The entrepreneur's past work experiences provided opportunity for growth and advancement, but he or she has a high interest in owning a business, and is constantly alert for new venture opportunities.

An example of Type 7 was Mr. 23 who worked in advertising and in his spare time developed his own innovative product ideas. With one of the ideas he started a company. He thought there would be a market for replacement collar stays, since he so often needed one. His idea centered on a unique package for the stays. Using the yellow pages he called manufacturers of collar stays and bought some. Then he spent a great deal of time developing his package and label. He went on the road to generate orders, then sold this item through manufacturer's representatives. He had no competitors since this was a rather small and unique market.

Type 8: Methodical Organizing

In order to establish this business the entrepreneur devotes a great deal of time to all the aspects of the business—planning, marketing, production, and finance. The entrepreneur is put in the position of having to learn the entire business from the ground up as the firm slowly takes form during the start-up period. The entrepreneur's previous work experiences provided great opportunities for job growth and salary increases, yet this individual has a high desire to own a business. The new venture is seen as risky since it is in an area in which the entrepreneur has little previous experience or expertise. The methodical aspect of the start-up is reflected in the entrepreneur's use of planning both in acquiring the skills and performing the tasks required for the new venture. The firm's products/services are similar to those of other firms, but the firm has some new twist, either in a slightly different way to manufacture the product or provide the service or by selling to a slightly different customer. This is a very competitive environment. Customers require highly technical and competent product/services, and there are many firms trying to meet these demands. The entrepreneur frequently deals with middlemen—retailers or purchasing agents—to reach customers. Much time and money is spent on advertising. The entrepreneur makes an initial part-time commitment to get the venture on its feet and earns money elsewhere to keep it afloat.

An example of Type 8 was Mr. 5 who started a company that manufactured collapsible baby strollers. He had a BA in English literature and an MBA in finance and marketing. His work experience was with a large food conglomerate in marketing. He quickly became dissatisfied with the corporate life-style. He decided to start a business on a path of "do-ability." The business would be in an industry meeting these criteria: (1) small industry, (2) not capital intensive, (3) history of a low rate of innovation, (4) little credit extension required of manufacturers to retailers, (5) industry of weak competitors. A number of industries were identified through extensive research. The children's furniture industry was chosen for a business start-up. Mr. 5 assembled consumer focus groups and asked them to identify children's furniture products that they were dissatisfied with. The old-fashioned baby stroller was most often identified. Mr. 5 had a collapsible baby stroller designed. It was the first of its kind. He sought out major retailers to carry the stroller. The firm devoted a great deal of time to meeting the needs of the large retailers, such as specialized packaging. Mr. 5's goal was to saturate the market channels before competitors entered. He contracted with another company for initial production of the stroller. The business plan estimated sales per year, and calculated break-even at a certain number of units per month. Within a year sales per month were three times break-even and Mr. 5 took over manufacture of the stroller.

DISCUSSION AND CONCLUSIONS

The underlying premise of this research is the belief that there is no single type of entrepreneur and that the organizations, behaviors, and the environments in which entrepreneurs create their businesses vary widely. These differences among entrepreneurs and their NBVs are what is significant and interesting. The taxonomy presented in this article is a modest beginning at uncovering frequently occurring combinations of NBVs while recognizing variation throughout the population of all NBVs. While taxonomies frequently require modifications and revisions as they are expanded and tested (McKelvey 1982), the taxonomic process was useful for revealing important aspects of the NBV creation process as well as for generating parsimony through the development of integrated profiles of similar types of NBVs.

Limitations of the Research

First, we are aware of a number of problems with the research. Although the sample was similar in many respects to the general population of individuals and firms, different methods of obtaining a sample may result in samples with different characteristics, thereby changing the characteristics of the taxonomy. A much larger sample would improve the reliability of any taxonomy and permit the use of more powerful statistical tests. Because of a lack of a detailed data base on new organizations which describes all four dimensions (individual, organizational, environment, and process) the generalizability of the sample to all new organizations can only be verified by similar future research based on different samples.

Second, the questionnaire was part of an overall research design that was cross-sectional, so that while we were able to describe new organizations, causal connections among the described elements could only be speculated upon, not shown. A longitudinal research approach will be necessary in order to discover these relationships. Also, the responses were based on the subjective perceptions and memories of the entrepreneurs and were taken at face value. Obviously, obtaining multiple respondents in a given organization would help to ascertain the validity of these descriptions.

Third, the factors and variables chosen to represent a new organization were dependent not only on the sample and questionnaire but on the method of factor analysis used. Other choices might have produced other models. Also, Miller (1978) discussed alternative techniques of cluster analysis that might have resulted in different ways of explaining the same data, that is, in different taxonomies.

Finally, the tests of the validity of the taxonomy, while statistically significant, point out a rather weak classification scheme if one were to verify the taxonomy through entrepreneurs selecting their own gestalt. Additional taxonomy development is clearly necessary for improving the reliability and validity of the NBV patterns generated.

Directions for Future Research

We do not want to imply that this taxonomy was generated to supercede other frameworks for differentiating entrepreneurial types. Every taxonomy of entrepreneurs begins with the same fundamental premise: All entrepreneurs are not the same. Taxonomy development is a method for identifying the most salient characteristics for differentiating among entrepreneurs as well as describing how each entrepreneurial type behaves. Although each taxonomy is created to emphasize specific differentiating variables, similarities among different taxonomies of entrepreneurs are not necessarily precluded. For example, the craftsman/opportunistic taxonomy developed by Smith (1967) and expanded and explored in further studies (Smith and Miner 1983; Peterson and Smith 1986; Woo et al. 1988) does not necessarily conflict with the taxonomy presented here. The two types of service firms (Type 3: Roll Over Skills/Contacts and Type 6: Aggressive Service) might be viewed as examples of the craftsman/opportunistic dichotomy. At this stage in the development of entrepreneurship as an area of study, no single taxonomy is likely to capture all of the important differentiating variables. In some respects this is because the phenomenon of entrepreneurship itself needs further refinement and description (Low and MacMillan 1988). The development of taxonomies is important for deliniating the fundamental characteristics of the phenomenon to be studied (McKelvey 1982). As entrepreneurship taxonomies became more detailed and comprehensive, so will our understanding of the entrepreneurship field. So we must continue to generate, develop, and eventually compare entrepreneurial taxonomies.

Research is needed on the mechanisms that influence variation in NBVs. Recognition of the depth and breadth of changes in a population of organizations due to NBVs should provide insights into the nature of organizational adaptation and the influence of environmental selection (Katz and Gartner 1988).

Throughout this research the emphasis on the quantitative aspects of the research may have overshadowed in the reader's mind the value and usefulness of the qualitative information provided by the entrepreneurs. We were able to draw upon the rich texture of their experiences in every phase of this research: in the development of the framework and questionnaire, in the cluster analysis and taxonomy development, and in the discussion that followed. However, only through the use of the questionnaire as a way of quantifying the entrepreneur's experiences could comparison and analysis of these experiences begin. Future research studies should continue to employ methods that combine both qualitative and quantitative approaches.

Implications

In some respects, the taxonomy of NBVs is a contingency theory about the process of NBV creation. The taxonomy uses variables from four perspectives on NBVs—individual, organizational, environmental, and process—as building blocks for the construction of integrated NBV profiles. Each NBV gestalt identifies a unique mix of entrepreneurial backgrounds and skills, organization structures and strategies, competitive environments, and start-up behaviors. Taken as a whole, the taxonomy portrays many different methods for starting an NBV. The taxonomy provides a useful framework for identifying critical aspects in the creation of a specific type of NBV. For the practitioner, the NBV taxonomy outlines a situational based framework by which an entrepreneur can determine the focus of organizational creation activities that should be undertaken based on all the other dimensions. For the potential entrepreneur, the NBV taxonomy provides an avenue to discover different possibilities for action. Confronted with a wide array of possibilities, individuals are more likely to ask, "What kind of entrepreneur am I?" rather than "Am I an entrepreneur?" The taxonomy may be useful for helping potential entrepreneurs match their skills, abilities, and interests to possible new venture types.

There is no "average" in entrepreneurship. Exploiting opportunities is more often doing things differently, rather than following the typical. By recognizing many different types of NBVs, we are more likely to see and appreciate the diversity inherent in entrepreneurship.

REFERENCES

Aldrich, H.E. 1979. *Organizations and Environments*. Englewood Cliffs, N.J.: Prentice Hall.

Anderberg, M.R. 1973. *Cluster Analysis for Applications*. New York: Academic Press.

Brockhaus, R.H. 1982. The psychology of the entrepreneur. In C.A. Kent, D.L. Sexton, and K.H. Vesper (Eds.) *Encyclopedia of Entrepreneurship*. Englewood Cliffs, N.J.: Prentice-Hall, pp. 39–56.

Brockhaus, R.H., and Horwitz, P.S. 1985. The psychology of the entrepreneur. In D.L. Sexton and R.W. Smilor (Eds.) *The Art and Science of Entrepreneurship*. Cambridge, Mass.: Ballinger.

Bruno, A.V., and Tyebjee, T.T. 1982. The environment for entrepreneurship. In C.A. Kent, D.L. Sexton, and K.H. Vesper (Eds.) *Encyclopedia of Entrepreneurship*. Englewood Cliffs, N.J.: Prentice-Hall, pp. 288–307.

Bureau of the Census. 1980. *Statistical Abstract of the United States, 1980,* 101st ed. Washington, D.C.: U.S. Government Printing Office.

Carland, J.W., Hoy, F., Boulton, W.R., and Carland, J.C. 1984. Differentiating entrepreneurs from small business owners: A conceptualization. *Academy of Management Review* 9(2):354–359.

Carsrud, A.L., Olm, K.W., and Eddy, G.C. 1985. Entrepreneurship: Research in quest of a paradigm. In D.L. Sexton and R.W. Smilor (Eds.) *The Art and Science of Entrepreneurship*. Cambridge, Mass.: Ballinger.

Cole, A.H. 1965. An approach to the study of entrepreneurship: A tribute to Edwin F. Gay. In H.G.J. Aitken (Ed.) *Explorations in Enterprise*. Cambridge, Mass.: Harvard University Press, pp. 30–44.

Collins, O.F., and Morre, D.G. 1964. *The Enterprising Man*. East Lansing, Mich.: Michigan State University.

Daling, J., and Taumura, H. 1970. Use of orthogonal factors for selection of variables in a regression equation: An illustration. *Applied Statistics* (Series C) 19:260–268.

Gartner, W.B. 1985. A conceptual framework for describing the phenomenon of new venture creation. *Academy of Management Review* 10(4):696–706.

Goronzy, F. 1970. A numerical taxonomy of business enterprises. In A.J. Cole (Ed.) *Numerical taxonomy*. New York: Academic Press.

Hagen, E.F. 1980. *The Economics of Development*, 3rd ed. Homewood, Ill.: Richard D. Irwin.

Hannan, M.T., and Freeman, J. 1977. The population ecology of organizations. *American Journal of Sociology* 82:929–964.

Hornaday, J., and Aboud, J. 1971. Characteristics of successful entrepreneurs. *Personnel Psychology* 24(2):141–153.

Infometrix, Inc. 1981. *ARTHUR 81: Users Manual for the January 1981 Revised Version*. Seattle, Wash.: Infometrix, Inc.

Katz, G., and Gartner, W. 1988. Properties of emerging organizations. *Academy of Management Review* 13(3):429–441.

Kilby, P. 1971. Hunting the heffalump. In P. Kilby (Ed.) *Entrepreneurship and Economic Development*. New York: Free Press, pp. 1–40.

Klastorin, T.D., and Ledingham, R. 1980. *Program CLAN: Documentation*. Working paper, Graduate School of Business Administration, University of Washington, Seattle.

Komives, J.L. 1972. A preliminary study of the personal values of high technology entrepreneurs. In A.C. Cooper and J.L. Komives (Eds.) *Technical Entrepreneurship: A Symposium*. 231–242. Milwaukee, Wis.: Center for Venture Management.

Leibenstein, H. 1968. Entrepreneurship and economic development. *American Economic Review*. 58(2):72–83.

Liles, P.R. 1974. *New Business Ventures and the Entrepreneur*. Homewood, Ill. Richard D. Irwin.

Lorr, M. 1983. *Cluster Analysis for Social Scientists*. San Francisco: Jossey-Bass.

Low, M.B., and MacMillan, I.C. 1988. Entrepreneurship: Past research and future challenges. *Journal of Management* 14:139–162.

Maidique, M. 1980. Entrepreneurs, champions and technological innovation. *Sloan Management Review*. 21:59–76.

McClelland, D. 1961. *The Achieving Society*. Princeton, N.J.: Van Nostrand.

McKelvey, B. 1975. Guidelines for the empirical classification of organizations. *Administrative Science Quarterly* 20:509–525.

McKelvey, B. 1982. *Organizational Systematics*. Berkeley, Calif.: University of California Press.

Miller, A., and Camp, B. 1985. Exploring determinations of success in new corporate ventures. *Journal of Business Venturing* 1:87–106.

Miller, D. 1978. The role of multivariate Q-techniques in the study of organizations. *Academy of Management Review* 3:515–531.

Miller, D. 1981. Toward a new contingency approach: The search for organizational gestalts. *Journal of Management Studies* 18:1–26.

Miller, D., and Friesen, P. 1978. Archetypes of strategy formulation. *Management Science* 24:921–933.

Miller, D., and Friesen, P. 1980. Archetypes of organizational transition. *Administrative Science Quarterly* 25:268–299.

Miller, D., and Friesen, P. 1984. *Organizations: A Quantum View*. Englewood Cliffs, N.J.: Prentice-Hall.

Miller, D., and Mintzberg, H. 1983. The case for configuration. In G. Morgan (Ed.) *Beyond Method*. Beverly Hills, Calif.: Sage.

Nie, N.H., Hull, C.H., Jenkins, J.G., Steinbreener, K., and Bent, D.H. 1975. *SPSS: Statistical Package for the Social Sciences*, 2nd ed. New York: McGraw Hill.

Palmer, M. 1971. The application of psychological testing to entrepreneurial potential. *California Management Review* 13(3):32–39.

Pennings, J.M. 1980. Environmental influences on the creation process. In J.R. Kimberly and R. Miles (Eds.) *The Organization Life Cycle. San Francisco: Jossey Bass, pp. 135–160*.

Pennings, J.M. 1982a. Organizational birth frequencies. *Administrative Science Quarterly* 27:120–144.

Pennings, J.J. 1982b. The urban quality of life and entrepreneurship. *Academy of Management Journal* 25:63–79.

Peterson, R.A., and Berger, D.G. 1971. Entrepreneurship in organizations: Evidence from the popular music industry. *Administrative Science Quarterly* 16:97–107.

Peterson, R., and Smith, N.R. 1986. Entrepreneurship: A culturally appropriate combination of craft

186 GARTNER ET AL.

and opportunity. In R. Ronstadt, J.A. Hornaday, R. Peterson, and K.H. Vesper (Eds.) *Frontiers of Entrepreneurship Research: 1986*. Wellesley, Mass.: Babson College, pp. 1–11.

Pfeffer, J., and Salancik, G.R. 1978. *The External Control of Organizations*. New York: Harper and Row.

Pinto, P.R., and Pinder, C.C. 1972. A cluster analytic approach to the study of organizations. *Organizational Behavior and Human Performance* 8:508–522.

Porter, M. 1980. *Competitive Strategy*. New York: Free Press.

Pugh, D.S., Hickson, D.J., and Hinnings, C.R. 1969. An empirical taxonomy of structures of work organizations. *Administrative Science Quarterly* 14:115–126.

Roberts, E.B., and Wainer, H.A. 1968. New enterprise on Rte. 128. *Science Journal* 4(12):78–83.

Samuel, Y., and Mannheim, B.F. 1970. A multidimensional approach toward a typology of bureaucracy. *Administrative Science Quarterly* 15:216–228.

Schumpeter, J.A. 1934. *The Theory of Economic Development*. Translated by R. Opie. Cambridge, Mass.: Harvard University Press.

Shapero, A., and Sokol, L. 1982. The social dimensions of entrepreneurship. In C.A. Kent, D.L. Sexton, and K.H. Vesper (Eds.) *Encyclopedia of Entrepreneurship. Englewood Cliffs, N.J.: Prentice-Hall, pp. 72–90.*

Siegel, S. 1956. *Nonparametric Statistics for the Behavioral Sciences*. New York: McGraw-Hill.

Smith, N.R. 1967. *The Entrepreneur and His Firm: The Relationship Between Type of Men and Type of Company*. East Lansing, Mich.: Bureau of Business and Economic Research, Michigan State University.

Smith, N.R., and Miner, J.B. 1983. Type of entrepreneur, type of firm, and managerial innovation: Implications for organizational life cycle theory. In *Frontiers of Entrepreneurship Research: 1983*. Wellesley, Mass.: Babson College, pp. 51–71.

Sneath, P.H.A., and Sokal, R.R. 1973. *Numerial Taxonomy*. San Francisco: Freeman.

Thorne, J.R., and Ball, J.G. 1982. Entrepreneurs and their companies: Smaller industrial firms. In K.H. Vesper (Ed.) *Frontiers of Entrepreneurship Research*. Wellesley, Mass.: Babson College, pp. 65–83.

Van de Ven, A.H. 1980. Early planning, implementation and performance of new organizations. In J.R. Kimberly and R. Miles (Eds.) *The Organization Life Cycle*. San Francisco: Jossey Bass, pp. 83–134.

Van de Ven, A.H., Hudson, R., and Schroeder, D.M. 1984. Designing new business startups: Entrepreneurial, organizational, and ecological considerations. *Journal of Management* 10(1):87–107.

Vesper, K.H. 1980. *New Venture Strategies*. Englewood Cliffs, N.J.: Prentice-Hall.

Ward, J.H. 1963. Hierarchical grouping to optimize an objective function. *Journal of the American Statistical Association* 58:236–244.

Williamson, O.E. 1975. *Markets and Hierarchies*. New York: Free Press.

Woo, C.Y., Cooper, A.C., and Dunkelburg, W.C. 1988. Entrepreneurial typologies: Definitions and implications. Paper presented at Babson Entrepreneurship Research Conference, Calgary, Canada.

Wortman, M.S. 1985. A unified framework, research typologies, and research prospectuses for the interface between entrepreneurship and small business. In D.L. Sexton and R.W. Smilor (Eds.) *The Art and Science of Entrepreneurship*. Cambridge, Mass.: Ballinger.

[7]

A PROFILE OF
NEW VENTURE SUCCESS
AND FAILURE
IN AN EMERGING
INDUSTRY

DONALD A. DUCHESNEAU
Natural Brands, Inc.

WILLIAM B. GARTNER
Georgetown University

EXECUTIVE SUMMARY

This study examined three types of factors: (1) the characteristics of the lead entrepreneur, (2) startup processes undertaken during the founding of the firm, and (3) firm behaviors after start-up, including management practices and strategic behaviors, associated with new venture success and failure. The research involved a field study of 26 small, young firms; 13 successful and 13 less, successful (or failed), each engaged in the distribution of fresh juices in eight metropolitan centers (about 30% of the total market) in the United States.

Both quantitative and qualitative data were collected through field work at each firm location. A statistical analysis of data collected in a structured questionnaire was the primary method for testing the factors. Case studies of all of the firms were developed to provide qualitative support for the quantitative findings of the study. Results from these analyses indicated significant differences between successful and unsuccessful firms in all three categories.

Lead entrepreneurs in successful firms were more likely to have been raised by entrepreneurial parents, have had a broader business and more prior startup experience, and believed they had less control of their success in business, than unsuccessful entrepreneurs. Successful entrepreneurs seek to reduce risk in their businesses. They work long hours, have a personal investment in the firm, and are good communicators. Successful firms were those initiated with ambitious goals. Lead entrepreneurs had a clear broad business idea which provided the adaptive torque required to overcome adversity, confrontation, and often, a troubled financial condition.

Effective startup or purchase required broad planning efforts that considered all aspects of the

Address correspondence to William B. Gartner, School of Business Administration, Old North Building, Georgetown University, Washington, D.C. 20057.

A version of this paper was presented at the 1988 Babson Conference on Entrepreneurship Research and is based on Dr. Duchesneau's dissertation, New Venture Success In An Emerging Industry. Fort Lauderdale, FL: Nova University, 1987.

Journal of Business Venturing 5, 297–312
© 1990 Elsevier Science Publishing Co., Inc., 655 Avenue of the Americas, New York, NY 10010

0883-9026/90/$3.50

industry and firm. Successful firms spent more time planning (237 hours) than unsuccessful firms (85 hours). The use of outside professionals and advisors for help in solving specific problems during startup was important for success as well as the advice and information provided by other industry participants, particularly customers and suppliers. Most ventures did not have written business plans.

Nearly all purchased firms failed. Buyers of competitively troubled firms were negatively displaced, generally unemployed managers who lacked broad management experience, and while often well educated, had no prior experience in purchasing a business.

Successful firms were found to be more flexible, participative, and adaptive organizations. These firms had employees who could perform the work duties of others and were likely to be managed in a way that provided these workers with the flexibility to modify their jobs to adapt to changing industry and organizational conditions. Lead entrepreneurs of successful firms were likely to spend more time communicating with partners, customers, suppliers, and employees than the lead entrepreneurs of unsuccessful firms.

Successful firms sought to become larger firms and embarked upon sales to broad sectors of the market. Successful firms achieved high market shares; with market shares came higher financial returns. Less successful firms were restricted to narrow market sectors consisting of smaller customers and those more difficult to service. While customer service remained an important concern, the commodity nature of fresh juices failed to support differentiation, and the narrowly focused firm was typified by high product costs and unprofitable operations.

INTRODUCTION

Why do some new ventures succeed while other new ventures fail?

This study suggests that new venture success is not solely influenced by a single type of factor, such as management, strategy, or industrial context. Instead, many factors influence new venture creation and performance in a complex web, in other words a "gestalt" (Gartner 1985; Miller and Friesen 1984), of interrelationships. We study three types of factors—(1) the characteristics of the lead entrepreneur, (2) start-up processes undertaken during the founding of the firm, and (3) firm behaviors after start-up involving organizational and industry practices—for the purposes of generating a profile of the many different variables which might be useful for differentiating between successful and unsuccessful young firms. This research stems from a study by Van de Ven et al. (1984), who examined 12 educational software companies (six low-performing and six high-performing) from three different approaches: entrepreneurial (background and characteristics of the founder of the new venture), organizational (processes by which the new venture is planned and structured), and ecological (environmental factors such as the political, economic, and structural conditions). While the software firms were provided with varying levels of support by a corporate sponsor, the Fresh Juice Distributors (FJDs) were involved in a more hostile and turbulent environment characterized by severe price competition. Our study is an expansion and modification of Van de Ven et al. (1984), which takes into account other studies that recognize the influence of a combination of many different factors affecting new venture performance (Buzzell and Gale 1987; Cooper 1970; Gartner 1985; Gartner et al. 1989; Sandberg 1986; Sandberg and Hofer 1987; Timmons et al. 1985; Vesper 1990).

This section will offer a brief overview of ideas on the factors that we believe influence new venture success. Subsequent sections of the paper describe the FJD industry, the sample of firms studied, the methodology employed for learning about firm success and failure, and a discussion of the significant findings generated from the research.

Since a number of thorough and thoughtful reviews of the entrepreneurship literature exist which comprehensively survey factors influencing the creation and success of new ventures (Bird 1989; Brockhaus 1982; Brockhaus and Horwitz 1986; Gartner 1989; Sandberg

1986; Vesper 1990; Wortman 1987), we limit our discussion of previous research (Table 1) to a limited selection of particular entrepreneurial characteristics that comprise the new venture success and failure profile (Tables 2 and 4). These variables were selected from a detailed and comprehensive discussion of research on factors that influence new venture creation and success found in Duchesneau (1987).

The Lead Entrepreneur

We posit that successful entrepreneurs are likely to: (1) have entrepreneurial parents, (2) obtain a broad range of managerial experiences, (3) seek to reduce risk, and (4) see firm success as within the sphere of their control.

Start-up Behaviors

Entrepreneurs that start successful new ventures are likely to: (5 and 6) identify a business idea that is clear and broad, (7) use a procedural and comprehensive planning process, (8) spend more time planning, (9) generate a broad plan which recognizes all of the functional areas, (10) undertake market research, (11) seek professional advice, and (12) purchase firms.

Firms Behaviors and Strategy

Successful new ventures are likely to have: (13) employees with diversified skills and abilities, (14) lead entrepreneurs who are solely in command, (15) utilized joint ventures, (16 and 17) lead entrepreneurs who encourage participative decision making at strategic and operational levels, (18) emphasis on high levels of communication, (19) started at higher levels of capitalization, and (20) strategies of aggressive entry to broad markets.

THE INDUSTRY AND SAMPLE

During the late 1970s, with the rising demand for fresh and natural foods, many new firms emerged as fresh juice distributors (FJDs) to process and distribute (or just distribute) fresh-squeezed (raw) juices. This industry has many of the characteristics of Porter's "emerging industry" type: technological and strategic uncertainty; poor and inadequate information about competitors and marketplace opportunities; high, but rapidly falling, product costs and selling prices; barriers in obtaining raw materials, capital, etc. (Porter 1980, pp. 221–225). In the FJD industry, barriers to market entry are low, and the product provided, fresh-squeezed juices, is perceived as a commodity. A FJD has little ability to command high prices through differentiation. In addition, fresh squeezed juices are themselves substitute products for long-established products such as juices from concentrate or fresh fruit squeezed on premises by the customer. In each market a relatively small number of institutional customers (primarily hotels or restaurants) consume an important, sometimes dominant, share of the total market. These customers consciously encouraged new firms to enter the industry to drive prices lower. The continual availability of high-quality products is a requirement for marketplace success. Access to citrus fruit can be a major problem because of unpredictable winter freezes in citrus-producing areas. By 1988, with industry growth rates of over 50% annually, over 90 firms had entered the industry, and a shakeout of

TABLE 1   A Selected Literature Review of New Firm Success Characteristics

Success Measure	Prior Support	Nonsupportive Findings
The Lead Entreprenuer		
1. Entrepreneurial Parents	Collins & Moore (1964); Copper (1971); Gilmore (1971); Mescon & Montari (1981); Shapiro (1972)	
2. Breadth of Management Experience	Buchele (1967); Van de Ven et al. (1984); Vesper (1990);	
3. Risk Reduction Behaviors	Collins & Moore (1967); Mitton (1984); Van de Ven et al. (1984); Webster (1976)	
4. Locus of Control	Brockhaus (1980); Brockhaus & Horwitz (1986); Frederickson & Mitchell (1984); Sandberg (1986)	Sandberg & Hofer (1982)
Start-up Behaviors		
5. Clarity of Business Idea	Timmons (1979, 1980); Van de Ven et al. (1984); Welch (1974)	
6. Breadth of Business Idea	Timmons (1979, 1980): Van de Ven et al. (1984); Welch (1974)	
7. Followed PPM	Delbec & Van de Ven (1971); Frederickson & Mitchell (1984); Van de Ven & Koening (1976); Van de Ven et al. (1984); Vesper (1980)	Frederickson & Mitchell (1984) (in turbulent enviroment) Ronstadt (1984)
8. Planning Time	Van de Ven et al. (1984)	
9. Planning Breadth	Frederickson & Mitchell (1984); Van de Ven et al. (1984)	
10. Market Research	Hills (1984); Hoad & Rasko (1964); Van de Ven et al. (1984); Timmons (1985)	
11. Used Professionals	Cooper (1982); Hoad & Rosko (1964); Liles (1974); Van de Ven et al. (1984); Woodward (1969)	
12. Purchase of Firm	Vesper (1990)	
Firm Behaviors and Strategy		
13. Employee Specialization	Lawrence & Lorsch (1967); Van de Ven et al. (1984)	
14. Single Person Strongly in Command	Collins & Moore (1967); Ronstadt (1984a); Van de Ven et al. (1984);	
15. Partnerships or Joint Venture Organization	Ronstadt (1984b); Thorne & Ball (1981); Timmons (1985)	Cooper (1980); Van de Ven et al. (1984); Collins & Moore (1967)
16. &17. Participative Decision Making	Van de Ven et al. (1984)	
18. Lead Entrepreneur	Van de Ven et al. (1984)	
19. High Year 1 Capitalization	Lamont (1969); Vesper (1980)	Goldstein (1984); Drucker (1985)
20. Aggressive Entry	Hobson & Morrison (1983); MacMillan & Day (1987); Miller & Camp (1985); Miller & Dess (1985)	

marginal firms became apparent. Total 1988 sales in the United States were estimated to be over $150 million.

The sample of 26 firms selected for this study consisted of 13 successful and 13 unsuccessful (or failed) firms, located in eight metropolitan centers with populations in excess of one million (each city was designated as a separate market) in the Southeast, Central, Southwest, and Pacific regions of the United States. Each of the 26 firms selected for this research was primarily in the business of distributing fresh orange juice to hotels, restaurants, and supermarkets. A FJD was defined as a person or firm that processes and distributes, or only distributes, fresh-squeezed (raw) juices as its primary or dominant line of business. The 13 successful firms were classified based on their financial returns for the 12 months preceeding the interview: three firms provided pre-tax profits and owners' salaries combined of over $35,000 annually but less than a 10% return on the firm's net worth; 10 firms had pre-tax profits and owners' salaries combined of over $35,000 annually and a return of more than 25% on the firm's net worth. Of the 13 unsuccessful firms, nine had discontinued operations, or were operated under court order or by creditors; and four had provided profits and owners salaries combined of less than $35,000 preceding the interview. Failed firms (those discontinuing operations) were included, provided that these firms were active on or since January 1, 1983. No firms older than seven years were encountered in the research effort. The study sample encompassed about 30% of the national population of FJDs and was choosen to represent a broad range of emerging FJD markets and new FJD ventures. Of the 26 firms studied: 7 were purchased and 19 were startups, 13 were early entrants and 13 were late entrants. Successful firms tended to be older (average age, 49 months) than less successful firms (average age, 32 months). The successful firms had average sales of $1,800,000 and nine employees, versus the less-successful or unsuccessful firms with average sales of $500,000 and four employees. The largest firm in the sample had annual sales in excess of $6,000,000, while the smallest firm had less than $200,000 in sales. While larger firm size was clearly identified with firm success, the attainment of such size and success was the concern of this study.

METHODOLOGY

Information on each of the 26 firms was collected during a four- to eight-hour visit at the respondent's place of business (or at an agreed-to meeting place for entrepreneurs of failed firms). Interviews with both successful and unsuccessful entrepreneurs were conducted from December, 1986 through June, 1987. During this visit the lead entrepreneur was interviewed, and for those entrepreneurs still in business, a tour of the firm's facilities was conducted. In addition to the visits, the lead author's role as an industry participant and founder of several FJDs provided unique access to other industry resources, such as information from partners, employees and managers, competitors, customers, and shipping sources. Two types of data were generated. A 15-page (116 question) questionnaire was filled out which provided quantitative information for analysis. This questionnaire was constructed from measures taken from research instruments used previously by Van de Van et al. (1984), for questions dealing with entrepreneurial characteristics and the process undertaken to start the firm, and by the Strategic Planning Institute's STR database of corporate ventures (Strategic Planning Institute 1978) and Miller and Dess's typology of competitive strategies (Miller and Dess 1985), for questions on the industry and the firm's strategic behaviors. In addition, a four- to eight-page case on each firm was written describing the firm's history as well as qualitative impressions about the lead entrepreneur, the process undertaken to start the firm, and the firm's strategic behaviors. The case narratives and questionnaire are described in Duchesneau (1987).

The two groups of firms (successful versus unsuccessful or failed) were compared using methods of analysis similar to methods employed by Van de Ven et al (1984), that is, univariate analysis of variation and correlations were generated to obtain insights into relationships among the different variables. Conclusions drawn from the results were based on both the statistical results from the questionnaire and the qualitative information provided in the cases and field research.

FINDINGS

Results from the univariate analysis of variation across the three dimensions of measures (lead entrepreneur, start-up processes, and firm behaviors) revealed significant differences between the two groups of firms. Table 2 provides a summary of some of the measures that were found to differentiate between successful and unsuccessful new firms in the sample studied. Table 3 shows correlations between these measures. A complete description of all of the significant and nonsignificant quantitative findings can be found in Duchesneau (1987).

TABLE 2 Characteristics of Successful and Unsuccessful Firms

Characteristic	Failure Mean	S.D.	Success Mean	S.D.	F	Sign. Level
The Lead Entrepreneur						
1. Entre. parents	1.38	.50	1.76	.44	4.28	.05
2. Breadth of m. exp	2.82	.77	3.70	1.04	5.93	.02
3. Risk reduction	2.07	.76	3.61	1.19	15.38	.00
4. Locus of control	4.69	.63	4.07	.95	3.76	.06
Start-up Behaviors						
5. Business idea	3.23	1.58	4.38	.96	5.01	.03
6. Breadth of vision	2.23	1.09	3.76	1.03	10.66	.00
7. Followed PPM	1.55	.54	2.12	.97	3.46	.07
8. Planning time	84.92	66.22	237.30	165.54	9.49	.00
9. Plan breadth	2.76	2.80	5.53	3.43	5.07	.03
10. Market research	1.46	.66	2.46	1.33	5.89	.02
11. Used professionals	1.38	1.55	2.61	.96	5.88	.02
12. Purchase of firm	1.53	.52	1.92	.27	5.55	.02
Firm Behaviors and Strategies						
13. Empl. specialization	3.61	1.04	2.30	.75	13.44	.00
14. Single command	4.69	.48	3.76	1.30	5.76	.03
15. Partnership	1.46	.52	1.92	.27	8.00	.01
16. Strategic d. m.	2.07	1.55	3.16	1.66	5.95	.02
17. Operational dec.	1.38	.76	2.76	1.36	10.18	.00
18. LE communication	2.87	.48	3.37	.45	7.11	.01
19. Year 1 capital	54.07	36.27	123.30	111.57	4.52	.05
20. Low cost/broad f.	1.07	.27	1.53	.51	8.00	.01

1. Did your parents own their own business? (1 = No, 2 = Yes)
2. Indicate the level of familiarity with skills required by this business, as supplied by the lead entrepreneur. (Average of scores on seven functional areas: 5 = completely familiar, to 1 = completely unfamiliar)
3. In the period during the start-up (or purchase) of your firm, what did you do to try to reduce risk? (Number of items mentioned: 5 = a great number, to 1 = none)

(*continued overleaf*)

TABLE 2   Characteristics of Successful and Unsuccessful Firms (*continued*)

4. At the time of the start-up (or purchase) of the firm, how did you see the success of this business as being in factors under your control versus factors beyond your control? (5 = mostly internal, to 1 = mostly external)

5. Were there special features or characteristics in your product or methods that you chose to focus on and that you felt were important to customers? Features described: (5 = concise, to 1 = vague)

6. Breadth of vision expressed: (1 = very narrow vision expressed, to 5 = very broad vision expressed)

7. Using procedures developed and described in Van de Ven et al. (1984), the degree to which the Program Planning Model (PPM) was followed: (based on averages to responses to three questions, each question a five-point scale with 1 = not followed, to 5 = closely followed)

8. Overall, how many weeks and hours per week were spent in planning this firm before its start-up or purchase? (# weeks × # average hours/week)

9. Indicate any areas covered in the written notes or business plan: (sum of 10 functional areas 0 = no, 1 = yes; total possible, 10)

10. Prior to the start-up or purchase of this firm did you try to identify your market and your competitors? How much research was done? (1 = no market or competitive assessment, to 5 = a great deal of market and competitive assessment.)

11. To what degree were professionals such as consultants, lawyers, accountants, etc. involved in the development of your business plan? (1 = not at all involved, to 5 = involved a great deal)

12. Was this firm purchased? (1 = yes, 2 = no)

13. How many of the people in this firm are qualified to do one another's jobs? (1 = none are qualified, to 5 = all or nearly all are qualified)

14. To what degree is there a single person in command of this company? (1 = to no extent, to 5 = to a great extent)

15. Is this firm organized as a joint venture or partnership? (1 = no, 2 = yes)

16. To what degree have partners, shareholders, or board members been involved in making decisions on developing goals and strategies for this firm? (1 = none, to 5 = very much)

17. To what degree have partners, shareholders, or board members been involved in making decisions on how work activities are to be performed in the firm? (1 = none, to 5 = very much)

18. During the past 6 months, how frequently have you communicated on business matters with the following: (Average of sum of five types: 1 = no contact, to 5 = more than once daily)

19. How much financial support was actually required during the first year after the purchase or start-up of this firm? (Actual amount in $'s)

20. Using criteria taken from the Start-up Data Form (Strategic Planning Institute), has this firm achieved lowest overall cost and broadest market scope? (1 = no, 2 = yes)

Comparisons between successful and unsuccessful entrepreneurs indicated that successful entrepreneurs were more likely to: (1) have entrepreneurial parents, (2) have a broad range of previous managerial experience, and (3) seek to reduce risk. Successful entrepreneurs were less likely to (4) see firm success as within the sphere of their control than the unsuccessful entrepreneurs. Entrepreneurs that started successful new ventures were more likely than unsuccessful entrepreneurs to: (5 and 6) identify a business idea that is clear and broad, (7) use a procedural and comprehensive planning process, (8) spend more time planning, (9) generate a broad plan which recognizes all of the functional areas, (10) undertake market research, and (11) seek professional advice. Unsuccessful entrepreneurs were more likely to (12) purchase firms. Successful new ventures were less likely to have: (13) employees with diversified skills and abilities and (14) lead entrepreneurs who were solely in command than unsuccessful new ventures. Successful entrepreneurs were more likely to: (15) utilize joint ventures, (16 and 17) encourage participative decision making at strategic and operational levels, and (18) emphasize high levels of communication. Successful

304   D.A. DUCHESNEAU AND W.B. GARTNER

TABLE 3   Correlation Matrix

	1	2	3	4	5	6	7	8	9	10	11	12	13	14	15	16	17	18	19	20
1 Entre. parents	1.000																			
2 Breadth of m. exp	.308	1.000																		
3 Risk reduction	.462	.697	1.000																	
4 Locus of control	-.258	-.081	-.279	1.000																
5 Business idea	.386	.433	.388	.097	1.000															
6 Breadth of vision	.561	.789	.766	-.133	.560	1.000														
7 Followed PPM	.294	.298	.514	-.221	.456	.455	1.000													
8 Planning time	.369	.408	.656	-.149	.501	.511	.370	1.000												
9 Planning breadth	.416	.540	.750	.090	.508	.703	.541	.715	1.000											
10 Market research	.316	.426	.689	-.025	.512	.640	.568	.429	.600	1.000										
11 Used professionals	.281	.515	.496	.033	.230	.640	.370	.263	.511	.222	1.000									
12 Purchase of firm	.182	.362	.347	.072	.103	.375	.023	.211	.368	.364	.438	1.000								
13 Empl. specialization	.041	-.307	-.377	.143	-.056	-.381	-.007	-.372	-.349	-.126	-.407	-.419	1.000							
14 Single command	-.183	-.266	-.211	.030	-.207	-.291	-.130	-.563	-.310	-.188	.079	-.197	.344	1.000						
15 Partnership	.104	-.013	.188	-.092	.208	.240	.211	.431	.383	.273	.120	.346	-.405	-.409	1.000					
16 Strategic d.m.	.014	.010	.170	-.119	.229	.209	.280	.562	.266	.215	.048	.147	-.432	-.724	.713	1.000				
17 Operational dec	.297	.060	.279	-.354	.249	.284	.248	.435	.281	.325	-.044	.310	-.359	-.707	.500	.691	1.000			
18 LE communication	.447	.167	.576	-.307	.249	.452	.320	.473	.463	.221	.539	.213	-.307	.090	.451	.264	.268	1.000		
19 Year 1 capital	.271	.464	.276	-.009	.334	.317	.119	.506	.340	-.113	.431	.111	-.247	-.230	.078	.150	-.054	.224	1.000	
20 Low cost/broad f.	.169	.150	.287	.136	.209	.125	.119	.335	.364	.252	.125	.368	-.058	-.216	.405	.205	.168	.226	.104	1.000

TABLE 4   A Profile of New Venture Success and Failure

Characteristic	Successful Firms	Unsuccessful or Failed Firms
The Lead Entrepreneur		
1. Entrepreneurial parents	Likely	Unlikely
2. Breadth of management experience	Broad	Narrow
3. Risk-reduction behaviors	Yes—cautious	No—impulsive
4. Locus of control	Moderately high	Very high
Start-up Behaviors		
5. Business idea	Clear	Vague
6. Breadth of vision	Broad	Narrow
7. Start-up behaviors	Procedural, comprehensive	Incomplete, sketchy
8. Time in planning	Lengthy	Brief
9. Planning breadth	Very broad	Narrow
10. Market research	Some	Little or none
11. Used professional advice	Yes, specific needs	Little or none
12. Purchased firm	No	Yes
Firm Behaviors and Strategy		
13. Employee specializaton	More	Less
14. LE'-s personal command	Low	High
15. Organizational format	Joint venture	Individual owner
16. Strategic decision making	Participative	Non-participative
17. Operational decisions	Participative	Non-participative
18. LE communication	Effective and Receptive	Less effective and guarded
19. Capital investment level	High*	Low
20. Lowest cost and service to broad markets	Yes	Seldom

*Low in early markets.

new ventures were more likely to have been (19) started at higher levels of capitalization, and to have utilized (20) strategies of aggressive entry into broad markets.

DISCUSSION

Table 4 summarizes some of the findings of the research in terms of successful and unsuccessful new venture practice. The discussion that follows focuses on this profile. This discussion is based on both the quantitative analysis and insights from the case studies.

The Lead Entrepreneur

Comparisons of successful and unsuccessful lead entrepreneurs revealed that successful lead entrepreneurs came from entrepreneurial families, and attained higher levels of: education, prior start-up and managerial experience, broad business skills, strong communication skills and propensities, self-confidence and reliance, resourcefulness, and caution, than the lead entrepreneurs of unsuccessful firms. These findings corroborate most of the results found in Van de Ven et al. (1984) as well as other studies that have evaluated entrepreneurial characteristics (Brockhaus 1982; Brockhaus and Horwitz 1986; Sandberg 1986).

Some researchers (Mescon and Montanari 1981; Timmons et al. 1985) have considered the value of family role models as an influence on new venture success. Based on both the quantitative and qualitative findings, we concur that previous family business experience appears to provide entrepreneurs with more realistic expectations from self-employment and the kinds of attitudes and behaviors necessary for surmounting the crises of entrepreneurship.

We suggest that the findings that prior start-up experience, managerial experience, higher education, and broad business skills were correlated to new venture success may indicate that these successful entrepreneurs have "street smarts"—an ability to learn from their mistakes. Entrepreneurial management in an emerging industry requires the application of knowledge learned in past situations to new but vaguely familiar problems. "Street smarts" comes from years of organizational situations—decision vignettes providing valuable patterns of problem recognition—which create a storehouse of personally integrated know-how to identify and solve new problems. Herbert Simon calls these patterns of recognition "chunks" and indicates that a large number of chunks are a requirement for expertness in a given field (Simon 1987). Without a large repertoire of chunks from prior education and experience, the lead entrepreneur is unlikely to muddle successfully through these problem situations. Inexperienced managers, those without prior start-up experience and broad business skills, resorted to a narrow range of behaviors learned from their prior experiences in mature and inflexible organizations. Such rigidity was tolerated in single-firm early markets, but punished under conditions of late market competition.

Start-up Behaviors

In successful firms, lead entrepreneurs had a clear broad business idea that provided organizational will to overcome adversity, confrontation, and often a troubled financial condition. A narrow or vague commitment from the entrepreneur(s) failed to provide the FJD with the adaptive torque required for survival. Successful firms were those initiated with ambitious goals—a case of "what you dream is what you get."

Among the procedures important to successful start-up are planning processes. Firms that used a planning process similar to the process outlined by Van de Ven et al. (1984) as the PPM Model (problem exploration, knowledge exploration, business plan development, and start-up on a small and incremental basis) were found to be more successful than those firms which followed a less comprehensive planning process. In this study, successful firms spent more time planning (237 hours) than unsuccessful firms (85 hours). Market and competitive research were required to identify opportunities and reduce marketplace risks, though the absolute level of market research was low for both groups of firms (successful firms undertook small efforts in market research, whereas unsuccessful firms undertook little or no market research). The use of outside professionals and advisors for help in solving specific problems during start-up was important for success. Successful new ventures also depended on the advice and information provided by other industry participants, particularly customers and suppliers. Successful entrepreneurs sought out information, that is, they were veridically aware (Webster 1976, 1977)—open to any information (good or bad) which could be used to help them improve their ventures' performance. Unsuccessful entrepreneurs were not truth seekers. They were personally rigid and less willing to recognize problems or accept advice from others.

Effective start-up or purchase required broad planning efforts that considered all aspects of the industry and firm. Most ventures (successful and unsuccessful) did not have written business plans. Successful entrepreneurs appeared to utilize personal planning notes, a written analysis of critical success factors used for personal decision making when evaluating a specific area of the business.

Purchased firms were predictive of the buyers' subsequent failure. Buyers invariably purchased competitively troubled firms. Buyers were often negatively displaced, unemployed managers. Buyers failed to realize the great financial risks of self employment. Buyers lacked broad management experience and, although often well educated, had no prior experience in purchasing a business. Sellers took purposive advantage of the buyer's inevitable lack of industry and competitive information. Buyers relied upon historical and financial information that had little predictive value in the face of new and strong competition. Inadequate market and competitive research was undertaken. The one buyer that used outside professionals in the purchase of his firm was the only purchased firm that was successful.

Firm Behaviors and Strategy

Successful firms were found to be more flexible, participative, and adaptive organizations. We were initially surprised to find that successful firms have more specialized employees than less successful firms. We had assumed that successful firms would be more "organic," that is, have fewer specialized employees, in order to adapt to changing environmental conditions. It seems that because successful firms were larger than unsuccessful firms (both in sales and in number of employees), successful firms were more likely to have reached a size that required individuals who had specialized skills. Lead entrepreneurs of successful firms were likely to spend more time communicating with partners, customers, suppliers, and employees than the lead entrepreneurs of unsuccessful firms.

Joint ventures appeared to be the organizational format most adaptive to changes in the industry. Partnerships, joint ventures, and shareholder agreements represented complex and sophisticated forms of firm ownership and participation in which resources (capital, access to raw materials and channels of distribution) could be rapidly acquired and exploited. Successful firms that employed such methods were comprised of individuals with greater business and start-up experience. Their industry experience and contacts enabled them to construct beneficial strategic alliances. The sole proprietorship or single shareholder firm was usually unsuccessful, in part because of the failure of purchased firms (which were all sole proprietorships). Sole proprietorships were managed by individuals who were less communicative and more guarded, less likely to take advice from professionals or others, and likely to rely upon strong personal control rather than participative decision-making processes. Sole proprietorships were likely to be outsiders, individuals who lacked a thorough knowledge of changes in the marketplace that could only be gained through a network of relationships with other industry participants.

Higher levels of initial capital were clearly associated with firm success, with the mean investment of $123,000 for successful new ventures versus $54,000 for unsuccessful firms. The higher-capitalized ventures were younger firms that had entered when the industry became more complex and capital intensive. In early markets, lower capital requirements were associated with success (Drucker 1985; Goldstein 1984, Thorne and Ball 1981). Later markets had high capital requirements to attain lowest product costs through investments in plant and equipment to achieve economies of scale. Marketplace survival in late markets often required "investment" in the form of sustained, unprofitable operations caused by unrealistic price competition—"price wars." Smaller firms and sole proprietorships were often unable or unwilling to sustain these losses and were closed or sold.

Because firms in the FJD industry sell commodities, that is, because all companies must compete by selling a high-quality fresh-squeezed juice, it was suggested that low-cost producers would be the most likely to survive price competition from rivals and other entrants. The ability to be a low-cost producer would involve selling the most product to the largest customers as well as to the largest number of customers. Companies restricted to high-cost positions or narrow focus were squeezed out of the marketplace.

Successful firms sought to become larger firms and embarked upon sales to broad sectors of the market. Successful firms achieved high market share; with market share came higher financial returns. Less successful firms were restricted to narrow market sectors consisting of smaller customers and those more difficult to service. While customer service remained an important concern, the commodity nature of fresh juices failed to support product differentiation, and the narrowly focused firm was typified by highest product costs and unprofitable operations. The nature of the marketplace pushes firms toward the low cost/broad focus strategy as a means of survival. Firms that were unable to achieve the low cost/broad focus strategy were faced with mediocre performance, exited by selling out, or failed.

Overall, these findings offer additional evidence that an aggressive entry strategy, that is, a strategy in which a firm enters an industry with a clear and broad vision that includes high market share objectives and profitability, a broad market focus and a correspondingly high capital investment for achieving its goals, generates higher market shares and profitability than less aggressive firms (Biggadike 1979; Hobson and Morrison 1983; MacMillan and Day 1987; Miller and Camp 1985).

LIMITATIONS AND DIRECTIONS FOR RESEARCH

The use of an in-depth case study methodology has benefits and disadvantages which influence the research results offered, yet the use of multiple measures and approaches (case studies, interviews, written histories, a quantitative questionnaire, the use of a panel of industry experts, and the collection of company records) may have minimized the introduction of error into the results generated. Univariate analysis of variance as a statistical method may not have captured some relationships among the variables, though a complete correlation matrix of all of the variables was generated and analyzed.

It should be emphasized that causality can not be inferred from the analysis of the quantitative data. We believe that the value of this field research does not depend solely on the quantitative measures, but rather on the broad qualitative inquiry used to understand the creation of successful organizations. It should also be noted that the inclusion of failed firms in the analysis was essential for identifying the practices and strategies of successful firms.

In-depth field research which recognizes the complex nature of the new venture process is likely to be fertile ground for the generation of useful theory and practice on the development of successful new ventures. We believe a very fruitful area for field research on new ventures will be to explore the nature and process of aggressive entry. Results in this study indicated that founders with prior entrepreneurial and managerial experience are more likely to think and act in ways which can build an organization with sufficient size and scope for aggressive entry. These prior experiences of aggressive entrepreneurs seem to be stepping stones which lead to the "big vision"—starting an organization with sufficient size and scope. Longitudinal field work, oral histories, and other historical methods would be useful for tracing how aggressive entrepreneurs acquire the chunks of knowledge necessary to imagine an ambitious new venture. In addition, in-depth field research would be useful for describing the complex process which entrepreneurs undertake to develop aggressive new ventures:

gathering the resources, forming a team and organization, and establishing a network of contacts, customers, advisors, and suppliers. Since many of the findings presented here both support and conflict with previous research on entrepreneurial characteristics, start-up behaviors, and firm characteristics and strategies, additional research should be undertaken to study new ventures in other emerging industries. As additional studies are undertaken, a more comprehensive model of the new venture process will emerge which may be able to identify the various contingencies that influence new venture success in specific industries.

CONCLUSIONS

A framework that outlined three types of factors: (1) the characteristics of the lead entrepreneur, (2) start-up processes undertaken during the founding of the firm, and (3) firm behaviors after start-up, including management practices and strategic behaviors, was used to generate a profile of variables associated with new venture success and failure.

Lead entrepreneurs in successful firms were more likely to have: broad business and prior startup experience, entrepreneurial parents, a high but moderated self-reliance, risk reducing behaviors, worked long hours, extensive communication efforts and ability, and a personal investment in the firm.

In successful firms, lead entrepreneurs had a clear, broad business idea that provided organizational will to overcome adversity, confrontation, and often a troubled financial condition. A narrow or vague commitment from the entrepreneur(s) failed to provide the adaptive torque required for survival. Successful firms were those initiated with ambitious goals.

Successful firms spent more time planning (237 hours) than unsuccessful firms (85 hours). The use of outside professionals and advisors for help in solving specific problems during start-up was important for success. Successful new ventures also depended on the advice and information provided by other industry participants, particularly customers and suppliers.

Effective start-up or purchase required broad planning efforts that considered all aspects of industry and firm. Such planning would likely be beneficial if developed into a written plan, but this research indicated that most ventures (successful and unsuccessful) did not have written business plans. Successful entrepreneurs appeared to utilize personal planning notes, a written analysis of critical success factors that entrepreneurs used for their own personal decision making.

Purchased firms were predictive of the buyers' subsequent failure. Buyers of competitively troubled firms were negatively displaced, generally unemployed managers. Buyers failed to realize the great financial risks of self employment. Buyers lacked broad management experience, and while often well educated, had no prior experience in purchasing a business.

Successful firms were found to be more flexible, participative, and adaptive organizations. Yet these firms were more likely to employ personnel with more specialized skills and abilities. Lead entrepreneurs of successful firms were likely to spend more time communicating with partners, customers, suppliers, and employees than the lead entrepreneurs of unsuccessful firms.

Higher levels of initial capital were clearly associated with firm success—with a mean investment of $123,000 for successful new ventures versus $54,000 for unsuccessful firms. The higher-capitalized ventures were younger firms that had entered when the industry became more complex and capital intensive. In early markets, lower capital requirements were associated with success. Later markets had high capital requirements to attain lowest product costs through investments in plant and equipment to achieve economies of scale.

Successful firms sought to become larger firms and embarked upon sales to broad sectors of the market. Successful firms achieved high market share; with market share came higher financial returns. Less successful firms were restricted to narrow market sectors consisting of smaller customers and those more difficult to service. While customer service remained an important concern, the commodity nature of fresh juices failed to support such differentiation, and the narrowly focused firm was typified by highest product costs and unprofitable operations.

This profile was generated to broadly distinguish between successful and unsuccessful new ventures. It is not our intention to suggest that all entrepreneurs must fit the "success" profile in order to build a successful business. As in any study involving the generation of results from comparing aggregations of "successes" to "failures," no clear-cut prescriptions can be offered that are guaranteed to work in every particular situation. As the results showed, no perfect correlations existed indicating that a particular factor was always related to new venture success. From our perspective, it appears to be part of the irony of entrepreneurship that successful new ventures often owe their survival to "luck"—some particular set of circumstances that could never be planned for, or counted on. This profile is, therefore, not a formula for success, but it does present characteristics that may identify critical start-up priorities for improving an entrepreneur's new venture success chances.

REFERENCES

Biggadike, R. 1979. The risky business of diversification. *Harvard Business Review* 57(3):103–111.

Bird, B.J. 1989. *Entrepreneurial Behavior*. Glenview, IL: Scott, Foresman.

Brockhaus, R.H. 1980. Risk taking propensity of entrepreneurs. *Academy of Management Journal* 23:509–520.

Brockhaus, R.H. 1982. The psychology of the entrepreneur. In C.A. Kent, D.L. Sexton, and K.H. Vesper, eds., *Encyclopedia of Entrepreneurship*. Englewood Cliffs, NJ: Prentice-Hall, pp. 39–56.

Brockhaus, R.H., and Horwitz, P.S. 1986. The psychology of the entrepreneur. In D.L. Sexton and R.W. Smilor, eds. *The Art and Science of Entrepreneurship*. Cambridge, MA: Ballinger.

Bruchele, R. 1967. *Business Policy in Growing Firms*. Scranton, PA: Chander Publishing Company.

Buzzell, R.D., and Gale, B.T. 1987. *The PIMS Principles*. New York: The Free Press.

Collins, O.F., and Moore, D.G. 1964. *The Enterprising Man*. East Lansing, MI: Michigan State University.

Cooper, A.C. 1970. The Palo Alto experience. *Industrial Research* 12(5):58–61.

Cooper, A.C. 1982. The entrepreneur-small business interface. In C.A. Kent, D.L. Sexton, and K.H. Vesper, eds., *Encyclopedia of Entrepreneurship*. Englewood Cliffs, NJ: Prentice-Hall, pp. 193–205.

Delbecq, A.L., and Van de Ven, A.H. 1971. A group process model for problem identification and program planning. *Journal of Applied Behavioral Science* 7:466–492.

Drucker, P.F. 1985. *Innovation and Entrepreneurship*. New York: Harper & Row.

Duchesneau, D.A. 1987. New venture success in an emerging industry. Ph.D. dis., Fort Lauderdale, FL: Nova University.

Fredrickson, J.W., and Mitchell, T.R. 1984. Strategic decision processes: Comprehensiveness and performance in an industry with an unstable environment. *Academy of Management Journal* 27:399–423.

Gartner, W.B. 1985. A conceptual framework for describing the phenomenon of new venture creation. *Academy of Management Review* 10(4):696–706.

Gartner, W.B. 1989. Who is an entrepreneur? Is the wrong question. *Entrepreneurship: Theory and Practice* 13(4):47–68.

Gartner, W.B., Mitchell, T.R., and Vesper, K.H. 1989. A taxonomy of new business ventures. *Journal of Business Venturing* 4(3):169–186.

Gilmore, J.B. 1971. An investigation of selected entrepreneurial model's ability to predict successful entrepreneurial activity. Ph.D. dis., Norman, OK: University of Oklahoma.

Goldstein, J. 1984. Undercapitalization as a winning entrepreneurial strategy. In J. Hornaday, F. Tarpley, J. Timmons, and K. Vesper, eds., *Frontiers of Entrepreneurship Research.* Wellesly, MA: Babson College, pp. 409–413.

Hills, G.E. 1984. Market analysis and marketing in new ventures: Venture capitalist's perceptions. In J.Hornaday, F. Tarpley, J. Timmons, and K.H. Vesper, eds., *Frontiers of Entrepreneurship Research.* Wellesley, MA: Babson College, pp. 43–54.

Hoad, W.M., and Rosko, P. 1964. *Management Factors Contributing to the Success and Failure of New Small Manufacturers.* Ann Arbor, MI: University of Michigan.

Hobson, E.L., and Morrison, R.M. 1983. How do corporate start-up ventures fare? In J.A. Hornaday, J.A. Timmons, and K.H. Vesper, eds., *Frontiers of Entrepreneurship Research.* Wellesley, MA: Babson College, pp. 390–410.

Lawrence, P.R., and Lorsch, J.W. 1967. *Organization and Environment: Managing Differentiation and Integration.* Homewood, IL: Richard D. Irwin.

Liles, P.R. 1974. *New Business Ventures and the Entrepreneur.* Homewood, IL: Irwin.

MacMillan, I.C., and Day, D.L. 1987. Corporate ventures into industrial markets: Dynamics of aggressive entry. *Journal of Business Venturing* 2(1):29–40.

Mescon, T., and Montanari, J. 1981. The personalities of independent and franchise entrepreneurs: An empirical analysis of concepts. *Journal of Enterprise Management* 3(2):149–159.

Miller, A., and Camp, B. 1985. Exploring determinants of success in corporate ventures. *Journal of Business Venturing* 1(1):87–106.

Miller, A., and Dess, G. 1985. The appropriateness of Porter's (1980) model of generic strategies as a method of classification and its implications for business unit performance. Working Paper No. 212, University of Tennessee, College of Business.

Miller, D., and Friesen, P.H. 1984. *Organizations: A Quantum View.* Englewood Cliffs, NJ: Prentice-Hall.

Mitton, D.G. 1984. No money, know-how, know who: Formula for managing venture success and personal wealth. In J. Hornaday, F. Tarpley, J. Timmons, and K.H. Vesper, eds., *Frontiers of Entrepreneurship Research.* Wellesley, MA: Babson College, 414–428.

Porter, M. 1980. *Competitive Strategy.* New York: The Free Press 1980.

Ronstadt, R. 1984a. *Entrepreneurship.* Dover, MA: Lord.

Ronstadt, R. 1984b. Ex-entrepreneurs and the decision to start an entrepreneurial career. In J. Hornaday, F. Tarpley, J. Timmons, and K.H. Vesper, eds., *Frontiers of Entrepreneurship Research.* Wellesley, MA: Babson College, 437–460.

Sandberg, W.R. 1986. *New Venture Performance.* Lexington, MA: Lexington Books.

Sandberg, W.R., Hofer, C.W. 1987. Improving new venture performance: The role of strategy, industry structure, and the entrepreneur. *Journal of Business Venturing* 2(1):5–28.

Shapiro, A. 1972. The process of technical company formation in a local area. In A.C. Cooper, J.L. Komives, eds., *Technical Entrepreneurship: A Symposium.* Milwaukee, WI: Center for Venture Management, pp. 63–95.

Simon, H.A. 1987. Making management decisions: The role of intuition and emotion. *Academy of Management Executive* 1(1):57–64.

Strategic Planning Institute. 1978. The Startup Data Manual. Cambridge, MA: Strategic Planning Institute.

Thorne, J.R., and Ball, J.G. 1981. Entrepreneurs and their companies: Smaller industrial firms. In K.H. Vesper, ed., *Frontiers of Entrepreneurship Research.* Wellesley, MA: Babson College, pp. 65–83.

Timmons, J.A. 1982. New venture creation: Models and methodologies. In C.A. Kent, D.L. Sexton, K.H. Vesper, eds., *Encyclopedia of Entrepreneurship.* Englewood Cliffs, NJ: Prentice-Hall, pp. 126–136.

Timmons, J.A., Smollen, L.C., and Dingee, A.L.M. 1985. *New Venture Creation,* 2nd ed. Homewood, IL: Richard D. Irwin.

Van de Ven, A.H., Hudson, R., and Schroeder, D.M. 1984. Designing new business startups: Entrepreneurial, organizational, and ecological considerations. *Journal of Management* 10:87–107.

Van de Ven, A.H., and Koening, R. 1976. A process model for program planning and evaluation. *Journal of Economics and Business* 28(3):161–170.

Vesper, K.H. 1990. *New Venture Strategies,* 2nd Edition. Englewood Cliffs, NJ: Prentice-Hall.

Webster, F.A. 1976. A model for new venture initiation: A disclosure on rapacity and the independent entrepreneur. *Academy of Management Review* 1:26–37.

Webster, F.A. 1977. Entrepreneurs and ventures: An attempt at classification and clarification. *Academy of Management Review* 2:54–61.

Welch, J.A. March 1974. Investing in the entrepreneur. Vail, CO: *Caruth Institute Proceedings*.

Woodworth, R.T. 1969. The entrepreneurial process and the role of accountants, bankers and lawyers. Seattle, WA: University of Washington.

Wortman, M.S. 1987. Entrepreneurship: An integrating typology and evaluation of the empirical research in the field. *Journal of Management* 13(2):259–279.

8

WHAT ARE WE
TALKING ABOUT
WHEN WE
TALK ABOUT
ENTREPRENEURSHIP?

WILLIAM B. GARTNER
Georgetown University

EXECUTIVE SUMMARY

The purpose of this research was to explore the underlying meanings researchers and practitioners have about entrepreneurship and to outline some themes that characterize the major issues and concerns that constitute the debate about entrepreneurship as a field of study.

The process used to identify the themes that characterize entrepreneurship took the form of a policy Delphi. This Delphi was constructed as a series of three questionnaires to elicit definitions of entrepreneurship that were then analyzed and evaluated. In the first phase, a one-page questionnaire asking for a definition of entrepreneurship was sent to leading academic researchers in entrepreneurship, to business leaders, and to politicians. The first questionnaire asked individuals: What is your definition of entrepreneurship? We received 44 responses (36 from academics, 8 from business leaders, and none from politicians) from the 280 individuals whom we invited to participate (a 16% response rate).

In phase 2, all of the entrepreneurship definitions from the first questionnaire were typed and sent back with a second questionnaire to the 44 respondents. The second questionnaire was generated through a content analysis of the entrepreneurship definitions. Ninety attributes were identified from the entrepreneurship definitions. The second questionnaire asked participants: How important is each attribute to your definition of entrepreneurship? Participants ranked the attributes from very important to unimportant. Of the 44 participants in phase 2, 41 responded to the second questionnaire (93% response rate). The responses from the second questionnaire were then evaluated and factor analyzed. The factor analysis sought to cluster the 90 attributes into a smaller set of factors (themes). The eight-factor solution was selected. The debate about what constitutes the nature of entrepreneurship can be characterized by these eight themes.

Address correspondence to Dr. William B. Gartner, Old North Building, School of Business Administration, Georgetown University, Washington, D.C. 20057.

A version of this paper was presented at the 1987 National Academy of Management meetings. The author gratefully acknowledges all participants who offered definitions and responded to two lengthy surveys.

The Entrepreneur. *The entrepreneur theme is the idea that entrepreneurship involves individuals with unique personality characteristics and abilities.*

Innovation. *The innovation theme is characterized as doing something new as an idea, product, service, market, or technology in a new or established organization.*

Organization Creation. *The organization creation theme described the behaviors involved in creating organizations.*

Creating Value. *This theme articulated the idea that entrepreneurship creates value.*

Profit or Nonprofit. *The profit/nonprofit theme is concerned with whether entrepreneurship involves profit-making organizations only.*

Growth. *At issue in this theme is the importance of growth as a characteristic of entrepreneurship.*

Uniqueness. *This theme suggested that entrepreneurship must involve uniqueness.*

The Owner-Manager. *This theme suggested that entrepreneurship involves individuals who are owners and managers of their businesses.*

The third phase of the Delphi asked the 41 participants to evaluate and comment on the eight factors generated in the second phase. Of the 41 participants in phase 3, 34 responded to the third questionnaire (83% response rate). Since no one agreed-upon definition of entrepreneurship appeared to emerge from the Delphi process, the researcher undertook a cluster analysis of the responses to the third questionnaire to uncover whether any similarities in viewpoints existed among the participants. The data was cluster analyzed using both hierarchical (complete linkage and single linkage) and K-means clustering techniques. Results from these analyses revealed two distinct clusters. The majority (79%) of the participants were clustered in group 1. The focus of this group seems to be on the characteristics of entrepreneurship. Group 1 looked at what happened in the situation. This group indicated that a situation was entrepreneurial if they could answer "yes" to these questions: Is there an entrepreneur involved? Is there innovation? Is there growth? Is there uniqueness? The other group, group 2, focused on the outcomes *of entrepreneurship. Group 2 saw a situation as entrepreneurial only if value was created or if someone gained.*

R ecent reviews of entrepreneurship research have indicated the lack of an agreed-upon definition of entrepreneurship and, more basic, a concern over what entrepreneurship constitutes as a field of study (Brockhaus 1987; Brockhaus and Horwitz 1985; Carsrud et al. 1985; Low and MacMillan 1988; Ronstadt et al. 1986; Sexton and Smilor 1985; Wortman 1985). Behind this concern is the worry that entrepreneurship has become a label of convenience with little inherent meaning. Labeling a research study as an entrepreneurship study does not seem to identify what will be studied and why. For example, the Entrepreneurship Division's Call for Papers for the 1989 National Academy of Management meeting illustrates the field of entrepreneurship with these words: "the creation and management of new businesses, small businesses and family businesses, and the characteristics and special problems of entrepreneurs." If we assume that all of these topics are entrepreneurial in nature, then what are the commonalities that link family businesses, small business management, and new ventures? Is entrepreneurship just a buzzword, or does it have particular characteristics that can be identified and studied?

The purpose of this research was to explore the underlying meanings researchers and practitioners have about entrepreneurship and to outline some themes that characterize the major issues and concerns that constitute the debate about entrepreneurship as a field of study.

The paper is divided into three sections. First, the Delphi process is outlined and the results from the Delphi are presented. Second, the Delphi process and results are explained and evaluated. Third, arguments are offered on the importance of continuing the discussion on what constitutes the field of entrepreneurship. This paper can only highlight some of the information generated from the entire Delphi process. For a complete description of the results please request the working paper "An Entrepreneurial Delphi" from the author.

METHOD AND RESULTS

The process used to identify the themes that characterize entrepreneurship took the form of a policy Delphi (Turoff 1975). This Delphi was constructed as a series of three questionnaires to elicit definitions of entrepreneurship that were then analyzed and evaluated. An important aspect of this Delphi was that each participant received feedback on what other participants wrote before responding to the next round. Also, participants could shift their views as additional information became available.

In the first phase, a one-page questionnaire asking for a definition of entrepreneurship was sent to leading academic researchers in entrepreneurship, to business leaders, and to politicians. The 91 academics were identified through Babson Entrepreneurship Research Conference publications, Academy of Management proceedings, and individuals known to the author. The 83 business leaders identified were from the mid-Atlantic region (one-half were the founders of companies in a wide range of industries with sales of over $1 million, and the other half were new venture development experts—lawyers, CPAs, and venture capitalists). The 109 politicians were members of the U.S. House and Senate who sat on committees addressing issues relevant to new business creation. This list was by no means exhaustive. The goal was to identify a broad spectrum of entrepreneurship researchers, practitioners, and policymakers so that many different views of the entrepreneurship field were likely to emerge.

The first questionnaire asked individuals: What is your definition of entrepreneurship? A follow-up questionnaire (with the same question) was mailed to individuals who did not respond to the first questionnaire. We received 44 responses (36 from academics, 8 from business leaders, and none from politicians) from the 280 individuals whom we invited to participate (a 16% response rate). The response rate for academics, business leaders, and politicians was 40%, 10%, and 0%, respectively. In subsequent phone calls to selected business leaders and politicians some reasons came to light for the poor response rate. Business leaders felt that defining entrepreneurship was not very practical and relevant to them. As one business leader remarked, "Why would I want to know what an entrepreneur is? I am one." The politicians wanted information on what they should be doing to improve policy on entrepreneurship, regardless of how entrepreneurship is defined.

In phase 2, all of the entrepreneurship definitions from the first questionnaire were typed and sent back with a second questionnaire to the 44 respondents. Some examples of the entrepreneurship definitions from the first questionnaire are listed in Table 1. The second questionnaire was generated through a content analysis of the entrepreneurship definitions. The definitions were broken down into separate attributes. For example this entrepreneurship definition:

> I most often define entrepreneurship as concerned with those activities associated with becoming an owner-manager of a new or small firm. This includes the starting of any firm, regardless of whether it is innovative. It also includes the purchasing of an established new or small firm. Entrepreneurship can also be defined to include the starting of new and typically innovative ventures within established organizations. This includes the starting of innovative ventures within established corporations, as well as in nonprofit or governmental organizations.

was segmented into the following attributes:

Activities associated with becoming an owner-manager of a firm

Creation of a new business

Innovative

Purchasing an existing business

Starts an innovative venture within an established organization

Creation of a not-for-profit business

Creation of a government organization

TABLE 1   Examples of Entrepreneurship Definitions

1. We think of entrepreneurship as the starting of new ventures. We avoid any implication of small or large. We view a new venture quite broadly. A new venture might be the buying of an old business: It is a new venture for the buyer. We prefer to stress the creation of new economic enterprises—the creation of wealth.

2. Entrepreneurs share financial risk, management risk, and, perhaps more importantly, *put their whole career on the line* in their pursuit of a *new, independent enterprise*. Essentially, they become inextricably intertwined with the new enterprise. In the early days of the new enterprise, *the overall enterprise* is not viable without the entrepreneur. . . . The enterprise should be a *for-profit* business. It should be a new venture although not necessarily a start-up. For example, a leveraged buy-out of a division of a large business is in most cases a new venture (even though no new products or services are created), and the lead entrepreneur meets the conditions of my "definition" of the entrepreneurial actor.

3. I most often define entrepreneurship as concerned with those activities associated with becoming an owner-manager of a new or small firm. This includes the starting of any firm, regardless of whether it is innovative. It also includes the purchasing of an established new or small firm. . . . Entrepreneurship can also be defined to include the starting of new and typically innovative ventures with established organizations. This includes the starting of innovative ventures within established corporations, as well as in nonprofit or governmental organizations.

4. The definition of entrepreneurship is a difficult one to achieve consensus on. Webster defines it as a profit-making undertaking. My definition is as follows: "An entrepreneur is a person who refines a creative idea and adapts it to a market opportunity, gathers resources to provide potentially for self-employment and/or profit." I feel that this definition addresses the original creative thought process. . . . Secondly, I dispute the idea that it has to be a "successful" venture in order for one to be classified as an entrepreneur. . . . Lastly I feel strongly that there is no profit motivation at most perhaps the goal of self-employment. . . . I do not necessarily feel comfortable with equating innovation with entrepreneurship since it does not always involve the same, or as many, skills. . . . The key word for me is initiation and implementation. I feel that a true entrepreneur is always the initiator and the implementor. He/she is the person who "puts it together and carries it off."

5. Entrepreneurship: The creation of a new venture. The new venture strategy possesses one or both of the following characteristics:
   - *An orientation toward significant and rapid growth*
   - *Innovative in product, service, technology, or market*

6. An entrepreneur is a leader who starts up his/her own profit or nonprofit enterprise. His/her most important (most severely tested) personality trait is commitment, which is manifested as perseverance or persistence. The entrepreneur is a risk taker—moderate, he/she says. But he/she may view risk in an entirely different light (according to different criteria) from the manager who take "moderate" risks.

7. I prefer the traditional definition of an owner-managed business. It seems to me that ownership makes a difference in the motivation and interests of the manager. . . . The "personality trait" approach to entrepreneurship is a hopeless direction for identification of succesful entrepreneurs. Although we may eventually be able to identify traits appropriate to entrepreneurship, we will not be able to predict success based upon these

(*continued overleaf*)

TABLE 1   *(Continued)*

traits. The reason is that human beings are capable of change in personality, and they do this when they are subjected to trauma. There is no trauma greater than threat to income survival, so we can expect much personality change to occur in the process of entrepreneurship. In fact, it may be that this personality change is exactly the phenomenon that underlies the assumption that owner-managers are more effective than hired managers. Existentialist philosophy is probably a better tool for understanding entrepreneurs than psychology.

8. Entrepreneurs are typically risk takers who have a vision that their need for achievement, power, and control over their life and enterprise can be best accomplished in a new environment under their direction and control. A stubborn determination, belief, and perseverance that they can and will achieve their goals and objectives in the face of adversity seems to be a requirement for the successful entrepreneur; they must also have the ability to challenge the common wisdom of logical intelligent advisors, friends, and associates who indicate that they will be unable to achieve their goals and objectives.

9. The act of innovation for commercial benefit within an autonomous organizational entity, be it a start-up, or an internal venture subsidiary.

10. Entrepreneurship is the sum of the qualities and activities of a person who establishes, and assumes the risk for, a new or innovative business venture. Entrepreneurs have special skills and talents, which include management skills and give them a "sixth sense" for business. Those personality traits and characteristics listed above, plus imagination, creativity, and long-term vision can probably be enhanced with experience, but I don't believe they can be taught or learned.

11. Innovative activity in combining resources to exploit a new technology, invention, source of supply, outlet, or consumer demand. The exercise of leadership to direct and inspire purposeful activity. The acceptance of personal responsibility for results and the risk of loss or gain of *personal capital*. The assumption of control over an enterprise as a whole.

12. Entrepreneurship is the process of designing and managing dynamic growth strategies for an organization.

In this way, 90 attributes were identified from the entrepreneurship definitions. The second questionnaire asked participants: How important is each attribute to your definition of entrepreneurship? Participants ranked the attributes from very important to unimportant. Of the 44 participants in phase 2, 41 responded to the second questionnaire (93% response rate). A summary of the attribute rankings is presented in Table 2.

The responses from the second questionnaire were then evaluated and factor analyzed. The factor analysis sought to cluster the 90 attributes into a smaller set of factors (themes). The eight-factor solution was selected. A description of the eight factors is provided in Table 3.

The third phase of the Delphi asked the 41 participants to evaluate and comment on the eight factors generated in the second phase. Of the 41 participants in phase 3, 34 responded to the third questionnaire (83% response rate). Table 4 presents a summary of the ratings, rankings, and correlations among these eight themes.

Since no one agreed-upon definition of entrepreneurship appeared to emerge from the Delphi process, the researcher undertook a cluster analysis of the responses to the third questionnaire to uncover whether any similarities in viewpoints existed among the participants. The data was cluster analyzed using both hierarchical (complete linkage and single linkage) and K-means clustering techniques (Anderberg 1973; Sneath and Sokal 1973). Results from these analyses revealed two distinct clusters (see Table 5). These clusters represent what appear to be two major viewpoints on how entrepreneurship might be defined.

20   W.B. GARTNER

TABLE 2   Highest and Lowest Entrepreneurship Definition Attribute Rankings

How important is each attribute to your definition of entrepreneurship?

3.48	The creation of a new business
3.34	New venture development
3.24	The creation of a new business that adds value
3.09	Integrates opportunities with resources to create product or service
3.09	Brings resources to bear on a perceived opportunity
3.07	Refines a creative idea and adapts it to a market opportunity
3.07	Innovative
1.97	Understands the government regulations influencing the business
1.97	Purchasing an existing business
1.95	A special talent that few have
1.92	Creation of a government organization
1.90	Destroys the status quo
1.87	The creation of a life-style business
1.82	The creation of a mom-and-pop business
1.68	Must be for-profit business
1.63	A leveraged buy-out
1.58	Extroverted
1.56	Egocentric behavior

4: Very important	A most relevant point. First-order priority. Has direct bearing on major issues.
3: Important	Relevant to the issue. Second-order priority. Significant impact but not until other items are treated.
2: Slightly important	Insignificantly relevant. Third-order priority. Has little impact.
1: Unimportant	No relevance. No priority. No measurable effect. Should be dropped as an item to consider.

DISCUSSION

Phase One

The generation of entrepreneurship definitions in the first phase of the Delphi process resulted in a wide range of viewpoints on what constitutes the field of entrepreneurship. The definitions in Table 1 were selected to show a diversity in viewpoints. Some definitions appear to be very simple (e.g., 1), while other definitions are more complex; that is, they identify many different constructs in one definition (e.g., 5). Some definitions seem to be similar (e.g., 3 and 7), while other definitions seem to be at opposite ends of the spectrum (e.g., 7 and 8). No obvious agreement as to the meaning of entrepreneurship was apparent from reading the definitions.

We had no expectations that participants would change their ideas about entrepreneurship when rating the 90 attributes in the second round. In many respects, the purpose of a policy Delphi was to help surface diversity of viewpoints on a subject, rather than work toward creating agreement. Our belief was that participants would see the results of the first round (the listing of all 44 definitions) and come to greater appreciation of the diversity of viewpoints. Yet, the participants probably would not change their views.

Phase Two

The analyses in the second phase of the Delphi were undertaken to determine specifically what similarities and differences in entrepreneurship definitions existed among the participants. By having each participant rate the same attributes, a quantitative profile for each participant could be constructed. These quantitative profiles could then be compared and contrasted. The first analysis sought to discover which attributes received the highest and lowest ratings by all of the participants (Table 2). The most important attributes describing entrepreneurship involved organization creation, innovation, and the acquisition and integration of resources. The least important attributes describing entrepreneurship were no-growth businesses, nonprofit businesses, and personality characteristics of the entrepreneur. These results are different from those found in a survey of 63 researchers at the Babson Entrepreneurship Research Conference in 1986 (Ronstadt et al. 1986). The Babson survey asked researchers to rank the top three areas according to highest interest. In both weighted and unweighted rankings, entrepreneurial characteristics and traits received the highest number of votes. But when researchers were asked for their two areas of least interest, entrepreneurial characteristics and traits was ranked third. The Babson results present a very mixed message on the importance of entrepreneurial traits. The Babson survey suggested that "some members see the topic (entrepreneurial traits) as relatively unproductive from a research standpoint and not very useful to practitioners" (p. xiv). In the Delphi ratings the definition of entrepreneurship seems to be a behavioral one (e.g., new venture development, integrates opportunities with resources to create product or service, brings resources to bear on a perceived opportunity) and not based on personality traits (e.g., egocentric behavior, extroverted, a special talent that few have). The next analysis explored this issue in greater detail.

The second analysis sought to cluster the 90 attributes into a smaller set of factors (themes). Many of the attributes were similar to each other (e.g., innovative, innovative product, innovative market, meets market demand in a new way), and the factor analysis sought to combine them. An eight-factor solution was chosen, which accounted for 67.3% of the variance in the responses. The primary goal of the factor analysis was to uncover a simple, parsimonious set of themes that articulated most of the basic ideas addressed in the 90 attributes. Statistical concerns were of secondary importance. The eight factors, the total variance accounted for by each factor, the eigenvalues, the frequencies for each attribute, and the correlations for the highest-loading attributes for each factor are presented in Table 3. Each factor (theme) is a view of entrepreneurship about which participants held strong beliefs—pro and con. When we think about entrepreneurship, our ideas center around these eight principal ideas or themes. These eight themes, therefore, represent eight issues which the participants strongly debated.

The Entrepreneur

The entrepreneur theme is the idea that entrepreneurship involves individuals with unique personality characteristics and abilities. Most of the attributes that described the entrepreneur (e.g., risk taking, locus of control, autonomy, perseverance, commitment, vision, creativity) correlated with this factor. It was not surprising that this theme captured 17% of the total variance. As previously mentioned, the Babson survey ranked entrepreneurial traits and characteristics as the topic of highest interest as well as the third least interesting. In both definitions and rankings from the Delphi, respondents' beliefs about the importance of the entrepreneur as a major theme in a definition of entrepreneurship showed great contrast. For example, definitions 7 and 10 in Table 1 showed respondents on opposite ends of the spectrum. Respondent 7 believed that personality traits are a hopeless direction for entrepreneurship, while respondent 10 believed that entrepreneurship was the special unteachable

TABLE 3 Entrepreneurship Factors

Factor 1 — The Entrepreneur, 17.4% V, 23.6 E

UN	SI	IM	VI	CORR	
17	17	34	32	.889	Assume management risk
12	27	29	32	.864	Assume financial risk
15	17	32	36	.847	Capacity for hard work
17	17	24	42	.847	Requires perseverance
17	10	34	39	.840	Perseverance
15	17	37	31	.833	A risk taker
24	34	22	20	.826	Assume social risk
17	17	24	42	.789	Requires commitment
24	30	24	22	.766	Willingness to sacrifice
12	17	37	34	.762	Risk taking
20	29	24	27	.758	Assume psychological risk
27	24	29	20	.689	Need for achievement
32	22	37	09	.622	Willingness to move quickly without full information
24	29	32	15	.621	Locus of control
22	20	37	21	.621	Requires autonomy
27	20	34	19	.617	Risk career
10	24	34	32	.608	Involves creativity (.475 on factor 2)
24	22	37	17	.599	Someone who wants to be his/her own boss
22	20	32	26	.576	Vision
20	20	37	23	.565	Ability to go out on one's own
41	22	24	13	.545	Self-assessment
27	27	32	14	.545	Creates self-employment

Factor 2 — Innovation, 12.0% V, 10.0 E

UN	SI	IM	VI	CORR	
15	29	41	15	.878	Innovation service
10	20	49	21	.840	Meets market demand in a new way
12	27	39	22	.825	Innovative product
12	32	37	19	.825	Innovative market
17	24	49	10	.791	Innovative technology
12	10	37	41	.744	Refines a creative idea and adapts it to a market opportunity
10	20	24	46	.697	Innovative
07	27	37	29	.680	Draws together resources in a new way
22	39	27	12	.653	Can occur in older organizations
24	17	41	18	.614	Starts an innovative venture within an established organization
17	32	37	14	.524	Convinces others to join the venture
32	32	29	17	.517	Corporate entrepreneurship
22	34	29	15	.503	Can occur in large organizations

Factor 3 — Organization Creation, 6.6% V, 5.8 E

UN	SI	IM	VI	CORR	
05	20	37	38	.744	Brings resources to bear on a perceived opportunity
07	22	24	47	.734	Integrates opportunities with resources to create product or service
07	29	39	25	.725	Gathers resources
20	20	29	31	.716	Must add value
05	22	46	27	.676	Mobilizes resources
22	37	20	21	.644	Creates incremental wealth
00	15	37	48	.639	New venture development
02	22	24	52	.538	The creation of a business that adds value

Factor 4 — Creating Value, 5.9% V, 5.3 E

UN	SI	IM	VI	CORR	
20	34	34	12	.784	The transformation of a business that adds value
02	05	34	59	.587	The creation of a new business
34	37	22	07	.547	Manages a growth strategy for an organization
27	29	17	27	.518	Process of breaking away from traditional procedures
46	27	17	10	.513	Destroys the status quo
17	24	39	20	.509	The creation of wealth
42	34	12	12	.502	A special talent that few have

(continued overleaf)

TABLE 3   *(continued)*

Factor 5 — Profit or Nonprofit 5.7% V, 4.9 E

UN	SI	IM	VI	CORR	
27	29	22	22	.777	Creation of a not-for-profit business
51	15	24	10	.767	Creation of a government organization

Factor 6 — Growth 6.1% V, 4.5 E

UN	SI	IM	VI	CORR	
34	27	32	07	.738	Involves rapid growth
20	22	44	14	.685	A growth-oriented undertaking
29	34	32	05	.662	Creates profit
63	12	17	08	.618	Must be for-profit business
56	29	10	05	.617	A leveraged buy-out
56	32	12	00	.540	Egocentric behavior
12	20	34	34	.510	The creation of a business growth intent on significant growth

Factor 7 — Uniqueness 8.7% V, 3.4 E

UN	SI	IM	VI	CORR	
27	34	22	17	.657	A special way of thinking
12	29	34	24	.623	A vision of accomplishment for an enterprise
15	32	38	14	.606	Creates a competitive advantage
07	22	49	22	.587	Identifies a market
17	34	32	17	.587	Provides a concept of a product or service
15	41	24	20	.566	Creates a unique combination
20	44	20	16	.554	Understands the requirements to accomplish goals
22	32	29	17	.530	Identifies others to join the venture
15	24	29	32	.517	Ability to see situations in terms of unmet needs
39	29	27	05	.506	Understands the government regulations influencing the business

Factor 8 — The Owner-Manager 4.9% V, 3.1 E

UN	SI	IM	VI	CORR	
49	24	22	05	.815	The creation of a mom-and-pop business
49	20	27	04	.736	The creation of a life-style business
34	39	22	05	.550	Purchasing an existing business
20	37	24	19	.525	Activities associated with becoming an owner-manager of a firm

V, variance; E. eigenvalue; UN, % unimportant; SI, %, slightly important; IM, % important; VI, % very important; CORR, correlation.

24   W.B. GARTNER

TABLE 4   Ratings, Rankings, and Correlations of Themes

	Rating[a]	Rank[b]	Score on Rank	ENT	INN	RIA	CV	FP	GRH	UNQ	OWN
							Correlations				
ENT	3.00	4	4.09	1.00							
INN	3.15	2	3.24	.42	1.00						
RIA	3.44	3	3.27	−.15	−.13	1.00					
CV	3.29	1	3.08	−.11	−.25	.07	1.00				
FP	1.50	8	7.24	−.03	−.05	.10	.23	1.00			
GRH	2.35	7	5.24	.30	.23	−.16	−.16	−.19	1.00		
UNQ	2.55	6	5.00	.26	.61	−.24	−.21	−.13	.35	1.00	
OWN	2.77	5	4.85	−.03	−.05	.22	.18	.38	−.09	−.18	1.00

ENT, The Entrepreneur; INN, Innovation; RIA, Organization Creation (Resource Integration and Acquisition); CV, Creating Value; FP, For Profit; GRH, Growth; UNQ, Uniqueness; OWN, The Owner-Manager.
[a]Very important = 4, not important = 1.
[b]Highest rank = 1, lowest rank = 8.

skills and talents of unique individuals. Almost 50% of the respondents rated characteristics of the entrepreneur as not important to a definition of entrepreneurship; that is, an average of the responses to the attributes listed in factor 1 (Table 3) found that 22% and 23% of the respondents ranked these attributes as unimportant and slightly important, respectively. Whether the entrepreneur is maligned and acclaimed, the entrepreneur theme has a prominent place in our thoughts about entrepreneurship. This result further supports the suggestion from the Babson survey that "perhaps the time may be ripe for debate on the subject"

TABLE 5   Summary Statistics for K-means Cluster Analysis

Variable	Between SS	df	Within SS	df	F ratio	Probability
ENT	2.87	1	31.12	32	3.96	.095
INN	6.54	1	21.72	32	9.63	.004
RIA	.66	1	21.72	32	.96	.332
CV	4.39	1	18.67	32	7.53	.010
FP	7.60	1	20.89	32	11.64	.002
GRH	10.04	1	23.72	32	13.54	.001
UNQ	8.59	1	33.78	32	8.13	.008
OM	10.52	1	29.52	32	11.37	.002

Variable	Cluster 1			Cluster 2	
	Mean	SD		Mean	SD
ENT	3.15	1.01		2.43	.73
INN	3.37	.82		2.29	.70
RIA	3.37	.87		3.71	.45
CV	3.11	.83		4.00	.00
FP	1.26	.52		2.43	1.40
GRH	2.63	.87		1.29	.70
OM	2.48	1.03		1.57	.49

(Ronstadt et al. 1986: xiv). The question that needs to be addressed is: Does entrepreneurship involve entrepreneurs (individuals with unique characteristics)?

Innovation

The innovation theme is characterized as doing something new as an idea, product, service, market, or technology in a new or established organization. Attributes that described various types of innovation correlated with this factor are listed in Table 3 (factor 2). The innovation theme had respondents who were either pro (definition 9) or con (definition 4) on its importance for defining entrepreneurship. It should be recognized that the attributes that described corporate entrepreneurship and older, larger organizations were also correlated to this factor. The innovation theme suggests that innovation is not limited to new ventures, but recognized as something which older and/or larger organizations may undertake as well (e.g., definition 3). Does entrepreneurship involve innovation?

Organization Creation

The organization creation theme described the behaviors involved in creating organizations. This theme described acquiring and integrating resource attributes (e.g., Brings resources to bear . . . , Integrates opportunities with resources . . . , Mobilizes resources, gathers resources) as well as attributes that described creating organizations (New venture development and The creation of a business that adds value). The results in Table 2 indicate that participants ranked new venture development and the creation of a business that adds value as the second and third most important attributes, respectively, of all the attributes describing entrepreneurship. But some participants (e.g., definitions 9, 10, and 12) indicated that organization creation was not necessary for entrepreneurship. Does entrepreneurship involve resource acquisition and integration (new venture creation activities)?

Creating Value

This theme articulated the idea that entrepreneurship creates value. The attributes in this factor indicated that value creation might be represented by transforming a business, creating a new business growing a business, creating wealth, or destroying the status quo. Does entrepreneurship involve creating value?

Profit or Nonprofit

The profit/nonprofit theme is concerned with whether entrepreneurship involves profit-making organizations only. Respondents had very different viewpoints on this theme. The first attribute correlated to this factor (Creation of a not-for-profit business) showed an even distribution of responses: very important (22%), important (22%), slightly important (29%), unimportant (27%). Most respondents felt that the second attribute (Creation of a government organization) was not an important characteristic of entrepreneurship: very important (10%), important (24%), slightly important (15%), unimportant (51%). These ratings and some of the definitions provided in Table 1 indicate that many people think that entrepreneurship can only be a for-profit undertaking (definition 2). But others believe that organization creation can be entrepreneurial whether it is for-profit or not (definitions 3 and 6). Does entrepreneurship involve profit-making organizations only?

Growth

At issue in this theme is the importance of growth as a characteristic of entrepreneurship. Most of the attributes in this factor described growth (e.g., Involves rapid growth, A growth-oriented undertaking, The creation of a business intent on significant growth), although two of the attributes described profits as well (Creates profits, Must be a for-profit business). The attribute ratings showed mixed results. For example, more than half of the respondents indicated that growth was not important to a definition of entrepreneurship by the ranking of the first attribute (Involves rapid growth): very important (7%), important (32%), slightly important (27%), unimportant (34%). Some definitions (e.g., 5 and 12) indicated that growth was one of the major characteristics of entrepreneurship. Does entrepreneurship involve growth-oriented organizations?

Uniqueness

This theme suggested that entrepreneurship must involve uniqueness. Uniqueness was characterized by attributes such as a special way of thinking, a vision of accomplishment, ability to see situations in terms of unmet needs, and creates a unique combination. Does entrepreneurship involve uniqueness?

The Owner-Manager

The ownership and management of an ongoing business was the last theme generated from the factor analysis. The four attributes correlated with this theme (The creation of a mom-and-pop business, The creation of a life-style business, Purchasing an existing business, Activities associated with becoming an owner-manager of a firm) point out that the management and ownership of an ongoing smaller organization is often tied to entrepreneurship. Most of the respondents did not feel that mom-and-pop type organizations were entrepreneurial: very important (5%), important (22%), slightly important (24%), unimportant (49%). But some of the definitions (e.g., 3 and 7) clearly identify the owner-manager as the most important characteristic of entrepreneurship. Does entrepreneurship involve owner-managed businesses?

Phase Three

The value of identifying these eight themes of entrepreneurship was that the diversity and complexity on the original 44 definitions of entrepreneurship could be simplified to some common concerns. The eight themes provided a way for individuals to reflect on their own definitions of entrepreneurship. The third part of the Delphi asked participants to carefully consider the importance of these eight themes to their ideas about entrepreneurship. One benefit of this was that it asked individuals to consider themes that they might not have brought up in their own definitions but that were articulated by others. As some of the written definitions indicate, many respondents focused solely on innovation or growth, without considering issues of uniqueness, value organization creation, profits, the entrepreneur, or the owner-manager. In addition, the questionnaire asked respondents to consider why they believe what they believe. Why is creating value important? Why must a company be innovative? Why must a company have growth? How important is the entrepreneur? Is a theme important to the participant because it is supported in the entrepreneurship literature or by the individual's experience? etc. Taking all of the participant's scores in total, the results from the rating and ranking of the eight themes (Table 4) appear to divide the themes into a high rated/ranked group (the entrepreneur, innovation, organization creation, and creating value), and a low rated/ranked group (for-profit, growth, uniqueness, and the owner-manager). Yet the only theme that was clearly a low-ranking theme was for-profit. A consensus from the participants appears to be that entrepreneurship can involve nonprofit organizations.

Two Viewpoints on Entrepreneurship

A cluster analysis was undertaken to discover whether the participants could be grouped together based on their rating of all eight themes; that is, whether the 34 participants represented 34 distinct views on entrepreneurship or a smaller number of viewpoints. Exactly the same two groups emerged from both the hierarchical clustering and the K-means clustering (Table 5). Participants in each of these two groups did not rate the eight themes exactly the same, but their ratings across the eight themes were more similar to participants in their group than to participants in the other group. One theme that showed no significant difference between the two groups was the resource acquisition and integration theme (new venture creation activities). Both groups indicated high ratings for this theme (this theme received the highest rating over the participants; Table 4). We might take from this result an indication that organization creation is one important aspect of entrepreneurship. For some individuals, it appears to be the only aspect of entrepreneurship, but for others, this theme is important only in the context of some of the other themes. After reading over each groups' written responses to the eight themes, two major viewpoints on how to see entrepreneurship became apparent.

The majority (79%) of the participants were clustered in group 1. The focus of this group seems to be on the *characteristics of entrepreneurship*. Participants rated the entrepreneur, innovation, growth, and uniqueness significantly higher than the other group. Group 1 looked at what happened in the situation. This group indicated that a situation was entrepreneurial if they could answer "yes" to these questions: Is there an entrepreneur involved? Is there innovation? Is there growth? Is there uniqueness? For this group, it appears that situations without these characteristics are not entrepreneurial situations.

The other group, group 2, focused on the *outcomes of entrepreneurship*. Participants ranked creating value, for profit, and owner-manager higher than the other group, while ranking the other themes much lower. Group 2 saw a situation as entrepreneurial only if value was created or if someone gained. For-profit and owner-manager were rated higher because group members felt that situations in which the entrepreneur could experience positive outcomes were likely to be entrepreneurial. For this group, it appears that situations where no value is created, or where no one gains, are not entrepreneurial situations.

IMPLICATIONS AND CONCLUSIONS

We need to give serious consideration to articulating our beliefs about entrepreneurship and to recognizing that these beliefs influence the kinds of questions we ask ourselves and others about this topic. For example, researchers who believe that entrepreneurship requires individuals with special personality characteristics are probably going to do research that explores these beliefs. Individuals who consider entrepreneurship to be the domain of owner-managers are likely to do research that is very different from individuals who believe that innovation and growth are important. Yet none of these domains are exclusive of the others, and a concern about one theme probably will overlap another.

Entrepreneurship is a very complex idea. The eight themes describe many different types of activities and states of existence. We need to be aware that when we talk about entrepreneurship we carry around a wide range of beliefs. Some of us may believe that entrepreneurship must involve risk-taking individuals who start new ventures that are innovative and experience rapid growth. Others may be concerned only about entrepreneurship as starting new ventures. What we must all be concerned about is making sure that when we talk about entrepreneurship we recognize that it has many different meanings attached to it.

A definition of entrepreneurship has yet to emerge. The views on entrepreneurship that have been articulated here reflect the robustness of a new field, budding with new ideas and thoughts, all competing for a prominent place in some future orthodoxy. No one definition of entrepreneurship need emerge. A definition of entrepreneurship that is so simple that it fails to reflect the thing we are concerned about does not have to be created. But if no existing definition can be agreed upon by most researchers and practitioners, then it is important to say what we mean. If many different meanings for entrepreneurship exist, then it behooves us to make sure that others know what we are talking about. The various themes of entrepreneurship expressed here seem to reflect different parts of the same phenomenon. The importance of this entrepreneurship Delphi is in helping us make explicit what we are talking about when we talk about entrepreneurship. Only by making explicit what we believe can we begin to understand how all of these different parts make up a whole.

REFERENCES

Anderberg, M.R. 1973. *Cluster Analysis for Applications*. New York: Academic Press.

Brockhaus, R.H. 1987. Entrepreneurial folklore. *Journal of Small Business Management* 25(3):1–6.

Brockhaus, R.H., and Horwitz, P.S. 1985. The Psychology of the entrepreneur. In D.L. Sexton and R.W. Smilor, eds., *The Art and Science of Entrepreneurship*. Cambridge, MA: Ballinger.

Carsrud, A.L., Olm, K.W., and Eddy, G.G. 1985. Entrepreneurship: Research in Quest of a paradigm. In D.L. Sexton and R.W. Smilor, eds. *The Art and Science of Entrepreneurship*. Cambridge, MA: Ballinger.

Low, M.B., and MacMillan, I.C. 1988. Entrepreneurship: Past research and future challenges. *Journal of Management* 14(2):139–162.

Ronstadt, R., Hornaday, J.A., Peterson, R., and Vesper, K.H. 1986. Introduction. In R. Ronstadt, J.A., Hornaday, R. Peterson, and K.H. Vesper, eds., *Frontiers of Entrepreneurship Research*. Wellesley, MA: Babson College.

Sexton, D.L., and Smilor, R.W. 1985. Introduction. In D.L. Sexton and R.W. Smilor, eds., *The Art and Science of Entrepreneurship*. Cambridge, MA: Ballinger.

Shapiro, A., and Sokol, L. 1982. The social dimensions of entrepreneurship. In C.A. Kent, D.L. Sexton, and K.H. Vesper, eds., *Encyclopedia of Entrepreneurship* Englewood Cliffs, NJ: Prentice-Hall.

Sneath, P.H.A., and Sokal, R.R. 1973. *Numerical Taxonomy*. San Francisco: Freeman.

Turoff, M. 1975. The policy Delphi. In H.A. Linstone and M. Turoff, eds., *The Delphi Method*. Reading, MA: Addison-Wesley.

Wortman, M.S. 1985. A unified framework, research typologies, and research prospects for the interface between entr·preneurship and small business. In D.L. Sexton and R.W. Smilor, eds., *The Art and Science of Entrepreneurship*. Cambridge, MA: Ballinger.

9

1042-2587-92-163$1 50
Copyright 1992 by
Baylor University

Acting As If: Differentiating Entrepreneurial From Organizational Behavior

William B. Gartner
Barbara J. Bird
Jennifer A. Starr

This paper suggests that entrepreneurship is the process of "emergence." An organizational behavior perspective on entrepreneurship would focus on the process of organizational emergence. The usefulness of the emergence metaphor is explored through an exploration of two questions that are the focus of much of the research in organizational behavior: "What do persons in organizations do?" (we will explore this question by looking at research and theory on the behaviors of managers), and "Why do they do what they do?" (ditto for motivation). The paper concludes with some implications for using the idea of emergence as a way to connect theories and methodologies from organizational behavior to entrepreneurship.

"The details are not details. They make the product. The connections, the connections, the connections."—Charles Eames

The purpose of this article is to propose some relationships between the entrepreneurship and organizational behavior disciplines. We suggest that thinking of entrepreneurship as the process of "emergence" offers a very fruitful metaphor for relating entrepreneurship to other disciplines. This paper uses the emergence metaphor to explore how the organizational behavior area might be connected to entrepreneurship by thinking about the organizational aspects of entrepreneurship—entrepreneurship as organizational emergence.

Connecting entrepreneurship to a discipline that is inherently multidisiplinary (organizational behavior) in a special issue of *Entrepreneurship Theory and Practice* that is devoted to exploring how various disciplines might offer new theoretical insights into the nature of entrepreneurship presented us with some interesting challenges. One challenge involved specifying the unique aspects of organizational behavior (vis-à-vis the other disciplines) as a focus of study. As Pfeffer (1985) points out, organizational behavior borrows from sociology, psychology, economics, political science, and anthropology. Identifying organizational behavior's specificity is, therefore, problematical. Weick (1979, p. 31) indicates that "organizational behavior" is inherently ambiguous:

. . . one is never certain whether it means behavior that occurs in a specific place, behavior with reference to some certain place, behavior controlled by an organization, behavior that creates an organization, or just what.

While Nord (1976) suggests that organizational behavior is connected to psychology *and* sociology, it is neither one nor the other. Organizational behavior is about organizations, a phenomenon that is not the sum of individual processes (e.g., need for affiliation), or the manifestation of a particular social process (e.g., transactions). Organizations are simultaneous individual and social phenomena (Katz & Kahn, 1966; Weick, 1979) that require a multitude of different disciplinary perspectives in order to see their natural complexities.

Besides the necessity of seeing organizations from a multitude of disciplines, another source of ambiguity stems from the multilevel nature of organizations; that is, talk about organizational behavior at any level of analysis (e.g., individual, group, organization, community, society) requires a recognition of the other levels as well.

In our review of the organizational behavior literature for ideas and methodologies that might lend more substance to the entrepreneurship area, we found that there is no dominant paradigm in organizational behavior, only a multitude of various perspectives and ideologies. Pfeffer concluded his review of the organizational behavior literature with the observation that organizational behavior was a form of "lay preaching" (Pfeffer, 1982, p. 293). If organizational behavior is, in fact, "lay preaching," it seems appropriate that this review be offered as a particular gospel about entrepreneurship: one of many possible sets of beliefs that might be true about entrepreneurship as a phenomenon.

Given the multilevel/discipline/ideology complexities inherent in organizational behavior, the ability to offer a comprehensive and detailed overview of all of the "organizational" factors that could be gleaned from all of the different disciplines and perspectives that comprise organizational behavior is beyond the scope of any one review. A "unified field theory" that would integrate such a diverse set of topics as personality, attitudes, motivation, group dynamics, roles, communication, decision making, structure, technology, environment, culture, power, leadership, and change about organizations does not exist. The organizational behavior area is just too large and complex. This review will, therefore, not be a primer on organizational behavior. A general overview of the field can be obtained by perusing any introductory organizational behavior undergraduate-level textbook. Current theory and research about organizational behavior can be found in journals (e.g., *Academy of Management Review, Journal of Management*) or books (e.g., *Annual Review of Sociology, Research in Organizational Behavior*) that systematically attempt to assess and review this field.

In Table 1, we outline the primary topics addressed in the organizational behavior area. This list is intended to convey the sense that organizational behavior encompasses a diverse set of topics that could be connected to entrepreneurial issues and concerns.

Our solution to the challenges of identifying the unique aspects of the organizational behavior area as well as attempting to relate the organizational behavior area to entrepreneurship is to offer this paper as a type of methodology for making those connections. This methodology involves using a metaphor about the nature of entrepreneurship (entrepreneurship as emergence) as a way to highlight how entrepreneurship researchers might approach any topic from an "entrepreneurial" point of view. In some respects, this methodology (subsuming a topic area into a new frame of reference) has been the strategy undertaken by researchers in organizational behavior. The organizational behavior topics we explore, behavior and motivation, are also important topics in other disciplines (i.e., anthropology, psychology, sociology, and social psychology). Organizational behavior researchers make a topic "organizational" by placing a person's behaviors and motivations within an organizational context. In the same vein, it is our goal to look at organizational phenomena and make them "entrepreneurial" by placing them within the context of emergence.

ENTREPRENEURSHIP AS ORGANIZATIONAL EMERGENCE

While there are many different ways that entrepreneurship might be defined (Bird, 1989; Carland et al., 1984; Cole, 1946; Gartner, 1990), one plausible view of the nature of entrepreneurship is to see it as an organizational phenomenon: the process of organization creation. We concur with Katz and Gartner (1988) that most theories about organizations assume, a priori, that organizations exist. In the language of the institutional theorists (Zucker, 1981), the existence of organizations is a "taken-for-granted aspect of everyday life" in most theoretical views of the organizational world. It would seem that the primary task of the entrepreneurial theorist is not to take organizations for granted, but to probe how and why organizations come into being. The connection, then, between entrepreneurship and organizational behavior is the link between the phenomenon of organizational emergence and the phenomenon of the already-in-existence organization.

The connection between these two phenomena occurs by viewing entrepreneurship as a type of organizing (Weick, 1979). In Weick's view, an organization is an on-going process of interactions among individuals—patterns of interlocked behaviors—and discourse about organizational behavior is a discussion of these *patterns* of individual interactions. We suggest that entrepreneurship's contribution to the discourse on organizational behavior is to explore how specific patterns of interlocked behavior are generated. The formation of organizations is fundamentally an "enacted" phenomenon (Weick, 1979), a particular form of a socially *constructed* reality (Berger & Luckman, 1967). Seeing entrepreneurship in this way, as a type of psycho-social (read: organizational) phenomenon that is focussed on "emergence" (Katz & Gartner, 1988), offers a way of connecting various entrepreneurship topics together. Topics such as corporate entrepreneurship, the management of rapid growth and innovation, and the pursuit of opportunity, can be seen as permutations of the process of emergence (Hansen & Wortman, 1989; Stevenson & Gumpert, 1985; Van de Ven, Angle, & Poole, 1989).

Since our primary thesis is that entrepreneurial behavior is "different" from organizational behavior, we intend to compare and contrast these two areas by describing the nature of individual behavior within the existing organization by looking at research and theory on the behaviors of managers, a form of organization behavior with individual behavior "within" the emerging organization (entrepreneurial behavior). We do this by discussing managerial work (Hales, 1986; Mintzberg, 1973; Stewart, 1967) and motivation (Landy & Becker, 1987; Vroom, 1964). We have chosen these two topic areas because they offer complementary approaches to the study of individual *behavior* in *organizational* contexts. The topic of managerial work delves into *what* activities are undertaken by managers. The topic of motivation delves into *why* these activities are undertaken.

DIFFERENCES BETWEEN EMERGING AND EXISTING ORGANIZATIONS

The purpose of this section is to outline how emerging organizations are different from existing organizations. If, as we have suggested earlier, the organizational behavior literature begins with the assumption that organizations exist, a priori, then our ideas about organization behavior are likely to be affected by these taken-for-granted assumptions.

The differences between emerging and existing organizations are not "differences in degree" across certain dimensions, but quantum differences (Miller & Friesen, 1984) between the two types. A quantum perspective views the change from an emerging

Table 1

An Outline of Organizational Behavior Topics*

I. Foundations of Individual Behavior
    A. Biographical characteristics: age, sex, marital status, tenure
    B. Ability: intellectual, physical
    C. Personality determinants and traits
    D. Learning

II. Perception and Individual Decision Making
    A. Perception: perceiver, target, situation
    B. Attribution theory
    C. Optimizing decision-making model
    D. The satisficing model
    E. The implicit favorite model

III. Values, Attitudes, and Job Satisfaction
    A. Values: theoretical, economic, aesthetic, social, political, religious
    B. Attitudes: satisfaction, involvement, commitment
    C. Consistency
    D. Cognitive dissonance theory

IV. Basic Motivation Concepts
    A. Hierarchy of needs theory
    B. Motivation–Hygiene theory
    C. Goal-setting theory
    D. Reinforcement theory
    E. Equity theory
    F. Expectancy theory

V. Applying Motivational Concepts
    A. Management by objectives
    B. Behavior modification
    C. Participative management
    D. Job redesign

VI. Group Behavior
    A. Reasons for joining: security, status, self-esteem, affiliation, power, goal-achievement
    B. Stages of development
    C. Structure: leadership, roles, norms, size, composition
    D. Member resources: abilities, personality characteristics
    E. Group processes and tasks
    F. External factors: strategy, authority structures, regulations, organizational resources, evaluation and
       reward systems, organizational culture, work setting

VII. Communication and Group Decision Making
    A. Communication process: distortion, feedback
    B. Formal and informal networks
    C. Group decision-making techniques
    D. Groupthink

VIII. Leadership
    A. Trait theories
    B. Behavioral theories: managerial grid
    C. Contingency theories: path goal theory, Fiedler model
    D. Implicit theories: attribution theory, charismatic leadership theory

IX. Power and Influence
    A. Bases and sources of power: reward, coercive, legitimate, referent, expert
    B. Dependency
    C. Tactics of power: assertion, persuasion, bridging, visioning, withdrawal

X. Conflict
    A. Sources of conflict
    B. Conflict process: potential opposition, cognition and personalization, behavior
    C. Intergroup relations

(continued overleaf)

Table 1

Continued

XI. Organizational Structure
   A. Division of labor
   B. Unity of command
   C. Authority and responsibility
   D. Span of control
   E. Departmentalization
   F. Size
   G. Technology
   H. Job design: enlargement, enrichment

XII. Organizational Change
   A. Forces for change: work force, technology, social trends, competition, world politics
   B. Resistance to change
   C. Managing change: Lewin's three step model, action research, organizational development

---

* Topics selected from Robbins (1991).

organization to an existing organization as radical and revolutionary (quantum), rather than evolutionary (Bygrave, 1989a,b). The process of change from the emerging organization to the existing organization is not the "growth" of certain variables, but an entirely new reconstitution, a "gestalt" (Miller & Friesen, 1984) of particular organizational characteristics and the interrelationships among them. Emerging organizations are not smaller, "incomplete" versions of existing organizations, but unique states of existence with organizational properties that are arranged in a fundamentally different way from an existing organization. We may observe the same structural characteristics and organizational processes in both types of organizations (emerging and established), but each type will make different connections among these variables. For example, the types of managerial work identified in most managerial work studies (Hales, 1986; Kotter, 1982; Mintzberg, 1973; Stewart, 1967) are similar to the types of work undertaken by entrepreneurs. However, managerial work is likely to be manifest (enacted, interpreted and retained) in a fundamentally different manner when compared to entrepreneurial work.

What, then, might be the "quantum" aspects of each organization type?

Emerging organizations are thoroughly equivocal realities (Weick, 1979) that *tend* towards non-equivocality through entrepreneurial action. In emerging organizations, entrepreneurs offer plausible explanations of current and future equivocal events as non-equivocal interpretations. Entrepreneurs talk and act "as if" equivocal events were non-equivocal. Emerging organizations are elaborate fictions of proposed possible future states of existence. In the context of the emerging organization, action is taken in expectation of a non-equivocal event occurring in the future. For example, Starr and MacMillan (1990) describe a Cuban American entrepreneur who secures the use of a friend's business resources (space, telephone, computer, copy machine, delivery van) during the start-up of a clothing import business and uses these resources to "amplify" (p. 84) the emerging business's size and legitimacy. The entrepreneur's use of the friend's business resources enables the emerging business to appear "as if" it were an existing business. If we assume that the interactions between the emerging business and other individuals are loosely coupled (Weick, 1976), it is likely that most outsiders will "see" the delivery van, conference space, telephone, etc. that the Cuban American borrowed as an existing business without immediate tests of its legitimacy. Outsiders would "take for granted" that these resources represented an existing business. Outsiders are then likely to respond to this emerging business "as if" it were an existing business: they will place orders, offer materials on credit, etc.

It is important to assert that we are not suggesting that appearances are reality, that acting "as if" an emerging business is an existing business will result in an existing business. In the case of the Cuban American's emerging business, the appearances of having the capabilities of an existing business does not insure that customers will place orders for imported clothing, or that the entrepreneur will be able to deliver the clothing if orders were placed.

An emerging business is embedded in an equivocal reality where the possible results of specific actions taken in the present can only have assumed future consequences. These equivocal actions are the phenomenon of "enactment" (Weick, 1979). Based on pragmatic ideas and values (Dewey, 1935; James, 1950), Weick (1979) argues that organizational phenomena begin with behaviors, that is, acting precedes thinking. Enactment occurs when uninterpreted action occurs. These uninterpreted behaviors are a source of variation of possible meanings that can be responded to in specific ways. Responses to equivocal behaviors (selection) constitute the second phase of a cycle of interactions (behavior–response–behavior) that form a double interact (Weick, 1979, chapter 4). In an initial double interact, an equivocal behavior will tend toward a repeated unequivocal behavior by the response offered to the initial action. A response to a behavior in an equivocal situation generates an interpretation of the initial action. When these original behaviors are undertaken again, they are now generated within the context of an "understanding" of a likely response (retention). For example, the actions of the Cuban American entrepreneur in setting up a display space (behavior) can begin a cycle of interactions when potential customers arrive (response), which would encourage the entrepreneur to undertake setting up the display space again (behavior). Enactment, then, is an "as if" phenomenon. Emergence begins with enactment. Equivocal behaviors are offered as a way of encouraging responses.

In contrast, the existing organization is bound-up in non-equivocal events. Individuals behave in a context of already determined (and interpreted) interactions. Individuals in existing organizations "take-for-granted" that certain interactions will occur and that these interactions will have a particular meaning to those individuals involved. Each individual has a role (Katz & Kahn, 1978) to perform, a constellation of specific behaviors and responses to specific situations. Existing organizations function because individuals, both within and around the organization, have an understanding of what appropriate behaviors are required in these cycles of interactions (Deal & Kennedy, 1982; McGrath & Kelly, 1986).

The knowledge of what to do (what the appropriate interactions among individuals are), and when to act, is what is generated in the process of organizational emergence. Much of the problem in talking about the nature of organizational emergence is the failure to recognize the variation in how and when the cycles of interactions are assembled. An entrepreneur can engage in a wide array of possible behaviors. These behaviors have some degree of equivocality. Either the situation, itself, is equivocal, or the entrepreneur will perceive equivocality. The entrepreneur will be uncertain as to the outcome of taking particular actions. Both the equivocal nature of emergence, itself, and the lack of knowledge of how specific unequivocal outcomes might be generated out of equivocal situations, is a critical source of variation.

Entrepreneurs face a wide variety of equivocal situations in the process of organizational emergence. At one extreme, entrepreneurs can purchase nearly unequivocal cycles of interactions by purchasing an established business or a franchise. In a franchise, the emergence process (the movement from equivocality to non-equivocality) is specified and programmed. At the other extreme, the process of emergence for new organizations in new industries is usually done in a more equivocal reality that requires more time for all individuals that might become involved in interactions to create, accept, and learn the appropriate behaviors (Aldrich, 1991). For example, the emergence of an organization that would be an independent start-up in a new industry might involve entrepreneurs that are unsure of how the organization might be structured, the nature and characteristics of the product or service to be offered, what particular manufacturing technology should be employed, and which customers should be contacted and how they might be approached. Other individuals are also unsure of an appropriate response to the emerging organization's actions. As investors reading the business plan, customers facing a prototype, or individuals considering employment in the new firm, they are engaged in the reduction of equivocality through their involvement in defining the routines of the emerging organization. Given the equivocal nature of the process of emergence, the process of organization formation appears to be inherently variable. The variation in the phenomenon of organization emergence has yet to be specified in a comprehensive manner.

BEHAVIOR IN EXISTING AND EMERGING ORGANIZATIONS

When organizations are seen as patterns of interlocked *behaviors* (Weick, 1979), knowledge about the behaviors themselves would obviously become important as a focus of study. Both entrepreneurship and organizational behavior scholars have sought to identify these "organizing" behaviors as well as develop theories connecting these behaviors to larger organizational processes. The format of this section is to review some of the literature on a specific aspect of research on individual behavior in organizations—managerial work (Mintzberg, 1973; Stewart, 1967), and show how this research might be applied to the generation of theory on the nature of entrepreneurial behavior.

Nearly all of the organizational behavior literature offers some insights into how and why individuals behave in organizational settings. Since our focus is on the nature of behavior itself as an organizational phenomenon, we have directed our attention to the research area that studies the behaviors themselves—managerial work. Scholars studying managerial work have focussed on describing the specific activities of managers. They have used these descriptions as building blocks for more comprehensive frameworks about the nature of individual behavior in organizational settings (Kotter, 1982; Mintzberg, 1973; Stewart, 1967). We use Hales' (1986) review and insights into over 30 empirical studies conducted on the nature of managerial work as a point of departure for discussing how entrepreneurship theory might be generated or improved.

The problems facing managerial work researchers appear to be very similar to the problems entrepreneurship researchers have encountered. First, managerial work researchers have selected a wide range of individuals as candidates for study, so the empirical evidence offers few clues as to how the managerial work school defines what is "managerial." While managerial work scholars seem to agree that a Chief Executive Officer's job is a "managerial job," senior, middle, and lower manager, as well as foreman jobs have also been studied as managerial work. This concern for defining a managerial job is similar to the debate in the entrepreneurship literature on differentiating entrepreneurs from other types of individuals (Carland, Hoy, Boulton, & Carland, 1984; Gartner, 1989). Hales suggests that an outcome of studying such a wide range of managerial jobs has been to identify a wide range of managerial activities. He points out that there seems to be agreement among a number of managerial work studies on broad categories of managerial activities: acting as figurehead, liaison, monitoring, allocating resources, handling disturbances, negotiating, innovating, planning, controlling, and directing (Hemphill, 1959; Kotter, 1982; Mintzberg, 1973; Pheysey, 1972; Sayles, 1964; Stewart, 1967). Hales posits that managerial work researchers have failed to offer a framework for differentiating managerial work from other types of work. At this point, no definitive characteristics of managerial work have been offered. This failure is primarily because researchers have failed to observe non-managerial work with the same degree of scrutiny.

Hales suggests that another problem with the managerial-work literature is that these studies rarely separate observable activities (what is actually done) from implied tasks (the intended or expected outcomes of the job). Observations of the day-to-day activities of managers are unlikely to uncover a manager's intentions or cognitive orientations. For example, most of the studies seem to suggest that managers do not "plan," and all of the studies reviewed describe managerial work as fragmented and brief. It appears that the failure to identify intentional behavior in these studies is the result of the methodologies employed. Managerial work research might be thought of as a "bottom up" look at managerial behavior where researchers focus on describing specific, concrete, identifiable activities. Once these activities are identified and described, frameworks are developed to show how these activities are related to higher order constructs about the nature of managerial work. This "bottom up" approach has tended to be a-theoretical (Fondas & Stewart, 1990).

Hales also suggests that managerial work researchers have generated very little empirical evidence about the differences between "good" and "bad" managerial work. He believes that, in general, there is little research that links specific managerial activities to the organization's performance or to specific expectations or demands for that managerial position. Hales links this concern about the expectations of good performance to the issue of "role demands" (Levinson, 1966). If a managerial job is a role that has particular situational criteria that must be played out in order for the role to be performed correctly, the managerial work literature offers little knowledge about whether managers are successful at performing their roles. Ironically, while foundation studies, such as Mintzberg (1973), Stewart (1967), and Kotter (1982), do not overtly suggest the specific characteristics of "good" managerial practice, many managerial training programs have been based on their findings. For example, what these researchers observed (the fragmented nature of the work day, little uninterrupted time, the use of non-written communications) has often been taught as what managers should do.

Entrepreneurship researchers can take solace from Hales' review by recognizing that managerial work researchers appear to have made no further progress in defining what is managerial, in differentiating managerial work from other types of work, and in linking specific managerial activities to successful or unsuccessful organizational performance. The concern for defining the phenomenon being studied, its unique characteristics, and the effects of these characteristics on other variables is not unique to entrepreneurship. These concerns are not easy to resolve. The managerial work research literature might be able to offer guidance to entrepreneurship researchers through the diverse methodologies used. Hales' review describes a broad array of data collection methods: self-recorded diaries, observations of critical incidents, checklists, self-administered questionnaires, interviews, activity sampling, analysis of appointment diaries and files, shadowing, and participant observation. The studies he identifies might serve as models for conducting research on entrepreneurs and entrepreneurial activities. As Aldrich (1990) indicates in his review of the methodologies used in entrepreneurship research, more diverse data collection methods, particularly qualitative and ethnographic methods, would add valuable and unique insights to understanding entrepreneurship.

Besides those studies identified by Hales, other researchers have sought to explore what managers do. One innovative approach to studying managers links the intentions of managers to their activities through the use of verbal protocols (Isenberg, 1984, 1986). Yet, even with the use of this methodology, Isenberg found it difficult to identify "rationality" in the decision-making processes of the executives studied. The general thought processes Isenberg (1984) identified—intuition, managing a network of inter-related problems, dealing with ambiguity, inconsistency, novelty, and surprise, and integrating action into the process of thinking—are probably not much unique to the work of senior managers.

Martinko and Gardner's (1985) overview of the methodologies employed in managerial work research identified problems with sample size, reliability checks (on observers' observations), coding methodology issues (problems with when an "activity" might have multiple meanings), and conceptual issues (determining effectiveness, identifying environmental and managerial variability, lacking a theory, failing to incorporate cognitive processes).

They suggest that managerial work research can be improved by using multiple category coding, cross-tabular analysis, complementary observation methods, as well as by capturing cognitive processes, developing coding schemes and micro-behavioral analyses, increasing sample sizes, and measuring performance. The concerns of Martinko and Gardner (1985) have been answered in a pioneering study that focuses on the processes of innovation and entrepreneurship (Van de Ven, Angel, & Poole, 1989). This book describes a research program that uses a detailed, process-oriented, cognitive, quantitative methodology that involves complementary observations and recognizes multiple categories. The book catalogues a number of projects that are insightful studies for describing individual behaviors and organizational processes. As a methodological primer, these studies will be benchmarks of how to conduct empirical research on managerial and entrepreneurial behaviors.

In summary, if the managerial work area is helpful as a model for how the entrepreneurship area might generate better theory, it is in offering an openness towards the use of more methodologies for describing the specific activities of individuals. The primary complaint about the managerial work area has been its a-theoretical orientation (Fondas & Stewart, 1990; Hales, 1986; Sharifi, 1988). Yet, this lack of a theoretical lens for viewing managerial activities appears to have freed the area to use diverse data-collection methods for describing what managers do. By not having a theory, researchers in the managerial work area seem to have taken more liberty to *describe* what actually occurs, rather than offer reasons for why such behaviors occur. In fact, in certain circumstances, a lack of theory is helpful when attempting to understand a phenomenon (Glaser & Strauss, 1967). It would seem difficult to generate a theory about the specific activities of entrepreneurs if little is known about what those specific activities actually entail. Theories about a phenomenon do require some information about what the elements of the phenomenon itself are composed of. We suggest that theories on entrepreneurial behavior would benefit from more studies that utilize a variety of data-collection methods that *describe* what entrepreneurs do. We concur with Aldrich's (1990) observation that the entrepreneurship area's pursuit of "rigor" has been narrowly construed to encompass only large sample sizes and the use of the latest sophisticated numerical analytical techniques, rather than an openness to use other methodologies that are likely to produce significant insights into the phenomenon.

The problems facing entrepreneurship researchers are similar to the problems faced by managerial work researchers. Both areas lack an agreed-upon definition of what the phenomenon entails, which has led to a variety of studies on different types of individuals. The focus on different types suggests a large degree of variation in the phenomenon studied, which has made it difficult to specify the unique aspects of managerial/ entrepreneurial work. Yet, managerial work researchers seem to be less concerned with the conceptual and theoretical problems with their area, and more willing to conduct field research. We might find it beneficial to be less "demanding" in our attempts to pursue a narrow view of "rigorous research" and spend more time with entrepreneurs as part of the theory-building process.

MOTIVATION IN EMERGING AND EXISTING ORGANIZATIONS

Even if we know, in detail, what entrepreneurs and managers do, this knowledge would not explain why these particular activities are undertaken or whether these activities lead to more- or less-successful outcomes in particular emerging or existing organizational situations. Theories of motivation focus on providing explanations for why individuals behave as they do (Bolles, 1975). Kelly Shaver and Linda Scott's "Person, Process, Choice: The Psychology of New Venture Creation," in the previous special issue of *Entrepreneurship Theory and Practice,* offers an overview of how social psychology provides insights into understanding factors that influence an individual's behavior. On the surface, the motivational issues addressed by social psychologists and organizational behaviorists are the same. Both groups start with the same fundamental orientation: $B = f(P, E)$, in Shaver and Scott's words, "meaning that behavior is a function of both person and environment." Since the "person" and the "environment" comprehensively include all phenomena that might influence behavior, it would seem that any unique claims that organizational behavior might make about understanding motivation would be subsumed under the broad reaches of social psychology. Most reviews of motivation found in organizational behavior-oriented publications (e.g., in *The Academy of Management Review* and in *Research in Organizational Behavior*) are predominantly written by social psychologists. What, then, is unique to the field of organizational behavior in regards to the study of motivation?

An organizational behavior perspective on motivation is likely to place a greater emphasis on the organizational factors that influence individual behavior. In the context of organizational behavior research, the environmental influences on an individual's motivation will be weighted towards organizational variables, such as the characteristics of the task to be accomplished, the way that tasks are coordinated among other individuals, and the goals of the organization that employ the individual. It appears that organizational behavior has an implicit ideology that focuses on how organizations influence individual behavior. The outcomes of organizational behavior research seem to suggest how the behavior of individuals might be manipulated in organizational settings. But, this is not to suggest that social psychologists are not as concerned with how social settings are manipulated by individual behavior. An organizational behavior perspective on motivation is, therefore, unique only in its implicit emphasis on organizational context regarding individual behavior.

Since the Shaver and Scott article offers a comprehensive overview of the motivational issues that influence an individual's behavior, vis-à-vis entrepreneurship (e.g., risk taking, locus of control, need for achievement), our contribution, from both organizational behavior and entrepreneurship perspectives, is to emphasize the emerging/ organizational factors that influence the motivations of individuals involved in organization creation. Our goal is not to provide a comprehensive analysis of how motivational theories in organizational behavior might be applied to entrepreneurship, but to demonstrate the usefulness of the idea of "emergence" as a way to shift theories used to explain behaviors in established organizations into the territory of the emerging organization. We use Landy and Becker's (1987) overview of the motivation literature, "Motivation Theory Reconsidered," as a framework for discussing why individuals behave as they do in emerging and established organizational settings.

Before delving into the motivation theories outlined in Landy and Becker (1987), it should be emphasized that the idea of emergence offers an important reorientation to viewing aspects of motivation in organizations. As we suggested in an earlier section of this article, organizational behavior assumes a "taken-for-granted" organization. Therefore, aspects of motivation are viewed and studied from a perspective that typically focuses on how individuals are motivated in a "taken-for-granted" non-equivocal situation (e.g., through organizational structure, rewards and punishments, changes in tasks and responsibilities). From an organizational behavior perspective, the antecedent factors that influence the motivation of entrepreneurs have typically been explored (e.g., traits and characteristics of the entrepreneur and the environment). In this context, the primary question asked is: What motivates entrepreneurs to start businesses? The entrepreneur's "motivation" is the dependent variable.

When viewing organizational phenomena through the lens of emergence, the entrepreneur is likely to be the independent variable because the entrepreneur is often critical to the process of changing the equivocality of interactions among a number of different individuals into the non-equivocal interactions of an organization. In emergence, the motivation equation is reversed. The question becomes: How do entrepreneurs motivate others? From the perspective of emergence, we will explore how Landy and Becker's framework of types of motivations can be used as a tool kit of ways that entrepreneurs influence others, rather than as factors that influence entrepreneurs to start businesses.

Landy and Becker (1987) suggest that the different theories of motivation are not competing or comprehensive theories of motivation, but mid-range theories (Pinder, 1984) that focus on a limited range of issues. They classify these theories into five types: *need* (e.g., Alderfer, 1972; Maslow, 1954); *reinforcement* (e.g., Skinner, 1971); *equity* (e.g., Goodman, 1977; Greenberg, 1989); *expectancy* (e.g., House, Shapiro, & Wahba, 1974; Vroom, 1964); and *goal* (Locke, Shaw, Saari, & Latham, 1981). Becker and Landy suggest that the five types of motivation theories are complementary. It is their view that each theory emphasizes different dependent variables. Each theory places differing priorities on such issues as choice, effort, satisfaction, performance, and withdrawal. We will provide a cursory description of each type of motivation theory and offer some suggestions for how these theories might be applied to the study of organizational emergence.

Need theories specify how certain needs might be satisfied. (See, e.g., Maslow's [1954] hierarchy of needs—physiological, safety, social, esteem, self-actualization; Herzberg, Mausner, & Snyderman's [1959] motivator and hygiene factors; McClelland's needs for achievement, power, and affiliation [Stahl, 1986].) Thus, the dependent variable in most needs-oriented studies is satisfaction. Landy and Becker (1987, p. 26) indicate that need-type theories are not very helpful for predicting behaviors such as effort and productivity because recent needs-oriented research suggests that individuals have different constellations of needs. In general, needs appear to play an indirect role as moderators in other motivational processes rather than as predictors of behavior.

The primary implication of current ideas about need-type theories of motivation for researchers interested in studying individuals involved in emerging organizations is that there is little likelihood that any needs will be found that can serve as predictors of behavior. In addition, there are too many types of entrepreneurs (Gartner, Mitchell, &

Vesper, 1989) to assume that a general profile of the needs of entrepreneurs can be specified. It might be appropriate to explore the different "satisfactions" that entrepreneurs receive when starting organizations. For example, Norman Smith's (1967) dichotomous profile of entrepreneurial types (craftsman and opportunistic) might be expanded to include other profiles of entrepreneurial needs. The study of needs as a motivational influence on organizational creation might be directed towards understanding how entrepreneurs seek to satisfy the needs of others. For example, instead of a profile of the needs of the entrepreneur, research could be directed to providing profiles of the needs of investors, new employees, suppliers, and buyers. Research might also explore how entrepreneurs go about discovering and satisfying each stakeholder's array of needs.

Landy and Becker (1987) emphasize that reinforcement-type theories of motivation focus on how to predict, control, and understand specific behaviors that are typically discrete parts of larger jobs. Since reinforcement-type theories often involve the study of rewards and punishments for specific behaviors, it would seem plausible that entrepreneurship research based on these theories might explore the specific reward/behavior linkages that stimulate entrepreneurial activity. For example, research could explore the kinds and frequency of feedback (i.e., rewards and punishments) given to entrepreneurs involved in seeking resources from investors. What kinds of feedback seem to discourage entrepreneurs from continuing to seek resources? What kinds of feedback encourage entrepreneurs? Conversely, research could focus on exploring the types and frequency of rewards offered by entrepreneurs as inducements to new employees, investors, suppliers, and buyers to participate in the start-up of an organization.

Equity theories focus on the "(1) tension or distress experienced by individuals who find themselves in inequitable situations, and (2) the strategies that individuals use to eliminate or reduce this tension or distress" (Landy & Becker, 1987, p. 27). In general, equity theories seem to be best for exploring an individual's sense of satisfaction in a situation that is perceived as being either equitable or unequitable. One useful application of equity theory to the study of entrepreneurship might be the exploration of perceptions of equity in negotiations for resources between entrepreneurs and investors. For example, it would be valuable to compare and contrast situations where entrepreneurs had different perceptions of whether they were being treated fairly (vis-à-vis other entrepreneurs) by venture capitalists. What happens to an entrepreneur's sense of satisfaction if the outcome of a negotiation results in an unfair deal for the entrepreneur? How do entrepreneurs go about determining what is equitable treatment? Researchers might also study how entrepreneurs manage a sense of equity in an emerging organization when employees might not share in the gains from a public stock offering. What happens to perceptions of equity when the entrepreneur becomes a multi-millionaire and founding employees continue to receive only a salary?

The process of emergence, the "as if" situation, appears to fit into the theoretical propositions of expectancy theory (Guest, 1984; Vroom, 1964). In expectancy theory, individuals make choices based on their assumptions and knowledge of various factors, such as skill level, effort, task complexity, and outcomes. Wanous et al. (1983) suggests that expectancy theory is most appropriate for modelling choices that involve thoughtful consideration of alternatives, costs, and benefits. They emphasize that expectancy theory is valuable for explaining major choices like the choice of a career or joining an organization, decisions that rank in significance to the decision to start a business. Entrepreneurship researchers might identify the expectancies of different entrepreneurs and how other factors (skill level, effort, task complexity) influence their perceptions of the feasibility of undertaking the start-up of a particular business. We suggest that the idea of "opportunity" (Herron & Robinson, 1990; Herron, Robinson, & McDougall,

1988; Stevenson & Gumpert, 1985) could be theoretically grounded in an expectancy-oriented model.

Entrepreneurs interact with different types of individuals who have different expectancies of the outcomes of interaction in an emerging organization. For example, entrepreneurs are often involved in selling to individuals such as purchasing agents (potential customers for the new firm's products or services) who are motivated to make purchases based on their organization's goals and objectives. Purchasing agents might be rewarded for purchasing products based on the lowest price, the convenience of daily deliveries, and knowledge of the product's previous satisfactory performance. In order for an entrepreneur to motivate a purchasing agent to buy the emerging organization's products/services, the entrepreneur needs some understanding of the purchasing agent's reasons for buying. Instead of asking entrepreneurs for their attributions for getting into business (Gartner, Gatewood, & Shaver, 1991), the organizational behavior researcher might ask others for their attributions for getting involved (interacting) with emerging organizations. Researchers might probe for the reasons individuals give for buying products from new companies, becoming an employee of a new organization, or investing in a new company. One might assume that entrepreneurs seek out the reasons other individuals offer for interacting with emerging organizations and utilize this knowledge in designing the interactions that start the organizing process.

Goal theory, much like reinforcement-type theories, has typically focussed on the study of behaviors that are specific and bounded. Solving arithmetic problems, assembling toys, and planting trees are simple and structured tasks compared to the larger and more complex tasks of starting a business. Even so, goal theory's fundamental proposition, "difficult goals that are accepted by the individual result in higher levels of performance than do easier goals accepted by the individual" (Landy & Becker, 1987, p. 23) is likely to have some application to entrepreneurship research. Studies of the goals (e.g., making the first sale, obtaining venture capital, developing the prototype) set by entrepreneurs as well as studies of the goals entrepreneurs establish for other individuals involved in the emerging organization might reveal that entrepreneurs who set higher goals are more likely to enable their emerging organizations to survive and grow larger than entrepreneurs without such goals.

Entrepreneurship researchers may be able to offer a unique perspective on motivation in organizational settings by specifying how motivations emerge. We suggest that entrepreneurs create a constellation of different motivational systems to involve different stakeholder groups in the organizing process. Entrepreneurs suggest (act "as if") to different individuals (e.g., potential buyers, suppliers, investors, employees, partners, governmental regulators) that certain outcomes (e.g., a better product, a significant new source of demand, a high rate of return, a rewarding and stable position, involvement, compliance with the law) will occur from the organizing process. Entrepreneurs, therefore, both seek out, as well as develop, motivations that will enable organizations to emerge.

If Weick's (1979) dictum, "How do I know what I think, until I see what I say?" is taken seriously in regards to how motivation is studied in emerging organizations, we are likely to see the motivations of the entrepreneurs, themselves, change during the process. The reasons why individuals become entrepreneurs may differ from the reasons they continue as entrepreneurs. The process of "enactment" generates reasons for prior behaviors. For example, an entrepreneur who begins the organizing process with the motivation to "make more money" may, after working long hours without a paycheck over many months or years to develop a new product, find a more reasonable explanation for these behaviors such as "by my own boss," or "develop a product that helps mankind.'' The equivocal nature of organizational emergence suggests that such factors as the motivations of the individuals involved are likely to be equivocal as well.

IMPLICATIONS AND DIRECTIONS FOR FUTURE RESEARCH

Our experience into delving into a segment of the organizational behavior literature has led to the following insights into the process of developing entrepreneurship theory. First, entrepreneurship researchers need not ''invent'' any new theories in our quest for developing theory about the nature of organizational emergence. There are countless ideas and perspectives on the nature of organizations (e.g., Table 1: leadership, participation, motivation, groups, organization development, power, teams, learning, socialization, etc.) that are likely to be useful for thinking about emerging organizations. Indeed, any organizational behavior topic seems ripe for use as an entrepreneurship research topic merely by asking: ''How is this __(e.g., construct, idea, hypothesis, proposition, finding, result) about established organizations different for an emerging organization?'' The gist of this article, therefore, is to suggest that just as organizational behavior takes a topic such as motivation and makes it an ''organizational behavior'' topic by focusing on the organizational influences of motivation, entrepreneurship makes a topic entrepreneurial by focussing on the topic's ''emerging'' characteristics.

When emerging and existing organizations are viewed as particular quantum states of equivocality/unequivocality, other processes in organizational behavior take on new interpretations. For example, the process of organization change for each organizational type (emerging or existing) can be seen as a movement towards its opposite. Change for an emerging organization is a movement towards more certain interpretations and more consistent cycles of interactions among individuals. Change for an existing organization is a movement towards equivocality, that is, away from singular interpretations for events and behaviors towards multiple meanings and a repertoire of actions (see, for example, Kurt Lewin's [1951] state of ''unfreezing''). We suspect that the creation of non-equivocality is likely to be different from the creation of equivocality. The process of change and the behaviors associated with undertaking change for each organizational type is likely to be different from the other.

We should borrow boldly. Where we can exercise some wisdom in the borrowing process is in knowing what, exactly, we are borrowing. The use of theories from organizational behavior will require a thorough understanding of the problems and limitations of these theories as well as how these theories have been linked to particular methodologies for the generation of empirical support. As Gartner (1989) pointed out in his suggestions for the improvement of research on entrepreneurial traits, the problem with most entrepreneurship trait research has been the thoughtless and shallow use of sophisticated theories and methodologies on individual traits and characteristics. Wise borrowing will require us to become active participants in the organization behavior area in order to be a part of the discourse in organization behavior (LaTour, 1987). It is likely that the attainment of such expertise by entrepreneurship researchers will also result in the entrepreneurship area providing new insights into the nature of organization behavior as well.

Second, we need to be more open to a broader array of research methodologies when studying entrepreneurial phenomena. We should be willing to conduct single case studies and recognize the different ways in which reliability and validity issues can be resolved with small samples. Many aspects of the phenomenon of entrepreneurship are not very likely to be understood with quantitative and survey method techniques. If we are going to be open to all kinds of ideas and disciplines in entrepreneurship, we might as well recognize that there are many legitimate methodologies for studying social phenomena. We need to give ourselves more room to figure out what is going on in entrepreneurship.

Our current methodologies do not let us explore very much of the "reality" of emergence. For example, we need to legitimate the use of oral histories as a way of gathering information on the nature of entrepreneurial activities. What people tell us about how they behaved is a reasonable beginning to understanding what they actually did. We must also realize it will be difficult to corroborate an entrepreneur's story through the use of stories from "outsiders." Since emerging organizations are equivocal phenomena, the actions and events of emergence are, by definition, open to a number of different interpretations and perspectives. The nature of equivocal realities requires us to appreciate the need for different viewpoints and perspectives as enhancements to an understanding of the phenomenon. Weick (1979) suggests that the appropriate response to equivocal phenomena is to develop and encourage requisite variety, that is, seeing and understanding require various ways of seeing and various ways of understanding. The nature of reliability and validity is therefore fundamentally different when studying equivocal phenomena.

CONCLUSIONS

The phenomenon of organizational emergence is different from the taken-for-granted world of the existing organization. Our theories about the nature of organizational behavior are much more comfortable with unequivocal phenomena, rather than with the equivocal realities that are the stuff of entrepreneurship. Much of the task of generating theory about entrepreneurship will be in understanding both worlds: emerging and existing, and in thoughtfully probing how connections between these two worlds can be made. We concur with Pfeffer (1982, p. 294):

> Possibly with a greater sensitivity to the range of approaches and perspectives available, greater awareness of the extent to which research and thinking about organizations has been affected by the context in which such theory was developed and the prevailing types and conditions of organizational and management problems, and some reminders about various criteria by which social science theory is evaluated, we can collectively get back to the task of pruning the garden of unproductive theory and growing some new, more useful varieties.

The garden of entrepreneurial theories is ready for a variety of seeds from many different disciplines and perspectives. As our field emerges, it might begin to look more like a weed patch, rather than a neatly cultivated garden. At this stage in our development, "weediness" should be encouraged. The fundamental property of emergence, equivocality, will require entrepreneurship theorists to acquire and appreciate a broad array of methodologies and theoretical approaches to understanding this phenomenon. In our acquisition of theoretical requisite variety, we may not, at this stage, possess the wisdom to accurately differentiate between weeds and flowers—those ideas that are intellectually vapid versus those ideas that will prove to be useful. Only through continued discussion, dialogue, and practice (both through empirical testing and actual use) can our theories about the nature of emergence be cultivated.

REFERENCES

Alderfer, C. P. (1972). *Existence, relatedness and growth: Human needs in organizational settings.* New York: Free Press.

Aldrich, H. E. (1990). Methods in our madness? Trends in entrepreneurship research. Paper presented at the State of the Art Research Conference on Entrepreneurship, Kenan Institute, University of North Carolina, Chapel Hill.

Aldrich, H. E. (1991). Fools rush in? Conditions affecting entrepreneurial strategies in new organizational populations. Paper presented at a conference on Theories of Entrepreneurship, University of Illinois, Champaign-Urbana.

Berger, P. L., & Luckman, T. (1967). *The social construction of reality.* Garden City, NY: Doubleday, Anchor Books.

Bird, B. J. (1989). *Entrepreneurial behavior.* Glenview, IL: Scott, Foresman and Company.

Bolles, R. C. (1975). *Theory of motivation* (2nd ed). New York: Harper & Row.

Bygrave, W. D. (1989a). The entrepreneurship paradigm (I): A philosophical look at its research methodologies. *Entrepreneurship Theory and Practice, 14*(1), 7-26.

Bygrave, W. D. (1989b). The entrepreneurship paradigm (II): Chaos and catastrophes among quantum jumps? *Entrepreneurship Theory and Practice, 14*(2), 7-30.

Carland, J. W., Hoy, F., Boulton, W. R., & Carland, J. C. (1984). Differentiating entrepreneurs from small business owners. *Academy of Management Review, 9,* 354-359.

Cole, A. H. (1946). An approach to the study of entrepreneurship: A tribute to Edwin F. Gay. *The Tasks of Economic History* (Supplement to the *Journal of Economic History*), 1-15.

Deal, T. E., & Kennedy, A. A. (1982). *Corporate cultures: The rites and rituals of corporate life.* Reading, MA: Addison-Wesley.

Dewey, J. (1935). The development of American Pragmatism. In J. Dewey (Ed.), *Studies in the history of ideas,* pp. 353-377. New York: Department of Philosophy, Columbia University.

Fondas, N., & Stewart, R. (1990). Developing role theory for research on managerial jobs and behavior. Working Paper MRP 90/1. Oxford: Templeton College.

Gartner, W. B. (1985). A conceptual framework for describing the phenomenon of new venture creation. *Academy of Management Review, 10,* 696-706.

Gartner, W. B. (1989). "Who is an entrepreneur?" is the wrong question. *Entrepreneurship Theory and Practice, 13*(4), 47-68.

Gartner, W. B. (1990). What are we talking about when we talk about entrepreneurship? *Journal of Business Venturing, 5*(1), 15-28.

Gartner, W. B., Gatewood, E., & Shaver, K. G. (1991). Reasons for starting a business: Not-so-simple answers to simple questions. In G. E. Hills & R. W. LaForge (Eds.), *Research at the marketing/entrepreneurship interface,* pp. 90-101. Chicago: University of Illinois at Chicago.

Gartner, W. B., Mitchell, T. R., & Vesper, K. H. (1989). A taxonomy of new business ventures. *Journal of Business Venturing, 4*(3), 169-186.

Glaser, B. G., & Strauss, A. L. (1967). *The discovery of grounded theory.* Chicago: Aldine.

Goodman, P. S. (1977). Social comparison process in organizations. In B. M. Staw & G. R. Salancik (Eds.), *New directions in organizational behavior*, pp. 97-132. Chicago: St. Clair.

Greenberg, J. (1989). Cognitive reevaluation of outcomes in response to underpayment inequity. *Academy of Management Journal, 32,* 174-184.

Guest, D. (1984). What's new in motivation. *Personnel Management,* May, 20-23.

Hales, C. P. (1986). What do managers do? A critical review of the evidence. *Journal of Management Studies, 23*(1), 88-115.

Hansen, E. L., & Wortman, M. S. (1989). Entrepreneurial networks: The organization in vitro. In F. Hoy (Ed.), *Proceedings '89,* pp. 69-73. Washington, DC: Academy of Management.

Hemphill, J. K. (1959). Job descriptions for executives. *Harvard Business Review, 37*(5).

Herron, L., & Robinson, R. B., Jr. (1990). Entrepreneurial skills: An empirical study of the missing link connecting the entrepreneur with venture performance. Paper presented at the National Academy of Management Meetings, San Francisco, CA.

Herron, L., Robinson, R. B., Jr., & McDougall, P. (1988). Evaluating potential entrepreneurs: The role of entrepreneurial characteristics and their effect on new venture performance. Paper presented at the National Academy of Management Meetings, Washington, DC.

Herzberg, F., Mausner, B., & Snyderman, B. *The motivation to work.* New York: John Wiley.

House, R. J., Shapiro, H. J., & Wahba, M. A. (1974). Expectancy theory as a predictor of work behavior and attitudes: A re-evaluation of empirical evidence. *Decision Sciences,* January, 481-506.

Isenberg, D. J. (1984). How senior managers think. *Harvard Business Review, 84*(6), 81-90.

Isenberg, D. J. (1986). Thinking and managing: A verbal protocal analysis of managerial problem solving. *Academy of Management Journal, 29,* 775-786.

James, W. (1950). *The principles of psychology* (vols. 1 & 2). New York: Dover.

Jenks, L. H. (1950). Approaches to entrepreneurial personality. *Explorations in Entrepreneurial History, 2,* 91-99.

Katz, J., & Gartner, W. B. (1988). Properties of emerging organizations. *Academy of Management Review, 13,* 429-441.

Katz, D., & Kahn, R. L. (1978). *The social psychology of organizations* (2nd ed.). New York: Wiley.

Kotter, J. (1982). *The general manager.* New York: Free Press.

Landy, F. J., & Becker, W. S. (1987). Motivation theory reconsidered. In L. L. Cummings & B. M. Staw (Eds.), *Research in organizational behavior, 9,* 1-38.

Latour, B. (1987). *Science in action.* Cambridge, MA: Harvard University Press.

Levinson, D. J. (1966). Role, personality and social structure. In L. A. Coser & B. Rosenberg (Eds.), *Sociological theory: A book of readings* (2nd ed.). New York: Collier Macmillan.

Lewin, K. (1951). *Field theory in social science.* New York: Harper & Row.

Locke, E. A., Shaw, K. N., Saari, L. M., & Latham, G. P. (1982). Goal setting and task performance: 1969-1980. *Psychological Bulletin, 90,* 125-152.

Martinko, M. J., & Gardner, W. L. (1985). Beyond structured observation: Methodological issues and new directions. *Academy of Management Review, 10,* 676-695.

Maslow, A. (1954). *Motivation and personality.* New York: Harper & Row.

McGrath, J. E., & Kelley, J. R. (1986). *Time and human interaction: Toward a social psychology of time.* New York: Guilford.

Miller, D., & Friesen, P. H. (1984). *Organizations: A quantum view.* Englewood Cliffs, NJ: Prentice Hall.

Mintzberg, H. (1973). *The nature of managerial work.* New York: Harper and Row.

Nord, W. R. (1976). *Concepts and controversy in organizational behavior.* Pacific Palisades, CA: Goodyear.

Pfeffer, J. (1982). *Organizations and organization theory.* Boston: Pitman.

Pfeffer, J. (1985). Organizations and organization theory. In G. Lindzey & E. Aronson (Eds.), *Handbook of social psychology* (3rd ed.). Westminster, MD: Random House.

Pheysey, D. C. (1972). Activities of middle managers—A training guide. *Journal of Management Studies, 9,* 158-171.

Pinder, C. C. (1984). *Work motivation.* Glenview, IL: Scott, Foresman.

Robbins, S. P. (1991). *Organizational behavior* (5th ed.). Englewood Cliffs, NJ: Prentice Hall.

Sayles, L. R. (1964). *Managerial behavior.* New York: McGraw-Hill.

Scharifi, S. (1988). *Managerial work: A diagnostic model.* Paper presented at the meeting of the British Academy of Management, Warwick University, England.

Skinner, B. F. (1971). *Contingencies of reinforcement.* East Norwalk, CT: Appleton-Century-Crofts.

Smith, N. R. (1967). *The entrepreneur and his firm: The relationship between type of man and type of company.* Lansing, MI: Bureau of Business and Economic Research, Graduate School of Business Administration, Michigan State University.

Stahl, M. J. (1986). *Managerial and technical motivation: Assessing needs for achievement, power, and affiliation.* New York: Praeger.

Starr, J. A., & MacMillan, I. C. (1990). Resource cooptation via social contracting: Resource acquisition strategies for new ventures. *Strategic Management Journal, 11,* 79-92.

Stevenson, H., & Gumpert, D. (1985). The heart of entrepreneurship. *Harvard Business Review, 85*(2), 85-94.

Stewart, R. (1967). *Managers and their jobs.* New York: McGraw-Hill.

Van de Ven, A. H., Angle, H. L., & Poole, M. S. (1989). *Research on the management of innovation.* New York: Harper & Row.

Vroom, V. (1964). *Work and motivation.* New York: Wiley.

Wanous, J. P., Keon, T. L., & Latack, J. C. (1983). Expectancy theory and occupational and organizational choices: A review and test. *Organizational Behavior and Human Performance, 32,* 66-95.

Weick, K. E. (1976). Educational organizations as loosely coupled systems. *Administrative Science Quarterly, 21,* 1-19.

Weick, K. E. (1977). Enactment processes in organizations. In B. M. Staw & G. R. Salancik (Eds.), *New directions in organizational behavior*. Chicago: St. Clair.

Weick, K. E. (1979). *The social psychology of organizing* (2nd ed.). New York: Random House.

Zucker, L. G. (1981). Organizations as institutions. In S. B. Bacharach (Ed.), *Perspectives in organizational sociology: Theory and research*. Greenwich, CT: JAI Press.

William B. Gartner is Associate Professor of Management at Georgetown University.

Barbara J. Bird is Associate Professor of Management at American University.

Jennifer A. Starr is Associate Professor of Management at Babson College.

A version of this paper was presented at the Interdisciplinary Conference on Entrepreneurship Theory, University of Baltimore, Baltimore, Maryland, January 17-19, 1991. The authors would like to thank Deborah Smith-Cook for her comments and insights in the preparation of the article.

[10]

WORDS LEAD TO DEEDS:

TOWARDS

AN ORGANIZATIONAL

EMERGENCE VOCABULARY

WILLIAM B. GARTNER
Georgetown University

EXECUTIVE SUMMARY

The words we use to talk about entrepreneurship influence our ability to think about this phenomenon, and subsequent to these thoughts, direct our actions towards research that might be conducted on this topic. This paper offers some words to be included in a lexicon on organizational emergence: being, circumstance, emerge, emergence, emergency, emergent evolution, equivocal, found, founder, genesis, and variation. These words are discussed and directions for research on organizational emergence are offered.

INTRODUCTION

The title for this paper stems from an epigram from Raymond Carver's (1992) "Meditation on a Line from Saint Teresa":

> Words lead to deeds . . . They prepare the soul, make it ready, and move it to tenderness. (p. 223)

Carver's meditation explores the importance of words as an avenue for steering thought towards action. He elegantly argues that words have as much power as deeds and that one should pay attention to what words, and how words, are used.

In "What are we talking about when we talk about entrepreneurship?" (Gartner 1990), I argued for the importance of making explicit the words we use for defining entrepreneurship. The article showed how different entrepreneurship researchers emphasized

Address correspondence to William B. Gartner, School of Business Administration, Old North Building, Georgetown University, Washington, D.C. 20057.

This article is based on "Aspects of Organizational Emergence," a presentation given at the Conference on Entrepreneurship Theory, University of Illinois at Urbana-Champaign, October 18–19, 1991. This conference was an opportunity to present some personal views on entrepreneurship theory development. As a result, this article lacks the argumentation that a *JBV* reader should expect from a normal science theory article. The author would like to thank Ivan Bull for his encouragement and support for developing the presentation, and two anonymous reviewers from *JBV* for their recommendations for helping to revise this presentation into some semblance of an article.

Journal of Business Venturing 8, 231–239

© 1993 Elsevier Science Publishing Co., Inc., 655 Avenue of the Americas, New York, NY 10010

0883-9026/93/$6.00

TABLE 1   Words about Organizational Emergence

Being:	(1) something that actually exists; (2) the qualities that constitute an existent thing: essence
Circumstance:	(1) a condition, fact, or event accompanying, conditioning, or determining another; (2) a piece of evidence that indicates the probability or improbability of an event
Emerge:	(1) to become manifest; (2) to rise from or as if from an enveloping fluid: come out into view; (3) to rise from an obscure or inferior condition; (4) to come into being through evolution
Emergence:	(1) the act or an instance of emerging
Emergency:	an unforeseen combination of circumstances or the resulting state that calls for immediate action
Emergent Evolution:	evolution which according to some biological and philosophical theories involves the appearance of new characteristics and qualities (as life and consciousness) at more complex levels of organization (as the cell or organism) which cannot be predicted solely from the study of less complex levels (as the atom or molecule).
Equivocal:	(1) subject to two or more interpretations; (2) of uncertain nature or classification
Found:	(1) to take the first steps in building; (2) to set or ground on something solid; (3) to establish (as an institution) often with provision for future maintenance
Founder:	n. one that founds or establishes
Founder:	v. (1) to become disabled; (2) to give way, collapse; (3) to sink below the surface of the water; (4) to come to grief, fail.
Genesis:	the origin or coming into being of something
Variation:	(1) the extent to which or the range in which a thing varies; (2) a measure of the change in data, a variable, or a function; (3) divergence in qualities of an organism or biotype from those typical or usual to its group

From: (Webster's 1988)

different words (e.g., creation, growth, innovation, uniqueness) in their personal definitions about entrepreneurship. These implicit and often unexpressed emphases on different words led to confusion. My intention was *not* to articulate a specific orthodoxy about the characteristics of entrepreneurship. Instead, my hope for generating explicit definitions was to highlight the critical features of this very complicated phenomenon. The choice of words we use to define entrepreneurship sets the boundaries for how we think about and study it. Language governs thought and action. The vocabulary used to talk about entrepreneurship is critical to the development of a theory about this phenomenon. The purpose of this paper is to expand on this initial thesis and offer some words (see Table 1) that, I believe, might be useful for developing entrepreneurship theory.

ORGANIZATIONAL EMERGENCE AS A TYPE OF ENTREPRENEURSHIP

The domain of entrepreneurship that interests me is focused on the phenomenon of organization creation. I am stuck on the same definition I offered in 1985, "New venture creation is the organizing (in the Weickian sense) of new organizations" (Gartner 1985, p. 697). What has changed for me since writing this definition, is some better sense of what, exactly, differentiates the phenomenon of organization creation from other organizational phenomenon.

Organization creation should be thought of in broad terms, much like Weick's definition of organizing, "To organize is to assemble ongoing interdependent actions into sensible sequences that generate sensible outcomes" (Weick 1979, p. 3). A number of labels have been used to indicate this time period in an organization's life: organizational

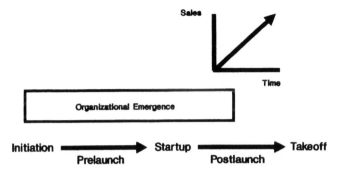

FIGURE 1   The organization creation process.

emergence (Gartner, Bird, and Starr 1992); the preorganization (Katz and Gartner 1988; Hansen 1990), the organization in-vitro (Hansen and Wortman 1989), pre-launch (McMullan and Long 1990), and start-up (Van de Ven, Angle, and Poole 1989; Vesper 1990). A diagram of the organization creation process (Figure 1) combines some of the aspects of these labels.

> "*Initiation* is the time when entrepreneurs decide to form a business venture (and if successfully launched becomes the birthday of the business), and *takeoff* is the time when the unit can do without the external support of its initiators and continue growing "on its own." The period between initiation and takeoff could be called *startup*, where the new unit must draw its resources, competencies, and technology from the founding leaders and external sources in order to develop the proprietary products, create a market niche, and meet the institutional standards established to legitimate the new business as an ongoing economic enterprise" (Van de Ven et al. 1989, p. 225).

> "Emerging organizations are thoroughly equivocal realities (Weick 1979) that *tend* towards non-equivocality through entrepreneurial action. In emerging organizations, entrepreneurs offer plausible explanations of current and future equivocal events as non-equivocal interpretation. Entrepreneurs talk and act "as if" equivocal events are non-equivocal. Emerging organizations are elaborate fictions of proposed possible future states of existence" (Gartner, Bird, and Starr 1992, p. 17).

The sensibility that should be captured from the labels in Figure 1 (organizational emergence, start-up, and pre-launch) and these two definitions is that the focus of organization creation is on those activities that enable persons to create an organization rather than on the behaviors involved in the growth, maintenance, or change of established organizations. Organization creation can take place in many different contexts: e.g., within established organizations (corporate entrepreneurship), as an independent activity, between organizations (joint ventures), as a private venture for personal gain, or as a community activity for public benefit (Gartner, in press). In whatever context studied, organization creation involves the formation of a new organization.

Yet, the word "creation" evokes some picture of a creator (typically the heroic version: e.g., Simon Bolivar, Henry Ford, Bill Gates, etc.) and some sense of the creator's intentions in this process. For example, though I've always enjoyed the rich images and poetic sensibility of this quote from Collins and Moore (1964) on the process of organization formation, I'm also bothered by the underlying heroic view on human action that it suggests:

> In this period of fear and doubt, however, these men found creativity. At a time when it became necessary for them to reorganize their lives and to re-establish their futures, they had the capacity not only to dream but to transmute their dreams to action. They created the business of which they were dreaming. Between the idea and the act falls the shadow. This shadow, which these men had to explore, and out of which they had to hammer a reality, lay immediately ahead. They had now to organize the universe around them in such a way that they could progress in establishing their new business. The first act in this direction is what we will call the act of creation (p. 164).

I gravitate towards a social constructionist view (Pfeffer 1982) which suggests that people act and then figure out what they've done (offer interpretations to themselves and others). If we ask people for explanations of "What has happened?" we will likely get different attributions for these occurrences, based on who was observing the event, and whether the event was viewed as a success or a failure (Kelly 1972; Weiner 1986; Weiner, Russell, and Lerman 1978). Individuals will attribute successful outcomes to internal causes (their own actions and thoughts), whereas unsuccessful outcomes will have external attributions (the environment). In addition, observers have a tendency to underestimate the influence of external factors and overestimate the influence of internal or personal factors when making judgments about the behavior of other individuals. In most situations where individuals are involved in the process of organization creation, the "doing" doesn't result in much of anything, e.g., most organizing doesn't result in organizations. If we only look at organizing that results in organizations we are likely to collect information on a very small number of organizing events, and these data will likely be biased towards internal attributions: individuals who are involved in successful organizing will attribute their success to their own actions. Compounding this bias will be the tendency for observers to concur with the "creators" internal attributions. Retrospective studies based on samples of organizing the result in organizations (e.g., Collins and Moore 1964) may fail to identify many of the activities that people do, as well as fail to provide some basis for comparison between what organizing activities result in organizations and what activities do not.

The use of the word "creation" seems to place undue attention on creators and what they thought they were doing in situations that may have had little to do with them. I believe that organization "creators" are an important part of the emergence of organizations, but I think we might see some interesting and important factors that are critical to this phenomenon if we direct some of our attention away from these individuals. I prefer to think of individuals involved in the process of organization creation as "founders." Whereas the noun form of founder describes a person who establishes something, the verb form of founder describes a type of failure. The double meaning of founder suggests the equivocal nature of creation as a process, rather than assuming that creation always is a successful outcome.

The "emerge" words listed in Table 1—emerge, emergence, emergency, emergent evolution—capture more of what I think occurs when organizations come into existence. I hope that the words "organizational emergence" will convey the image of organizations becoming manifest, that is, organizational emergence is the process of how organizations make themselves "known" (how they come out into view; how they come into existence). I also want to alert readers to the definition of emergent evolution and suggest possible connections to evolutionary ideas in organizational sociology (e.g., Aldrich 1979; Hannan and Freeman 1989). All organizations have a history. In an evolutionary context, "history matters" (Aldrich 1990, p. 20), and an understanding of the process of organizational emergence requires that we see that

"Foundings occur within a space–time context in which the order of events is a critical part of the process." Time, as a fundamental aspect of organizing, has to be accounted for (Bird 1992).

The idea of emergent evolution can also be connected to the idea of inferiority as a phenomenological foundation for genesis (Hillman 1975). In emergence, the whole becomes greater than the sum of its parts. Finally, I hope that the words organizational emergence bring to mind the word: emergency—"an unforeseen combination of circumstances or the resulting state that calls for immediate action." When I think about organizational emergence I can see both *unforeseen* circumstances as well as immediate *action* as fundamental characteristics of the phenomenon.

What should be noticed when looking at Figure 1 is that the phenomenon of organizational emergence occurs before the organization exists. If emergence occurs before the organization exists, then the phenomenon is not a new organization. Organizational emergence is the process of organizing that results in a new organization. One implication of this view is that: *emergence is not newness.* The problems that new organizations encounter (e.g., liability of newness, Stinchcombe 1965) are not the same problems that are encountered by emerging organizations. The evolutionary aspects of emergence are a different set of social phenomena.

An appropriate analogy for comparing organizational emergence to the new organization is to consider the difference between establishing a relationship (e.g., dating) versus being in a relationship (e.g., marriage). Individuals in a relationship often forget how difficult it is to find a person to be in a relationship with. The skills of finding a person and establishing the context for developing an ongoing relationship (e.g., generating trust, cooperation, and understanding) are different than maintaining the new relationship itself. It would seem to me that the reasons for failing to establish a relationship are different from the reasons for why new relationships fail. I suggest that an appropriate model for understanding the process of founding an organization might be to explore the academic literature on establishing individual relationships, such as the "falling in love" literature (e.g., Brown 1987, Fine 1985, Scarf 1987, Soble 1990, and Walsh 1991).

Organizational emergence focuses on those factors that lead to, and influence, the development of an organization. The primary questions in studying organizational emergence involve the issue of genesis: How did this organization come into existence? Why did this organization come into existence? Where did this organization come into existence? When did this organization come into existence (and when did certain activities occur in the emergence process)? Who and what was involved when this organization came into existence?

ORGANIZATIONAL EMERGENCE IS DEPENDENT ON VARIATION

I feel a strong affiliation to scholars in organizational sociology, not only because I admire the theoretical and methodological rigor of their work, but because they specify "variation" as a fundamental aspect of their theoretical model. Their interest in variation is primarily at the population and community levels and their focus of attention has been on the effect of selection processes on aspects of organizational diversity (Hannan and Freeman 1989, p. 17). Where I believe scholars studying organization emergence can contribute to the discourse in organizational ecology is in describing the sources, types, and degrees to which variation occurs in the development of new organizations. I agree with Hannan and Freeman's view that a critical aspect of a society's ability to adapt will hinge on its stock of different populations of organizations (1989, p. 7). Because selection processes "select" from the "variation" available, it would seem critical to continually promote a wide range of possible organizational forms in order to insure the greatest degree of flexibility for adaptation. It would seem to me that the sources of variation that result in new organizational forms occur at a time before the selection pressures on new organizations begin—at emergence.

It is difficult to sort through the essential similarities and differences among emerging organizations. The problem faced by researchers studying entrepreneurship is the tendency to focus on comparisons of averages between groups, whereas what seems to be critical to an understanding of the phenomenon of emergence is the deviations among all of the cases within the entrepreneurial sample. An under-appreciated aspect of Karl Vesper's book, *New Venture Strategies* (1980), is its emphasis on cataloguing all of the various ways that people get into business as well as all of the different types of businesses that these individuals start. This book was an important impetus for my dissertation research on a taxonomy of ways that individuals start organizations (Gartner, Mitchell, and Vesper 1989). I have a personal saying that I evoke whenever I read studies attempting to compare and contrast a group of entrepreneurs with other types of persons—There is no average in entrepreneurship! It seems to be a contradiction to talk about "average entrepreneurs," that is, to lump a bunch of people together who seem to be involved in processes that generate wide ranges of variation in their organization formation experiences and then compare the "average" of their experiences to the average of some other group of individuals.

In many respects, my concern reflects what has been suggested by other organizational scholars (e.g., Pinder and Moore 1979) about the need for mid-range theories that reflect contingent relationships rather than offering a "One Best Way" type of model. Aggregating data inherently involves trade-offs between one's ability to speak about specific details in a particular situation versus talking about general trends across all situations. Yet, I am also suggesting that organizational emergence is, at its core, about variation. Each emerging organization is different from all previous organizations. These differences, no matter how subtle, need to be considered.

ORGANIZATIONAL EMERGENCE AS: BEING AND CIRCUMSTANCE

I am very intrigued with how the intentions of entrepreneurs play a role in organizational emergence (Bird 1988). Though a certain goal orientation (being) seems to play an important part in the organization formation process, I'm continually confronted with the importance of circumstance, especially those situations that seem to be random yet critical to whether or not something actually occurs. I am going to suggest a fictional study of an entrepreneurial event as an example of the dynamics between being (an entrepreneur) and the circumstances that occur in order for things to work out. The fictional study is Max Apple's short story, "Peace" (Apple 1989):

> "Peace" is about Jay Wilson, the co-founder of a mail-order business in Tallahassee, Florida that specializes in "bargains," mostly inexpensive junk: pellet snakes, sparklers, paper American flags, Uncle Sam masks, and rubber beer can holders, that are imported from the Far East and sold via their nineteen page catalogue. Jay, longing for the excitement of New York City sells his 1/2 interest in the business to his partner, Leo, and with the proceeds, about $60,000, sets out to meet with Abraham Huang, an entrepreneur who had made millions from distributing Rubik's Cube. Jay has been pen pals with Abraham after reading "a small item about him in *Business Week*." Mr. Huang shows Jay warehouses full of merchandise (all priced under $3.49, "real numbers"): bottle openers, flower-shaped ice cube trays, squeezable change purses. At one warehouse Jay finds crates of *Star Wars* swords that had originally sold retail for $7.95, but now can be purchased for 10 cents each—600,000 of them. An opportunity or a dog? Jay calls his ex-partner for advice. "Buy 'em," he said, "then stab yourself 600,000 times." Maybe Jay could sell them for 2 to 3 dollars a piece, probably, at worse he could unload them for 25 cents each and still make a 150 percent profit.

Before the big decision, Jay's back goes out (tension). He goes to see a chiropractically trained masseuse, Lucy Fishman, that he falls in love with (and she with him). Jay buys the swords, $60,000 for the lot, plus $1,500 a month for storage. It doesn't take Jay long to learn the swords are "dead." "They're not worth the storage," a Brooklyn toy distributor told him. "I turned them down for a nickel. I wouldn't even take them for free." No one wants these swords. As the months pass the storage costs eat away at the remainder of Jay's capital, and he moves in with Lucy. In fact, Lucy has to give Jay money to pay the storage costs. Jay spends his days selling swords at a wooden table at the corner of Amsterdam and Ninety-sixth Street for $3.00 each. He sells few. Jay seeks out Abraham, furious:

" . . . You set me up. You knew how much cash I had. You led me straight to those swords and set the price just at the top of my budget. Did you get the whole sixty?"

"No," Huang said, "only half."

"You bastard."

"Not bastard. Straight business."

"You knew nobody wanted them. You offered them all over town."

"All over the world," Huang said. "Dime. Very cheap price. Require very big risk. . . ."

"You just took my money," Jay said. "You knew I'd never be able to sell."

"No. I knew Abraham Huang could not sell. Maybe Jay Wilson sell. This is business." (p. 60)

Day after day, few swords sell. Prospects for even selling enough swords to continue to pay the storage costs look grim. One very hot day, in desperation, Jay abandons the ninety swords he had brought to sell on the street, and begins to run the 25 blocks to his Lucy's apartment up on 125th. At 121st street, his eye catches a procession of robed individuals entering an auditorium at Union Theological Seminary. Jay follows them. In the cool of the auditorium, he listens as Reverend Lamberts talks about an "enormous undertaking of the church—the sponsorship of an International Day of Peace." After the sermon,

" . . . he rushed to the platform; he needed to know the day of the International Day of Peace . . .

and the outcome:

Seventy-five thousand assembled in Tokyo's Olympic stadium, 8,000 in London's Albert Hall. End zone to end zone they filled Soldier Field in Chicago, and 120,000 stood in the São Paulo soccer stadium. In Moscow and Kuala Lumpur, in select locations throughout the world, men and women made contemporary the words of the prophet. Nearly 600,000 blades, freshly stamped "Turn *Star Wars* into ploughshares," were raised and then dropped at exactly noon. . . . At $2 apiece, the National Council of Churches considered the swords a bargain, a small price for international symbolism . . ." (p. 61)

The chance occurrence—of Jay seeing the procession and taking the time to listen to the sermon—is the kind of experience which, from my observations of the formation of organizations, is the rule, not the exception. I suppose some other opportunity would have come along for Jay to unload the 600,000 swords. Certainly Jay had the motive to be aware of any possibilities to sell the swords. But, having the motive does not necessarily mean one has the opportunity. Intentions are not necessarily operationalizable without the necessary circumstances. Chance is critical to success and the "lucky" ones seem to be invariably posed to take hold of the opportunities that chance provides.

Weick (1979, p. 246), makes the point that "the most important decisions are often the least apparent," and in various parts of his book suggests that small occurrences often become significant influences on an organization's behaviors. As observers, we tend to look for big causes for big outcomes while it might be more likely that a big outcome began with a very tiny cause. In our pursuit of the sublime reasons for the causes of organizational emergence, we should remember Mies van der Rohe's aphorism: "God is in the details," particularly the small ones.

I believe that the interaction of being and circumstance is likely to be noticed when we observe "small wins" (Weick 1984). Weick's article offers a logic for how seemingly small actions can be the basis for a pattern of achievement:

> A small win is a concrete, complete, implemented outcome of moderate importance. By itself, one small win may seem unimportant. A series of wins at small but significant tasks, however, reveals a pattern that may attract allies, deter opponents, and lower resistance to subsequent proposals. Small wins are controllable opportunities that produce visible results (Weick 1984, p. 43).

While "Peace" ends with the "big win" of selling 600,000 swords, we can also trace the "small wins" that carried Jay from Florida to 121st Street in New York City: showing up, writing letters, meeting strangers, and calling people on the phone. The nature of opportunity, therefore, seems to hinge on such ever-so-slight behaviors: a letter of admiration, a warehouse tour, hanging around the sidewalk. If there is some single differentiating factor that seems to separate those individuals involved in organizational emergence from other types of people, it is likely to stem from this tautological idea: entrepreneurs organize, painters paint, singers sing, dancers dance, teachers teach, etc. My answer to those individuals who ask me: "Am I an entrepreneur?" is: "If you are starting an organization, you are an entrepreneur, if you are not starting one, then you're not." Who we are is what we do.

It would seem that a productive way to explore the process of organizational emergence is to follow entrepreneurs around using the same type of methodology as Mintzberg's study of managers (1973). Do entrepreneurs initiate more phone calls than managers? Do entrepreneurs meet with more people than managers? What kinds of people do entrepreneurs meet with? The knowledge we would gain from the day-to-day observation of entrepreneurs would be extremely valuable.

CONCLUSION

I believe that we cannot behave in ways we cannot imagine. I suggest that the possibilities for new behaviors (e.g., the ability to be innovative, the ability to generate new types of organizations) is dependent on generating new words to talk about what we see and experience. The search for new words to describe emergence is one of the primary tasks of developing a theory of organizational emergence. Yet this search for a new vocabulary of emergence will be difficult, because:

> . . . one has only learnt to get the better of words
> For the thing one no longer has to say, or the way in which
> One is no longer disposed to say it. And so each venture
> Is a new beginning, a raid on the inarticulate . . . (Eliot 1943, p. 31)

Words are windows for seeing what was earlier hidden or missing. The variety of words we use to talk about organizational emergence will provide us with the requisite variety to see and understand the variation in this phenomenon.

REFERENCES

Aldrich, H. 1979. *Organizations and Environments.* Englewood Cliffs, NJ: Prentice-Hall.

Aldrich, H. 1990. Using an ecological perspective to study organizational founding rates. *Entrepreneurship: Theory and Practice* 14 (3):7–24.

Apple, M. February 1989. Peace. *Harper's Magazine.* 278:56–61.

Bird, B.J. 1988 Implementing entrepreneurial ideas: the case for intention. *Academy of Management Review* 13 (3):442–453.

Bird, B.J. 1992. The operation of intentions in time: the emergence of the new venture. *Entrepreneurship: Theory and Practice* 17 (1):11–20.

Brown, R. 1987. *Analyzing Love.* New York: Cambridge University.

Carver, R. 1992. *No Heroics, Please.* New York: Vintage.

Collins, O.F., and Moore, D. G. 1964. *The Enterprising Man.* East Lansing, MI: Michigan State University.

Eliot, T.S. 1943. *The Four Quartets.* New York: Harcourt Brace Jovanovich.

Fine, R. 1985. *The Meaning of Love in Human Experience.* New York: Wiley.

Gartner, W.B. 1985. A Framework for Describing and Classifying the Phenomenon of New Venture Creation. *Academy of Management Review* 10 (4):696–706.

Gartner, W.B. 1990. What are we talking about when we talk about entrepreneurship? *Journal of Business Venturing* 5 (1):15–28.

Gartner, W.B., Bird, B.J., and Starr, J.A. 1992. Acting as if: differentiating entrepreneurial from organizational behavior. *Entrepreneurship: Theory and Practice* 16(3):13–31.

Gartner, W.B., Organizing the voluntary organization. *Entrepreneurship: Theory and Practice* 17 (2) (in press).

Gartner, W.B., Mitchell, T.R., and Vesper K.H. 1989. A taxonomy of new business ventures. *Journal of Business Venturing* 4 (3):169–186.

Hannan, M.T., and Freeman, J. 1989. *Organizational Ecology.* Cambridge, MA: Harvard University Press.

Hansen, E.L. 1990. Entrepreneurial networks: their effect on new organization outcomes. Unpublished Doctoral Dissertation. Knoxville, TN: University of Tennessee.

Hansen, E.L., and Wortman, M.S. 1989. Entrepreneurial networks: the organization in vitro. In F. Hoy, ed., *Best Papers Proceedings.* Washington, D.C.: Academy of Management, pp. 69–73.

Hillman, J. 1975. *Re-Visioning Psychology.* New York: Harper & Row.

Katz, J., and Gartner, W.B. 1988. Properties of emerging organizations. *Academy of Management Review* 13 (3):429–441.

Kelly, H.H. 1972. Attribution in social interaction. In E. Jones et al., eds., *Attribution: Perceiving the Causes of Behavior.* Morristown, NJ: General Learning Press.

McMullan, W.E., and Long, W.A. 1990. *Developing New Ventures.* San Diego, CA: Harcourt Brace Jovanovich.

Mintzberg, H. 1973. *The Nature of Managerial Work.* New York: Harper and Row.

Pfeffer, J. 1982. *Organizations and Organization Theory.* Boston, MA: Pitman.

Pinder, C., and Moore, L.F. 1979. *Middle Range Theory and the Study of Organizations.* Leiden, Netherlands: Martinus Nijhoff.

Scarf, M. 1987. *Intimate Partners: Patterns in Love and Marriage.* New York: Random House.

Soble, A. 1990. *The Structure of Love.* New Haven, CT: Yale University Press.

Stinchcombe, A.L. 1965. Social Structure and Organizations. In James G. March, ed., *Handbook of Organizations.* Chicago: Rand McNally pp. 142–193.

Van de Ven, A.H., Angle, H.L., and Poole, M.S. 1989. *Research on the Management of Innovation.* New York: Harper and Row.

Vesper, K.H. 1980. *New Venture Strategies* Englewood Cliffs, NJ: Prentice-Hall.

Vesper, K.H. 1990. *New Venture Strategies (2nd Ed.)* Englewood Cliffs, NJ: Prentice-Hall.

Walsh, A. 1991. *The Science of Love.* Buffalo, NY: Prometheus Books.

Webster's Ninth New Collegiate Dictionary. 1988. Springfield, MA: Merriam-Webster Inc.

Weick, K. 1979. *The Social Psychology of Organizing* (2nd ed.) Reading, MA: Addison-Wesley.

Weick, K. 1984. Small wins. *American Psychologist* 39 (1):40–49.

Weiner, B. 1986. *An Attributional Theory of Motivation and Emotion.* New York: Springer-Verlag.

Weiner, B., Russell, D., and Lerman, D. 1978. Affective consequences of causal ascriptions. In J.H. Harvey, W. Ickes, and R.F. Kidd, eds., *New Directions in Attribution Research* (vol. 2). Hillsdale, NJ: Lawrence Erlbaum Associates, pp. 59–90.

ELSEVIER

A LONGITUDINAL STUDY OF COGNITIVE FACTORS INFLUENCING START-UP BEHAVIORS AND SUCCESS AT VENTURE CREATION

ELIZABETH J. GATEWOOD
University of Houston

KELLY G. SHAVER
College of William and Mary

WILLIAM B. GARTNER
San Francisco State University

EXECUTIVE SUMMARY

The purpose of this study was to explore whether certain cognitive factors of potential entrepreneurs (as measured by a personal efficacy scale and the kinds of reasons people offer for their decision to undertake efforts to start a business) can be used to predict their subsequent persistence in business start-up activities and in new venture creation success. Two hypotheses were tested:

H1: *Potential entrepreneurs who offer internal and stable explanations for their plans for getting into business (e.g., "I have always wanted to own my own business") should be more likely to persist in actions that lead to successfully starting a business.*
H2: *Potential entrepreneurs with high personal efficacy scores should be more likely to persist in actions that lead to successfully starting a business.*

The beginning pool of subjects for this research consisted of 142 consecutive preventure clients (47 women, 95 men) of a Small Business Development Center between October 1990 and February 1991. As part of their initial consultation, these individuals were asked to explain their decision to enter business. These responses were coded on the basis of a detailed procedure derived from the attributional model (Weiner 1985). Potential entrepreneurs also responded to a locus-of-control questionnaire: Paulhus (1983) Spheres of Control Scale. In February 1992, all 142 people were sent a follow-up

Address correspondence to Elizabeth J. Gatewood, SBDC, University of Houston, 5th Floor, 1100 Louisiana Street, Houston, TX 77002.

Journal of Business Venturing 10, 371–391
© 1995 Elsevier Science Inc.
655 Avenue of the Americas, New York, NY 10010

questionnaire designed to assess the extent of their new venture development activity in the intervening year. Responses from 85 individuals were available for this analysis.

The follow-up questionnaire listed 29 separate activities involved in starting a business. These activities were grouped into five major categories: gathering market information, estimating potential profits, finishing the groundwork for the company, structuring the company, and setting up business operations. The measure of success at getting into business was operationalized by the question: "Have you completed the first sale (defined as having delivered the product or service and collected the payment from your customer)?"

An analysis of the results found that H1 (internal/stable attributions, e.g., "I have always wanted to be my own boss") was supported for female potential entrepreneurs, whereas external/stable attributions (e.g., "I had identified a market need") were significant for male potential entrepreneurs. SIC code classifications revealed no significant differences in the sorts of businesses being contemplated by women and men. H2 (personal efficacy) was not supported.

Those activities that focused on setting up business operations (e.g., purchasing materials, hiring employees, producing the product/service, distributing the product) distinguished potential entrepreneurs who had started businesses from those who had not.

We believe that one of the important features of this research is the use of a longitudinal research design. By measuring attributions before these potential entrepreneurs had started (or not started) their businesses, we can make stronger claims for a causal relationship between initial attributions and each individual's subsequent success or failure in business start-up. Given all of the events and activities that occur between an individual's attributions for getting into business and the actual start-up, the attributional findings about male and female potential entrepreneurs have important implications for future research and practice. Men and women do have different reasons for getting into business that appear to be significant indicators of their future ability to start a business successfully. We believe that the development of measures focusing on details of the attributional model (i.e., perceptions of skills, abilities, the difficulty of the task, luck, and the value of the opportunity) will likely lead to a more comprehensive and accurate conception of the factors that influence entrepreneurial persistence. We offer some suggestions for how the use of an attributional model might influence the selection, counseling, and training of potential entrepreneurs.

INTRODUCTION

Creating a new business is a process fraught with difficulty and failure (Reynolds and Miller 1992; Van de Ven 1992b; Venkataraman et al. 1990). We suggest that the cognitive orientation (i.e., ways of thinking) of potential entrepreneurs will have a significant influence on their willingness to persist in entrepreneurial activity in the face of these difficulties. For example, it seems reasonable to assume that individuals who believe they can control the environment through their actions will be more likely to persist in entrepreneurial activities when difficulties in the start-up process are encountered (Brockhaus and Horwitz 1986). This study will explore two kinds of cognitive factors that might influence entrepreneurial persistence. One cognitive factor concerns the reasons that potential entrepreneurs offer when contemplating getting into business. Weiner, Russell, and Lerman (1978) note that three dimensions of causal explanation – the locus of causality (which is not the same construct as the locus of control), the stability of the presumed causes, and the intentions of the actors in the situation – will have significant effects on persistence. For example, individuals will persist in an activity if they attribute the reasons for their successes to internal, stable, and intentional factors while attributing their failures to external, variable, or accidental factors. Research in a variety of educational and occupational settings has indicated the importance of these three dimensions [see (Weiner 1985) for a review]. Building on this literature we argue that potential entrepreneurs who offer internal/stable reasons (e.g., "I've always wanted to own my own business," "I want the autonomy and independence to do what I like through self-employment") are more likely to persist through the difficulties and failures of getting into business.

The second cognitive factor that will be studied is the personal efficacy dimension of locus of control (Collins 1974; Levenson 1981; Rotter 1966; Strickland 1989). The idea behind exploring locus of control as a predictor is a view of successful entrepreneurs as people who have an intense desire to control their own destinies, at least in an economic sense. Thus, individuals with a high locus of control would be likely to persist in starting a business (Brockhaus and Horwitz 1986).

CONCEPTUAL DEVELOPMENT

The focus of this research is on some of the individual level factors (cognitions and actions) that influence the process of starting a new business. A number of researchers have labeled this time period in an organization's life as organizational emergence (Gartner 1993; Gartner, Bird, and Starr 1992), the preorganization (Hansen 1990; Katz and Gartner 1988), the organization in vitro (Hansen and Wortman 1989), prelaunch (McMullan and Long 1990), and start-up (Van de Ven, Angle, and Poole 1989; Vesper 1990). Previous research on the process of starting a business indicates that entrepreneurial activities and the results of these activities are complicated, chaotic, and prone to failure (Bygrave 1989; Cooper and Gascon 1992; Longsworth 1991). The primary focus of this study was to discover what cognitive factors might influence an individual's persistence in entrepreneurial activities despite the uncertain odds of start-up success.

The underlying premise of this research is that some individuals are more likely to start a business, no matter what difficulties they encounter, because of their cognitive orientation regarding the nature of the business start-up. An entrepreneur's persistence influences two aspects of the process of starting a business: (1) the activities undertaken to start a business, and (2) success at starting a business. In general, one would assume that the more time and effort one devotes toward accomplishing a task, the more likely it is that the achievement of this task will occur. Yet, the start-up of a business appears to consist of problems and difficulties that are unforeseen at the outset and often uncontrollable once these activities are undertaken (Van de Ven et al. 1989). Success at getting into business is, therefore, not only due to the amount of time and effort devoted to entrepreneurial activities, but also to some exercise of will toward achievement of this elusive goal. If one views persistence in terms of the adage, "Where there's a will, there's a way," then it becomes a plausible assumption that potential entrepreneurs with the will (the "right" cognitive orientation) to get into business will find a way to achieve this objective.

Shaver and Scott (1991) suggest that certain cognitive factors of potential entrepreneurs are likely to affect their subsequent success. Recognizing that the start-up of an organization is composed of a series of discontinuous changes (Bygrave 1989), Shaver and Scott specify that:

> No matter how the sequence from initial idea to new company is segmented, the social cognition approach argues that the explanations potential founders offer for prior segments will affect the likelihood of the final discontinuous change (p. 34).

In other words, how entrepreneurs think about themselves and their situation will influence their willingness to persist towards the achievement of their goal. This study looks at two different cognitive factors likely to have some bearing on an entrepreneur's persistence at

TABLE 1 Causes of Success and Failure

Stability	Locus of Causality	
	Internal	External
Stable	Ability	Task Difficulty
Variable	Effort	Luck

starting a business: the explanations offered for wanting to try, and the individual's belief about personal efficacy.

Attributions of Causality

The social psychological study of the attribution of causality is based on the work of Heider (1958), who first argued that task performance would depend on the balance between personal force – the capabilities associated with the individual, and environmental force – the dispositional characteristics of the external surroundings. Key elements of personal force are ability, intention, and effort. Key elements of the environmental force are task difficulty and luck. The success or failure of an intentional action depends on the relationships among ability, effort, task difficulty, and luck. These four causes can be arrayed in a two-by-two table (Table 1). One dimension represents what is known in the literature (Weiner 1986) as locus of causality (not to be confused with *locus of control* to which we refer below). Presumed locus of causality is either internal to the person or external. The other dimension represents the presumed stability of the factor involved. Presumed stability is either stable or variable. For example, ability is internal and stable, whereas luck is external and variable. A substantial amount of research has confirmed the influence of these dimensions on perceptions of likely success in a variety of domains (see Weiner 1985). Particularly important for the present purposes is the consistent finding that higher levels of achievement motivation are associated with the presence of internal and stable attributions for task success. Entrepreneurial success has often been linked to achievement motivation [see a review by Johnson (1990)], so it is reasonable to expect that attribution processes will also be linked to entrepreneurial behavior. The attribution principles involved in Weiner's model have been generalized beyond contemporary American culture to societies, such as in the People's Republic of China, usually considered to have economic and social conditions dramatically different from those in the United States (Stipek, Weiner, and Li 1989). In short, the attributional model appears sufficiently robust to be extended from educational achievement settings to entrepreneurship, and from a capitalist economic structure to other economic systems.

The four specific causes – ability, effort, task difficulty, and luck – are attributed only after the fact of a success or failure. In prospective research, like that reported here, it is pointless to ask people to explain a success or failure that has not yet occurred. On the other hand, the causal *dimensions* of stability and locus can be used to characterize a person's account of plans for the future as well as the person's explanations for events in the past. Moreover, we believe that the dimensions used in the explanation of plans are the more likely dimensions to be used in the later explanations offered for the outcome.

What should be ascertained from this discussion of attribution theory is that internal/stable attributions of success will significantly affect entrepreneurial persistence. If this reasoning is correct, then:

> *H1:* Potential entrepreneurs who offer internal and stable explanations for their plans for getting into business should be more likely to persist in actions that lead to successfully starting a business.

Locus of Control

The logic for using locus of control as a measure for identifying potential successful entrepreneurs was specified by Brockhaus and Horwitz (1986) in their review of the psychology of the entrepreneur:

> Individuals who cannot believe in their ability to control the environment through their actions would be reluctant to assume the risks that starting a business would entail (p. 27).

Although many investigators have used locus-of-control scales to study entrepreneurs, (e.g., Ahmed 1985; Begley and Boyd 1987; Brockhaus 1980; Cromie and Johns 1983; Venkatapathy 1987), the results of these studies have been mixed (Brockhaus and Horwitz 1986). In most of these studies locus of control has been assessed with the Rotter (1966) Internal-External Locus of Control Scale. One reason for the empirical confusion regarding locus of control might be that the Rotter measure is multidimensional, and not all of its dimensions are equally plausible as predictors of entrepreneurial activity. For example, several factor analyses of the Rotter scale have identified a "political responsiveness" factor and a "personal efficacy" factor (e.g., Collins 1974; Levenson 1981; see also a review by Strickland 1989). Whereas beliefs about personal efficacy make intuitive sense as possible predictors of entrepreneurial behavior, beliefs about the responsiveness of the political system seem less clearly related to entrepreneurial activity. Shaver and Scott (1991) suggested that the Paulhus (1983) Spheres of Control Scale subscale specific to personal efficacy was a preferable alternative for research in entrepreneurship. Paulhus (1983) describes several validity studies of the entire 30-item Spheres of Control subscale of 10 items. On the chance that prior inconsistencies in locus-of-control research might have been instrument-specific, we used the Paulhus SOCS Personal Efficacy subscale. We suggest the following hypothesis:

> *H2:* Potential entrepreneurs with high personal efficacy scores should be more likely to persist in actions that lead to successfully starting a new business.

Other Factors Influencing Start-Up Success

Although a certain cognitive orientation toward entrepreneurship might influence one's readiness to persist in entrepreneurial action, previous research has shown that some entrepreneurial activities (e.g., planning, networking, selling, finding resources) are more likely to result in a successful start-up than are others (Cooper 1993; Duchesneau and Gartner 1992; Hills 1984; Van de Ven et al. 1984; Vesper 1990). Being willing and able to persist in entrepreneurial activities may not lead to the successful creation of a business if persistence merely results in potential entrepreneurs engaging in the wrong activities. For example, a critical activity in starting a business is likely to be "finding potential customers." If a potential entrepreneur devotes a substantial amount of time to planning, but no time to finding potential customers, a new business may not be created. We suggest that entrepreneurial activities are, therefore, an important mediating variable between an entrepreneur's cognitive orientation and subsequent start-up success.

We undertook a review of the entrepreneurship literature (e.g., Duchesneau and Gartner 1992; Gartner 1988; Gartner and Starr 1993; Timmons 1990; Van de Ven et al. 1984; Vesper 1990) to identify specific entrepreneurial activities that might lead to the successful start-up of a business. Using the list of activities generated from this literature review, we engaged a focus group of SBDC counselors in a discussion and evaluation of these activities in terms of their perceived efficacy in real-world settings. From these discussions we generated a summary list of 29 separate entrepreneurial activities (see Appendix 1) grouped into five major categories: gathering market information, estimating potential profits, finishing the groundwork for the business, developing the structure of the company, and setting up business operations. Rather than propose a series of hypotheses of which activities might be significant for successfully starting a business, we sought to measure these activities in the study and to see which activities proved to be significant.

Finally, we sought to explore gender as a mediating factor that might influence the cognitive orientations of these potential entrepreneurs, their entrepreneurial activities, and start-up success. Overviews of the effect of gender in entrepreneurship have offered mixed results (Bird 1993; Brush 1992), though Brush (1992) suggests that the results from a comprehensive study of women-owned businesses in 24 countries shows that women follow different approaches to venture creation because of different occupational, social, and educational experiences. Some studies (Brush 1990; Chaganti 1986; Geoffe and Scase 1983; Scott 1986) have found that women business owners are motivated to create their own businesses out of a desire to have flexibility in their work and family schedules, and that the process of business founding may be different for female entrepreneurs (Belcourt, Bourke, and Lee-Gosselin 1991; Fischer, Reuber, and Dyke 1993; Sexton and Bowman-Upton 1990). Yet, other studies have not found gender to be a significant differentiating characteristic. The need for achievement, independence, job satisfaction, and economic necessity seemed to be shared by men and women, alike (Chaganti 1986; Hisrich and Brush 1983, 1985; Longstreth, Stafford, and Maudlin 1987; Schwartz 1979). This controversy in the literature precludes our offering specific hypotheses regarding the role that gender might play in our research, but it also suggests that gender will need to be taken into account in our analysis of the data.

METHOD

Subjects

The beginning pool of participants for this research consisted of 142 individuals (47 women, 95 men) who were preventure clients of a Small Business Development Center (SBDC) in a large southwestern metropolitan area between October 1990 and February 1991. None of these consecutive 142 participants refused to complete the initial questionnaires. Preventure clients of an SBDC are obviously different from the general population in that they have taken one concrete step in the direction of organizing a new business venture. They are also different from sophisticated repeat-entrepreneurs who would not require the services offered by SBDCs. On the other hand, SBDC clients represent an important segment of the population to which we hope our findings will generalize—individuals seeking to start businesses.

As part of their initial consultation at the SBDC, all 142 preventure clients were asked to explain the reasons why they chose to enter business and to complete a locus of control scale. These two measures (described in detail below) were the psychological variables involved in the study.

In February of 1992 all 142 participants were sent a follow-up questionnaire designed to assess the extent of their new venture development activity during the intervening year. This follow-up questionnaire asked for the hours devoted to each of 29 business start-up activities and asked whether there had been sales, whether the entrepreneur was involved full-time in the business, and whether there were additional employees of the business. Individuals who did not return this questionnaire were sent a second one. Individuals who

TABLE 2   Reasons for Getting Into Business

1st Reason #	%	2nd Reason #	%	1+2 Combined #	%	
53	37%	15	17%	68	29%	I had identified a market need
34	24%	7	8%	41	18%	I wanted the autonomy and independence to do what I like through self-employment
14	9%	27	30%	41	18%	I wanted to make more money
15	11%	19	21%	34	16%	I wanted to use my knowledge and experience
11	8%	6	7%	17	7%	Enjoyment through self-employment
3	2%	8	9%	11	5%	I wanted to show I could do it
12	9%	8	8%	20	7%	Other (e.g., opportunity to learn, needed a job, an opportunity to be creative, provide jobs for others, avoid taxes, God's will)
142	100%	90	100%	232	100%	Totals

did not return the second questionnaire were then sent a third questionnaire by certified mail, and an attempt was made to contact them by telephone. Of the 142 participants, 30 individuals could not be reached by mail or phone, and 27 individuals who were contacted did not complete the follow-up questionnaire.

Initial Attributional Coding

To examine the relationship between attributional processes and business success, we asked all 142 potential entrepreneurs to tell us why they want to enter business. Specifically, we explained that we were interested in their decision-making processes, and then we asked them the two questions shown below:

1. What business are you thinking of starting?
2. Why would you start this business?

All answers to the question, "Why would you start this business?" were subjected to attributional coding and were subsequently analyzed. To conserve space, we report only a summary of people's first two answers in Table 2. Some potential entrepreneurs gave more than five explanations.

All verbatim answers to the "Why?" question were coded according to a detailed procedure derived from the attributional model described previously. This coding protocol is an extension of attributional coding procedures first described by Harvey et al. (1980). Two of the authors of this study, each acting independently, first separated every answer into the number of separate explanations it contained. Then for each separate explanation, the coder first decided whether the explanation identified a factor internal to the person or a factor in the external environment. Once the internal/external decision had been made, the coder then decided whether the explanation identified a stable characteristic (one that would not, or could not, change in the immediate short-term) or a variable characteristic (one that would, or could, change in the immediate short-term). For example, "I have always wanted to be my own boss" is an internal-stable reason for going into business, whereas "there is a large market demand for this product" is an external stable reason for going into business.

As a result of the three-step coding process, each separate explanation was first identified and then placed into one of the four coding categories constructed from the combination of internal/external and stable/variable. Reliabilities for coding were computed separately for each step in the process. The Pearson correlations reflecting intercoder reliability for parsing answers into separate explanations was 0.95; reliability for the internal/external step was 0.95; reliability for the stable/variable step was 0.85. These reliabilities show a very high degree of agreement in the content coding. The few disagreements in coding that did arise were resolved by discussions among all three authors.

Based on previous research on the importance of attributions for success (Weiner 1985), the primary measures for the present study were the numbers, for each individual in the study, of internal/stable attributions and external/stable attributions offered in their statements answering the question "Why would you start this business?" It was predicted that this attribution measure would be related to persistence, both in terms of sustained business start-up activity and in terms of actually getting into business. In other words, we predict that potential entrepreneurs who gave internal/stable attributions for getting into business would persist in the activities involved in starting a business and that persistence would lead to starting a business that actually made sales.

Locus of Control

Empirically, locus of control has in the entrepreneurship literature been assessed using the Rotter (1966) Internal-External Locus of Control Scale. As has been argued elsewhere (Shaver and Scott 1991), this measure is not well-suited to the study of the founding of new business ventures. A better alternative is the Paulhus (1983) Spheres of Control Scale, specifically, the subscale having to do with personal efficacy. As noted earlier, this subscale has sufficient reliability and validity and has the added advantage of containing only 10 items, thus minimizing the time that subjects must devote to its completion.

Assessment of Business Start-Up Activity

The follow-up questionnaire began with a listing of the 29 separate activities involved in starting a business, grouped into the categories described earlier. Recall that the categories were: gathering market information (six items), estimating potential profits (four items), finishing the groundwork for the business (three items), developing the structure of the company (seven items), and setting up business operations (nine items). Respondents were asked to indicate which of the 29 separate activities they performed, and to provide an *estimate* of the hours they had devoted to each activity. Respondents were also asked to give an estimate of the total hours per week they were currently spending on the business activities described earlier.

Success at Getting Into Business

The measure of success at getting into business was operationalized by the question: "Have you completed the first sale (defined as having delivered the product or service and collected the payment from your customer)?" If respondents answered affirmatively as to whether or not they were in business, then they were asked to provide the date of their first sale and the number of their full-time and part-time employees. First sale was used as the measure of successfully getting into business based on Katz and Gartner's (1988) properties of emerging organizations framework. They offer theoretical justifications for using measures of exchange (i.e., date of first sale) as appropriate indicators of successful business start-up. In addition,

TABLE 3   Comparisons of Respondents to Nonrespondents

Subject gender:	Females		Males	
Response:	NonResp	Respond	NonResp	Respond
n^a:	15	31	40	54
Age category[b]	3.20	3.45	2.80	3.11
	(1.01)	(1.23)	(0.97)	(0.74)
Experience category[c]	1.73	1.87	2.50	2.11
	(1.16)	(1.15)	(1.45)	(1.31)
Education category[d]	3.27	3.61	3.53	3.98
	(1.28)	(1.28)	(1.13)	(1.11)
Spheres of Control	56.47	56.65	57.13	56.82
	(8.63)	(6.40)	(9.26)	(6.09)
Business pers-stable	0.93	1.39	0.80	1.07
	(1.28)	(1.20)	(0.82)	(1.01)

Note: Figures in parentheses are standard deviations.
[a] Numbers of nonrespondents reduced by two missing cases.
[b] Age categories: 1 (under 21), 2 (21 to 29), 3 (30 to 39), 4 (40 to 49), 5 (50 to 59), 6 (60 and over).
[c] Experience as years in field: 1 (<1 year), 2 (1 to 3 years), 3 (3 to 5 years), 4 (>5 years).
[d] Education categories: 1 (not a high school grad), 2 (high school grad), 3 (some college), 4 (college degree), 5 (some graduate school), 6 (graduate degree).

Reynolds and Miller's (1992) study of new firm gestation indicators concludes that "Date of first sale appears a suitable indicator of 'birth' if only one event is to be used" (p. 405).

RESULTS

In Appendix 2 we provide a detailed description of the plan used for data analysis.

Representativeness of the Respondents

The final sample of 85 respondents constituted nearly 60% of the total of 142 individuals who participated in the initial assessment of reasons for entering business, and nearly 76% of the individuals for whom there were valid addresses or telephone numbers. Comparisons of the 85 respondents to the 57 nonrespondents on various demographic measures are shown in Table 3. These mean scores were subjected to a 2 × 2 (Subject Gender × Response) analysis of variance, which revealed no significant differences between respondents and nonrespondents. The relatively high response rate and the lack of differences between the two groups gives us confidence that the respondents were representative of the total sample.

Cognitive Factors and Business Start-Up Activities

Pearson correlations among the two cognitive factors (internal/stable attributions and Spheres of Control scores) and the five category measures of business start-up activity are shown in Table 4. All significance tests are two-tailed, based on 85 subjects. Two features of these correlations are immediately apparent. First, among the business start-up activities, the first four—assessing the market, estimating the profits, completing the groundwork, and structuring the company—were all highly intercorrelated. But only one of these (assessing the market) was significantly correlated with setting up business operations. The second feature of the correlations is that the Spheres of Control Scale scores were not correlated with any organizing activity, whereas personal attributions correlated significantly with structuring the company.

TABLE 4 Correlations Among Business Start-Up Activities and Psychological Variables

	PRO	GRD	STR	OPE	SOC	ATT
Assessing market	0.70[c]	0.30[b]	0.49[c]	0.32[b]	−0.07	0.16
Estimating profits (PRO)		0.52[c]	0.81[c]	0.18	0.02	0.13
Completing groundwork (GRD)			0.46[c]	0.12	0.02	0.15
Structuring company (STR)				0.16	0.07	0.27[b]
Setting up operations (OPE)					0.02	0.10
Spheres of Control score (SOC)						0.04
Personal stable attributions (ATT)						

Note: Significance tests are two-tailed, based on $n = 85$.
[a] $p < .05$.
[b] $p < .025$.
[c] $p < .001$.

This is especially interesting given the fact that the attribution measure has a highly restricted range, whereas the locus of control measure has a substantial range.

Business Start-Up Activity and Getting Into Business

The five categories of business start-up activities can be considered part of the process that takes place between the intention to start a business and making the first sale. As we noted earlier, this process may be quite different for females than for males. Consequently, we examined the five categories of business start-up activity separately for females and males, also considering whether sales have actually been made. The five business start-up activity category scores are shown in Table 5 separately for females and males who have, or have not, made sales.

The activity measures are properly regarded as a within-subjects variable, so we performed a $2 \times 2 \times 5$ (Gender × Sale × Activity) multivariate analysis of variance, with repeated measures on the last factor. Because the various activity measures were differentially correlated with one another, a multivariate statistical test was appropriate. The analysis revealed no significant interaction between gender and either entrepreneurial activity or sales. There was a significant interaction between sales and activity, Wilks' lambda = 0.84, $p <$

TABLE 5 Mean Scores for Business Start-Up Activities by Gender and Sales

Subject Gender:	Females		Males	
Sales:	No Sales	Sales	No Sales	Sales
n:	20	11	38	16
Assess market	12.05	39.77	23.61	25.19
	(13.55)	(85.73)	(43.52)	(15.48)
Estimate profits	10.88	22.30	26.43	25.55
	(15.03)	(45.10)	(54.78)	(26.81)
Complete ground work	54.00	79.50	71.54	54.58
	(154.41)	(106.83)	(166.53)	(71.05)
Structure company	8.83	12.56	24.73	22.77
	(17.04)	(17.45)	(76.03)	(31.19)
Set up operations	3.45	58.16	3.56	65.01
	(9.49)	(71.85)	(12.16)	(89.92)

Note: Figures in parentheses are standard deviations.

.01 (approximate F = 3.80, with 4 and 78 df)[1]. This interaction is best understood by examining the differences between activity levels of respondents who made sales and respondents who had not made sales. For four of the activity categories this difference score (mean activity score for those with sales minus the mean activity score for those without sales) was low, or even negative (assessing market difference = 11.50 hours, estimating profits different = 3.16 hours, completing groundwork difference = −0.076 hours, structuring company difference = −0.64 hours). Indeed, a 2 × 2 × 4 (Gender × Sales × Activity) MANOVA on these four activities showed no significant sales × activity interaction. For the remaining category, however, there was an impressive difference between respondents with sales and respondents without sales (mean difference = 58.7 hours). This difference is even more impressive expressed as a ratio than as a mean difference: Compared to respondents without sales, respondents with sales devoted 17.8 times the hours to setting up business operations.

Some elements in the setting up operations category, such as installing and adjusting the product or service, or training customers, would be expected to occur only in very rare cases unless sales had been made. Consequently, it might be the case that the sale/no sale difference for the category could be an artifact produced by the greater time devoted to activities that would normally only follow sales. To check this possible explanation, we examined the activity mean scores for all elements of the category (Table 6). A 2 × 2 (Gender × Sale) multivariate analysis of variance of the elements shown in Table 6 revealed a significant multivariate effect for sale, Wilks' lambda = 0.67, $p < .001$ (approximate F value = 3.95, with 9 and 73 df). Examination of the corresponding univariate tests revealed a significant sale effect for every separate element except the first one – securing a location. Therefore, respondents who made sales differed from those who did not make sales on activities that normally precede sales (e.g., purchasing supplies, leasing equipment) as well as on activities that normally follow sales (e.g., installation and adjustment, training of customers).

Cognitive Factors and Getting Into Business

Hypotheses regarding the two cognitive factors (attributions, beliefs in personal efficacy) included in the research can be tested directly in two ways. First, the cognitive factors can be correlated to each of the five general categories of business start-up activity. These correlations appear in Table 4. As noted before, all of these correlations were positive, but only the correlation between attributions and structuring the company reached conventional levels of significance. The second direct way to test the relationship between attributions and success at starting a business is to compare respondents who made sales to respondents who did not make sales, and ask whether these two groups of individuals had different attributional patterns at the beginning of this process. Mean scores for the attributions and the Spheres of Control scores are shown in Table 7.

Each cognitive factor was subjected to a 2 × 2 (Gender × Sales) analysis of variance. For personal stable attributions there was a significant interaction between gender and sales, $F(1, 81) = 5.41, p < .025$. Among female respondents, but not among male respondents, the personal stable attributions were higher among those who subsequently made sales than among those who did not subsequently make sales. Almost the reverse pattern was obtained for external stable attributions, which also showed a significant interaction between gender

---

[1] In this design, both the Pillai-Bartlett trace and the Hotelling trace produce exactly the same approximate F value as the Wilks' lambda, so we have elected to use the more familiar Wilks measure.

TABLE 6   Mean Scores for Elements in Setting up Operations by Gender and Sales

Subject Gender:	Females		Males	
Sales:	No Sales	Sales	No Sales	Sales
n:	20	11	38	16
Secure a location	1.00	9.91	9.90	9.06
	(2.77)	(23.99)	(31.01)	(16.01)
Purchase supplies	2.65	8.73	1.24	31.44
	(5.59)	(11.92)	(4.25)	(59.35)
Lease equipment	1.35	4.76	0.76	20.19
	(3.92)	(8.09)	(2.79)	(27.05)
Hire employees	1.05	26.36	1.18	38.13
	(3.69)	(72.43)	(6.50)	(80.35)
Produce prd./serv.	11.50	101:46	1.42	65.56
	(36.31)	(299.51)	(6.66)	(130.76)
Distrib. prd./serv.	2.25	63.84	0.90	162.13
	(8.96)	(178.54)	(4.18)	(453.87)
Market prd./serv.	9.25	160.45	15.29	191.13
	(35.78)	(237.73)	(81.03)	(372.43)
Install and adjust	0.00	32.36	0.63	28.88
	(0.00)	(90.01)	(3.89)	(59.97)
Train customers	2.00	30.09	0.68	41.56
	(8.94)	(89.83)	(3.90)	(149.31)

Note: Figures in parentheses are standard deviations.

and sales $F(1, 81) = 3.96$, $p < .05$. Males who had subsequently made sales showed the highest frequency of external stable attributions. Finally, the analysis of Spheres of Control scores produced no significant differences.[2]

There are two possible explanations for the attributional differences. First, there is the stereotyped view that females start service businesses (where presumably sheer persistence is more important than know-how or outside financing), whereas males start technological businesses in which external forces are more important than internal desires. This alternative can be tested by comparing the SIC code distributions for females and males. If the stereotype is true, and is the explanation for our differences, then the female respondents should have been under-represented in such areas as manufacturing and transportation (both capital-intensive) and overrepresented in service businesses. We combined the manufacturing and transportation SIC categories (all codes beginning with 2 or 3) into a single cell; maintained wholesale and retail business as a second cell (codes beginning with 5); combined finance, insurance, and real estate (codes beginning with 6) with the two service categories (codes 7 and 8); and examined the participation of females and males in each of the three cells. The chi-squared analysis showed no significant difference in the participation of females and

---

[2] Paulhus (1983) reports several cross-validation samples in which the subscale alpha reliabilities range from 0.75 to 0.80. In our sample, the entire personal efficacy subscale produced an alpha reliability of only 0.48, suggesting that the scale might have been operating differently in our context. For this reason, we elected to factor analyze responses on the (sub)scale. A principle components factor analysis with varimax rotation produced four factors (respectively four items, three items, two items, and one item) that together accounted for 65% of the variance. Only the first of these had a satisfactory Chronbach's alpha (0.78). This four-item factor, which we call Diligence, included "when I get what I want it's usually because I worked hard for it," "My major accomplishments are due to my hard work and ability," "When I make plans I am almost certain to make them work," and "I can learn almost anything if I put my mind to it."

Both control measures (the 10-item scale and the four-item Diligence subscale) were subjected to a 2 × 2 (Gender × Sales) analysis of variance. The results of these analyses revealed no significant differences based on gender, sales, or their interaction for either the 10-item or four-item measure of locus of control.

TABLE 7 Mean Scores for Psychological Variables by Gender and Sales

Subject Gender:	Females		Males	
Sales:	No Sales	Sales	No Sales	Sales
n:	20	11	38	16
Personal stable	1.10	1.91	1.18	0.81
	(1.11)	(1.22)	(1.04)	(0.91)
External stable	0.45	0.27	0.37	0.81
	(0.69)	(0.47)	(0.59)	(0.83)
Spheres of Control	57.30	55.46	56.76	56.94
	(6.85)	(5.48)	(5.91)	(6.70)

Note: Figures in parentheses are standard deviations.

males across the three cells, χ^2 (2, N = 82) = 1.30, p = NS. Thus, the differential importance of personal attributions to women does not appear to be related to the general kinds of businesses being started by men and women.

A second explanation for the attributional differences, also based on a stereotyped view of females and males in the workforce, is that females can afford the "luxury" of following their internal desires, because in doing so they would become the second breadwinner in a family. In contrast, males, who by this view are the primary breadwinners in a family, would need to concentrate on the external environment in order to ensure the success of their planned businesses. The difficulty with this alternative is that it leads us to expect consistently more external attributions from men regardless of whether or not they had actually made sales, but there was no gender main effect on external stable attributions.

Alternative Conceptions of Getting Into Business

Throughout the article we have defined "getting into business" as having made a sale and collected money from a customer. There are, however, other ways in which an entrepreneur's seriousness toward getting into business might be measured, such as hours devoted to the business or hiring employees. We examined both of these alternative ways of assessing an entrepreneur's seriousness about the business. Specifically, we first split the sample into those respondents devoting 30 or more hours per week to the business and those devoting 29 or fewer hours per week. A 2 × 2 (Gender × hours) analysis of variance on personal stable attributions showed the same interaction obtained with sales as the cross-cutting variable, $F(1,80) = 3.71, p < .06$. A similar Gender × Hours analysis of variance on external stable attributions produced a strong trend comparable to the interaction obtained with sales as the cross-cutting variable, $F(1,80) = 2.91, p < .10$. Next, we split the data according to the presence of at least one full-time employee (who might be the founder) or at least one part-time employee who is not the founder. A 2 × 2 (Gender × Employee) analysis of variance on personal stable attributions showed a nearly significant interaction comparable to that obtained with sales $F(1,81) = 3.65, p < .06$. A similar Gender × Employee analysis of variance on external stable attributions showed a nearly significant interaction comparable to that obtained with sales, $F(1,81) = 3.80, p < .06$. Thus, despite the fact that the particular individuals involved changed slightly from one grouping to another, the overall attributional results remain essentially the same: whatever the definition used for "getting into business," females who successfully start businesses have higher internal stable attributions, whereas males who successfully start businesses have higher external stable attributions.

DISCUSSION

The Value of an Attributional Approach for Research and Practice

The use of attributional measures to predict entrepreneurial persistence in business start-up activities and in business start-up success shows much promise as a viable approach to understanding the cognitive factors that influence potential entrepreneurs. The following discussion highlights the results and offers some suggestions for how the use of an attributional approach might be of benefit to research and practice.

The attributional measures used in this study – counts of the number of internal/stable and external/stable causes – proved significant for predicting both persistence in activities and persistence for success in business creation. We found that the internal attribution measure was significantly correlated to some entrepreneurial activities measured in this study – structuring the company. We also found that the attributional measure was useful for predicting success at getting into business. Females with internal and stable reasons for getting into business (e.g., "I've always wanted to own my own business," "I want the autonomy and independence to do what I like through self-employment") were more likely to start businesses that generated sales. Males with external and stable reasons for getting into business (e.g., "I had identified a market need") were more likely to start businesses that generated sales.

The finding that females with internal and stable reasons for getting into business are more likely to start a business that generates sales runs counter to a view of entrepreneurs as opportunists. In the attributional framework, opportunities are external causes for getting into business (i.e., opportunities are not internal characteristics of individuals.) We believe that a more detailed exploration of the perceptions of entrepreneurial success or failure using the attributional framework outlined in Table 1 will lead to a better understanding of the causes of entrepreneurial persistence. For example, because internal and stable attributions suggest a focus on internal needs and abilities, the result about internal/stable attributions and success at getting into business seems to indicate that females undertake entrepreneurial activity because they perceive they have the desire, skills, and abilities to be successful, and women stop entrepreneurial activity when they perceive they don't have the desire, skills, and abilities to be successful. If this is true, then, training programs might be of value for enhancing female potential entrepreneurs' perceptions of their desires for starting a business, as well as their abilities at successfully starting a business.

Individuals who enter business for internal/stable reasons such as "I wanted the autonomy and independence to do what I like through self-employment" may also have more knowledge of the value of entrepreneurship versus those that fail. It is likely that individuals who perceive a high payoff (e.g., financial, emotional, social) for getting into business may be more likely to persist at difficult tasks than those who perceive fewer rewards. The relationship between the types of efforts undertaken (for example, efforts to explore the value of the opportunity by spending time marketing and getting customer orders) and perceptions of the value and difficulty of the entrepreneurial opportunity might also be explored. Results presented in Table 6 suggest that undertaking marketing activities influences efforts to begin operations. It is likely that individuals who have undertaken more activities to understand the market might have more favorable perceptions of the value of the opportunities they face and more favorable perceptions of their abilities to complete successfully the tasks required.

Other aspects of the attribution framework might also be explored for clues to why some potential entrepreneurs start businesses and why others do not. For example, entrepreneurs must believe that their abilities and effort can meet the perceived demands of the tasks involved in starting a business. Research may find that individuals stop entrepreneurial activity because they perceive that the necessary tasks required to get into business are too difficult. Or research may explore whether there is an interactive effect between a potential entrepreneur's perceptions of skills, abilities, and task difficulty. For example, successful entrepreneurs may choose "easier" new ventures that *match* their skills and abilities to the perceived difficulty of getting into business. Or successful entrepreneurs who perceive they lack the skills or abilities to be successful at a difficult new venture may *shift* their attention to easier opportunities (less difficult tasks).

The findings about female and male potential entrepreneurs offers additional evidence that gender makes a difference (Belcourt, Bourke, and Lee-Gosselin 1991; Brush 1992; Fischer, Reuber, and Dyke 1993; Sexton and Bowman-Upton 1990). Our findings are consistent with those that have found that women decide to become entrepreneurs for such reasons as self-fulfillment (Thompson and Hood 1991) and as a way to actualize personal goals that focus on family (Birley 1989, Chaganti 1986; Orr 1992). Moreover, our results contribute to the view that gender is not merely a demographic descriptor of the characteristics of a sample of entrepreneurs, but an important differentiating factor. If female and male potential entrepreneurs with similar success in starting ventures have persisted for different reasons, then selection and training need to account for this difference.

For example, assuming that new venture success depends on both personal commitment and a viable market opportunity, entrepreneurship training might be used to enhance a potential entrepreneur's strengths with complementary skills and knowledge. Training for females who offer internal/stable reasons for getting into business might be oriented toward identifying viable market opportunities. On the other hand, training for males who offer external/stable reasons for getting into business might be oriented toward exploring their personal commitment toward entrepreneurship. We believe that training that recognizes the different reasons for why successful potential entrepreneurs are willing to persist in entrepreneurial activity is more likely to result in the creation of successful and sustainable new firms because such training builds on a potential entrepreneur's strengths by affirming a person's reasons to persist.

In summary, the attributional framework is based on a substantial body of theory and empirical research that can be adapted to the particular needs and issues of entrepreneurship researchers. Using the attributional framework offers a new way to think about the specific causes of entrepreneurial persistence, as the interaction between locus of causality (internal/external) and stability (stable/variable): ability, effort, task difficulty, and luck. Besides the benefits for improving research on entrepreneurs by grounding these explorations in a rich base of prior theory and empirical evidence, we believe the application of the attributional framework to entrepreneurial problems is likely to influence the selection, counseling, and training of potential entrepreneurs. For example, perceptions of the difficulty of getting into business can be changed through exposure to cases, stories and interactions with successful entrepreneurs (e.g., If that person can get into business, then I can get into business too!). And in many instances, appropriate exposure to the difficulties of entrepreneurship may help individuals to decide not to pursue this endeavor. Especially in light of the results for attributions, the low predictive validity of the Paulhus Spheres of Control personal efficacy subscale comes as a surprise. Obviously the low reliability of this scale in our sample reduces the measure's potential for predictive validity. In the future it might be better to develop locus-of-control items specific not only to personal efficacy, but also to the domain of entrepreneurial business.

Business Start-Up Activities

The results from this study show that both groups (those who were successful and those who were not successful at getting into business) devote the same amount of time to gathering information, estimating profits, completing know-how, and structuring the company. Yet those individuals who were successful at getting into business take the next step and devote effort to beginning operations (see Tables 5 and 6). This result suggests a number of lines of inquiry.

Because both successful and unsuccessful entrepreneurs devote nearly the same amount of time to exploring an opportunity – gathering marketing information, estimating potential profits, finishing the groundwork, and structuring the company – the critical difference between success and failure at getting into business, might be the nature of the opportunity itself. It is likely that not all opportunities that entrepreneurs encounter are similar. Some opportunities are likely to be "bad" opportunities (new ventures with a low probability of sufficient rewards for the efforts and investments necessary), whereas other opportunities are likely to be "good" opportunities. Successful entrepreneurs may be luckier than unsuccessful entrepreneurs (encounter better opportunities) or successful entrepreneurs may perceive opportunities differently than unsuccessful entrepreneurs.

As we suggested earlier, individuals who are successful at getting into business might have skills and abilities that better match the opportunities they face than unsuccessful entrepreneurs. Successful entrepreneurs may be wise to begin operations because they have the necessary capabilities. Unsuccessful entrepreneurs may be wise to abandon efforts to begin operations because they lack the necessary skills.

Future research might also focus on how potential entrepreneurs go about solving certain kinds of new venture tasks. For example, successful entrepreneurs may perceive the scale of certain tasks differently than unsuccessful entrepreneurs. Successful entrepreneurs may be more global in confronting the tasks of getting into business, or they may accomplish tasks better by breaking them into smaller pieces. Unsuccessful entrepreneurs may be overwhelmed by the number and difficulty of the tasks they face because they lack an ability to break down this complex experience into a series of small accomplishable achievements.

Some behaviors that entrepreneurs undertake are likely to be more beneficial for getting into business than others. Some behaviors, such as selling, are likely to improve a potential entrepreneur's knowledge of the value and difficulty for achieving a given opportunity. In addition, effort expended on some activities is likely to improve one's skills and abilities so that some tasks become easier to accomplish over time.

We believe that a critical aspect of business start-up behavior involves the interplay of action and its effect on knowledge. Individuals successful at getting into business appear to be eager learners who use new knowledge to adapt to new and changing circumstances. A study of entrepreneurial activities necessitates a methodology that identifies behaviors over time and the events that both influence and are influenced by these activities (Van de Ven 1992a, 1992b).

CONCLUSIONS

We believe that one of the important features of this research is the use of a longitudinal research design. By measuring attributions *before* these potential entrepreneurs had started (or not started) their businesses, we can make stronger claims for a causal relationship between these initial attributions and each individual's subsequent success in starting a venture. Given all of the events and activities that occur between an individual's attributions for getting into business and the actual start-up, the finding that female potential entrepreneurs who offered internal and stable attributions ("I want to be my own boss") for getting into business, and male potential entrepreneurs who offered external and stable attributions ("I had identified a market need"), actually succeeded at getting into business, is a significant result. Attributions matter. If research in entrepreneurship is going to focus on the individual, and if researchers believe that the attitudes, motivations, intentions, and cognitions of entrepreneurs are an important factor in determining entrepreneurial success, then prospective research designs must become the norm, rather than the exception.

REFERENCES

Ahmed, S.U. 1985. nAch, risk-taking propensity, locus of control, and entrepreneurship. *Personality and Individual Differences* 6:781–782.

Begley, T.M., and Boyd, D.P. 1987. Psychological characteristics associated with performance in entrepreneurial firms and smaller businesses. *Journal of Business Venturing* 2(1):79–93.

Belcourt, M., Burke, R., and Lee-Gosselin, H. 1991. *The Glass Box: Women Business Owners in Canada*. Ottawa: The Canadian Advisory Council on the Status of Women.

Bird, B.J. 1993. Demographic approaches to entrepreneurship: the role of experience and background. *Advances in Entrepreneurship, Firm Emergence, and Growth*. 1:11–48.

Birley, S. 1989. Female entrepreneurs: are they really different? *Journal of Small Business Management* 27(1):32–37.

Brockhaus, R.H. 1980. Risk-taking propensity of entrepreneurs. *Academy of Management Journal* 23:509–520.

Brockhaus, R.H., and Horwitz, P.S. 1986. The psychology of the entrepreneur. In D.L. Sexton and R.W. Smilor, eds., *The Art and Science of Entrepreneurship*. Cambridge, MA: Ballinger, pp. 25–48.

Brush, C.G. 1990. Women and enterprise creation: barriers and opportunities. In S. Gould and J. Parzen, eds., *Enterprising Women: Local Initiatives for Job Creation*. Paris: OECD.

Brush, C.G. 1992. Research on women business owners: past trends, a new perspective and future directions. *Entrepreneurship: Theory and Practice* 16(4):5–30.

Bygrave, W.D. 1989. The entrepreneurship paradigm (II): chaos and catastrophes among quantum jumps. *Entrepreneurship: Theory and Practice* 14(2):7–30.

Chaganti, R. 1986. Management in women-owned enterprises. *Journal of Small Business Management* 24(4):18–29.

Collins, B.E. 1974. Four components of the Rotter Internal-External scale: belief in a difficult world, a just world, a predictable world, and a politically responsive world. *Journal of Personality and Social Psychology* 29:381–391.

Cooper, A.C. 1993. Challenges in predicting new firm performance. *Journal of Business Venturing* 8(3):241–254.

Cooper, A.C., and Gascon, F.J.G. 1992. Entrepreneurs, processes of founding, and new firm performance. In D.L. Sexton and J.D. Kasarda, eds., *The State of the Art of Entrepreneurship*. Boston: PWS–Kent, pp. 301–340.

Cromie, S., and Johns, S. 1983. Irish entrepreneurs: some personal characteristics. *Journal of Occupational Behavior* 4:317–324.

Duchesneau, D.A., and Gartner, W.B. 1990. A profile of new venture success and failure in an emerging industry. *Journal of Business Venturing* 5(5):297–312.

Fischer, E.M., Reuber, A.R., and Dyke, L.S. 1993. A theoretical overview and extension of research on sex, gender, and entrepreneurship. *Journal of Business Venturing* 8(2):151–168.

Gartner, W.B. 1988. "Who is an entrepreneur?" is the wrong question. *American Journal of Small Business* 12(4):11–32.

388 E.J. GATEWOOD ET AL.

Gartner, W.B. 1993. Words lead to deeds: toward an organizational emergence vocabulary. *Journal of Business Venturing* 8(3):231–240.

Gartner, W.B., Bird, B.J., and Starr, J.A. 1992. Acting as if: differentiating entrepreneurial from organizational behavior. *Entrepreneurship: Theory and Practice.* 16(3):13–31.

Gartner, W.B., and Starr, J.A. 1993. The nature of entrepreneurial work. In S. Birley and I.C. MacMillan, eds., *Entrepreneurship Research: Global Perspectives.* Amsterdam: North-Holland, pp. 35–67.

Hansen, E.L. 1990. Entrepreneurial networks: their effect on new organization outcomes. Unpublished Doctoral Dissertation. Knoxville, TN: University of Tennessee.

Hansen, E.L., and Wortman, M.S. 1989. Entrepreneurial networks: the organization in vitro. In F. Hoy, ed., *Best Papers Proceedings.* Washington, DC: Academy of Management, pp. 69–73.

Harvey, J.H., Yarkin, K.L., Lightner, J.M., and Town, J.P. 1980. Unsolicited interpretation and recall of interpersonal events. *Journal of Personality and Social Psychology* 35:55–568.

Heider, F. 1958. *The Psychology of Interpersonal Relations.* New York: Wiley.

Hisrich, R.D., and Brush, C.G. 1983. The woman entrepreneur: implications of family, educational, and occupational experience. *Frontiers of Entrepreneurship Research.* Wellesley, MA: Babson College, pp. 255–270.

Hisrich, R.D., and Brush, C.G. 1985. Women and minority entrepreneurs: a comparative analysis. *Frontiers of Entrepreneurship Research.* Wellesley, MA: Babson College, pp. 566–572.

Johnson, B.R. 1990. Toward a multidimensional model of entrepreneurship: the case of achievement motivation and the entrepreneur. *Entrepreneurship: Theory and Practice* 14(3):39–54.

Katz, J.A., and Gartner, W.B. 1988. Properties of emerging organizations. *Academy of Management Review* 13(3):429–441.

Levinson, H. 1981. Differentiating among internality, powerful others, and chance. In H.M. Lefcourt, ed., *Research With the Locus of Control Construct: Assessment Methods.* Vol. 1. New York: Academic Press, pp. 15–63.

Longsworth, E.K. 1991. *The Anatomy of a Start-Up.* Boston: Inc. Publishing.

McMullan, W.E., and Long, W.A. 1990. *Developing New Ventures.* San Diego, CA: Harcourt Brace Jovanovich.

Orr, E. 1992. Assessment of Title II Demonstration Projects for Women Business Owners. Washington, DC: Small Business Administration. Contract SBA 4137-WIB89.

Paulhus, D. 1983. Sphere-specific measures of perceived control. *Journal of Personality and Social Psychology* 44:1253–1265.

Reynolds, P., and Miller, B. 1992. New firm gestation: conception, birth, and implications for research. *Journal of Business Venturing* 7:405–418.

Rotter, J.B. 1966. Generalized expectancies for internal versus external control of reinforcement. *Psychological Monographs* 80(Whole No. 609).

Sexton, D.L., and Bowman-Upton, N. 1990 Female and male entrepreneurs: psychological characteristics and their role in gender-related discrimination. *Journal of Business Venturing* 5:29–36.

Shaver, K.G., and Scott, L.R. 1991. Person, process, choice: the psychology of new venture creation. *Entrepreneurship: Theory and Practice* 16(2):23–45.

Stipek, D., Weiner, B., and Li, K. 1989. Testing some attribution-emotion relations in the People's Republic of China. *Journal of Personality and Social Psychology* 56:109–116.

Strickland, B.R. 1989. Internal-external control expectancies: from contingency to creativity. *American Psychologist* 44:1–12.

Timmons, J. 1990. *New Venture Creation.* 3rd ed. Homewood, IL: R.D. Irwin.

Thompson, J.K., and Hood, J.N. 1991. A comparison of social performance in female-owned and male-owned small businesses. Presented at the Annual Academy of Management Meetings, Entrepreneurship Division, Miami, Florida, August.

Van de Ven, A.H. 1992a. Suggestions for studying strategy process: a research note. *Strategic Management Journal* 13:169–188.

Van de Ven, A.H. 1992b. Longitudinal methods for studying the process of entrepreneurship. In D.L. Sexton and J.D. Kasarda, eds., *The State of the Art of Entrepreneurship.* Boston: PWS-Kent Publishers, pp. 214–242.

Van de Ven, A.H., Hudson, R., and Schroeder, D.M. 1984. Designing new business start-ups: entrepreneurial, organizational, and ecological considerations. *Journal of Management* 10:87–107.

Van de Ven, A.H., Venkataraman, S., Polley, D., and Garud, R. 1989. Processes of new business creation in different organizational settings. A.H. Van de Ven, H.L. Angle, and M.S. Poole, eds., *Research on the Management of Innovation.* New York: Harper and Row, pp. 221–297.

Venkatapathy, R. 1984. Locus of control among entrepreneurs: a review. *Psychological Studies* 29: 97–100.

Venkataraman, S., Van de Ven, A.H., Buckeye, J., and Hudson, R. 1990. Starting up in a turbulent environment: a process model of failure among firms with high customer dependence. *Journal of Business Venturing* 5:277–296.

Vesper, K.H. 1990. *New Venture Strategies.* 2nd ed. Englewood Cliffs, NJ: Prentice Hall.

Weiner, B. 1985. An attributional theory of achievement motivation and emotion. *Psychological Review* 92:548–573.

Weiner, B., Russell, D. and Lerman, D. 1978. Affective consequences of causal ascriptions. In J.H. Harvey, W. Ickes, and R.F. Kidd, eds., *New Directions in Attribution Research.* Vol. 2. Hillsdale, NJ: Lawrence Erlbaum Associates, pp. 59–90).

APPENDIX 1   Client Follow-up Questionnaire

This questionnaire is a follow-up to your visit(s) to the Small Business Development Center (SBDC). As part of your visit approximately a year ago, we asked you to indicate the reasons you were considering going into business for yourself. At that time, we noted that your answers could help us improve out services to clients, but to do that we need to find out what kinds of activities you have been involved in since visiting the SBDC. Would you please take a few moments to tell us about your activities and the progress of your business?

1.   Listed below are activities that might be involved in trying to start a business. Would you please place a check mark in the space before *any* activities you undertook during the past year? then for each checked activity, please *estimate* the total number of hours you spent on that activity.

a.   Gathering Marketing Information: Hours

_____   on the industry   _____
_____   on who would be my customers   _____
_____   on firms that could be my suppliers   _____
_____   on the *existing* competitors to my product or service   _____
_____   on possible entrants (my *potential* competitors)   _____
_____   on products or services that could serve as a substitute for mine   _____

b.   Estimating My Potential Profits:

_____   gathering information on the cost of raw materials, wages, and salaries   _____
_____   gathering information on costs for rents, leases, equipment   _____
_____   making sales/revenue projections   _____
_____   establishing a price for my product or service   _____

c.   Finishing the Groundwork for My Product or Service
_____   getting the know-how or technical expertise to make the product or deliver the service   _____
_____   refining the business idea, enhancing or improving the business idea   _____
_____   getting into the business network (joining trade organizations, bulletin boards, or clubs)   _____

(continued)

390 E.J. GATEWOOD ET AL.

APPENDIX 1 *Continued*

d.   Developing the Structure of My Company:
_____   developing financial statements (income and cash flow statements, break-even analysis)   _____
_____   seeking financing   _____
_____   gathering information on legal requirements (permits, licenses, legal corporate entity)   _____
_____   arranging for legal assistance or accounting assistance   _____
_____   developing goals and objectives (business plan, organization structure, strategic plan)   _____
_____   choosing a business name, legally incorporating, getting state and federal tax numbers   _____
_____   developing a logo and letterhead, printing stationery and business cards   _____

e.   Setting up Business Operations:
_____   securing a location   _____
_____   purchasing raw materials and supplies   _____
_____   purchasing or leasing equipment or furniture   _____
_____   hiring and training employees, developing personnel policies   _____
_____   producing the product or service package   _____
_____   distributing the product or service   _____
_____   marketing the product or service   _____
_____   supporting customers with installation and adjustment of the product   _____
_____   supporting customers with training on the product or service   _____

2.   Approximately how many hours per week are you now devoting to the business described   _____
     on the other side?

3.   If you have completed your first sale (delivered the product or service and collected the   _____
     payment from your customer), please tell us the DELIVERY DATE:

4.   Including yourself, how many full-time employees does your business now have?   _____

5.   Including yourself, how many part-time employees does your business now have?   _____

6.   If the business you have been describing here is NOT the same business you discussed
     with us in your visit to the SBDC, please tell us what the business is:

APPENDIX 2 Overall Analysis Plan

Wherever there were analysis choices to be made, we chose the route that would retain the maximum number of subjects. Two such choices were necessary. First, there was the question of missing data. Four subjects checked business activities in which they had participated, but provided no hour estimates for those activities. In each of these instances, the overall mean score for the particular activity checked was inserted, so that the case could be retained.

The second analysis choice that could have reduced the sample arose because of the assumptions underlying the statistical tests to be used. Specifically, the correlation procedures and multiple analyses of variance (MANOVAS) assume that the underlying distributions of scores are essentially normal in form. But whenever individuals are asked to indicate how many hours they might have spent on each of 29 separate activities during the preceding year, the result is likely to be a distribution with a substantial positive skew. There is a logical lower limit (zero hours), but the upper limit might be in excess of 2000 hours (eight hours per day for 240 working days devoted to only one activity), and indeed, we received several activity time estimates that exceeded 1000 hours. Either the data from such outliers can be excluded, or the data can be transformed to reduce the variance and minimize the positive skew of the distributions. Eliminating any scores that exceeded $+3.5$ standard deviations from the overall mean would have reduced the number of cases by 9, and more importantly would have cost us valuable information from individuals who were particularly active in their attempts to establish a business. For this reason, we elected to retain all cases, using a square root transformation (appropriate when the means and variances are proportional) to reduce the skewness of the distributions. Analyses were performed on both the transformed and the nontransformed scores, and in all cases the two methods produced equivalent statistical conclusions. Consequently, to keep as close to the original data as possible, we report below only the nontransformed scores.

As noted earlier, the 29 business organizing activities were grouped into five major categories. To simplify presentation of the results, an average score was computed for each category. This score was computed by adding up the hours a respondent spent on any activity in the category and then dividing by the number of separate activities in the category, whether or not a particular respondent had performed all activities. In this way, the average hours spent on completing the groundwork, for example, can be directly compared to the average hours spent structuring the company, despite the fact that the former category contains only three elements whereas the latter category contains seven elements. Dividing by the number of elements assumes, of course, that all elements within a category are at the same level of specificity, and this assumption may not be justified. To examine this possibility, we conducted parallel analyses of the *sums* of activity in each of the five categories. This analysis produced the same results as those reported below for the category means. Finally, we conducted multiple analyses of variance on the elements within each category, and report the mean scores for elements on which there were substantial differences across subject groups.

Our first hypothesis, that internal stable attributions will be positively related to venture creation, is clearly directional. But our other expectations for the outcome of the study could not be stated as directional predictions. Consequently, to minimize confusion we have elected to use two-tailed statistical tests throughout.

[12]

EXPLORING START-UP EVENT

SEQUENCES

NANCY M. CARTER
Marquette University

WILLIAM B. GARTNER
San Francisco State University

PAUL D. REYNOLDS
Babson College

EXECUTIVE SUMMARY

This research analyzed new venture start-up activities undertaken by 71 nascent entrepreneurs. Nascent entrepreneurs are individuals who were identified as taking steps to found a new business but who had not yet succeeded in making the transition to new business ownership. Longitudinal data for the study comes from a secondary data analysis of two representative samples, one of 683 adult residents in Wisconsin (Reynolds and White 1993) and the other of 1016 adult residents of the United States (Curtin 1982). These surveys were conducted between 1992 and 1993, and the nascent entrepreneurs were reinterviewed six to 18 months after their initial interview.

Three broad questions were addressed: (1) What activities do nascent entrepreneurs initiate in attempting to establish a new business? (2) How many activities do nascent entrepreneurs initiate during the gestation of the start-up? and (3) When are particular activities initiated or completed?

Between the first and second interview, 48% of the nascent entrepreneurs reported they had set up a business in operation. Over 20% had given up and were no longer actively trying to establish a business. Almost a third of the respondents reported they were still trying to establish a firm.

As a way to summarize the results and as a springboard toward some insights into the implications of this research for practice and future research, we developed the following activity profiles of the three types of nascent entrepreneurs studied. These profiles are offered as a combination of both fact and some intuition about the findings.

STARTED A BUSINESS. Nascent entrepreneurs who were able to start a business were more aggressive in making their businesses real. They undertook activities that made their businesses tangible to others: they looked for facilities and equipment, sought and got financial support, formed a legal entity, organized a team, bought facilities and equipment, and devoted full time to the business. Individuals who started businesses seemed to act with a greater level of intensity. They undertook more activities than those individuals who did not start a business. The pattern of activities seem to indicate that individuals who started firms put themselves into the day-to-day process of running an ongoing business as quickly as they could and that these activities resulted in starting firms that generated sales (94%

Address correspondence to Nancy M. Carter, School of Business Administration, Marquette University, 606 North 13th St., Milwaukee, WI 53233.

Journal of Business Venturing 11, 151–166
© 1996 Elsevier Science Inc.
655 Avenue of the Americas, New York, NY 10010

0883-9026/96/$15.00
SSDI 0883-9026(95)00129-8

of the entrepreneurs) and positive cash flow (50% of the entrepreneurs). What is not known is how successful or profitable these new firms will be over time. For example, 50% of the firms that were started had not reached positive cash flow and these firms may have been started by individuals who were foolhardy and rushed into operation of a business that would not be sustainable.

GAVE UP. The pattern of activities for the group of entrepreneurs who gave up seem to indicate that these entrepreneurs discovered that their initial idea for their businesses would not lead to success. The finding that the activity of developing a model or prototype differentiated individuals who gave up from those who were still trying would suggest that those who gave up had "tested" their ideas out and found that they would not work according to their expectations. Nascent entrepreneurs who gave up seemed to be similar in their activity patterns compared with those who started their firms, that is, individuals who gave up pursued the activities of creating a business in an aggressive manner at the beginning of the process. But as the business unfolded over time, these entrepreneurs decreased their activities and then ceased start-up activities. This group of individuals might be seen as either having the wisdom to test their ideas out before jumping into something that might lead to failure or lacking the flexibility to find more creative ways to solve the problems that they were confronted with.

STILL TRYING. It would seem that those who are still trying are not putting enough effort into the start-up process in order to find out whether they should start the business or give up. Those still trying had undertaken fewer activities than individuals in the other two groups. The still trying entrepreneurs were devoting their short-term efforts toward activities internal to the start-up process (e.g., saving money and preparing a plan) and less effort toward activities that would make the business real to others. The still trying entrepreneurs may be all talk and little action. Or these still trying entrepreneurs might be involved in developing businesses that take longer for these particular opportunities to unfold. (It should be noted that there was no industry effect across the three groups.)

Our advice to individuals considering business start-up is that the results seem to provide evidence that nascent entrepreneurs should aggressively pursue opportunities in the short-term, because they will quickly learn that these opportunities will either reveal themselves as worthy of start-up or as poor choices that should be abandoned. Individuals who do not devote the time and effort to undertaking the activities necessary for starting a business may find themselves perennially still trying, rather than succeeding or failing.

What entrepreneurs do in their day-to-day activities matters. The kinds of activities that nascent entrepreneurs undertake, the number of activities, and the sequence of these activities have a significant influence on the ability of nascent entrepreneurs to successfully create new ventures. This study suggests that the behaviors of nascent entrepreneurs who have successfully started a new venture can be identified and differentiated from the behaviors of nascent entrepreneurs who failed. We believe that future studies will more precisely identify the kinds of behaviors appropriate for certain new venture conditions. If such contingency information can be generated, entrepreneurship research is likely to have significant benefits for entrepreneurship practice, education, and public policy.

INTRODUCTION

This study focused on nascent entrepreneurs and the process of organization creation. Other terms for this period of time are: organizational emergence (Gartner, Bird, and Starr 1992); the preorganization (Katz and Gartner 1988; Hansen 1990), the organization in vitro (Hansen and Wortman 1989), prelaunch (McMullan and Long 1990), gestation (Reynolds and Miller 1992; Whetten 1987), and start-up (Van de Ven, Angle, and Poole 1989; Vesper 1990). Organization creation involves those events before an organization becomes an organization, that is, organization creation involves those factors that lead to and influence the process of starting a business.

Reynolds (1994) estimates that nearly 4% of working age adults in the United States are, at any one time, actively involved in the process of starting a business. He found that nearly 10% of the nascent entrepreneurs in his study reported a new firm in place within 12 to 18 months of initial contact, whereas it took, on average, over two years before nascent entrepreneurs indicated they had given up on efforts to start a business. Coupled with Birch's (1987) findings that, on average, over one million businesses are founded in the United States each year, substantial efforts are undertaken and resources utilized (both successfully and unsuccessfully) to create new organizations.

This study explored the activities undertaken by nascent entrepreneurs during the organization creation process. Three broad questions were addressed: (1) What activities do nascent entrepreneurs initiate in attempting to establish a new business? (2) How many activities do nascent entrepreneurs initiate during the gestation of the start-up? and (3) When are particular activities initiated or completed?

LITERATURE REVIEW

A number of scholars have offered frameworks for exploring the characteristics of the organization creation process. Gartner (1985) outlined a framework of four dimensions that should be accounted for when studying new ventures: the individuals involved in the creation of the new venture, the activities undertaken by those individuals during the new venture creation process, the organizational structure and strategy of the new venture, and the environmental context of the new venture. Van de Ven et al. (1989) suggested that researchers explore the business creation process by looking at " (1) how a business idea (or strategy) emerges over time, (2) when and how different functional competencies are created to develop and market the first proprietary product, (3) when and how these functional competencies are redeployed to develop subsequent new products in a family of products believed to result in a sustainable business, and (4) how these business development efforts both influence and are constrained by organization and industry contexts" (pp. 224–225). Vesper (1990) argued that a new company is composed of five key ingredients: (1) technical know-how, (2) a product or service idea, (3) personal contacts, (4) physical resources, and (5) customer orders, and he offers some insights into various start-up sequences that occur among the five key ingredients. Katz and Gartner (1988) explored the organization theory and entrepreneurship literature to identify a theoretical and empirically based framework for identifying the properties that would indicate an organization in the process of creation. Their literature review found that most theories on organizations assume complex properties that occur only after organizations achieve some particular size (e.g., Mintzberg 1979; March and Simon 1958; Miles 1980), rather than some minimal set of characteristics that might differentiate an emerging organization from other types of social situations. Katz and Gartner (1988) suggested four emergent properties that would be indicators that an organization is in the process of coming into existence: *intention* to create an organization, assembling *resources* to create an organization, developing an organizational *boundary* (e.g., incorporation), and *exchanges* of resources across the boundary (e.g., sales).

Subsequent empirical explorations (Reynolds and Miller 1992; Reynolds and White 1993, Reynolds 1994) of the Katz and Gartner (1988) framework have found that no one pattern or sequence of events is common to all emerging organizations. Whereas the most common first event in the creation of an organization is a personal commitment by individuals involved in the new venture (five out of six new firms), some emerging organizations (two in five) reported the first event as having sales, whereas others began with hiring or financial support (one in four). The most common last events in the creation of an organization were likely to be hiring first employees and first sales income (one-half of new ventures), financial support (two in five), and a major personal commitment to the venture (one in four new ventures). In general, the average time a firm was in the process of emergence was one year, though 20% completed gestation within one month, and 90% completed gestation within three years. In contrast, Van de Ven et al. (1989) in a study of high-technology ventures found that entrepreneurs engaged in a set of activities for nearly four years before business initiation.

We sought to reexamine the literature on entrepreneurial behaviors and develop linkages between certain cogent entrepreneurial behaviors and their efficacy for organization creation. The theoretical and empirical literature on entrepreneurial behaviors is very diverse, and few efforts have been undertaken to identify and validate a set of comprehensive and parsimonious behaviors necessary to create new businesses (Gatewood, Shaver, and Gartner 1995; Gartner and Starr 1993). As discussed in the methodology section, we had available for analysis 14 activity measures taken from two previous studies of nascent entrepreneurs (see Table 1). The theoretical basis for our exploration is grounded in Weick's theory of organizing (Weick 1979). In Weick's view, an organization is an ongoing process of interactions among individuals. We see the process of organization formation as analogous to Weick's process of "enactment"—the generation of specific patterns of interlocked behaviors among individuals. In general, one would expect that some behaviors would be more effective in enacting an organization compared to others. For example, Aldrich and Fiol (1994) suggest that entrepreneurs seek to gain cognitive legitimacy for their organizations by developing trust among those involved in the start-up. In broad terms, a view of organization formation as "enactment" would assume that entrepreneurs who were involved in behaviors that demonstrated to others that the emerging business was "real" would be more likely to create an organization (Gartner, Bird, and Starr 1992, p. 17). For example, a behavior such as buying facilities and equipment might be a more significant indicator to others that a nascent business is real than undertaking a behavior such as planning. Buying facilities may show others that the entrepreneur has made a significant commitment to creating a new business compared to what might be a less public demonstration of commitment like planning. A fully developed logic for linking theoretical ideas about organizing with specific hypotheses and measures awaits development.

Our primary objective was to explore the three questions listed earlier: What activities were undertaken? How many activities were undertaken? When were these activities undertaken? It was our assumption that nascent entrepreneurs who were able to get a business up and running undertook different behaviors (or sequences of behaviors) in starting their businesses than those nascent entrepreneurs who failed to start a business. What specific behaviors or sequences of behaviors would result in the successful creation of a business would be discovered through exploration of the survey responses.

METHODOLOGY

Source of Data

Longitudinal data for the study comes from a secondary data analysis of two representative samples, one of 683 adult residents in Wisconsin (Reynolds and White 1993) and the other of 1016 adult residents of the United States (Curtin 1982). Data had been collected in these two studies through a procedure that starts with a random selection of households, followed by a random selection of an adult member of the household. During the course of a phone interview these randomly selected adults were asked: "Are you, alone or with others, now trying to start a business?" If they answered yes, they were asked if they had "given serious thought to the new business" and whether a number of different activities associated with starting a new firm had been initiated or completed. They were also asked the month and year all reported actions were initiated. Those that reported two or more firm gestation behaviors were considered nascent entrepreneurs. Follow-up interviews were completed on both samples. When the follow-up sample was restricted to autonomous start-ups and franchises, data were available for 71 nascent entrepreneurs. Subsidiaries, branches, or purchases of another business were excluded from the study.

Measures

Precursor Activities

During the phone interviews the nascent entrepreneurs were asked about a series of activities associated with the gestation process. For each activity respondents indicated whether the activity was: (1) not yet initiated; (2) initiated; (3) complete; or (4) not relevant. If the behavior had been initiated or completed they were asked to indicate the month and year of initiation and/or completion. The entrepreneurs also were asked if the new business was included in any of the standard lists of businesses: Dun and Bradstreet files, unemployment insurance files, social security files, or the federal tax return listing. At the time of the second interview the respondents were again asked to indicate the status of the start-up activities and whether they were included on the various standard lists of businesses. We classified 14 of the activities as precursor behaviors that entrepreneurs commonly undertake to establish a new business (e.g., develop a business plan, look for facilities or equipment or location, ask for funding). The activities and their intercorrelations are displayed in Table 1.

Using the dates associated with when the activities were initiated, a time frame of firm development was constructed. An activity was considered initiated if the entrepreneur reported in either of the two interviews that they had initiated or completed the activity. Each activity was categorized according to the length of time separating its initiation or completion from that of the earliest reported activity. The time scale was separated into categories beginning with the first month of activity and progressing by quarter through the fourth year. Thus, for example, a value of 1 corresponded to activities that were initiated during the first month of the firm's development, a value of 2 to activities within the first quarter, and 3 to activities undertaken during the 2 quarter, etc. A value of 17 accordingly, represented activities initiated in the fourth quarter of the fourth year and 18 represented activities corresponding to the 5th year of activity. All activities commencing in the fifth year were grouped together. This measure was used to examine the sequencing of the start-up activities.

We created three measures from the time scale. First, each activity was dummy coded to designate whether the respondent reported initiating or completing the behavior (1 = yes; 0 = no). This information was used to examine what activities entrepreneurs engaged in during their firms' development. Second, a count was made of the total number of activities initiated (range possible; 0 = 14). This measure was used to assess the rate of activity initiation. Third, each category of the time scale was assigned a value designating the time period in which the action was initiated. Values ranged from 1 (corresponding to activities initiated within a month of the first behavior) to 18 (corresponding to the 5th year of activity). Thus, for example, a value of 3 signified activities that were initiated during the second quarter of the first year of the firm's development, whereas a value of 16 represented activities initiated in the third quarter of the fourth year. This measure was used to examine the sequencing of start-up activities.

TABLE 1 Pearson Product Correlation Coefficients for Activities Initiated or Completed within Five Years of Initiating First Start-Up Behavior

	1	2	3	4	5	6	7	8	9	10	11	12	13
1. Organized team													
2. Prepared plan	0.16												
3. Bought facilities/equip	-.13	-.08											
4. Rented facilities/equip	-.06	-.11	-.05										
5. Looked for facilities	.08	.10	.29^a	.08									
6. Invested own money	-.02	.12	.57^b	-.02	.38^b								
7. Ask for funding	-.06	.08	.27^a	.02	.28^a	.30^a							
8. Got financial support	-.07	.05	.34^b	.07	.30^a	.26^a	.61^a						
9. Developed models	.22	.10	-.05	-.14	.23^a	-.02	-.05	-.01					
10. Devoted fulltime	.01	-.16	.17	.27^a	.18	-.11	.15	.22	.12				
11. Applied license/patent	.10	.18	.33^a	.02	.26^a	.33^b	.14	.19	.09	.21			
12. Formed legal entity	.39^b	.24^a	.13	-.09	.02	.13	.22	.21	.29^a	-.01	.22		
13. Hired employees	.12	.13	.29^a	.18	.22	.14	.12	.25^a	-.08	.39^b	.21	.16	
14. Saved money to invest	.23	.10	.07	-.20	.15	.03	.03	.03	.02	-.01	-.15	.09	.07

^{a} $p < .05$.
^{b} $p < .01$.

Start-up Indicators

During the second interview, the respondents were asked a self-perception measure of the current status of the development of their firm: (1) still working on putting the business in place; (2) given up, do not expect to start that business; (3) the business is now in operation, up and running. Responses to this question were used to group the entrepreneurs into one of three outcome categories that we refer to as "outcome status." Additionally, several other start-up indicators were assessed. Using the same scale as that used to assess the precursor behaviors, respondents were asked to indicate whether their business was included on four standard business listings (i.e., Dun and Bradstreet files, unemployment insurance files, social security files, or the federal tax return listing), whether they had received any money from the sales of goods or services, and if they had achieved a positive cash flow (monthly revenues exceeded the monthly expenses). If they responded "yes," they were asked to indicate the date when the start-up indicator first happened.

Analytical Techniques

Discriminant analysis and one-way analysis of variance were used to test whether there were significant differences among the three outcome categories. Additionally, descriptive statistics were displayed to illustrate sequencing of the start-up activities. The discriminant variables (precursor activities) were entered stepwise according to the Wilks' lambda criterion. Stepwise analysis was appropriate, because the relationship between the discriminant variables and the status outcomes was not known from previous research. The functions were rotated using varimax rotation to aid in the interpretation of the functions' meanings.

RESULTS

Table 2 shows the outcome status of the gestation efforts. Between the first and the second interview, 48% of the nascent entrepreneurs reported they had put a business into operation, up and running. Over 20% had given up and were no longer actively trying to establish the new venture. Almost a third of the respondents reported they were still trying to establish a firm.

Table 3 reports the results of a forward stepwise discriminant analysis used to examine whether the kinds of activities nascent entrepreneurs initiate varies by outcome status. The discriminant analysis revealed that the first discriminant function had an eigenvalue of 0.279 accounting for 62.7% of the variance, with a canonical correlation of 0.467. The second discriminant function had an eigenvalue of 0.166, accounting for 37.3 percent of the variance. Wilks' lambdas prior to extraction of each function were 0.67 and 0.86. Both lambdas were significant at .005 or less.

The first function, which explained the most variance, differentiated the entrepreneurs who were still actively trying to start businesses from the other two groups. These nascent entrepreneurs were least likely to get financial support or to buy facilities or equipment. In

TABLE 2   Outcome Status at Time of Second Interview

Fledgling new firm, started	34 (48%)
Still actively trying to establish firm	21 (30%)
Not actively trying – Gave up	16 (22%)
Total	71

158   N.M. CARTER ET AL.

TABLE 3   Results of Discriminant Analysis: Activities Initiated within Five Years of First Behavior

Variable	Function 1	Function 2
Canonical discriminant funcitons evaluated		
at group means (centroids)		
Started businesses	.658	−.497
Gave up, not actively trying	−.084	.739
Still actively trying	−.720	−.254
Rotated standardized discriminant		
function coefficients		
Bought facilities/equipment	.658	−.498
Got financial support	.604	.555
Developed models	−.000	.789
Correctly classified 63%		

contrast, nascent entrepreneurs who had started businesses were most likely to have bought facilities or equipment and to have obtained financial support. The second function separated entrepreneurs who gave up and were no longer actively trying to establish a new business from the other two groups. Those who gave up were more likely to get financial support and to have developed models or prototypes.

Table 4 provides further insight into the kinds of activities nascent entrepreneurs in the three outcome status groups initiated. A review of the precursor activities that did not statistically discriminate the groups indicates that a substantial percentage of all entrepreneurs in the study reported having saved and invested their own money in the start-up, having looked for equipment or facilities, and having organized a start-up team.

A review of the start-up indicators shows that over 90% of the entrepreneurs who had

TABLE 4   Percentage of Activities Initiated within Five Years of First Behavior

	Started (n = 34)	Gave Up (n = 16)	Still Trying (n = 21)	Total (n = 71)
Discriminating activities				
Bought facilities, equipment	85	50	43	65
Got financial support	47	44	5	34
Developed models/prototypes	15	44	14	21
Other precursor activities				
Organized start-up team	68	56	48	59
Devoted full time	47	38	14	35
Asked for funding	53	44	10	38
Invested own money	91	81	67	82
Looked for facilities/equipment	82	81	52	73
Applied license/patent	71	56	38	58
Saved money to invest	68	56	67	65
Prepared plan	53	56	43	51
Formed legal entity	49	45	36	28
Hired employees	32	6	10	20
Rented facilities, equipment	24	19	19	21
Start-Up indicators				
Sales	94	50	48	70
Positive cash flow	50	19	19	34
D&B credit listing	6	6	5	5
Unemployment insurance	24	0	0	11
FICA	47	0	0	22
Filed federal tax	71	6	19	41

TABLE 5 Summary of Analysis of Variance for Total Number of Activities Initiated

Source	df	MS	F	p
Outcome status	2	114.35	9.75	.0002
Error	68	398.89		

a business in operation at the time of the second interview had sales from goods or services, 71% had filed federal income tax returns, and 50% reported having a positive cash flow. These rates far exceed those of the other two groups.

We used a one-way analysis of variance to examine whether the total number of activities entrepreneurs initiate varies across the outcome status groups. The results reported in Table 5 indicate a statistical difference. Pairwise comparisons of the means revealed that the average total number of precursor activities initiated by entrepreneurs who have a business operating (mean = 8.00) are significantly greater than the number initiated by entrepreneurs who gave up (mean = 6.56), or those who are still trying (mean = 5.05).

Figure 1 plots the initiation of activities across the time scale. The trends indicate that entrepreneurs who started businesses initiated more activities at all time periods measured. Entrepreneurs who eventually gave up were similar in their rate of activity to those who got a business started through the first year. However, after the first year, the rate of initiation by those who eventually gave up began to taper off. Those who reported they were still trying to establish a business initiated significantly fewer activities across all time periods than either of the other two groups.

To further analyze the trends we recalculated the scores plotted in Figure 1 as a percentage of total activities initiated by their group. The results indicate that by the end of the first year, almost two-thirds of all activities that would be initiated by each of the groups already had been undertaken. We then sought to determine whether the kinds of activities initiated early in the developmental process varied by outcome status.

The analytic techniques that could be employed to address this issue were limited. The number of activities initiated early in the process resulted in the time scale variable being highly skewed to the left. We relied on median values to examine the sequencing of activities initiated during the first year. The results are displayed in Table 6.

The results from this analysis provide further insight into the apparent passive approach of entrepreneurs still in the gestation process. During the first six months of start-up, these entrepreneurs focused on saving money to invest in the business, preparing a business plan, and organizing a start-up team. In contrast, entrepreneurs who got a business operating looked for and bought facilities or equipment, invested their own money, prepared a business plan, asked for and got financial support, organized a start-up team, formed a legal entity, and devoted full time to the business. Table 7 displays additional information about the sequencing patterns. The data indicates that six months after initiating their first start-up activity, 50% of the entrepreneurs who reported staring a business had received money from sales. Entrepreneurs who had given up and were no longer actively trying to establish a business appear to be somewhat less aggressive than those who started operations. Those who gave up were distinct in their early efforts by developing models or prototypes. By the sixth month, only 25% of this latter group had money from sales.

It should also be noted that we conducted analyses to determine whether the results were affected by industry. There was no industry effect among the three groups of nascent entrepreneurs (i.e., started, gave up, trying to start). For example, developing a model or prototype is an activity that differentiates those nascent entrepreneurs who gave up from those

160   N.M. CARTER ET AL.

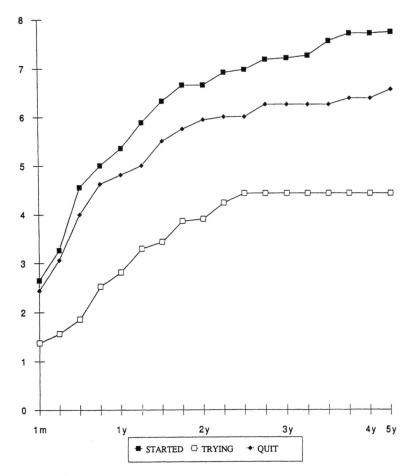

FIGURE 1   Number of activities initiated since first start-up behavior.

nascent entrepreneurs who continued to try and, therefore, it seemed plausible that those entrepreneurs who had developed a model and gave up would likely be in industries that are in manufacturing or other types of industries that might be more capital intensive than service industries. Yet, of the 14 nascent entrepreneurs who indicated they had initiated or completed models or prototypes, nearly seven of these individuals were in the gave up category in such industries as: one in nondurable manufacturing, one in restaurants/bars/clubs, two in consumer services, and three in business services.

DISCUSSION

As way to summarize the results and as a springboard toward some insights into the implications of this research for practice and future research, we developed the following activity profiles

TABLE 6 Sequencing of Startup Activities[a,b]

Year 1	Started (n = 34)	Gave up (n = 16)	Still Trying (n = 21)
1st month	Looked for F + E	Asked for funding Developed models Saved money to invest Organized start-up team	
1st quarter	Invested own money Asked for funding Got financial support Prepared plan	Invested own money Got financial support	Saved money to invest
2nd quarter	Formed legal entity Organized team Bought F + E Devoted full time	Prepared plan Bought F + E	Prepared plan Organized team
3rd quarter	Hired employees	Looked for F + E	Invested own money Looked for F + E Applied for L/P
4th quarter	Saved money Rented F + E Applied for L/P	Devoted full time Applied for L/P	Bought F + E

[a] Categorized by median value of those who had initiated the activity.
[b] Median values reported only if more than five entrepreneurs in the group had initiated activity.

of the three types of nascent entrepreneurs studied. These profiles are offered as a combination of both fact and some intuition about the findings.

Profiles of Types of Nascent Entrepreneurs

Started A Business

Nascent entrepreneurs who were able to start a business were more aggressive in making their businesses real, that is, they undertook activities that made their businesses tangible to others: they looked for facilities and equipment, sought and got financial support, formed a legal entity, organized a team, bought facilities and equipment, and devoted full time to the business. Individuals who started businesses seemed to act with a greater level of intensity. They undertook more activities than those individuals who did not start their businesses. The pattern of activities listed in Table 5 seem to indicate that individuals who started firms put themselves into the day-to-day process of running an ongoing business as quickly as they could and that these activities resulted in starting firms that generated sales (94% of the entrepreneurs) and positive cash flow (50% of the entrepreneurs). What is not known is how successful or profitable these new firms will be over time. For example, the 50% of the firms started that have not reached positive cash flow may be firms started by individuals who were foolhardy and rushed into operation of a business that could not be sustained.

Gave Up

The pattern of activities for the group of entrepreneurs who gave up seems to indicate that these entrepreneurs discovered that their initial idea for their businesses would not lead to

TABLE 7   Percentage of Entrepreneurs Initiating Activity within the First Year of Initial Start-Up Behavior

	Started				Gave Up				Still Trying			
	1mo	3mo	6mo	12mo	1mo	3mo	6mo	12mo	1mo	3mo	6mo	12mo
Discriminating activities												
Bought facilities, equip.	32	38	53	59	19	25	25	31	14	14	14	24
Developed models	0	0	6	6	25	31	38	38	0	0	0	10
Got financial support	21	24	27	32	19	25	38	38	0	0	0	0
Other precursor activities												
Organized start-up team	24	32	44	56	31	31	31	38	19	24	24	33
Devoted full time	15	18	29	29	0	6	19	19	10	10	10	10
Asked for funding	24	27	41	44	25	38	44	44	0	0	0	10
Invested own money	41	53	68	71	31	44	56	63	24	24	29	38
Looked for facilities	44	47	59	65	13	19	38	63	10	14	19	33
Applied license/patent	12	15	27	35	6	13	19	31	10	10	14	24
Saved money to invest	18	24	32	41	38	38	44	50	29	33	38	48
Prepared plan	18	27	32	38	25	25	38	44	19	19	24	33
Formed legal entity	6	9	21	27	6	6	6	13	0	5	10	14
Hired employees	3	6	9	21	0	0	0	0	0	0	0	0
Rented facilities, equip.	9	9	12	12	6	6	6	13	5	5	5	5
Start-up indicators												
Sales	29	35	50	65	13	19	25	31	10	14	14	19
Positive cashflow	15	15	21	32	6	6	13	13	5	10	10	10
D&B credit listing	0	0	3	6	6	6	6	6	5	5	5	5
Unemployment insur.	3	3	12	15	0	0	0	0	0	0	0	0
FICA	15	12	27	32	0	0	0	0	0	0	0	0
Filed federal tax	15	15	27	41	0	6	6	6	5	5	10	14

success. The finding that the activity of developing a model or prototype differentiated individuals who gave up from those who were still trying would suggest that those who gave up had tested their ideas out and found that they would not work according to their expectations. Nascent entrepreneurs who gave up seemed to be similar in their activity patterns compared with those who started their firms, that is, individuals who gave up pursued the activities of creating a business in an aggressive manner at the beginning of the process. But as the business unfolded over time, these entrepreneurs decreased their activities and then ceased start-up activities. This group of individuals might be seen as either having the wisdom to test their ideas out before jumping into something that might lead to failure or lacking the flexibility to find more creative ways to solve the problems that they were confronted with.

Still Trying

It would seem that those who are still trying are not putting enough effort into the start-up process in order to find out whether they should start the business, or give up. The still trying had undertaken fewer activities than individuals in the other two groups. The still trying entrepreneurs were devoting their short-term efforts toward activities internal to the start-up process (e.g., saving money and preparing a plan) and less effort toward activities that would make the business real to others. The still trying entrepreneurs may be all talk and little action. Or, these still trying entrepreneurs might be involved in developing businesses that take longer for these particular opportunities to unfold. (Yet, as noted earlier, there was no industry effect.)

Implications for Practice

In terms of advice to individuals considering starting a business, it would seem that the results provide evidence that nascent entrepreneurs should aggressively pursue opportunities in the short-term, because they will quickly learn that these opportunities will either reveal themselves as worthy of start-up or as poor choices that should be abandoned. Individuals who do not devote the time and effort to undertaking the activities necessary for starting a business may find themselves perennially still trying, rather than succeeding or failing. It would seem that a certain level of effort and activity is necessary to determine success or failure in starting a business.

Consultants, advisors, and investors involved in helping nascent entrepreneurs may find in these results evidence that entrepreneurs are action oriented rather than passive. Individuals who do not begin a business or reach a decision to abandon efforts to start a business within a year are likely to remain in a constant state of abeyance, thereby wasting the valuable time and resources of advisors that could be devoted to helping individuals who will actually undertake the activities to discover whether they can start a business.

These findings may lead to a better diagnostic to help nascent entrepreneurs and entrepreneurship advisors determine whether these nascent entrepreneurs should abandon their efforts at start-up sooner, change their activities, or continue their efforts. The analytical results may also be useful for the development of a set of indicator variables for use in identifying those nascent entrepreneurs who are likely to develop ventures that have the potential for substantial growth in sales and employment.

Implications and Directions for Research

Given that this study was based on an analysis of secondary data, the measures available for analysis were not as comprehensive or as specific as we would have liked. In future longitudinal studies of nascent entrepreneurs, the measures in these studies should capture additional information about various factors and behaviors that might influence the venture start-up process. For example, it would be valuable to explore the expectations of these nascent entrepreneurs regarding their perceptions of the future success of their ventures and their subsequent activities. It would also be valuable to explore whether nascent entrepreneurs expect to start their firms quickly (i.e., in less than six months) compared with other nascent entrepreneurs that may expect the start-up process to take longer. One reason that some firms may take longer to create may involve acquiring substantial financial resources or the procurement of government licenses or regulatory approval. Some nascent entrepreneurs may also expect to start firms that grow more rapidly compared with other nascent entrepreneurs.

A number of start-up behaviors (e.g., gathering marketing information on competitors and customers, acquiring know-how or expertise, seeking advice from mentors and advisors, and the activities involved with selling, marketing, and distribution) were not explored in this research and might have a significant influence on the outcome of the start-up process. It might also be appropriate to develop measures of the activities that reflect estimates of the number of hours the nascent entrepreneur devoted to a particular activity between the date of inception and its completion.

It would also be of value to collect additional information on the types of ventures that nascent entrepreneurs are planning to create. Characteristics of these emerging ventures that would be appropriate to study would include: strategy (e.g., pricing policy, perceived distinctive competence) and industry characteristics (e.g., growth rates, technological change, competition, power of suppliers and buyers, and barriers to entry). In addition, the firms that were started should be studied to find out if they were successful in the long run.

A larger effort at identifying and tracking nascent entrepreneurs is critical to generating a sample size sufficient for the statistical power necessary to identify the nuances inherent in the business start-up process. With a sample of size of 71 cases, a division of these cases into even a few groups quickly eliminates the use of many statistical and analytical tools. We believe there are many factors that are likely to have a significant moderating affect on the activities of nascent entrepreneurs (e.g., previous experience and background of the entrepreneur, the venture's strategy, the venture's industry) that will likely surface when a larger sample size is available for analysis.

Finally, we offer some speculations for future research based on the three profiles that were generated from the quantitative analyses of the data. The differences in the number of activities initiated among the three groups (started a business, gave up, and still trying) might suggest that "enacting" an organization, that is, taking venture creation actions that are visible to others (e.g., buying facilities and equipment, forming a legal entity) is more likely to result in an ongoing business. We believe that future empirical research on nascent entrepreneurs could lead to an operationalization of the actions involved in enactment. Empirical research on entrepreneurship could therefore inform Weick's theory on organizing. The finding that the "still trying" group undertakes fewer activities might suggest that a critical factor for differentiating individuals who get into business from those that do not involves action rather than planning, or "doing" rather than "thinking about it." It might be useful to explore how nascent entrepreneurs undertake planning and whether entrepreneurs who get into business use planning as a springboard for action, compared to those "still trying" who may use planning as a form of procrastination. The finding that those individuals who "gave up" undertook a similar number of activities in the first year compared with those who got into business should be explored through case studies and in-depth interviews. It would be very valuable to uncover how entrepreneurs make judgments about the potential success of a new venture, and whether those who "gave up" were more discerning in their ability to spot fatal flaws in a new business, or whether those who "gave up" were less creative in surmounting perceived potential problems. If, as Gartner, Bird, and Starr (1992) suggest, entrepreneurial action transforms equivocal events into nonequivocal interpretations and interactions, the impact of circumstance on the process and outcomes of business formation is important and deserves careful study. For example, MacMillan and Katz (1992) point out that entrepreneurial events are often idiosyncratic, obscure, and infrequent. In-depth longitudinal case studies are necessary to explore the effects of chance occurrences, such as how the sharing of a limousine ride to the airport with a stranger leads to the formation of a tea company (Ziegler, Rosenzweig, and Ziegler 1992) on the process of organization formation.

CONCLUSIONS

What entrepreneurs do in their day-to-day activities matters. The kinds of activities that nascent entrepreneurs undertake, the number of activities, and the sequence of these activities have a significant influence on the ability of nascent entrepreneurs to successfully create new ventures. This study suggests that the behaviors of nascent entrepreneurs who have successfully started a new venture can be identified and differentiated from the behaviors of nascent entrepreneurs who failed. We believe that future studies will more precisely identify the kinds of behaviors appropriate for certain new venture conditions. If such contingency information can be generated, entrepreneurship research is likely to have significant benefits for entrepreneurship practice, education, and public policy.

REFERENCES

Aldrich, H.E., and Auster, E.R. 1986. Even dwarfs started small: Liabilities of age and size and their strategic implications. *Research in Organizational Behavior* 8:165-198.

Aldrich, H.E., and Fiol, C.M. 1994. Fools rush in? The institutional context of industry creation. *Academy of Management Review* 19(4):645-670.

Birch, D.L. 1987. *Job creation in America.* New York: The Free Press.

Curtin, R. 1982. Indicators of consumer behavior: The University of Michigan Surveys of Consumers. *Public Opinion Quarterly* 46:340-362.

Gartner, W.B. 1985. A conceptual framework for describing the phenomenon of new venture creation. *Academy of Management Review* 10(4):696-706.

Gartner, W.B., Bird, B.J., and Starr, J.A. 1992. Acting as if: Differentiating entrepreneurial from organizational behavior. *Entrepreneurship: Theory and Practice* 16(3):13-31.

Gartner, W.B. and Starr, J.A. 1993. The nature of entrepreneurial work. In S. Birley and I.C. MacMillan, eds., *Entrepreneurship Research: Global Perspectives.* Amsterdam: North-Holland, pp. 35-67.

Gatewood, E.J., Shaver, K.G., and Gartner, W.B. 1995. A longitudinal study of cognitive factors influencing start-up behaviors and success at venture creation. *Journal of Business Venturing* 10(5):371-391.

Hansen, E.L. 1990. Entrepreneurial networks: Their effect on new organization outcomes. Unpublished doctoral dissertation. Knoxville, TN: University of Tennessee.

Hansen, E.L., and Wortman, M.S. 1989. Entrepreneurial networks: The organization in vitro. In F. Hoy, ed., *Best Papers Proceedings.* Washington, DC.: Academy of Management, pp. 69-73.

Katz, J., and Gartner, W.B. 1988. Properties of emerging organizations. *Academy of Management Review* 13(3):429-442.

March, J.G., and Simon, H.A. 1958. *Organizations.* New York: Wiley.

MacMillan, I.C., and Katz, J.A. 1992. Idiosyncratic milieus of entrepreneurial research: The need for comprehensive theories. *Journal of Business Venturing* 7:1-8.

McMullan, W.E., and Long, W.A. 1990. *Developing New Ventures.* San Diego, CA: Harcourt Brace Jovanovich.

Miles, R.H. 1980. *Organizational Behavior.* Glenview, IL: Scott Foresman.

Mintzberg, H. 1979. *The Structuring of Organizations.* Englewood Cliffs, NJ: Prentice-Hall.

Reynolds, P. 1992. Predicting new-firm births: Interactions of organizational and human populations. In D.L. Sexton and J.D. Kasarda, eds., *The State of the Art of Entrepreneurship.* Boston: PWS-Kent, pp. 268-297.

Reynolds, P. 1994. Reducing barriers to understanding new firm gestation: Prevalence and success of nascent entrepreneurs. Paper presented at the Academy of Management Meetings, Dallas, TX (August).

Reynolds, P., and Miller, B. 1992. New firm gestation: Conception, birth, and implications for research. *Journal of Business Venturing* 7:405-417.

Reynolds, P., and White, S. 1993. Wisconsin's entrepreneurial climate study. Milwaukee, WI: Marquette University Center for the Study of Entrepreneurship. Final Report to Wisconsin Housing and Economic Development Authority.

Stinchcombe, A.L. 1965. Social structure and organizations. In J.G. March, ed., *Handbook of Organizations.* Chicago, IL: Rand McNally, pp. 142-193.

166 N.M. CARTER ET AL.

Van de Ven, A.H., Angle, H.L., and Poole, M.S. 1989. *Research on the Management of Innovation.* New York: Harper and Row.

Vesper, K.H. 1990. *New Venture Strategies,* 2nd ed. Englewood Cliffs, NJ: Prentice Hall.

Whetten, D.A. 1987. Organizational growth and decline processes. *Annual Review of Sociology* 13: 335–358.

Ziegler, M., Rosenzweig, B., and Ziegler, P.1992. *The Republic of Tea.* New York: Doubleday.

ELSEVIER

RESEARCH NOTE

PREDICTING NEW VENTURE SURVIVAL: AN ANALYSIS OF "ANATOMY OF A START-UP." CASES FROM *INC.* MAGAZINE

WILLIAM B. GARTNER
University of Southern California

JENNIFER A. STARR
Suffolk University

SUBODH BHAT
San Francisco State University

EXECUTIVE SUMMARY

This article tests the insights and predictions of venture success as offered by reporters and experts in Inc. *magazine, to the predictions generated from an analysis of data from a venture screening questionnaire. The venture screening questionnaire, consisting of 85 items covering four broad categories: (1) Individual Characteristics; (2) Entrepreneurial Behaviors; (3) Strategy; and (4) Environment, was used to evaluate 27 "Anatomy of a Start-up" articles from* Inc. *magazine. The creation of the questionnaire was guided by the following premises:*

Individual Characteristics. *We hypothesized that the chances of venture survival would be improved if: (1) entrepreneurs had substantial knowledge and ability at the beginning of the start-up story; (2) entrepreneurs gained knowledge and ability during the start-up process; and (3) entrepreneurs continued to demonstrate substantial knowledge and ability at the end of the start-up story.*

Entrepreneurial Behaviors. *We hypothesized that entrepreneurs who expended more effort in any*

Address correspondence to Dr. W.B. Gartner, University of Southern California, The Entrepreneur Program, Bridge Hall One, Marshall School, Los Angeles, CA 90089-1421. E-mail: wgartner@marshall.usc.edu

The authors would like to thank Bruce Hunter, Hon-Kiong Chia, and Mark Claussen for analyzing the case studies, and the editor and reviewers for their suggestions for improving this manuscript.

Journal of Business Venturing **14**, 215–232
0883-9026/99/$–see front matter
PII S0883-9026(97)00063-3

216   W.B. GARTNER, J.A. STARR, AND S. BHAT

of the following activities would be in new ventures that survived compared to entrepreneurs who ex-
pended less effort: Finding and Refining the Opportunity—*comprised of 9 different activities, such as,*
defining the purpose of the business, planning, analyzing competitors; Acquiring Resources and Help—
comprised of 15 different activities, such as, finding investors, getting advice from lawyers, getting a loan,
acquiring technical expertise; Operating the Business—*comprised of 5 different activities, such as, deal-*
ing with distributors, managing the day to day operations of the business; Identifying and Selling to Customers—*comprised of 5 different activities, such as, identifying specific customers to sell to, selling to*
customers, managing sales channels; Outside of the Business Issues—*comprised of 4 different activities,*
such as, dealing with family problems, spouse, and friends.

Strategy and Environment. *The strategy and environment variables were characteristics requiring*
comparisons of the relative performance of new firms vis-à-vis other competitors and their industry char-
acteristics, much like the questions used in PIMS research: first to entry, degree of innovation, rate of
industry growth, size of market, relative price, and relative quality. There were 28 questions in this section
of the instrument. We hypothesized that niche oriented strategies and high growth environments might
be strategy and environmental characteristics common to startups that survived.

In total, there were 85 questions that comprised the venture screening questionnaire.

New Venture Survival. *The measure of new venture survival for this study was a determination*
of whether the new venture described in each Inc. *magazine article (Longsworth 1991) was still in opera-*
tion as of January 1995. This date is nearly 4 years after the last case study that we analyzed was published
(September 1990), and nearly 7 years after the first case study was published (February 1988). We were
able to determine that of the 27 new ventures profiled in the "Anatomy of a Startup" series published
in Longsworth (1991), 17 of these ventures were still in operation.

A discriminant analysis was performed that resulted in seven variables that correctly classified 85%
of the cases into new venture survivors or non-survivors. New ventures that survived were more likely
to have: (1) entrepreneurs who gained knowledge and ability during the founding process; who devoted
greater efforts to (2) dealing with suppliers; (3) analyzing potential new entrants and who (4) devoted
less time to determining the identity of the business; businesses that had (5) "fundable" resource require-
ments (6) focused on products or services that were designed or produced to order; and (7) were in high
growth industries. The classification accuracy of the model was much better than industry experts (55%
correct), competitors (55% correct), venture capitalists and financiers (40% correct), and customers
(38% correct).

Even though the discriminant analysis was better able to predict venture survival or non-survival
compared to the experts, there are significant limitations to the reliability and validity of this one particular
model, and the data set used. The primary value of this exercise involves making obvious the variables
that observers use to make judgments about predicting venture success. One of the frustrations we experi-
enced in analyzing the expert's predictions was our inability to glean consistent and general "rules of
thumb" about new venture success from their observations. We conclude by discussing the value of aca-
demic research on new venture success predictors vis-à-vis other avenues of inquiry and expertise: popular
journalism and practice.   © 1998 Elsevier Science Inc.

INTRODUCTION

Can the survival of a new venture be predicted?

One of the engaging aspects of the "Anatomy of a Start-up" articles that began
to appear in *Inc.* magazine beginning in February, 1988, was the commentary by venture
experts on whether the new venture described in the article would likely survive. The
"Anatomy of a Start-up" articles were written by journalists as profiles of ongoing new
venture start-ups. When these articles were written the journalists did not know whether
the new venture start-ups would succeed or fail. As George Gendron, Editor-in-Chief
of *Inc.* magazine, explained:

TABLE I Advice From *Inc.* Magazine

1. *If Cash Is King, Flexibility Is God.* "What has made or broken many of the companies we've watched, though, is this: the ability (or inability) to recognize and react to the completely unpredictable."
2. *Nobody Likes Your Product As Much As You Do.* "The most successful entrepreneurs worked hard to assess the need for their offerings; others acted on blind faith, and for them the start-up process has been particularly rocky."
3. *If You Don't Have Experience, Buy It.* "The strongest companies were led by people with experience in their industries."
4. *Your Competitors Aren't Dumb.* "Competitors are to be respected. ... When start-ups ignore that, they turn arrogance into red ink."
5. *It Isn't the Sales. It's the Sales Cycle.* "... what a lot of companies repeatedly miscalculated was the sales cycle—the length of time between the first sales pitch to the customer and that customer's actual purchase."
6. *Don't Underestimate How Much Time Simply Being the Boss Will Eat Up.* "Those who delegated well didn't get overwhelmed by minutiae. Others got buried."

> Each month we scout the start-up landscape for the most compelling business plans we can find: those that tell us something new about the world in which we do business or about the start-up process itself. One of *Inc.*'s writers takes the material and works it into publishable form—including a summary of the business plan narrative, a biography of the founder, detailed financial projections and all. Then (and here's the fun part), we locate the toughest, most seasoned, most skeptical experts—investors, industry analysts, even potential competitors—send them our write-up, and let them play venture capitalist. Will the new venture succeed? What are the hidden pitfalls that have been overlooked? How could the plan be changed to increase its chances of survival? (Longsworth 1991, p. iv)

What we found intriguing about these articles was the wide variation in the experts' opinions about the criteria for predicting new venture survival as well as *Inc.* magazine's insights (Brokaw 1991), about new venture survival/success predictors [e.g., "the most successful entrepreneurs worked hard to assess the need for their offerings," (p. 55); "the strongest companies were led by people with experience in their industries," (p. 57). See Table 1]. The insights offered by the venture experts and Brokaw (1991) prompted us to explore whether a systematic framework for assessing new ventures generated from the academic literature in entrepreneurship might result in a more comprehensive and accurate model for predicting the survival of the "Anatomy of a Start-up" ventures. In other words, could academically derived venture screening criteria be used to "beat the experts" at predicting new venture survival?

In addition, we were interested in exploring the use of publicly available data (i.e., magazine articles) as a source of information for analyzing new venture survival. The use of widely available articles from magazines as a source of data would solve some of the problems identified by Katz (1988, 1989) regarding the need to make data sets widely available to all researchers, and provide for inexpensive access to information on new ventures for research and teaching.

This article is divided into four sections. The first section offers a brief overview of some of the academic literature on new venture survival predictors and describes key aspects of the venture screening questionnaire. The second section describes how the venture screening questionnaire was used to analyze "Anatomy of a Start-up" articles from *Inc.* magazine. The third section presents results from an exploration of the data and a discussion of these findings. The final section of the paper concludes with

218   W.B. GARTNER, J.A. STARR, AND S. BHAT

some observations about the venture screening questionnaire's usefulness as a method for research on predicting new venture survival.

NEW VENTURE SCREENING CRITERIA

As Cooper and Gascon (1992) indicate, one of the central issues in the academic literature on entrepreneurship focuses on criteria for predicting successful new ventures. A significant amount of research has been conducted to address this issue (e.g., Bull and Willard 1993; Buzzell and Gale 1987; Covin and Slevin 1990; Duchesneau and Gartner 1990; Gartner 1985; Herron and Robinson 1993; Low and MacMillan 1988; MacMillan, Siegel, and Subba Narasimha 1985; Merrifield 1987; Miller and Camp 1985; Roure and Keeley 1990; Sandberg and Hofer 1987, Timmons 1994; Van de Ven, Hudson, and Schroeder 1984; Vesper 1990). The number of new venture success predictors that have been suggested by academic researchers is substantial (Cooper 1993). For example, Timmons (1994) lists over 100 different items, in a 40 page venture opportunity screening guide, that he suggests are useful for discerning new venture success.

Yet research on the efficacy of specific venture success criterion indicates a mixed set of results with few consistent findings (Cooper 1993; Gartner 1988; VanderWerf 1989). In addition, research on new venture success has tended to focus on evaluating the characteristics of a new venture opportunity at a particular point in time, rather than on evaluating the process that entrepreneurs undertake to change (or adapt to) situations to enhance new venture survival. As comprehensive overviews of the venture success/survival literature already exist (Cooper and Gascon 1992; Cooper 1993), the focus of this literature review will be on the logic we used for the selection of questions/ variables for the venture screening questionnaire and a brief history of the questionnaire's development. A copy of the venture screening questionnaire is available from the lead author.

The framework used to organize the various new venture survival variables is based on Gartner's (1985) framework for categorizing variables that describe new venture creation into four dimensions: individual characteristics, entrepreneurial behaviors, strategy, and environment. This framework is similar to other categorizations of the kinds of characteristics that influence new venture creation (e.g., Eisenhardt and Schoonhoven 1990; Sandberg and Hofer 1987; Stuart and Abetti 1987; Timmons 1994; Van de Ven et. al., 1984; Vesper 1990). While recognizing the importance of individual, firm, and environmental characteristics that influence new venture success, our study was oriented towards exploring the behaviors of the entrepreneurs: a critical part of the entrepreneurial process is the ability of entrepreneurs, over time, to change their behaviors to modify their circumstances into viable opportunities. A major focus of the venture screening questionnaire, was, therefore, to explore which behaviors may have aided entrepreneurs in their quest to get the odds of venture survival in their favor.

Individual Characteristics

The primary variables explored in this section of the questionnaire focused on the "experience" of the entrepreneurs involved in the development of the new venture. Experience, as defined in this study, is the knowledge or ability of an individual due to circumstances in a particular job, organization, or industry (Hill 199; McCall, Lombardo, and Morrison 1988). Based on previous research on the benefits and liabilities of entrepreneurial experience (Cooper and Gascon 1992; Starr and Bygrave 1992; Starr, Bygrave and Tercanli 1993; Stuart and Abetti 1990), questionnaire items were included to identify the level of knowledge and ability the entrepreneur (or team of entrepreneurs) had attained at both the beginning and the end of the start-up stories. By identifying levels of knowledge and ability at both the beginning and end of the stories, we hoped to surface information on whether new venture success might be influenced by the aptitude of these entrepreneurs to learn.

Although many studies had treated the knowledge and ability of entrepreneurs as something static and monolithic (e.g., prior industry, entrepreneurial, or managerial experience), we see the capacity of entrepreneurs to learn new knowledge and gain abilities during the start-up process as critical to new venture success. As entrepreneurs involve themselves in the changing circumstances of their new venture creation, they either learn from these circumstances or do not. It is possible that the knowledge and abilities gained before or during start-up could be a liability and a hindrance to success in some industries if the competitive dynamics change and these changes are not recognized (Starr and Bygrave 1992).

We believe that gains in knowledge and ability, even over a short period of time, should be recognizable in the case studies analyzed. In addition, we believe that an entrepreneur's knowledge and ability should not be considered in some broad manner, like years of previous industry experience, but as specific kinds of knowledge and ability that entail aspects of the functions of a business. Certain kinds of functional expertise may be more relevant to new venture success than other kinds.

Entrepreneurs were rated on seven kinds of knowledge/ability in the venture screening questionnaire: (1)*Marketing/Sales:* knowledge of customers and how to sell to them, (2) *Finance & Accounting:* knowledge of resources required to run the type of business the new venture is in, and the ability to monitor and control these resources, (3) *Operations:* how to make the products or provide the services, (4) *Technical Knowledge:* knowledge of industry standards and practices, (5)*Management:* ability to productively use employees, consultants, and other paid experts, (6) *Administration:* planning and MIS, and (7) *Street Smarts:* practical and "real world" knowledge of how an industry really works and how to survive as a new business in this industry.

The level of an entrepreneur's knowledge/ability was rated on a scale of 1 (no knowledge/ability: Novice/Newcomer); 2 (some knowledge/ability: Apprentice); 3 (average knowledge/ability: Journey person); 4 (above average knowledge/ability: Mentor); to 5 (Expert). Ratings of the levels of the entrepreneurs' knowledge/ability were taken for both the beginning and end of the start-up stories, and a composite measure of the change in the knowledge/ability ratings of the entrepreneur(s) was generated (Ending Knowledge/Ability Rating—Beginning Knowledge/AbilityRating = Knowledge/Ability Gained).

We hypothesized that: (1) entrepreneurs with more knowledge/ability (e.g., mentor or expert level) at the beginning of the start-up story would be in new ventures that survived than entrepreneurs with less; (2) entrepreneurs who gained knowledge/ability during the start-up would be in new ventures that survived; and (3) entrepreneurs with more knowledge/ability at the end of the start-up story would be in new ventures that survived than entrepreneurs who had less.

Entrepreneurial Behaviors

It is our view that entrepreneurial behaviors are the primary determinant of venture survival, that is, what entrepreneurs do during the venture creation process changes the odds toward venture survival (Carter, Gartner, and Reynolds 1996; Gartner 1988; Gartner, Bird, and Star 1992). Based on a previous review of the literature on entrepreneurial behavior (Gartner and Starr 1992), and subsequent empirical investigations on the nature of entrepreneurial behavior (Gartner & Starr 1993a, 1993b; Gatewood Shaver, and Gartner, 1995), we developed a list of five kinds of entrepreneurial activities: (1) Finding and Refining the Opportunity: comprised of 9 different activities, such as, defining the purpose of the business, planning, analyzing competitors; (2) Acquiring Resources and Help: comprised of 15 different activities, such as, finding investors, getting advice from lawyers, getting a loan, acquiring technical expertise; (3) Operating the Business: comprised of 5 different activities, such as, dealing with distributors, managing the day to day operations of the business; (4) Identifying and Selling to Customers: comprised of 5 different activities, such as, identifying specific customers to sell to, selling to customers, managing sales channels; (5) "Outside of the Business" Issues: comprised of 4 different activities, such as, dealing with family problems, spouse, and friends.

For each behavior, an evaluation of the level of effort the entrepreneurs expended on these activities was required. The level of effort was determined by rating the entrepreneur (or team) on the amount of time and intensity expended by the end of the start-up story. Ratings were determined by comparing the entrepreneur to the other 26 start-up stories that were read. Ratings were assigned scores of: 1 (this activity was not undertaken); 2 (little effort); 3 (an "average" amount of effort); 4 (more than average); or 5 (a great deal of effort: top 5%).

We hypothesized that entrepreneurs who expended more effort [e.g., were rated as expending 4 (more than average), or 5 (a great deal of effort)] in any of the activities would be in new ventures that survived compared with entrepreneurs who expended less effort.

Strategy and Environment

As suggested by Cooper (1993), much of the entrepreneurship literature, and particularly the literature on new venture strategy, has focused on identifying variables that predict new firm performance. For this study, as a basis for developing questions that could be used by observers to code the "Anatomy of a Start-up" articles, we chose variables based on the constructs explored and substantiated in the corporate venturing literature (e.g., Buzzell and Gale 1987; Dean, Meyer, and DeCastro, 1993; MacMillan and Day 1987; Miller and Camp 1985), for example: first to entry, degree of innovation, rate of industry growth, size of market, relative price, and relative quality. The corporate venturing approach typically uses PIMS variables that measure firm characteristics in relationship to other competitors and these firms' industry characteristics. This is not to suggest that the remainder of the new venture strategy literature was ignored, but to identify where the questions for the questionnaire used in this study were procured. There were 28 questions in this section of the instrument.

Given the diversity of strategies and environments described in the "Anatomy of a Start-up" articles, we hypothesized one broad strategic and one broad environmental characteristic that might differentiate between surviving and non-surviving ventures: (1) surviving ventures would likely choose niche strategies; and (2) surviving ventures would likely be in high growth industries.

In total, there were 85 questions that comprised the venture screening questionnaire.

New Venture Survival

The measure of new venture survival for this study was a determination of whether the new venture described in each *Inc.* magazine article (Longsworth 1991) was still in operation as of January 1995. This date is nearly 4 years after the last case study that we analyzed was published (September 1990) and nearly 7 years after the first case study was published (February 1988). Although a variety of measures exist for indicating new-venture success (Brush and VanderWerf 1992; Sapienza, Smith, and Gannon 1988), we posit that a venture's ability to survive at least 4 years is a key indicator. To determine whether a company had survived, the ventures described in the case articles were contacted to determine whether they were in operation. For companies that could not be readily located, we queried *Inc.* magazine reporters who may have kept up contact with these organizations or their founders. We were able to determine that of the 27 new ventures profiled in the "Anatomy of a Start-up" series published in Longsworth (1991), 17 of these ventures were still in operation.

USING THE VENTURE SCREENING QUESTIONNAIRE

As described earlier, the "Anatomy of a Start-up" articles were written by journalists as profiles of on going new venture start-ups. Each "Anatomy of a Start-up" article was 12 to 18 pages in length and provided a "summary of the business plan narrative, a biography of the founder, detailed financial projections, and all" (Longsworth 1991, p. iv). The 27 "Anatomy of a Start-up" articles describe a wide variety of new ventures in such industries as services (Landmark Legal Plans, Inc., Buddy Systems, Inc., Blackstone Bank and Trust Co.), restaurants and food service (The O! Deli Corp., Sieben's River North Brewery, Inc., Pizza Now!, Inc.), manufacturing (Microfridge, Inc., Appliance Control Technology, Inc., Animalens, Inc.), and media (Sports Band Network, Sanctuary Recording, Inc.). Although the "Anatomy of a Start-up" articles portray a diversity of types of new ventures, these cases are not intended to represent a generalizable sample that would reflect the population of all new ventures. Of the 27 cases used in this analysis, there were 17 new ventures that were still in operation as of January 1995. A listing of the survivors and non-surviving ventures is provided in Table 2.

Based on a previous evaluation process described in Miller and Friesen (1984), three MBA students were trained by the researchers to evaluate the *Inc.* magazine articles using the venture screening questionnaire. As a way to generate interrater reliability, the lead researcher met with the students to discuss similarities and differences among the ratings given by each of the three individuals on a scoring of three of the cases. The group discussed the process of evaluating each case and worked to develop a consensus regarding how ratings for each question in the questionnaire would be applied in various circumstances. The three MBA students then read the remaining 24 articles in *Anatomy of a Start-up: Why Some New Businesses Succeed and Others Fail* (Longsworth 1991) and completed a questionnaire for each article. The MBA students were told not to read the last chapter of the book, where the outcomes of the 27 cases were discussed. After rating the remaining 24 cases, the MBA students were required to meet together to reach an agreement on a team rating on all 85 variables for each of the cases. When there was a significant difference on the numerical rating on a specific variable among the three students, the students were asked to reach a consensus. Significant differences on the numerical ratings [a significant difference was defined in

222   W.B. GARTNER, J.A. STARR, AND S. BHAT

TABLE 2   *Anatomy of a Start-up:* Survivors and Failures

Survivors	Failures
Queen Anne Inn	Associated Video Hut Inc.
City Year, Inc.	Blackstone Bank and Trust Co.
The O! Deli Corp.	Sanctuary Recording, Inc.
Wall Street Games	Landmark Legal Plans, Inc.
MicroFridge, Inc.	Oualie, Ltd.
Appliance Control Technology, Inc.	The National
Rusmar, Inc.	Sieben's River North Brewery, Inc.
Gruenberg Video Group, Inc.	Crescent City Communications Co.
R. W. Frookies	Keener-Blodee, Inc.
Filmstar, Inc.	SportsBand Network
Carousel Systems, Inc.	
Pizza Now!, Inc.	
Plastic Lumber Co.	
American DreamCar, Inc.	
Animalens, Inc.	
Buddy Systems	
Neugoren, Inc.	

Miller and Friesen (1984) as instances when Likert scale scores differed by at least two (e.g., 3 to 5, 2 to 4), or when opposites were chosen on a bi-polar scale] occurred on less than 10% of the questions. The group meetings to generate the team ratings for the cases lasted from 1.5 to 2 hours for each case. These team ratings were then entered into a data matrix for subsequent analyses.

Method of Analysis

Given the number of variables used in the analyses (85) versus the number of cases (27) analyzed, a variable reduction strategy was employed. First we compared the mean ratings on each of the predictor variables between the survival and non-survival groups. We noted that the mean ratings for each variable were not significantly different (a = 0.05) between the survival and non-survival groups with the notable exception of the variable "Growth." Because we wished to identify a wider set of variables that could predict survival or non-survival, we decided to consider those variables that displayed the widest absolute different in means such that the correlations among them were not high. In addition, it was found that the measures for gaining knowledge/ability (computed as the difference between the knowledge/ability scores at the beginning and at the end of the start-up cases) for the seven kinds of knowledge/ability were highly correlated with each other. A factor analysis revealed that all of these variables loaded on the same factor. For these two reasons, a new composite knowledge/ability change variable was created (Change in Knowledge/Ability) that was constructed as the mean of the seven knowledge/ability change measure means. Fourteen variables with the widest difference in means between the survivor and non-survivor groups were identified (See Table 3). We then chose to use discriminant analysis, a technique that allows for the identification of variables that best discriminate between two or more groups.

RESULTS AND DISCUSSION

The discriminant analysis resulted in a discriminant function that was statistically significant (Wilks' Lambda = 0.228, $p < 0.001$), suggesting a meaningful difference on the

TABLE 3   Means and Standard Deviations for Top Fourteen Variables

Variables	Survivor		Non-Survivor	
	Mean	S.D.	Mean	S.D.
Growth	3.71	0.47	2.78	0.83
Funding Needs	3.00	0.00	3.22	0.67
Change in K/A	1.22	0.96	1.03	1.25
Identity	3.86	0.53	4.22	0.44
Suppliers	3.64	0.50	3.33	0.50
Entrants	3.21	0.70	3.00	0.00
Distribution	3.50	0.76	3.33	0.71
Selling	3.93	0.62	3.65	0.73
Standard	1.57	1.45	1.00	0.00
Innovative Process	2.86	1.23	3.44	0.88
Patents	3.00	2.08	1.89	1.76
Competition	2.07	0.73	2.22	0.44
Aggressive	2.71	0.73	3.00	1.41
Price	2.57	1.28	3.33	1.00

Growth: *Is this business in a growing industry?* (1)Declining industry: Growth in industry sales is negative; (2) Slow growth industry: Growth is less than growth in economy; (3) Average growth: Growth is same as growth in economy; (4) Better than average; (5) A rapidly growing industry.

Funding Needs: *Are the resource requirements for this business?* (1) Low: The entrepreneur or team has the personal resources to fund the venture; (3) Moderate: The entrepreneur or team can raise the funds for the venture; (5) High: The resources required for the venture are so high that funding is unlikely.

Change in K/A (Knowledge/Ability): *Sum [(Ending K/A Score -Beginning K/A Score) for the 7 kinds of K/A]/7.*

At the *beginning* of the case, how would you rate the level of Knowledge/Ability of the lead entrepreneur (or team) has in this industry? At the *end* of the case, how would you rate the level of Knowledge/Ability of the lead entrepreneur (or team) has in this industry?: (1) No K/A: Novice/newcomer; (2) Some K/A (bottom 25%): Apprentice; (3) Average K/A (middle 50%): Journey Person; (4) Above average K/A (75% to 95%): Mentor; (5) This person (team) is an expert (top 5%): Expert.

(1) In marketing/sales? (market research and evaluation, market planning, product pricing, sales management, direct selling, customer service, distribution management)

(2) In finance? (accounting, capital budgeting, cash flow management, credit and collection management, short term financing, long term financing)

(3) In operations? (manufacturing management, inventory control, cost analysis and control, quality control, production scheduling and flow, purchasing, job evaluation)

(4) In technical knowledge of the product/service? (e.g., knowledge of industry standards and practices, specific knowledge of how to make the product or provide the service)

(5) In management? (leadership/vision, conflict management, teamwork, interpersonal skills)

(6) In administration? (planning, decision making, project management, negotiations, MIS, personnel administration)

(7) In "Street Smarts"? Practical and real work knowledge of how industry really works and how to survive as a new business in this industry.

Compared to the other cases in the *Anatomy of a Start-up* book, by the *end* of the case, how much effort (as indicated by time and intensity) was devoted to the following activities: (1) This activity was *not* undertaken; (2) Little effort (bottom 25%); (3) An "average" amount of effort (middle 50%); (4) More than average (75%to 94%); (5) A great deal of effort (top 5%)

Identity: *Determining the identity of the business (e.g., Who are we?)*

Suppliers: *Dealing with already established suppliers or subcontractors*

Entrants: *Analyzing potential new entrants*

Distribution: *Dealing with distributors*

Selling: *Determining how to sell to customers*

Standard: *Are the products/services of this business:* (1) More or less standardized for all customers?; (5) Designed or produced to order for individual customers?

Innovative Process: *Indicate the degree of innovation, relative to the norms of this industry, of the PRODUCTION/SERVICE PROCESS used by this business. If you are not sure whether was any innovation, write down 3.* (1) Major innovation; (3) Incremental innovation; (5) Similar Offering.

Patents: *Does this business benefit to a significant degree from patents, trade secrets, or other proprietary methods of productionor operation?* (1) No; (5) Yes.

Competition: *How would you rate the advantage of this businesses products/services relative to the products or services of its competitors?* (1) VERY STRONG advantage over competitive or substitute products; (2) MODERATE advantage; (3) MATCHED existing competitive or substitute products; (4) SOMEWHAT INFERIOR; (5) VERY INFERIOR to competitive or substitute products.

Aggressive: *Did this business aggressively attempt to enter this market (i.e., spend more than competitors on marketing, selling, advertising, etc. in order to become the firm with the largest share of the market)?* (1) LESS AGGRESSIVE, sought a small share of the market; (3) SAME aggressiveness as other competitors; (5) MORE AGGRESSIVE than other competitors, sought the largest share of the market.

Price: *Are the PRICES for this business's products or services higher or lower than similar products/services of competitors or substitutes?* (1) Prices are MUCH LOWER than competitors; (2) Prices are LOWER than competitors; (3) Prices are about the SAME as competitors; (4) Prices are HIGHER than competitors; (5) Prices are MUCH HIGHER than competitors.

TABLE 4   Standardized Canonical Discriminant Function Coefficients

Variable	Coefficient
Identity	−0.86145
Entrants	0.42922
Suppliers	0.74645
Growth	1.01971
Standard	0.63297
Funding Needs	−0.84676
Change in K/A	0.35479

discriminant score between the survivor and non-survivor groups. The discrimination between the two groups was possible with only seven variables: change in knowledge/ability (CHANGE IN K/A), determining the identity of the business (IDENTITY), analyzing potential competitors (ENTRANTS), dealing with already established suppliers (SUPPLIERS), the standardized or customized nature of the product (STANDARD), the "fundability" the new venture (FUNDING NEEDS), and the rate of industry growth (GROWTH), with the additional seven variables used being redundant. This discriminant function correctly classified 85.2% of the cases, another demonstration of its differentiating power.

Next we examined the relative discriminating power of the seven variables (see Table 4 for the standardized discriminant function coefficients for the variables). All variables were effective discriminators of venture success or failure, but GROWTH, IDENTITY, FUNDING NEEDS, SUPPLIERS, and STANDARD were particularly useful. It should be noted that some caution must be taken in interpreting the relative importance of these variables in light of possible correlation's among them.

It should be noted that this discriminant analysis generated a set of variables that served to differentiate between survivors and non-surviving firms. These variables, taken as a whole, are measures that might be appropriate as a way to predict subsequent venture's survival. A single measure, by itself, is less useful for differentiating between surviving and non-surviving firms. The following discussion of each of the individual variables that proved to be a significant predictor, should be considered in this context.

Individual Characteristics

The hypotheses that entrepreneurs with more knowledge/ability at the beginning, or at the end of the case, were in surviving firms, were not supported. None of the "beginning" or "ending" measures of knowledge/ability predicted venture success or failure. This study appears to confirm overviews of research on prior experience and its effect on start-up success that indicate that prior experience is not a consistent predictor (Cooper and Gascon 1992). Indeed, a close reading of the venture cases suggests that prior industry experience may often be a liability rather than a benefit. Starr and Bygrave (1992) suggest that entrepreneurs with prior experience can suffer from biases and blinders, strong ties, the "success syndrome," and the liabilities of staleness, sameness, priciness, and costliness that make it difficult to navigate the uncharted waters of a new venture start-up. For example, the lead entrepreneur in the article about the chair manufacturing company, Keener-Blodee, Inc., had "expert" level knowledge/ability in the furniture industry, yet his "big company" furniture background was a major hindrance in providing him with the skills to run a start-up company with meager capital. Because he didn't know how to start and run a small company, Keener-Blodee quickly ran out of cash when sales and cash flow were not sufficient to cover the high overhead the company carried. The dictum that industry experience is crucial for venture success (Brokaw 1991) may be appropriate in a limited number of circumstances. Industry experience may be of value in managing functional aspects of the business where the "rules of the game" have not changed. Given that an inherent aspect of entrepreneurship is often changing the rules of the game, knowledge of yesterday's rules may not lead to future success.

The "change in knowledge/ability" measure was found to be one of the predictors of venture success. Given that this measure is the difference between beginning and ending knowledge/ability scores, it should be recognized that individuals with beginning knowledge/ability scores of "expert" would have a knowledge/ability change score of zero or negative. This result might be an indication that potential entrepreneurs who are perceived to "not have all the answers" (i.e., are not experts) at the beginning of the start-up process are more likely to have flexibility, "the ability (or inability) to recognize and react to the completely unpredictable." (Brokaw 1991, p. 54). It should also be noted that the seven "change in knowledge/ability" measures were highly correlated, which might suggest a "halo effect" among specific kinds of changes in knowledge/ability. Also, it might have been difficult, from the information provided in these articles, for the raters to have made more specific judgments about differing types of functional expertise a particular entrepreneur, or team, might possess.

Entrepreneurial Behaviors

Very few of the entrepreneurial behavior measures proved to be significant predictors of subsequent venture survival. Of the 38 variables that measured different entrepreneurial behaviors, only three measures were significant predictors. Entrepreneurs who devoted more effort to: (1) working with established suppliers or subcontractors and (2) analyzing potential new entrants were more likely to start a new venture that survived. Entrepreneurs who devoted less effort to: (3) determining the identity of their business were more likely to start a new venture that survived. Analyzing potential new entrants is one aspect of surveying the marketplace for competitive threats.

It seems that this analysis supports the insights from *Inc.* magazine: "Competitors are to be respected. . . . When start-ups ignore that, they turn arrogance into red ink" (Brokaw 1991, p. 67). Working with established suppliers or subcontractors may be interpreted as a measure of the entrepreneur's ability to focus on internal issues that impact the new venture's expenses and costs of goods sold.

There are a number of speculations appropriate for explaining the incidence of entrepreneurs devoting less effort toward determining the identify of their firm. Entrepreneurs with more complete and specific visions of the future of their organizations might be more able to accomplish the specific tasks necessary for venture survival (Duchesneau and Gartner 1990). Another explanation might be that ventures where entrepreneurs needed to reformulate their new venture's identity are likely to have initially chosen a competitive strategy that wasn't working in the marketplace, which would, therefore, require greater effort to revise the venture's identity. Assuming the liabilities of newness and smallness (Aldrich and Auster 1986), the resources available for adaptation are likely to be minimal, prompting failure because the new firm could not survive long enough to find a viable niche.

Strategy and Environment

Two strategic variables and one environmental variable proved to be significant predictors of new venture survival. New ventures that survived focused on customized products or services, thereby supporting the hypothesis that new ventures pursuing a niche strategy would be more likely to survive. New ventures that were started in growing industries were more likely to survive, thus supporting many previous studies (MacMillan et al. 1987; Merrifield 1987; Stuart & Abetti 1987) demonstrating this effect. New ventures started with the venture team's personal resources or readily available funding were more likely to survive is an intriguing finding. This measure is a subjective evaluation of the observer's view of the new venture's need for funding and the ability of its entrepreneurs to satisfy the venture's funding needs. For example, some of the ventures that survived needed funding that could be satisfied easily through the entrepreneur's personal savings and easily available credit (e.g., the entrepreneurs in "Queen Anne Inn" could fund the renovations to the inn through their personal savings and through mortgages on the property), while other ventures required substantially more funding, but the entrepreneur had the capabilities for acquiring these resources through joint ventures, stock sales, and other fund raising mechanisms (e.g., the entrepreneur in "R.W. Frookies" sold stock to suppliers and distributors as a way to raise capital and lower his production and distribution costs).

The failed ventures seemed to need resources that were far beyond the capabilities of the entrepreneurs to raise, but this result may also reflect a perception by the raters that some ventures required such a substantial amount of resources to become viable that the possibility of generating a reasonable return on the investment appeared unlikely (e.g., Sieben's River North Brewery required such a substantial investment in equipment for a brewing beer, that generating profits from beer sales as a brew-pub, would not be sufficient to repay investors.)

The different aspects of the "fundability" of a venture (i.e., the entrepreneur's ability to raise funds, the resource needs of the venture, the rates of return required by different investors, and the ability of the venture to generate income to repay investors) needs more study to analyze these interactions. It would be particularly valuable to ascertain how entrepreneurs might make changes in their ventures' strategies vis-à-vis their ability to acquire funding.

Comparing Predictions

We were curious as to whether the discriminant analysis was more accurate at predicting venture survival than the experts' predictions offered in the *Inc.* magazine articles. We grouped experts into four categories for comparison: industry experts, competitors, venture capitalists and financiers, and customers. We classified a non-survival prediction based on whether the expert specifically indicated the venture would not survive. If there seemed to be doubt as to whether the expert predicted survival or non-survival, the prediction was classified as a prediction of venture survival.

Given that 17 of 27 ventures survived (63% survival rate), we thought it prudent to bias the expert predictions toward predicting survival, rather than failure in instances where there might be any ambiguity. For many of these ambiguous predictions, the experts offered a qualification, such as "Yes, the venture may succeed, if the entrepreneur makes the following changes. . . ." In predictions where experts offered a qualification, we specified these predictions as: predicting survival. For all 27 cases analyzed there were a total of 114 predictions made by the experts: 36 by industry experts, 29 by competitors, 25 by venture capitalists and financiers, and 24 by customers.

In matching the predictions of these experts to the actual survival or non-survival of these new ventures, we found that industry experts correctly predicted survival or non-survival in 55% of the predictions, competitors in 55% of the predictions, venture-capitalists and financiers in 40% of the predictions, and customers in 38% of the predictions. In reviewing the predictions, we were struck with the frequency in the number of qualifications given by the industry experts and competitors. Both industry experts and competitors were likely to predict the survival of a venture if certain characteristics of the venture could be modified. Venture capitalists and financiers, on the other hand, were more likely to predict the non-survival of a venture, without offering any recommendations for how the venture might be changed to improve its chances for survival.

We speculate that one reason that venture capitalists and financiers were less accurate in their predictions of venture survival is an inherent bias toward assuming that most ventures do not survive because they might believe that entrepreneurs are incapable of making changes in their ventures. Resource providers may believe they have little ability to make changes in a new venture, beyond the decision to fund, so they may make a determination about a venture's ability to survive based on the existing situation. Industry experts and competitors may be more inclined to take the role of the entrepreneur, and therefore, seek to identify how the present situation might be modified to enhance a venture's chances of survival. It seems that the optimism of the industry experts and competitors that obstacles could be overcome was indeed, a more accurate predictor.

An implication of these "Anatomy of a Start-up" cases may be that entrepreneurs do find ways to solve obstacles that stand in the way of success. On the other hand, since firms in this sample were more likely to survive (63% survivors), a different sample of firms with higher rates of non-survivors might likely tip the scales for predicting non-survival in favor of the more pessimistic resource providers.

CONCLUSIONS

This research examined scholarly and practitioner predictions of venture success using an idiosyncratic dataset: *Inc.* magazine articles. Before offering any further insights about the findings, we believe it is prudent to identify some of the limitations of this approach.

Limitations of the Research

As was noted earlier, the *Inc.* magazine articles are unlikely to be a generalizable and representative set of cases depicting all new venture start-ups. The start-ups profiled may represent an editorial bias toward depicting successful start-ups in growth oriented businesses (*Inc.*—"The Magazine for Growing Companies") rather than depicting successful small start-ups or start-ups in more stable markets that might be successful.

The actual events, behaviors, and experiences depicted in these *Inc.* start-ups have been filtered through the biases of: the entrepreneurs' stories as told to the *Inc.* reporters, the reporters' interests in creating an engaging article for *Inc.* magazine readers, and the magazine's editorial stance that guides what key issues might be explored or described in articles that are published.

Whether the measures reflect the actual events and occurrences of a particular start-up is, therefore, open to some speculation. Few variables seemed to have power to differentiate between survivors and non-survivors. Either most variables don't matter, that is both surviving and non-surviving start-ups may behave in similar ways and exist in similar circumstances, or the ability of raters to ascertain subtle differences in various start-up cases may be limited. One might speculate that the lack of significant differences in mean scores between survivors and non-survivors across most variables in the questionnaire may indicate an inability of the raters to ascertain more than gross differences among various start-ups. So, what could have been observed (the information presented in the *Inc.* article), and what was ascertained (the rater's ability to correctly perceive specific information about each start-up), are both subject to significant bias.

One can't help but notice that each *Inc.* start-up story does appear to provide enough information for people to offer a judgment about a start-up's likely success. But was the information consistently presented in the same level of detail, and on the same level of comprehensiveness across all articles? Was the information consistently reliable, given that over a dozen different writers were authors of these stories? Some concern is warranted.

The expert's predictions, as depicted in the articles, and as measured in this study, may be unreliable. It could be that anyone will offer speculation about the future of a business based on little information, or inconsistent information, and, therefore, these predictions by the experts were naive guesses, rather than predictions based on some sort of heuristic or reasoned assessment that would be representative of a group norm (i.e., a venture capitalist's perspective). One might suggest that the experts' opinions were solicited in order to generate some controversy in an article to make it more interesting to read. More reasoned, or more cautious predictions by certain experts may not have been published because they appeared to be less interesting to readers. Rarely did an expert have an opportunity to comment on more than one start-up case, while our model is based on an evaluation of 27 cases.

Group prediction percentages, for each type of expert, were based on an aggregate of individual predictions for specific start-ups. Each expert, given an opportunity to evaluate all 27 cases individually, may have made a more accurate percentage of correct predictions. The data used—articles and expert commentaries—have significant limitations that warrant some skepticism regarding certain findings. But, certain aspects of this study merit recognition.

Implications for Scholarship and Practice

This research stems from prior efforts to ascertain the critical factors that experts use to make judgments about venture success (MacMillan, Siegel, and SubbaNarasimha 1985; MacMillan, Zemann, and SubbaNarasimha 1987; Merrifield 1988; Roure and Kelley 1990), but with a difference in the type of information analyzed: magazine articles rather than business plans. The choice of magazine articles as a source of data for this study grew out of our interest in finding materials in the popular press that students could readily find for practicing venture screening skills. Implicit in this interest is a perspective that individuals can be trained to identify critical success factors in the start-up situations they encounter.

As in other academic studies of new venture success (Cooper 1993), the primary value of this exercise involves making "more obvious" the significant variables that observers use to make judgments about predicting venture success. One of the frustrations we experienced in analyzing the expert's predictions in the magazine articles was our inability to glean consistent and general "rules of thumb" for making predictions about new venture success from their observations. The experts tended to speak to the specifics of the particular venture opportunity, rather than to general principles that might be used to guide other entrepreneurs in other situations. In other words, the reasons given by the start-up experts lacked "theory."

We would assume that the advantage of academic research on new venture success predictors is a body of knowledge, "rules of thumb," a theory or theories to explain why certain factors affect certain circumstances, that might be used as guidelines that could improve an entrepreneur's chances for success. This study, therefore, began with a belief that academic research can lead to knowledge, that, in all likelihood, can be taught and learned, and prove to be useful for enabling individuals to better undertake entrepreneurial activities.

The 85 variable screening questionnaire offered a way to comprehensively focus on many of the details concerning the start-up of a business that might be overlooked in a cursory overview of an entrepreneurial story. Paying attention to the details involved in a start-up might be one important aspect of learning about entrepreneurship. Yet only a few of these variables appeared to be important for differentiating between surviving and non-surviving firms. Knowing which details to pay attention to is an important aspect of developing the knowledge necessary to improve an entrepreneur's ability to improve odds of new venture survival.

The use of the venture screening questionnaire as a way to predict new venture survival could be significantly improved to achieve this objective. First, the venture screening questionnaire could be compared to other methods of prediction to see whether the venture screening questionnaire helped individuals better predict venture survival. Such a test might be accomplished by assigning individuals to different "conditions" where some individuals would receive the venture screening questionnaire as an aid, while other individuals would make their predictions without using the venture screening questionnaire. A comparison of the prediction accuracy between the two groups might indicate that individuals using the venture screening questionnaire were able to correctly identify surviving vs. non-surviving potential ventures. Second, the venture screening questionnaire, itself, can be improved. Given the low discriminating power of most of the items in the questionnaire, most items should be dropped. The validity of the seven variables identified to predict venture success needs further exploration. Third, there should be comparisons conducted with other venture screening exercises (e.g., Merrifield 1987; Roure & Keeley 1990) to determine the strengths and weaknesses of these approaches. Finally, we encourage more effort toward generating venture screening questionnaires through in-depth field studies (e.g., Hisrich and Jankowicz 1990).

We suggest that venture screening questionnaires be applied to other start-up cases that can be found in business case books, biographies, autobiographies, newspaper articles, and published oral histories. These sources provide a rich database of information that can be analyzed, not only for the knowledge that researchers can gain through careful reading, evaluation, discussion, and analysis, but also through the cumulative benefits of generating information that can be aggregated, quantified, and analyzed in a more rigorous manner.

Although the writers and editors of *Inc.* magazine probably did not expect their ideas to be the subject of a scholarly empirical test, the ideas of journalists writing for the practitioner audience are ripe for exploration and analysis. The results of our analyses were not completely consistent with the advice from *Inc.* magazine (see Table 1). Our findings seem to support the *Inc.* advice that entrepreneurs be flexible (point 1), and understand their competitors (point 4) and customers (point 2). Our findings do not support *Inc.*'s belief that "the strongest companies were led by people with experience in their industries" (point 3). *Inc.*'s remaining two issues, "it's the sales cycle" (point 5), and "being the boss" (point 6), did not surface as variables significant in our analyses.

Finally, we hope that this academic approach toward gleaning wisdom from these various stories of start-ups from *Inc.* magazine, might be viewed as "scholarship of application" (Boyer 1990), where researchers attempt to apply theory and knowledge in useful and meaningful ways. There is substantial empirical evidence about the nature of new venture start-ups in scholarly journals that can be used as evidence to test the ideas proffered by journalists and other writers about the phenomenon of entrepreneurship. To assume that academic research will, by osmosis, reach the consciousness of journalists, entrepreneurs, and public policy makers, is a bit optimistic. The community of academic researchers in entrepreneurship will not likely influence the public's beliefs and behaviors about entrepreneurship without a more concerted effort to develop bridges between the academic and practitioner worlds. Certainly, there are many ways to develop these bridges. We believe that part of this process involves engaging the imagination of the "non-scholarly world" in their everyday realm: using popular books, magazines, and newspaper articles about entrepreneurship as the fodder for scholarly analysis.

REFERENCES

Aldrich, H.A. and Auster, E. 1986. Even dwarfs started small: Liabilities of age and size and their strategic implications. *Research in Organizational Behavior* 8:165–198.

Argyris, C. and Schon, D. 1978. *Organizational Learning: A Theory of Action Perspective.* Reading, MA: Addison-Wesley.

Boyer, E.L. 1990. *Scholarship Reconsidered: Priorities of the Professoriate.* Princeton, NJ: The Carnegie Foundation for the Advancement of Teaching.

Brokaw, L. 1991. The truth about start-ups. In E.K. Longsworth, ed., *Anatomy of a Start-up: Why Some New Businesses Succeed and Others Fail.* Boston: Inc. Publishing.

Brush, C.G. and VanderWerf, P.A. 1992. A comparison of methods and sources for obtaining estimates of new venture performance. *Journal of Business Venturing* 7:157–170.

Bull, I. and Willard, G.E. 1993. Towards a theory of entrepreneurship. *Journal of Business Venturing* 8(3):183–196.

Buzzell, R.D. and Gale, B.T. 1987. *The PIMS Principles.* New York: Free Press.

Carter, N.M., Gartner, W.B., and Reynolds, P.D. 1996. Exploring start-up event sequences. *Journal of Business Venturing* 11:151–166.

Cooper, A.C. 1993. Challenges in predicting new firm performance. *Journal of Business Venturing* 8(3):241–254.

Cooper, A.C. and Gascon, F.J.G. 1992. Entrepreneurs, processes of founding, and new-firm performance. In D.L. Sexton and J.L. Kasarda, eds. *The State of the Art of Entrepreneurship.* Boston: PWS-Kent Publishing.

Covin, J.G. and Slevin, D.P. 1990. New venture strategic posture, structure, and performance: An industry life cycle analysis. *Journal of Business Venturing* 5(2):123–135.

Dean, T.J., Meyer, G.D., and DeCastro, J. 1993. Determinants of new-firm formations in manufacturing industries: Industry dynamics, entry barriers, and organizational inertia. *Entrepreneurship: Theory and Practice* 17(2):49–60.

Duchesneau, D.A. and Gartner, W.B. 1990. A profile of new venture success and failure in an emerging industry. *Journal of Business Venturing* 5(5):297–312.

Eisenhardt, K.M. and Schoonhoven, C.B. 1990. Organizational growth: Linking founding team, strategy, environment, and growth among U.S. semiconductor ventures, 1978–1988. *Administrative Science Quarterly* 35:504–529.

Gartner, W.B. 1985. A conceptual framework for describing the phenomenon of new venture creation. *Academy of Management Review* 10(4):696–706.

Gartner, W.B. 1988. Who is an entrepreneur? Is the wrong question. *American Journal of Small Business* 12(4):11–32.

Gartner, W.B., Bird, B.J., and Starr, J.A. 1992. Acting as if: Differentiating entrepreneurial from organizational behavior. *Entrepreneurship: Theory and Practice* 16(3):13–32.

Gartner, W.B. and Starr, J.A. 1993a. The nature of entrepreneurial work. In S. Birley and I.C. MacMillan, eds., *Entrepreneurship Research: Global Perspectives.* Amsterdam: Elsevier, 35–67.

Gartner, W.B. and Starr, J.A. 1993b. A methodology for identifying entrepreneurial behaviors. Paper presented at the Third Global Conference on Entrepreneurship Research, Lyon, France, March.

Gatewood, E.J., Shaver, K.G., and Gartner, W.B. 1995. A longitudinal study of cognitive factors influencing start-up behaviors and success at venture creation. *Journal of Business Venturing* 10(5):371–391.

Herron, L. and Robinson, R.B., Jr. 1993. A structural model of the effects of entrepreneurial characteristics on venture performance. *Journal of Business Venturing* 8(3):281–294.

Hill, L.A. 1992. *Becoming a Manager.* Boston: Harvard Business School Press.

Hisrich, R.D. and Jankowicz, A.D. 1990. Intuition in venture capital decisions: An exploratory study using a new technique. *Journal of Business Venturing* 5(1):49–62.

Katz, J.A. 1988. Entrepreneurship researchers and research entrepreneurs: Problems in the equitable sharing of data. *Journal of Business Venturing* 3(2):89–96.

Katz, J.A. 1989. Penurious strategies for parsimonious research: "Little guy" alternatives for "big buck" research. *Journal of Business Venturing* 4(6):361–366.

Longsworth, E.K. 1991. *Anatomy of a Start-up: Why Some New Businesses Succeed and Others Fail.* Boston: Inc. Publishing.

Low, M.B. and MacMillan, I.C. 1988. Entrepreneurship: Past research and future challenges. *Journal of Management* 14(2):139–161.

MacMillan, I.C. and Day, D.L. 1987. Corporate ventures into industrial markets: Dynamics of aggressive entry. *Journal of Business Venturing* 2(1):29–40.

MacMillan, I.C., Siegel, R., and SubbaNarasimha, P.N. 1985. Criteria used by venture capitalists to evaluate new venture proposals. *Journal of Business Venturing* 1(1):119–128.

MacMillan, I.C., Zemann, L. and SubbaNarasimha, P.N. 1987. Criteria distinguishing successful from unsuccessful ventures in the venture screening process. *Journal of Business Venturing* 2:123–137.

McCall, M.W. Jr., Lombardo, M.M., and Morrison, A.M. 1988. *The Lessons of Experience.* Lexington, MA: Lexington Books.

Merrifield, D.B. 1987. New business incubators. *Journal of Business Venturing* 2:277–284.

Merrifield, D.B. 1988. Industrial survival via management technology. *Journal of Business Venturing* 3:171–185.

Miller, A. and Camp, B. 1985. Exploring determinants of success in corporate ventures. *Journal of Business Venturing* 1(1):87–106.

Miller, D. and Friesen, P. 1984. *Organizations: A Quantum View.* Englewood Cliffs, NJ: Prentice-Hall.

Roure, J.B. and Keeley, R.H. 1990. Predictors of success in new technology based ventures. *Journal of Business Venturing* 5(4):201–220.

Sandberg, W.R. and Hofer, C.W. 1987. Improving new venture performance: The role of strategy, industry structure, and the entrepreneur. *Journal of Business Venturing* 2(1):5–28.

232   W.B. GARTNER, J.A. STARR, AND S. BHAT

Sapienza, H.J., Smith, K.J., and Gannon, M.J. 1988. Using subjective evaluations of organizational performance in small business research. *American Journal of Small Business* 12(3):45–54.

Sudikoff, J.P. 1994. Street smarts. *Inc.* 16 (3):23.

Starr, J.A. and Bygrave, W.D. 1992. The second time around: The outcomes, assets and liabilities of prior start-up experience. In S. Birley and I.C. MacMillan, eds., *International Perspectives on Entrepreneurship Research.* Amsterdam: Elsevier.

Starr, J.A., Bygrave, W.D., and Tercanli, D. 1993. Doesexperience pay? Methodological issues in the study of entrepreneurial experience. In S. Birley and I.C. MacMillan, eds., *Entrepreneurship Research: Global Perspectives.* Amsterdam: Elsevier.

Stuart, R. and Abetti, P.A. 1987. Start-up ventures: Towards the prediction of initial success. *Journal of Business Venturing* 2:215–230.

Timmons, J.A. 1994. *New Venture Creation* (4th ed). Homewood, IL: Irwin.

Van de Ven, A.H., Hudson, R., and Schroeder, D.M. 1984. Designing new business startups: Entrepreneurial, organizational,and ecological considerations. *Journal of Management* 10:87–107.

VanderWerf, P.A. 1989. Achieving empirical progress in an undefined field. *Entrepreneurship: Theory and Practice* 14(2):45–58.

Vesper, K.H. 1990. *New Venture Strategies.* Englewood Cliffs, NJ: Prentice-Hall.

[14]

ELSEVIER   Journal of Business Venturing 18 (2003) 13–39

The career reasons of nascent entrepreneurs☆

Nancy M. Carter[a,*,1], William B. Gartner[b], Kelly G. Shaver[c,2],
Elizabeth J. Gatewood[d,3]

[a]*Graduate School of Business, University of St. Thomas, TMH 470-1000 LaSalle Ave., Minneapolis,
MN 55403-2005, USA*
[b]*Lloyd Greif Center for Entrepreneurial Studies, Bridge Hall One, Marshall School of Business,
University of Southern California, Los Angeles, CA 90089-0801, USA*
[c]*Psychology Department, College of William and Mary, Williamsburg, VA 23187, USA*
[d]*Johnson Center for Entrepreneurship and Innovation, Indiana University, 501 Morton Street, Suite 108,
Bloomington, IN 47404, USA*

Received 30 April 2001; received in revised form 30 October 2001; accepted 30 October 2001

Abstract

This paper explores the reasons that nascent entrepreneurs offered for their work and career choices and compares those responses to the reasons given by a group of nonentrepreneurs. Six separate factors accounted for 68% of the variance: self-realization, financial success, roles, innovation, recognition, and independence. The factor scores of nascent entrepreneurs and nonentrepreneurs were not significantly different on self-realization, financial success, innovation, and independence. Nascent entrepreneurs rated reasons concerning roles and recognition significantly lower than nonentrepreneurs. Finally, gender differences in reasons also emerged; male nascent entrepreneurs and nonentrepreneurs rated financial success and innovation higher than did females, regardless of their group of origin.
© 2002 Elsevier Science Inc. All rights reserved.

☆ A version of this paper was presented at the Babson/Kauffman Entrepreneurship Research Conference, Wellesley, MA, June 2000.
* Corresponding author. Tel.: +1-651-962-4407; fax: +1-651-962-4410.
E-mail addresses: wgartner@marshall.usc.edu (W.B. Gartner), nmcarter@stthomas.edu (N.M. Carter), kgshav@attglobal.net (K.G. Shaver), gatewood@indiana.edu (E.J. Gatewood).
[1] Tel.: +1-651-962-4407; fax: +1-651-962-4410.
[2] Tel.: +1-757-221-3885; fax: +1-757-221-3896.
[3] Tel.: +1-812-855-4248; fax: +1-812-855-2751.

1. Executive summary

This paper explores the reasons that nascent entrepreneurs offered for their work and career choices and compares these responses to the reasons given by a group of nonentrepreneurs.

A substantial concern about the validity of research on the reasons for business start-up has hinged on the problem of retrospection, that is, interviewing entrepreneurs about their reasons for entrepreneurship long after they are in business. To address this concern we examined the reasons that individuals offered for choosing independent business start-up while they were in the initial stages of forming a business. In addition, our research compared these nascent entrepreneurs with a representative comparison sample of individuals who were not actively engaged in independent business creation.

Based on prior research, we identified six categories of reasons that individuals give for starting businesses: The first category, *innovation*, involved reasons that describe an individual's intention to accomplish something new; the second category, *independence*, described an individual's desire for freedom, control, and flexibility in the use of one's time; *recognition* described an individual's intention to have status, approval, and recognition from one's family, friends, and from those in the community; *roles* described an individual's desire to follow family traditions or emulate the example of others; *financial success* involved reasons that describe an individual's intention to earn more money and achieve financial security; and *self-realization* described reasons involved with pursuing self-directed goals.

We offered a number of ideas that support the view that nascent entrepreneurs have similar reasons for career choice as working age adults in the general population. Based on this viewpoint, we tested the following hypothesis:

> *Hypothesis 1:* Nascent entrepreneurs and a comparison group of nonentrepreneurs have similar scores on the six kinds of career reasons (innovation, financial success, independence, recognition, roles, and self-realization).

Research on the differences between men and women indicated that there are significant differences in their career choices, and that theoretical models that described the career paths of men are less suited to the experiences of women. There appeared to be significant differences in the reasons that compel men and women to pursue entrepreneurial careers, especially if more weight was given to the results of prospective studies. Therefore, we suggested:

> *Hypothesis 2:* Women (nascent entrepreneurs and the comparison group) rate the six kinds of career reasons differently than men (nascent entrepreneurs and the comparison group).

The data for this research were obtained from the Panel Study of Entrepreneurial Dynamics (PSED), a national database of nascent entrepreneurs who were in the process of starting companies. The analysis was conducted on the reduced PSED data set of 558 nascent entrepreneurs and comparison group participants. Eighteen items from the mail survey of the PSED database (items G1a–r) were selected for coding and analysis. We first tested the predictive validity of our model by subjecting the data to a principal components factor

N.M. Carter et al. / Journal of Business Venturing 18 (2003) 13–39　　15

analysis (listwise deletion of missing values, varimax rotation) with the analysis directed to produce six factors. The rotation required eight iterations to converge. The six factors that were produced account for more than 68% of the variance and show truly remarkable similarity to the theoretical dimensions—only two of the items were out of place.

The Group × Reasons interaction tested the primary hypothesis of the research, that nascent entrepreneurs and a comparison group have similar scores on career reasons. The ANOVA revealed a significant Group × Reasons interaction, $F(5,2770) = 28.25$, $P < .0001$. The findings provided mixed support for accepting Hypothesis 1. There was no significant difference between nascent entrepreneurs and the comparison group on four of the scales (self-realization, financial success, innovation, and independence). There was a significant difference between nascent entrepreneurs and the comparison group on two of the scales (recognition and roles). The analysis also showed a significant main effect for group, with overall scores lower for nascent entrepreneurs than for the comparison group $F(1,554) = 5.57$, $P < .02$, but this difference was most likely a consequence of the significant interaction.

In addition to the significant Group × Reasons interaction, the $2 \times 2 \times 6$ (Group × Gen-Gender × Reasons) repeated measures ANOVA on the weighted scale values also showed a highly significant main effect difference among the reasons' mean scores, with independence having the overall highest scores and roles having the overall lowest scores, $F(5,2770) = 292.20$, $P < .0001$. This ordering of the six sets of reasons made it clear that the significant differences between nascent entrepreneurs and the control group occurred on scales that were rated as less important by both groups (such as roles). On scales that were highly rated (such as independence, financial success, and self-realization), there were no significant differences between the two groups. Finally, the analysis showed a small but significant difference between men and women, with men having higher scores on financial success and innovation than women, regardless of their group of origin, $F(5,2770) = 2.67$, $P < .02$. This finding partially supported Hypothesis 2. It is important to note that although the score women assigned to financial success was lower than that given by men, women still saw financial success as an important reason in career choice and equal in their ranking to self-realization.

Nascent entrepreneurs are both similar to, and different from, the general population. Entrepreneurs were similar to nonentrepreneurs on four scales: independence financial success, self-realization, and innovation. Both entrepreneurs and nonentrepreneurs rated independence, financial success, and self-realization as more important than recognition, innovation or roles. The differences that were found between nascent entrepreneurs and nonentrepreneurs were on the scores that both groups ranked lower than the others: roles and recognition. Nascent entrepreneurs offered reasons for getting into business that were less likely to take the validation of others into account. There were differences in reasons for career choice by gender. Males (entrepreneurs and nonentrepreneurs) rated financial success and innovation higher than females (entrepreneurs and nonentrepreneurs) as a reason for choosing a career.

An issue that should not be underestimated in this study is the fact that this research was based on interviews with a representative sample of individuals in the process of starting a business and that this sample of nascent entrepreneurs was compared to a control group that is generalizable to the population of the United States. These nascent entrepreneurs were offering reasons for getting into business before the success (or failure) of their efforts was determined. Because these findings are based on prospective reasons, rather than retrospective reasons, we believe the results of this study should take precedence over any previous studies where retrospective reasons for start-up were offered. The overall results of our research argue against considering entrepreneurs to be qualitatively different from individuals who pursue other career options.

2. Introduction

The creation of new independent businesses accounts for between one fourth to nearly one third of the variation in economic growth in many industrialized countries (Davidsson et al., 1994; Reynolds, 1994; Reynolds and Maki, 1990; Reynolds et al., 2000). Discovering the factors that influence an individual's choice to pursue independent business creation might, therefore, lead to insights that would have an impact on economic growth and development. There is a long history of specifying various personal characteristics, cognitions, and social conditions that influence an individual's choice to pursue entrepreneurial activity (Aldrich, 1999; Carroll and Mosakowski, 1987; Gartner, 1988, 1989; Katz, 1992; Kolvereid, 1996a,b; Krueger et al., 2000; Shaver and Scott, 1991; Simon et al., 2000). This article focuses on a specific set of cognitions, namely the reasons individuals offer for undertaking entrepreneurial activity.

A substantial concern about the validity of research on reasons for business start-up has hinged on the problem of retrospection, that is, interviewing entrepreneurs about their reasons for entrepreneurship long after they are in business (Gartner, 1989; Shaver and Scott, 1991). Retrospective accounts, particularly when describing prior intentions, have been shown to have a significant self-justification bias. Such bias seriously undermines any confidence that the initial reasons an individual gives for an action accurately describes their undertaking subsequent actions, or outcomes of those actions (Golden, 1992; Huber and Power, 1985). To address this concern we examined the reasons that individuals offered for choosing independent business start-up while they were in the initial stages of forming a business. These nascent entrepreneurs offered prospective accounts for their choice of entrepreneurship, rather than retrospective reminiscences. In addition, our research compared these nascent entrepreneurs with a representative comparison sample of individuals who were not actively engaged in independent business creation.

This article is structured in the following manner. Prior research on reasons that entrepreneurs offered for starting businesses is explored and summarized. An attempt is made to link these prior research efforts to theories that might explain the reasons for choosing entrepreneurship versus other types of work. Based on the results of previous empirical studies of entrepreneurial reasons, and the theoretical justifications generated, variables were identified for use in a questionnaire. Hypotheses are offered for why nascent entrepreneurs would rate reasons for starting new businesses differently from (or similarly to) other individuals' ratings of reasons about their work careers. The critical problem of retrospective reporting was remedied by using data from the PSED. The PSED is a survey of individuals who were identified while they were in the process of starting their businesses. The survey also collected information from a comparison group identified in such a way that the individuals in the group represented the population of individuals in the United States. Responses from the nascent entrepreneurs and the comparison group were analyzed, described, and discussed. Implications for research and practice are offered.

3. Prior research and hypotheses

As outlined in Kolvereid (1996a), the reasons that potential entrepreneurs offer for getting into business should have a significant influence on whether they actually engage in entrepreneurial activity (Ajzen, 1991; Krueger and Brazeal, 1994; Krueger and Carsrud, 1993). Reasons that individuals offer for getting into business (or not) matter, because reasons are traditionally considered to be the basis of intentions (Anscombe, 1956; Shaver, 1985). New businesses are not created by accident. The effort and time involved in starting a business would suggest that entrepreneurial actions are clearly intentional. Indeed, a number of studies of the new venture creation process described individuals persisting at a variety of activities over a period of months, or years, in order to achieve the creation of a new firm (Carter et al., 1996; Gatewood et al., 1995; Reynolds and Miller, 1992; Reynolds and White, 1997). When obstacles arise in connection with any of these activities, entrepreneurs must find ways to overcome them. In summary, new venture creation is action that involves repeated attempts to exercise control over the process, in order to achieve the desired outcome. By this description, new venture creation constitutes a sort of behavior that social psychologists, for nearly 50 years, have regarded as intentional (Heider, 1958).

3.1. Reasons for getting into business

Academic research on the reasons entrepreneurs offer for starting businesses has a long history of prior empirical and theoretical efforts. We offer a chronology of the progression of these efforts as a way to show how we have extended ideas from this previous research and how we arrived at the reasons for the variables used in the present study. Many of the initial research efforts on reasons entrepreneurs offer for starting businesses stemmed from work undertaken by Sari Scheinberg and colleagues. This research has been labeled as the Society of Associated Researchers of International Entrepreneurship (SARIE) research (Alange and Scheinberg, 1988; Birley and Westhead, 1994; Blais and Toulouse, 1990; Dubini, 1988; Scheinberg and MacMillan, 1988; Shane et al., 1991). Initially, the theoretical justification for the list of reasons used in these empirical studies (Scheinberg and MacMillan, 1988) was based on a wide variety of sources, such as: need for independence (Friberg, 1976; Hofstede, 1980), need for material incentives (Friberg, 1976), desire to escape or avoid a negative situation (Collins and Moore, 1955; Cooper, 1971; Friberg, 1976; Hagen, 1962; Shapero, 1975), need for social approval (Friberg, 1976; Maslow, 1943; McClelland, 1961; Vroom, 1967), and a drive to fulfill personal values or norms (Friberg, 1976). A list of 38 statements (reasons), based loosely on different aspects of these theories, was generated for the SARIE research. Scheinberg and MacMillan (1988) sought to discover the differences among entrepreneurs in how they might rate these reasons. Over 1400 independent business owners/founders in 11 countries were surveyed. Subsequent explorations of this data began a quest to develop what might be labeled as an "empirically based" theory about the reasons entrepreneurs offered for business creation.

Scheinberg and MacMillan (1988) conducted a factor analysis of the 38 items and found six broad factors of reasons for business creation that they called: need for approval, perceived instrumentality of wealth, communitarianism, need for personal development, need for independence, and need for escape. In comparing entrepreneurs by country, they found that the reasons for business creation varied. For example, U.S. and Australian entrepreneurs scored highest on the "need for independence" factor, whereas entrepreneurs from Italy, Portugal, and China scored highest on "communitarianism." Scandinavian countries, such as Sweden, Norway, and Denmark had entrepreneurs who offered low scores on the instrumentality of wealth factor. In a follow-up study, Shane et al. (1991) sought to extend the model developed by Scheinberg and MacMillan (1988) by focusing on nationality and gender of the entrepreneur. In hopes of improving the response rate, they reduced the original 38 "reasons" items to 21 and added two questions on tax considerations. They surveyed 597 owner–managers in three of the 11 countries, Great Britain, New Zealand, and Norway, and identified four broad factors that explained an entrepreneur's reasons for business creation. They called these four factors: recognition, independence, learning, and roles. They identified a number of nationality and gender differences but no overall main effect for any specific item. Based on these two previous explorations, Birley and Westhead (1994) administered a questionnaire with 23 reasons items to 405 owner–managers of independent businesses in the United Kingdom. A factor analysis of the 23 reasons produced seven factors that the authors labeled: need for approval, need for independence, need for personal development, welfare considerations (in terms of contributing to a sense of community), perceived instrumentality of wealth, tax reduction, and following role models. Each of these studies involved surveys of individuals who had already started firms.

Although the preponderance of research exploring the reasons entrepreneurs offer for starting new business can be attributed to the SARIE efforts, there have been other academic studies on the topic. Kolvereid (1996a) explored the reasons given for self-employment versus organizational employment using a group of 372 Norwegian business-school gradu-ates. He designed a classification scheme that posited 11 types of reasons for choosing between self-employment and organizational employment: security, economic opportunity, authority, autonomy, social environment, work load, challenge, self-realization, participation in the whole process, avoid responsibility, and career. He found that individuals who were self-employed were more likely to choose economic opportunity, authority, autonomy, challenge, self-realization, and participate in the whole process, compared to those choosing organizational employment. Although many of Kolvereid's classifications were consistent with those of the SARIE studies, his effort did not build directly on these earlier studies. His research methodology however, was consistent with the earlier retrospective approach— surveying people years after their occupational choices had been made.

N.M. Carter et al. / Journal of Business Venturing 18 (2003) 13–39   19

In one of the few prospective studies on reasons offered for getting into business, Gatewood et al. (1995), asked 142 preventure clients from a small business development center (SBDC) their reasons for choosing to start a business. Most respondents provided no more than two distinct answers to this open-ended question. Although there were obviously differences in individual wording, six kinds of answers accounted for 93% of the first two reasons offered, and five of the categories reflected the categories of the SARIE studies. These reasons were identification of a market need (29% of the total), autonomy and independence (an additional 18%), a desire to make more money (18%), a desire to use knowledge and experience (16%), the enjoyment of self-employment (7%), and a desire to show that it could be done (5%).

All of these studies suggest that entrepreneurs offer a variety of reasons for getting into business. Table 1 displays our attempt to synthesize the reasons generated by the SARIE studies and the research of others as a way to show the continuity that exists among these prior research efforts. The listing, shown in Table 1, is intended as a post hoc parsimonious synthesis of the SARIE studies, which essentially became an empirically derived theory of the reasons entrepreneurs offer for getting into business. The order of the categories listed in Table 1 corresponds to the order of the factor weights in each related empirical analysis.

The first category in Table 1, labeled innovation, involves reasons that describe an individual's intention to accomplish something new (McClelland, 1961; McClelland and Winter, 1969). The category contains items Shane et al. (1991) considered as "learning" and what Birley and Westhead (1994) and Sheinberg and MacMillan (1988) considered as "need for personal development." The second category, independence, describes an individual's desire for freedom, control, and flexibility in the use of one's time (Schein, 1978; Smith and Miner, 1983). Items in this category were consistently identified in all three of the SARIE studies. The third category we labeled recognition and combined two categories of items from the previous research: recognition and need for approval. Items in this category describe an individual's intention to have status, approval, and recognition from one's family, friends, and other people in the community (Bonjean, 1966; Nelson, 1968). The fourth category, roles, contains items from Shane et al. (1991) that describe an individual's desire to follow family traditions or emulate the example of others (Hofstede, 1980). The last category, financial success, involves reasons that describe an individual's intention to earn more money and achieve financial security (Knight, 1987). Although Shane et al. (1991) did not find a financial success factor, the other two studies (Birley and Westhead, 1994; Scheinberg and MacMillan, 1988) did, which they labeled as "perceived instrumentality of wealth."

In addition to the five categories identified from the SARIE studies and described in Table 1, evidence in previous research on gender in entrepreneurship (e.g., Brush, 1992; Carter, 1997; Fischer et al., 1993) led us to believe a sixth factor, self-realization, should be added to the classification scheme. There is evidence that men are more likely to seek to create financial wealth, whereas women are more likely to pursue other types of goals that center on personal interests. Women are seen as experiencing more complexity in making career choices because of their need to balance employment, childcare, and housing. Fulfilling multiple roles requires women to consider time and space constraints as they make

Table 1
Categories of entrepreneurship reasons

	Innovation	Independence	Recognition	Roles	Financial success
Schienberg and MacMillan (1988)	Need for personal development m. To develop an idea for product/business h. To keep learning c. To be innovative and in the forefront of new technology *. Direct contribution to success of company	Need for independence *. Control of my own time b. To have greater flexibility for private life f. Freedom to adapt my own approach to work	Need for approval e. Be respected by friends l. Achieve something and get recognition a. Achieve higher position in society *. Increase status of family in society *. Have more influence in community		Perceived instrumentality of wealth k. Desire to have high earnings *. Needed more money to survive g. Give self and family security *. Access to indirect benefits
Shane et al. (1991)	Learning m. To develop an idea for a product c. To be innovative and in the forefront of new technology h. To continue learning	Independence *. To control my own time b. To have greater flexibility for my personal and family life f. To have considerable freedom to adapt my own approach to work	Recognition a. To achieve a higher position for myself in society *. To have more influence in my community e. To be respected by friends l. To achieve something and get recognition for it *. To increase the status and prestige of my family	Roles d. To continue a family tradition *. To have more influence in my community i. To follow the example of a person I admire	
Birley and Westhead (1994)	Need for personal development c. To be innovative and be in the forefront of technological development m. To develop an idea for a product h. To continue learning	Need for independence f. To have considerable freedom to adapt my own approach to my work b. To have greater flexibility for my personal and family life *. To control my own time	Need for approval a. To achieve a higher position for myself in society e. To be respected by friends *. To increase the status and prestige of my family l. To achieve something and get recognition for it k. Desire to have high earnings *. To have more influence in my community	Follow role models i. To follow the example of a person I admire	Perceived instrumentality of wealth g. To give myself, my spouse, and children security *. To contribute to the welfare of my relatives

The letters (a - m) in correspond to the item letters used in our analyses (presented in Table 2). The table, therefore, links the questions used in this study with those of prior research.
* Item not used in subsequent analyses for this research.

N.M. Carter et al. / Journal of Business Venturing 18 (2003) 13–39   21

economic and social decisions in concert (Gilbert, 1997). One explanation for gender differences in career development is that differing societal expectations for men and women lead to divergence in work preferences (Harriman, 1985). Sex-role socialization experiences teach young girls what roles are appropriate, or not. These experiences are seen as constricting career choices, compromising career potential (Gottfredson, 1981) and influencing women's beliefs, attitudes and self-conceptions that ultimately affect their work interests and choices (Farmer, 1997). Several studies of choices involving the start-up of a business support this perspective (Brush, 1992; Buttner and Moore, 1997; Carter, 1997; Gatewood et al., 1995), but others provide evidence that the entrepreneurial career choice is gender blind (Fagenson, 1993). Adding variables to constitute a self-realization factor, therefore, seemed to be an appropriate way to test which viewpoint was more plausible. Moreover, adding this factor appeared to offer a more comprehensive list of the types of reasons that might differentiate between nascent entrepreneurs and others.

3.2. Are the career reasons of nascent entrepreneurs different?

A cursory review of the literature may lead to the conclusion that entrepreneurs offer different reasons for getting into business than other people give for having jobs. Many of the prior studies implicitly assumed a difference, but only Kolvereid (1996a) directly compared the reasons of entrepreneurs with the reasons given by adults choosing other careers. Unfortunately, his study was retrospective in nature. We could find not one prospective study that compared the reasons of individuals in the process of getting into business with the career reasons of other individuals. The validity of retrospective surveys of successful entrepreneurs for accurately ascribing the prospective reasons offered by nascent entrepreneurs is doubtful. As suggested earlier, such retrospective reminiscences are likely to be biased and inaccurate depictions of what may have actually occurred in the past (Golden, 1992; Huber and Power, 1985). In addition, it is unlikely that surveys of established business owners would accurately capture the diversity of ratings on career reasons. Surveying successful entrepreneurs about their retrospections of start-up reasons could have a significant "left-censored" bias. Specifically, entrepreneurs who attempted to start businesses but quit, or those who started businesses that no longer exist, would not be in the sample. Such samples may reflect only a small proportion of the individuals who represent the phenomenon of interest.

We believe that—*when questions are asked before the fact*—the reasons offered by potential entrepreneurs for getting into business will not be significantly different from the reasons offered by a similar comparison group of individuals in other types of careers. Such reasons as to lead, to achieve something, to earn income, to grow and learn, to challenge oneself, to be respected, to attain a higher position for oneself, would likely be the kinds of reasons that anyone might offer for choosing any kind of job (Fagenson, 1993; Kanter, 1977; Powell, 1988). In this way, the differences among entrepreneurs may be as great as the differences among nonentrepreneurs, and vice versa (Gartner, 1985; 1988). Even setting aside the retrospective bias argument, we believe that the previous findings of differences between the career choice reasons of entrepreneurs and others are flawed. They are likely to

22   *N.M. Carter et al. / Journal of Business Venturing 18 (2003) 13–39*

represent a historical artifact. We speculate that the "job of entrepreneurship" as a career, has changed over time. The SARIE studies were originally undertaken in the mid-1980s and early 1990s, and the samples used involved entrepreneurs from a variety of countries. At that time in history, an individual's chance of self-employment as a career probably reflected an option perceived as more of an "outlier" than other career choices. In the current decade, the choice of entrepreneurship as a career in the United States is likely to be perceived quite differently compared to 20 years ago. Entrepreneurship, today, may be perceived to be more like other jobs.

As a starting point for comparing nascent entrepreneurs to people in the general population, we follow a logic that assumes that the prospective reasons of these nascent entrepreneurs are *not* different than the reasons of others. Therefore, we suggest the following hypothesis:

> *Hypothesis 1:* Nascent entrepreneurs and a comparison group have similar scores on the six kinds of career reasons (innovation, financial success, independence, recognition, roles, and self-realization).

3.3. Gender differences in reasons for getting into business

Research on the differences between men and women indicate that there are significant differences in their career choices, and that theoretical models that describe the career paths of men are less suited to the experiences of women (Farmer, 1997; Farmer et al., 1995; Larwood and Gattikers, 1989). Some studies of job preferences revealed that women want work that is intellectually stimulating and provides opportunities for personal and professional growth (Bigoness, 1988; Brenner and Tomkiewicz, 1979). Brush (1992) found women business owners tend to balance economic goals with other kinds of goals, such as personal enjoyment and helping others. Sexton and Bowman-Upton (1990) found that female business owners scored lower on energy level and risk taking and higher on autonomy and change than male business owners. Fischer et al. (1993) found that on three motivational factors (financial, lifestyle, and social/recognition) women scored higher than men on financial motivation, a result they found "somewhat unexpected" (p. 162). Buttner and Moore (1997) found that "pull factor" reasons, such as seeking challenge and self-determination, were more important to women than to men. Conversely, in a comparison of the values of entrepreneurs and managers, Fagenson (1993) found more similarities among women and men than differences. Women were found to value equality more than men, and men tended to value family security more than women, but the greater differences were found between entrepreneurs and managers. Entrepreneurs were found to value self-respect, freedom, a sense of accomplishment, and an exciting life more than did managers.

Although the findings are mixed, there appear to be significant differences in the reasons that compel men and women to pursue entrepreneurial careers, especially if more weight is given to the results of prospective studies like those of Gatewood et al. (1995) and Carter (1997). In their study of preventure clients, Gatewood et al. found that nascent women entrepreneurs who offered internal reasons (e.g., "I always wanted to be my own boss") and nascent men entrepreneurs who offered external reasons (e.g., "I had identified a market need") were more likely to start businesses than entrepreneurs who gave other types of reasons. In a study of 92 nascent entrepreneurs, Carter used a list of reasons similar to the list of reasons used in this study and generated a set of four factors: autonomy or independence, task interest, wealth or income, and a desire to stay in the community. She found that nascent men entrepreneurs rated wealth and prestige higher than nascent women entrepreneurs. Both men and women rated the autonomy factor higher than the other factors. Women appeared to place a higher value on staying in the community, relative to their rating on wealth.

Extrapolating from these findings, we argue that the reasons men and women offer for choosing careers are different whether they choose self-employment, or another career option. We hypothesize:

Hypothesis 2: Women (nascent entrepreneurs and the comparison group) rate the six kinds of career reasons differently than men (nascent entrepreneurs and the comparison group).

Taken together, our hypotheses suggest that reasons offered by entrepreneurs for getting into business will be similar to the reasons offered by nonentrepreneurs for having jobs, but in either case the reasons given by women will differ from those given by men. Implicit in these two hypotheses is our belief that any differences between entrepreneurs and nonentrepreneurs in their career reasons may be driven by differences in a failure to account for the proportion of gender in the samples. Typically, men started businesses at rates that were two to five times higher than women (Reynolds et al., 2000). Previous samples of entrepreneurs were likely to have significantly more men than women compared to a sample of people who have jobs. The proportion of men and women needs to be recognized when analyzing samples of entrepreneurs and nonentrepreneurs. If the gender variable is controlled, there may not be any differences in reasons between entrepreneurs and others, but women may offer different reasons than men.

4. Method

4.1. Sample

The data for this research were obtained from the PSED, a national database of individuals who were in the process of starting companies. The Institute for Social Research at the University of Michigan administers the PSED (, http://projects.isr.umich.edu/psed/). Detailed descriptions of the methods and sampling used to generate the PSED can be found in Reynolds (2000). PSED data used in this study involve three different samples of individuals, all of whom were initially identified through a random-digit dialing (RDD) telephone survey procedure conducted in two phases.

In the first phase, Market Facts Inc., telephoned households through their TeleNation surveys, which involve a minimum of 1000 completed interviews of adults (500 female, 500 male) 18 years of age or older over a 3-day period. Up to three attempts were made on each selected telephone number. During 1998 to 1999, through successive waves of phone calls, an initial sample of RDD calls were made, totaling 31,261 individuals (15,662 females and 15,599 males). Two questions in the telephone screening were designed to identify people who might be starting businesses (either as autonomous start-ups or as something being done in cooperation with a current employer).

- Are you, alone or with others, now trying to start a business?
- Are you, alone or with others, now starting a new business or new venture for your employer? An effort that is part of your job assignment?

A respondent could answer "no" or "yes" to either question, thereby placing him- or herself into one of four categories (no start-up activity, start-up activity in conjunction with an employer, autonomous start-up activity, or both kinds of start-up activity). For purposes of this research, only individuals falling into the autonomous start-up category were considered eligible for the designation "nascent entrepreneur." Two additional questions asked in the telephone screening were used to separate those people actively involved in autonomous start-up from those who were perhaps thinking about it, but not actively involved. These questions inquired (a) whether the respondent anticipated becoming an "owner" (in whole or in part) of the business being developed, and (b) whether there had been any ongoing business organizing activity during the immediately preceding 12 months. Affirmative answers to both questions were necessary for individuals to be considered "nascent entrepreneurs." The result was a total of 1494 nascent entrepreneurs (561 females, 933 males) eligible for the longer telephone interviews conducted by the University of Wisconsin Survey Research Laboratory (UWSRL).

In the second phase of the research, respondents who met the inclusion criteria were called by the UWSRL and were interviewed extensively by telephone. At the conclusion of these telephone interviews, participants were sent a detailed mail questionnaire. One of the early questions in the telephone interview asked whether the business being organized had achieved sufficient cash flow for 3 months to pay expenses and the owner–manager's salary. If the answer was affirmative, as it was for some 27% of the people contacted (Reynolds, 2000), then the activity was considered an "infant business" no longer in the organization stage and the respondent was dropped from the overall telephone interview sample.

4.1.1. Oversample of women

The Entrepreneurial Research Consortium (ERC), which consisted primarily of academic institutions, financed the original data collection for the PSED. Additional financial support was later obtained from the National Science Foundation (NSF), but these funds were earmarked for the specific purposes of generating a telephone oversampling of women and minorities. (Note: As the funds for oversampling of minorities arrived well into the research process, the only oversampling included in the present data set was the oversampling for women.) The 1494 eligible nascent entrepreneurs (NEs) noted above consequently fell into the four categories formed by the intersection of respondent gender with source of support (ERC or NSF). The ERC funds were used to collect information from both female and male respondents, whereas the NSF funds were used to collect telephone information *only* from females. Interviews were completed with 148 ERC females (51.41% of the original group of eligible NE females), 222 ERC males (46.64% of the originally eligible NE males), 154 NSF females (56.62% of the originally eligible NE females) and 45 of the 457 NSF males. Although the NSF funds were intended for interviewing only females, sometimes females screened by Market Facts reported on start-up activities that were being undertaken by males in the household. When UWSRL conducted the phone interview, the person most responsible for the start-up initiative was asked to provide information on the start-up. A comparison of variables that identified the sex of the founder of a solo start-up or that of team members, the first names of respondents, and interview notes made at the conclusion of the phone interview were used to ascertain the correct identification of the respondent's sex.

At the end of the telephone interview, respondents were asked to volunteer their first name and address, so that they could be sent a mail questionnaire and a US$25 payment for taking part in the telephone interview. Not all respondents agreed to provide a name and address. Respondents were also offered a payment of an additional US$25 for completion of the mail survey. Some respondents who agreed to answer the mail questionnaire did not, and some respondents did not answer all of the questions we used. Thus, our sample consisted of nascent entrepreneurs starting independent business ventures who answered questions on the mail questionnaire that were of interest in the present study. The category sizes were as follows: 108 ERC females, 149 ERC males, 97 NSF females, and 30 NSF males. The total of 384 represented an overall response rate for our questions of 39% of the originally eligible individuals engaged in start-up activities.

The comparison group for the present research was the initial comparison group of 119 females and 104 males. However, this comparison group actually included four people (two females and two males) who at the 1-year follow-up interview indicated that they had started businesses. We eliminated these four people from the comparison group on the grounds that their answers to the "reasons" questions most probably dealt with their intended start-up, rather than their (current) work for others. The resulting group of 219 completed a shorter version of the telephone interview, with 174 (89 female, 85 male) also completing the questions of interest here.

4.2. Use of weights

The PSED data set comes with "post-stratification weights for each respondent based on estimates from the U.S. Census Bureau's Current Population Survey (Reynolds, 2000). The post-stratification scheme was based on gender, age, household income, and the four National Census Regions [Northeast, South, Midwest, and West]. The scheme produces a total of 144 cells for weighting adjustments" (p. 177). The weights are essential for drawing conclusions intended to generalize to the entire U.S. population. According to Reynolds (p. 181), "any analysis should be completed with a weighted sample. .... This is a reflection of the number of procedures employed in the sampling and data collection that increased the yield and efficiency of the procedures." Details about the creation and application of weights in this research are described in Appendix A.

4.3. Measures of reasons

Eighteen items from the mail survey of the PSED database (items G1a–r) were selected for coding and analysis. Twelve of these items were adopted from the SARIE survey. Ten are a subset of the 14 items Shane et al. (1991, p. 445) found significant in their factor analysis comparing the reasons of entrepreneurs in Britain, New Zealand, and Norway. From their findings we selected and adapted items with factor scores greater than .50 from each of their four factor constructs. Three items represent innovation (m—to develop an idea for a product, c—to be innovative and in the forefront of technology, h—to grow and learn as a person) (alphabetic designations as listed in Tables 1 and 2). Two items represent independence (b— to have greater flexibility for my personal and family life, f—to have considerable freedom to adapt my own approach to work). Three items represent recognition (a—to achieve a higher position for myself in society, e—to be respected by my friends, l—to achieve something and get recognition for it). Moreover, two items represent roles (d—to continue a family tradition, i—to follow the example of a person I admire). We also adapted two items from other SARIE studies (Birley and Westhead, 1994; Scheinberg and MacMillan, 1988) having to do with financial success (g—to give myself, my spouse, and children financial security; k—to earn a larger personal income). In addition to these two items, we added two items to the financial success category (n—to have a chance to build great wealth or a very high income; j—to build a business my children can inherit). Finally, we added four items (items o, p, q, r) to represent the pursuit of self-realization that can motivate individuals to become entrepreneurs (o—fulfill a personal vision; p—to lead and motivate others; q—to have the power to greatly influence an organization; r—to challenge myself).

The 18 items were asked in the following manner. For the nascent entrepreneurs, the items were preceded by this question: "To what extent are the following reasons important to you in establishing this new business?" For the comparison group, the items were preceded by this question: "To what extent are the following important to you in your decisions about your work and career choices? " Both groups responded to each item on a 1 to 5 scale: 1, *to no extent*; 2, *little extent*; 3, *some extent*; 4, *great extent*; 5, *to a very great extent*.

4.4. Corrections for missing item responses

The total number of respondents for the 18 questions varied by question, from a low of 578 for the item having to do with "build a business my children can inherit" to a high of 586 for two of the items, one of which was "financial success." Across the 18 items, different respondents omitted different items. The result was that there were only 558 individuals who answered all 18 items. It is these 558 people (384 nascent entrepreneurs, 174 comparison

Table 2
Factor loadings for reasons items: six factor solution, $N = 558$

G1 #	Factor:	1 Self-Realization	2 Financial Success	3 Roles	4 Innovation	5 Recognition	6 Independence
	Sum of squared rotated loadings:	2.60	2.41	1.98	1.98	1.75	1.50
	Percentage variance accounted for:	14.43	13.40	11.01	10.98	9.72	8.32
	Cronbach α:	.78	.76	.73	.63	.60	.58
r	To challenge myself	**.77**	a				
o	To fulfill a personal vision	**.68**					
h	Grow and learn as a person	**.66**					.37
p	To lead and motivate others	**.65**			.33		
q	Power to influence an organization	**.41**			.48		
k	Earn a larger personal income		**.81**				
g	Financial security		**.80**				
n	Build great wealth, high income		**.66**		.35	.38	
j	Build business children can inherit		**.61**[b]		.31		
d	To continue a family tradition			**.78**			
i	Follow example of a person I admire	.38		**.72**			
e	To be respected by my friends			**.64**		.60	
c	Innovative, forefront of technology				**.78**		
m	To develop an idea for a product				**.72**		
l	Achieve something, get recognition					**.78**	
a	Gain a higher position for myself		.31	.32		**.54**	
b	Get greater flexibility for personal life						**.79**
f	Free to adapt my approach to work	.34					**.68**

[a] Factor loadings smaller than .30 have been suppressed.
[b] Cronbach alpha shown for this factor is with item j removed to increase the reliability of the remaining scale.

group individuals) whose answers were factor analyzed to determine the underlying structure of the items.

5. Analysis and results

5.1. Model testing

As noted earlier, the 18 items in this section of the PSED were developed on the basis of prior research to reflect six categories of the reasons people might choose one career path over another: innovation (items c, h, m), independence (items b, f,) recognition (items a, e, l), roles (items d, i), financial success (items g, j, k, n), and self-realization (items o, p, q, r). See Table 2 for a listing of the reasons items.

We first tested the predictive validity of this model by subjecting the data to a principal components factor analysis (listwise deletion of missing values, varimax rotation) with the analysis directed to produce six factors. The analysis was conducted on the reduced PSED data set of 558 nascent entrepreneurs and comparison group participants. Because the test of validity intended no between-group contrasts, the factor analysis was conducted on raw scores, not weighted scores. This analysis accounted for a total of over 68% of the variance, and the rotation required eight iterations to converge. The six factors produced showed truly remarkable similarity to the theoretical dimensions—only two of the items (h and e) were out of place. As shown in Table 2, the first factor, self-realization, involved five items (Cronbach α reliability of the scale=.78), the second, financial success, involved three items (Cronbach α=.76 for the three-item scale, dropping item j), the third, roles, involved three items (α=.73), and the remaining factors (innovation achievement, recognition, and independence) had two items apiece (α levels, respectively, .63, .60, and .58). Two of the 18 items (q and e) had cross-loadings that exceeded the usual rejection criterion of $\pm.40$, but in each case the Cronbach α for the scale would have been reduced or eliminated by dropping them. To retain as many items as possible, we used this reliability criterion (which led us to drop item j), rather than the cross-loading criterion. It is always difficult to obtain high Cronbach α levels when scales consist of only two items, and because the last three scales were an identical match to their conceptual counterparts, we elected to use them despite their marginal reliabilities. To test the hypotheses we calculated values for each of the six reason scales by summing the items in each scale and dividing by the number of items associated with the scale.

5.2. Comparisons of reasons

Because the number of participants was reduced due to missing data on the reasons questions, the mail questionnaire weights to be applied to factor scores prior to conducting the ANOVA were adjusted so that they summed to 205, 179, 89, and 85, respectively. The weighted scores, by groups, are shown in Table 3, which also indicates the number of participants in each group and the standard deviation of the adjusted mail questionnaire

N.M. Carter et al. / Journal of Business Venturing 18 (2003) 13–39

Table 3
Mean scores for six weighted[a] reasons by groups

	Nascent entrepreneurs		Comparison group		Total
	Female $n = 205$ $wt_{S.D.} = 0.28$	Male $n = 179$ $wt_{S.D.} = 0.30$	Female $n = 89$ $wt_{S.D.} = 0.38$	Male $n = 85$ $wt_{S.D.} = 0.71$	
Independence					
M	4.23	4.10	4.06	4.18	4.15
S.D.	1.78	1.34	1.76	2.97[b]	1.89
Financial success					
M	3.68	3.92	3.77	3.98	3.82
S.D.	1.74	1.37	1.54	2.66	1.78
Self-realization					
M	3.67	3.56	3.77	3.68	3.65
S.D.	1.59	1.21	1.54	2.43	1.63
Recognition					
M	2.76	2.71	3.34	3.33	2.92
S.D.	1.44	1.31	1.66	2.84	1.74
Innovation					
M	2.61	2.74	2.70	2.91	2.71
S.D.	1.54	1.31	1.45	2.37	1.62
Roles					
M	1.96	1.88	2.94	2.98	2.24
S.D.	1.12	.90	1.49	2.42	1.48

[a] Each individual's reasons factor scores were multiplied by the individual's demographic weight for the mail questionnaire, with the original mail questionnaire weights corrected to sum to the total n by group and gender. Thus within each of the four Group × Gender cells, the mean of the corrected weights is 1.0.

[b] The larger standard deviations for weighted means in this column reflect the fact that as a group, it also has the highest standard deviation for mail questionnaire weights.

weights. The weights were more variable among males in the comparison group than among participants in any of the other three groups, so the standard deviations of weighted factor scores were also higher in this group. High within-subject variability, of course, acts to reduce the likelihood of finding statistically significant differences across groups, so the ANOVA on weighted scale values can be regarded as a relatively conservative test of the hypotheses.

The weighted scores were subjected to a $2 \times 2 \times 6$ (Group × Gender × Reasons) analysis of variance with repeated measures on the reasons variable. The primary hypothesis of the research was tested by the Group × Reasons interaction, as weighted score patterns of entrepreneurs were compared with the weighted score patterns of the comparison group participants. The ANOVA revealed a significant Group × Reasons interaction, $F(5,2770) = 28.25$, $P < .0001$. On four of the clusters of reasons for occupational choice—self-realization, financial success, innovation, and independence—the largest mean difference between participant groups (averaged across gender within group) was less than .15. On the remaining two clusters of reasons, recognition and roles, scores for nascent entrepreneurs (both female and male) were substantially lower than comparable scores for the comparison group (.6 lower for recognition, over 1 point lower for roles). The findings provide mixed support for accepting Hypothesis 1 that nascent entrepreneurs and a comparison group have similar sets of reasons for their career choices. There was no significant difference between nascent entrepreneurs and the comparison group on four of the scales (self-realization, financial success, innovation, and independence). There was, however, a significant difference between nascent entrepreneurs and the comparison group on two of the scales (recognition and roles). Men in the process of starting a business assigned the lowest score of either group, across all reasons categories to the role scale. Apparently, the influence of role models on their career choice is minimal compared to other reasons.

It is important to note that this group-based difference on motives having to do with public views of one's behavior (external validation and roles) was a very robust finding. For example, if the analyses were conducted using the unweighted mean scores from the six scale values, rather than the weighted scores, there was a significant Group × Reasons interaction; with the same two clusters of reasons showing a difference between nascent entrepreneurs and people in the comparison group. Or, if the factor analysis was conducted so that the "minimum eigenvalue" criterion was used to terminate the factor analysis, rather than specifying the six factors that tests the theoretical criterion, the result was four factors (accounting for 58% of the variance) instead of the six reported here. One of those four factors consisted of items e, d, i, and a (four of the five items that constituted Factors 3 and 5 in the six-factor solution). A 2 × 2 × 4 (Group × Gender × Reasons) repeated measures ANOVA computed on these four reasons categories showed a significant Group × Reasons interaction with the only difference occurring on the e–d–i–a cluster, with the scores for nascent entrepreneurs again lower than those for comparison individuals.

In addition to the significant Group × Reasons interaction, the 2 × 2 × 6 repeated measures ANOVA on weighted scale values also showed a highly significant main effect difference among the six types of reasons, with independence having the overall highest scores and roles having the overall lowest scores, $F(5,2770) = 292.20$, $P < .0001$. This ordering makes it clear that the significant differences between nascent entrepreneurs and the control group occurred on the scales that were rated as less important to both groups (such as roles). On scales that were highly rated (such as independence achievement, financial success, and self-realization), there were no significant differences between the two groups. It should also be noted that the mean scores for the nascent entrepreneurs tended to be lower overall than scores in the control group $F(1,554) = 5.57$, $P < .019$. This difference, however, is most probably attributable to the two scales shown to be significantly different in the Group × Reasons interaction.

Finally, the analysis showed a small but significant difference between men and women on some of the weighted scale values, with men having higher scores on financial success and innovation than women, regardless of their group of origin, $F(5,2770) = 2.67$, $P < .02$. This finding partially supports Hypothesis 2 that women would have differences in the six kinds of reasons compared to men.

Although the score women assigned to financial success was lower than that given by men, women still saw financial success as an important reason in career choice, equal in importance to them as self-realization. As illustrated in Table 3, the score for women on financial success, like the score for men, is their second highest ranking, exceeded only by the desire for independence. This finding supports the results of Fischer et al. (1993) who found that financial success motivated women. Similarly, it is noteworthy that the mean score that nascent women entrepreneurs gave independence was the highest assigned by all groups, across all reasons. This is similar to the results of Carter (1997), who found that both men and women starting businesses desired autonomy and independence, but for women it was their highest work value. Similarly, Gatewood et al. (1995) found that nascent women entrepreneurs often reported "want[ing] to be my own boss" as the reason for starting their ventures, and Buttner and Moore (1997) found self-employed women were most motivated by self-determination.

6. Discussion

Implicit in prior research on the reasons entrepreneurs offer for getting into business was an assumption that entrepreneurs pursued entrepreneurial activity because of greater interest in such reasons as financial success, independence, and self-actualization. Entrepreneurs were assumed to offer such reasons because they wanted "more of" these reasons than individuals who were pursuing jobs. Entrepreneurs wanted more financial success, more independence, and more self-actualization than others. Yet, surprisingly, prior studies offered no specific tests of this assumption. Previous studies were typically retrospective (surveying only successful entrepreneurs long after they had started their firms) and often failed to compare the reasons of entrepreneurs with other individuals. Are the reasons for starting businesses similar for nascent entrepreneurs compared to the general population?

The present study reveals that nascent entrepreneurs were both similar to, and different from, the general population. Entrepreneurs were similar to nonentrepreneurs in the kinds of reasons they offered for career choice on self-realization, financial success, innovation, and independence. Both entrepreneurs and nonentrepreneurs rated independence, financial success, and self-realization as more important than recognition, innovation or roles. In fact, as measured by a composite of the six scales, nonentrepreneurs scored higher than nascent entrepreneurs on these dimensions. Overall, these findings argue against considering entrepreneurs to be qualitatively different from individuals who pursue other career options. In reasons for career choice, entrepreneurs do not seem to fit the stereotype held about them in the popular wisdom (Shaver, 1995).

The two between-group differences that were obtained were on the scale values that both nascent entrepreneurs and nonentrepreneurs ranked low: roles and recognition. By comparison to the nonentrepreneurs, nascent entrepreneurs offered reasons for getting into business that were less influenced by external validation from others: the respect of friends, family traditions, the examples of others, achieve something and get recognition, and gain a higher position for myself.

There were differences in reasons for career choice by gender. Males (entrepreneurs and nonentrepreneurs) rated financial success and innovation higher than females (entrepreneurs and nonentrepreneurs) as a reason for choosing a career. This finding was consistent with previous research by Carter (1997) and Gatewood et al. (1995).

In summary: (1) nascent entrepreneurs were more similar to nonentrepreneurs than they were different. The primary exception is in terms of desiring recognition or external validation: nascent entrepreneurs were less likely to do so; and (2) males were different from females. Males were more likely to seek financial success and opportunities to create new products or technology than women.

6.1. Concerns

There might be a concern that the way the reasons for career choice were presented to the nascent entrepreneurs and the control group influenced their responses. Nascent entrepreneurs were asked "To what extent are the following reasons important to you in establishing this new business?" while the comparison group was asked "To what extent are the following important to you in your decisions about your work and career choices?" The nascent entrepreneurs were asked to offer a prospective account of their reasons for undertaking the new task of developing a new business, while the comparison group may have interpreted their question to account for their decision to stay in their current job, rather than provide reasons for why they would decide to choose a career. Although there may be some semantic nuances between the ways these two questions were presented, we believe that those individuals in the comparison group were offering a logic for their current career *choice*: their reasons for staying in their current position would reflect their reasons for choosing to stay in their current position.

Given that the control group of individuals was selected to represent the population of adults in the United States, it should contain a certain number of individuals who report being self-employed. When screened during the Market Facts interview, these individuals would have responded that they were not at the time of the interview, "alone or with others attempting to start a new business." Instead, these individuals may have been self-employed for a number of years. We would expect their responses to the *reason* questions to reflect their present work status, as managers/owners of the businesses, rather than as nascent entrepreneurs explaining why they are considering self-employment as a career option. As owners, their responses should be similar to others in the control group.

To test this supposition we first determined if there were self-employed individuals in the control group. Both nascent entrepreneurs and control group respondents were asked about their occupational status during their phone interviews. Specifically, respondents were asked, "In terms of current work activity, are you involved in any of the following?" Response options included: working for others (full time vs. part time); a small business owner or self-employed; a manager of a business; a homemaker; retired; student (full time vs. part time); or unemployed. Multiple responses for the categories were allowed. Thirty-nine individuals in the control group reported they were small business owners or self employed, and of these, 16 indicated they also worked full time for others while being self-employed.

To determine whether these individuals might change the outcome of the analyses, we removed the self-employed individuals from the control group data and reran the factor analysis and repeated measures analysis of variance. The factor structure remained essentially the same, and the six-cluster repeated measure analysis (weighted) revealed the same reasons by group interaction as before, $F(5,2570) = 24.89$, $P < .0001$, and the same reasons by gender interaction as before $F(5,2570) = 2.83$, $P < .02$. The findings generated from all of these analyses offer remarkably similar results.

6.2. Implications

If one agrees with the generalizability of this sample of nascent entrepreneurs and the comparison group, these findings offer an important answer to some questions about differences between entrepreneurs and nonentrepreneurs. Overall, it would appear that nascent entrepreneurs offer reasons for starting businesses that are similar to the reasons offered by nonentrepreneurs for choosing jobs: independence, self-realization, financial success, innovation. Business start-up or "a job in an organization" are both pathways to meeting the same goals. This finding has significant implications for research and practice.

We believe that the findings presented here challenge prior beliefs and theories that suggest that individuals will choose entrepreneurship because they desire higher levels of financial success, self-realization, and independence compared to other individuals. The evidence presented here does not support this view. The desire for financial success, self-realization, and independence is important it seems, to nearly everyone, not just to nascent entrepreneurs. We would hope that one important message from the evidence presented here is that nascent entrepreneurs are not, in terms of their reasons for career choice, very different than others.

These findings should be encouraging evidence for those who suggest that there may be other kinds of cognitive and behavioral factors that affect an individual's decision to start a firm versus the choice of some other career. For example, Krueger et al. (2000) argued that perceived self-efficacy and perceived feasibility of accomplishing new business creation would have a significant impact on career choice. From our perspective, this argument is one about the likely effectiveness of a process, rather than a difference in the intent behind the process. Entrepreneurship educators should take note. The perception of the feasibility of business creation can be modified through education, training, and feedback (Gatewood, 1993; Gatewood et al., 2001). Individuals can be taught knowledge, skills, and behaviors to improve their effectiveness in the tasks necessary for business creation. Knowledge and skills may have more of an impact on an individual's choice of starting a business than any assumed innate desire. Greater insights about the factors influencing an individual's choice to pursue entrepreneurial activity could lead to better designed economic growth and development programs.

The consistency of the factors generated in this study of nascent entrepreneurs to those reported in the previous retrospective studies (Birley and Westhead, 1994; Scheinberg and MacMillan, 1988; Shane et al., 1991) give us confidence in the validity of the items associated with the six factor solution (self-realization, financial success, roles, innovation, recognition, and independence). Given that the 18 items used in this study did not completely correspond to the 23 items used by Birley and Westhead (1994) and Shane et al. (1991) or the 38 motivational items used in Scheinberg and MacMillan (1988), the degree of consistency can be viewed as some triumph. We believe that any differences in the results between the present and previous studies are more likely a function of sample selection. For example, although Birley and Westhead (1994) and Shane et al. (1991) used the same items for analysis, their factor results were different. Shane et al. (1991) did not find a consistent factor for entrepreneurs in their three-country study on the financial success items. We believe that the sampling procedures used in the PSED mitigates any affects on the factor analyses that might be caused by a selection bias, either in the selection of nascent entrepreneurs or in the selection of the comparison group.

The selection of a sample of individuals to represent nascent entrepreneurs and the sample of individuals to represent the general population is critical. This study surveyed entrepreneurs in the process of starting firms, and their reasons are likely to offer a concurrent logic for their actions. It is doubtful whether surveying individuals who had successfully started businesses would accurately capture the diversity of ratings on career reasons. As we noted earlier, a sample of successful entrepreneurs surveyed about their retrospections of start-up reasons may have a significant "left-censored" bias, in that all entrepreneurs who attempted to start businesses but quit, or who started businesses that no longer exist, would not be in the sample. In addition, retrospective "stories" may tell us more about the present views of entrepreneurs than about views they held at the time of venture creation (Golden, 1992; Huber and Power, 1985). Given these two important limitations, it is not surprising that studies involving successful entrepreneurs produced some of the "facts" that are now called into question by an improved methodology. Finally, this study not only surveyed individuals in the process of starting firms, it also provided a comparison group whose characteristics generalized to the population of individuals in the United States. We believe that this attention to the characteristics of the sample of entrepreneurs and the comparison group is an important standard for other researchers who desire to make generalizations about their findings.

6.3. Speculations

Our speculation that previous research findings about the reasons individuals give for starting a business may be flawed because of their retrospective bias, or because of their historical setting, appear to be supported. Nascent entrepreneurs are not unlike others making career choices, perhaps in large part because the "job of entrepreneurship" as a career choice has changed. Similarly, the fact that we found only limited differences in the reasons between men and women (only differences on *some* of the reasons) may also be time dependent. The finding may be a harbinger that career paths and interests of men and women are converging. Differences in gender may represent a social milieu that reflects a moment in time that, as time passes, will likely change. The findings presented here, therefore, should be viewed in the context of time and place (Aldrich, 1999).

Some scholars may disagree with our perspective that an entrepreneur's retrospective reasons for starting a business may not be an accurate depiction of that entrepreneur's reasons at the time of start-up. It might be plausible that the reasons entrepreneurs offer are stable over a long period of time. We suggest that both views will be subject to testing when longitudinal data from the PSED becomes available.

It should also be noted that at the time of submission of this article, no determination had been made regarding the outcome of the start-up efforts of the nascent entrepreneurs that were sampled for this study. Based on prior longitudinal studies of nascent entrepreneurial efforts (Carter et al., 1996; Gatewood et al., 1995; Reynolds and Miller, 1992; Reynolds and White, 1997), there is a high probability that many of these nascent entrepreneurs will not be successful in starting their companies. It might be plausible that the scores and ratings of reasons offered by nascent entrepreneurs who successfully start businesses may be different from nascent entrepreneurs who give up, or are still trying. In addition, successful nascent entrepreneurs may have scores and ratings of reasons that are different from the comparison group. An analysis of forthcoming longitudinal data from the PSED should offer insights about this issue.

7. Conclusions

These research results provide evidence that the reasons nascent entrepreneurs offered for starting a business are very similar to the career reasons of other individuals on such dimensions as self-realization, financial success, innovation and independence. The career reasons of nascent entrepreneurs were more similar to individuals choosing jobs, than they were different.

One issue that should not be underestimated in this study is the fact that this research is based on interviews of a representative sample of individuals in the process of starting a business. Moreover, the reasons offered for getting into business are prospective, rather than retrospective. These nascent entrepreneurs are offering their reasons for getting into business *before* the success (or failure) of their efforts are determined. Because these findings are based on prospective reasons, rather than retrospective accounts, we believe the results of this study should take precedence over previous studies where retrospective explanations for start-up have been offered. In short, the stereotype of the highly independent, financially driven, self-actualized entrepreneur may be nothing more than a distillation of the retrospective stories that entrepreneurs have told researchers in the past. In addition, this study systematically compared nascent entrepreneurs to a representative sample of nonentrepreneurs, a comparison that no other study, heretofore, has accomplished. The choices involved in sampling individuals to represent entrepreneurs matter, and any challenges to the findings presented here will require as thoughtful a process as this study for identifying individuals who are starting businesses. The identification of a comparison group matters as well, and questions about the generalizability of a study's findings necessitates some way to link the characteristics of the comparison sample to the population at large. We believe that this study marks a turning point in research on entrepreneurship, particularly for research on individuals involved in the process of starting businesses.

Acknowledgements

This material is based upon work supported by the National Science Foundation under Grant No. 9809841. Any opinions, findings, and conclusions or recommendations expressed in this material are those of the author(s) and do not necessarily reflect the views of the National Science Foundation.

The authors thank Paul Reynolds, Coordinator of the Entrepreneurial Research Consortium (ERC), for his tireless efforts on the Panel Study of Entrepreneurial Dynamics (PSED); Elizabeth Crosby and Nikhil Aggarwal for their research assistance; and two anonymous reviewers for their comments and insights during the revision process. The ERC has provided support for the development of the PSED with supplemental funding from the National Science Foundation [Nancy M. Carter, Principal Investigator, Grant SBR-9809841]. Support for the development and analysis of the PSED data used in this study was provided to Kelly G. Shaver and William B. Gartner from the Kauffman Center for Entrepreneurial Leadership. Support for the preparation of this paper was provided to Kelly G. Shaver and Nancy M. Carter from the Entrepreneurship and Small Business Research Institute (ESBRI).

Appendix A. Application of weights

When Reynolds (2000) states that "any analysis" should use weighted scores, we understand him to mean any analysis that involves comparisons between or among groups of respondents, where such factors as gender and nascent status are used to define the groups. By contrast, when there are *no* comparisons *across* demographically defined groups, the weights are superfluous. Specifically, for example, for the within-subjects factor analysis of the reasons variables, weights were not applied to the variable scores. Once the factor analysis (which was based on a total, nonsubdivided sample) was done, however, we applied the weighting system to the resulting factor scores, as we were then going to compare those factor scores across demographically defined groups of respondents.

The actual weights used in the PSED data set were significantly modified from the original Market Facts weights (Reynolds, 2000, p. 177). Specifically, because 144 weighting categories were too many for the size of the sample, this number was reduced to 32 (the factorial combination of two levels of respondent sex, four Census regions, two levels of household income, and two levels of respondent age). Second, the final weights were computed separately for the comparison group and for females and males within the entrepreneur groups. This was done to take into account the fact that the selection probabilities within the entrepreneur groups were different for females and males (because of the NSF-male empty interview cell). Within demographic groups the weights have always been normalized, so that the sum of weights for any particular subsample (e.g., nascent entrepreneur males) was equal to the total number of respondents in that subsample. Thus the phone interview weights sum to the number of respondents in the phone interviews, and the mail interview weights sum to the (smaller) number of participants who returned the mail survey. Following this logic, we modified the mail questionnaire weights in each of the four (nascent/comparison by female/male) respondent categories to reflect the fact that not all people who returned the mail questionnaire actually answered all items of interest to us. Thus our weights, like those for the overall phone survey and the overall mail survey, summed to the final cell sizes: 205 nascent females, 179 nascent males, 89 comparison group females, 85 comparison group males.

References

Ajzen, I., 1994. The theory of planned behavior. Organ. Behav. Hum. Decis. Processes 50, 179–211.

Alange, S., Scheinberg, S., 1988. Swedish entrepreneurship in a cross-cultural perspective. Frontiers of Entrepreneurship Research, Wellesley, MA: Babson College, 1–15.

Aldrich, H.E., 1999. Organizations Evolving. Sage, London.

Anscombe, G.E.M., 1956. Intention. Basil Blackwell, London.

Bigoness, W., 1988. Sex differences in job attribute preferences. J. Organ. Behav. 9, 139–147.

Birley, S., Westhead, P., 1994. A taxonomy of business start-up reasons and their impact on firm growth and size. J. Bus. Venturing 9, 7–31.

Blais, R.A., Toulouse, J.M., 1990. National, regional or world patterns of entrepreneurial motivation? An empirical study of 2,278 entrepreneurs and 1,733 non-entrepreneurs in fourteen countries on four continents. J. Small Bus. Entrepreneurship 7, 3–20.

Bonjean, C.M., 1966. Mass, class and the industrial community: a comparative analysis of managers, businessmen, and workers. Am. J. Sociol. 72 (2), 149–162.

Brenner, O.C., Tomkiewicz, J., 1979. Job orientation of males and females: are sex differences declining? Pers. Psychol. 32, 741–749.

Brush, C.G., 1992. Research on women business owners: past trends, a new perspective and future directions. Entrepreneurship Theory Pract. 2 (1), 1–24.

Buttner, E.H., Moore, D.P., 1997. Women's organizational exodus to entrepreneurship: self-reported motivations and correlates with success. J. Small Bus. Manage. 35 (1), 34–46.

Carroll, G.R., Mosakowski, E., 1987. The career dynamics of self-employment. Administrative Sci. Q. 32, 570–589.

Carter, N.M., 1997. Entrepreneurial processes and outcomes: the influence of gender. In: Reynolds, P.D., White, S.B. (Eds.), The Entrepreneurial Process. Westport, CT: Quorum Books, pp. 163–178.

Carter, N.M., Gartner, W.B., Reynolds, P.D., 1996. Exploring start-up event sequences. J. Bus. Venturing 11 (3), 151–166.

Collins, D.F., Moore, D.G., 1955. The Enterprising Man. Double Day, New York.

Cooper, A., 1971. The Founding of Technologically Based Firms. Center for Venture Management, Milwaukee, WI.

Davidsson, P., Lindmark, L., Olofsson, C., 1994. New firm formation and regional development in Sweden. Reg. Stud. 28 (4), 395–410.

Dubini, P., 1988. The influence of motivations and environment on business start-ups: some hints for public policies. J. Bus. Venturing 4, 11–26.

Fagenson, E.A., 1993. Personal value systems of men and women entrepreneurs versus managers. J. Bus. Venturing 8, 409–430.

Farmer, H.S., 1997. Gender differences in career development. In: Farmer, H.S. & Associates (Eds.), Diversity and Women's Career Development. Thousand Oaks, CA: Sage Publications, pp. 127–160.

Farmer, H.S., Wardrop, J., Anderson, M., Risinger, R., 1995. Women's career choices: focus on science, math and technology careers. J. Couns. Psychol. 42, 155–170.

Fischer, E.M., Reuber, A.R., Dyke, L.S., 1993. A theoretical overview and extension of research on sex, gender, and entrepreneurship. J. Bus. Venturing 8, 151–168.

Friberg, M., 1976. Is the salary the only incentive for work? (in Swedish). Sociol. Forsk. 1.

Gartner, W.B., 1985. A framework for describing and classifying the phenomenon of new venture creation. Acad. Manage. Rev. 10 (4), 696–706.

Gartner, W.B., 1988. Who is an entrepreneur? is the wrong question. Am. J. Small Bus. 12 (4), 11–32.

Gartner, W.B., 1989. Some suggestions for research on entrepreneurial traits and characteristics. Entrepreneurship Theory Pract. 14 (1), 27–38.

Gatewood, E.J., 1993. The expectancies in public sector venture assistance. Entrepreneurship Theory Pract. 17 (2), 91–95.

Gatewood, E.J., Shaver, K.G., Gartner, W.B., 1995. A longitudinal study of cognitive factors influencing start-up behaviors and success at venture creation. J. Bus. Venturing 10, 371–391.

Gatewood, E.J., Powers, J.B., Shaver, K.G., Gartner, W.B., 2001. The effects of perceived entrepreneurial ability on task persistence (Working paper).

Gilbert, M.R., 1997. Identity, space and politics: a critique of the poverty debates. In: Jones, J.P., Nast, H.J., Roberts, S.M. (Eds.), Thresholds in Feminist Geography: Difference, Methodology, Representation, pp. 29–45.

Golden, B., 1992. The past is the past—or is it? The use of retrospective accounts as indicators of past strategy. Acad. Manage. J. 35 (4), 848–860.

Gottfredson, L., 1981. Circumscription and compromise: a developmental theory of occupational aspirations. J. Couns. Psychol. 28, 545–579.

Hagen, E.E., 1962. On the Theory of Social Change: How Economic Growth Begins. Dorsey Press, Homewood, IL.

Harriman, A., 1985. Women/Men/Management. Praeger, New York.

Heider, F., 1958. The Psychology of Interpersonal Relations. Wiley, New York.

Hofstede, C., 1980. Culture's Consequences: International Differences in Work Related Values. Sage, Beverly Hills, CA.

Huber, G., Power, D., 1985. Retrospective reports of strategic-level managers: guidelines for increasing their accuracy. Strategic Manage. J. 6, 171–180.

Kanter, R., 1977. Men and Women of the Corporation. Basic Books, New York.

Katz, J.A., 1992. A psychological cognitive model of employment status choice. Entrepreneurship Theory Pract. 17 (1), 29–37.

Knight, R.M., 1987. Can business schools produce entrepreneurs? Frontiers of Entrepreneurship Research, 603–604.

Kolvereid, L., 1996a. Organizational employment versus self-employment: reasons for career choice intentions. Entrepreneurship Theory Pract. 20 (3), 23–31.

Kolvereid, L., 1996b. Prediction of employment status choice intentions. Entrepreneurship Theory Pract. 21 (1), 47–58.

Krueger Jr., N.F., Brazeal, D.V., 1994. Entrepreneurship potential and potential entrepreneurs. Entrepreneurship Theory Pract. 19 (3), 91–104.

Krueger, N.F., Carsrud, A.L., 1993. Entrepreneurial intentions: applying the theory of planned behavior. Entrepreneurship Reg. Dev. 5 (4), 315–330.

Krueger, N.F., Reilly, M.D., Carsrud, A.L., 2000. Competing models of entrepreneurial intentions. J. Bus. Venturing 15, 411–432.

Larwood, L., Gattikers, U., 1989. A comparison of the career paths used by successful men and women. In: Gutek, B., Larwood, L. (Eds.), Women's Career Development, pp. 129–156.

Maslow, A.H., 1943. A theory of human motivation. Psychol. Rev., 370–396 (July).

McClelland, D.C., 1961. The Achieving Society. Free Press, New York.

McClelland, D.C., Winter, D.G., 1969. Motivating Economic Achievement. Free Press, New York.

Nelson, J.I., 1968. Participation and integration: the case of the small businessman. Am. Sociol. Rev. 33 (3), 427–438.

Powell, G., 1988. Women and Men in Management. Sage, Beverly Hills.

Reynolds, P.D., 1994. Autonomous firm dynamics and economic growth in the United States 1986–1990. Reg. Stud. 28 (4), 429–442.

Reynolds, P.D., 2000. National panel study of U.S. business startups: background and methodology. In: Katz, J.A. (Ed.), Advances in Entrepreneurship, Firm Emergence, and Growth, vol. 4, Stanford, CT: JAI Press, pp. 153–227.

Reynolds, P.D., Maki, W.R., 1990. Business volatility and economic growth. Final Project Report. Small Business Administration, Contract SBA, Washington, DC, 3067-OA-99, May 1990.

Reynolds, P.D., Miller, B.A., 1992. New firm gestation: conception, birth, and implications for research. J. Bus. Venturing 7, 1–14.

Reynolds, P.D., White, S.B., 1997. The Entrepreneurial Process. Greenwood Publishing, Westport, CT.

Reynolds, P.D., Hay, M., Bygrave, W.D., Camp, S.M., Autio, E., 2000. Global Entrepreneurship Monitor: 2000 Executive Report. Kauffman Center for Entrepreneurial Leadership, Kansas City.

Schein, E.H., 1978. Career Dynamics: Matching Individual and Organizational Needs. Addison-Wesley, Readings, MA.

Scheinberg, S., MacMillan, I.C., 1988. An 11-country study of motivations to start a business. In: Kirchoff, B.A., Long, W.A., McMullan, W.E., Vesper, K.H., Wetzel, W.E. (Eds.), Frontiers of Entrepreneurship Research, Wellesley, MA: Babson College, pp. 669–687.

Sexton, D.L., Bowman-Upton, N., 1990. Female and male entrepreneurs: psychological characteristics and their role in gender-related discrimination. J. Bus. Venturing 5, 29–36.

Shane, S., Kolvereid, L., Westhead, P., 1991. An exploratory examination of the reasons leading to new firm formation across country and gender. J. Bus. Venturing 6, 431–446.

Shapero, A., 1975. The displaced uncomfortable entrepreneur. Psychol. Today, 83–88 (November).

Shaver, K.G., 1985. The Attribution of Blame: Causality, Responsibility, and Blameworthiness. Springer-Verlag, New York.

Shaver, K.G., 1995. The entrepreneurial personality myth. Bus. Econ. Rev. 41 (3), 20–23.

Shaver, K.G., Scott, L.R., 1991. Person, process, choice: the psychology of new venture creation. Entrepreneurship Theory Pract. 16 (2), 23–45.

Simon, M., Houghton, S.M., Aquino, K., 2000. Cognitive biases, risk perception, and venture formation: how individuals decide to start companies. J. Bus. Venturing 15 (2), 113–134.

Smith, N.R., Miner, J.B., 1983. Type of entrepreneur, type of firm, and managerial innovation: Implications for organizational life cycle theory. Frontiers of Entrepreneurship Research. Wellesley, MA: Babson College, 51–71.

Vroom, V.H., 1967. Work and Motivation. Wiley, New York.

7.   The language of opportunity[1]

William B. Gartner, Nancy M. Carter and Gerald E. Hills

'To imagine a language is to imagine a form of life.'
Wittgenstein

INTRODUCTION

What do we talk about when we talk about opportunity? Our purpose in presenting a paper on opportunity at the Movements of Entrepreneurship workshop, knowing that there would be subsequent debate, discussion and dialogue and the time to undertake a revision of the paper (presented here), was to attempt to thoughtfully provoke a patient, intellectual 'pause' in what seems to be a movement to embrace the word 'opportunity' as a critical attribute of entrepreneurship. The advantage of the Movements workshop process has been the serendipity that has occurred between the initial inception of the paper and the product you see here. This chapter is the outcome of many different ideas and individuals that have met at this particular intellectual juncture (as will be noted later). Do not expect to find us at this place, again, in subsequent work on this topic. We can see many different pathways ahead, and we are likely to take a number of diverse directions in our exploration of opportunity as a topic of study.

There appears to be a bandwagon (Abrahamson, 1996) in the entrepreneurship literature for positing 'opportunity' as a fundamental aspect of the phenomenon of entrepreneurship (Gaglio, 1997; Kirzner, 1997; Venkataraman, 1997; Shane and Venkataraman, 2000; Gaglio and Katz, 2001). This heightened interest in the idea of opportunity has resulted in thoughtful discussion about definitions of the attributes of opportunity and explorations of the processes by which opportunity occurs, as well as the beginnings of specifying the value of the concept of opportunity to entrepreneurial studies (Erikson, 2001; Shane and Venkataraman, 2001; Singh, 2001; Zahra and Dess, 2001; Schoonhoven and Romanelli, 2001). Such a debate is healthy for helping all scholars clarify their assumptions about the characteristics of opportunity vis-à-vis entrepreneurship so that these ideas can be tested and their merit proven (Gartner, 2001).

Therein lies the rub. While there is some systematic evidence about the nature of opportunity by which current ideas can be tested (Kaish and Gilad, 1991; Busenitz, 1996; Hills and Schrader, 1998; Singh, Hills and Lumpkin, 1999; Shane, 2000), the interpretations of these results is, at best, equivocal (Gaglio and Katz, 2001).

It is our fear that current theoretical speculations about the nature of opportunity may direct us towards beliefs about this phenomenon that have little basis in fact (since little evidence, at this point, exists to support any one viewpoint), and such beliefs may make it more difficult to pursue other lines of reasoning or undertake empirical explorations that may lead toward more fruitful insights (Van Maanen, 1995a; 1995b; Martin and Frost, 1996; Pfeffer, 1997). In other words, if scholars talk about opportunity in certain ways, it is likely that our language will constrain our ability to consider other possible meanings that might be used by others, particularly those individuals who engage in the phenomenon of opportunity: entrepreneurs. What do they talk about when they talk about opportunity? In addition, we believe that the meanings that scholars use to construct a language about opportunity will also constrain their ability to see other possible facts about this phenomenon. You cannot see something if you cannot talk about it (Weick, 1979).

It became very apparent from the subsequent debate and discussion of the first version of the opportunity paper at the Movements conference (a paper entitled 'Entrepreneurial Opportunities are Enacted!') that our approach towards discussing the idea of opportunity has an inherent North American bias. Our citations are primarily from North American journals. The scholars we cite are primarily North Americans. Given that the evidence we use comes from North American entrepreneurs, support for our perspective on the nature of opportunity also promotes a North American perspective. We point this bias out, not only to indicate that the paper could be connected to the context of European scholars and their work on the nature of language, meaning, and scholarship (Czarniawska, 1997; 1998; Chan, 2000; Fournier and Grey, 2000; Ogbor, 2000; Hardy, Phillips and Clegg, 2001), but also to suggest that our ideas about opportunity are likely to limit the discourse on opportunity, as well. If we succeed in showing that the current scholarly discussion of opportunity has been somewhat limited (using our rather narrow North American perspective), then, it is likely that a more expansive knowledge of non-North American scholarship would lead to an even larger vocabulary about opportunity, as a phenomenon.

This chapter explores the following arguments. Discussions about the nature of opportunity are discussions about how circumstances external to the entrepreneur are construed. Most scholars currently pursue a line of reasoning about the nature of opportunity that suggests that opportunities are, so to speak, concrete realities waiting to be noticed, discovered, or observed by entrepreneurs (Kirzner, 1979; Shane, 2000; Shane and Venkataraman, 2000). We label this viewpoint the 'opportunity discovery' perspective. Such a perspective uses the economics literature to emphasize the importance of alertness, observation and the informational asymmetries among all individuals who are pursuing their best interests (Hayek, 1945; Arrow, 1974). We argue that such a view tells only one side of the story and that pursuing this line of reasoning, exclusively, may ignore important characteristics of opportunity, as a phenomenon. We propose another alternative. We argue that in many circumstances, opportunities are enacted, that is, the salient features of an opportunity only become apparent through the ways that entrepreneurs make sense of their experiences (Weick, 1979; Gartner, Bird and Starr, 1992; Sarasvathy, 2001). Indeed, we suggest that merely by talking about opportunities as a part of the circumstances of entrepreneurship, scholars invoke a way of making sense of the phenomenon of entrepreneurship that provokes entrepreneurs to see their experiences in a certain way. Entrepreneurs may talk about 'discovering opportunities' because that is the way we (academic scholars) talk about opportunity. We believe that 'opportunity enactment' perspective provides another way to talk about opportunity without using the dominant logic of economics. We suggest that the 'opportunity enactment' perspective stems from insights offered from the strategic identity and organization theory literatures, and that recognizing the contributions of these streams of research offers a number of ideas about how opportunities emerge and are pursued in organizations (Daft and Weick, 1984; Dutton and Jackson, 1987; Jackson and Dutton, 1988; Dutton, 1993b; Thomas, Clark and Gioia, 1993; Hill and Levenhagen, 1995; Gioia, Schultz and Corley, 2000; Scott and Lane, 2000). In the opportunity enactment perspective, opportunities are seen to emerge out of the imagination of individuals by their actions and their interactions with others. Conceptualizing entrepreneurship and opportunity as an emergent cognitive and social process is not new to the field of entrepreneurship (Shaver and Scott, 1991; Gartner, Bird and Starr, 1992; Gartner, 1993), yet social psychological approaches to the study of this phenomenon seem to have been lost in the current fashion for an economic rationality to this process.

OPPORTUNITIES ARE …

According to *Webster's* dictionary (1988, p. 828), opportunity is defined as: 'a favourable junction of circumstances, or a good chance for advancement or progress'. In this definition, then, opportunity depends on circumstances, and *Webster's* (1988, p. 242) defines circumstance as: 'a condition, fact, or event accompanying, conditioning or determining another, or a piece of evidence that indicates the probability or improbability of an event, or the sum of essential and environmental factors'. At least in the vernacular, then, opportunities seem to be 'favourable events'. How 'favourable events' are theoretically construed and, operationalized and studied, should be an important aspect of academic discussion with regard to the nature of opportunity.

In broad terms, 'favourable events' can be taken to mean 'the environment', which would be anything that is not, substantially, about the entrepreneur. (This assumption implies that one can separate the entrepreneur's experience from the entrepreneur. More on this later.) Academic scholarship on the nature and characteristics of environments has a long intellectual history and the breadth and depth of theory and empirical research on this topic is substantial (Hawley, 1950; Hall, 1972; Pfeffer and Salancik, 1978; Aldrich, 1979; Pfeffer, 1982; Meyer and Scott, 1983; Scott, 1992; Carroll and Hannan, 2000). Without appearing to be too simplistic, we suggest that a fundamental controversy among scholars who study entrepreneurial and organizational environments have centred on whether environments are best understood by employing subjective or objective measures (Scott, 1992, p. 141). Those scholars that put forward the use of subjective measures believe that the decisions of individuals (organizations) will be based on their perceptions of the salient features of an environment, irrespective of how an environment might be objectively measured (Lawrence and Lorsch, 1967; March and Olson, 1976; Weick, 1979). Individuals (organizations) will act based on what they know. In contrast, scholars who suggest objective measures posit that irrespective of an individual's (organization's) perceptions of the environment, the characteristics of an environment will have a substantive impact on the outcomes of an individual's (organization's) choices (Pfeffer and Salancik, 1978; Carroll and Hannan, 2000). The outcomes of an individual's (organization's) choices are likely to be affected by forces that may be outside of the perceptions and control of the individuals (organizations) affected. It is within this broad dichotomy of 'subjective versus objective' views of the environment that we will compare and contrast the 'opportunity discovery' and 'opportunity enactment' perspectives and suggest the type of language that each perspective might use in depicting the phenomenon of opportunity.

Discovered

The primary way that environments have been described from an opportunity discovery perspective has been to theorize and explore how entrepreneurs are involved with the recognition of and search for information (Kaish and Gilad, 1991; Busenitz, 1996; Gaglio, 1997; Shane and Venkataraman, 2000; Gaglio and Katz, 2001). In the opportunity discovery perspective, scholars have tended to believe that information (facts, knowledge, data) exists irrespective of the individuals who would have this information in their brains. This perspective is essentially, what constitutes 'an objective view of the environment'. In an objective view of the environment, information, just 'is'. Information exists without a context of how and why individuals relate and interact to it. Much of the debate for entrepreneurship scholars who have an objective view about the environment involves a discussion of *how* individuals recognize this objective information. The debate appears to hinge on whether individuals are seen to have an imperfect ability to access or process information (Arrow, 1974) or whether individuals are merely ignorant that such information exists (Kirzner, 1997). In either case, individuals are, in some fashion, inadequate to the task of accessing or understanding information in order to recognize and pursue opportunities. In the more extreme view of these two cases, Kirzner (1997) suggests that market processes are full of 'errors' in perceptions, and that entrepreneurial opportunities only occur when alert entrepreneurs correct these 'errors' by noticing and grasping them (pp. 70–71). Through a series of mental gymnastics, Kirzner (1997) suggests that alert individuals discover opportunities by *surprise*:

> What distinguishes *discovery* (relevant to hitherto unknown profit opportunities) from *successful search* (relevant to the deliberate production of information which one knew one lacked) is that the former (unlike the latter) involves that surprise which accompanies the realization that one had overlooked something in fact readily available...*The notion of discovery, midway between that of the deliberately produced information in standard search theory, and that of sheer windfall gain generated by pure chance, is central to the Austrian approach.* (p. 72)

Alert individuals are open to the possibility of 'unthought-of knowledge', (Kirzner, 1997, p. 74) and it is in this type of knowledge where profitable opportunities lie. Kirzner's view of opportunity typifies an objective view of the world, where opportunities are separate from individuals. Opportunities are waiting for individuals to see, what could have always been seen, but wasn't. Non-alert individuals are essentially blind. Opportunities are in the environment; just not visible to those who are not alert. Conversely, only alert individuals will be able to see opportunities that already exist. Shane and Venkataraman (2000) seem to best express this objective perspective about information as it is construed in their conception of 'opportunity':

> To have entrepreneurship, you must first have entrepreneurial opportunities. Entrepreneurial opportunities are those situations in which new goods, services, raw materials, and organizing methods can be introduced and sold at greater than their cost of production (Casson, 1982). Although recognition of entrepreneurial opportunities is a subjective process, the opportunities themselves are objective phenomena that are not known to all parties at all times. (p. 220)

Much like Kirzner (1997), Shane and Venkataraman (2000) assume an environment where people have different beliefs about the accuracy of information about various market factors. From their perspective, it is in the asymmetry of beliefs about the objective environment where opportunities are discovered, and subsequently exploited. In their framework, individuals who discover opportunities are likely to possess valuable information that others do not have (Venkataraman, 1997) or have cognitive abilities to process information in ways that others cannot (Sarasvathy, Simon and Lave, 1998). In any case, a fundamental premise of Shane and Venkataraman's (2000) logic assumes that objective information about an opportunity exists regardless of any individual's ability to access this information or accurately perceive it. Others are following this bandwagon. For example, Gaglio and Katz (2001) have recently presented a schema of the entrepreneurial alertness process, where alert individuals are hypothesized to have a more accurate and veridical perception of the environment. Again, inherent in Gaglio and Katz's logic is a view of the environment where opportunities are an objective reality, where accurately seeing an opportunity, is indeed, possible. Let us not underestimate this insight. From the opportunity discovery perspective, opportunities are real and concrete. The question of whether an opportunity will be identified is, therefore, nearly tautological. If an opportunity is discovered, an alert individual accurately saw it, if an opportunity is not discovered, then, no individual was alert enough.

In terms of the language that would depict the opportunity discovery perspective, obviously, the word 'discovery' is critical to how scholars describe the process of how individuals become involved with opportunities (Kirzner, 1985; 1997). The word, 'discovery' suggests that information can be found, noticed, made visible, exposed, or seen. We believe that the language of discovery implies that objective information is outside of the individual, who, through some process of awareness, is able to see what, heretofore was not apparent or obvious. Opportunity discovery, therefore, involves seeing, in its many forms, the objective characteristics of circumstances. While scholars conjecture that entrepreneurs discover opportunities, do entrepreneurs, in fact, discover them? Do entrepreneurs talk about discovery when they talk about opportunity? We would initially, at this point, suggest that if entrepreneurs do in fact, discover opportunities, we would expect that their language would reflect the use of such 'discovery' words as: see, notice, find, look. These words would be indicative of actions that individuals would undertake to recognize an opportunity as something that is objectively outside of themselves. Later on in the chapter we will 'see' whether entrepreneurs use discovery-oriented language when talking about their opportunities.

Enacted

The primary way that environments have been described from an opportunity enactment perspective has been to theorize and explore how entrepreneurs make sense of their circumstances through 'organizing' (Weick, 1979; Gartner, 1985; 1993; Gartner, Bird and Starr, 1992; Levenhagen, Porac and Thomas, 1993; Hill and Levenhagen, 1995). In the opportunity enactment perspective, opportunities are an *outcome* of the sensemaking activities of individuals (Daft and Weick, 1984; Dutton and Jackson, 1987; Jackson and Dutton, 1988; Dutton, 1993b; Thomas, Clark and Gioia, 1993; Hill and Levenhagen, 1995; Gioia, Schultz and Corley, 2000; Scott and Lane, 2000). In this perspective, environments are equivocal, that is, individuals will construct their circumstances through scanning, interpretation, and action (Daft and Weick, 1984; Thomas, Clark and Gioia, 1993). Environments are socially constructed, subjective *and* the product of an individual's (organization's) actions, rather than viewed as a set of fixed circumstances that must be responded to. As Weick (1979) suggests, 'The concept of the *enacted environment* is not synonymous with the concept of a *perceived environment* ... managers construct, rearrange, single out, and demolish many "objective" features of their surrounding ... The organizing model is based on the view that order is imposed rather than discovered, on the grounds that action defines cognition' (pp. 164–5). Indeed, Weick (1979) tends to put the enactment perspective in diametrical opposition to an objective view:

> The enactment perspective implies that people in organizations should be more self-conscious about and spend more time reflecting on the actual things they *do*. If people imagine that the environment is separate from the organization and lies out there to be scanned so that effective responses can be produced, then they will spend their resources outfitting themselves with the equivalents of high-powered binoculars to improve acuity. If people recognize that they create many of their own environments, then all of that effort to improve acuity is irrelevant. The organization concerned about its own enactment needs to discover ways to partial out the effects of its own interventions from the effect that would have happened had the observer never obtruded in the situation in the first place ... If environments are enacted then there is no such thing as a representation that is true or false, there simply are versions that are more and less reasonable (pp. 168–9).

From an enactment perspective, it is not about 'seeing' it is about 'sensemaking' (Weick, 1995). The gist of an enactment perspective is not to deny that certain concrete characteristics of an individual's (organization's) circumstances exist and have an impact. An enactment perspective does not deny the physics of gravity, for example. Rather, the opportunity enactment perspective offers sensitivity towards viewing an environment as having features that are determined by the scope of an individual's (organization's) actions. This perspective transports us to a very different appreciation of how and why an opportunity would occur. In the opportunity enactment perspective, opportunities emerge (Gartner, 1993), that is, opportunities will come into existence out of the day-to-day activities of individuals. If an entrepreneur recognizes an opportunity, as such, it would be only as an aspect of the retrospective sense making that follows action (i.e., How can I know what I think until I see what I say? [Weick, 1979, pp. 133–43]). What the idea of retrospective sensemaking implies is that the 'discovery' of an opportunity would merely be a realization, and therefore, a labelling of an ongoing set of entrepreneurial activities, one of which would be, 'the recognition of an opportunity'. In the opportunity enactment perspective, 'discovery' is a bracketing of a cacophony of experiences and activities that entrepreneurs are engaged in. That is, opportunities would be described as occurring from (as a part of, out, or after) activities that individuals are already involved in.

In terms of the language that would depict the opportunity enactment perspective, we would suggest that individuals would describe their actions and the circumstances surrounding their actions. Opportunities would be the result of what individuals do, rather than the result of what they see. In addition, opportunities would be recognized as occurring within a stream of other events and activities. We would expect that entrepreneurs would likely talk about the occurrence of an opportunity retrospectively, that is, entrepreneurs would make sense of the experience of opportunity recognition as an emergent process, where the opportunity that is recognized is an outgrowth of actions already taken.

WHAT DO ENTREPRENEURS SAY ABOUT OPPORTUNITY?

The way in which these ideas about the two perspectives about the nature of opportunity will be explored will be to analyse data from surveys of nascent entrepreneurs from the Panel Study of Entrepreneurial Dynamics (PSED). Specifically, we will investigate some of the written responses from an open-ended question on the PSED mail questionnaire that asks nascent entrepreneurs how the original idea for starting their businesses was developed. In addition, we will present some data about the kinds of initial activities that nascent entrepreneurs undertake vis-à-vis differences in whether nascent entrepreneurs specified that they had an idea first, or the desire to start a business first, or both.

The PSED is a sample of nascent entrepreneurs who were identified using a random-digit dialling process to all United States households with telephones from summer 1998 through to winter 2000. This research built on earlier efforts by Paul Reynolds and colleagues to study nascent entrepreneurs in Wisconsin (Reynolds and White, 1993; 1997), as well as a national sample of nascent entrepreneurs who were identified from a study that was 'piggy-backed' on to the University of Michigan Institute for Social Research Survey of Consumer Attitudes (Curtin, 1982; Reynolds, 1997). The research design for the PSED involves: (1) a procedure for identifying and interviewing nascent entrepreneurs and a comparison group; and (2) the content of the interviews. The details involved in undertaking the PSED research effort are/were substantial, and readers interested in this study are referred to Reynolds (2000) and Shaver, Carter, Gartner and Reynolds (2001). Reynolds (2000) provides a detailed overview and history of the development of all aspects of the research design as of 1999. Shaver, et al (2001) describes the details of the various cohorts of nascent entrepreneurs and the comparison group that were sampled through 2000 (e.g., an overall sample labelled the mixed gender sample, a comparison group sample, an over sample of women, an over sample of minorities, and a minority comparison group over sample) as well as the specific decision rules for selecting the nascent entrepreneurs used in the study presented here. The PSED data sets are administered and maintained by the University of Michigan Institute for Social Research (ISR). The web site for the project is (http://projects.isr.umich.edu/psed/).

When an adult 18 years of age or older is contacted on the telephone, and agrees to respond to a survey, a questionnaire, primarily about marketing issues and consumer preferences was administered. A set of two items was randomly inserted into this survey (the questions could appear at the beginning, middle or end of the survey) to determine whether the respondent might qualify as a nascent entrepreneur:

1. Are you, alone or with others, now trying to start a new business?
2. Are you, alone or with others, now starting a new business or new venture for your employer? An effort that is part of your job assignment?

Individuals targeted for one of the nascent entrepreneur sub-samples who answered 'yes' to the first are labelled as 'independent nascent entrepreneurs'; people answering affirmatively to the second are labelled as 'corporate nascent entrepreneurs', individuals answering positively to both are labelled 'both'. All of these individuals were considered candidates for the nascent entrepreneur interview if they met three additional criteria:

1. They expect to be owners or part owners of the new firm.
2. They have been active in trying to start the new firm in the past 12 months.
3. The effort is still in the start-up or gestation phase and is not a new firm.

The first two criteria were included as part of the commercial marketing interview questionnaire.

Those individuals who met the two criteria (full or part ownership and start-up activity in the past 12 months) were invited to participate in 'a national study of new businesses being conducted through the University of Wisconsin' and told that a cash payment would be provided. Names and phone numbers of potential nascent entrepreneurs were forwarded from Market Facts to the University of Wisconsin Survey Research Laboratory (UWSRL) along with basic socio-demographic information on respondents and their households as well as the county and state in which the phone was located. The UWSRL contacted these individuals for a detailed interview about their business start-up efforts. A number of modifications were undertaken to the sample of nascent entrepreneurs and the comparison group contacted and surveyed. Details of these changes are described in Shaver, Carter, Gartner and Reynolds (2001). The final sample of respondents in the PSED, for this research effort, numbers 1,216 people: 715 'fully autonomous', 102 'partially autonomous', and 399 (without involvement in a start-up) in the comparison group. Full autonomy is defined as a start-up effort with no corporate sponsorship or ownership by any 'non-persons'. Partial autonomy is defined as a start-up effort with any type of business sponsorship (such as a franchise or multilevel marketing business) or any ownership by 'non-persons', provided that such ownership is less than 51 per cent.

Walking the Walk

The individuals that are nascent entrepreneurs in the PSED represent a particular ontological understanding about the nature of entrepreneurial activity. The initial question that qualifies individuals for identification as nascent entrepreneurs is a query about whether they are currently engaged in activities to *start a business*. The sample reflects the population of individuals, at a moment in time, who perceive that they are attempting to start firms, and who also indicate they have engaged in certain firm start-up activities, within the past 12 months. The sample, therefore, would reflect all of the variations in a particular type of entrepreneurial activity (firm start-up) at the time of the survey. The primary purpose of the PSED is to explore the prevalence of firm creation activity in the United States; as well as to depict the variation in activities (as well as human, social and financial capital endowments) among individuals engaged in the firm start-up process. Such a sample should identify the entire distribution of individuals engaged in firm start-up activity, so, for example, some individuals might indicate they are in the first few weeks of the firm start-up process while other individuals may have engaged in start-up activities for a period of time, and may be close to having a firm 'up and running'. Determining *where* an individual is, in terms of the activities that might lead to the formation of a firm, is, in itself, an interesting and puzzling issue. Suffice to say, from looking at some of the empirical evidence that has been analysed from the PSED, there is significant *variation* in: when individuals begin certain start-up activities relative to their own start-up effort; which activities occur; the sequence of these activities; the endowments of human, social and financial capital these individuals begin with; the goals of these individuals; and the kinds (types, sizes, strategies) of firms that each nascent entrepreneur envisions as an outcome of the start-up process. There is no typical entrepreneurial situation. It should be noted that the survey was conducted in a way that individuals would describe the sequence of business start-up events and activities that occurred before the survey was conducted so that details of the entire firm creation process would be depicted. These individuals were then subsequently reinterviewed over a two-year period to ascertain their activities and experiences. We believe that the sample of individuals identified and surveyed in the PSED would be helpful for generating insights into firm start-up processes, overall, particularly as this phenomenon involves the experiences of a random sample of individuals involved with opportunities. Whether individuals encounter opportunities through 'discovery' or through 'enactment' should be a question that, we believe, can be empirically tested with this data.

Some entrepreneurship scholars have pointed out the creation of organizations is but one of many ways in which entrepreneurs exploit opportunities (Gaglio, 1997; Gaglio and Katz, 2001; Shane and Venkataraman, 2000). The use of the nascent entrepreneurs in the PSED would, therefore, not be representative of all entrepreneurial activity. For example, individuals who decide to sell or license their opportunities are not included. Be that as it may, we would suggest that the PSED does provide a good starting point for exploring how an important class of individuals (those who exploit opportunities through firm creation) talk about the opportunities they are involved with.

Talking the Talk

The nascent entrepreneurs who completed the phone survey were also asked to complete an eight-page mail survey and return it for a payment of $25. Of the 480 individuals who returned the mail survey, approximately 443 individuals responded to the following open-ended question: Briefly, how did the original idea for starting a business develop? The responses to this question were then added to the PSED data set as SPSS string variables. We used a 'word count' programme, called the Web Frequency Indexer, (found at http://www.georgetown.edu/cball/webtools/web_freqs.html) to count all of the words that were offered by these nascent entrepreneurs in response to the question. Overall, there were 6,717 total words used in response to this question, so, on average, each respondent wrote approximately 15 words. There were 1,407 unique words. The top ten most frequently used words to describe how the business idea developed were: 'I' (311 times mentioned), 'to' (304), 'and' (251), 'a' (248), 'the' (176), 'my' (173), 'for' (171), 'of' (146), 'in' (114), 'business' (113). The top ten most frequently used verbs to describe the kinds of activities involved in how the business idea developed were: 'was' (81 times mentioned), 'wanted' (70), 'work' (69), 'own' (60), 'have' (52), 'working' (47), 'need' (44), 'had' (40), 'decided' (31) and 'make' (29). We were particularly interested in identifying words that would suggest that nascent entrepreneurs discovered their opportunities. We found 38 statements with verbs that might indicate discovery: 'saw' (17 times mentioned), 'find' or 'found' (13), 'looking' (4) and 'notice' (4). There was no mention of Kirzner's (1997) favourite words 'discover' or 'surprise' in any of the 443 statements. It would appear that the word counts indicate that nascent entrepreneurs use discovery verbs infrequently for describing how their opportunities occurred. Only 38 statements out of 443 statements (9 per cent) included discovery verbs.

We found that our European colleagues were a bit puzzled as to why anyone would count all of the words offered by these entrepreneurs when the meaning of these words would likely be imbedded in the particular combination of words used by each entrepreneur. That is, meanings are individually-based, and, only after understanding each individual, would one attempt efforts at aggregation. Counting all of the words seems to be a good example of how many North American scholars would seek a broad quantitative methodology for exploring what would appear to be a specific qualitative affect. 'Why not conduct indepth interviews with a number of entrepreneurs to find out what they really were thinking? Wouldn't indepth interviews more likely identify the underlying thought processes and activities these individuals were actually experiencing?' We offer this rationale for counting all of the words. The entrepreneurs who responded to this survey represent a sample of the entire population of all individuals actively engaged in business creation activities. The 443 statements, therefore, represent all of the possible variation in statements to the question: How did the original idea for starting a business develop? What these statements in aggregate form offer, is a broad portrayal of the phenomenon of how business ideas evolve.

If we think of all of the 6,717 words as a painting, let's say, of a landscape, we can explore whether the landscape was primarily composed of red pigments, or blue, or yellow. It would be like counting all of the coloured dots in a Seurat painting to be able to say that the painting is primarily 'blue-based' or 'red-based'. While this might, on the surface, appear to lead to a somewhat shallow and superficial sense of what a Seurat painting is, such an exploration does in fact result in finding out a significant amount of information about what attracts us to particular paintings (Wypijewski, 1997). Most people are, in fact, more attracted to 'blue' paintings than they are to paintings that are primarily composed of gold, orange, peach or teal colours (Wypijewski, 1997, pp. 12–13). Counting words offers much the same type of knowledge. What we know from the word counts is that the landscape of words that characterize the evolution of business ideas is not, primarily based on 'discovery' words. Indeed, the words used by these entrepreneurs appear to depict the evolution of business ideas as based, primarily, on words that depict themselves and their desires. 'I' 'wanted' 'my' 'own' 'business'. The word counts describe the overall effect of the phenomenon of how business ideas evolve, as a whole. But not, particular instances, or a specific rationale for how one business idea evolves.

Since we believe the sample depicts all of the variation in descriptions of how business ideas evolve, it would be likely that some statements do actually offer evidence of a discovery approach. Indeed, here are a few examples:

- 'It was an impulse. I went to a seminar I liked what I *saw* so I did it.'
- 'I *saw* an ad for an idea in the paper and wanted to expound.'
- 'I was watching television and *saw* some advertisement.'

These statements seem to reflect Kirzner's perspective that opportunity recognition occurs to these individuals as an almost sudden surprise. These statements appear to indicate that some individuals see opportunities as objective realities outside of themselves and their situations.

But, many of these nascent entrepreneurs appear to be using discovery verbs retrospectively, that is, they appear to 'see' as a way to make sense of their experience as a nascent entrepreneur in the process of starting a firm. For example, the 'discovery' of an opportunity often appears to occur among other kinds of experience and activities:

- 'Don't *find* traditional jobs interesting and suited to my talents and creativity. Years of research has given me access to information and processes I want to share.'
- 'I have always loved cooking and decorating cakes. *Found* I have an artistic flare and decorate cakes differently than most.'
- 'Working for another company I *saw* too many mistakes being made. Thought I could do that better.'
- 'Working in the business, I *saw* a need to take an area of it in a different direction, that didn't exist.'
- 'While working for and with another agency we *found* the management and bookkeeping skills lacking and decided to start a business with proper management and people skills.'
- 'By being an artist and *noticing* how easy it was working graphics on computers. Why work for a salary when one can earn what one wants?'

In these statements, did nascent entrepreneurs encounter opportunities that were 'out there', that is, separate from their ongoing experiences and interests, or did these opportunities emerge from the day-to-day activities of these individuals? Or, is the activity of 'seeing' or 'finding' a way for nascent entrepreneurs to bracket (Weick, 1979, p. 153) a stream of ongoing activities? In Table 7.1, we provide a list of the 38 statements that use the words 'saw', 'find + found', 'looking', and 'notice' for readers to make their own interpretations.

Intentions in the Activities of Nascent Entrepreneurs

There is other evidence in the PSED that might shed some light on this conundrum of whether opportunities are discovered or enacted. In Table 7.2, nascent entrepreneurs were asked whether the business idea, or the decision to start a business, came first. These results would indicate there is no preponderance of evidence for either view. A little more than a third of the respondents (35 per cent) indicated that the idea came first; while 44.5 per cent indicated the desire to start came first, and 20 per cent indicated that both the desire and idea came at the same time. In Table 7.3 we present data that identifies the kinds of behaviours that these nascent entrepreneurs first undertook in the process of starting a business. These results are most surprising, not for the finding that 55 per cent of nascent entrepreneurs first 'spent a lot of time thinking about starting a business', but that the other 45 per cent of the nascent entrepreneurs were first engaged in activities that did not involve a conscious interest in start-up. From looking over the list of the first behaviour activities that these nascent entrepreneurs indicated they were engaged in, it would appear that many entrepreneurs found themselves in the process of starting a business before they had given much thought to what these activities meant. In Table 7.4, we cross-tabulate the responses in Table 7.2 with the data in Table 7.3 to see whether we can ferret out any differences among those nascent entrepreneurs who 'have an idea first' compared to those nascent entrepreneurs who indicated a 'desire to start first'. As was shown in Table 7.3, a large proportion of nascent entrepreneurs first spent time thinking about starting a business, so it would not be a surprise that 50 per cent of these individuals desired to start a business first. If we attempt to generate a profile of differences between those who have the idea/opportunity first, compared to those who had a desire to start first, we offer the following insights. In proportion to the other two groups (idea and both), for those who had a desire to start a business first, it appears that these nascent entrepreneurs first undertook actions to 'prepare' themselves for aspects of the start-up process: some spent time thinking about the business, some took classes, some saved money, and some devoted full-time effort to the start-up. In proportion to the other two groups (desire and both) for those who had the idea/opportunity first, it appears that these nascent entrepreneurs were more likely to first undertake actions that involved the start-up process, itself: some defined a market opportunity, some purchased materials and supplies, some filed federal tax returns and some arranged for child care.

We believe that the primary 'take aways' from studying the results in Tables 7.2, 7.3 and 7.4 would be an appreciation that the phenomenon of entrepreneurial activity is very diverse, and that for many nascent entrepreneurs, a broad range of start-up activities are occurring before they appear to 'discover' their opportunity, if indeed, whether many of these nascent entrepreneurs ever

Table 7.1   Descriptions with 'opportunity discovery' verbs

Written responses to: Briefly, how did the original idea for starting a business develop?

SAW

I *saw* a need for certain types of equipment not yet in use in my profession.

I *saw* (noticed) an unfulfilled need in the multiply-handicapped children I was teaching, and I felt I could provide the product and create the market.

I *saw* the concept elsewhere and developed on it.

It was an impulse. I went to a seminar I liked what I *saw* so I did it.

I *saw* an ad for an idea in the paper and wanted to expound.

After the ADA passed I *saw* how people were taking advantage of it and using it to benefit themselves rather than who it was meant for.

Not happy with services given. *Saw* ways to improve on service and technology.

Needed a job and *saw* a need.

I was watching television and *saw* some advertisement.

My father had a small construction company and I *saw* the amount of money and independence. You could have both.

Saw a business similar to what I would like to open.

I was young and having trouble keeping a job. I *saw* an infomercial. I didn't believe in what they said but it sparked an idea in me that grew.

I *saw* a need in the day-to-day workings at the company I used to work for.

I *saw* a lot of other people doing it and making money so I thought why can't I?

Working for another company I *saw* too many mistakes being made. Thought I could do that better.

Saw ad for new system.

Working in the business, I *saw* a need to take an area of it in a different direction, that didn't exist.

FIND + FOUND

Class was available and affordable and I had been wanting to *find* something else to do besides legal secretary work.

I was injured and had to *find* a new way to make a living.

Don't *find* traditional jobs interesting and suited to my talents and creativity. Years of research have given me access to information and processes I want to share.

Could not *find* the product in our area at reasonable prices.

Table 7.1   (continued)

While working for and with another agency we *found* the Management and Bookkeeping skills lacking and decided to start a business with proper management and people skills.

I worked in the business several months and *found* it gave me fulfilment.

We wanted to start a home-based business. After some research we *found* this company to have the best business strategy.

I had a strong desire to do public speaking and also wanted to *find* a way to help troubled kids and young adults.

I have always loved cooking and decorating cakes. *Found* I have an artistic flare and decorate cakes differently than most.

While researching an old doll to *find* value I came to realize the huge interest in buying and selling toys from 50s through to the 80s. Thus I decided to buy up toys (stock) for an old toy store.

I have been having trouble *finding* some items to use in jewellery-making and also came up with an idea for a new item.

Tired of retirement, so I did some research of small businesses, to *find* something I could do on my own.

I was laid off my job in 1992 and had a hard time *finding* another.

LOOKING

My friend and I were talking about how we needed a restaurant in our business park and how it would be a good opportunity for someone starting one in our area and we started *looking* in to the possibility.

Looking at the way corporate America is downsizing, I thought I should get something going for myself to generate additional income.

Working for others does not work! I was and am *looking* (as others) for an opportunity where I have control of my destiny or keep trying.

I was *looking* for a way to generate extra income.

NOTICE

I saw (*noticed*) an unfulfilled need in the multiply-handicapped children I was teaching, and I felt I could provide the product and create the market.

When I was employed by different households I *noticed* they needed a hands-on cleaning service.

I was toying with the idea of starting up my own business when I *noticed* the ad and checked into it.

By being an artist and *noticing* how easy is working graphics on computers. Why work for a salary when one can earn what one wants?

Table 7.2   Which came first? Idea or desire?

Question (A2): Which came first for you, the business idea or your decision to start some kind of business?

Frequency	Per cent	Response
194	35.3	Business idea or opportunity came first
244	44.5	Desire to start a business came first
111	20.1	Idea or opportunity and desire to have a business came at the same time
549	100.0	

'discover' an opportunity, at all. Overall, we do not believe there is a preponderance of support for a belief that most entrepreneurs see opportunities in an objective way, that is, there is not very much evidence that opportunities are discovered in the manner assumed by some academic scholars (Kirzner, 1997; Shane and Venkataraman, 2000; Gaglio and Katz, 2001). Others may interpret the evidence we have presented in a different manner.

CONCLUSIONS

Our intention is to question the movement of entrepreneurship scholarship towards its current fascination with the phenomenon of opportunity and a belief that opportunities are discovered. There is, it seems, a sense that the interest in opportunity has much the same cachet as previous searches for the elusive entrepreneur. Are opportunity and the opportunity discovery perspective, the new Heffalump (Kilby, 1971)?

We are concerned that pursuing a belief in the opportunity discovery perspective will mean ignoring a significant portion of entrepreneurial activity. Ideas about opportunity discovery that have little empirical support could be used to ignore the empirical evidence that does exist. Should for example, Kirzner's ideas (Kirzner, 1997) drive empirical explorations of entrepreneurial activity, or, should the evidence from empirical explorations of entrepreneurial activity inform us about the relevance of Kirzner's ideas? The answer to this issue is of great importance to phenomenon-based studies of entrepreneurship, such as the PSED. How and why certain activities and events are defined as 'entrepreneurial' has been a continual problem with defining scholarly activity in the entrepreneurship area (Gartner, 1985; 1988; 1990;

120   *Moving concepts*

Table 7.3   Distribution of most frequent first behaviours

FIRST BEHAVIOURS

	N^1	$\%^2$
Spent a lot of time thinking about starting business	404	57
Took classes or workshops on starting business	115	16
Saving money to invest in business	109	15
Invested own money in business	98	14
Developed model or procedures for product/service	82	12
Defined market opportunities	58	8
Raw materials, inventory, supplies purchased	52	7
Business plan prepared	50	7
Start-up team organized	40	6
Major items like equipment, facilities or property purchased, leased	24	3
Filed federal tax income tax return	17	2
Marketing or promotional activities started	17	2
Arranged childcare or household help to allow time for business	16	2
Devoted full time to business	13	2
Credit from supplier established	14	2
Projected financial statements developed	9	1
Bank account opened exclusively for this business	9	1
Received money, income or fees from sale of goods or services	8	1
Applied for patent, copyright or trademark	8	1
Asked financial institutions or people for funds	5	>1
Hired employees or managers	2	>1
Paid federal social security taxes (FICA)	3	>1
Monthly revenues exceeded monthly expenses	2	>1
Business has own phone listing	1	>1
Business has own phone line	2	>1
Paid state unemployment insurance	1	>1
Paid managers who are owners a salary	0	0
Business listed with D&B (Dunn and Bradstreet)	0	0

Notes:
1. Total doesn't sum to number of eligible nascent entrepreneurs (715) since some respondents indicated simultaneous first behaviours.
2. Percentage of 715 eligible nascent entrepreneurs who reported item as one of first behaviours.

1993; 2001; Venkataraman, 1997; Shane and Venkataraman, 2000). We hope that all perspectives about the nature of entrepreneurship will be given careful consideration by all parties interested in improving scholarship in this area.

We believe that the kinds of questions that scholars ask nascent entrepreneurs may significantly affect the kinds of answers we obtain (Sudman and Bradburn, 1982). We believe that by asking nascent entrepreneurs whether they

Table 7.4   Distribution of most frequent first behaviour by A2 (Desire/Idea)

| | Which Came First | | | |
	Idea/ Opp	Desire to Start	Both Same Time	Total N
Spent a lot of time thinking about starting business	32%	50%	18%	266
Took classes or workshops on starting business	28%	49%	23%	83
Saving money to invest in business	37%	49%	15%	74
Invested own money in business	39%	51%	11%	57
Developed model or procedures for product/service	38%	48%	14%	50
Defined market opportunities	46%	32%	22%	41
Raw materials, inventory, supplies purchased	47%	30%	23%	30
Business plan prepared	34%	44%	22%	32
Start-up team organized	24%	44%	32%	25
Major items like equipment, facilities or property purchased, leased	46%	46%	9%	11
Filed federal tax income tax return	40%	20%	40%	15
Marketing or promotional activities started	30%	50%	20%	10
Arranged childcare or household help to allow time for business	46%	27%	27%	11
Devoted full time to business	30%	60%	10%	10
Credit from supplier established				
Projected financial statements developed				
Bank account opened exclusively for this business				
Received money, income or fees from sale of goods or services				
Applied for patent, copyright or trademark				
Asked financial institutions or people for funds				
Hired employees or managers				
Paid federal social security taxes (FICA)				
Monthly revenues exceeded monthly expenses				
Business has own phone listing				
Business has own phone line				
Paid managers who are owners a salary				
Paid state unemployment insurance				
Business listed with D&B (Dunn and Bradstreet)				

Notes:
1. Sample size reduction comes from moving to mail survey data for A2 on opportunities.
2. Percentages reported only when 'first' behaviour was reported by ten, or more, respondents.

'discovered' their opportunities forces them to conceptualize their past experiences to account for 'discovery' having occurred, even if it didn't. If some other process has taken place, a question about discovery is unlikely to uncover it. There may be more unobtrusive ways of probing the nature of opportunity. In addition, there may be more appropriate methodologies for exploring the nature of entrepreneurial activity, overall (Gartner and Birley, 2002).

We suggest that in the talk that entrepreneurs offer about how their ideas for their businesses developed; opportunities may be enacted by individuals rather than recognized through discovery. At this point, given the evidence and ideas we have presented, it might appear that enactment is merely 'not-discovery', that is, if evidence were sparse for support of the discovery perspective, then, we might surmise enactment occurs. We are not, at this point, willing to suggest that entrepreneurial activities that appear to be 'not-discovery' in nature, is strong evidence for the enactment perspective. But, we would like others to entertain the thought that there are significant problems with a belief that opportunities, for most entrepreneurs, are objective phenomenon.

What do entrepreneurs talk about when they talk about opportunity? Do they, in fact, actually talk about opportunity? How should the experiences of entrepreneurs, particularly those individuals involved in the start-up of businesses, be understood, and made sense of, by scholars who study this phenomenon? Opportunity, as an objective phenomenon, may be an artifact of previous academic beliefs and theories that have little relationship to the actual events and experiences of entrepreneurial individuals. We wonder whether the academic focus on 'discovery' forces an a priori sensemaking on a nascent entrepreneur's responses. For example, if scholars believe that opportunities are discovered, and, therefore, ask the question: 'How did you discover your opportunity?' won't the responses from nascent entrepreneurs be a self-fulfilling prophecy? We believe that the language we use to explore and understand the events we observe will shape what we actually can find and know. When scholars use words like 'opportunity recognition' or 'opportunity discovery', these words immediately demarcate aspects of the phenomenon of entrepreneurship that may not actually exist, or occur. (Did Columbus discover America?) Talking about discovery assumes that there is something to be discovered. If entrepreneurship scholars talk about opportunity recognition and discovery, we are likely to find it. If the vocabulary that signifies opportunity tends to describe entrepreneurial activity in terminology that identifies enactment, our understanding of this phenomenon may be very different. (What occurred as Columbus sought to find a passage to China? He bumped into Cuba.) 'Opportunity', 'opportunity discovery', and 'opportunity recognition' may be words that make sense to entrepreneurship scholars, but to few others outside our community.

Serendipity

To talk about 'favourable circumstances' allows us to become aware of them, in our own situations. Concurrent to the Movements of Entrepreneurship workshop, which was planned to celebrate the fifth anniversary of ESBRI, was the centennial celebration of the Nobel Prizes, which was exhibited at the new

Nobel Museum in Stockholm. One hundred years of creativity and innovation represented in banners, displays and films. We couldn't help but be moved by the parade of banners representing every individual who has been celebrated for their scientific discoveries and creative efforts by receiving the Nobel Prize. It should not be surprising that a central theme of this centennial celebration of the Nobel Prize was an exploration of this question: How and why did these creative efforts occur? The parallels to the issues addressed in the ESBRI conference on Movements in Entrepreneurship couldn't have been more germane. While there were many ideas and insights that we gathered from this experience, one particular insight seemed to best comment on our current odyssey with the nature of opportunity: serendipity. One of the activities involved in the Nobel centennial celebration was the joint publication by *The Kenyon Review* and *Stand Magazine* of a series of essays on various facets of creativity and discovery by Nobel Prize winners. One particular essay by Robert Friedel entitled 'Serendipity is no accident' (Friedel, 2001), offers a final commentary on some of our opportunity conundrums.

While we tend to think of serendipity as 'accidental discovery', Horace Walpole actually coined the word 'serendipity' when he attributed his experience of a surprising discovery of the similarities in the fairy tale 'The Three Princes of Serendip'. The fairy tale describes a series of situations where three princes make rather surprising (but correct) deductions about their observations of events. As Friedel points out, 'Insight is every bit as important as the accident. Simply to stumble upon something of value is not serendipity; that requires a mental capacity that goes beyond the obvious' (2001, p. 38). Serendipity is about discovery with insight. Friedel offers three ways in which serendipitous discovery occurs: Columbian, Archimedean, and Galilean. Columbian serendipity is 'when one is looking for one thing, but finds another thing of value, and recognizes that value' (p. 39). Archimedean serendipity is 'finding sought-for results, although by routes not logically deduced but luckily observed' (p. 40). In other words, this kind of serendipity is similar to Pasteur's statement: 'in observation, chance favours only prepared minds'. ('Dans les champs de l'observation, le hazard ne favorise que les ésprits préparés.') Finally, Galilean serendipity involves the use of 'new instruments or capabilities to generate surprises' (p. 40). In Galileo's case, it was his use of the telescope that enabled him to be surprised by what he saw when he looked at the night sky. A number of examples are offered from the endeavours of Nobel Prize winners in recent decades to show how these three approaches are still currently manifest in scientific activity. Friedel ends his essay by positing that serendipity is fundamental to discovery: 'The end of surprise would be the end of science' (p. 45).

While Friedel gleans from his observations and examples of serendipity the aspect of 'surprise', much like Kirzner (1997), we see that serendipity begins with action. What is a fundamental commonality among the three types of serendipity (Columbian, Archimedean, and Galilean) that Friedel offers is the pursuit of scientific activity. Scientists 'do' science, and, in the process of scientific activity, they are more likely to make the kinds of observations that truly contain some new insight. When there is an element of surprise in science, it can only stem from the groundwork already undertaken through years of scientific work. It is such an obvious insight, but one that seems to get lost in the overwhelming joy of insight and discovery. We tend to forget about all of the scientific work that is necessary for a scientific discovery to occur. Friedel does not offer any examples of individuals serendipitously discovering something insightful in science by individuals who were not scientists or who had not undertaken years of scientific work. Scientific action is critical to scientific observation. Without action, there is no insight.

We suggest that a belief in the importance of opportunity to entrepreneurship will need to be predicated on an appreciation of the necessity of entrepreneurial activity. There is some irony in the observation that Friedel devotes his entire essay to describing a variety of scientific activities as the bases for discovery (to prove the idea that 'serendipity is no accident'), yet he seems to slip into the celebration of 'surprise', as the culmination of his thoughts on the process of discovery. He could have just as well celebrated the importance of all of the mundane activities in science that provided the foundation for generating new insights. Yet, in the end, he becomes enamoured with surprise. Entrepreneurship scholars should be vigilant about falling into the same trap. In entrepreneurship, it is entrepreneurial activity that matters. The favourable circumstances that entrepreneurs are likely to recognize are a product of their own initiative. The serendipity that occurs when opportunities are recognized stem from an entrepreneur's own experiences. Without action, there is no insight. As scholars, we should be willing to make ourselves available to the surprise of what we can see in the experiences of entrepreneurs. Let us not be caught up in the celebration of the insights of these entrepreneurs (that is, how they perceived how they recognized their opportunities) without appreciating the multitude of mundane and minute actions that are the underpinning of their recognition of favourable circumstances.

NOTE

1. This material is based upon work supported by the National Science Foundation under Grant No. 9809841. Any opinions, findings, and conclusions or recommendations expressed in this material are those of the author(s) and do not necessarily reflect the views of the National Science Foundation.

References

Abrahamson, E. (1996a), 'Management fashion', *Academy of Management Review*, **21**, pp. 254–85.

Abrahamson, Eric (1996b), 'Technical and aesthetic fashion', in Barbara Czarniawska and Guje Sevón (eds), *Translating Organizational Change*, Berlin: de Gruyter, pp. 117–37.

Aldrich, H.E. (1979), *Organizations and Environments*, Englewood Cliffs, NJ: Prentice-Hall.

Arrow, K. (1974), 'Limited knowledge and economic analysis', *American Economic Review*, **64** (1), pp. 1–10.

Busenitz, L.W. (1996), 'Research on entrepreneurial alertness', *Journal of Small Business Management*, **34** (4), pp. 35–44.

Carroll, G.R. and G.R. Hannan (2000), *The Demography of Corporations and Industries*, Princeton, NJ: Princeton University Press.

Chan, A. (2000), 'Redirecting critique in postmodern organization studies: The perspective of Foucault', *Organization Studies*, **21** (6), pp. 1059–75.

Curtin, R. (1982), 'Indicators of consumer behavior: The University of Michigan survey of consumers', *Public Opinion Quarterly*, **46**, pp. 340–62.

Czarniawska, B. (1997), 'A four times told tale: Combining narrative and scientific knowledge in organization studies', *Organization*, **4** (1), pp. 7–30.

Czarniawska, B. (1998), *A Narrative Approach to Organization Studies*, Thousand Oaks, CA: Sage.

Daft, R.L. and K.L. Weick (1984), 'Toward a model of organizations as interpretation systems', *Academy of Management Review*, **9** (2), pp. 284–95.

Dutton, J.E. (1993a), 'Interpretations on automatic: A different view of strategic issue diagnosis', *Journal of Management Studies*, **30** (3), pp. 339–57.

Dutton, J.E. (1993b), 'The making of organizational opportunities: An interpretive pathway to organizational change', *Research in Organizational Behavior*, **15**, pp. 195–226.

Dutton, J.E. and S.E. Jackson (1987), 'Categorizing strategic issues: Links to organizational action', *Academy of Management Review*, **12** (1), pp. 76–90.

Erikson, T. (2001), 'The promise of entrepreneurship as a field of research: A few comments and some suggested extensions', *Academy of Management Review*, **26** (1), pp. 12–13.

Fournier, V. and C. Grey (2000), 'At the critical moment: Conditions and prospects for critical management studies', *Human Relations*, **53** (1), pp. 7–32.

Friedel, R. (2001), 'Serendipity is no accident', *The Kenyon Review*, **23** (2), pp. 36–47.

Gaglio, C.M. (1997), 'Opportunity identification: Review, critique and suggested research directions', in J.A. Katz and R.H. Brockhaus (eds), *Advances in Entrepreneurship, Firm Emergence and Growth*, Greenwich, CT: JAI Press, pp. 139–202.

Gaglio, C.M. and J.A. Katz (2001), 'The psychological basis of opportunity identification: Entrepreneurial alertness', *Journal of Small Business Economics*, **16** (2), pp. 95–111.

Gartner, W.B. (1985), 'A framework for describing and classifying the phenomenon of new venture creation', *Academy of Management Review*, **10** (4), pp. 696–706.

Gartner, W.B. (1988), 'Who is an entrepreneur? Is the wrong question', *American Journal of Small Business*, **12** (4), pp. 11–32.

Gartner, W.B. (1990), 'What are we talking about when we talk about entrepreneurship?', *Journal of Business Venturing*, **5** (1), pp. 15–28.

Gartner, W.B. (1993), 'Words lead to deeds: Towards an organizational emergence vocabulary', *Journal of Business Venturing*, **8** (3), pp. 231–40.

Gartner, W.B. (2001), 'Is there an elephant in entrepreneurship? Blind assumptions in theory development', *Entrepreneurship Theory and Practice*, **25** (4), pp. 27–39.

Gartner, W.B. and S. Birley (2002), 'Introduction to the special issue of qualitative methods in entrepreneurship research', *Journal of Business Venturing*, **17**, pp. 387–95.

Gartner, W.B., B.J. Bird and J. Starr (1992), 'Acting as if: Differentiating entrepreneurial from organizational behavior', *Entrepreneurship Theory and Practice*, **16** (3), pp. 13–32.

Gioia, D.A., M. Schultz and K.G. Corley (2000), 'Organizational identity, image, and adaptive instability', *Academy of Management Review*, **25** (1), pp. 63–81.

Hall, R.H. (1972), *Organizations: Structures and Processes*, Englewood Cliffs, NJ: Prentice-Hall.

Hardy, C., N. Phillips and S. Clegg (2001), 'Reflexivity in organization and management theory: A study of the product of the research "subject"', *Human Relations*, **54** (5), pp. 531–60.

Hawley, A. (1950), *Human Ecology*, New York: Ronald Press.

Hayek, F.A. (1945), 'The use of knowledge in society', *The American Economic Review*, **35** (4), pp. 519–30.

Hill, R.C. and M. Levenhagen (1995), 'Metaphors and mental models: Sensemaking and sensegiving in innovative and entrepreneurial activities', *Journal of Management*, **21** (6), pp. 1057–74.

Hills, G.E. and R. Schrader (1998), 'Successful entrepreneur's insights into opportunity recognition', *Frontiers of Entrepreneurship Research*, Wellesley,

MA: Babson College, pp. 30–43.

Jackson, S.E. and J.E. Dutton (1988), 'Discerning threats and opportunities', *Administrative Science Quarterly*, **33**, pp. 370–87.

Kaish, S. and B. Gilad (1991), 'Characteristics of opportunity searches of entre-preneurs versus executives: Sources, interests, general alertness', *Journal of Business Venturing*, **6** (1), pp. 45–61.

Kilby, P. (1971), 'Hunting the Heffalump', in P. Kilby (ed.), *Entrepreneurship and Economic Development*, New York: Free Press.

Kirzner, I.M. (1979), *Perception, Opportunity, and Profit*, Chicago: University of Chicago Press.

Kirzner, I.M. (1985), *Discovery and Capitalist Process*, Chicago: University of Chicago Press.

Kirzner, I.M. (1997), 'Entrepreneurial discovery and the competitive market process: An Austrian approach', *Journal of Economic Literature*, **35** (1), pp. 60–85.

Lawrence, P.R. and J.W. Lorsch (1967), 'Organization and environment: Managing differentiation and integration', Boston: Graduate School of Business, Harvard University.

Levenhagen, M.J., J.F. Porac and H. Thomas (1993), 'Emergent industry leadership and the selling of technological visions: A social constructionist view', in G. Johnson and J. Hendry (eds), *Strategic Thinking, Leadership, and the Management of Change*, New York: John Wiley.

March, J.G. and J.P. Olsen (1976), *Ambiguity and Choice in Organizations*, Bergen, Norway: Universitetsforlaget.

Martin, J. and P. Frost (1996), 'The organizational culture war games: A struggle for intellectual dominance', in S. Clegg, C. Hardy and W. Nord (eds), *Handbook of Organization Studies*, pp. 599–621, London: Sage.

Meyer, J.W. and W.R. Scott (1983), *Organizational Environments: Ritual and Rationality*, Beverley Hills, CA: Sage.

Ogbor, J.O. (2000), 'Mythicizing and reification in entrepreneurial discourse: Ideology-critique of entrepreneurial studies', *Journal of Management Studies*, **37** (5), pp. 605–35.

Pfeffer, J. (1982), *Organizations and Organization Theory*, Marshfield, MA: Pitman.

Pfeffer, J. (1997), *New Directions for Organization Theory*, New York: Oxford University Press.

Pfeffer, J. and G.R. Salancik (1978), *The External Control of Organizations*, New York: Harper and Row.

Reynolds, P.D. (1997), 'Who starts new firms? Preliminary explorations of firms-in-gestation', *Small Business Economics*, **9**, pp. 449–62.

Reynolds, P.D. (2000), 'National panel study of U.S. business startups:

Background and methodology', in J.A. Katz (ed.), *Advances in Entrepreneurship, Firm Emergence, and Growth*, vol. 4, Stamford, CT: JAI Press, pp. 153–227.

Reynolds, P.D. and S.B. White (1993), *Wisconsin's Entrepreneurial Climate Study*, Milwaukee: Marquette University Center for the Study of Entrepreneurship.

Reynolds, P.D. and S.B. White (1997), *The Entrepreneurial Process*, Westport, CT: Greenwood Publishing.

Sarasvathy, S.D. (2001), 'Causation and effectuation: Towards a theoretical shift from economic inevitability to entrepreneurial contingency', *Academy of Management Review*, **26** (2), pp. 243–63.

Sarasvathy, S.D., H. Simon and L. Lave (1998), 'Perceiving and managing business risks: Differences between entrepreneurs and bankers', *Journal of Economic Behavior and Organization*, **33**, pp. 207–25.

Schoonhoven, C.B. and E. Romanelli (2001), *The Entrepreneurship Dynamic: Origins of Entrepreneurship and the Evolution of Industries*, Stanford, CA: Stanford University Press.

Scott, S.G. and V.R. Lane (2000), 'A stakeholder approach to organizational identity', *Academy of Management Review*, **25** (1), pp. 43–62.

Scott, W.R. (1992), *Organizations: Rational, Natural and Open Systems*, 3rd edn, Englewood Cliffs, NJ: Prentice-Hall.

Shane, S. (2000), 'Prior knowledge and the discovery of entrepreneurial opportunities', *Organization Science*, **11** (4), pp. 448–69.

Shane, S. and S. Venkataraman (2000), 'The promise of entrepreneurship as a field of research', *Academy of Management Review*, **25** (1), pp. 217–26.

Shane, S. and S. Venkataraman (2001), 'Entrepreneurship as a field of research: A response to Zahra and Dess, Singh and Erikson', *Academy of Management Review*, **26** (1), pp. 13–16.

Shaver, K. and L. Scott (1991), 'Person, process, choice: The psychology of new venture creation', *Entrepreneurship Theory and Practice*, **16** (2), pp. 23–45.

Shaver, Kelly G., Nancy M. Carter, William B. Gartner and Paul D. Reynolds (2001), 'Who is a nascent entrepreneur? Decision rules for identifying and selecting entrepreneurs in the panel study of entrepreneurial dynamics', paper presented at the *Babson College Kauffman Foundation Entrepreneurship Research Conference*, Jönköping, Sweden, June.

Singh, R.P. (2001), 'A comment on developing the field of entrepreneurship through the study of opportunity recognition and exploitation', *Academy of Management Review*, **26** (1), pp. 11–12.

Singh, R.P., G.E. Hills and G.T. Lumpkin (1999), 'New venture ideas and entrepreneurial opportunities: Understanding the process of opportunity recognition', proceedings of *United States Association for Small Business and Entrepreneurship National Meeting*, San Diego, pp. 657–71.

Sudman, S. and N.M. Bradburn (1982), *Asking Questions: A Practical Guide to Questionnaire Design*, San Francisco: Jossey-Bass.

Thomas, J.B., S.M. Clark and D.A. Gioia (1993), 'Strategic sensemaking and organizational performance: Linkages among scanning, interpretation, action, and outcomes', *Academy of Management Journal*, **36** (2), pp. 239–70.

Van Maanen, J. (1995a), 'Fear and loathing in organization studies', *Organization Science*, **6**, pp. 687–92.

Van Maanen, J. (1995b), 'Style as theory', *Organization Science*, **6**, pp. 133–43.

Venkataraman, S. (1997), 'The distinctive domain of entrepreneurship research: An editor's perspective', in J.A. Katz and R.H. Brockhaus (eds), *Advances in Entrepreneurship, Firm Emergence and Growth*, vol. 3, Greenwich, CT: JAI Press, pp. 119–38.

Webster's Ninth New Collegiate Dictionary (1988), Springfield, MA: Merriam-Webster.

Weick, K.E. (1979) (2nd edn), *The Social Psychology of Organizing*, New York: McGraw-Hill.

Weick, K.E. (1995), *Sensemaking in Organizations*, Thousand Oaks, CA: Sage.

Wypijewski, J. (1997), *Painting by Numbers: Komar and Melamid's Scientific Guide to Art*, New York: Farrar, Straus and Giroux.

Zahra, S. and G.G. Dess (2001), 'Entrepreneurship as a field of research: Encouraging dialogue and debate', *Academy of Management Review*, **26** (1), pp. 8–10.

[16]

Small Business Economics (2006) 27: 23–40
DOI 10.1007/s11187-006-0020-0

© Springer 2006

Research article

The Effects of Pre-venture Plan Timing and Perceived Environmental Uncertainty on the Persistence of Emerging Firms

Jianwen Liao
William B. Gartner

ABSTRACT. This paper explores the effects of when pre-venture planning occurs (early or late) in the sequence of activities accomplished during the process of new business emergence, and the moderating effects of environmental context (the degree of perceived financial, competitive and operational uncertainty), on the persistence of emerging business startup efforts. Using data from the U.S. Panel Study of Entrepreneurial Dynamics (PSED), our analyses found a strong main effect for business planning: Nascent entrepreneurs who completed a business plan were 2.6 times more likely to persist in the process of business emergence than those who did not complete a plan. In addition, the likelihood of venture persistence increased when nascent entrepreneurs engaged in planning early in the sequence of start-up activities in perceived uncertain financial and competitive environments, while venture persistence increased when nascent entrepreneurs engaged in planning late in a sequence of activities in perceived certain financial and competitive environments.

KEYWORDS: nascent entrepreneurs, Panel Study of Entrepreneurial Dynamics, pre-venture planning

1. Introduction

Entrepreneurial action is necessary to assemble the resources and capabilities required for new firms to come into existence (Gartner, 1985; Katz and Gartner, 1988; Shaver and Scott, 1991;

Final version accepted on March 17, 2006

Jianwen Liao
Northeastern Illinois University
5500 N. St. Louis, Chicago, IL, 60625, USA

William B. Gartner
Spiro Center for Entrepreneurial Leadership
Clemson University
345 Sirrine Hall, Clemson, SC, 29634-1305, USA
E-mail: gartner@clemson.edu

Reynolds and Miller, 1992; Carter et al., 1996; Alvarez and Busenitz, 2001; Delmar and Shane, 2003, 2004; Gartner and Carter, 2003; Honig and Karlsson, 2004). Yet, all entrepreneurs have limitations for undertaking a variety of organizing activities simultaneously (Aldrich, 1999; Bhide, 2000). Since the formation of new organizations evolves through a sequence of venture activities over time, it would be reasonable to assume that some venture creation activities would be more beneficial to engage in before others (Gartner and Carter, 2003). There is a long history of thought in the entrepreneurship area that suggests that entrepreneurs should engage in business planning early in the process of venture formation as a way to guide these new venture creators towards activities that are more useful for starting new firms (e.g., Fry and Stoner, 1985; Mancuso, 1985; Henderson, 1988). Indeed, while there has been some concern about devoting too much time to business planning or making the business planning process too sophisticated (Bhide, 1994; Gumpert, 2003), there is a strong belief that it is better to engage in some type of planning early in the venture development process, rather than later (Bhide, 2000). Recent research on the role of pre-venture planning in venture creation appears to support this view. For example, studies by Delmar and Shane (2003, 2004), and Honig and Karlsson (2004) suggest that nascent entrepreneurs should engage in pre-venture planning early because they were likely to use pre-venture planning as a way to generate legitimacy and therefore enhance venture persistence (Meyer and Rowan, 1977). Delmar and Shane (2004) indicate "Our evidence suggests that completing business plans and establishing a legal entity early in the life of a new venture are advantageous to new ventures because these activities facilitate the transition to other firm organizing activities" (p. 406).

Yet, business planning early in the formation of new ventures may not be effective in all environmental contexts (Castrogiovanni, 1996). For example, Matthews and Scott (1995) found that as perceived environmental uncertainty increased, new entrepreneurial and small firms were less likely to engage in business planning. They suggested that entrepreneurs who perceive highly uncertain environments may be less likely to engage in planning because they believe that planning efforts will not provide any information that can be usefully acted on. From a social constructionist perspective, Baker and Nelson (2005) identified entrepreneurs who enacted the creation of necessary resources for venture development and growth rather than rely on perceived environmental constraints. They suggest that entrepreneurs construct their businesses and environments through action:

> *The bricoleurs in our study did not view opportunities as objective and external to the resources and activities of the firm. Rather, the processes of discovering opportunities and enacting resources were often one and the same, with both the resource environment and the opportunity environment idiosyncratic to the specific firm and constructed through processes of bricolage. (Baker and Nelson, 2005: 358)*

They make a case for Weick's view that action is necessary for sensemaking to occur (Weick, 1979) which would imply that planning before taking action to explore the environment (certain or uncertain) would be premature.

We explore how both the emerging venture's context and the benefits of planning will affect when nascent entrepreneurs should engage in pre-venture planning to increase the chances that efforts to continue the process of venture creation will persistence. Different contexts are likely to require different times for when planning should occur. And, different perspectives on the planning process may offer alternative views of when planning might be initiated. For example, in contrast to the views of Matthews and Scott (1995), an alternative explanation for the need for planning early in uncertain environments could posit that nascent entrepreneurs who start businesses that require outside investment or significant support from outside stakeholders (i.e., situations that are perceived as a highly uncertain financial environment) would likely engage in planning early as a way to acquire these resources. Nascent entrepreneurs who don't need resources from others may therefore be less inclined to write a plan early in the startup process. Or, in uncertain competitive environments, nascent entrepreneurs may believe that early pre-venture planning may help them better understand which actions they might find of value as a guide to undertaking future activities. In more stable environments, nascent entrepreneurs may find that they need to better understand their prior efforts, so they engage in pre-venture planning later in the startup process as a way to learn about what they have done. In those situations, pre-venture planning takes on Weick's (1979) dictum, "How do I know what I think until I see what I say?" And, still other nascent entrepreneurs may find the complexity of their startup operations to be such that early pre-venture planning may help them more efficiently undertake the necessary actions for venture persistence. The value of pre-venture planning for venture persistence, then, is likely to be dependent on a variety of factors which could be explained from alternative perspectives.

In the following sections of the paper, we suggest hypotheses about how certain contexts will influence the efficacy of when pre-venture planning occurs as a way to increase the probability that new venture creation efforts will continue. Similar to Castrogiovanni's (1996) ideas on the effects of perceived uncertainty on pre-venture planning, we suggest that nascent entrepreneurs are likely to plan early when they perceive high degrees of financial, competitive and operational uncertainty, and plan late when they perceive low degrees of financial, competitive and operational uncertainty. These hypotheses are operationalized and tested using data from the U. S. Panel Study of Entrepreneurial Dynamics (Gartner et al., 2004). Based on the results generated, we offer insights into the value of pre-venture planning to increase the persistence of emerging firms, in general, as well as insights into when nascent entrepreneurs should engage in pre-venture planning under certain perceived environmental conditions.

2. Theoretical framework and hypothesis development

A comprehensive review of the pre-venture planning literature (Castrogiovanni, 1996) indicates that a broader range of factors than those explored by Delmar and Shane (2003, 2004) may influence the organizing process, which may differentially affect the efficacy of pre-venture planning on venture persistence. Castrogiovanni suggested that many interrelated dimensions are likely to affect the value of pre-venture planning on venture persistence: the background and capabilities of the nascent entrepreneur; the nature and purpose of pre-venture planning for the nascent entrepreneur; the types of businesses that might be more likely to need pre-venture planning; the environmental context and kinds of industries that might lead nascent entrepreneurs to engage in planning; the value and outcomes of pre-venture planning to subsequent activities, and likelihood that new ventures would be created and grow. Castrogiovanni organizes these factors in a framework of two dimensions that would affect the degree to which pre-venture planning would occur and be of value to the emerging venture's persistence: planning context and planning benefits. Planning context comprises such factors as the environmental and founding conditions of the emerging venture. Environmental conditions would take into consideration the uncertainty and munificence of the emerging venture's context. Founding conditions would consider the founder's knowledge and the emerging venture's need for resources beyond the founder's personal funds.

2.1. *Environmental uncertainty*

Environmental uncertainty is a central construct in the inquiry of relationships between an organization and its environment (Aldrich, 1999). Environmental uncertainty is generally referred to as the difference between the amount of information required to perform a task and the amount of information possessed by an individual or an organization (Galbraith, 1973). In a review of the literature and research on environmental uncertainty, Milliken (1987) developed a general definition of environmental uncertainty as "an individual's perceived inability to predict (an organization's environment) accurately because of a 'lack ... of information' or 'an inability to discriminate between relevant and irrelevant data'" (p. 136). Milliken further proposed three types of uncertainty – state, effect and response uncertainty. *State uncertainty* is referred to as perceived environmental uncertainty, which is defined as the inability to understand or to predict the state of the environment due to a lack of information or a lack of understanding of the interrelationships among environmental elements. *Effect uncertainty* is defined as an inability to predict what the consequences of environmental changes will be on the organization. *Response uncertainty* is referred to as an inability to predict the likely consequences of a response choice.

This research effort, as in other explorations of new venture planning and uncertainty (Delmar and Shane, 2003, 2004; Matthews and Human, 2000, 2004), focuses on state uncertainty. We look at state uncertainty as we believe these three types of uncertainty may differentially impact the timing of business planning. For example, if response uncertainty is high – knowing that actions (i.e., planning) will less likely lead to a desired effect, nascent entrepreneurs would more likely to delay planning to a later stage. However, if state uncertainty is high, nascent entrepreneurs may plan early by searching for additional information to reduce the perception of unpredictability. Using prior convention, we will refer to state uncertainty simply as "environmental uncertainty" throughout this paper.

Matthews and Human (2000, 2004) have explored three kinds of environmental uncertainty that are likely to affect the creation of new firms: financial, competitive and operational. Financial uncertainty describes the nascent entrepreneur's perceptions of the likelihood of obtaining start-up and working capital, bank loans and investors. That is, when nascent entrepreneurs indicate high levels of financial uncertainty, they cannot predict with certainty that they will have the resources they need to start their ventures. Competitive uncertainty involves the nascent entrepreneur's perception of environmental factors that affect the strategic viability of the new firm: such as the likelihood the emerging firm will attract customers, successfully compete with other firms, keep up with technological advances in the industry, and comply with government regulations. Basically, these variables would constitute how a new firm would follow the "rules of the game" in a particular industry. Operational uncertainty involves the nascent entrepreneur's perception of the likelihood the emerging venture can be efficient in such activities as: obtaining raw materials, attracting employees, and obtaining supplies. If key aspects of the emerging business cannot be put into place in a cost effective manner, then, the emerging venture is likely to offer products or services at higher (less competitive) prices than its competitors. Perceptions of high operational uncertainty would indicate that nascent entrepreneurs felt less likely to be able to reduce the costs of actions to start an emerging firm, as well as reduce the costs of actions to coordinate the operation of a fledgling firm. These three types of environmental uncertainty (financial, competitive, and operational) are examined in our analyses.

2.2. *Uncertainty and business plan timing*

There are two opposing viewpoints regarding the effects of uncertainty on whether to plan early or late in the process of organization creation. On one side, some researchers find business planning should occur early under conditions of high environmental uncertainty. This perspective views the reduction of uncertainty through access to high quality information as one of the major objectives of business planning (Fuller, 1996). Labeled as "the information uncertainty perspective" (Swamidass and Newell, 1987: 514), these authors argue that

environmental uncertainty increases the need for information gathering and processing, therefore business planning. This line of reasoning is evident both in the prescriptive and empirical literature in the strategy area (i.e., Miller and Frisen, 1983; Ansoff, 1984). For example, Miller and Friesen (1983) conclude that strategic planning is a means to counter the resulting unpredictability arising from constant changes in external environments. Matthew and Scott (1995) found evidence that entrepreneurial ventures (ventures with a high goal and future orientation) are actually more likely continue to plan in the face of increasing uncertainty.

On the other side, some researchers argue business planning may be delayed, postponed and even nullified in the face of environmental uncertainty. Environmental changes make information needed in the strategic planning process quickly obsolete (Bourgeois and Eisenhardt, 1988), so that high environmental uncertainty will likely render planning efforts futile. In this perspective, with high environmental uncertainty, the focus should be on short-term quick responses rather than purposeful and deliberate planning activities. Bhide (1994) suggests that under conditions of environmental uncertainty, entrepreneurs focus on actions that are based largely on intuition. His research found that when entrepreneurs faced increasing environmental uncertainty, they tended to postpone business planning efforts in order to pursue other activities.

As mentioned earlier, Castrogiovanni (1996) provides a comprehensive overview of the literature on pre-venture planning that suggests two broad factors affecting the value of the degree of business planning on business persistence: planning context and planning benefits. The planning context involves environmental and founding conditions. In terms of environmental conditions, he argues that the degree of environmental uncertainty will positively influence the degree of pre-venture planning while the degree of environmental munificence will be negatively correlated with the degree of pre-venture planning. In terms of founding conditions, he argues that the founder's preexisting knowledge of the business will be negatively correlated with the degree of pre-venture planning while the business' need for capital beyond the founder's investment will be positively correlated to the degree of pre-venture planning.

Based on the three types of environmental uncertainty encountered by nascent entrepreneurs (Matthews and Human, 2000, 2004) we propose some hypotheses about how these different types of uncertainty would affect whether entrepreneurs engage in business planning early or late in the process of venture creation. We suggest that nascent entrepreneurs who perceive a high degree of financial uncertainty are likely to engage in planning early to obtain the necessary resources to create the firm. Nascent entrepreneurs would create a plan as a way to legitimate the viability of the prospective new business with those stakeholders with the resources required to develop the venture (Delmar and Shane, 2003, 2004; Honig and Karlsson, 2004). In situations of financial uncertainty, a nascent entrepreneur is likely to believe that the acquisition of resources early in the startup process will enable other startup activities to occur. For example, a nascent venture may need resources to pay employees to engage in product development and marketing. Without resources early on in the startup process, these other start-up activities are unlikely to be undertaken. We would assume that by engaging in planning efforts early in the start-up process, nascent entrepreneurs would expect to reduce their financial uncertainty by attracting various resource providers to the fledgling new venture. We would also assume that nascent entrepreneurs who expressed high financial certainty (indicated they had a high likelihood of obtaining resources) would plan late (vis-à-vis other startup activities). Since they were certain they could obtain resources (or had resources already in place), they would not need to write a plan early to obtain resources they already had or knew they could get. We posit:

H1a: Planning early in situations of perceived high financial uncertainty is likely to increase the likelihood of new venture persistence.
H1b: Planning late in situations of perceived financial certainty is likely to increase the likelihood of new venture persistence.

We believe that nascent entrepreneurs who perceive a high degree of competitive uncertainty would be engaged in "sense making," that is, nascent entrepreneurs would focus on understanding how the game is played in the situation they find themselves in Weick (1995). Such variables as attracting customers, competing with other firms, technology changes and complying with government regulations are all issues where a nascent entrepreneur would need to understand how these issues are interrelated, and which variables would likely affect the emerging firm at a particular moment in time. As Castrogiovanni points out, nascent entrepreneurs engage in sense making, through the planning benefit of learning, as a way to understand their competitive situation. Early pre-venture planning, therefore, might help nascent entrepreneurs better understand what subsequent actions to take for directing their emerging firms. In certain competitive environments, nascent entrepreneurs assume they already know the rules of the game, so they would have less need to plan to figure out what to do, indeed, their goal would be to act first. We posit:

H2a: Planning early in situations of perceived high competitive uncertainty is likely to increase the likelihood of new venture persistence.
H2b: Planning late in situations of perceived competitive certainty is likely to increase the likelihood of new venture persistence.

Early pre-venture planning might assist nascent entrepreneurs who perceive highly uncertain operational environments identify how they can more effectively take actions to enable their emerging firms to operate more efficiently. In contrast, nascent entrepreneurs in perceived certain operational environments would likely plan late since they have an understanding of how their activities might lead to operational efficiencies. We posit:

H3a: Planning early in situations of perceived high operational uncertainty is likely to increase the likelihood of new venture persistence.

H3b: Planning late in situations of perceived operational certainty is likely to increase the likelihood of new venture persistence.

In general, in situations where nascent entrepreneurs perceive uncertainty (financial, competitive and operational), we suggest that they are more likely to engage in pre-venture planning early in the process of new firm start-up. Perceptions of certain environments are likely to prompt nascent entrepreneurs to plan late (after they accomplish other start-up activities). Since, by the definition we have used here – "certain environments" are situations where nascent entrepreneurs believe they have sufficient knowledge – it begs the question as to whether entrepreneurs perceiving certain environments would see any need to engage in planning at all (Indeed, it may be the case that the activity of planning has no influence on a nascent entrepreneur's ability to develop a new venture, particularly in environments where nascent entrepreneurs are certain about the characteristics of their environments. In these situations, the act of planning would take time and effort away from other tasks that may be more necessary for creating a new business. We offer this final hypothesis to explore whether the absence of planning may increase the likelihood of persistence in the creation of new ventures:

H4: The absence of planning in situations of perceived environmental certainty (financial, competitive, and operational) is likely to increase the likelihood of new venture persistence.

3. Research methods

3.1. Sampling procedures

The data for this study were obtained from the Panel Study of Entrepreneurial Dynamics (PSED). The PSED is a longitudinal data set of individuals in the process of starting businesses who were identified from a random digit dialing telephone survey of 64,622 adults in the United States (Reynolds and Curtin, 2004). Details of the survey process and descriptions of specific items in the questionnaires used for the initial

and follow-up interviews can be found in the *Handbook of Entrepreneurial Dynamics* (Gartner et al., 2004).

To qualify as "nascent entrepreneurs," that is, individuals who were in the process of starting a business, respondents answered "yes" to the following two questions: (1) Are you, alone or with others, now trying to start a new business? (2) Are you, alone or with others, now starting a new business or new venture for your employer? Is the effort a part of your job assignment? In addition, respondents needed to meet three additional criteria. First, they expected to have some share in the ownership of the business. Second, they were involved in activities to start the new firm in the last 12 months. Third, the effort was still in the start-up or gestation phase and was not an infant firm (Shaver et al., 2001). Based on these selection criteria, the number of cases available for analysis was 817.

A number of arguments have been offered that strongly urge researchers interested in the activities of nascent entrepreneurs to use cohorts of individuals initiating firms within the same time frame (Delmar and Shane, 2003, 2004; Gartner and Carter, 2003). Based on analyses of firm startup markers completed by each respondent at the initial interview: Gartner et al. (2003) suggested that a cohort of nascent entrepreneurs who first began startup activities within 2 years of the initial interview date would be appropriate as a similar time frame cohort when studying nascent entrepreneurs in the PSED dataset. We applied the 2-year time frame selection criteria, which resulted in a cohort of 361 nascent entrepreneurs.

Follow-up surveys were conducted at intervals of 12- (R wave), 24- (S wave), and 36- (T wave) months to evaluate the status of these start-up efforts. Because of a significant loss in number of respondents in the S wave and T wave follow-ups (see Reynolds and Curtin, 2004), we selected nascent entrepreneurs who had responded at the first follow-up (R wave). This provided us with a cohort of 276 nascent entrepreneurs who reported their status as: operating business – 83, active start-up – 71, inactive start-up – 59 and no longer worked on – 63. We labeled the first two categories as "continuing startups" and the latter two as "discontinued startups."

The PSED dataset comes with post-stratification weights for each respondent based on estimates from the U.S. Census Bureau's Current Population Survey (Curtin and Reynolds, 2004). The post-stratification scheme was based on gender, age, ethnic background and educational attainment. Applying these weights for analyses are essential for the generalizability of any studies related to PSED data set. According to Curtin and Reynolds (2004: 492) "Weights should be used in all types of analyses." As per their suggestions for using these weights, we adjusted the weights to reflect the reduction in the number of cases due to missing and not applicable responses.

3.2. *Measures*

3.2.1. *Persistence*
Following the suggestions of Delmar and Shane (2003, 2004) we considered organizing efforts that resulted in a new firm or were still ongoing, to be an indicator of emerging firm persistence. In the follow-up data collection (R wave), which occurred approximately 1 year after the initial interview, nascent entrepreneurs were asked about the status of their startup efforts. Responses fell into four categories – "operating business," "active startup," "inactive startup," and "no longer worked on." The first two categories were coded as "continuing startups" (1), while the last two categories were "discontinued startups" (0). In our final sample of those nascent entrepreneurs who reported information on startup status at the R wave: 56.9% were coded as "continuing startups" while 43.1% were coded as discontinued startups.

3.2.2. *Business planning*
In the initial interview (Q wave) and first follow-up (R wave) of data collection, nascent entrepreneurs were asked if they engaged in a list of 26 start-up activities (Gartner et al., 2004). The measure for the activity of business planning used for this study were items Q111 and R111: "A business plan usually outlines the markets to be served, the products or services to be provided, the resources required, including money, and the expected growth and profit for the new

business. Has a business plan been prepared for this start-up?" Nascent entrepreneurs who reported "yes" on this business planning activity measure were coded as "1," while those who reported "no" were coded as "0."

3.2.3. *Business plan timing*
Business planning may occur at any point along a sequence of start-up activities. When nascent entrepreneurs were interviewed about the 26 start-up activities, they were asked whether each specific activity had been completed (yes or no). If a nascent entrepreneur said "yes," a month and year was also provided for when that activity occurred. Calculating whether business planning was early or late in the sequence of start-up activities was determined as the time (in months) from the date in which any one of the 26 start-up activities were initiated to the date when business planning occurred. This number was divided by the total gestation time, which is determined as the time (in months) between the dates of the earliest and latest activities indicated from responses in both the Q and R waves.

3.2.4. *Perceived environmental uncertainty*
To ascertain perceptions of environmental uncertainty, we used an 11-item measure from PSED mail survey (Matthews and Human, 2004). Each variable used a five-point Likert scale to assess respondents' perceptions of the environmental context for entrepreneurship. These items are related to these nascent entrepreneurs' perceptions of their ability to understand or to predict the state of various environmental conditions due to lack of information or uncertainty about that environment. The question for the 11-item scale reads: "Considering the economic and community context for the new firm, how certain are you that the new business will be able to accomplish each of the following?" The response scale was anchored by (5) – "very high certainty" to (1) – "very low certainty" including a category for (8) – "does not apply." A principal components factor analysis with varimax rotation was conducted on the responses to the 11-item measure and three factors were extracted with eigenvalues greater than one. As suggested by Matthews and Human (2004), we labeled these

three factors as "Financial Uncertainty," "Competitive Uncertainty," and "Operational Uncertainty." Cumulatively they account for approximately 53% of the variance. Cronbach's alphas for the three factors were 0.758, 0.705 and 0.682. Our results were consistent with Matthew and Human's (2004) factor analysis of responses from nascent entrepreneurs completing the mail questionnaire items at the initial interview stage (Q wave). The composite factor values from our factor analysis were used (see Table I).

3.2.5. *Control variables*

Prior research has argued that persistence of new ventures depends on the founder's human capital (Bates, 1990; Bruderl et al., 1992; Castrogiovanni, 1996). Following Delmar and Shane (2004), we control for five dimensions of human capital: education, industry experience, managerial experience, prior startup experience and venture team size. For education, nascent entrepreneurs were asked "what is the highest level of education you have completed so far?" Responses were coded on an ordinal scale from 0 to 9, with 0 – "up to eighth grade" to 9 – "LLD, MD, Ph. D and EDD degree." Studies suggest that entrepreneurs with more industry

experience are less likely to terminate their new ventures (Bates, 1990). We measure industry experience as the total years of full-time paid work experience in any field within the industry these nascent entrepreneurs were starting their emerging firms in. For managerial experience, nascent entrepreneurs were asked to respond to the question "For how many years, if any, did you have any managerial, supervisory or administrative responsibilities." Consistent with Bruderl and Preisendorfer (1998), we control for prior startup experience and venture team size. Prior startup experience was measured by the number of startups a nascent entrepreneur has been involved with. We coded "0" for first time entrepreneurs and "1" for those who have had prior startup experience. Lechler (2001) in a review of research on ventures formed by teams versus solo-founders indicated that teams are more successful. Team size is measured as the number of members in the initial venture team at the time of the initial interview. Finally, we control for the industry and an entrepreneur's growth aspiration. Growth aspiration was operationalized as expectations of whether nascent entrepreneurs wanted to grow their ventures to a size "as large as possible" or "at a manageable level." Matthews and Human

TABLE I
Factor analysis of perceived environmental uncertainty

Item number	Items	Factors		
		Financial uncertainty	Competitive uncertainty	Operational uncertainty
QD1c	Obtain start-up capital:	**0.862**	0.049	0.027
QD1d	Obtain working capital:	**0.831**	0.242	−0.022
QD1f	Obtain a banks help	**0.718**	0.033	0.194
QD1k	Obtain venture capitalists' help	**0.499**	0.058	0.458
QD1f	Attract customers	0.094	**0.702**	0.036
QD1g	Compete with other firms:	0.113	**0.679**	0.073
QD1h	Comply with local, state, and federal regulations	−0.041	**0.700**	0.058
QD1i	Keep up with technological advances	0.221	**0.574**	0.221
QD1a	Obtain raw materials	0.004	−0.067	**0.779**
QD1b	Attract employees	0.267	0.213	**0.535**
QD1e	Deal with distributors	−0.002	0.368	**0.554**
	Eigenvalue (> 1)	2.343	2.024	1.508
	Percentage of variance	21.303	18.398	13.707
	Cumulative percentage	21.303	39.701	53.408
	Cronbach's alpha	0.758	0.705	0.682

(2000) found that perceptions of operational uncertainty were highly correlated to growth aspirations. We control for industry by using SIC code information reported in the dataset, which we coded into 10 broad industry sectors: 1 for agriculture, forest and fishing, 2 for mining, 3 for construction, 4 for manufacturing, 5 for transportation and communication, 6 for wholesale, 7 for retail, 8 for business services, 9 for consumer and service, and 10 for health care and education.

3.3. Models

A series of logistic regression models were employed to determine the impact of business planning, the timing of business planning and the moderating effects of the various dimensions of environmental uncertainty on the probability of venture persistence. Binary logistic regression was used because it restricts the range of the dependent variable to a value between 0 and 1, which is appropriate for investigating the likelihood or probability of persistence. We first created a base model of logistic regression, which includes all our control variables and environmental uncertainty variables. We subsequently added business planning, timing of business planning and the cross products of timing of business planning and the three dimensions of environmental uncertainty independently. We then tested for the significance of the difference between the full models and the nested base model by using Chi-square tests. A significant Chi-square test means additional variance of probability of persistence explained by the added-on predictors.

4. Results

Table II lists means, standard deviation and correlations for our control variables, moderators and independent variables.

As indicated in model 1 of Table III, education, industry experience and team size have significant and positive coefficients, suggesting that nascent entrepreneurs with more years of education, industry experience and who started with a team will have a higher probability of

persistence in the startup process. Surprisingly, we failed to detect any significant impact of prior startup experience on venture persistence as predicted in previous studies (i.e., Bruderl et al., 1992). Furthermore, we also found that venture persistence is independent of industry sector.

Model 2 of Table III shows that the coefficient for business planning is 0.961 ($p < 0.01$) with an odd ratio of 2.614. It suggests that nascent entrepreneurs who completed a business plan were 2.614 times more likely to persist than those who did not. It should be noted that we also tested the interaction effects between business planning and the three dimensions of environmental uncertainty: financial, competitive and operational. All of these interaction effects were not statistically significant, suggesting a strong and independent effect of business planning on startup persistence. In a cross tabulation of business planning with persistence rate, nascent entrepreneurs who completed a business plan had a persistence rate of 66.7%, while those without a business plan had a persistence rate is 41.7%. Hypothesis 4 was, therefore, not confirmed. Planning is critical to continuing the process of venture emergence, no matter what the perception of the environment is, and whether planning occurs early or late in the venture creation process.

Model 3 tests the independent effect of the timing of business planning, overall, on venture persistence. The Chi-square change is not statistically significant ($\Delta\chi^2 = 0.885$; df = 1). Models 4, 5 and 6 test the cross products between timing of business planning and financial uncertainty, competitive uncertainty and operational uncertainty. Models 4 and 5 show that the impact of business planning on persistence is moderated by perceived financial uncertainty ($\Delta\chi^2 = 6.813$; df = 1; $p < 0.01$) and perceived competitive uncertainty ($\Delta\chi^2 = 11.381$; df = 1; $p < 0.01$). But we failed to detect any moderating effect for perceived operational uncertainty ($\Delta\chi^2 = 0.119$; df = 1).

We conducted additional analyses to interpret the interaction effect between the timing of business planning and financial and competitive uncertainty. First, variable means in Models 4 and 5 were substituted for all predictors except for the timing of business planning, the uncertainty

Jianwen Liao and William B. Gartner

TABLE II

Descriptive statistics: means, standard deviation and correlation matrix

	N	Mean	STD	1	2	3	4	5	6	7	8	9	10	11	12	13
Continued vs. discontinued	276	0.558	0.498	1.000												
Education	274	4.693	2.008	0.164***	1.000											
Startup experience	276	0.188	0.392	0.037	0.059	1.000										
Industry experience	273	16.300	10.578	0.078	0.184***	0.066	1.000									
Managerial experience	266	7.925	8.168	0.054	0.198***	0.144**	0.615***	1.000								
Team size	273	1.908	1.069	0.144**	0.222***	-0.408***	0.064	0.091	1.000							
Industry	271	7.336	2.000	-0.020	0.160***	0.020	-0.065	-0.070	-0.048	1.000						
Growth aspiration	273	1.791	0.407	-0.001	0.042	-0.008	0.082	0.102*	-0.111*	0.171***	1.000					
Financial uncertainty	203	2.165	1.257	0.084	-0.041	-0.078	-0.066	-0.049	0.250***	-0.017	-0.013	1.000				
Competitive uncertainty	205	3.767	0.991	0.065	-0.008	0.088	-0.001	-0.052	0.062	0.001	-0.206	0.295***	1.000			
Operational uncertainty	203	2.159	1.383	-0.071	-0.129**	-0.120	-0.045	-0.063	0.155**	-0.160**	-0.158**	0.316***	0.347***	1.000		
W/without planning	276	0.620	0.486	0.250***	0.149**	-0.100*	0.107*	0.094	0.258***	-0.089	-0.110*	0.049	0.118*	0.051	1.000	
Timing business planning	172	0.498	0.334	-0.108	-0.070	-0.081	0.059	-0.084	0.101	0.004	-0.062	0.125	0.003	0.069	0.114	1.000

*$p \leq 0.1$; **$p \leq 0.05$; ***$p \leq 0.01$.

TABLE III

Main and interaction effects of timing of business, process and environment variables on persistence

Variable	Model 1 β	Model 1 Exp(β)	Model 2 β	Model 2 Exp(β)	Model 3 β	Model 3 Exp(β)	Model 4 β	Model 4 Exp(β)	Model 5 β	Model 5 Exp(β)	Model 6 β	Model 6 Exp(β)
Intercept	-2.049**	0.129	-2.115	0.121	-0.106	0.900	-1.974	0.139	-5.892**	0.030	-0.290	0.748
Education	0.171*	1.186	0.134	1.143	0.088	1.092	0.164	1.178	0.068	1.071	0.087	1.091
Startup experience	0.395	1.484	0.425	1.529	0.687	1.987	0.616	1.851	0.763	2.145	0.673	1.960
Industry experience	0.0389*	1.040	0.033	1.033	0.031	1.031	0.028	1.028	0.031	1.032	0.029	1.030
Managerial experience	-0.038	0.963	-0.038	0.963	-0.0363**	0.963	-0.0733**	0.929	-0.075*	0.928	-0.0724*	0.930
Team size	0.343*	1.409	0.262	1.299	0.367	1.444	0.349	1.417	0.427	1.533	0.364	1.438
Industry	0.171	1.187	0.168	1.183	0.197	1.218	0.297	1.346	0.073	1.076	0.220	1.246
Growth aspiration	-0.056	0.946	-0.036	0.965	0.027	1.027	0.029	1.029	0.100	1.105	0.024	1.024
Financial uncertainty	0.145	1.156	0.156	1.168	0.127	1.135	0.811**	2.249	0.146	1.157	0.120	1.127
Competitive uncertainty	0.197	1.218	0.127	1.136	-0.167	0.846	-0.129	0.879	1.224**	3.399	-0.164	0.848
Operational uncertainty	-0.188	0.829	-0.180	0.835	-0.040	0.961	-0.083	0.920	-0.033	0.967	0.048	1.049
W/without Biz planning			0.961***	2.614								
Timing of Biz planning							2.420**	11.242	12.041***	169610.95	-0.217	0.805
Timing of Biz planning × financial uncertainty							-1.380***	0.252				
Timing of Biz planning × competitive uncertainty									-3.175***	0.042		
Timing of Biz plan × operational uncertainty											-0.175	0.840
Δχ²	17.434		8.222		0.885		6.813		11.321		0.119	
d.f	10		1		1		1		1		1	
α≤	0.05		0.01		n.s.		0.01		0.01		n.s.	

* $p \leq 0.1$; ** $p \leq 0.05$; *** $p \leq 0.01$.

variable and the cross products between the two variables. The result was a reduced equation with the two predictors and their cross product. Second, we followed the procedure of Cohen and Levinthal (1990), in that we selected values for high and low of the uncertainty variable as one standard deviation above zero point and one standard deviation below zero point respectively. Substituting each of these values into the reduced equation yielded the following two sets of linear equations (Depicted in Figures 1a, b).

Model 4. Timing of Business Planning × Financial Uncertainty
When Financial Uncertainty is high (means + 1 std)

$$In[p/(1-p)] = 2.653 - 3.214 * \text{ Timing of business planning}$$

When Financial Uncertainty is low (means – 1 std)

$$In[p/(1-p)] = 0.102 + 1.313 * \text{ Timing of business planning}$$

Model 5. Timing of Business Planning × Competitive Uncertainty
When Competitive Uncertainty is high (means + 1 std)

$$In[p/(1-p)] = 2.389 - 3.417 * \text{ Timing of business planning}$$

When Competitive Uncertainty is low (means – 1 std)

$$In[p/(1-p)] = -0.271 + 2.339 * \text{ Timing of business planning}$$

where p is the probability of persistence.

Figure 1a indicates that the impact of timing of business planning on persistence depends on the degree of financial uncertainty. Specifically, planning early would increase venture persistence under highly uncertain financial environments. By contrast, planning late would increase venture persistence under more certain financial environments. This confirms hypotheses 1a and 1b.

Figure 1b indicates that perceived competitive uncertainty moderates the relationship between timing of business planning and the probability of persistence. Specifically, planning early significantly increased the surviving probability under uncertain competitive environments. By contrast, planning late would be more effective when the competitive environment is relatively certain. This confirms hypotheses 2a and 2b.

As mentioned earlier, we found no relationship between operational uncertainty and the timing of business planning, therefore, hypotheses 3a and 3b were not confirmed. We also tested the interaction effects between business planning (with or without) and the three types of environmental uncertainty. In all three logistic regression models, the added interaction terms were not statistically significant, therefore lending no support for Hypothesis 4. It therefore suggests that the effect of business planning is independent of environmental conditions.

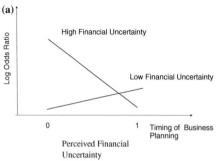
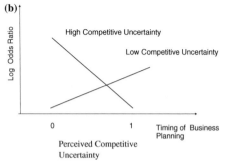

Figure 1. (a, b) Moderating effects of financial and competitive uncertainty.

Because the measure of persistence separates nascent entrepreneurs into two groups consisting of discontinued startups (inactive and those who gave up) versus continuing startups (those still active in trying to start a business and those who started businesses), there may be characteristics in the continuing startup group (between the "still active" group and those who started businesses group) which might affect these results. Carter et al. (1996) suggested that the "still active" group may consist of a number of nascent entrepreneurs who simply do not engage in enough activities to determine whether their entrepreneurial efforts could be a success or a failure. One might, think of some of these "still active" nascent entrepreneurs as "dabblers" compared to those nascent entrepreneurs who were able to get a new business in operation. We tested the logistic regression models for a recoded sample of the "in-business" group, coded as "1" and the "still active" group, coded as "0". To our surprise, we failed to detect any significant impact on business planning, and its interactions with uncertainty variables on the rate difference between "still active" and "in-business."

Finally, while the measure used for business planning (Q111 and R111) in this study describes what a business plan contains, and then asks whether such a plan has been prepared, there is likely to be varying degrees to which these plans are actually formalized. Matthews et al. (2003) argue that all entrepreneurs engage in planning, to some degree, throughout the venture creation process as an ongoing inherent cognitive orientation of individuals involved in undertaking new activities. From their perspective, the completion of a business plan may be achieved in varying degrees of formalization, from something that is in the entrepreneurs' head to a formally prepared plan. This logic was explored in the PSED research program. For those nascent entrepreneurs who answered "yes" to Q111 or R111, respondents were then asked in Q114: "What is the current form – (1) unwritten or in your head, (2) informally written, (3) formally prepared, (4) both 1 and 2, (5) Don't know, or (6) Something else?" In Table IV we report a cross tabulation of the three types of business plan formalization (unwritten, informal, and formally prepared) by whether these plans were accomplished early or late in the venture creation process. Surprisingly, only about a third of those who responded to this question indicated that they completed a formally prepared business plan. So, while nascent entrepreneurs may indicate that they complete a business plan (i.e., Q111: "A business plan usually outlines the markets to be served, the products or services to be provided, the resources required, including money, and the expected growth and profit for the new business. Has a business plan been prepared for this startup?"), it is less likely to be in the formalized format many scholars and consultants would

TABLE IV
Business plan timing (early or late) by plan formalization

Respondent count	Business plan formalization			Total
Business plan timing	Unwritten/in head	Informally written	Formally prepared	
Early	15	42	21	78
Late	11	30	34	75
Total	26	72	55	153
χ^2 test	0.615	3.769*	4.786**	

*$p < 0.1$, **$p < 0.01$.
Note: Three respondents in the planned early category reported "something else".
One respondent in the planned early category reported "don't know".
One respondent in the planned early category reported both "unwritten and informally written".
One respondent in the planned late category reported both "unwritten and informally written".

suggest (Gumpert, 2003). In addition, these results indicate that there is a weak statistical relationship ($p < 0.1$) suggesting that when nascent entrepreneurs plan early they are more likely to complete informal plans, and a strong statistical relationship ($p < 0.01$) suggesting that when nascent entrepreneurs plan late they are more likely to complete formally prepared plans. We found these results somewhat counter-intuitive, and we will discuss them in the next section.

5. Discussion and conclusions

This study looked at nascent entrepreneurs in the process of starting companies to determine whether the completion of a business plan improved the likelihood of venture creation persistence. In addition, we studied whether these nascent entrepreneurs' perceived environments had any moderating effect on whether planning efforts occurring either early or late in the venture development process also improved the likelihood of venture creation persistence. The results of this study indicate a significant main effect for the completion of a business plan for increasing the likelihood of persistence (i.e., establishing a new firm or continuing to engage in startup activities) irregardless of the emerging venture's context. Pre-venture planning does matter. It is better, in general, to complete a business plan during the process of venture creation, than to not plan. This result is in line with recent research (Delmar and Shane, 2003, 2004; Honig and Karlsson, 2004) that found that business planning increases persistence in the venture creation process as well as increasing the likelihood of success at starting new ventures.

We should also note that a nascent entrepreneur's level of education and industry experience had an affect on persistence, while other control variables, such growth aspirations and team size did not. The finding that industry experience increases the likelihood of persistence is also consistent with previous research (Parker, 2004).

The emerging venture's context does seem to moderate the effect on venture persistence for when pre-venture planning occurs in the process

of venture creation. Nascent entrepreneurs completing business plans early in the startup process in highly uncertain financial and competitive environments were more likely to persist in the venture creation process than those who planned late. And, nascent entrepreneurs completing business plans late in the startup process in certain financial and competitive environments were more likely to persist in the venture creation process than those who planned early. Operational uncertainty does not appear to affect the impact of business planning on the persistence of emerging firms.

These results would seem to support prior theory and evidence (Castrogiovanni, 1996; Delmar and Shane, 2004) and some practitioner wisdom that early business planning can be beneficial. What this research shows, though, is that not all emerging ventures will benefit from planning early.

Before offering any additional thoughts about issues of planning early or late in different environmental contexts, it is important to look closely at what each of the three uncertainty measures, actually measures (see Table I). In this study, "financial uncertainty" ascertains these nascent entrepreneurs' perceptions of their ability to accomplish the acquisition of financial resources for the emerging venture. A "less certain" financial environment means that the nascent entrepreneur is less certain of obtaining startup capital, working capital, help from a bank, or assistance from a venture capitalist. "Competitive uncertainty" ascertains these nascent entrepreneurs' perceptions of their ability to attract customers, compete with other firms, comply with government regulations and keep up with technological advances. And "operational uncertainty" focuses on perceptions of whether nascent entrepreneurs can accomplish such tasks as obtaining raw materials, attracting employees, and deal with distributors. Ratings of "very low certainty" indicate environments were nascent entrepreneurs are less confident they have the information from their economic and community context to determine whether their firms can accomplish financial, competitive, and operational activities.

Given these descriptions of the three types of environments, we believe that our findings show that early business planning is more helpful in situations where nascent entrepreneurs need to acquire financial resources that may enable subsequent organizing activities to occur (thereby leading to venture persistence), and where nascent entrepreneurs need to make sense of more uncertain competitive environments (thereby leading to venture persistence). We would have thought that one of the reasons for completing a business plan early in the venture creation process in conditions of financial uncertainty, would be for the purposes of raising financial resources from others, and, that such planning would likely involve the completion of a formally prepared business plan. The results in Table IV temper this assumption. For those respondents indicating the degree of business plan formalization, nearly 75% of those nascent entrepreneurs who planned early (78 respondents), completed a plan that was "unwritten" (15 respondents) or "informal" (42 respondents). If formally prepared business plans are necessary for acquiring financial resources, most nascent entrepreneurs who planned early were not taking this route. How these "unwritten and informal" business plans were used, then, is an issue that needs further exploration.

We believe that the completion of a business plan early in the venture formation process seems to help nascent entrepreneurs reduce "state" uncertainty (Milliken, 1987). In completing "unwritten and informal" business plans, as well as formally prepared plans, nascent entrepreneurs gain information to help them better understand their situations through the process of planning. We would surmise that planning early to reduce uncertainty enables nascent entrepreneurs to more effectively identify what other actions to accomplish.

In some respects, we can use the finding that success at venture persistence for nascent entrepreneurs who perceive more certain financial and competitive environments, and who plan later, as evidence that in situations where there is less need to reduce state uncertainty, the process of completing a business plan is less necessary at the beginning of the startup process.

The finding that operational uncertainty had no effect on planning, and no effect on planning

early or late, as it pertains to persistence, is subject to some speculation. Given that the variables that consist of this measure are composed of activities that often have alternative sources of supply (i.e., raw materials, employees, distributors), the knowledge that choices exist for acquiring these resources might be more important than the value of gaining knowledge of what specific choices might be available. That is, the state uncertainty for operational aspects of the new venture may be perceived as something that the entrepreneur has more control over, where being either certain or uncertain of operational issues may have less impact. Both financial and competitive uncertainty may seem to be areas where reducing certainty is perceived to have more impact on the emerging firm's survival.

5.1. *Limitations and suggestions for future research*

As is in the use of any secondary dataset, one of the problems with using the PSED is that one can only use the questions that were asked. The business planning questions in the PSED are, at best, crude measures of business planning and the business planning process. It would be helpful to know more about the specific kinds of activities (e.g., preparing pro-forma income statements and capital budgets, identifying specific customers) that nascent entrepreneurs undertook during the process of business planning, and the amount of time and effort devoted to these activities. The evidence in Table IV is disconcerting in that a large number of nascent entrepreneurs completed business plans that were "in their head/unwritten" or "informally written." An exploration of what constitutes a completed "unwritten" business plan would be a helpful insight. It would also be helpful to know more about the reasons nascent entrepreneurs engaged in business planning. Few questions are asked in the PSED that attempt to explore why nascent entrepreneurs engage in the activities they do. Providing reasons for planning activities would generate many insights as to whether business plans were used to raise capital, etc. It would be valuable to supplement the PSED cases with matching in-depth case studies of nascent entrepreneurs (i.e., finding nascent entrepreneurs who have similar demographic, start-up and venture characteristics) to identify more of the details and logic used by these individuals for how and why they planned.

Some concerns have been raised about the endogenous aspects of perceived uncertainty and planning, in that, the process of planning, itself, would seem to increase a nascent entrepreneurs' awareness of uncertainty in the environment. Or, the lack of planning may suggest an "ignorance is bliss" effect, where perceptions of a certain environment reflects a lack of due diligence on the part of some nascent entrepreneurs. Our efforts to untangle the influence of planning activities on perceptions of uncertainty through analyses of when the perception measures were asked in the sequence of other venture creation activities, was inconclusive. Further analyses on the timing of planning activities and the administration of perceptual questions about the environment need to be undertaken to determine their interactive effects.

Business planning is only one of many activities that nascent entrepreneurs may undertake during the startup process. As shown in Delmar and Shane (2003: 1177), business planning appears to be significantly correlated to organizing activities, overall. This might suggest that those nascent entrepreneurs engaged in business planning may also be simultaneously engaged in completing other kinds of startup behaviors that may also affect persistence. This study explored whether business planning occurred early or late as measured by a ratio of: the months between when the first startup activity occurred and when business planning occurred, and the months between when the first startup activity and last startup activity occurred. We did not explore the number of startup activities that may have occurred, when each startup activity occurred, or the sequence of each startup activity, and how the number, timing, and sequence of other startup activities may affect the value of business planning for venture persistence.

And, finally, the process of business planning, itself, is likely to involve undertaking a number of activities that may be beneficial for persistence. The process of planning is more than the process of generating the plan, itself. If the business plan "outlines the markets to be served, the products and services to be provided, and the resources required..." then nascent entrepreneurs would have needed to engage in a variety of behaviors to generate this information. Parsing out what entrepreneurs do when they plan is likely to provide insights into how "doing" informs "thinking" when planning.

A number of other features of an emerging venture's context may also affect the value and timing of business planning. A nascent entrepreneur's perception of uncertainty may be affected by the knowledge resources available. Nascent entrepreneurs vary in their level of social and business contacts (Aldrich and Carter, 2004), as well as their knowledge of government help (Dennis and Reynolds, 2004) that could help in reducing uncertainty. Nascent entrepreneurs who perceive more certain environments may also have more social, business and government support.

6. Conclusions

In general, pre-venture business planning significantly increases the likelihood that emerging firm formation efforts will continue and/or become new firms. Under certain perceived environments, pre-venture planning increases the likelihood of emerging firm persistence in situations where nascent entrepreneurs perceive higher levels of financial and competitive uncertainty. We suggest that the uncertainty measures used in this study may reflect these nascent entrepreneurs' confidence in their ability to both acquire resources (financial uncertainty) and compete against other firms (competitive uncertainty). When nascent entrepreneurs indicate they are less uncertain about their financial and competitive situations, they may be indicating that they lack confidence in the knowledge they currently have. Engaging in pre-venture planning would likely increase a nascent entrepreneur's knowledge, and thereby reduce uncertainty. In contrast, for those nascent entrepreneurs who were confident about their knowledge of their competitive and financial situation, engaging in pre-venture business planning would not be perceived as a way to enhance knowledge they already have. Planning for these entrepreneurs would be less relevant to their business formation activities early on their venture creation efforts. Yet, as the emerging venture develops, nascent entrepreneur do plan (i.e., late planning) which increases the chances the emerging venture will persist.

Planning is important to the process of venture creation, and research should be undertaken to explore more of the details of the planning process as well as the specific activities these individuals engage in. Since the information gained from planning is likely to be gained from other activities (i.e., contacting customers, evaluating competitors, talking with investors), it is critical that we develop better ways to systematically observe entrepreneurial behavior over time. The PSED is the first step in developing generalizable data on the process of new business creation.

References

Aldrich, H., 1999, *Organizations Evolving*, London: Sage.

Aldrich, H. E. and N. M. Carter, 2004, Social Networks, in W. B. Gartner, K. G. Shaver, N. M. Carter and P. D. Reynolds (eds.), *Handbook of Entrepreneurial Dynamics*, Thousand Oaks, CA: Sage Publications, 324–335.

Alvarez, S. A. and L. W. Busenitz, 2001, 'The Entrepreneurship of Resource-Based Theory', *Journal of Management* 27(6), 755–775.

Ansoff, H. I., 1984, *Implanting Strategic Management*, New Jersey: Prentice Hall.

Baker, T. and R. E. Nelson, 2005, 'Creating Something from Nothing: Resource Constructions through Entrepreneurial Bricolage', *Administrative Science Quarterly* 50, 329–366.

Bates, T., 1990, 'Entrepreneur Human Capital Inputs and Small Business Longitivity', *Review of Economic Statistics* 72(4), 551–559.

Bhide, A., 1994, 'How Entrepreneurs Craft Strategies that Work', *Harvard Business Review* March-April, 150–161.

Bhide, A., 2000, *The Origin and Evolution of New Businesses*, New York: Oxford University Press.

Bourgeois, L. J. and K. Eisenhardt, 1988, 'Strategic Decision Process in High Velocity Environments: Four Cases in the Microcomputer Industry', *Management Science* 34(7), 816–835.

Bruderl, J. and P Preisendorfer, 1998, 'Network Support and the Success of Newly Founded Businesses', *Small Business Economics* 10, 213–225.

Bruderl, J., P. Preisendorfer and R. Ziegler, 1992, 'Persistence Chances of Newly Founded Business Organizations', *American Sociological Review* 57, 227–302.

Carter, N., W.B. Gartner and P.D. Reynolds, 1996, 'Exploring Startup Event Sequences', *Journal of Business Venturing* 11(3), 51–166.

Castrogiovanni, G. J., 1996, 'Pre-startup Planning and the Persistence of New Small Businesses: Theoretical Linkages', *Journal of Management* 22(6), 801–822.

Cohen, W. M. and D. A. Leventhal, 1990, 'Absorptive Capacity: A New Perspective On Learning and Innovation', *Administrative Science Quarterly* 35, 128–152.

Curtin, R. T. and P. D. Reynolds, 2004, Appendix B: Data Documentation, Data Preparation, and Weights, in W. B. Gartner, K. G. Shaver, N. M. Carter and P. D. Reynolds (eds.), *Handbook of Entrepreneurial Dynamics*, Thousand Oaks, CA: Sage Publications, 477–494.

Delmar, F. and S. Shane, 2003, 'Does Business Planning Facilitate the Development of New Ventures?', *Strategic Management Journal* 24, 1165–1185.

Delmar, F. and S. Shane, 2004, 'Legitimating First: Organizing Activities and the Persistence of New Ventures', *Journal of Business Venturing* 19, 385–410.

Dennis, W. J. and P. D. Reynolds, 2004, Knowledge and Use of Assistance, in W. B. Gartner, K. G. Shaver, N. M. Carter and P. D. Reynolds (eds.), *Handbook of Entrepreneurial Dynamics*, Thousand Oaks, CA: Sage Publications, 336–351.

Fry, F. L. and C. R Stoner, 1985, 'Business Plans: Two Major Types', *Journal of Small Business Management* 23(1), 1–6.

Fuller, M., 1996, 'Strategic Planning in an Era of Total Competition', *Planning Review* 24(3), 22–27.

Galbraith, J., 1973, *Designing Complex Organizations*, Reading, MA: Addison-Wesley.

Gartner, William B., 1985, 'A Framework for Describing and Classifying The Phenomenon of New Venture Creation', *Academy of Management Review* 10(4), 696–706.

Gartner, W. B. and N. M. Carter, 2003, Entrepreneurial Behavior and Firm Organizing Processes, in Z. J. Acs and D. B. Audretch (eds.), *Handbook of Entrepreneurship Research*, Boston: Kluwer Academic Publishers, 195–221.

Gartner, W. B., N. M. Carter and P. D. Reynolds, 2004, Business Startup Activities, in W. B. Gartner, K. G. Shaver, N. M. Carter and P. D. Reynolds (eds.), *Handbook of Entrepreneurial Dynamics*, Thousand Oaks, CA: Sage Publications, 285–298.

Gartner, W. B., N. M. Carter, B. M. B. Lichtenstein and K. Dooley (2003), When are New Firms Founded? Paper presented at the annual meeting of the Academy of Management, Seattle, WA.

Gartner, W. B., K. G. Shaver, N. M. Carter and P. D. Reynolds, 2004, *Handbook of Entrepreneurial Dynamics*, Thousand Oaks, CA: Sage Publications.

Gumpert, D. E., 2003, *Burn Your Business Plan*, Needham, Ma: Lauson Publishing.

Henderson, J. W., 1988, *Obtaining Venture Financing*, Lexington, MA: Lexington Books.

Honig, B. and T. Karlsson, 2004, 'Institutional Forces and the Written Business Plan', *Journal of Management* 30(1), 29–48.

Katz, J. and W.B. Gartner, 1988, 'Properties of emerging Organizations', *Academy of Management Review* 13(3), 429–442.

Lechler, T., 2001, 'Social Interaction: A Determinant of Entrepreneurial Team Venture Success', *Small Business Economics* 16(4), 263–278.

Mancuso, J. R., 1985, *How to Write a Willing Business Plan*, Englewood Cliffs, NJ: Prentice-Hall.

Matthews, C., M. Baucus and M. Ford, 2003, 'To Plan Or Not To Plan, is that Really The Question?' Presentation at the Babson Kauffman Entrepreneurship Research Conference, Glasgow, Scotland.

Matthew, C. and S. Human, 2000, *The Little Engine that Could: Uncertainty and Growth Expectations of Nascent Entrepreneurs. Frontiers of Entrepreneurship Research*, Wellesley, MA: Babson College 55–66.

Matthew, C. and S. Human, 2004, The Economic and Community Context for Entrepreneurship: Perceived Environmental Uncertainty, in W. B. Gartner, K. G. Shaver, N. M. Carter and P. D. Reynolds (eds.), *Handbook of Entrepreneurial Dynamics*, Thousand Oaks, CA: Sage Publications, 421–429.

Matthew, C. H. and S. G. Scott, 1995, 'Uncertainty and Planning in Small and Entrepreneurial Firms: An Empirical Assessment', *Journal of Small Business Management* **33**(4), 34–52.

Meyer, J. and B. Rowan, 1977, 'Institutional Organizations: Formal Structure as Myth and Ceremony', *American Journal of Sociology* **83**, 340–363.

Miller, D. and P. H Friesen, 1983, 'Strategy-Making and Environment: The Third Link. Strategic', *Management Journal* **4**(3), 221–235.

Milliken, F., 1987, 'Three Types of Uncertainty about Environment: State, Effect and Response Uncertainty', *Academy of Management Review* **12**, 133–143.

Parker, S. C., 2004, *The Economics of Self-Employment and Entrepreneurship*, Cambridge: Cambridge University Press.

Reynolds, P. D. and R. T. Curtin, 2004a, Appendix A: Data Collection, in W. B. Gartner, K. G. Shaver, N. M. Carter and P. D. Reynolds (eds.), *Handbook of Entrepreneurial Dynamics*, Thousand Oaks, CA: Sage Publications, 453–475.

Reynolds, P. D. and B. A. Miller, 1992, 'New Firm Gestation: Conception, Birth, and Implications for Research', *Journal of Business Venturing* **7**, 1–14.

Shaver, K. G., N. M. Carter, W. B. Gartner and P. D. Reynolds, 2001, *Who is a Nascent Entrepreneur? Decision Rules for Identifying and Selecting Entrepreneurs in the Panel Study of Entrepreneurial Dynamics (PSED). Frontiers of Entrepreneurship Research*, Wellesley, MA: Babson College 122.

Shaver, K. G and L. R. Scott, 1991, 'Person, Process, Choice: The Psychology of New Venture Creation', *Entrepreneurship Theory and Practice* **16**(2), 23–45.

Swamidass, P. M. and W. T. Newell, 1987, 'Manufacturing Strategy, Environmental Uncertainty and Performance: A Path Analytic Model', *Management Science* **33**(4), 509–524.

Weick, K. E., 1979, *The Social Psychology of Organizing*, 2 Englewood Cliffs, NJ: Prentice Hall.

Weick, K. E., 1995, *Sensemaking in Organizations*, Thousand Oaks, CA: Sage Publications.

10

A "Critical Mess" Approach to Entrepreneurship Scholarship

W. B. Gartner

It is a capital mistake to theorize before one has data.
Insensibly one begins to twist the facts to suit theories,
instead of theories to suit facts.

Arthur Conan Doyle

My perspective on future trends in the field of entrepreneurship focuses on an idea, that, at the current moment, seems to be intriguing, to me, and, I hope, of interest to others. My fascination with entrepreneurship is in entrepreneurship, itself. By "entrepreneurship, itself," I mean I am curious about the study of all things that seem to be about entrepreneurship, as a phenomenon. But I am not, necessarily, curious about studying entrepreneurship solely from a phenomenological perspective. The idea that is presented, here, explores the approach that I take to the study of entrepreneurship, which is labeled the "critical

213

214   *A "Critical Mess" Approach to Entrepreneurship Scholarship*

mess." The idea of the "critical mess" is less of a coherent methodology for studying entrepreneurship, and more of a nuance toward the kinds of facts and theories that one might use for understanding what "entrepreneurship, itself," actually is, or might be.

I may be, at this moment in the history of the FSF–NUTEK Awards, unique among the award winners in that my research on entrepreneurship does not seem to be easily categorized into a particular disciplinary perspective, such as economics, sociology, or psychology. By starting with the question, "What is entrepreneurship?" the answers to exploring this question begin with descriptions of the phenomenon. From description, one might then begin to offer ideas as to "why" aspects of the phenomenon behave as they do. (This approach, I believe, is somewhat similar to naturalistic inquiry (Lincoln and Guba, 1985), but, as I hope to show, also different, in that I'm less concerned with the facts generated from direct personal experience.) As the quote that begins this article suggests, the primacy of facts should drive the search for theory that can make sense of those facts. The trend that is currently occurring in entrepreneurship scholarship is for many scholars to import a theory from another discipline and then go in search of facts to support it. When scholars are grounded in the facts of their own discipline and the facts found in the entrepreneurship area, then, the application of theories from other disciplines results in the kinds of insightful ideas that other FSF–NUTEK award winners have found. But, when scholars are not well grounded in the facts of a particular discipline (e.g., "non-disciplined trained" entrepreneurship scholars who inappropriately apply a theory from a discipline outside of entrepreneurship), or when scholars are not well grounded in the facts of entrepreneurship (e.g., "disciplined trained" scholars who inappropriately apply entrepreneurship facts to their theories), we get confusion, rather than insight. My approach is to ask scholars to devote substantially more time to collecting and being "mindful" (Langer, 1979) of facts about entrepreneurship, before identifying a theory to find causal linkages among these facts. The remainder of this article will describe the "critical mess" approach, and then, offer other analogies as attempts to capture the sensibility in the perspective I propose.

10.1 The "Critical Mess" Approach

I came across the label "critical mess" in reading an article on book collecting in *The New Yorker* magazine that Sue Birley and I subsequently used as an analogy for the value of qualitative research in the field of entrepreneurship (Gartner and Birley, 2002, p. 394).

> Finally, we offer an insight about the nature of qualitative research which might be considered as a parting trifle, but we believe contains some truth which bears consideration: the "critical mess theory." In qualitative research there is typically an immersion into the muddled circumstances of an entrepreneurial phenomenon that is cluttered and confusing. Part of the difficulty of generating and reporting the findings of a qualitative research effort seems to stem from the experience of being in such an untidy reality. Qualitative researchers seem to get overwhelmed with too much information, rather than too little. Yet, it is in this experience of information overload that a certain knowledge and wisdom often occurs. One can often tell which researchers in our field have spent considerable time intensively involved with entrepreneurs. The knowledge and insights that stem from all of their research just seem to ring a bit truer and clearer. We borrow a label for this sensibility of immersion from a profile of Michael Zinman, a bibliophile and Michael Reese's insights into Zinman's strategy for collecting books:
>
>> "You don't start off with a theory about what you're trying to do. You don't begin by saying, 'I'm trying to prove x.' You build a big pile. Once you get a big enough pile together – the critical mess – you're able to draw conclusions about it. You see patterns... People who have the greatest intuitive feel for physical objects start from a relationship with

216   *A "Critical Mess" Approach to Entrepreneurship Scholarship*

> the objects and then acquire the scholarship, instead of the other way around. The way to become a connoisseur is to work in the entire spectrum of what's available – from utter crap to fabulous stuff. If you're going to spend your time looking only at the best, you're not going to have a critical eye." (Singer, 2001, p. 66).

Qualitative researchers are likely to be the connoisseurs of entrepreneurship scholarship only in that they are more likely to immerse themselves to a greater depth and in a wider variety of situations where entrepreneurship occurs. We encourage all entrepreneurship scholars to develop a critical eye in their efforts to explore entrepreneurship, and hope that more work will be undertaken to utilize qualitative methods for seeking such an understanding.

The "critical mess" label has captured my imagination for providing a way for me to talk about the diverse ways I have looked at entrepreneurship, itself (Gartner, 2004). My original research sought to create a "critical mess" of information (based on data from 106 questionnaires and "mini-cases" written from in-depth interviews) that resulted in a typology of ways that individuals start businesses (Gartner *et al.*, 1989), and I have used similar quantitative/qualitative "messes" to look at individuals starting businesses during the evolution of the fresh-squeezed orange juice industry (Duchesneau and Gartner, 1990), and the stories of entrepreneurs in magazine articles (Gartner *et al.*, 1999). Probably the biggest quantitative/qualitative "critical mess" is the Panel Study of Entrepreneurial Dynamics (PSED), which is a longitudinal generalizable sample of individuals in the process of starting businesses (Gartner *et al.*, 2004). I have also been interested in how the imagination, through fiction, provides insights into entrepreneurship: for example, the *Music Man* as "corporate entrepreneur" (Gartner *et al.*, 1985), *Pilgrim's Progress* as an entrepreneurial odyssey (Gartner *et al.*, 1987; and studies of the importance of human volition through entrepreneurial action using the films

Ikiru (Gartner, 1990b) and *The Man Who Planted Trees* (Gartner, 1993b). And, I have been interested in how entrepreneurship scholars make sense of entrepreneurship as an academic field (Gartner, 1990a, 2001), and how poetry and art might offer a language for describing the process of organizing (Gartner, 1993a). This eclectic selection of examples is a mess: no one particular theoretical perspective, no one particular kind or type of data, and fiction seems to have as much value for providing insights into entrepreneurship, as empirical facts. There is much to recommend for taking this approach.

I find that scholars who use a rather narrow disciplinary focus in the field of entrepreneurship often lack the "critical eye" that comes from creating a "critical mess." It is all too easy to use the "fabulous stuff" in one's own discipline without attending to the "utter crap" that might be found in other disciplines or in other research findings in one's own discipline, as well. Without a deep and comprehensive understanding and appreciation of the breadth and complexity of entrepreneurship scholarship (as well as other non-scholarly work about entrepreneurship), it is easy to generate results that seem to look right (given the theory and evidence used), yet are wrong to anyone with a broader knowledge of the phenomenon of entrepreneurship, itself.

10.2   Conventional Wisdom versus Esoteric Knowledge

In somewhat the same vein, Davis (1971) in "That's Interesting!" suggests this conflict about acquiring a broad range of facts versus a focus on theory is inherent between laypersons with "conventional wisdom" and experts with "esoteric knowledge":

> "Intellectual specialties were formed when various groups of self-styled experts began to accept those propositions which had refuted the assumptions of laymen. As an intellectual speciality developed, what began merely as a proposition which refuted a taken-for-granted assumption of the common-sense world now became a taken-for-granted assumption in its own right. When an intellectual speciality reached maturity – and

> this is the important point – all propositions generated
> within it are referred back not to the old baseline of
> the take-for-granted assumption of the common-sense
> world, but to the new baseline of the take-for-granted
> assumption of the intellectual speciality itself (Davis,
> 1971, p. 330).

Something gets lost when the focus of research on entrepreneurship
sticks too closely to the "esoteric knowledge" a narrow disciplinary
perspective. A finding can be right and interesting to a scholar within
a specific theoretical perspective, but, wrong or obvious to the practitioner and scholar with a broader and messier knowledge of the phenomenon. If scholarship in the field of entrepreneurship emphasizes the
search for answers using narrow disciplinary approaches, we may find
ourselves irrelevant to the issues facing those persons involved in the
broader phenomenon of entrepreneurship, itself.

10.3   Hedgehogs versus Foxes

Another metaphor that captures aspects of the "critical mess" approach
from the perspective of a cognitive orientation is Isaiah Berlin's expo-
sition on the hedgehog and the fox (Berlin, 1993, p. 1):

> There is a line among the fragments of the Greek
> poet Archilochus which says: 'The fox knows many
> things, but the hedgehog knows one big thing'. Scholars
> have differed about the correct interpretation of these
> dark words, which may mean no more than that the
> fox, for all his cunning, is defeated by the hedgehog's
> one defense. But, taken figuratively, the words can be
> made to yield a sense in which they mark one of the
> deepest differences which divide writers and thinkers,
> and, it may be, human beings in general. For there
> exists a great chasm between those, on one side, who
> relate everything to a single central vision, one system
> less or more coherent or articulate, in terms of which
> they understand, think and feel – a single, universal,

organizing principle in terms of which alone all that they are and say has significance – and, on the other side, those who pursue many ends, often unrelated and even contradictory, connected, if at all, only in some *de facto* way, for some psychological or physiological cause, related by no moral or aesthetic principle; these last lead lives, perform acts, and entertain ideas that are centrifugal rather than centripetal, their thought is scattered or diffused, moving on many levels, seizing upon the essence of a vast variety of experiences and objects for what they are in themselves, without consciously or unconsciously, seeking to fit them into, or exclude them from, any one unchanging, all-embracing, sometimes self-contradictory and incomplete, at times fanatical, unitary inner vision. The first kind of intellectual and artistic personality belongs to the hedgehogs, the second to the foxes . . . ."

This dichotomy (the fox of "many things" versus the hedgehog of "one big thing") has actually been the subject of much serious academic study in regards to the kinds of cognitive styles individuals use for making judgments and forecasts (*cf.*, Suedfeld and Tetlock, 2002). In general, the "fox" cognitive style appears to lead to better predictions and judgments compared to the "hedgehog" style. Indeed, Tetlock (2005), in a summary of 20 years of research on the judgment of political experts, describes a number of ways that foxes appear to differ from hedgehogs that would seem to bolster the value of the "critical mess" approach.

Foxes are more skeptical about the use of theory to explain the past or predict the future. One of the problems with applying theory is that application requires judgment about which theories would actually be relevant in particular situations. Yet, theorists tend to seek parsimony in their explanations, so that "one size fits all" more often becomes "all sizes fit one." By being more mindful of all of the facts that accumulate in the "critical mess" there is less of a temptation to seize on a singular explanation.

220   *A "Critical Mess" Approach to Entrepreneurship Scholarship*

Foxes tend to qualify predictions with disconfirming evidence. A "critical mess" of information is more likely to keep one humble when positing a particular theory to explain these facts. This sensibility is also, I believe, a characteristic of the practitioner's conventional wisdom. The day-to-day bombardment of disparate facts stemming from being in the phenomenon of entrepreneurship does not often lend itself to "a theory" that can encompass one's particular situation.

Foxes are more likely to see the ironic aspects of the phenomenon, in that irony enables one to see the double meanings as well as the paradoxes imbedded in the situation. An example that comes to mind about the irony inherent in entrepreneurship would be the paradox of entrepreneurs as self-seeking individuals. We assume that entrepreneurs are more likely to be self-actualizers, individuals who "do their own thing" yet, those individuals we are likely to suggest as exemplars of entrepreneurship (e.g., Bill Gates and Richard Branson) are wildly successful because they provide goods and services that other people want. So, success in entrepreneurship at "doing your own thing" requires that this doing be about solving other people's problems. Indeed, I believe that entrepreneurship is actually based more in irony than other "personal"-oriented activities, such as the creation of art (*cf.*, Hjorth). Entrepreneurship, inherently involves the "other." Entrepreneurial activity requires transaction and interaction (Katz and Gartner, 1988) among a variety of people, while it is possible to create art without patrons, buyers or an audience. A "critical mess" approach that begins with the phenomenon, itself, is more likely to recognize the many different facets of particular entrepreneurial actions and their many possible meanings. Probably the best proponents of an ironical approach to the study of entrepreneurship are works by Hjorth (2003) and Steyaert (1995, 1997), where their ability to explore the subtle dualities in the phenomenon of entrepreneurship are magical.

Foxes are more likely to see the "and" among competing points of view rather than posit the "either/or." I suggest that one important feature of a "critical mess" approach is a willingness to see entrepreneurship across multiple levels of analysis (Davidsson and Wiklund, 2001). So, for example, it is valuable to be able to see that individual action takes place within a social and environmental context, and, to appreciate how the individual might influence the social/environment and vice versa.

Finally, a quote from Tetlock (2005, p. 118) on some problematic aspects of the hedgehog approach:

> "... hedgehogs dig themselves into intellectual holes. The deeper they dig, the harder it gets to climb out and see what is happening outside, and the more tempting it becomes to keep on doing what they know how to do; continue their metaphorical digging by uncovering new reasons why their initial inclination, usually too optimistic or pessimistic, was right. Hedgehogs are thus at continual risk of becoming prisoners of their preconceptions, trapped in self-reinforcing cycles in which their initial ideological disposition stimulates thoughts that further justify that inclination, which, in turn, stimulates further supportive thoughts."

The challenge, then, is to keep oneself open to a variety of facts and ideas that may become apparent through mindful experience (Langer, 1979). I find that my greatest challenge as an entrepreneurship researcher [as in re- (go back) search- (and look)] is to pay attention to entrepreneurship scholarship across a wider venue of disciplines and perspectives, and to read comprehensively, rather than selectively.

10.4 Complicate Yourself!

The title of my speech at the FSF–NUTEK award ceremony was "Entrepreneurship in Two Words of Less" and the presentation was based on four slogans that I had printed on T-shirts to both show and give away. (I find that there are fewer technical glitches with showing a T-shirt compared to using a computer to display PowerPoint slides.) The four slogans were: [ ] THINK; Aspire Higher; Fail *forward;* and Complicate Yourself! Social psychologists will be familiar with "Complicate Yourself!" as the final section heading in Weick's *Social Psychology of Organizing* (Weick, 1979). My "takeaway" from Weick's

222   *A "Critical Mess" Approach to Entrepreneurship Scholarship*

"Complicate Yourself!" slogan is that complex phenomena require complex people:

> "... the complicated individual can sense variations in a larger environment, select what need *not* be attended to, what will *not* change imminently, what *won't* happen, and by this selection the individual is able to amplify his control variety. He safely (that is, insightfully) ignores that which will not change, concentrates on that which will, and much like the neurotic psychiatrist is able to anticipate significant environmental variation when and where it occurs. Complicated observers take in more. They see patterns that less complicated people miss, and they exploit these subtle patterns by concentrating on them and ignoring everything else."
> (Weick, 1979, 193)

The phenomenon of entrepreneurship is complicated (Gartner, 1985), and, for this reason, I believe, the "critical mess" approach is a necessary bromide to narrower disciplinary perspectives. As I suggested at the beginning of this article, those entrepreneurship scholars with an omnivorous willingness to collect facts and ideas: both good and bad; "utter crap to fabulous stuff;" micro and macro; individual, firm and environment; esoteric knowledge and conventional wisdom; the pedantic and amateur; policy and personal, are more likely to develop the discernment so necessary for finding the key nuggets of insight about entrepreneurship as a phenomenon. The challenge, then, for entrepreneurship scholars, is to be willing to build their own "big pile" of knowledge, facts, theories, experiences, and insights about the phenomenon of entrepreneurship, and to be at peace with the realization that much of what one collects is "utter crap." The process of developing insight is not efficient. And, there is no guarantee that there will be fabulous stuff buried within one's mess. But, such efforts are necessary.

References

Berlin, I. (1953/1993), *The Hedgehog and the Fox: An Essay on Tolstoy's View of History*. Chicago: Ivan R. Dee Publisher.

Davidsson, P. and J. Wiklund (2001), 'Levels of analysis in entrepreneurship research: Current research practices and suggestions for the future'. *Entrepreneurship Theory and Practice* **25**(4), 81–100.

Davis, M. S. (1971), 'That's interesting! Towards a phenomenology of sociology and a sociology of phenomenology'. *Philosophy of the Social Sciences* **1**, 309–344.

Duchesneau, D. A. and W. B. Gartner (1990), 'A profile of new venture success and failure in an emerging industry'. *Journal of Business Venturing* **5**(5), 297–312.

Gartner, W. B. (1985), 'Did River City really need a boy's band?'. *New Management* **3**(1), 28–34.

Gartner, W. B. (1987), 'A pilgrim's progress'. *New Management* **4**(4), 4–7.

Gartner, W. B. (1990a), 'To live: The obligation of individuality. A review of the film Ikiru, directed by Akira Kurosawa'. *The Organizational Behavior Teaching Review* **14**(2), 138–143.

Gartner, W. B. (1990b), 'What are we talking about when we talk about entrepreneurship?'. *Journal of Business Venturing* **5**(1), 15–28.

Gartner, W. B. (1993a), 'Can't see the trees for the forest. A review of the film *The Man Who Planted Trees*, directed by Frederick Back'. *Journal of Management Education* **17**(2), 269–274.

Gartner, W. B. (1993b), 'Words lead to deeds: Towards an organizational emergence vocabulary'. *Journal of Business Venturing* **8**(3), 231–240.

Gartner, W. B. (2001), 'Is there an elephant in entrepreneurship? Blind assumptions in theory development'. *Entrepreneurship Theory and Practice* **25**(4), 27–39.

Gartner, W. B. (2004), 'Achieving "critical mess" in entrepreneurship scholarship'. In *Advances in Entrepreneurship, Firm Emergence, and Growth*, J. A. Katz and D. Shepherd (eds.), Vol. 7, pp. 199–216. Greenwich, CT: JAI Press.

Gartner, W. B. and S. Birley (2002), 'Introduction to the special issue on qualitative methods in entrepreneurship research'. *Journal of Business Venturing* **17**(5), 387–395.

Gartner, W. B., T. R. Mitchell, and K. H. Vesper (1989), 'A taxonomy of new business ventures'. *Journal of Business Venturing* **4**(3), 169–186.

Gartner, W. B., K. G. Shaver, N. M. Carter, and P. D. Reynolds (2004), *Handbook of Entrepreneurial Dynamics: The Process of Business Creation*. Thousand Oaks, CA: Sage Publications.

Gartner, W. B., J. A. Starr, and S. Bhat (1999), 'Predicting new venture survival: An analysis of "anatomy of a startup". Cases from *Inc. Magazine*'. *Journal of Business Venturing* **14**, 215–232.

Hjorth, D. (2003), *Rewriting Entrepreneurship: For a New Perspective on Organizational Creativity*. Copenhagen: CBS Press.

Katz, J. and W. B. Gartner (1988), 'Properties of emerging organizations'. *Academy of Management Review* **13**(3), 429–442.

Langer, E. J. (1979), *The Power of Mindful Learning*. Cambridge, MA: Perseus Publishing.

Lincoln, Y. S. and E. G. Guba (1985), *Naturalistic Inquiry*. Beverly Hills, CA: Sage Publications.

Singer, M. (2001), 'The book eater'. *The New Yorker* February **5**, 62–71.

Steyaert, C. (1995). Perpetuating entrepreneurship through dialogue. A social constructionist view. Unpublished doctoral dissertation. Katholieke Universiteit Leuven. Department of Work and Organizational Psychology.

Stayaert, C. (1997), 'A qualitative methodology for process studies of entrepreneurship: Creating local knowledge through stories'. *International Studies of Management and Organization* **27**(3), 13–33.

Suedfeld, P. and P. E. Tetlock (2002), 'Individual differences in information processing'. In *Blackwell Handbook of Social Psychology: Intra-individual Processes*, A. Tesser and N. Schwarz (eds.), pp. 284–304. Oxford: Blackwell Publishers.

Tetlock, P. E. (2005), *Expert Political Judgment.* Princeton: Princeton University Press.

[18]

Available online at www.sciencedirect.com

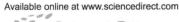

ScienceDirect

JOURNAL
of BUSINESS
VENTURING

ELSEVIER

Journal of Business Venturing 22 (2007) 613–627

Entrepreneurial narrative and a science of the imagination

William B. Gartner *

Spiro Center for Entrepreneurial Leadership, 345 Sirrine Hall, Clemson University, Clemson, SC 29634-1345, United States

Abstract

This article is an introduction to a special issue on entrepreneurial narrative that provides theoretical and empirical links between scholarship in narrative and entrepreneurship as well as demonstrates how theories and methods in narrative may be applied to the study of entrepreneurship as a phenomenon. A conjecture that narrative perspectives might lead to a "science of the imagination" is offered.
© 2006 Elsevier Inc. All rights reserved.

Keywords: Entrepreneurial narrative; Qualitative research; Case method; Science of the imagination

1. Executive summary

This article is an introduction to a special issue on entrepreneurial narrative. A simple definition of narrative approaches is: an analysis of the stories that people tell. The special issue consists of seven articles. The first article is Terry Allen's story, told in 1984, or how he started a toy store, in Rutland, Vermont, in 1965. The *Toy Store(y)* serves as the basis for six articles that apply narrative approaches.

The goal of the special issue on entrepreneurial narrative is to provide theoretical and empirical links between scholarship in narrative and entrepreneurship as well as demonstrate how theories and methods in narrative may be applied to the study of entrepreneurship as a phenomenon. Narrative approaches and narrative methodologies are

---

* Tel.: +1 864 656 0825; fax: +1 864 656 7237.

  E-mail address: gartner@clemson.edu.

0883-9026/$ - see front matter © 2006 Elsevier Inc. All rights reserved.
doi:10.1016/j.jbusvent.2006.10.003

reflexive, that is, in the process of analyzing other people's stories, we, as researchers, are also looking into the mirror of our own stories of how and why our research is conducted. To describe how and why the articles in this special issue analyzed a particular story told by an entrepreneur, from a reflexive point of view, a discussion of the evolution of this special issue is offered, and reasons are provided for why the *Toy Store(y)* in particular, serves as the focus of these narrative analyses.

This introduction is not a summary of the articles in the special issue. Rather, the introduction points out three broad insights that seem to characterize all six narrative analyses: (1) Stories are never complete, in and of themselves. Stories are told in a particular context, to particular listeners, by a particular story teller, for particular purposes. When a story is subject to various narrative approaches, a variety of insights can be gained as to what is really being said and why, as well as what wasn't said which might be. (2) Stories are told in the larger context of other stories and ideas: "larger voices." To listen/read a story offers an opportunity to engage in how a story interrelates to other "larger voices" that readers/listeners bring with them. To call upon these "larger voices" through narrative approaches has value analytically and creatively. (3) Narrative approaches come with their own epistemology, theories, and methods that must be met on their own terms. As this occurs, narrative approaches will play an increasing role in entrepreneurship scholarship.

Readers of the six entrepreneurial narratives might be skeptical of articles where, at points in their development, there is an allowance for "fiction." That is, when there are "unknowns" in the knowledge of specific "facts as given," the authors of these narrative analyses are likely to provide "facts as made." There might be a fear that narrative approaches might lead to taking normative paradigmatic scholarship down the rabbit hole of treating all knowledge as "fiction." This is not actually the case, and rather than setting up a struggle of either/or between paradigmatic approaches and narrative approaches, their inherent similarities are recognized as ways in which knowledge is gained through the application of skill.

The label, "science of the imagination" is suggested as another promise for what entrepreneurship (and specifically, entrepreneurial narrative) might offer as a contribution to scholarship. The narrative of entrepreneurship is the generation of hypotheses about how the world might be: how the future might look and act. The articles in this special issue not only probe how entrepreneurs generate and modify their visions of the future, the scholars in these articles generate and modify alternative visions of the future, as well. There is a skill here, in these six entrepreneurial narratives, that is subtle, but very critical for understanding how the imagination works.

This article concludes with a suggestion that narrative approaches offer ways for both scholars and practitioners to "tell back" entrepreneurial stories. The process of "telling back" surfaces the models we use to talk about entrepreneurship. Narrative approaches not only uncover the models we currently use to talk about entrepreneurship, they give us new ways to talk this phenomenon, as well.

2. Introduction

The aim of this special issue on entrepreneurial narrative is to provide theoretical and empirical links between scholarship in narrative and entrepreneurship as well as

W.B. Gartner / Journal of Business Venturing 22 (2007) 613–627   615

demonstrate how theories and methods in narrative may be applied to the study of entrepreneurship as a phenomenon. I believe that embedded in this aspiration is a sense that narrative approaches surface tensions in "how things are currently done" in entrepreneurship scholarship. I will also suggest that narrative perspectives in the study of entrepreneurship might also lead to the genesis of a science of the imagination. The aim, then, of this special issue is rather far reaching and hitting this target requires a certain amount of deftness, not only on the part of the authors writing for the special issue, but, of our readers, as well. Given that a variety of readers may encounter this special issue (i.e., experts in narrative with little knowledge of entrepreneurship, experts in entrepreneurship with little knowledge of narrative, experts in narrative and entrepreneurship, and novices in both entrepreneurship and narrative scholarship), it was a challenge to select papers and engage authors in revisions that met these multiple goals.

I believe that much of the tension in reading the articles in this special issue will be due to the inherent conflict between "insiders" and others, that is, between expert specialists in specific intellectual domains and those less knowledgeable (Davis, 1971). Demonstrating knowledge and expertise to one group is often irrelevant or obvious to another. One of the major strength's of the *Journal of Business Venturing* has been its constant admonition to scholars to translate theories and results based on insider expertise for a larger domain of individuals (both practitioners and scholars) with less know–how. Yet, in practice, this has meant that both sides must stretch: the novice to undertake an effort to learn aspects of a scholar's insights and methods, and, the expert to let go of a certain precision, nuance and language that only insiders can see and appreciate. Otherwise, I sense, there is dissatisfaction from each end of the continuum, and not much learning. It behooves readers, then, to bring along fewer expectations and more alertness to the ideas, methods and insights offered in these articles.

The remainder of this article will describe: the evolving logic for how this special issue came to be; highlight from my perspective, some of the insights and ideas posited in the articles in this special issue; and offer some speculations about how the study of entrepreneurial narrative might provide the basis for a science of the imagination.

3. From a story to a narrative analysis

It is very easy to complicate the scholarly area that is connoted by such terms as discourse, narrative, and story (Grant et al., 1998; Rhodes and Brown, 2005). I will offer this rather simplistic description of what narrative approaches do: they involve analyzing the stories that people tell. Hosking and Hjorth (2004: 265) offer a more elaborate description:

- "Story construction is a process of *creating* reality
- in which self/story teller is clearly *part of* the story.
- Narratives are relational realities, socially constructed, not individual subjective realities.
- Narratives are situated — they are con-textualized in relation to multiple local–cultural–historical acts/text.
- Inquiry may articulate multiple narrative and relations.
- Change-work works with multiple realities and power relations, for example, to
- facilitate ways of relating that are open to possibilities."

There is much discussion about what a story or narrative consists of, whether all stories are narratives or whether all narratives are stories, and any number of other conundrums that scholars in this field can quickly mire themselves in (Grant et al., 2004). Be-that-as-it-may, without getting quickly lost in what are, actually, important semantic issues involved with the labels narrative scholars use to describe aspects of these types of research, narrative approaches provide some very powerful tools for exploring what entrepreneurs (or others) say about what they do.

If there seems to be one archetypal characteristic of narrative approaches and narrative methodologies (e.g., Boje, 2001; Gabriel, 2004; O'Connor, 1997) that permeates this perspective, it would be their reflexivity (Fletcher, 2007). That is, in the process of analyzing other people's stories, we, as researchers, are also looking into the mirror of our own stories of how and why our research is conducted on these other people's stories (Czarniawska, 1997). To describe how and why the articles in this special issue analyzed a particular story told by an entrepreneur, from a reflexive point of view, then, requires some discussion of the evolution of this special issue. While this discussion might seem egocentric, it speaks to the spirit of recognizing the importance of the context in which narrative analyses take place.

First, it is worth noting the difficulty of describing the origin of this special issue "after the fact." Writing now, about the evolution of an idea that was not, at the outset, labeled as "entrepreneurial narrative" to this outcome as a set of articles on entrepreneurial narrative in the *Journal of Business Venturing*, is much of the difference suggested by Bourdrieu (1977) between *opus operatum* — sense making about the process after it is over, as a finished task, and *modus operandi* — sense making about the process while one is still in it. This description is *opus operatum*, with much of the messiness, wrong turns, waiting, ambiguity, and my own stupidity, ignorance and confusion-missing. Since Fletcher (2007) also writes about how this special issue evolved, it may be well worth comparing these two accounts.

I believe that the origin of this special issue, did, actually, begin with this initial question: Is it the researcher, or the "data," that makes for the generation of insights when undertaking qualitative research? If one, for example, looks at Pitt's (1998) analysis of interview material from two entrepreneurs, are the insights gained from his reading of these entrepreneurs due to: the source material the two entrepreneurs provided; Pitt's process of uncovering this source material; Pitt's analyses; or ("all of the above," or "something else," and/or...)? This question is, actually, a fantasy about viewing researchers separate from their research [i.e., "How can we know the dancer from the dance?" (Yeats, 1956)]. Yet, in my own neurotic way (Adler, 1917), I would treat both quantitative and qualitative information "as if" (Vaihinger, 1924/1952) they were sought, collected, interpreted and analyzed irrespective of the researcher. What makes this question "neurotic" is treating the fiction of "research separate from the researcher" as fact (that is, fact as "given" rather than as "made").[1] Research (quantitative or qualitative) is not "fact as given," yet, I continue to hold on to this neurotic fantasy that "data" is separate from the researcher and the research

---

[1] The author thanks Ellen O'Conner for her comments on this section and for offering Giambattista Vico's insight that the term "fact" in Latin is "factum" which means "made." Yet, as she points out, we now, tend to think of "fact" as something that is "given."

W.B. Gartner / Journal of Business Venturing 22 (2007) 613–627   617

process. While I was generally aware of many scholars who had poked holes in this fantasy (e.g., Geertz, 1988; Hatch, 1996; Van Maanen, 1988 — I offer only a few citations rather than a comprehensive bibliography to signal my knowledge of mostly North American writers and their sensibilities), it simply is, for me, hard to let go of this fiction. I tend to believe that the quantitative data in the Panel Study of Entrepreneurial Dynamics (Gartner et al., 2004) is "fact as given" rather than a fairly complicated social construction of the beliefs of over 100 scholars submitting questions for a questionnaire, phone survey specialists probing for responses, respondents interpreting these survey questions (e.g., "What does completing a business plan 'in my head' mean?") and scholars selecting questions for analysis and interpreting their results. It was not hard for me to segue from my fantasy that quantitative data (i.e. the PSED—that can be studied by many scholars with the assumption that this research is separate from the researchers who created this data and analyze it) to considering this question: What would happen if a variety of scholars studied the same qualitative "data"? If the qualitative "data" was held constant, would we see variation in the insights generated? If so, would the differences in insights be due to theories, methods, or other issues idiosyncratic to the scholars, themselves?

While Hillman (1983: 111) suggests that: "To be sane we must recognize our beliefs as fictions, and see through our hypotheses as fantasies," I couldn't let go of this goal of getting a number of scholars to look at the same qualitative data. My background is strongly influenced by what might be labeled as the "Harvard approach" (Contardo and Wensley, 2004) to analyzing qualitative data as represented in the case method (Barnes et al., 1994; Naumes and Naumes, 1999), and with many years of both creating and using cases for teaching, and with experience with case competitions (as a writer, judge, and team sponsor), the idea of taking qualitative data and comparing how scholars analyzed this material, seemed an obvious and valuable exercise. And, while the *Harvard Business Review* in the "Case Study" section of their magazine offers a comparative evaluation of case material from the viewpoints of a variety of practitioners and scholars, I had not seen an academic journal attempt to publish a series of scholarly articles analyzing the same material. This concept, therefore, seemed worth pursuing.

While I was attending the first "Movements in Entrepreneurship" workshop in Sweden, in June 2001, I mentioned this idea (about having a number of scholars look at the same qualitative data) to Denise Fletcher, and suggested that I had a transcription of a story that an entrepreneur had told me that I thought could serve as the basis for the "data" to analyze. She indicated that the idea and story sounded intriguing, and to send her the transcript. I did.

Now, what the previous paragraph just omits, is my recollection of another, larger dialogue occurring between us on: the "problem" of qualitative researchers publishing their work in North American based academic journals; the issues of validity and reliability in case research that quantitative-oriented journal reviewers seemed to have with manuscripts that didn't have numbers; and the general lack of knowledge and interest of most North American scholars in the history and philosophy of the science embedded in qualitative entrepreneurship scholarship. I was, then, completing a special issue for the *Journal of Business Venturing* on qualitative research with Sue Birley (Gartner and Birley, 2002), and the above issues seemed most salient based on this insight from that experience: The knowledge and skills of many European entrepreneurship researchers in the area of qualitative scholarship were far and ahead of their North American counterparts. My sense was (is) that North American scholars who are not steeped in the rich European traditions and methods of qualitative scholarship simply lack clues to the kinds of significant contributions that qualitative scholarship can make.

As Fletcher (2007) describes in her article, there was email correspondence about: the history of the transcription of the entrepreneur's story of the founding of a toy store, which in these articles, is labeled as the "Toy Story," the "Toy Store" or the "Toy Store(y);" and the reasons for why I thought this story might be of value for scholarly analysis. And, subsequently, she wrote a manuscript about this story and sent it to me. The arrival of this manuscript was the inflection point for knowing that there were other scholars who would take the risk of analyzing the story of the "Toy Store," and, that the story seemed to be sufficient for a "Call for Papers."

Starting with the knowledge that Denise Fletcher and I had of which scholars might have some interest and capability to explore the *Toy Store(y)*, I began to contact individuals to ascertain their willingness to develop a manuscript that would be considered for presentation at the Lloyd Greif Symposium on Emerging Organizations, which was an event that I held at the University of Southern California. In addition, besides their manuscript submissions to the symposium, both Chris Steyaert and Daniel Hjorth provided numerous connections to qualitative researchers who might have important contributions to make. From this variety of contacts, manuscripts were submitted, some were selected (decisions were make by the special issue editor), and authors of those selected papers met in February 2004 to present and discuss their work. This special issue then took form as papers were reworked and revised.

A number of reasons (in the retrospection of *opus operatum*) can be offered for why the "Toy Store(y)" was selected as the focus of the analyses in this special issue. First, the story is a transcription of an entrepreneur's presentation told in a classroom setting, similar to the format in many university entrepreneurship courses where entrepreneurs serve as "living cases." Second, the story is, I believe, typical of the genre of stories that entrepreneurs tell in classroom settings, and, it would not be out of the ordinary for a successful entrepreneur to tell a story based on a distant experience that reflected how the entrepreneur underwent a "rite of passage" from a naïve to sophisticated entrepreneur (Smith and Anderson, 2004). Third, the story is typical of the structure of an entrepreneur's story that would end with explicit "lessons" of the kind "Do what I say, not what I do" yet, much of the insights that can be gleaned from the story capture implicit and tacit knowledge about what the entrepreneur actually does. Fourth, there are a number of situations described in the story that are rich in their implications about the values, ethics, character, thoughts, motivations and behaviors of the story's protagonists. Fifth, there is, as in many Harvard-type cases, a "trick" or insight in the story where the application of a bit financial acumen would likely lead a reader to a different conclusion as to the financial straights the entrepreneur tells us he is in [see Baker (2007) for an exploration of this insight]. And, finally, the story, from my perspective, was engaging, and, it seemed that part of the reason I sought to have the story explored was to better understand why it was engaging. So, all-in-all, there seemed to be enough material in the *Toy Store(y)* for other scholars to work with that could likely lead to some keen insights about the nature of entrepreneurship. If you have not already done so, I suggest that you read *The Toy Store(y)* (Allen, 2007) in this issue before reading anything

W.B. Gartner / Journal of Business Venturing 22 (2007) 613–627   619

further in this article or any of the other articles. *The Toy Store(y)* article serves as the "data" upon which all of the other articles are focused.

4. The possibilities of narrative

It would be hubris on my part to make claims that I have substantial expertise in the scholarship of narrative and its application to entrepreneurship. I believe the articles in this special issue are exemplars of the richness, complexity, and depth of narrative scholarship as applied to the entrepreneurship field. I believe that my contribution to this special issue, and to entrepreneurship scholarship, as a whole, is in my role as an amateur (as in the Latin root "lover of") of entrepreneurship (Gartner, 2004). I am interesting in the phenomenon of entrepreneurship, in whatever form and manifestation (Gartner, 1985, 1993). The implication of this, then, is that I am devoted to looking at the phenomenon of entrepreneurship, at hand, and open to gaining whatever knowledge and skills necessary to make sense of what is within my grasp, and the stories that entrepreneurs tell about their ventures is more often in my day-to-day experience, than not. To explore the story that an entrepreneur tells about the creation of a business, puts me into the scholarship of narrative, but not as one who seeks to use an already gained expertise in narrative ideas and methods.

The review process, then, for the development of these articles, involved sending the manuscripts out to all of the participants in the symposium, as well as to other colleagues I thought might help provide me with insights, with the goal of encouraging these authors to provide better clarity and understanding of narrative approaches for "non-narrative" trained scholars. As mentioned earlier, the ability to write an article that both speaks to scholars in narrative, as well as to outsiders to this tradition, is a challenge that these authors have met.

My intention in this section of the article is to offer my sense of some of the important issues and ideas that are addressed in the articles in this special issue, as I have come to appreciate them. I believe this perspective will be of value to the "typical" reader of the *Journal of Business Venturing*: a reader who has knowledge of entrepreneurship scholarship, is more likely to be using quantitative methods for exploring the phenomenon of entrepreneurship, and, a reader who is likely to wonder about the value of narrative ideas and methods for entrepreneurship scholarship, as a whole. It should also be recognized that the articles speak for themselves, and that the few thoughts I offer merely hint at a cornucopia of insights that can be gleaned from careful study.

4.1. Not the "whole story"

My analysis of the *Toy Store(y)* accepts this story, "as is" — this is, as a story told by Terry Allen: nothing more and nothing less. Yet, in every analysis in this issue, scholars challenge this "as is" assumption. Indeed, Steyaert (2007) begins his article with "I can safely assume that this is not the whole story..." The narrative approach recognizes that a story is never the whole story. Any story is embedded in a context which involves recognizing: when and where the story was written (e.g., how might this story be influenced by the time period of 1965, by the location of the story in Rutland, Vermont in 1965); who is telling the story (e.g., what do we know and don't know about Terry Allen, the "author" of this story, and, what about other characters in this story, such as John Simmons, the other entrepreneur, or the wives, or the banker, or the toy supplier, or...), what is in this story (e.g., what information does the author of this story provide, what is omitted, what else could the story say, and why wasn't it said?); and why the story is being told (e.g., what are the author's intention's in telling this story, what were the intentions of the special issue editor in having this story told, rather than another?).

Each of the articles in this special issue both explores and challenges the context of the whole story of the *Toy Store(y)*. As O'Connor (2007) posits, "We want the real goods," beyond the literal and superficial level of the story "as is." Her article provides an overview of the problems of the using the Harvard Case Method approach which assumes a reliable representation of events and an assumption that events depicted in cases are the "facts" rather than interpretations or assumptions. The *Toy Store(y)* is of a genre, a type of writing, that has its own format and logic that is followed by both the author and the reader, and that the genre cannot, as a format, be able to contain the "whole story." I find that O'Connor's analysis of Terry Allen's own lesson of the toy story "I don't know what we learned from this thing, except that if you don't know anything it pays to be absolutely lucky" very perceptive in how she demonstrates that Allen did learn during the events of the story about how to make money from the genesis of the toy store idea. To talk about luck is to place this story in the genre of other entrepreneurship stories where both Allen and the reader not only assume luck, but, also fail to devote the effort to pursue paths to elucidate how entrepreneurship does occur. Insights into how Terry Allen gains this knowledge does not come easily without narrative methodologies that can parse out the interlocking logics this escapade offers.

Fletcher (2007), through the use of the narrative approach of reader response theory, explores the context of the *Toy Store(y)* itself, as products of: the author, Terry Allen; the special issue editor, Bill Gartner; and the article author, Denise Fletcher. As readers, we expect that there is a way in which stories will be told, and, we embrace a story about entrepreneurship that satisfies certain assumptions and beliefs. Fletcher (2007) offers the idea of the "stretchiness" of entrepreneurship, in that stories "stretch" beyond an author's own telling into a larger social construction that is based both on the author's story and on what others bring to their reading of this story, as well. The "whole story," then, must recognize the social, political, philosophical, and inter- and intra-personal context of the story and how it subsumes this story into something else that is no longer just the author's story, alone.

Both Baker (2007) and Ahl (2007) suggest other stories that could be told in conjunction with Allen's story of the *Toy Store(y)* as a well of capturing more of the "whole story." While Ahl's narrative analysis is grounded in a post-structuralist feminist perspective, and could be viewed as, primarily, an exploration of gender issues in entrepreneurship research and education, I see the value of her analysis in exploring this question: "Who else should be speaking?" I find her observation that all of the men in Allen's story have names, and the women do not, as a critical example into Ahl's feminist perspective that men in Allen's story have, through their implicit identification, more value and importance than the women. Yet, the women have a critical story to tell, not only as co-investors in this venture, but also as partners and managers of the store's operations. Issues of gender, then, are also issues about how power and influence are exercised and described, which then implies that some individuals may be more privileged to both tell stories and to be listened to.

W.B. Gartner / Journal of Business Venturing 22 (2007) 613–627   621

Baker, in his application of the idea of bricolage (Baker and Nelson, 2005) to the events of the *Toy Store(y)* suggests a series of other stories told by characters identified in Allen's story as a way to show that the intentions and processes of bricolage can occur outside the specific intentions of the entrepreneur. This idea of "network bricolage" (Baker, Miner, Eesley, 2003), and the stories Baker offers to portray this idea, provide another example of Allen's toy story as not being the "whole story." While Terry Allen offers a story that makes him the primary agent that manipulates other characters towards his goals, Ted Baker offers stories that make these other characters the primary agents who manipulate Terry Allen towards their goals. As examples to demonstrate the similarities and differences among bricolage, "resource seeking," and improvisation, Baker's use of the narrative approach provides a way to surface how the use of bricolage may often be unrecognized, and therefore, untold, by entrepreneurship scholars and practitioners.

4.2. "Larger voices calling"

While all of the articles in this special issue recognize a broader context of social, political, relational, institutional, etc. characteristics that envelop Terry Allen's particular telling of a business startup story, both Hjorth (2007) and Steyaert (2007) point to, what I would term, "larger voices" the inform us of deeper sensibilities and strategies in the nature of entrepreneurship. Hjorth (2007) uses the character of Iago, from Shakespeare's *Othello* to speak outside of managerial and institutional perspectives embedded in our normative views of what entrepreneurship is and how it occurs. Initially, I found the Iago/Roderigo dialogue somewhat incongruous with Terry Allen's toy story, yet, further meditation on Iago's words and Hjorth's exegesis of the drama of entrepreneurship, made apparent to me, how the comprehensive demands of narrative approaches offer an understanding of human nature, not just the nature of entrepreneurship. Rather than narrative approaches serving our normative rationality of thinking of narrative as data for the grist of management scholarship (e.g., Pentland, 1999), narrative approaches can fundamentally alter our world view of what entrepreneurship is vis-à-vis the whole person. By pointing out what Iago speaks, Hjorth yearns for what Allen leaves unspoken to the audience that expects the "enterprise discourse." I believe that Hjorth (2007) is right in his view that "For entrepreneurship the art, politics, ethics, aesthetics of organization creation is, I suggest, central."

Steyaert (2007) very subtly probes (through the use of the philosophy of Nietzsche, literary studies, the humanities, sociology and anthropology) issues about how the individual is construed in entrepreneurship scholarship. He suggests that "'who is the entrepreneur?' is not the wrong question, it is a right question wrongly formulated." and crafts an approach to the individual using the narrative alternative. In order to use narrative approaches now (as in this special issue), Steyaert playfully recognizes what it would mean to have used narrative approaches then (Gartner, 1988), when one form of the discussion of the role of the entrepreneur in entrepreneurship was taking place. Entrepreneurial narratives are told in the larger context of a culture of personal narratives in which we all tell our stories in one form or another. "Larger voices" may inform us of the many ways of (who, what, where, why and when) of story telling, yet Steyaert (2007) asks us to consider narrative approaches as a way to "resign from analyzing and interpreting stories too much and perhaps invest in completing them, playing along, rearrange them, etc." Narrative approaches, then, not only have value analytically, but also, creatively.

4.3. "Attention must be paid"

As I suggested earlier, while one might consider the usefulness of narrative approaches in regards to how they might be applied to normative quantitative scholarship in entrepreneurship, it might be more appropriate to consider how narrative approaches are valid and insightful, in and of themselves. By implication, once one considers narrative approaches on their own terms, the "terms" of this scholarship, are indeed costly for the quantitative scholar to acquire. I find that the authors in this special issue grapple with the difficulty of bringing readers into their realm of expertise and insight, and, that competence in their areas is often broader, deeper, and more complicated than the foundations of quantitative scholarship. I have not, for example, read recently in a quantitatively based article how authors felt the necessity of explaining multiple linear regression and its various nuances and applications to an analysis of their data, yet, approaches to narrative, at least for now do seem to require more explanation. Given the format and genre of journal articles, this lack of the easy shorthand of common citations, methods, and terminology in narrative approaches might appear to put the publication of articles using narrative analyses at a "competitive disadvantage" to more easily understandable articles from a normative quantitative perspective. I am less inclined to believe this. My view is based less on whether scholars find some relative advantage in using particular qualitative or quantitative methodologies to enhance their ability to publish, and more on the insight that "attention must be paid" to narrative in entrepreneurship.

I find Bruner's (1986: 11) idea of two modes of thought (i.e., "a good story and a well-formed argument") particularly helpful in suggesting that a focus on narrative is not about narrative's relative value to what Bruner labels as the paradigmatic or logico-scientific approach. The narrative approach is a comprehensive way of understanding the world. It is ontologically complete.

> "The imaginative application of the narrative mode leads instead to good stories, gripping drama, believable (thought not necessarily "true") historical accounts. It deals in human or human-like intention and action and the vicissitudes and consequences that mark their course. It strives to put its timeless miracles into the particulars of experience, and to locate the experience in time and place. Joyce thought of the particularities of the story as epiphanies of the ordinary. The paradigmatic mode, by contrast, seeks to transcend the particular by higher and higher reaching for abstraction, and in the end disclaims in principle any explanatory value at all where the particular is concerned." (Bruner, 1986: 13)

Without belaboring the differences between these two modes of thought, the point I believe worth making here is that an understanding of the phenomenon of entrepreneurship begs for the narrative mode. Therefore, significant growth in the application and publication of narrative scholarship is inevitable.

5. A science of the imagination

One might be skeptical of a series of papers where, at points in their development, there is an allowance for fiction. That is, when there are "unknowns" in the knowledge of specific "facts as given," the authors of these narrative analyses are likely to provide "facts as made." It would seem, then, that a drift towards the recognition and use of narrative approaches places the entrepreneurship scholar in the solipsistic bind of reading "science fiction" (creating facts to serve a fiction) or reading "fiction science" (seeing the process of creating facts as a fiction). There might be a fear that narrative approaches might lead to taking logio-scientific scholarship down the rabbit hole of treating all knowledge as "fiction." This, I believe, is not actually the case, and rather than setting up a struggle of either/or between logio-scientific approaches and narrative approaches, it seems more appropriate to consider their inherent similarities. Ormizton and Sassower (1989) point out that the word *science* comes from the Latin word *scientia*, which means "knowledge" or *scire* meaning "to know."

> "Scire has its roots in *skei*, which means "to cut" or "to split." Knowledge, then, is understood as the ability, the skill "to separate one thing from another, "to discern." In the Greek, such separation is related to *skhizein* meaning "to split" into many parts, which is the root for *schizo-* and *schism*. Thus, the ability to discern differences, or what Plato calls in *The Republic* a certain kind of "mindfulness" is related to another Latin root *skel*, which also means "to cut" but which is more directly related to a concept developed later in the Old Norse where *reason, knowledge* and *incisiveness* are comprehended by *skil*, a precursor to our contemporary term *skill*." (p. 5).

The focus on the etymology of *science*, here, is to suggest to the logio-scientifically oriented scholar that all knowledge requires the acquisition of a skill to discern it. The skills of logio-scientific and narrative approaches are both, hard won, and both, not easily dismissed. To acquire knowledge about the nature of entrepreneurship is to be mindful of the phenomenon's many parts.

I do believe that a focus on entrepreneurial narratives might actually provide a unique contribution to narrative scholarship, normative logio-scientific entrepreneurship scholarship, and to scholarship in science, as well. I posit that normative science tends to hold up as the culmination of the scientific method the standard of falsifiability (Popper, 1959): for an idea to be a scientific idea, it must be testable. I will risk this speculation that the scientific process obsesses on the selection of non-falsifiable ideas. In most cases, less concern is offered for how ideas are generated for falsifiable testing [Campbell (1987) being a significant exception]. Yet, in the Popperian world of falsifiability, the process of science requires the generation of ideas:

> "Bold ideas, unjustified anticipations, and speculative thought, are our only means for interpreting nature: our only organon, our only instrument, for grasping her. And we must hazard them to win our prize." (Popper, 1959: 280).

The process of how ideas come into existence, is, an inherent aspect of entrepreneurial narrative. To study Terry Allen's story, for example, is to struggle not only with how an idea originates and becomes, but also with how narrative scholars struggle, themselves, with how ideas originate and become (in their study of how their own ideas originate and become when reading Terry Allen's story). The reflexiveness of narrative scholarship speaks to a "double doubling" of idea creation as both subject and process, twice (both as the object of study, and in the study of the study of the object).

The label, "science of the imagination" is suggested, then, as another promise (Shane and Venkataraman, 2000) for what entrepreneurship (and specifically, entrepreneurial narrative) might offer as a contribution to scholarship. What I find intriguing about the Terry Allen story, is not only how the entrepreneurs constellate the toy store idea "as if" (Gartner, Bird and Starr, 1992; Vaihinger, 1952) it were an on going business, but also how these entrepreneurs suggest various permutations of the idea's manifestation: "What if?" There is, in Allen's toy story, an imagination of the future in most of the actions these entrepreneurs undertake: "What if" we start a toy store? "What if" we get toys on consignment? "What if" we rent a space... get a loan, buy more toys, corner the market on Marvel Mustangs...? The narrative of entrepreneurship is the generation of hypotheses about how the world might be: how the future might look and act. The articles in this special issue not only probe how entrepreneurs generate and modify their visions of the future, the scholars in these articles generate and modify alternative visions of the future, as well. "What if" the reader's knowledge and experience were taken into account in the reading of the toy story? "What if" the women or the banker told their stories of the toy story? "What if" we were to consider all of the paths not taken, and write these unlived lives, as lived? There is a skill here, in these six entrepreneurial narratives, that is subtle but very critical for understanding how the imagination works.

6. Conclusion

I had originally thought to end this introduction with the idea that entrepreneurship scholars face a "story deficit." That is, while we (academic entrepreneurship scholars) currently live in a world that offers a variety of stories by and about entrepreneurs, the arena of academic entrepreneurship scholarship seems to lack much recognition and discussion of entrepreneurship stories. Ask yourself, what stories do you call upon to talk about entrepreneurship? While I can name dozens of entrepreneurs, I doubt whether I could actually tell much about their stories. I have logico-scientific descriptions, explanations, categories, concepts, and hypotheses about entrepreneurs, but, frankly, I don't have many stories to tell. Maybe you do.

While it might be appropriate to surmise that narrative approaches might challenge us to collect more stories, I now believe that the issue is not a "story deficit" but a deficit in how entrepreneurship stories are told. The articles that comprise this special issue show us that there are a variety of narrative approaches that offer a multitude of insights into just one story told by an entrepreneur. I would conjecture there might be ten times the six articles in this special issue that could talk about Terry Allen's story. I hope that this special issue might encourage more scholars to engage in narrative approaches and work to surmount the difficulties of the journal publication process.

These special issue articles represent, in a more sophisticated form, Bruner's (1986: 6–7) idea of "telling back" a story:

> "One gets a sense of the psychology of genre by listening to readers "tell back" a story they have just read or spontaneously "tell" a story about a "happening" in their

own lives. "Telling back" a Conrad story, one reader will turn it into a yarn of adventure, another into a moral tale about duplicity, and a third into a case study of a *Doppelganger*. The text from which they started was the same...

> But stories, in Paul Ricouer's phrase, are "models for the redescription of the world." But the story is not by itself the model. It is, so to speak, an instantiation of models we carry in our own minds. An undergraduate seminar in which I once participated interpreted *Hamlet* as an account of the bungling of a Danish prince who had become 'sword happy" at his German university and who was so inept at killing the man he hated that he did in his wisest friend, Polonius, in the process. Yet, this student admitted, the play was a "tragedy," but it was also a bungle (he was in engineering — with a passion.)"

And so, in these six entrepreneurial narratives, Terry Allen is "told back:" through a culture of personal narratives, confronted with the Harvard case method; within the interrelationships of a set of readers and writers; as a misogynist; as a bricolager; and mute vis-à-vis Shakespeare's Iago. Every telling is an aspect, another facet, of a more multi-dimensional perspective on the nature of entrepreneurship.

And, the process of "telling back" is not only of value as a scholarly exercise. Denise Fletcher (2007) offers images of students' readings of the toy story, as a way to stretch our imaginations of what narrative approaches might offer.

> "At best, education can only be undertaken as an experiment — an attempt to engage others by recollecting – responding or reacting – to the constellation of textual phrasings or connections. The perpetuation of a specific tradition, or fostering disciplines, is not the issue." (Ormizton and Sassower, 1989: 133).

I hope that this special issue engages you in new ways of knowing and talking about entrepreneurship.

Acknowledgements

The generosity of Lloyd Greif, and the Lloyd Greif Center for Entrepreneurial Studies at the Univeristy of Southern California made possible this article, and all of the articles in this special issue through the funding of the 5th Annual Greif Symposium on Emerging Organizations held in February 2004. All of the scholars in this special issue (Helene Ahl, Ted Baker, Denise Fletcher, Daniel Hjorth, Ellen O'Conner, and Chris Stayeart) played significant roles in the evolution of this special issue, particularly in improving my knowledge and appreciation of narrative approaches. Suna Sorensson provided substantial insights and thoughtful reviews of the six manuscripts and this introduction.

References

Adler, A., 1917. The Neurotic Constitution. (B. Glueck and J. E. Lind. Trans.). Moffat Yard, New York.
Ahl, H., 2007. Sex business in the toy store: A narrative analysis of a teaching case. Journal of Business Venturing 22 (5), 673–693.
Allen, T., 2007. A toy store(y). Journal of Business Venturing 22 (5), 628–636.

Baker, T., 2007. Resources in play: Bricolage in the *Toy Store(y)*. Journal of Business Venturing 22 (5), 694–711.

Baker, T., Nelson, R.E., 2005. Creating something from nothing: resource construction through entrepreneurial bricolage. Administrative Science Quarterly 50, 329–366.

Barnes, L.B., Christensen, C.R., Hansen, A.J., 1994. Teaching and the Case Method: Text, Cases, and Readings. Harvard Business School Publishing, Boston.

Boje, D.M., 2001. Narrative Methods for Organizational and Communication Research. Sage Publications, London.

Boudrieu, P., 1977. Outline of a Theory of Practice (Translated by R. Nice). Cambridge University Press, Cambridge.

Bruner, J., 1986. Actual Minds, Possible Worlds. Harvard University Press, Cambridge, MA.

Campbell, D.T., 1987. Blind variation and selective retention in creative thought as in other knowledge processes. In: Radinitzky, G., Bartley III, W.W. (Eds.), Evolutionary Epistemology, Rationality, and the Sociology of Knowledge. Open Court Publishing Company, La Salle, IL, pp. 91–114.

Contardo, I., Wensley, R., 2004. The Harvard Business School story: avoiding knowledge by being relevant. Organization 11 (2), 211–231.

Czarniawska, B., 1997. A four times told tale: combining narrative and scientific knowledge in organization studies. Organization 4 (1), 7–30.

Davis, M.S., 1971. That's interesting! Towards a phenomenology of sociology and a sociology of phenomenology. Philosophy of the Social Sciences 1, 309–344.

Fletcher, D., 2007. 'Toy Story:' The narrative world of entrepreneurship and the creation of interpretive communities. Journal of Business Venturing 22 (5), 649–672.

Gabriel, Y., 2004. Narratives, stories and texts. In: Grant, D., Hardy, C., Oswick, C., Putnam, L. (Eds.), The Sage Handbook of Organizational Discourse. Sage Publications, London, pp. 61–78.

Gartner, W.B., 1985. A framework for describing and classifying the phenomenon of new venture creation. Academy of Management Review 10 (4), 696–706.

Gartner, W.B., 1988. Who is an entrepreneur? Is the wrong question. American Journal of Small Business 12 (4), 11–32.

Gartner, Wiliam B., 1993. Words lead to deeds: towards an organizational emergence vocabulary. Journal of Business Venturing 8 (3), 231–240.

Gartner, W.B., 2004. Achieving "critical mess" in entrepreneurship scholarship. In: Katz, J.A., Shepherd, D. (Eds.), Advances in Entrepreneurship, Firm Emergence, and Growth, vol. 7. JAI Press, Greenwich, CT, pp. 199–216.

Gartner, W.B., Birley, S., 2002. Introduction to the special issue on qualitative methods in entrepreneurship research. Journal of Business Venturing 17 (5), 387–395.

Gartner, W.B., Bird, B.J., Starr, J., 1992. Acting as if: differentiating entrepreneurial from organizational behavior. Entrepreneurship Theory and Practice 16 (3), 13–32.

Gartner, W.B., Shaver, K.G., Carter, N.M., Reynolds, P.D., 2004. Handbook of Entrepreneurial Dynamics: The Process of Business Creation. Sage Publications, Thousand Oaks, CA.

Geertz, C., 1988. Works and Lives: The Anthropologist as Author. Stanford University Press, Stanford.

Grant, D., Hardy, C., Oswick, C., Putnam, L. (Eds.), 2004. The Sage Handbook of Organizational Discourse. Sage Publications, London.

Grant, D., Keenoy, T., Oswick, C., 1998. Introduction: organizational discourse: Of diversity, dichotomy, and multidisciplinarity. In: Grant, D., Keenoy, T., Oswick, C. (Eds.), Discourse and Organization. Sage, London, pp. 1–13.

Hatch, M.J., 1996. The role of the researcher: an analysis of narrative position in organizational theory. Journal of Management Inquiry 5, 359–374.

Hillman, J., 1983. Healing Fiction. Spring Publications, Woodstock, CN.

Hjorth, D., 2007. Lessons from Iago: Narrating the event of entrepreneurship. Journal of Business Venturing 22 (5), 712–732.

Hosking, D., Hjorth, D., 2004. Relational constructionism and entrepreneurship: some key notes. In: Hjorth, D., Steyaert, C. (Eds.), Narrative and Discursive Approaches in Entrepreneurship. Edward Elgar, Cheltenham, UK, pp. 255–268.

Naumes, W., Naumes, M., 1999. The Art and Craft of Case Writing. Sage Publications, Thousand Oaks, CA.

O'Connor, E., 1997. Telling decisions: the role of narrative in organizational decision making. In: Shapira, Z. (Ed.), Organizational Decision Making. Cambridge University Press, New York, pp. 304–323.

O'Connor, E.S., 2007. Reader beware: Doing business with a store(y) of knowledge. Journal of Business Venturing 22 (5), 637–648.

Ormizton, G.L., Sassower, R., 1989. Narrative Experiments. University of Minnesota Press, Minneapolis, MN.

Pentland, B.T., 1999. Building process theory with narrative: from description to explanation. Academy of Management Review 24 (4), 711–724.

Pitt, M., 1998. A tale of two gladiators: 'reading' entrepreneurs as texts. Organization Studies 19 (3), 387–414.

Popper, K.R., 1959. The Logic of Scientific Discovery. Basic Books, New York.

Rhodes, C., Brown, A.D., 2005. Narrative, organizations and research. International Journal of Management Reviews 7 (3), 167–188.

Shane, S., Venkataraman, S., 2000. The promise of entrepreneurship as a field of research. Academy of Management Review 25 (1), 217–226.

Smith, R., Anderson, A.R., 2004. The devil is in the e-tail: forms and structures in the entrepreneurial narratives. In: Hjorth, D., Steyaert, C. (Eds.), Narrative and Discursive Approaches in Entrepreneurship. Edward Elgar, Cheltenham, pp. 125–143.

Steyaert, C., 2007. Of course that is not the whole (toy) story: Entrepreneurship and the Cat's Cradle. Journal of Business Venturing 22 (5), 733–751.

Vaihinger, H., 1952. The Philosophy of "as if" (C.K. Ogden, Trans.). London: Routledge. (Original English work published 1924).

Van Maanen, J., 1988. Tales of the Field: On Writing Ethnography. University of Chicago Press, Chicago.

Yeats, W.B., 1956. Among school children. The Collected Poems of W.B. Yeats. MacMillan, New York.

1

Entrepreneurship as Organizing

Emergence, Newness, and Transformation

William B. Gartner and Candida G. Brush

Besides a number of comprehensive reviews of the entrepreneurship field, a variety of multidisciplinary perspectives for observing, studying, and understanding entrepreneurship has yielded a large number of views on the nature of the entrepreneurship scholarship.[1–14] Many of these scholars argue that this growing body of entrepreneurship research is not well synthesized and many research findings appear to be in disagreement with each other.[15–22] Using an evolutionary framework based on Weick, we categorize research articles used by Busenitz et al., in their survey of the field to show one possible approach to understanding and organizing entrepreneurship scholarship.[23, 24]

We view entrepreneurship as an organizational phenomenon, and more specifically, as an organizing process. Without belaboring the etymology of the word *entrepreneurship*, its root, *entreprendre* (i.e., go ahead, take in hand, undertake, take a hold of) is fundamentally about organizing (as in a "generic category of assembly rules").[25–31] *Organizing* involves planning and coordination of resources, people, ideas, market mechanisms as well as the establishment of routines, structures, and systems.[32–35] Organizing processes are accomplished through interactions among people, continually reaccomplished and renewed over time.[36] At the same time, organizing in entrepreneurship is socially embedded and context specific, where the entrepreneur (organizer) interacts with internal and external environments.[37, 38]

The process of organizing is not a singular event, but one that consists of a sequence of activities: enactment, selection, and retention.[39] We propose that the phenomenon of entrepreneurship is evident in cycles between the activities of enactment, selection, and retention of this organizing framework. We believe that the phenomenon of entrepreneurship is most often found in the transitional states in the evolution of an organization's structure and process. A diagram of this

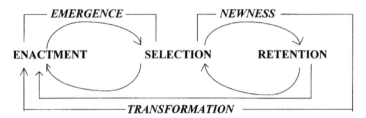

Figure 1.1.   Cycles of entrepreneurial activity—emergence, newness, and transformation.

process (Figure 1.1) identifies *emergence, newness,* and *transformation* as labels for cycles of these pair-wise organizing activities. Emergence is a cycle of activities between enactment and selection; newness is a cycle of activities between selection and retention; and transformation is a cycle of activities between retention and enactment. This framework has a subtle but significant difference from the organizing model described by Weick, because it includes a feedback loop between enactment and selection.[40] The labels (emergence, newness, and transformation) are not substitutes for Weick's concepts (enactment, selection, and retention), but an elaboration of this model that suggests where entrepreneurial processes are likely to occur, and where entrepreneurship scholarship has focused its efforts. At the same time, while we recognize that Weick's model is intended to be inter-personal and intraorganizational, the larger context of evolutionary thought about organizations (e.g., Aldrich, 1999) may allow us to imply that this framework of ours would also be applicable to population and macro levels of analysis, as well. Our framework shifts the focus to organizing processes rather than the organi-zation, and therefore is not rooted in age, structure, or size assumptions, such as life cycle or organizational development models.[41, 42] So, for example, in our view, these processes of emergence, newness, and transformation may occur in a variety of settings that may not have been traditionally seen as entrepreneurial.

The format of the chapter is as follows. The concepts of emergence, newness, and transformation are outlined, and inferences to ideas in the organizational sciences are made. We then provide a way to categorize entrepreneurship re-search into the three types of organizing processes—emergence, newness, and transformation—and suggest that many of the disparate findings in the entre-preneurship literature are due to differences in the type of organizing phenomena studied. Suggestions are offered for how entrepreneurship research might be influenced through the use of this framework.

EMERGENCE

Organizational emergence is the process of organization creation, which is an unfolding of organizing activities involving both enactment and selection.[43]

Other terms for this period of time are: the *preorganization,* the *organization in vitro, prelaunch, launch, gestation, inception,* and *start-up.*[44–54]

Organizational emergence involves those events and activities before an organization becomes an organization, that is, organizational emergence includes those factors that lead to, and influence the creation and development of the organization. Organizational emergence is where vision, which connects possibilities, moves from vague to clear in imagery, taking on form and meaning.[55] Tacit knowledge becomes explicit or shared.[56] The value associated with the new reality is being discovered and exploited.[57] This process involves the entrepreneur's perception of opportunity structures, or gaps in the market, that are met by acquisition and the management of resources (land, labor, and capital) and information networks.[58] In this phase, entrepreneurs perceive and identify relevant resources and opportunities in the environment, then "coordinate activities that involve different markets ... (that is, they are) an inter-market operator."[59] Each organizing process is chaotic and disorderly, often including networking, resource borrowing or sharing, boundary establishment, and legitimating activities.[60–63]

In organizational emergence, there is significant interplay between the processes of enactment and selection. As entrepreneurs undertake the tasks of organization creation, they also recognize and attempt to adapt to various selection mechanisms.[64] For example, entrepreneurs must convince prospective investors of the viability of their ideas, which requires these entrepreneurs to understand the investor's criteria for investing in new opportunities.[65, 66] Organizational emergence might, therefore, be viewed as purposeful, though the capabilities of entrepreneurs to comprehend the selection mechanisms operating might also be perceived as limited or nonexistent.[67, 68]

The process of emergence occurs before the organization exists. It is likely, therefore, that the process of emergence does not always result in an organization. The outcome of organizational emergence could be an organization or a failed attempt at creating an organization, or something else.[69] Conversely, the existence of a new organization is, therefore, not equivalent to attempts at start-up, or the process of emergence. In particular, the problems of new organizations (e.g., the liability of newness, lack of legitimacy) are not the same problems encountered in the process of becoming a new organization.[70–73] In emergence, entrepreneurs must craft a vision and set direction where none existed before, identify, attract, and acquire resources, and gain the commitment of participants, developing trust, and engaging them to join the organization.[74–77] At emergence, knowledge is often tacit and individual, so that making knowledge explicit and shared is a significant challenge. The creation of systems, roles, and responsibilities, where none previously existed is a perplexity for generating an administrative framework of effective procedures and social contracts in the venture.[78–80]

Observers of ecological analyses of organizational foundings have recognized this dichotomy between the process of starting a business (founding attempts), and the existence of new organizations (organization foundings).[81–85]

Owing to the dearth of data on preorganizing processes, organizational ecologists rarely distinguish successful events from nonevents in the founding process. Instead, ecological researchers concentrate their attention on the times between the appearance of operational start-ups—that is, successful new entities that being to product goods and services. A sample selection bias ensues because many emerging organizations fail before they start operations: some potential founders fail to incorporate, and newly incorporate entities may be unable to commence production.[86-88]

An organization founding is recognized when there is an appearance of an organizational start-up, such as at the time of incorporation. However, the study of organization foundings fails to recognize attempts at founding that did not result in an operational start-up.[89]

NEWNESS

The circumstances of organizational *newness* involve the process of facing the pressures of selection and developing established routines. This phase of development is also referred to as: survival and stability, growth and direction, survival and success, survival, founding, and expansion.[90-96] New organizations have gained some measure of legitimacy through stakeholder exchanges and relationships, control and management of resources, and acceptability or legitimacy.[97] In newness, an organization's direction is articulated through resource commitments.[98] Procedures for managing resource deployment are developed.[99] The individual human and social assets become increasingly institutionalized in the organization.[100, 101] An organization may add people, requiring incentives for insuring commitment, as well as mechanisms for transferring knowledge.[102, 103] Internal organizational processes and routines are improved and more formalized procedures and structures are developed.[104, 105] Some organizing activities are associated with the development of internal policies, knowledge transfer, and specialization of labor, while other activities involve external interactions in implementing product/market strategies, acquiring new resources, and extending networks.[106] The new venture is focused on surviving in the short term, and achieving performance in the longer run, although the organization may become stable or decline.

The challenges of newness are complex. New organizations face difficulties associated with their liability of newness, and size influencing perceived legitimacy in the eyes of external constituents, which may affect a new organization's ability to obtain resources.[107-111] Competitive threats may challenge a new organization to stick to or modify its vision, while decisions involving resource allocation, combination, and development into unique assets present additional dilemmas.[112, 113]

Having emerged through the transition from idea to existence, the new organization faces continuing selection problems, as well as opportunities for substantial growth and success.[114-117] These distinct sets of challenges reflect two contrasting viewpoints to studying new firms. The ecological approach is, in some respects, a more pessimistic viewpoint on organizational survival, in that, implicit in the name, "the liabilities of newness," is significant evidence that newer and smaller firms have high rates of failure.[118] Strategic approaches that study the differential characteristics of a select number of more or less successful new organizations appear to be more optimistic, in taking a perspective that appears to reflect the optimism of these business owners.[119, 120] From either perspective, much of this research has had a "disproportionate pre-occupation among contributors with issues of success and failure, survival and death, and the relative economic performance of firms."[121]

TRANSFORMATION

Transformation is the way that an organization changes its established routines through enactment. Transformation involves a metamorphosis from an existing vision that produces changes in the products and services, customers/clients, channels, skills, margins, competitive advantage, and people.[122] For instance, the organization takes on a new strategic direction or way of carrying out its activities. Organizational transformations are therefore, profound changes in an organization with revitalizing potential that may or may not be realized. The following terms are descriptive of organizational transformation:

- Organizational change—which is a change in the key patterns of the organizational system, or shifts in the way the organization is related to its environment, especially patterns by which the organization imports energy, raw materials, and transforms inputs, or changes in patterns of differentiation, coordination and integration, structures, human resources, and policies and procedures
- Transformative change—which cuts through the mental and organizational barriers
- Punctuated equilibrium—which refers to a nonlinear shift in strategies, structures, and/or processes, such that the current resource configuration is rapidly transformed[123-126]

In organizational transformation, the challenge is to set a new direction, to abandon an orientation rooted in the present, and adopt a new orientation rooted in the future.[127] In circumstances where there has been a delegitimization and disengagement of a previous vision, organizational transformation occurs when there is the need to identify new resources and develop new means to acquire and allocate these.[128] The fixed definition of its structure, patterns of behavior, and cognitive understanding are revised either through endogenous pressures or exogenously generated pressures.[129] Challenges of transformation may include structural changes (e.g., mergers, acquisitions, going public), personnel and leadership changes. Adjustments to the loss of some personnel or integration of others, as well as resistance to change means that a transformation challenge can include developing renewed trust and commitment.[130] The organization is faced with continual dilemmas of how to revise or destroy existing processes, policies, and procedures to make it possible for new knowledge creation.[131]

DISCUSSION

By viewing entrepreneurship as different types of organizing, we offer a relatively simple way to categorize entrepreneurship research that crosses a variety of disciplinary perspectives and units of analysis. In Tables 1.1, 1.2, and 1.3, we provide examples of empirical research in entrepreneurship that illustrate differences among the three different cycles of entrepreneurial activity by level of analysis. The examples for these tables were taken from Busenitz, West, Shepherd, Nelson, Zacharakis, and Chandler, who generated, from their perspective, a comprehensive list of ninety-seven top-tier journal articles on the topic of entrepreneurship, based on an evaluation of articles from seven journals: *Academy of Management Journal* (AMJ), *Academy of Management Review* (AMR), *Administrative Science Quarterly* (ASQ), *Journal of Management* (JOM), *Management Science* (MS), *Organization Science* (OS), and *Strategic Management Journal* (SMJ).[132] We looked at the empirical articles only, of which eighty-eight of the ninety-seven articles analyzed data, either quantitatively or qualitatively. No articles from the AMR or other theoretical articles from the other six journals are included in the tables. Table 1.4 provides a summary of the percentages of empirical articles that could be categorized into the three categories of emergence, newness, and transformation (which were 22, 53, and 25 percent, respectively).

An important implication of this framework, for entrepreneurship scholars, is recognizing the apparent divergence of entrepreneurship research into the study of three very different organizational phenomena. As described in previous sections, the problems and issues of emergence, newness, and transformation are fundamentally different from each other. It might be appropriate, therefore, for entrepreneurship scholars to consider the value of choosing sides; that is, entrepreneurship scholars might find value in identifying with one of the three entrepreneurial types (emergence, newness, and transformation), and speaking to scholars who are doing research on that organizational type. Developing the paradigm of entrepreneurship requires some consensus on the phenomenon studied.[133] We believe that entrepreneurship is too broad a topic area for entrepreneurship scholars to meaningfully address all of the core issues in this field.[134] It is unlikely that scholars, focused on any of these three entrepreneurial phenomena, can, at this point, bridge the inherent differences (research questions, methodologies, problems, etc.) among these three types. The entrepreneurship field might be strengthened if scholars were to narrow their views on the domain

Table 1.1.   Empirical Emergence Articles in Busenitz et al. (2003) by Level of
Analysis (LOA)

Citation	Journal	Sample Size	LOA	Description of Data
Arend (1999)	SMJ	NA	Environment	Emergence of entrepreneurs in the technology field
Baum and Haverman (1997)	ASQ	614	Firm	Transient hotels operating in Manhattan from 1898 to 1990
Begley, Boyd (1987)	JOM	471	Individual	Managers and entrepreneurs in New England
Boeker (1989)	ASQ	53	Firm	Semiconductor industry from 1958 to 1985
Budros (1994)	OS	62	Firm	NY life insurance companies from 1894 to 1904
Carroll and Mosa kowski (1987)	ASQ	2172	Individual	Study of self-employment in Germany
Cooper, Dunkelberg (1986)	SMJ	1756	Individual	Degrees of entrepre- neurship and paths to ownership
Day (1994)	OS	136	Firm	Championing in internal corporate ventures
Dowling and McGee (1994)	MS	52	Firm	New ventures in telecom- munications equipment
Feeser and Williard (1990)	SMJ	42	Individual	Founding strategies in computer industry
Frese, Kring, Soose, Zempel (1996)	AMJ	1623	Individual	Personal initiative in East and West Germany
Garud, Van de Ven (1992)	SMJ	719	Event	Development of a new venture within a corporation
Kazanjian, Drazin (1989)	MS	71	Firm	Emergence and growth in computer/electronics firms
Louis et al. (1989)	ASQ	818	Individual	Academic entrepreneur- ship in life sciences
Luo (1997)	OS	116	Firm	International joint ventures in manufacturing, 1988–1991
McDougall et al. (1994)	SMJ	123	Firm	New ventures in high- growth industries
Morris et al. (1993)	JOM	84	Firm	Computer software firms attempting IPOs in 1983–1984

(*continued*)

Table 1.1.   (*continued*)

Citation	Journal	Sample Size	LOA	Description of Data
Naman and Slevin (1993)	SMJ	122	Firm	"Fit" in entrepreneurial-style strategic management
Sedaitis (1998)	OS	9	Environment	Community exchange markets in Russia, 1991–1993
Shane (1996)	JOM	89	Environment	Entrepreneurship activity in United States, 1899–1988

Academy of Management Journal—AMJ, *Academy of Management Review*—AMR, *Administrative Science Quarterly*—ASQ, *Journal of Management*—JOM, *Management Science*—MS, *Organization Science*—OS, and *Strategic Management Journal*—SMJ.

of their scholarship. For example, the concept of entrepreneurial orientation is essentially strategic in nature, having to do with the "processes, practices, and decision-making activities that lead to new entry."[135, 136] Since the ideas of entrepreneurial orientation stem primarily from the strategic management literature, it might be appropriate to view the entrepreneurial orientation construct within the phenomenon of organizational newness, rather than assuming that this construct applies to organizational emergence, and transformation, as well. Furthermore, this should lead to enhanced external validity of studies by bounding the research domain so that it would be possible to replicate studies, achieve convergence, and generalize findings.[137]

We propose that the organizing framework permits application or testing of a variety of theories, rooted either in social sciences or economics.[138] Each category is comprehensive enough to include relevant factors, and open ended enough to permit debates and competing ideas. By specifying the domain of study, we believe that researchers can study core dimensions of each of the three types of organizational processes but not be limited by their choice of theory.[139–141]

An aspect of the emergence–newness–transformation categorization of entrepreneurship research is path dependence among these types of organizational phenomena. New firms are the result of the emergence process, but the dependent variable (the new firm) cannot be used to predict the initial process (firm emergence). As Aldrich and Kenworthy suggest, the abundance of studies of new firms and comparative lack of studies of emerging firms, indicate that we know little about the ways the organizations are created, and therefore, little about why new firms are structured and behave as they do.[142] Understanding the struggle of new organizations, as they unfold and seek to survive, is unlikely to provide insights into which and why certain organizational possibilities did not reach viability. Few entrepreneurship studies are longitudinal, hence the circumstances

Table 1.2. Empirical Newness Articles in Busenitz et al. (2003) by Level of Analysis (LOA)

Citation	Journal	Sample Size	LOA	Description of Data
Ariño and de la Torre (1998)	OS	2	Firm	Joint venture case study
Barringer and Bluedorn (1999)	SMJ	169	Firm	Corporate entrepreneurship in manufacturing
Baum and Singh (1994)	OS	682	Firm	Day-care centers in Toronto
Begley and Boyd (1987)	JOM	471	Individual	Members of Smaller Business Association of New England
Boeker (1989)	ASQ	53	Firm	Semiconductor firms in 1985
Bracker et al. (1986)	SMJ	555	Firm	Dry-cleaning businesses
Bracker et al. (1988)	SMJ	217	Firm	Electronic businesses
Bracker and Pearson (1986)	SMJ	188	Firm	Dry-cleaning businesses
Bracker, Pearson, and Keats (1988)	SMJ	73	Firm	Small firms
Browning et al. (1995)	AMJ	54	Individual	Founding and current leaders of SEMATECH
Cooper et al. (1986)	SMJ	1756	Firm	National Federation of Independent Business members
Covin and Slevin (1989)	SMJ	161	Firm	Small manufacturing firms
Dean, Brown, and Bamford (1998)	SMJ	302	Firm	Small and large manufacturing firms
Dess, Lumpkin, and Covin (1997)	SMJ	96/32	Individual	Entrepreneurial strategy making within firms
Dickson and Weaver (1997)	AMJ	433	Firm	Norwegian firms
Dodge, Fullerton, and Robbins (1994)	SMJ	645	Firm	Small business firms
Dollinger and Golden (1992)	JOM	486	Firm	Small manufacturing firms
Dowling and McGee (1994)	MS	52	Firm	New entrants in telecommunications
Eisenhardt et al. (1996)	OS	102	Firm	Semiconductor firms, 1978–1985
Feeser et. al. (1990)	SMJ	78	Firm	High- and low-growth computing firms

(continued)

Table 1.2. (*continued*)

Citation	Journal	Sample Size	LOA	Description of Data
Fiegenbaum and Karnani (1991)	SMJ	3000	Firm	Small firms in eighty-three different industries
Gersick (1994)	AMJ	1	Individual	Temporal pacing in group projects
Gimeno et. al. (1997)	ASQ	1547	Firm	New businesses in the United States
Horwitch and Thietart (1987)	MS	641	Firm	Business units in consumer and industrial goods
Kalleberg et al. (1991)	AMJ	411	Firm	Small firms in Indiana
Lafuente and Salas (1989)	SMJ	360	Individual	Entrepreneurs in small Spanish firms
Larson (1992)	ASQ	4	Firm	Interfirm alliances
Luo (1997)	OS	116	Firm	International joint ventures in China
McDougall et al. (1994)	SMJ	123	Firm	High- and low-growth new ventures
McGee (1995)	SMJ	210	Firm	High-technology new ventures
McGee, Dowling, and Megginson (1995)	SMJ	210	Firm	High-technology new ventures
Merz and Sauber (1995)	SMJ	370	Firm	Small firms
Miller (1987)	AMJ	97	Firm	Small- and mid-size companies
Mosakowski (1991)	SMJ	122	Firm	Entrepreneurial firms in computing industry
Mosakowski (1993)	JOM	86	Firm	Entrepreneurial software firms
Naman et al. (1993)	SMJ	82	Firm	Small- and medium-sized high-tech firms
Roberts and Hauptman (1987)	MS	26	Firm	New biomedical firms formed 1968–1975
Robinson et al. (1998)	SMJ	115	Firm	New manufacturing ventures
Romanelli (1989)	ASQ	174	Firm	Mini-computer firms, 1957–1981
Sapienza and Korsgaard (1996)	AMJ	162	Individual	Entrepreneurs and venture capitalists (VCs)
Schoonhover et al. (1990)	ASQ	98	Firm	Semiconductor firms, 1978–1985
Sedaitis (1998)	OS	293	Firm	Russian firms in commodities, 1991–1993

(*continued*)

Table 1.2. (*continued*)

Citation	Journal	Sample Size	LOA	Description of Data
Segev (1987)	MS	126	Firm	Kibbutzes
Shan (1990)	SMJ	278	Firm	New start-ups
Shane and Foo (1999)	MS	1292	Firm	New franchisors in United States 1979–1996
Shepherd (1999)	MS	66	Individual	VCs in Australia
Zahra (1996)	AMJ	127	Firm	Entrepreneurial activity in Fortune 500

Academy of Management Journal—AMJ, *Academy of Management Review*—AMR, *Administrative Science Quarterly*—ASQ, *Journal of Management*—JOM, *Management Science*—MS, *Organization Science*—OS, and *Strategic Management Journal*—SMJ.

surrounding organizational emergence and development, and associated sequences of activities over time are poorly understood. Cases, qualitative studies, and panel studies are infrequently used to explore ways that firms emerge, survive newness, and move through transition.

As can be seen in Table 1.4, firm-level studies are in the majority for each of the three cycles, and, overall, 75 percent of all studies in Tables 1.1, 1.2, and 1.3 focus on firm-level issues. This finding may be a reflection of the journals selected in the Busenitz et. al. study, that is, the seven journals tend to focus on firm-level issues, compared with other disciplinary journals that might tend toward the individual level (e.g., *Journal of Applied Psychology*), or the environment (*American Economic Review* or *American Journal of Sociology*).[143] Paradoxically, while the emergence–newness–transformation framework describes the entrepreneurship field as three disparate research foci, the earlier sections of this chapter indicate that there are ample connections to other research streams within the organizational sciences. There are also some implicit affinities within the entrepreneurship field where stronger links among researchers can be made. For example, family business, as a topic area, can be viewed, within the emergence–newness–transformation framework as having links to aspects of organizational transition, such as the management and ownership succession from one generation to another.[144–146] Small business research would have links to organizational newness.[147] Some research topics are likely to span across the three organizational types. Franchising, for example, can be viewed as a way for individuals to organize; as a strategy for growth and survival; and as a way for radical change to occur.[148–150]

The recognition of levels of analysis in the framework suggests new directions for research beyond the organization.[151] Networks, industries, and communities move through sequences of emergence, newness, and transformation. For example, networking can lead to new connections, new patterns of venturing, and commerce in response to perceived opportunities. Challenges to legitimacy

Table 1.3.   Empirical Transformation Articles in Busenitz et al. (2003) by Level of Analysis (LOA)

Citation	Journal	Sample Size	LOA	Description of Data
Barringer et al. (1999)	SMJ	169	Firm	Manufacturing firms
Birkinshaw (1997)	AMJ	124	Firm	Medium- and large-sized U.S.-based businesses in ten industries
Boeker (1989)	AMJ	51	Firm	Semiconductor firms in Silicon Valley
Browning, Beyer, and Shetler (1995)	AMJ	66	Individual	Semiconductor industry in the United States
Day (1994)	OS	136	Firm	Internal corporate ventures, Fortune 1000
Dess et al. (1997)	AMJ	96	Individual	Executives from thirty-two diversified firms
Dickson et al. (1997)	AMJ	433	Firm	Norwegian manufacturing firms, 6–500 employees
Drazin, Kazanjian	AMJ	109	Individual	CEO succession in tech firms
Farjoun (1994)	OS	12781	Firm	Firms in 222 industries
Galunic and Eisenhardt (1996)	OS	80	Individual	Divisions inside high-technology firms
Horwitch and Thietart (1987)	MS	641	Firm	Businesses with high R&D expenditures
Miller (1987)	AMJ	97	Firm	Small- and medium-sized firms in Quebec
Norburn and Birley (1988)	SMJ	953	Individual	Top executives in largest 150 U.S. firms
Ocasio (1999)	ASQ	108	Firm	Publicly held industrial corporations
Pennings, Barkema, and Douma (1994)	AMJ	462	Firm	Dutch firms
Richardson (1996)	OS	14	Firm	Fashion apparel industry
Rosenblatt et al. (1993)	OS	1	Firm	Small school district
Russel and Russel (1992)	JOM	77	Firm	Strategic business units
Segev (1987)	MS	252	Individual	Top two executives of 126 kibbutz-owned enterprises

(*continued*)

Table 1.3. (*continued*)

Citation	Journal	Sample Size	LOA	Description of Data
Stopford and Baden-Fuller (1994)	SMJ	10	Firm	Firms in four different industries in the United Kingdom
Thompson and Horowitz (1993)	MS	2	Firm	One cooperative and one entrepreneurial firm
Welbourne et al. (1999)	AMJ	360	Firm	U.S. firms that went public in 1993

Academy of Management Journal—AMJ, *Academy of Management Review*—AMR, *Administrative Science Quarterly*—ASQ, *Journal of Management*—JOM, *Management Science*—MS, *Organization Science*—OS, and *Strategic Management Journal*—SMJ.

confront early entrants as the industry emerges.[152, 153] From another perspective, industries emerge or are reformed due to technological innovation, shifts in relative cost relationships, new consumer needs, or other economic or social changes that elevate a new product or service to the level of a potentially viable business opportunity.[154, 155] At this stage, there are no rules of the game, and industry structural factors are uncertain, in contrast with mature or declining industries where barriers to entry and exit, and bases of competition are defined.[156] Yet, current research in the field infrequently examines these more macro units of analysis.

The framework, therefore, is not intended as a way to exclude various types of entrepreneurial research; rather, the framework helps clarify what kind of entrepreneurship research is being conducted, and suggests gaps where new research might be carried out in the future. In addition, the framework offers ways to expand our view of entrepreneurial phenomena at different levels of analysis and as different kinds of organizing processes. We believe that the field of entrepreneurship is more likely to build a distinct body of knowledge, if entrepreneurship scholars can

Table 1.4. Summary of Organizing Type by Level of Analysis for Busenitz et al. (2003)

Organizing Type —> Level of Analysis	Emergence	Newness	Transformation	Total (percentage)
Individual	6	7	6	19 (22%)
Firm	10	40	16	66 (75%)
Environment	3	0	0	3 (3%)
Total (percentage)	19 (22%)	47 (53%)	22 (25%)	88 (100%)

link their specific contribution within the wider context of all entrepreneurship research.[157, 158] This framework may offer such a possibility.

NOTES

1. L. W. Busenitz et al., "Entrepreneurship in Emergence: Past Trends and Future Directions," *Journal of Management* 29, no. 3 (2003): 285–308.

2. H. Aldrich and T. Baker, "Blinded by the Cites? Has There Been Progress in Entrepreneurship Research?" in *Entrepreneurship 2000*, eds. D. L. Sexton and R. W. Smilor (Chicago: Upstart Publishing, 1997), 377–400.

3. M. B. Low and I. C. MacMillan, "Entrepreneurship: Past Research and Future Challenges," *Journal of Management* 14, no. 2 (1988): 139–161.

4. See, for example, S. Birley and I. C. MacMillan, *Entrepreneurship Research: Global Perspectives* (Amsterdam: North-Holland, 1993).

5. G. E. Hills, *Marketing and Entrepreneurship: Research Ideas and Opportunities* (Westport, CT: Quorum, 1994).

6. L. Herron et al., "Entrepreneurship Theory from an Interdisciplinary Perspective: Volume 1," *Entrepreneurship: Theory and Practice* 16, no. 2 (1991).

7. L. Herron et al., "Entrepreneurship Theory from an Interdisciplinary Perspective: Volume 2," *Entrepreneurship: Theory and Practice* 16, no. 3 (1992).

8. G. D. Libecap, *Advances in the Study of Entrepreneurship, Innovation, and Economic Growth*, Vol. 6 (Greenwich, CT: JAI Press, 1993).

9. J. A. Katz and R. H. Brockhaus, *Advances in Entrepreneurship, Firm Emergence, and Growth*, Vol. 1 (Greenwich, CT: JAI Press, 1993).

10. D. L. Sexton and J. D. Kasarda, *The State of the Art of Entrepreneurship* (Boston: PWS-Kent, 1992).

11. D. L. Sexton and R. Smilor, *Entrepreneurship 2000* (Boston: Upstart Publishing, 1997).

12. M. Hitt et al., *Strategic Entrepreneurship: Creating a New Mindset* (Oxford, UK: Blackwell, 2003).

13. S. Alvarez et al., *Handbook of Entrepreneurship Research: Disciplinary Perspectives* (Berlin: Springer, 2005).

14. Z. Acs and D. Audretsch, *Handbook of Entrepreneurship Research: An Interdisciplinary Survey and Introduction* (London: Kluwer, 2003).

15. S. Alvarez et al., *Handbook of Entrepreneurship Research: Disciplinary Perspectives* (Berlin: Springer, 2005).

16. Z. Acs and D. Audretsch, *Handbook of Entrepreneurship Research: An Interdisciplinary Survey and Introduction* (London: Kluwer, 2003).

17. R. Amit et al., "Challenges to Theory Development in Entrepreneurship Research," *Journal of Management Studies* 30, no. 5 (1993): 815–834.

18. I. Bull and G. E. Willard, "Towards a Theory of Entrepreneurship," *Journal of Business Venturing* 8 (1993): 183–195.

19. G. T. Lumpkin and G. G. Dess, "Clarifying the Entrepreneurial Orientation Construct and Linking It to Performance," *Academy of Management Review* 21 (1996): 135–172.

20. S. Shane and S. Venkataraman, "The Promise of Entrepreneurship as a Field of Research," *Academy of Management Review* 25 (2000): 217–226.

21. S. Venkataraman, "The Distinctive Domain of Entrepreneurship Research," *Advances in Entrepreneurship, Firm Emergence and Growth, Vol. 3* (Greenwich, CT: JAI Press, 1997), 119–138.

22. Aldrich and Baker, 1997.

23. K. E. Weick, *The Social Psychology of Organizing,* 2nd ed. (New York: Random House, 1979).

24. Busenitz et al., 2003.

25. See, for example, Baumol (1993), Bull and Willard (1993), and Herbert and Link (1988) for discussions of a history of entrepreneurship definitions; and Amit, Glosten, and Muller (1993) and Gartner (1990, 1993) for recent interpretations. W. J. Baumol, "Formal Entrepreneurship Theory in Economics: Existence and Bounds," *Journal of Business Venturing* 8 (1993): 197–210.

26. Bull and Willard, 1993.

27. R. F. Herbert and A. N. Link, *The Entrepreneur* (New York: Praeger, 1988).

28. W. B. Gartner, "Words Lead to Deeds: Towards an Organizational Emergence Vocabulary," *Journal of Business Venturing* 8 (1993): 231–240.

29. W. B. Gartner, "What Are We Talking about When We Talk about Entrepreneurship?" *Journal of Business Venturing* 5 (1990): 15–28.

30. D. Crookall, "Editorial: Entrepreneurship Education," *Simulation and Gaming* 25, no. 3 (1994): 333–334.

31. Weick, 1979, p. 235.

32. S. W. Becker and G. Gordon, "An Entrepreneurial Theory of Formal Organizations, Part I: Patterns of Formal Organizations," *Administrative Science Quarterly* 11 (1966): 315–344.

33. H. Leibenstein, "Entrepreneurship and Development," *American Economic Review* 58, no. 2 (1968): 72–83.

34. J. Ronen, ed., *Entrepreneurship* (Lexington, MA: Lexington Books, 1982).

35. S. Shane, *A General Theory of Entrepreneurship: The Individual-Opportunity Nexus* (Cheltenham, UK: Edward Elgar, 2003).

36. J. E. Pfeffer, *Organizations and Organization Theory* (Cambridge, MA: Ballinger, 1982).

37. Shane and Venkataraman, 2000.

38. N. Nohria and R. Gulati, "Firms and Their Environments," in *The Handbook of Economic Sociology,* eds. N. J. Smelser and R. Swedberg (Princeton, NJ: Princeton University Press, 1994).

39. Weick, 1979, pp. 119–146.

40. Weick, 1979, pp. 45, 132–137.

41. N. C. Churchill and B. Lewis, "The Five Stages of Small Business Growth," *Harvard Business Review* (1983): 30–50.

42. S. Hanks et al., "Tightening the Life-Cycle Construct: A Taxonomic Study of Growth Stage Configurations in High-Technology Organizations," *Entrepreneurship Theory and Practice* 18 (1994): 5–29.

43. W. B. Gartner et al., "Acting as if: Differentiating Entrepreneurial from Organizational Behavior," *Entrepreneurship: Theory and Practice* 16 (1992): 13–32.

44. J. Katz and W. B. Gartner, "Properties of Emerging Organizations," *Academy of Management Review* 13 (1988): 429–442.

45. E. L. Hansen, "Entrepreneurial Networks: Their Effect on New Organization Outcomes." Unpublished doctoral dissertation (Knoxville, TN: University of Tennessee, 1990).

46. E. L. Hansen and M. S. Wortman, "Entrepreneurial Networks: The Organization in Vitro," in *Best Papers Proceedings*, ed. F. Hoy (Washington, DC: Academy of Management, 1989), 69–73.

47. W. E. McMullan and W. A. Long, *Developing New Ventures* (San Diego, CA: Harcourt Brace Jovanovich, 1990).

48. G. L. Lippitt and W. H. Schmidt, "Crisis in Developing Organizations," *Harvard Business Review* 45 (1967): 101–122.

49. P. Reynolds and B. Miller, "New Firm Gestation: Conception, Birth, and Implications for Research," *Journal of Business Venturing* 7 (1992): 405–417.

50. D. A. Whetten, "Organizational Growth and Decline Processes," *Annual Review of Sociology* 13 (1987): 335–358.

51. M. Scott and R. Bruce, "Five Stages of Growth in Small Businesses," *Long Range Planning* 20 (1987): 45–52.

52. N. M. Carter et al., "Exploring Start-Up Event Sequences," *Journal of Business Venturing* 11 (1996): 151–166.

53. A. H. Van de Ven et al., *Research on the Management of Innovation* (New York: Harper and Row, 1989).

54. K. H. Vesper, *New Venture Strategies*, 2nd ed. (Englewood Cliffs, NJ: Prentice-Hall, 1990).

55. P. Nutt and R. Backoff, "Organizational Transformation," *Journal of Management Inquiry* 6 (1997): 235–254.

56. I. Nonaka, "A Dynamic Theory of Organizational Knowledge Creation," *Organization Science* 5 (1994): 14–37.

57. Ronen, 1982.

58. W. Glade, "Approaches to a Theory of Entrepreneurial Formation," *Explorations in Entrepreneurial History* 4 (1966): 245–259.

59. Leibenstein, 1968.

60. H. E. Aldrich, *Organizations Evolving* (Thousand Oaks, CA: Sage, 1999).

61. N. M. Carter et al., "Discontinuance Among New Firms in Retail: The Influence of Initial Resources, Strategy and Gender," *Journal of Business Venturing* 12 (1997): 125–145.

62. Katz and Gartner, 1988.

63. F. Delmar and S. Shane, "Legitimating First: Organizing Activities and the Survival of New Ventures," *Journal of Business Venturing* 19 (2004): 385–410.

64. Aldrich, 1999.

65. J. Kaplan, *Startup* (Boston: Houghton Mifflin, 1995).

66. R. J. Kunze, *Nothing Ventured* (New York: HarperBusiness, 1990).

67. B. Bird, "Implementing Entrepreneurial Ideas: The Case for Intention," *Academy of Management Review* 13 (1988): 442–453.

68. H. E. Aldrich and A. L. Kenworthy, "The Accidental Entrepreneur: Campbellian Antinomies and Organization Foundings," in *Variations in Organization Science*, eds. J. A. C. Baum and B. McKelvey (Thousand Oaks, CA: Sage, 1999), 19–33.

69. Ronen, 1982.

70. A. L. Stinchcombe, "Social Structure and Organizations," in *Handbook of Organizations* (Chicago: Rand McNally, 1965), 142–193.

71. Meyer and Rowan, 1977.

72. P. Reynolds, "Reducing Barriers to Understanding New Firm Gestation: Prevalence and Success of Nascent Entrepreneurs," paper presented at the Academy of Management Meetings, Dallas, Texas (August 1994).

73. Delmar and Shane, 2004.

74. E. H. Shein, *Organizational Culture and Leadership* (San Francisco: Jossey Bass, 1987).

75. P. Nutt and R. Backoff, "Creating Vision," *Journal of Management Inquiry* 6 (1997): 308–328.

76. M. M. Stone and C. G. Brush, "Planning in Ambiguous Contexts: The Dilemma of Meeting Needs for Commitment and Demands for Legitimacy," *Strategic Management Journal* 17 (1996): 633–652.

77. Van de Ven, 1993.

78. Becker and Gordon, 1966.

79. Penrose, *The Theory of the Growth of the Firm* (New York: John Wiley and Sons, 1959).

80. Aldrich, 1999.

81. H. E. Aldrich and G. Wiedenmeyer, "From Traits to Rates: An Ecological Perspective on Organizational Foundings," in *Advances in Entrepreneurship, Firm Emergence and Growth*, Vol. 1, eds. J. Katz and R. Brockhaus (Greenwich, CT: JAI Press, 1993), 145–195.

82. T. L. Amburgey and H. Rao, "Organizational Ecology: Past, Present and Future Directions," *Academy of Management Journal* 39 (1996): 1265–1286.

83. M. T. Hannan and G. R. Carroll, *Dynamics of Organizational Populations* (New York: Oxford University Press, 1992).

84. M. T. Hannan and J. Freeman, "The Ecology of Organizational Founding Rates: The Dynamics of Foundings of American Labor Unions, 1836–1975," *American Journal of Sociology* 92 (1987): 910–943.

85. M. T. Hannan and J. Freeman, *Organizational Ecology* (Cambridge, MA: Harvard University Press, 1989).

86. H. E. Aldrich et al., "The Impact of Social Networks on Business Foundings and Profit," in *Frontiers of Entrepreneurship Research*, eds. N. Churchill, J. Hornaday, O. J. Krasner, and K. Vesper (Wellesley, MA: Babson College, 1986): 154–168.

87. Hannan and Carroll, 1992.

88. Amburgey and Rao, 1996, pp. 1272–1273.

89. Katz and Gartner, 1988.

90. G. L. Lippitt and W. H. Schmidt, "Crisis in Developing Organizations," *Harvard Business Review* 45 (1967): 101–122.

91. L. E. Grenier, "Evolution and Revolution as Organizations Grow," *Harvard Business Review* 50 (1972): 37–46.

92. D. Miller and P. Friesen, *Organizations: A Quantum View* (Englewood Cliffs, NJ: Prentice Hall, 1984).

93. Churchill and Lewis, 1983.

94. Scott and Bruce, 1987.

95. Aldrich and Weidenmeyer, 1994.

96. Hanks et al., 1994.

97. Delmar and Shane, 2004.

98. M. J. Dollinger, *Entrepreneurship: Strategies and Resources*, 2nd ed. (Englewood Cliffs, NJ: Prentice Hall, 1999).

99. Becker and Gordon, 1966.

100. W. Boeker, "Organizational Origins: Entrepreneurial and Environmental Imprinting at the Time of Founding," in *Ecological Models of Organizations*, ed. G. R. Carroll (Cambridge, MA: Ballinger, 1988), 33–51.

101. K. G. Shaver and L. R. Scott, "Person, Process, Choice: The Psychology of New Venture Creation," *Entrepreneurship: Theory and Practice* 16 (1991): 23–47.

102. Nonaka, 1994.

103. Shane, 2003.

104. R. Quinn and C. Cameron, "Organizational Life Cycles and Shifting Criteria of Effectiveness: Some Preliminary Evidence," *Management Science* 29 (1983): 33–51.

105. Quinn and Cameron, 1983.

106. D. Ireland et al., "A Model of Strategic Entrepreneurship: The Construct and its Dimensions," *Journal of Management* 29 (2003): 963–989.

107. Aldrich and Weidenmeyer, 1993.

108. A. L. Stinchcombe, "Social Structure and Organizations," in *Handbook of Organizations*, ed. J. G. March (Chicago: Rand McNally, 1965), 142–193.

109. H. E. Aldrich and E. R. Auster, "Even Dwarfs Started Small: Liabilities of Age and Size and Their Strategic Implications," *Research in Organizational Behavior* 8 (1986): 165–198.

110. Arrow, 1982.

111. H. E. Aldrich and C. M. Fiol, "Fools Rush In? The Institutional Context of Industry Creation," *Academy of Management Review* 19 (1994): 645–670.

112. C. G. Brush, P. G. Greene, and M. M. Hart, "From Initial Idea to Unique Advantage: The Entrepreneurial Challenge of Constructing a Resource Base," *Academy of Management Executive* 15, no. 1 (2001): 64–80.

113. Ireland et al., 2003.

114. Aldrich and Auster, 1986.

115. A. L. Stinchcombe, "Social Structure and Organizations," in *Handbook of Organizations*, ed. J. G. March (Chicago: Rand McNally, 1965), 142–193.

116. Aldrich, 1999.

117. A. C. Cooper, "Challenges in Predicting New Firm Performance," *Journal of Business Venturing* 8 (1993): 241–253.

118. Hannan and Carroll, 1992.

119. A. C. Cooper et al., "Entrepreneurs' Perceived Chances for Success," *Journal of Business Venturing* 3 (1988): 97–108.

120. Ireland et al., 2003.

121. S. Venkataraman, "Associate Editor's Note," *Journal of Business Venturing* 9 (1994): 3–6.

122. Nutt and Backoff, 1997.

123. G. E. Ledford et al., "The Phenomenon of Large Scale Organizational Change," in *Large Scale Organizational Change*, eds. A. M. Mohrman et al. (San Francisco: Jossey Bass, 1989), 1–32.

124. R. Kanter, *The Changemasters: Innovation and Productivity in the American Corporation* (New York: Simon and Schuster, 1983).

125. E. Romanelli and M. L. Tushman, "Organizational Transformation as Punctuated Equilibrium: An Empirical Test," *Academy of Management Journal* 37, no. 5 (1994): 1141–1166.

126. C. Gersick, "Time and Transition in Work Teams," Academy *of Management Journal* 29 (1988): 9–41.

127. G. Hamel and C. K. Prahalad, *Competing for the Future* (Boston: Harvard Business School Press, 1994).

128. H. Mintzberg, "Patterns in Strategy Formation," *Management Science* 24, no. 9 (1978): 934–948.

129. H. Tsoukas and R. Chia, "On Organizational Becoming," *Organization Science* 12 (2002): 567–582.

130. Kanter, 1983.

131. Nonaka, 1994.

132. Busenitz et al., 2003.

133. J. E. Pfeffer, "Barriers to the Advance of Organizational Science: Paradigm Development as a Dependent Variable," *Academy of Management Review* 18 (1993): 599–620.

134. C. B. Brush, I. M. Duhaime, W. B. Gartner, A. Stewart, J. Katz, M. A. Hitt, S. Alvarez, G. D. Meyer, and S. Venkataraman, "Doctoral Education in the Field of Entrepreneurship," *Journal of Management* 29, no. 3 (2003): 309–331.

135. Lumpkin and Dess, 1996.

136. Lumpkin and Dess, 1996, p. 136.

137. D. Brinberg and J. McGrath, *Validity and the Research Process* (Newbury Park, CA: Sage, 1985).

138. Brush et al., 2003.

139. D. A. Whetten, "What Constitutes a Theoretical Contribution?" *Academy of Management Review* 14, no. 4 (1989): 490–495.

140. D. Ulrich and J. Barney, "Perspectives in Organizations: Resource Dependence, Efficiency and Population," *Academy of Management Review* 9 (1984): 471–481.

141. R. Dubin, *Theory Building* (New York: Free Press, 1978).

142. Aldrich and Kenworthy, 1999.

143. Busenitz et al., 2003.

144. W. C. Handler, "Succession in Family Business: A Review of the Research," *Family Business Review* 7 (1994): 133–158.

145. R. A. Litz, "The Family Business: Towards Definitional Clarity," *Family Business Review* 8 (1995): 71–82.

146. T. Habbershon et al., "A Unified Systems Perspective of Family Firm Performance," *Journal of Business Venturing* 18, no. 4 (2003): 451–465.

147. Aldrich and Auster, 1986.

148. P. J. Kaufmann, "Franchising and the Choice of Self-Employment," *Journal of Business Venturing* 14 (1999): 345–362.

149. T. Jambulingam and J. R. Nevin, "Influence of Franchisee Selection Criteria on Outcomes Desired by the Franchisor," *Journal of Business Venturing* 14 (1999): 363–396.

150. J. Stanworth and J. Curran, "Colas, Burgers, Shakes, and Shirkers: Towards a Sociological Model of Franchising in the Market Economy," *Journal of Business Venturing* 14 (1999): 323–344.

151. P. Davidsson and J. Wiklund, "Levels of Analysis in Entrepreneurship Research: Current Research Practices and Suggestions for the Future," *Entrepreneurship Theory and Practice* 25 (2001): 81–100.

152. Aldrich and Fiol, 1994.

153. Aldrich, 1999.

154. M. E. Porter, *Competitive Strategy: Techniques for Analyzing Industries and Competitors* (New York: Free Press, 1980).

155. C. B. Schoonhoven and E. Romanelli, *The Entrepreneurship Dynamic: Origins of Entrepreneurship and the Evolution of Industries* (Stanford, CA: Stanford University Press, 2001).

156. Porter, 1980.

157. Shane and Venkataraman, 2000.

158. Venkataraman, 1997.

20

Strategic Entrepreneurship Journal
Strat. Entrepreneurship J., **2**: 301–315 (2008)
Published online in Wiley InterScience (www.interscience.wiley.com). DOI: 10.1002/sej.62

OPPORTUNITIES AS ATTRIBUTIONS: CATEGORIZING STRATEGIC ISSUES FROM AN ATTRIBUTIONAL PERSPECTIVE

WILLIAM B. GARTNER[1]*, KELLY G. SHAVER[2], AND JIANWEN (JON) LIAO[3]
[1]*Spiro Institute for Entrepreneurial Leadership, College of Business and Behavioral Science, Clemson University, Clemson, South Carolina, U.S.A.*
[2]*Department of Management and Entrepreneurship, School of Business and Economics, College of Charleston, Charleston, South Carolina, U.S.A.*
[3]*Stuart School of Business, Illinois Institute of Technology, Chicago, Illinois, U.S.A.*

This study explores the label 'opportunity' in the strategic issue literature as a point of departure for offering an attributional framework for categorizing opportunities entrepreneurs offer as they undertake efforts to start businesses. The strategic issue literature broadly labels opportunities as being positive and controllable and involving potential gain. We demonstrate that this is similar to an attribution theory approach. In preparing this article, the authors analyzed open-ended questions from the Panel Study of Entrepreneurial Dynamics (PSED). Entrepreneurs were more likely to offer attributions about their opportunities that can be categorized as dependent on their abilities (internal and stable attributions) and efforts (internal and variable attributions). Copyright © 2009 Strategic Management Society.

INTRODUCTION

A number of scholars suggest that the idea of *opportunity* is a fundamental and critical aspect of the phenomenon of entrepreneurship (Alvarez and Barney, 2007; Buenstorf, 2007; Casson and Wadeson, 2007; Companys and McMullen, 2007; Gaglio and Katz, 2001; Kirzner, 1997; McMullen, Plummer, and Acs, 2007; Plummer, Hayne and Godesiabois, 2007; Shane, 2000; Shane and Venkataraman, 2000; Shepherd, McMullen, and Jennings, 2007, Stevenson, 1983; Stevenson and Gumpert, 1985; Stevenson and Jarillo, 1990). Indeed, one of the entrepreneurship

Keywords: opportunity; attribution theory; strategic issue; PSED
*Correspondence to: William B. Gartner, Spiro Institute for Entrepreneurial Leadership, College of Business and Behavioral Science, Clemson University, 326 Sirrine Hall, Clemson, S.C. 29634-1305, U.S.A. E-mail: gartner@clemson.edu

field's core definitions focuses on opportunity. As Stevenson (1983: 3) writes 'From our perspective, entrepreneurship is an approach to management that we define as follows: *the pursuit of opportunity without regard to resources currently controlled.*' Yet, recent discussions about characteristics of opportunity, as an aspect of the phenomenon of entrepreneurship (e.g., Alvarez and Barney, 2007; Plummer *et al.*, 2007; McMullen *et al.*, 2007; Shepherd *et al.*, 2007) appears to be somewhat myopic in regards to the relevance of contributions from strategic management research to this discourse.

We will explore strategic management scholarship that focuses on *strategic issue identification* (e.g., Dutton, Stumpf, and Wagner, 1990; Panzano and Billings, 1994; Thomas, Clark and Gioia, 1993; Thomas and McDaniel, 1990), a topic that examines how and why situations are interpreted as opportunities, rather than ignored or interpreted as threats. It is our contention that the strategic issue identification literature provides a strong theoretical and empirical basis for understanding what opportunities are and how opportunities are constructed. In addition, we propose that the strategic issue identification perspective is fundamentally based on a social psychological perspective (Heider, 1958; Kelley, 1973; Rosch, 1978; Rosch *et al.*, 1976). The identification of opportunities stems from the perceptions of decision makers, and these individuals will use cognitively based frameworks for generating explanations for their decisions (Gooding and Kinicki, 1995). Opportunities are, therefore, a consequence of making sense of situations (Daft and Weick, 1984; Dutton and Jackson, 1987; Jackson and Dutton, 1988; Thomas *et al.*, 1993). We suggest that using an attributional approach (Dweck, Chiu, and Hong, 1995; Heider, 1958; Kelley, 1973; Shaver, 1985; Weiner, 1985) to examine the nature of opportunity brings the discourse about the characteristics of opportunity (Alverez and Barney, 2007; McMullen *et al.*, 2007; Plummer *et al.*, 2007) into a larger arena of proven theory and empirical evidence about how individuals make sense of their situations. We posit that the way opportunities are framed in the strategic issue identification literature is very similar to how individuals frame events in attribution theory. Therefore, an attributional perspective and its methods can be applied to categorizing how opportunities are constructed. After making these links between the issue identification theory and evidence with attribution theory, we offer a framework about how individuals will frame their descriptions of opportunities in attributional terms. Using secondary data from the Panel Study of Entrepreneurial Dynamics (Gartner *et al.*, 2004), we explore whether the attributional framework we propose can categorize various opportunity statements offered by individuals in the process of starting new businesses, and we find that these entrepreneurs are more likely to offer certain types of attributions to describe their opportunities. We suggest that this study provides evidence that entrepreneurial action stems from the resources that are within these entrepreneurs' immediate control (Alvarez and Busenitz, 2001; Barney, 1991; Baker and Nelson, 2005; Sarasavathy, 2001, 2008), as well as from their own efforts and activities.

STRATEGIC ISSUE IDENTIFICATION

There is a significant body of theory and empirical evidence from the field of strategic management—

here labeled as the *strategic issue identification* literature—that has explored how managers make sense of their situations and then determine whether these events are opportunities that may be acted on. We suggest that this scholarship has gone unrecognized in current discussions about the nature of opportunity and its impact on entrepreneurial action (c.f. Alvarez and Barney, 2007; McMullen *et al.*, 2007; Plummer *et al.*, 2007), and that a failure to recognize this scholarship leaves a fundamental gap in already established links between strategic management and entrepreneurship scholarship. It is our intention to reintroduce this literature into current discussions regarding entrepreneurship and opportunity identification as a very viable and fruitful way to pursue theory development and empirical research on this topic.

Daft and Weick (1984) suggest that the primary task of managers is to offer interpretations of events and formulate actions based on these interpretations. This interpretive view of managerial decision making has been elaborated on by a number of scholars (e.g., Cowan, 1990; Dutton, Walton, and Abrahamson, 1989; Weick, 1979), and Dutton (1990) has specifically developed it to apply to how and why managers construct opportunities.

Dutton (1990) posits that organizational actions are based on interpretations (Dutton and Duncan, 1987; Ginsberg, 1990; Isabella, 1990, Pondy and Mitroff 1979); that issues are ambiguous and equivocal, so that the labels ascribed through interpretations are powerful devices for generating direction and motivation (Dutton, Fahey, and Narayanan, 1983; Weick, 1979); and that motivations to construct issues are influenced in many different ways (Dutton and Ashford, 1990; Nelson, 1979). Dutton (1990) offers the term *constructing* for describing the activities that individuals undertake to develop meanings and legitimate particular issues. She uses this instead of *sensemaking* or *interpretation* to suggest that individuals actively engage in the process of issue identification rather than passively perceive events and situations.

The labeling of an issue matters. For example, Dutton (1990) explores whether an event, such as finding a parking space or coming up for a tenure review, would be acted upon differently if the event were labeled as a threat or an opportunity. Based on prior research (Dutton and Jackson, 1987), individuals who encounter events labeled as opportunities are more likely to feel they have the personal competence and access to the means to resolve the issue, as well as the autonomy to determine whether to resolve the issue. Threats, on the other hand, tend to invoke feels of depression and anxiousness, the need to act quickly, and a desire to minimize damages. Determining whether circumstances would be labeled as opportunities or threats or are ignored, then, has important implications for how individuals respond to their circumstances. There are similarities in this approach to both prospect theory (Tversky and Kahneman, 1981) and issues about cognition in decisions, overall (Markus and Zajonc, 1985).

Dutton and Jackson (1987) suggest that decision makers generate schemata (Bartlett, 1932; Piaget, 1952) to categorize their perceptions of their situations. Dutton and Jackson (1987: 80) indicate that a *strategic issue* is a type of schema: a 'superordinate-level category that signifies an important environment event, trend, or development for which future resolution will be sought.' They specify that the labels of *threat* and *opportunity* are the primary categories by which managers interpret their situations. Dutton and Jackson conceptualize an opportunity as an event that is perceived as a positive situation where some benefit is likely and the decision maker has some control. A threat is perceived as a negative situation where a loss is likely and the decision maker has little control. In addition, Dutton and Jackson (1987) suggested that responses to perceived threats were likely to be internal, whereas responses to perceived opportunities were likely to be external to the organization.

When Jackson and Dutton (1988) empirically explored these ideas in later research, their results suggested that decision makers were more likely to label ambiguous events as threats. This is 'despite the prominence of folk wisdom that individuals do better if they frame issues as opportunities' (Dutton, 1990: 200). What is relevant about this finding is that perceptions of threat reduce actions involving information search and increase the likelihood of habitual responses (Staw, Sandelands, and Dutton, 1981). Correspondingly, Thomas *et al.* (1993) found that managers who were more likely to engage in environmental scanning were more likely to interpret events as being positive and controllable. Identifying events as opportunities or threats will influence subsequent behavior.

There are some important findings in the Jackson and Dutton (1988) article that have applicability to current discussions about the nature of opportunity. In their study, they provide a map of 56 issue attributes that are either consistent or discrepant with the labels of opportunity and threat. Issue characteristics that are clearly associated with opportunities are 'positive, may gain, won't lose, resolution is likely, have the means to resolve the issue, have autonomy to act, have a choice whether to act, and feeling qualified' (Jackson and Dutton, 1988: 375). Issue characteristics that are clearly associated with threats are: 'may lose and won't gain, personal loss from acting on the issue is likely, others constrain actions, negative, and feeling under qualified' (Jackson and Dutton, 1988: 375). Opportunities, then, from the strategic issue perspective, are

'. . . *positive issues. There is a high potential for gain without loss and successful resolution of such issues is considered likely; feelings of control are likely to be high because resources are available for resolving the issue; in addition, respondents associated opportunities with feelings of being qualified, having autonomy to take action, and having the freedom to decide whether to act'* (Jackson and Dutton, 1988: 375–376).

Subsequent research has explored in more detail the characteristics of opportunities, as well as how certain issues are labeled as *opportunities* (Anderson and Nichols, 2007; Barr, 1998; Barr and Glynn, 2004; Denison *et al.*, 1996; Dutton *et al.*, 1990; Highhouse and Paese, 1996; Highhouse, Mohammed, and Hoffman, 2002; Highhouse, Paese, and Leatherberry, 1996; Highhouse and Yuce, 1996; Kuvas, 2002; Milliken and Lant, 1991; Mohammed and Billings, 2002; Thomas *et al.*, 1993).

What is an opportunity?

Based on the three strategic interpretation dimensions of threat/opportunity (positive-negative, gain-loss, and controllable-uncontrollable) identified in Jackson and Dutton (1988), Thomas and McDaniel (1990) developed a 15-item questionnaire to measure the characteristics of opportunities and threats. Their factor analyses of scores from these items suggested a two-factor solution, where the positive-negative and gain-loss dimensions (which were correlated, $r = 0.90$) were collapsed into a single dimension they labeled as *positive gain*. Opportunities, in this model would be interpreted as situations with a high positive gain and high controllability. Anderson and Nichols (2007)—in a factor analysis of the same 15 items in a longitudinal study of 69 managers facing issues involved with the effects of e-commerce on their businesses and industries—found a three-factor solution of positive gain, controllability, and threat. In this categorization, issues would be opportunities when they are perceived as having high positive gain and high controllability, and are not threats. Opportunities and threats appear to be distinct from gain and loss reference points. Both Highhouse and Paese (1996) and Highhouse and Yuce (1996) found that when decision makers were presented with options that were framed as losses, perceived risk taking was seen as an opportunity, while when options were framed as gains, perceived risk taking was seen as a threat. Highhouse and Yuce (1996) suggest that losses and gains are seen to be status quo reference points for decision makers, while threats and opportunities are truly interpretations of issues. Mohammed and Billings (2002) developed a 30-item scale that took into account issue characteristics such as urgency, duration, visibility, responsibility, feasibility, understanding, capability, and interdependence (Dutton *et al.*, 1990), as well as items measuring loss/gain, uncontrollable/controllable, and negative/positive attributes of threat and opportunity (Dutton and Jackson, 1987; Jackson and Dutton, 1988). Through a factor analysis, Mohammed and Billings (2002) generated a two-factor solution of dimensions of opportunity and threat. The 10 items that loaded on the opportunity dimension described issues where the respondent can take action, has control over resources and the situation, has knowledge and skills to resolve the situation, and the situation is positive. When Mohammed and Billings (2002) tested for whether beliefs about self-efficacy would moderate perceptions of threats and opportunities, they found that individuals with high self-efficacy scores were more likely to categorize issues as opportunities.

Information search

In both Thomas and McDaniel (1990) and Thomas *et al.* (1993), organizations with higher levels of information scanning and use of information were more likely to interpret issues as having potential gains that were controllable. Having more information available was positively related to perceptions of controllability for both opportunity and threat labels (Kuvaas, 2002). Anderson and Nichols (2007) separated information search into two dimensions: time involved in search and the diversity of information sought. They found that managers who spent more time searching for information saw ambiguous

issues as more of a threat, while increasing the diversity of information sought tended to influence managers to see ambiguous issues as less of a threat. Increases in information search and the diversity of information gathered had no influence on whether managers perceived ambiguous issues as opportunities. Anderson and Nichols (2007) suggest that managers who do not seek diverse information sources merely reinforce preexisting views if they spend more time in information search (e.g., the threat rigidity hypothesis, Staw *et al.*, 1981).

Time and action

Highhouse *et al.* (2002) found that the time frame of when a threat or opportunity is presented matters. In the near term, decision makers were more likely to perceive threat and opportunity issues equally, while in the long term, threats were perceived to be less likely to occur. When they explored the interaction of perceptions of control with time, threats were seen to be more controllable the further away in time they were. Thomas *et al.* (1993) found that managers were more likely to take action when issues were perceived as controllable, and that there was no effect on whether issues were perceived as a positive gain.

Strategic issues as opportunities

Our reading of the strategic issue identification literature suggests two key characteristics of opportunity: *Opportunities are perceived as positive situations that are controllable.* Describing opportunities as positive situations that are controllable is similar to Stevenson and Gumpert's (1985: 86) opportunity definition that 'to be an entrepreneurial opportunity, a prospect must meet two tests: it must represent a desirable future state, involving growth or at least change; and the individual must believe it is possible to reach that state' and to Stevenson and Jarillo's (1990: 23) subsequent reinterpretation:

> 'Opportunity is defined here as a future situation which is deemed desirable and feasible. Thus, opportunity is a relativistic concept; opportunities vary among individuals and for individuals over time, because individuals have different desires and they perceive themselves with different capabilities. Desires vary with current position and future expectations. Capabilities vary depending upon innate skills, training and the competitive

environment. Perceptions of both desires and capabilities are only loosely connected to reality.'

Opportunities are viewed, then, as desirable (e.g., the construct of positive/gain) and feasible (e.g., the construct of controllability). While all strategic issue identification studies have emphasized *positive gain* as an important characteristic of opportunity, we see the characteristic of *controllability* as one of the key characteristics that emerges from these studies as well. It is this issue of controllability that we will explore further in the next section of the article.

Finally, we do offer a note of caution in regard to categorizing issues into threats or opportunities. It should be noted that the process of labeling events as opportunities or threats may be driven more by the agenda of academics than by the labels that individuals actually provide (Sudman and Bradburn, 1982). For example, other research has focused on developing empirically based classification schemes of perceptions of problems without the use of an *a priori* theoretical approach (Cowan, 1990; Smith, 1995). In his atheoretical generation of problem categories, Smith noted that the concepts of threat and opportunity were not obvious in language used by managers, and he implied that these two labels might not be the primary constructs by which strategic issues are differentiated.

Yet, the research on strategic issue identification does suggest that managers interpret events by generating various categories as a way to make sense of the myriad of details that constitute their situations. The labels that managers offer for categorizing their perceptions of events may, however, vary depending on how researchers explore this topic. Consequently, there appear to be a variety of ways that researchers may interpret managers' sensemaking (Gergen, 1999; Potter and Wetherell, 1987). We suggest another way in which managers interpret and categorize their situations that uses attributional approaches (Gooding and Kinicki, 1995). After outlining some of the basic tenets of attribution theory, we offer a framework describing the kinds of attributions entrepreneurs might offer about their opportunities.

CATEGORIZING STRATEGIC ISSUES FROM AN ATTRIBUTIONAL PERSPECTIVE

Attribution theory attempts to offer a scientific account of the way people explain their own actions and the actions of others (Heider, 1958; Kelley, 1973; Shaver, 1985, Weiner, 1985). Attribution theory began with the work of Heider (1958), who argued that the production of effects depends on a particular combination of personal force and environmental force. Heider proposed that task success requires: (1) an intention to perform the task; (2) exertion in the direction of the intention; and (3) a condition described as *can*, which represents a personal level of ability that exceeds the difficulty of the task. Intention, exertion, and ability are all internal to the person. Task difficulty and luck are external. These elements were later described by Weiner and his associates (see Weiner, 1985, for a review) as being represented by two dimensions: locus of causality and stability of the cause. Locus of causality describes whether a factor influencing task success is internal or external to the person. It is important to note that in the social psychological literature *locus of causality* is normally distinguished from *locus of control*, a personal disposition originally identified by Rotter (1966). Stability of the cause describes whether a potential cause is capable of immediate change. So, for example, a person's ability is both internal and stable, because ability does not change from moment to moment. By contrast, effort is internal and variable, because the extent to which a person tries can change moment to moment. Among the major external causes, task difficulty is a stable factor. Luck is an external factor that varies.

Several studies have used attributional approaches to explore managerial decision making (e.g., Bettman and Weitz, 1983; Clapham and Schwenk, 1991; Gooding and Kinicki, 1995; Salancik and Meindl, 1984). These studies have tended to portray managers as offering self-serving biases (Weary and Arkin, 1981) when interpreting their situations. That is, managers offer internal attributions for positive events and provide external attributions for negative events. Entrepreneurship scholars have made a similar point (Baron, 1998, 2007).

Because an opportunity is labeled as a positive situation and the decision maker has some control, we expect that entrepreneurs who described opportunities would be more likely to make attributions that were internal, that is, describe opportunities as issues that are within their control. Internal attributions involve either issues describing ability (internal/stable) and/or effort (internal/variable). An entrepreneur can control ability and effort. They cannot control situations outside themselves, such as task difficulty (external/stable) or luck (external/variable).

Strat. Entrepreneurship J., **2**: 301–315 (2008)
DOI: 10.1002/sej

From an attributional perspective, we would suggest that t*he descriptions of opportunities offered by entrepreneurs will be predominantly internal.*

Items that load on the opportunity dimension in Mohammed and Billings (2002: 1262), for example, describe primarily internal attributions:

I can take action on this situation (internal/ variable attribution)

I can now take action to being to resolve this situation (internal/variable attribution)

I have the knowledge necessary to resolve this situation (internal/stable attribution)

I am capable of dealing with this situation (internal/stable attribution)

This situation is positive (external/stable attribution)

Indeed, of the 10 items that loaded on Mohammed and Billings' (2002) opportunity dimension, eight of these items begin with *I* and describe either actions the individuals can take or knowledge and capabilities these individuals have. Correspondingly, the items developed in Thomas *et al.* (1993: 269), while focusing on organizational issues, primarily have an *internal* orientation, as well (i.e., 'To what extent would your hospital feel it has the capability to address the situation?') Opportunities, therefore, are likely to be seen as positive situations where entrepreneurs believe they can do something about them. Opportunities are both desirable and feasible. Entrepreneurs believe they have the ability or can undertake the effort to make a difference in these situations. We suggest that the idea of controllability in the strategic issue literature is, in many respects, similar to the idea of feasibility in entrepreneurship but with this important caveat: the feasibility of an opportunity is an assessment that entrepreneurs make based on internal attributions. Entrepreneurs judge whether they have the ability and can undertake the effort necessary to pursue their desires.

In order to ascertain whether opportunities can be categorized, primarily as internal attributions, we explore statements that entrepreneurs offer about the opportunities that lead to developing their businesses.

METHOD

Sample

We used data from the Panel Study of Entrepreneurial Dynamics (PSED), which is a national longitudinal sample of 64,622 U.S. households that were contacted to find individuals who were actively engaged in starting new businesses (Gartner *et al.*, 2004). Data for the PSED were collected in three stages. The first stage involved a telephone survey of households to create two samples—nascent entrepreneurs and a comparison group—that were representative of the national population of adults 18 years of age and older. In the second stage of the process, individuals in these two samples responded to a detailed phone interview and then completed a mail questionnaire. The third stage involved follow-up interviews (phone and mail questionnaires) with these nascent entrepreneurs. This has been done three times for portions of the sample, at 12, 24, and 36 months after the first interview.

This study analyzes data from the *ERC Mixed-Gender* sample of 438 nascent entrepreneurs (Gartner *et al.*, 2004). A complete description of our sample is shown in Table 1, which identifies the sex of the respondents and shows whether their enterprises are fully or partially autonomous (material participation by another business). As the table shows, we have *complete* information—at least one opportunity and at least one problem—from 242 of the original 438 (55 percent). Current information

Table 1.   ERC mixed-gender respondents (RTYPE 10) at each stage of research

Respondent sex:	Female		Male		Total
Autonomy:	Full	Partial	Full	Partial	
Original interview	144	26	235	33	438
Completed mail	112	20	160	21	313
Follow-up status	119	22	168	26	335
Answered all	89	13	123	17	242

Strat. Entrepreneurship J., **2**: 301–315 (2008)
DOI: 10.1002/sej

about the dataset, code books, and questionnaires is available for public use and can be found at: www.psed.info or http://projects.isr.umich.edu/psed/.

We account for sex as a variable in our analyses because previous research in entrepreneurship has found that men and women offer different reasons for their decisions to start new businesses (Brush, 1992; Buttner and Moore, 1997; Carter, 1997; Fischer, Reuber, and Dyke, 1993). And more specifically to an attributional perspective, Gatewood, Shaver, and Gartner (1995) found that women are more likely to offer internal reasons for starting businesses (e.g., *I always wanted to be my own boss*) while men were likely to offer external reasons (e.g., *I had identified a market need*). We account for problems that nascent entrepreneurs identify and categorize them attributionally as well, primarily as a validation check on whether our coding scheme and analyses would be able to differentiate among opportunities and other types of issues. This will be discussed in more detail later in the article.

Initial attributional coding

This study used open-ended items on opportunities (A1) in the mail questionnaire and problems (Q107) in the phone interview. The opportunity question was a written response to: *Briefly, how did the original idea for starting a business develop?* The problem question was a verbal response to: *What major problems have you had in starting this business?*

All responses to the problem and opportunity questions were coded according to a detailed procedure derived from the attributional model described above. This coding protocol is an extension of attributional coding procedures first described by Harvey, *et al.* (1980) and later elaborated on by others (e.g., Anderson, Krull and Weiner, 1996; Grier and McGill, 2000; Schulman, Castellon, and Seligman, 1989), and specifically applied to the PSED entrepreneurs by Shaver *et al.* (2001).

Acting independently, one of the authors of this study and an undergraduate research assistant parsed every answer into the number of separate explanations it contained. For each separate explanation, the coder first decided whether the explanation identified a factor internal to the person or a factor in the external environment. Once the internal/external decision had been made, the coder then decided whether the explanation identified a stable characteristic (one that would not, or could not, change in the immediate short term) or a variable characteristic (one that would, or could, change in the immediate short term). For example, identifying *superior skills* is an internal-stable attribution for an opportunity, whereas *competition* is an external-variable attribution for a problem. An extensive report of the coding procedures is described by Shaver *et al.* (2001).

As a result of the three-step coding process, each separate explanation was identified and then placed into one of the four coding categories constructed from the combination of external/internal and stable/variable. Reliabilities for coding were computed separately for each step in the process. The Pearson correlation reflecting intercoder reliability for parsing answers into separate explanations was 0.95, reliability for the external/internal step was 0.97, and reliability for the stable/variable step was 0.98. These reliabilities show a high degree of agreement in the content coding. The few disagreements in coding that did arise were resolved by discussions among the two authors and the research assistant. All separately parsed elements were coded into the four attributional categories. Tables 2 and 3 provide examples of the first 10 opportunity and problem responses, respectively, information about how each response was parsed (indicated by a / to denote how we divided a response), and the attributional codes for each statement (E = External, I = Internal, V = Variable, S = Stable). We confined our analyses to the first-mentioned opportunity or problem.

RESULTS

Attributional characteristics of opportunities

The attributional codes for first-mentioned opportunities and problems are presented in Table 4. A chi-square test on the row total for first opportunity was highly significant, χ^2 ($df = 3$) = 39.17, $p < 0.0005$. The internal and stable category was the most frequent, with internal and variable not far behind. Thus, the following statement was supported: *The descriptions of opportunities offered by entrepreneurs will be predominantly internal.* Interestingly, there was also an interaction between attribution category and respondent sex, χ^2 ($df = 3$) = 7.65, $p = 0.054$. Specifically, females were less likely than males to describe internal opportunities as variable.

Table 2.   Ten examples of opportunity responses and their attributional codes

RESPID	RESPONSE to Mail (A1)—Briefly, how did the original idea for starting a business develop?	E/I #1	S/V #1	E/I #2	S/V #2	E/I #3	S/V #3	E/I #4	S/V #4	E/I #5	S/V #5
328100001	Offshoot of my full-time employment.	I									
328100002	I wrote an article for an in service newspaper. / I rewrote it plus expanded it. / I decided to rewrite it again and make it a pamphlet, which I am selling.	I	S	I	S		S				
328100003	Observing firms that could not or would not offer services as a package, / that I could offer.	E	V	I	S						
328100004	From working for a sound equipment shop delivering goods. / I decided to go into the courier business for myself.	I	S	I	S						
328100006	A relative gave me the idea.	E	S								
328100007	I was senior instructor when the government-funded school was closed in a budget reduction. / A friend wanted to let me offer the energy conservation I had taught for the state through his remodeling company. / I wanted to stay involved in a very narrow field, / and thought a market existed.	E	S	E	S	I	V	E	S		
328100008	Wanted a job to supplement retirement.	I	V								
328100010	Because my mother just popped up and said 'We need to make some more money. Real money.'	E	V								
328100012	My husband has always been able to work with wood and, / due to his disability, he can no longer work out. / He wants to develop a business he likes and / is good at so that / he can add additional income to the family.	I	S	I	S	I	S	I	S	E	V
328100013	Desire for family security.	I	V								

Strat. Entrepreneurship J., **2**: 301–315 (2008)
DOI: 10.1002/sej

Table 3.   Ten examples of problem responses and their attributional codes

RESPID	RESPONSE to Phone (Q107)—What major problems have you had in starting this business?	E/I #1	S/V #1	E/I #2	S/V #2	E/I #3	S/V #3	E/I #4	S/V #4	E/I #5	S/V #5
328100001	Money … start-up cash. to buy equipment. Microchips and video cameras.	E	V								
328100002	Getting advertisements in the right media. Writing good advertisements. Copy.	I	V	I	V						
328100003	1. Marketing. / 2. Getting foot in the door. / But I'm striving to develop a strong business plan.	I	V	I	V	I	V				
328100004	The major problem is trying to maintain income to just do this job. / By starting to try to get (word) out (business card, / marketing, etc., and getting enough clientele).	E	V	I	V	E	V				
328100005	Financial: got to have money to make money.	E	V								
328100006	Getting customers.	E	V								
328100007	Getting the word out. / Creating credibility. / Educating. / Finding interested customers.	I	V	I	V	I	V	E	V		
328100009	Finding a place—ae (almost everywhere)? No	I	V								
328100010	Customers (men women). Customers in general. When you start something new, you have to have clientele. / And the clientele is not great (women 'not great') / because there are not as many people as you suspected there would be.	E	V	E	V	E	S				
328100011	Nothing, because information is there. / Brokerage firms always looking for new investments. / You play like Monopoly before you are ready to do it.	E	S	E	S	E	V				

310   *W. B. Gartner, K. G. Shaver, and J. Liao*

Table 4.   Attributions for first-mentioned opportunity and first-mentioned problem, respondents classified by sex

Coding target/sex	Attributional coding				Total
	External		Internal		
	Stable	Variable	Stable	Variable	
First opportunity					
Females	18	30	41	29	118
Males	17	29	60	64	170
Total	35	59	101	93	288
First problem					
Females	9	52	2	44	107
Males	17	79	9	48	153
Total	26	131	11	92	260

Table 5.   Attributions for first-mentioned opportunity compared to attributions for first-mentioned problem

Coding for first opportunity		Coding for first problem			
		External		Internal	
		Stable	Variable	Stable	Variable
External	Stable	3	22	1	6
	Variable	3	32	3	18
Internal	Stable	13	34	3	40
	Variable	7	43	4	28

As for problems (also shown in Table 4), the first accounts given by nascent entrepreneurs were most likely in attributional terms to be variable (external and internal), χ^2 $(df = 3) = 146.49$, $p < 0.0005$. The most frequent attributional category was external and variable, with internal and variable the second-most used category. The attribution category by respondent sex comparison was not significant, χ^2 $(df = 3) = 4.66$, $p < 0.2$.

One of the major objectives of this research was to determine whether respondents' descriptions of opportunities were *data driven* or determined by the cognitive structures of the respondents, regardless of the data. If the latter is true, then people who regard opportunities as constant features of the themselves (attributional coding of *internal/stable or variable*) also ought to regard problems as constant features of themselves (again, *internal/stable or variable*). The same is true for the other three attributional patterns.

There is a substantial amount of research in social psychology—derived from Dweck's distinction between *entity theorists* and *incremental theorists*—to support the argument that people's world views lead them to think that people and events are either as they are or susceptible to alteration (Dweck *et al.*, 1995; Dweck and Leggett, 1988). Taking this position seriously in regard to the present research would lead to the prediction that a person who considered an opportunity to be internal and stable would have essentially the same view of a problem. In more specific terms, an array consisting of attributions for opportunities on one dimension and attributions for problems on the other would be expected to have high scores down the principal diagonal, with the off-diagonal cells being mostly zeroes. Just that sort of array is shown in Table 5, and even though the chi-squared value was not significant, χ^2 $(df = 9) = 14.04$, $p < 0.15$, it is clear from inspection that only 66 of the 260 entries fell on the principal diagonal.

Strat. Entrepreneurship J., **2**: 301–315 (2008)
DOI: 10.1002/sej

Consequently, the data in the present research did not conform to the *two world views* idea. As noted earlier, opportunities were internal (both stable and variable) and problems were variable (both external and internal). In other words, the respondents' views about opportunities and problems were *data driven*, not *cognitive structure driven*. Although this outcome did not conform to the idea that there are two fundamental world views, it *was* consistent with quite a bit of research on what personality and social psychology have for years called the *person x situation interaction* (see Bowers, 1973; Funder and Colvin, 1991; Mischel, 1968; Mischel and Peake, 1982).

DISCUSSION

In this study, entrepreneurs offered different interpretations for opportunities and problems—opportunities were internal (stable and variable) and problems were variable (internal and external). Entrepreneurs saw opportunities as originating from within, either as a product of their abilities (internal/stable attributions) or their effort (internal/variable attributions). Opportunities were, therefore, perceived to be within the control of the individual—*ability* is a characteristic I already have, while *effort* is something that I can do. Opportunities were, therefore, interpretations about how entrepreneurs perceive themselves—the value of their abilities and effort—rather than interpretations about the importance of their external circumstances. In contrast, entrepreneurs perceived problems as variable (internal or external). In the attributional framework, problems involve either lack of *effort* (internal/variable attributions) or bad *luck* (external/variable attributions). Much like the perception of some opportunities, some problems require exertion to overcome (internal/variable attributions). Problems that involve luck (external/variable) imply that nascent entrepreneurs saw some problems as beyond their control, which is probably an accurate depiction of many circumstances in the development of a new venture.

As we noted earlier, our research findings support the general thrust of research in the strategic identity literature says individuals label opportunities in different ways than they label threats (Anderson and Nichols, 2007; Barr, 1998; Barr and Glynn, 2004; Denison *et al.*, 1996; Dutton and Jackson, 1987; Dutton *et al.*, 1990; Highhouse and Paese, 1996; Highhouse *et al.*, 1996; Highhouse *et al.*, 2002;

Highhouse and Yuce, 1996; Jackson and Dutton, 1988; Kuvas, 2002; Milliken and Lant, 1991; Mohammed and Billings, 2002; Thomas *et al.*, 1993). This study also appears to confirm Howard Stevenson's thoughts on the nature of opportunity as perceptions of situations that are both desirable and feasible (Stevenson and Gumpert, 1985; Stevenson and Jarillo, 1990). Perceptions of feasibility hinge on an individual's beliefs about his/her capabilities and efforts to pursue situations that are desirable. Projects are thought to be unfeasible when individuals believe they do not have the capabilities or cannot provide the necessary effort. Mohammed and Billings (2002) demonstrate that increasing beliefs about one's own self-efficacy significantly increases one's ability to frame situations as opportunities. This insight implies that entrepreneurship training that increases the entrepreneurial capabilities of individuals as well as encourages them to engage in more effort also increases their perceptions of labeling their situations as opportunities.

We should note that an important aspect of exploring how individuals think about opportunity involves an appreciation of how questions about opportunity are asked. In this research project, individuals were asked, *Briefly, how did the original idea for starting a business develop?* By asking how—that is, by asking about a *past* process of opportunity development—individuals were significantly more likely to point to their own abilities and efforts. Yet, in a related research project (Gartner and Shaver, 2004), 1,686 owner/managers of firms were asked to provide written responses to the question, *What is the biggest opportunity facing your business?* Their responses were predominantly attributions that were external and stable, that is, opportunities were seen as long-term and unchangeable situations they could exploit. We bring this up to suggest that the nature of opportunity, as perceived by those individuals pursuing opportunities, is viewed as a fairly complex phenomenon. If we attach the *what* and *how* together, we see that the nature of opportunity involves individuals who, through their abilities and efforts, pursue perceived favorable circumstances. So, in Gartner and Shaver (2004) opportunities are *out there*, but based on this current research, opportunities appear to be recognized and actualized because of an individual's capabilities and effort.

We make this point about the internal and external tensions in the perceptions of opportunities because of discussions in the entrepreneurship field as to whether opportunities are created or discovered (Acs and Audretsch, 2003; Alvarez and Barney, 2007; Gartner, Carter, and Hills, 2003). As Dutton (1990) suggests, there is a reciprocal influence between individuals and objects (events, developments, and trends). Objective realities external to individuals do affect whether these individuals notice, perceive, and act on them. Individuals do choose (or not) to interact with objects, which implies that they can create and develop them in particular ways. Opportunities, then, are both created and discovered: dependent on individual capabilities and efforts melded to perceptions of changing events and circumstances.

FUTURE RESEARCH

This study demonstrated that an attributional categorization scheme could classify entrepreneurs' statements about the development of ideas that lead to business creation efforts as opportunities that were primarily internal attributions. Further research could be conducted to explore various moderators that may affect differences in these attributions. As internal attributions are construed to be issues involving capabilities and effort, individual characteristics (such as education, experience, amount of time devoted to the start-up effort, and measures of specific activities over time) could be explored as factors influencing perceptions of opportunities. If opportunities have components of both desirability and feasibility, it might be possible, given the variety of items offered in the PSED, to ascertain what entrepreneurs perceive as desirable about the opportunities they seek, and to then, explore whether there may be significant interactions between these two constructs as entrepreneurs decide to move forward. As the PSED is a longitudinal dataset that tracks individuals during the process of venture creation to outcomes (e.g., quit the process, continue to work at starting a business, establish a business, etc.), there would be much value in exploring whether the kinds of opportunities described by these entrepreneurs impacted the likelihood of venture creation efforts leading to established ventures.

CONCLUSIONS

We believe this study makes a number of contributions to the current discourse on the nature of opportunity. First, we reintroduce an ongoing stream of

strategic management scholarship—the strategic issue literature—to suggest that the strategic management field already has a significant body of theory and evidence about what opportunities are and how they are recognized. Second, we suggest that a major stream of research in social psychology (attribution theory) can be used to understand and explore the nature of opportunity, as well. Third, we make links between the strategic issue literature and attribution theory to demonstrate some underlying constructs in regard to the nature of opportunity. Finally, we posit that the two primary characteristics of opportunities identified in the strategic issue literature (positive/gain and controllability) are similar to the two original core issues used for describing opportunity in the entrepreneurship literature (desirability and feasibility).

The idea of opportunity, as a construct that has meaning both in strategic and entrepreneurial terms, needs further development and definition, both empirically and theoretically. This study suggests that there are other disciplinary traditions (attribution theory), and strategic management perspectives (the strategic issue literature) that can offer insights into the discourse on opportunity that have not yet been a part of the dominant discussion. We also believe in the value of offering empirical evidence that explores opportunity as a way to ascertain whether our scholarly ideas *fit* with the experiences of individuals in the world. We want to reemphasize a point made earlier—that when Smith (1995) undertook an empirical exploration of 1,376 problem definitions, his evidence found little to suggest that individuals thought in such concepts as *threat* and *opportunity*. While we, as scholars, may offer the label of *opportunity* for the experience that entrepreneurs encounter, they rarely use words such as *discover* or *create* to describe situations academics might construe as entrepreneurial opportunities (Gartner *et al.*, 2003). Opportunity, as a label for an objective phenomenon, may be an artifact of previous academic beliefs and theories that have little relationship to the actual events and experiences of entrepreneurial individuals. The kinds of questions that scholars ask themselves (and entrepreneurs) will significantly affect the kinds of answers obtained (Sudman and Bradburn, 1982). We wonder whether asking entrepreneurs if they *discovered* or *created* their opportunities forces them to conceptualize their past experiences to account for *discovery* or *creation* having occurred, even if they did not. If some other process has taken place, a question about discovery

Strat. Entrepreneurship J., **2**: 301–315 (2008)
DOI: 10.1002/sej

or creation is unlikely to uncover it. There is an opportunity, then, to devote more attention to the language used to talk about the nature of opportunity (Bruner, 1986). If we seek a science of the imagination (Gartner, 2007; Schendel and Hitt, 2007), approaches to understanding the phenomenon of opportunity may depend on ideas, methods, and observations that are not within the repertory of our current scholarly norms.

REFERENCES

Acs ZJ, Audretsch DB. 2003. Editor's introduction. *Handbook of Entrepreneurship Research*. Kluwer Academic Publishers: Boston, MA; 3–20.

Alvarez SA, Barney J. 2007. Discovery and creation: alternative theories of entrepreneurial action. *Strategic Entrepreneurship Journal* **1**(1–2): 11–26.

Alvarez SA, Busenitz LW. 2001. The entrepreneurship of resource-based theory. *Journal of Management* **27**(6): 755–775.

Anderson CA, Krull DS, Weiner B. 1996. Explanations: processes and consequences. In *Social Psychology: Handbook of Basic Principles*, Higgins ET, Kruglanski AW (eds). Guilford: New York; 271–296.

Anderson MH, Nichols ML. 2007. Information gathering and changes in threat and opportunity perceptions. *Journal of Management Studies* **44**(3): 367–387.

Baker T, Nelson R. 2005. Creating something from nothing: resource construction through entrepreneurial bricolage. *Administrative Science Quarterly* **50**: 329–366.

Barney J. 1991. Firm resources and sustained competitive advantage. *Journal of Management* **17**(1): 99–120.

Baron RA. 1998. Cognitive mechanisms in entrepreneurship: why and when entrepreneurs think differently than other people. *Journal of Business Venturing* **13**: 275–294.

Baron RA. 2007. Behavioral and cognitive factors in entrepreneurship: entrepreneurs as the active element in new venture creation. *Strategic Entrepreneurship Journal* **1**(1–2): 167–182.

Barr PS. 1998. Adapting to unfamiliar environmental events: a look at the evolution of interpretation and its role in strategic change. *Organization Science* **9**: 644–699.

Barr PS, Glynn MA. 2004. Cultural variations in strategic issue interpretation: relating cultural uncertainty avoidance to controllability in discriminating threat and opportunity. *Strategic Management Journal* **25**(1): 59–67.

Bartlett FE. 1932. *Remembering*. Cambridge University Press: Cambridge, U.K.

Bettman JR, Weitz BA. 1983. Attributions in the board room: causal reasoning in corporate annual reports. *Administrative Science Quarterly* **28**: 165–183.

Bowers KS. 1973. Situationism in psychology: an analysis and a critique. *Psychological Review* **80**: 307–336.

Bruner J. 1986. *Actual Minds, Possible Worlds*. Harvard University Press: Cambridge, MA.

Brush CG. 1992. Research on women business owners: past trends, a new perspective and future directions. *Entrepreneurship Theory and Practice* **2**(1): 1–24.

Buenstorf G. 2007. Creation and pursuit of entrepreneurial opportunities: an evolutionary perspective. *Small Business Economics* **28**: 323–337.

Buttner EH, Moore DP. 1997. Women's organizational exodus to entrepreneurship: self-reported motivations and correlates with success. *Journal of Small Business Management* **35**(1): 34–46.

Carter NM. 1997. Entrepreneurial processes and outcomes: the influence of gender. In *The Entrepreneurial Process*, Reynolds PD, White SB (eds). Quorum Books: Westport CT; 163–178.

Casson M, Wadeson N. 2007. The discovery of opportunities: extending the economic theory of the entrepreneur. *Small Business Economics* **28**: 285–300.

Clapham SE, Schwenk CR. 1991. Self-serving attributions, managerial cognition and company performance. *Strategic Management Journal* **12**(3): 219–229.

Companys YE, McMullen JS. 2007. Strategic entrepreneurs at work: the nature, discovery, and exploitation of entrepreneurial opportunities. *Small Business Economics* **28**: 301–322.

Cowan DA. 1990. Developing a classification structure of organizational problems: an empirical investigation. *Academy of Management Journal* **33**(2): 366–390.

Daft RL, Weick KE. 1984. Toward a model of organizations as interpretation systems. *Academy of Management Review* **9**(2): 284–295.

Denison DR, Dutton JE, Kahn JA, Hart SL. 1996. Organizational context and the interpretation of strategic issues: a note on CEOs' interpretations of foreign investment. *Journal of Management Studies* **33**: 453–474.

Dutton JE. 1990. The making of organizational opportunities: an interpretive pathway to organizational change. *Research in Organizational Behavior* **15**: 195–226.

Dutton JE, Ashford S. 1990. Selling issues to the top management team. Paper presented at the meeting of the National Academy of Management, San Francisco, CA.

Dutton JE, Duncan RB. 1987. The creation of momentum for change through the process of strategic issue diagnosis. *Strategic Management Journal* **8**(3): 279–295.

Dutton JE, Fahey L, Narayanan VK. 1983. Toward understanding strategic issue diagnosis. *Strategic Management Journal* **4**(4): 307–323.

Dutton JE, Jackson SE. 1987. Categorizing strategic issues: links to organizational action. *Academy of Management Review* **12**(1): 76–90.

Dutton JE, Stumpf S, Wagner D. 1990. Diagnosing strategic issues and investment of resources. In *Advances in*

Strategic Management, Lamb R, Shrivastava P (eds). JAI Press: Greenwich, CT; 143–167.

Dutton JE, Walton E, Abrahamson E. 1989. Important dimensions of strategic issues: separating the wheat from the chaff. *Journal of Management Studies* **14**: 79–396.

Dweck CS, Chiu C, Hong Y. 1995. Implicit theories and their role in judgments and reactions: a world from two perspectives. *Psychological Inquiry* **6**: 267–285.

Dweck CS, Leggett EL. 1988. A social-cognitive approach to motivation and personality. *Psychological Review* **95**: 256–273.

Fischer EM, Reuber AR, Dyke LS. 1993. A theoretical overview and extension of research on sex, gender, and entrepreneurship. *Journal of Business Venturing* **8**: 151–168.

Funder DC, Colvin CR. 1991. Explorations in behavioral consistency: properties of persons, situations, and behaviors. *Journal of Personality and Social Psychology* **60**: 773–794.

Gaglio CM, Katz JA. 2001. The psychological basis of opportunity identification: entrepreneurial alertness. *Journal of Small Business Economics* **16**(2): 95–111.

Gartner WB. 2007. Entrepreneurial narrative and a science of the imagination. *Journal of Business Venturing* **22**(5): 613–627.

Gartner WB, Carter NM, Hills GE. 2003. The language of opportunity. In *New Movements in Entrepreneurship*, Steyaert C, Hjorth D (eds). Edward Elgar: London, U.K.; 103–124.

Gartner WB, Shaver KG. 2004. Opportunities as attributions: the enterprise-serving bias. In *Research in Entrepreneurship and Management: Opportunity Identification and Entrepreneurial Behavior*, Vol. 4, Butler JE (ed). IAP: Greenwich, CT; 29–46.

Gartner WB, Shaver KG, Carter NM, Reynolds PD. 2004. *Handbook of Entrepreneurial Dynamics: The Process of Business Creation.* SAGE Publications: Thousand Oaks, CA.

Gatewood EJ, Shaver KG, Gartner WB. 1995. A longitudinal study of cognitive factors influencing start-up behaviors and success at venture creation. *Journal of Business Venturing* **10**: 371–391.

Gergen KJ. 1999. *An Invitation to Social Construction.* SAGE Publications: London, U.K.

Ginsberg A. 1990. Connecting diversification to performance: a sociocognitive approach. *Academy of Management Review* **15**(3): 514–535.

Gooding RZ, Kinicki AJ. 1995. Interpreting event causes: the complementary role of categorization and attribution processes. *Journal of Management Studies* **32**: 1–22.

Grier SA, McGill AL. 2000. How we explain depends on whom we explain: the impact of social category on the selection of causal comparisons and causal explanations. *Journal of Experimental Social Psychology* **36**: 545–566.

Harvey JH, Yarkin KL, Lightner JM, Town JP. 1980. Unsolicited interpretation and recall of interpersonal events. *Journal of Personality and Social Psychology* **38**: 551–568.

Heider F. 1958. *The Psychology of Interpersonal Relations.* Wiley: New York.

Highhouse S, Mohammed S, Hoffman JR. 2002. Temporal discounting of strategic issues: bold forecasts for opportunities and threats. *Basic and Applied Social Psychology* **24**(1): 43–56.

Highhouse S, Paese PW. 1996. Problem domain and prospect frame: choice under opportunity versus threat. *Personality and Social Psychology Bulletin* **22**: 124–132.

Highhouse S, Paese PW, Leatherberry T. 1996. Contrast effects on strategic-issue framing. *Organizational Behavior and Human Decision Processes* **65**: 95–105.

Highhouse S, Yuce P. 1996. Perspectives, perceptions and risk-taking behavior. *Organizational Behavior and Human Decision Processes* **65**: 159–167.

Isabella L. 1990. Evolving interpretations as change unfolds: how managers construct key organizational events. *Academy of Management Journal* **33**(1): 7–41.

Jackson SE, Dutton JE. 1988. Discerning threats and opportunities. *Administrative Science Quarterly* **33**: 370–387.

Kelley HH. 1973. The processes of causal attribution. *American Psychologist* **28**: 107–128.

Kirzner I. 1997. Entrepreneurial discovery and the competitive market process: an Austrian approach. *Journal of Economic Literature* **35**: 60–85.

Kuvaas B. 2002. An exploration of two competing perspectives on informational contexts in top management strategic issue interpretation. *Journal of Management Studies* **39**(7): 977–1001.

Markus H, Zajonc RB. 1985. The cognitive perspective in social psychology. In *Handbook of Social Psychology* (3rd edn), Lindzey G, Aronson E (eds). Random House: New York; 137–230.

McMullen JS, Plummer LA, Acs ZJ. 2007. What is an entrepreneurial opportunity? *Small Business Economics* **28**: 273–283.

Milliken F, Lant T. 1991. The impact of an organization's recent performance history on strategic persistence and change: the role of managerial interpretations. In *Advances in Strategic Management,* Vol. 7, Shrivastava P, Huff A, Dutton J (eds). JAI Press: Greenwich, CT; 129–156.

Mischel W. 1968. *Personality and Assessment.* Wiley: New York.

Mischel W, Peake PK. 1982. Beyond déjà vu in the search for cross-situational consistency. *Psychological Review* **89**: 730–755.

Mohammed S, Billings RS. 2002. The effect of self-efficacy and issue characteristics on threat and opportunity categorization. *Journal of Applied Social Psychology* **32**(6): 1253–1275.

Nelson B. 1979. Setting the public agenda: the case of child abuse. In *The Policy Cycle*, Wildavsky A (ed). SAGE Publications: Thousand Oaks, CA.

Panzano PC, Billings RS. 1994. The influence of issue frame and organizational slack on risk decision making: a field study. *Academy of Management Best Paper Proceedings*: 377–381.

Piaget J. 1952. *The Origins of Intelligence in Children*. International Universities Press: New York.

Plummer LA, Hayne JM, Godesiabois J. 2007. An essay on the origins of entrepreneurial opportunity. *Small Business Economics* **28**: 363–379.

Pondy L, Mitroff I. 1979. Beyond open systems models of organizations. In *Research in Organizational Behavior*, Staw BM (ed). JAI Press: Greenwich, CT; 3–39.

Potter J, Wetherell M. 1987. *Discourse and Social Psychology: Beyond Attitudes and Behavior*. SAGE Publications: London, U.K.

Rosch E. 1978. Principles of categorization. In *Cognition and Categorization*, Rosch E, Lloyd B (eds). Lawrence Erlbaum: Hillsdale, NJ; 27–48.

Rosch E, Mervis C, Gray W, Johnson D, Boyes-Braem P. 1976. Basic objects in natural categories. *Cognitive Psychology* **8**: 382–439.

Rotter JB. 1966. Generalized expectancies for internal versus external control of reinforcement. *Psychological Monographs* **80**: 1–28.

Salancik GR, Meindl JR. 1984. Corporate attributions as strategic illusions of management control. *Administrative Science Quarterly* **29**: 238–254.

Sarasavathy S. 2001. Causation and effectuation: toward a theoretical shift from economic inevitability to entrepreneurial contingency. *Academy of Management Review* **26**(2): 243–263.

Sarasavathy S. 2008. *Effectuation: Elements of Entrepreneurial Expertise*. Edward Elgar: Cheltenham, U.K.

Schendel D, Hitt MA. 2007. Comments from the editors: introduction to volume 1. *Strategic Entrepreneurship Journal* **1**(1–2): 1–6.

Schulman P, Castellon C, Seligman ME. 1989. Assessing explanatory style: the content analysis of verbatim explanations and the attributional style questionnaire. *Behavioral Research Therapy* **27**(5): 505–512.

Shane S. 2000. Prior knowledge and the discovery of entrepreneurial opportunities. *Organization Science* **11**(4): 448–469.

Shane S, Venkataraman S. 2000. The promise of entrepreneurship as a field of research. *Academy of Management Review* **25**(1): 217–226.

Shaver KG. 1985. *Attribution of Blame: Causality, Responsibility, and Blameworthiness*. Springer-Verlag: New York.

Shaver KG, Gartner WB, Crosby E, Bakalarova K, Gatewood EJ. 2001. Attributions about entrepreneurship: a framework and process for analyzing reasons for starting a business. *Entrepreneurship Theory and Practice* **26**(2): 5–32.

Shepherd DA, McMullen JS, Jennings PD. 2007. The formation of opportunity beliefs: overcoming ignorance and reducing doubt. *Strategic Entrepreneurship Journal* **1**(1–2): 75–95.

Smith GF. 1995. Classifying managerial problems: an empirical study of definitional content. *Journal of Management Studies* **32**(5): 679–706.

Staw BM, Sandelands L, Dutton JE. 1981. Threat-rigidity effects in organizations: a multi-level analysis. *Administrative Science Quarterly* **26**: 501–524.

Stevenson HH. 1983. A perspective on entrepreneurship. Working paper, Harvard Business School, Boston, MA.

Stevenson HH, Gumpert DE. 1985. The heart of entrepreneurship. *Harvard Business Review* **85**(2): 85–94.

Stevenson HH, Jarillo JC. 1990. A paradigm of entrepreneurship: entrepreneurial management. *Strategic Management Journal* **11**(Summer): 17–27.

Sudman S, Bradburn NM. 1982. *Asking Questions: A Practical Guide to Questionnaire Design*. Jossey-Bass: San Francisco, CA.

Thomas JB, Clark SM, Gioia DA. 1993. Strategic sense-making and organizational performance: linkages among scanning, interpretation, action, and outcomes. *Academy of Management Journal* **36**(2): 239–270.

Thomas JB, McDaniel RR. 1990. Interpreting strategic issues: effects of strategy and the information-processing structure of top management teams. *Academy of Management Journal* **33**: 286–306.

Tversky A, Kahneman D. 1981. The framing of decisions and the psychology of choice. *Science* **211**(30): 453–458.

Weary G, Arkin RM. 1981. Attributional self-presentation. In *New Directions in Attribution Research*, Harvet JH, Ickes W, Kidd RF (eds). Lawrence Erlbaum: Hillsdale, NJ; 223–246.

Weick K. 1979. *The Social Psychology of Organizing*. Addison-Wesley: Reading, MA.

Weiner B. 1985. An attributional theory of achievement motivation and emotion. *Psychological Review* **92**: 548–573.

Article

International Small Business Journal
28(1) 6–19
© The Author(s) 2010
Reprints and permission: http://www.
sagepub.co.uk/journalsPermission.nav
DOI: 10.1177/0266242609351448
http://isb.sagepub.com

A new path to the waterfall: A narrative on a use of entrepreneurial narrative

⑤SAGE

William B. Gartner
Clemson University, USA

Abstract
The limitations of the paradigmatic mode of thought as an approach for describing and understanding the nature of entrepreneurial intentions and actions and their interrelationships with circumstance is explored by showing how the author's previous empirical scholarship often fails to offer insights into the intention/action/circumstance condition (IACC) in entrepreneurship. As a way to understand and describe the IACC in entrepreneurship, the rubric 'narrative' is offered as a 'solution.' The author suggests a particular narrative gambit (the 'new path') for studying entrepreneurship.

Keywords
critical mess theory, entrepreneurial narrative, methodological critique, new paths

Introduction

When the Editors of the *International Small Business Journal* (*ISBJ*) offered me an opportunity to write an annual review article – 'It is envisaged that this paper would broadly constitute a considered overview of the development of the "field" of entrepreneurship, the current state of affairs and some considerations regarding the potential for future research areas/issues/challenges/ opportunities etc.' – my initial reaction was that I am not above the entrepreneurship field in such a way as to have an overview. I am, as Eliot (1934: 26) would suggest, in between lost and found: "in the middle," "in a dark wood," "risking enchantment." My current scholarship is unfamiliar to me; it is reflected in other lines in Eliot's poem (1934: 30) in which he recognizes the failure of one's past words to talk about where one is now or will be.

So, my willingness to write an article for *ISBJ* in response to the Editors' query is therefore, an idiosyncratic description of how I find myself in this middle of the way in the entrepreneurship field, a speculation as to why I have arrived in the middle, and some thoughts as to why my efforts to find a way out of this bramble by forging a 'new path' for myself may be perceived as 'risking enchantment'.

Corresponding author:
William B. Gartner, Spiro Professor of Entrepreneurial Leadership, Spiro Institute for Entrepreneurial Leadership,
345 Sirrine Hall, Clemson University, Clemson, SC 29634-1345, USA.
Email: gartner@clemson.edu

In the middle

Somewhat concurrent to winning the FSF/Nutek Award in 2005 for intellectual contributions to research in entrepreneurship and small business, I was engaged in some self-reflection about my research efforts in the entrepreneurship field (Gartner, 2004a, 2006a,b). My approach to understanding entrepreneurship begins with the phenomenon of entrepreneurship itself (Gartner, 1985a). I believe the way to grasp the phenomenon of entrepreneurship is by omnivorously confronting the 'critical mess' of it ('it' being 'entrepreneurship'). The idea of the 'critical mess' first showed up in Gartner and Birley (2002: 393):

> 'finally, we offer an insight about the nature of qualitative research which might be considered as a parting trifle, but we believe contains some truth which bears consideration – the 'critical mess theory.' In qualitative research there is typically an immersion into the muddled circumstances of an entrepreneurial phenomenon that is cluttered and confusing. Part of the difficulty of generating and reporting the findings of a qualitative research effort seems to stem from the experience of being in such an untidy reality. Qualitative researchers seem to get overwhelmed with too much information, rather than too little (Yin, 2008). Yet, it is in this experience of information overload that a certain knowledge and wisdom often occurs. One can often tell which researchers in our field have spent considerable time intensively involved with entrepreneurs. The knowledge and insights that stem from all of their research just seem to ring a bit truer and clearer. We borrow a label for this sensibility of immersion from a profile of Michael Zinman, a bibliophile, and Michael Reese's insights into Zinman's strategy for collecting books: You don't start off with a theory about what you're trying to do. You don't begin by saying, 'I'm trying to prove x', you build a big pile. Once you get a big enough pile together – the critical mess – you're able to draw conclusions about it. You see patterns ... People who have the greatest intuitive feel for physical objects start from a relationship with the objects and then acquire the scholarship, instead of the other way around. The way to become a connoisseur is to work in the entire spectrum of what's available – from utter crap to fabulous stuff. If you're going to spend your time looking only at the best, you're not going to have a critical eye. (Singer, 2001: 66)

> Qualitative researchers are likely to be the connoisseurs of entrepreneurship scholarship only in that they are more likely to immerse themselves to a greater depth and in a wider variety of situations where entrepreneurship occurs. 'We encourage all entrepreneurship scholars to develop a critical eye in their efforts to explore entrepreneurship, and hope that more work will be undertaken to utilize qualitative methods for seeking such an understanding' (Gartner and Birley, 2002: 394).

This critical mess approach is both theoretically and empirically agnostic (Miller, 2007) in regards to paths to understanding the phenomenon. The critical mess reflects both a sense of a method for understanding and describing entrepreneurship, as well as a sensibility for what the phenomenon of entrepreneurship. The method in the critical mess is that there is no one particular method. The sensibility of the critical mess is that there is no one particular entrepreneurial characteristic (Gartner, 1985a) that can capture the nature of entrepreneurship; the phenomenon of entrepreneurship is often more complicated and complex than we tend to espouse. And, I believe that critical insights into entrepreneurship tend to get lost when one depends on certain methods. The irony is that the method that I primarily depended on (labeled here as the 'paradigmatic' mode [Bruner, 1986]) has typified much of my research and therefore limited my ability to see entrepreneurship as the comprehensive and complex phenomenon that it is:

the paradigmatic or logico-scientific (mode) attempts to fulfill the ideal of a formal, mathematical system of description and explanation. It employs categorization or conceptualization and the operations by which categories are established, instantiated, idealized, and related one to the other to form a system … Its domain is defined not only by observables to which its basic statements relate, but also by the set of possible worlds that can be logically generated and tested against observables – that is, it is driven by principled hypotheses … The imaginative application of the paradigmatic mode leads to good theory, tight analyses, logical proof, sound argument, and empirical discovery guided by reasoned hypothesis. (Bruner, 1986: 12–13)

My story as a scholar suggests that my research using the paradigmatic mode did not bring me closer towards describing and understanding the entrepreneurial phenomenon. My experience of entrepreneurial phenomena did not fit general principles; that is, there is not, inherently for any particular entrepreneurial situation, a way to understand it through an idealized solution. I am not suggesting that the paradigmatic model is a 'dead end' for studying entrepreneurship. There is still a great need for good theory, tight analyses, logical proof, sound argument and empirical discovery guided by reasoned hypothesis for many aspects of the phenomenon of entrepreneurship. I am suggesting that the paradigmatic mode, for me, has serious limitations for helping me understand what entrepreneurship is. For the most part, I have reached the end of where this research approach can take me. I am in the middle.

Getting to the middle

While it might appear that I am tied to a belief that entrepreneurship is about 'business creation' (Gartner, 1985a, 1988), a careful reading of these articles, and others (i.e. Gartner, 1990b; Gartner et al., 2006), would suggest that I believe entrepreneurship is a very broad topic area. Entrepreneurship scholars have a wide range of views and beliefs about what the phenomena of entrepreneurship are which all have some value. For my own purposes, I have attempted to explore a small aspect of the entrepreneurship field: business creation. I hope readers can see the difference between suggesting that entrepreneurship is business creation and suggesting that business creation is a part of the field of entrepreneurship (to clarify, then, I believe that business creation is a part of the field of entrepreneurship).

My original research effort involved collecting stories that entrepreneurs told about their experiences starting new businesses, as well as developing a quantitative scoring system to categorize questionnaire responses from these individuals into similar types of startup 'gestalts' (Gartner, 1982). This effort was a 'critical mess' of qualitative and quantitative muddling among 106 interviews and questionnaire responses. As described in Gartner (2008), my initial training with Karl Vesper (for a sense of this perspective, see Vesper [1980]), and my initial research efforts undertaken in my dissertation (Gartner, 1982), led me to this insight about the nature of entrepreneurship:

The process also left me believing that the phenomenon of entrepreneurship was, then, a struggle with seeing how many different ways that different kinds of individuals, in different settings, could start different kinds of businesses. There wasn't one, or 'an' entrepreneurial type. Indeed, I could see that each entrepreneur was inherently unique, and that only through efforts to create groupings of these unique entrepreneurs could one suggest that there were types and kinds of entrepreneurs. But, these groupings were intellectual and statistical artifacts of my research to make sense of the diversity that I saw. Variation is, inherently, a fundamental characteristic of entrepreneurship. (Gartner, 2008: 359)

Another way to say this is the aphorism: 'there is no average in entrepreneurship.' Now, this is not to say that one cannot create 'averages' among various measures that might characterize aspects of entrepreneurship; rather, I suggest that the creation of averages tends to mask the wide range of differences that exist in entrepreneurial phenomena (Gartner, 1985a, 1988). This perspective (that variation is inherent in entrepreneurial phenomena) tends to be missed in reading my work.

The article, 'Who is an Entrepreneur? Is the Wrong Question' (Gartner, 1988), for example, should be read as a plea for entrepreneurship scholars to recognize the great diversity of individuals involved in entrepreneurial activities, and by implication, the insight that it is unlikely that scholars will be able identify a particular entrepreneurial 'type' (Gartner, 2004b). There are too many different kinds of entrepreneurs engaging in many different ways to act entrepreneurially in a wide variety of different circumstances. So, to compare 'the entrepreneur', to 'the manager', or 'the average person', does not for me, make much sense. The stories that I had collected in Gartner (1982) spoke to me of an interplay between an entrepreneur's thoughts, actions, and the circumstances encountered. These stories had unique perspectives about how individuals lived out a complex interplay of their intentions, coupled with actions and the interactions with their specific circumstances. Gartner (1988) is recognition that observations of entrepreneurs, when studied in an in-depth comprehensive way (that also recognizes the researcher in the research), were more likely to generate insights suggesting the inherent uniqueness and variation among these individuals, rather than surface significant differences between entrepreneurs and other 'types' of individuals.

It has always surprised me that I am identified as someone who dismisses the trait approach for studying entrepreneurship. I do not dismiss using 'traits' or other characteristics of individuals as a way to describe entrepreneurs. I am concerned when specific 'traits' or other characteristics are used to differentiate between some group of individuals called 'entrepreneurs' in a study, and another group of entrepreneurs called 'managers' or 'others,' etc. I see that there are too many different kinds of entrepreneurs to reasonably talk about an 'entrepreneurial type' versus another 'type.' I sense that the use of 'traits' merely provides an easy label for broadly identifying one kind of entrepreneur rather than engaging in more reflective and in-depth assessments of the phenomenon of a particular entrepreneurial situation and a description of kinds of entrepreneurs. In reading Gartner (1988) I would always pair it with Gartner (1985a). There are many different kinds of entrepreneurs (Gartner, 1988) and these many different kinds of entrepreneurs undertake many different ways to develop a variety of firms in a variety of environments (Gartner, 1985a).

I think one loses this sense of the breadth and depth of the variety of entrepreneurial phenomena as soon as there is a focus on a particular variable. Yet, the focus on a particular variable or on a few variables was a major thrust of much of my empirical efforts in the entrepreneurship field. Reconciling my need for theories that celebrate uniqueness and variation with empirical explorations that, by their methods, inherently sought out commonalities, proved to be very, very difficult to navigate. For example, the framework for accounting for differences in entrepreneurial phenomena (Gartner, 1985a) was quickly published, but, the quantitative exploration of this framework (Gartner et al., 1989), met with significant resistance, and was published four years later (after many rejections). I took from this experience a sense that it was 'OK' to present ideas about the nature of variation, but, an empirical attempt to demonstrate the nature of this variation was less so. The publication of Gartner et al. (1989) was somewhat of a 'mercy' publication in the *Journal of Business Venturing*. I believe that Ian McMillan stepped in and allowed the manuscript to be published even though the reviews were not sufficiently positive. Many of the negative

10   *International Small Business Journal 28(1)*

reviews of the manuscript stemmed from a perspective that suggested that the manuscript should have used approaches to find common factors among all of the cases, rather than attempt to group them into types. So, pointing out that there are many different types of entrepreneurs seemed to be less interesting to reviewers than methods that might lead to finding an 'ideal way' that entrepreneurs, in general, might use. It seemed to me, at the time, that research that focused on 'differences' (i.e. variation and uniqueness) tended to be of less interest as a dominant logic in academic entrepreneurship scholarship.

I am sure that some readers are thinking that this discussion is merely a play on Thorngate's (1976) idea that a theory of social behavior cannot be simultaneously general, accurate, and simple. Maybe I nuance this trade-off. For me, the issue is more about the nature of variation in a social phenomenon versus its 'average.' If there is no average in entrepreneurship then, why would one use methods that explore averages? This, to me, is the conundrum of my research efforts. My methods in these quantitative studies are at odds with my ideas. What the 'Gartner, et. al. (1989)' experience taught me was that the way to play the game of academic scholarship when quantitative methods were applied required projects that would utilize some form of regression for the most part or, some other statistical tool that would compare the means and standard deviations of one group with another. When I review such efforts as Carter et al. (1996), Duchesneau and Gartner (1990), Gatewood et al. (1995), and Gartner et al. (1999), what becomes apparent, to me, is that these articles carefully skirt around issues that I had originally considered in my early research. These quantitatively-based articles describe actions or characteristics of individuals that in general increase the chances of some individuals to create or sustain their entrepreneurial activities. These articles suggest that there is an ideal or general way for entrepreneurs to start businesses or, that certain activities in certain situations might lead to the ongoing success of a business. But, there is very little discussion on the variety of start-up phenomena that was actually found in the samples used. Most quantitative methods do not allow for that. The variation in these studies was masked by focusing on means (rather than on what might be going on when looking at the standard deviations). None of these studies could adequately capture the 'interactive mechanisms' of the startup process itself, even though this was exactly what these articles, in various ways, sought to capture. Many of these quantitative articles sought to link particular individual behaviors with success in the business formation process, but these explorations are very crude markers of the start-up process over time. When I talk to entrepreneurs, they invariably describe a series of events where their initial intentions are challenged and modified through a series of circumstances, some of which seem to be governed more by luck, than by purpose. It is difficult to model these interactions over time, if at all, since the independent variables often become the dependent variables, and vice versa. These quantitative studies are, in most respects, Thorndike's trade-off of looking for solutions that were general and simple while my concerns in the 'theory' articles tended to be more about accuracy and simplicity.

If my intention was to find answers to issues about how individuals navigated through the complexity of a phenomenon that accounted for aspects of: themselves (the individual), how they went about the process, the kind of business they decided to engage in, and, the context (environment) in which these actions take place, then my quantitative empirical studies were not likely to find answers in the way that my theories and ideas posited. I say this not to denigrate the insights these studies provide about broad activities that, on average, the groups in these samples as a whole seemed to utilize that led to 'success'. The frustration is more that these quantitative studies, inherently, would always generate insights that lacked a nuanced understanding of entrepreneurship. They could never be accurate. But, more important, these studies could never portray the interdependent interactive aspects of individuals over time, engaging with, and responding to, their circumstances. 'On average' mashes together all of the differences among a group of individuals that sweeps away the specific characteristics and activities of specific individuals that were critical in their specific situations. This, I suppose, is the primary dilemma with Gartner et al. (1989). The creation of 'gestalts' of entrepreneurships appeared to be a poor compromise among accuracy, generalizability and simplicity. One cannot have all three simultaneously as a satisfactory answer.

I continued to pursue explorations of the nature of entrepreneurs that focus on business creation using similar methods, but more recently, with a more comprehensive, in-depth and generalizable sample of entrepreneurs: the Panel Study of Entrepreneurial Dynamics (PSED; Gartner et al., 2004). The PSED has been nearly a 15-year effort (accounting for the initial efforts to raise money, involve scholars in the process, develop questionnaires, and undertake studies with the responses generated from the longitudinal survey). Yet, by using quantitative methodologies in the paradigmatic mode (e.g. Liao and Gartner, 2006, 2008; Lichtenstein et al., 2007; Reynolds et al., 2004), these efforts provide similar results to what was found in earlier studies. Generalizable principles – 'on average' – are offered in these studies, but the nuances of particular entrepreneurial situations, the nuances that actually characterize how individuals go about thinking through, over time, the complications of utilizing their capabilities and resources as they are both informed by, and seek to change their circumstances, is 'averaged' away.

No secure foothold

My experience, as reflected in the aforementioned quantitative studies in the paradigmatic mode, did not bring me closer towards describing and understanding the entrepreneurial phenomenon I encountered. So, concurrently, I attempted to grapple with the nature of entrepreneurship using another approach. I used fictional stories, e.g. 'The Music Man' (Gartner, 1985b), 'Pilgrim's Progress' (Gartner, 1986) and the 'Ikuru' (Gartner, 1990a) to explore aspects of how intention and action interplay with circumstance to comprise the entrepreneurial experience. While these articles begin to suggest the temporal complexities and interactions among intentions, actions and circumstances, the problem with them is that they do not have a language for explaining how the entrepreneurial experience unfolds. To explore specific situations that involve human agency over time, another mode of understanding is required – 'narrative knowing', as (Polkinghorne, 1988) observes:

> Narrative is a form of 'meaning making.' It is a complex form which expresses itself by drawing together descriptions of states of affairs contained in individual sentences into a particular type of discourse. This drawing together creates a higher order of meaning that discloses relationships among states of affairs. Narrative recognizes the meaningfulness of individual experiences by noting how they function as parts of a whole. Its particular subject matter is human actions and events that affect human beings, which it configures into wholes according to the roles these actions and events play in bringing about a conclusion. Because narrative is particularly sensitive to the temporal dimension of human existence, it pays special attention to the sequence in which actions and events occur. (Polkinghorne, 1988: 36)

My encounter with narrative as a set of theories and methods for understanding entrepreneurship did not begin until 2004. So, an article, such as Gartner (1993), which uses the short story *Peace* (Apple, 1989), is devoid of a foundation in narrative scholarship. Now I drown in the vastness of narrative scholarship (e.g. Atkinson, 1998; Bamberg, 2007; Bruner, 1986; Clandinin, 2007; Cobley, 2001;

Elliott, 2005; Herman, 2009; Herman & Vervaeck, 2005; Martin, 1986; McAdams et al., 2001; Mishler, 1999; Polkinghorne, 1988), its application to organization scholarship (e.g. Boje, 1991, 2001; Czarniawska, 1997, 1999; Gabriel, 2000; Green et al., 2009; Pentland, 1999; Phillips, 1995) and its use in the field of entrepreneurship (e.g. Chen et al., 2009; Downing, 2005; Fletcher, 2006; Hjorth & Steyaert, 2004; Martens et al., 2007; Pitt, 1998; Rae, 2004). These citations are by no means comprehensive but a reflection of my limited familiarity with the narrative literature. I intend these citations to serve as a signal that whatever I have been reading about narrative is unlikely to be what others have read. And, frankly, the narrative field is currently so big and diverse that it defies easy ways to make sense of itself (Smith, 2007). So, I come to the field of narrative studies and to the path of narrative studies in entrepreneurship from a different set of readings than others. Indeed, I am sure that my perspective on narrative does not offer a comprehensive and detailed reflection of narrative inquiry in entrepreneurship studies. Be that as it may, beyond my initial musings that offered 'just so stories' for making inquiries into entrepreneurial phenomenon (Gartner, 1985b, 1986, 1990b, 1993), I see that, now, narrative scholarship is a significant and primary mode for exploring entrepreneurship. And I believe narrative scholarship can best address issues in entrepreneurship that are concerned with entrepreneurial intentions and actions and their interrelationships with circumstance (as defined in the earlier Polkinghorne quotation). Yet, how did I come to find 'narrative' as a way to understand and describe the phenomenon of entrepreneurship?

Gartner (2007) describes an event that occurred in 2004 where scholars with different narrative perspectives met to explore a specific entrepreneurial story (Allen, 2007); the gist of this event being that I invited a number of colleagues to write about an entrepreneur's account of starting a toy store. I expected that there would be convergence in their analyses. Instead, the story prompted a divergence of perspectives and insights (see *Journal of Business Venturing* 22[5]). The insight offered in Gartner (2007) is not that narrative scholarship is important as a mode for exploring and understanding entrepreneurship – narrative scholarship is important – this should be taken for granted. The primary insight is that various narrative methods, when applied to a specific entrepreneurial narrative, yield a cornucopia of insights into entrepreneurial phenomena. I believe this event is connected to the 'critical mess' because this particular approach (focusing on a specific text using various narrative methods) provides larger opportunities for various theories about the nature of a specific entrepreneurial phenomenon to have their say. Just as there is variation in entrepreneurial phenomena, there is variation in the ways we can analyze a specific entrepreneurial situation. The 'text,' matters, in so far as a particular text, a particular narrative, grounds all of the narrative explorations in the same set of words. These words then, undergo various interpretations, and through these interpretations and analyses we come to more thoroughly understand entrepreneurship (Campbell, 1975; March et al., 1991; Weick, 1979: 37–9). I guess this could be summed up as a story of how I expected one thing and got another. But, the experience has taken on a 'risking enchantment' sensibility in my life. I had an experience that 'enchanted' me, but I am not sure, to this day, how or why, and I am still attempting to understand the ramifications of what that experience means. I am all the way in the middle.

As I read the literature on narrative, I believe one of the key aspects of this approach is a focus on texts, rather than on specific theories or methodologies. By way of analogy, if one is a Shakespearean scholar, the focus is primarily on the texts of Shakespeare, not on what particular methods or approaches or theories one might have about these texts. Theories and methods only illuminate aspects of the text. But, the text, itself, is always at the basis of any analysis. So, Shakespearean scholars are identified by their focus on Shakespearean texts; they speak to each other as a community of scholars focused on these texts. What these scholars have in common then, are the Shakespearean texts themselves. I believe that the variation of insights about the same text is where major gains in our understanding of entrepreneurship are likely to occur. I would like narrative scholarship in entrepreneurship to coalesce around specific 'texts' rather than around particular narrative theories or methodologies. For example, Murfin (1989) offers a variety of critical approaches to Joseph Conrad's *Heart of Darkness*, which, I believe, taken as a whole, provides a richer understanding of the story. This is where I am, but I am not sure whether I have a secure foothold in which to move forward (if there is such a thing as forward when one is in the middle).

A new path to the waterfall

For me, in my way to get out of the middle way, I intend to engage in narrative projects that offer the entire text for readers to study when I engage in using particular narrative methods. Now, particular articles might not be able to include the entire text analyzed, but somewhere (e.g. either posted as a document on the web, published as a book, or made available as a manuscript), I want readers to have an opportunity to read what I am writing about. By way of analogy, if a scholar were to offer an analysis of a new unknown manuscript of a Jane Austen novel and the analyst were to offer this critique using brief quotations from the unknown manuscript and then not make available the entire text for other readers to read, what would we make of such an analysis? I would be wondering, 'Why these quotes? Why not other quotes from the manuscript? What is missing that I am not able to read?' I think one of the major advantages of much of the genre of literary criticism is that critics look at texts that other readers can read for themselves. Readers are not left guessing about what the critic is not looking at, or could have looked at, and therefore readers can make their own judgments about how (and why) the critic analyzed the text. This would seem to fit into a phenomenological approach, a 'critical mess' approach that allows readers to engage in the researcher's experience of entrepreneurship in that particular situation.

Implications of the 'new path' for quantitative scholarship

It should be noted that this preference for providing readers with the entire text used as the basis of narrative analyses has significant implications for quantitative studies as well. I believe that one of the great weaknesses of much of my earlier quantitative scholarship is the failure to provide opportunities for readers to see the data that was used in these studies. By data, I mean, all of the data that was used to construct a dataset that was subsequently analyzed and reported in the journal article. This would include the questionnaires used, the research protocols used, and all of the raw data collected from these questionnaires. The failure to provide readers with opportunities to see all of the data is, I believe, asking the scientific community to trust me in ways that are incredibly naïve. Again, using the Jane Austen metaphor, would you, as a reader of a criticism of a new unknown Jane Austen novel, be willing to believe an analysis of this new unknown novel without the opportunity of reading it? So, should readers of scientific journal articles based on quantitative studies believe analyses where the data is not made available for the reader to 'read'? I believe the standards for sharing data used in the publication of quantitative studies would not meet the minimal standards of evidence required by literary scholars. Who would believe a scholar that has built a career offering analyses of novels that no other reader had the opportunity to read? Yet, much of the quantitative scholarship published in most entrepreneurship (as well as management, organization theory, organization behavior, etc.) journals provide readers with little evidence for making claims generated through various quantitative analyses.

Now, I am not suggesting that individuals using quantitative approaches (myself included) are engaged in fraudulent behaviors by not making their data available for others to read. But, I do find that when datasets are made available for other scholars to analyze, it is often the case that significant 'interpretive' issues arise about how the data was collected, used, and analyzed. This has certainly been the case with the PSED (see http://www.psed.info and http://projects.isr.umich.edu/psed) where the data is publicly available for scholars to read and interpret in various ways and indeed, various interpretations of this data have occurred. For example, various interpretations have been used for what dependent measures of 'success' represent. In studies determining whether a nascent entrepreneur's efforts lead to venture 'success' this has been measured as: (1) a judgment made by the nascent entrepreneur indicating that a new business is 'currently operating'; (2) an indication from the nascent entrepreneur that the effort has generated sales; (3) a judgment made by the nascent entrepreneur that the start-up effort is still in process (this measure is used because if an entrepreneur is still engaged in starting a business there is the possibility of a new business, while, if the entrepreneur is not engaged in the startup effort, there cannot be a new business); (4) a nascent entrepreneur's judgment that the new venture has generated cash flow to pay for salaries for the owners; and, (5) a nascent entrepreneur's judgment that the new venture has reached breakeven. All of these measures can be measures of 'success' at venture creation, but on face value they would seem to indicate different perspectives and interpretations on exactly what success is for the academic scholar engaged in these studies. And, each measure of success often provides different 'answers' as to what independent variables might be correlated with success. I could go on and on about the way in which specific questions are worded in the PSED dataset appears to affect responses and how the sequence of questions asked appears to affect responses, as well.

What occurs when 'data' is not made public is that significant interpretive issues regarding how other scholars might read the data collected in a particular quantitative study are ignored. Without opportunities for readers to see all of the information that goes into the research process (particularly the raw data used for analyses), the reader relies (I believe) too heavily on a researcher's singular analysis of a 'text'. I believe there are too many opportunities for *false readings*, *misinterpretations*, and *flawed analyses* that cannot be identified because no other scholar has an opportunity to 'read' this data. At some point I believe, quantitative researchers should offer access to the primary data used in their analyses (for example, within one year of publication of an article in a journal, the data used in that journal article should be made public for other scholars to access and analyze). Other researchers must have the opportunity to undertake their own analyses of this data and make their own judgments regarding a researcher's findings and insights.

An invitation

As I mentioned earlier, my preference, in engaging in narrative approaches to entrepreneurship, involves an exploration of specific texts. Researchers then bring to a specific text their ideas, theories and methods as the basis for what might be seen as comparative analyses of the text. What I found in Gartner (2007) was that no two researchers engage in the analysis of a text in the same way. What I believe occurs when a number of scholars look at the same text from their own individual perspective and method is a tremendously rich understanding of the phenomenon of entrepreneurship. A 'text-based' approach to scholarship in entrepreneurship, I believe, may be able to build a more thoughtful and cohesive community of entrepreneurship scholars linked to these common texts rather than to common narrative methods or theories.

Anyway, I think such an effort is worth a try

As a way to move this 'text-based' effort forward, I have begun the process of creating a new journal, *EN:TER – Entrepreneurial Narrative: Text, Ethnomethodology & Reflexivity*. Similar to the *Journal of Business Venturing* special issue on entrepreneurial narrative (22[5]), the focus of each issue is on a specific text that scholars analyze using whatever perspective and approach they feel is appropriate. The first issue (forthcoming in 2010) focuses on the book, *The Republic of Tea* (Zeigler et al., 1992). This book is a series of faxes sent among three entrepreneurs as they developed the idea for a business selling tea. I believe the book is worth exploring by many scholars since it provides: (1) a longitudinal portrayal of the process of organization emergence, (2) multiple authors involved in articulating what the business is and will become and (3) a reflexive commentary (by these authors) on their actions and motivations. I have found few other books with this level of detail, told in 'real time'. The first issue contains nine articles providing very different ways to read *The Republic of Tea*. I think that this collective effort, once published, will provide a strong exemplar of how other texts might be approached in the future.

I will also mention that one problem that *EN:TER* will address, as a journal, is the need for a forum to continue discussions and analyses, both of the text analyzed and also of the analyses published. This feature extends beyond 'Letters to the Editor' that a few journals nominally provide regarding articles previously published. I see each published issue of the journal where a text is initially explored as version 1.0, with subsequent published editions (e.g. 1.1, 1.2, 1.3, etc.) of additional analyses and commentaries. I believe that a scholarly community requires more opportunities for dialogue and that as writers and readers, we need a place to engage in more direct writing and reading exchanges. The Internet provides us with unprecedented opportunities to engage each other in real time. I find the typical journal process for publishing articles and then generating responses to these articles (via publishing other articles) takes too long given these new communication processes. There needs to be a better forum for enhancing interactions. My ultimate goal, in developing this new journal, is to enable other scholars to champion entrepreneurial texts they believe should be studied as well as their methods and ideas about the nature of entrepreneurship via their analyses of these texts. If all goes according to 'plan' (my imaginary view of what the future might be like), then other scholars will serve as Editors of the journal and serve as monitors of the subsequent dialogue among other researchers willing to read and write about specific texts.

Finally, I see the process of having scholars analyze similar texts as furthering the sensibility of the 'critical mess' (Gartner, 2004a, 2006a,b). Alone, I cannot begin to fathom all of the nuances and insights that a particular entrepreneurial phenomenon might offer. But as a group, with many different approaches and perspectives applied to a specific entrepreneurial phenomenon, we better see the richness and complexity in specific entrepreneurial situations that do justice to what these phenomena actually are (I realize, that, broadly, this is what the community of entrepreneurship scholars already is [Gartner et al., 2006], but I would prefer to have a community of scholars talking more specifically about the same 'text' as a way to compare and contrast their different perspectives).

The phenomenon of entrepreneurship is complicated (Gartner, 1985a) and for this reason, I believe, the 'critical mess' approach is a necessary bromide to narrower disciplinary perspectives. As I suggested at the beginning of this article, those entrepreneurship scholars with an omnivorous willingness to collect facts and ideas, both good and bad – 'utter crap to fabulous stuff' – micro and macro, individual, firm and environment, esoteric knowledge and conventional wisdom, the pedantic and amateur, policy and personal, are more likely to develop the discernment so necessary for finding the key nuggets of insight about entrepreneurship as a phenomenon. The challenge then, for entrepreneurship scholars, is to be willing to build their own 'big pile' of knowledge, facts, theories, experiences, and insights about the phenomenon of entrepreneurship and to be at peace with the realization that much of what one collects is 'utter crap'. The process of developing insight is not efficient. And, there is no guarantee that there will be fabulous stuff buried within one's mess. But, such efforts are necessary (Gartner, 2006a: 82).

I do not imagine this multitude of voices reading shared texts as a chorus; such an articulation will be a cacophony. More dissonance in the entrepreneurship field is needed (Hjorth et al., 2008; Hjorth and Steyaert, 2009; Jones and Spicer, 2010). Yet, offering a variety of approaches and understandings of entrepreneurship will not lead to anarchy as a way to build community in entrepreneurship scholarship. I believe we, as scholars in the entrepreneurship field, can meet on the common ground of the 'text' I realize that disputes about what 'texts' should be common ground will arise in the normal process of things. This is to be expected.

Is this new path to the waterfall a dream (Carver, 1989: 19)? I think not. I feel a shift in the momentum of how we, as scholars looking at entrepreneurship, seek to understand it. But, I'm still in a dark wood.

Acknowledgements

The author would like to thank the Editors of *ISBJ*, and particularly Susan Marlow for providing an opportunity to idiosyncratically wander across the field of entrepreneurship, and to Alistair R. Anderson, Robert Blackburn, Denise Fletcher, Patricia Greene, Ellie Hamilton, Daniel Hjorth, Helle Neegaard and Susan Marlow for very helpful comments on an earlier draft of this article: my apologies for not doing justice to these perceptive insights.

References

Adler PS, Forbes LC, and Willmott H (2007) Chapter 3: Critical management studies. *The Academy of Management Annals* 1: 119–179.

Allen T (2007) The Toy Story. *Journal of Business Venturing* 22: 628–638.

Alvesson M, Hardy C, and Herley B (2008) Reflecting on reflexivity: Reflexive textual practices in organization and management theory. *Journal of Management Studies* 45: 480–501.

Apple M (1989) Peace. *Harper's Magazine* 278(February): 56–61.

Atkinson R (1998) *The Life Story Interview.* Thousand Oaks, CA: SAGE.

Bamberg M (2007) *Narrative: State of the Art.* Amsterdam: John Benjamins.

Boje DM (1991) The storytelling organization: A study of story performance in an office-supply firm. *Administrative Science Quarterly* 35: 106–126.

Boje DM (2001) *Narrative Methods for Organizational and Communication Research.* Thousand Oaks, CA: SAGE.

Brown AD (2006) A narrative approach to collective identities. *Journal of Management Studies.* 43: 731–753.

Bruner J (1986) *Actual Minds, Possible Worlds.* Cambridge, MA: Harvard University Press.

Campbell DT (1975) 'Degrees of freedom' and the case study. *Comparative Political Studies.* 8: 178–193.

Carter NM, Gartner WB, and Reynolds PD (1996) Exploring start-up event sequences. *Journal of Business Venturing* 11: 151–166.

Carver R (1989) Looking for work. *A New Path to the Waterfall.* New York: Atlantic Monthly Press, 19.

Chen X, Yao X, and Kotha S (2009) Entrepreneur passion and preparedness in business plan presentations: A persuasion analysis of venture capitalists' funding decisions. *Academy of Management Journal* 52: 199–214.

Clandinin DJ (2007) *Handbook of Narrative Inquiry: Mapping a Methodology*. Thousand Oaks, CA: SAGE.

Cobley P (2001) *Narrative*. London: Routledge.

Contardo I, Wensley R, (2004) The Harvard Business School story: Avoiding knowledge by being relevant. *Organization* 11: 211–231.

Czarniawska B (1997) *Narrating the Organization: Dramas of Institutional Identity*. Chicago, IL: University of Chicago Press.

Czarniawska B (1999) *Writing Management: Organization Theory as a Literary Genre*. Oxford: Oxford University Press.

Davis M (1971) 'That's interesting!' Towards a phenomenology of sociology and a sociology of phenomenology. *Philosophy of the Social Sciences* 1: 309–344.

Davis M (1986) 'That's classic!' The phenomenology and rhetoric of successful social theories. *Philosophy of the Social Sciences*. 16: 285–301.

Downing S (2005) The social construction of entrepreneurship: Narrative and dramatic processes in the coproduction of organizations and identities. *Entrepreneurship Theory and Practice* 29: 185–204.

Duchesneau DA, Gartner WB, (1990) A profile of new venture success and failure in an emerging industry. *Journal of Business Venturing* 5: 297–312.

Eliot TS (1943) *Four Quartets*. New York: Harcourt Brace & Company.

Elliott J (2005) *Using Narrative in Social Research: Qualitative and Quantitative Approaches*. London: SAGE.

Fletcher DE (2006) Entrepreneurial processes and the social construction of opportunity. *Entrepreneurship and Regional Development* 18: 421–440.

Gabriel Y (2000) *Storytelling in Organizations: Facts, Fictions and Fantasies*. Oxford: Oxford University Press.

Gartner WB (1982) *An Empirical Model of the Business Startup, and Eight Entrepreneurial Archetypes*. Seattle, WA: University of Washington.

Gartner WB (1985a) A framework for describing and classifying the phenomenon of new venture creation. *Academy of Management Review* 10(4): 696–706.

Gartner WB (1985b) Did River City really need a boy's band? *New Management* 3: 28–34.

Gartner WB (1986) The Oz in organization. *New Management* 4: 14–21.

Gartner WB (1988) Who is an entrepreneur? Is the wrong question. *American Journal of Small Business* 12: 11–32.

Gartner WB (1990a) To live: The obligation of individuality. A Review of the Film Ikiru, directed by Akira Kurosawa. *The Organizational Behavior Teaching Review* 14: 138–143.

Gartner WB (1990b) What are we talking about when we talk about entrepreneurship? *Journal of Business Venturing* 5: 15–28.

Gartner WB (1993) Words lead to deeds: Towards an organizational emergence vocabulary. *Journal of Business Venturing* 8: 231–240.

Gartner WB (2004a) Achieving 'Critical Mess' in entrepreneurship scholarship'. In: Katz JA and Shepherd D (eds) *Advances in Entrepreneurship, Firm Emergence, and Growth*. Greenwich, CT: JAI Press, 199–216.

Gartner WB (2004b) The edge defines the (w)hole: Saying what entrepreneurship is (not). In: Steyaert C and Hjorth D (eds) *Narrative and Discursive Approaches in Entrepreneurship*. London: Edward Elgar, 245–254.

Gartner WB (2006a) A 'Critical Mess' approach to entrepreneurship scholarship. In: Lundstrom A and Halvarsson S (eds) *Entrepreneurship Research: Past Perspectives and Future Prospects, Foundations and Trends in Entrepreneurship* 2: 73–82.

Gartner WB (2006b) Entrepreneurship, psychology and the 'Critical Mess'. In: Baum JR, Michael F and Baron RA (eds) *The Psychology of Entrepreneurship*. Mahwah, NJ: Lawrence Erlbaum Associates, 325–334.

Gartner WB (2007) Entrepreneurial narrative and a science of the imagination. *Journal of Business Venturing* 22: 613–627.

Gartner WB (2008) Variations in entrepreneurship. *Small Business Economics* 31: 351–361.

Gartner WB, Bird BJ, and Starr J (1992) Acting as if: Differentiating entrepreneurial from organizational behavior. *Entrepreneurship Theory and Practice* 16: 13–32.

Gartner WB, Birley S (2002) Introduction to the special issue on qualitative methods in entrepreneurship research. *Journal of Business Venturing* 17: 387–395.

Gartner WB, Davidsson P, and Zahra SA (2006) Are you talking to me? The nature of community in entrepreneurship scholarship. *Entrepreneurship Theory and Practice* 30: 321–331.

Gartner WB, Mitchell TR, and Vesper KH (1989) A taxonomy of new business ventures. *Journal of Business Venturing* 4: 169–186.

Gartner WB, Shaver KG, Carter NM, et al. (2004) *Handbook of Entrepreneurial Dynamics: The Process of Business Creation*. Thousand Oaks, CA: SAGE.

Gartner WB, Starr JA, and Bhat S (1999) Predicting new venture survival: An analysis of 'Anatomy of a Startup' cases from Inc. magazine. *Journal of Business Venturing* 14: 215–232.

Gatewood EJ, Shaver KG, and Gartner WB (1995) A longitudinal study of cognitive factors influencing start-up behaviors and success at venture creation. *Journal of Business Venturing* 10: 371–391.

Grant R, Perren W, (2002) Small business and entrepreneurial research: Meta-theories, paradigms and prejudices. *International Small Business Journal* 20: 185–211.

Green SE Jr, Li Y, and Nohria N (2009) Suspended in self-spun webs of significance: A rhetorical model of institutionalization and institutionally embedded agency. *Academy of Management Journal* 52: 11–36.

Herman D (2009) *Basic Elements of Narrative*. Chichester: Wiley-Blackwell.

Herman L, Vervaeck B (2005) *Handbook of Narrative Analysis*. Lincoln: University of Nebraska Press.

Hjorth D, Jones C, and Gartner WB (2008) Recreating/recontextualising entrepreneurship. *Scandinavian Journal of Management* 21: 81–84.

Hjorth D, Steyaert C (2004) *Narrative and Discursive Approaches in Entrepreneurship*. Cheltenham: Edward Elgar.

Hjorth D, Steyaert C (2009) Moving entrepreneurship: An incipiency. In: Hjorth D and Steyaert C (eds) *The Politics and Aesthetics of Entrepreneurship*. Cheltenham: Edward Elgar.

Jones C, Spicer A, (2009) *Unmasking the Entrepreneur*. Cheltenham: Edward Elgar.

Katz J, Gartner WB, (1988) Properties of emerging organizations. *Academy of Management Review* 13: 429–441.

Liao J, Gartner WB, (2006) The effects of pre-venture plan timing and perceived environmental uncertainty on the persistence of emerging firms. *Small Business Economics* 27: 23–40.

Liao J, Gartner WB, (2008) The influence of pre-venture planning on new venture creation. *Journal of Small Business Strategy* 18: 1–21.

Lichtenstein BB, Carter NM, Dooley KJ, et al. (2007) Complexity dynamics of nascent entrepreneurship. *Journal of Business Venturing* 22: 236–261.

March JG, Sproull LS, and Tamuz M (1991) Learning from samples of one or fewer. *Organization Science* 2: 1–13.

Martin W (1986) *Recent Theories of Narrative*. Ithaca, NY: Cornell University Press.

Martens ML, Jennings JE, and Jennings PD (2007) Do the stories they tell get them the money they need?: The role of entrepreneurial narratives in resource acquisition. *Academy of Management Journal* 50: 1107–1132.

McAdams DP, Josselson R, and Lieblich A (2001) *Turns in the Road: Narrative Studies of Lives in Transition*. Washington, DC: American Psychological Association.

McClelland DC (1961) *The Achieving Society*. New York: The Free Press.

Michler EG (1999) *Storylines: Craftartists' Narratives of Identity*. Cambridge, MA: Harvard University Press.

Miller D (2007) Paradigm prison, or in praise of atheoretic research. *Strategic Organization* 5: 177–184.

Murfin R (1989) *Joseph Conrad, Heart of Darkness: A Case Study in Contemporary Criticism*. New York: St. Martin's Press.

Pentland BT (1999) Building process theory with narrative. From description to explanation. *Academy of Management Review* 24: 711–724.

Phillips N (1995) Telling organizational tales: On the role of narrative fiction in the study of organizations. *Organization Studies* 16: 625–649.

Pitt M (1998) A tale of two gladiators: 'Reading' entrepreneurs as texts. *Organization Studies* 19: 387–414.

Polkinghorne DE (1988) *Narrative Knowing and the Human Sciences*. Albany: State University of New York Press.

Rae D (2004) Practical theories from entrepreneurs' stories: Discursive approaches to entrepreneurial learning. *Journal of Small Business and Enterprise Development* 11: 195–202.

Reynolds PD, Carter NM, Gartner WB, and Greene PG (2004) The prevalence of nascent entrepreneurs in the United States: Evidence from the Panel Study of Entrepreneurial Dynamics. *Small Business Economics* 23: 263–284.

Rhodes C, Brown AD, (2005) Narrative, organizations and research. *International Journal of Management Reviews* 7(3): 167–188.

Singer M (2001) The book eater. *The New Yorker* (5 February): 62–71.

Smith B (2007) The state of the art in narrative inquiry: Some reflections. *Narrative Inquiry* 17: 391–398.

Thorngate W (1976) 'In general' vs. 'it depends:' some comments on the Gergen-Schlenker debate. *Personality and Social Psychology Bulletin* 2: 404–410.

Vesper KH (1980) *New Venture Strategies*. Englewood Cliffs, NJ: Prentice Hall.

Weick KE (1979) *The Social Psychology of Organizing: 2nd Edition*. New York: Random House.

Ziegler M, Rosenzweig B, and Ziegler P (1992) *The Republic of Tea*. New York: Currency Doubleday.

Zucker LG (1987) Institutional theories of organization. *American Review of Sociology* 13: 443–464.

Zucker LG (1989) Combining institutional theory and population ecology: No legitimacy. No history. *American Sociological Review* 54: 542–545.

Yin RK (2008) *Case Study Research: Design and Methods* London: SAGE.

BEGIN You start where you are,
ANYWHERE not where you want to be
There are two mistakes one can make along the
road to truth: Not going all the way and not starting

Come on! Play!
Invent the world! **RISK**
Invent reality! ENCHANTMENT

ACT "as if" and it will become
always so as to increase the number of choices

The voyage of discovery lies not in finding
new landscapes, but in having new eyes **PAY**
Traditions are solutions to yesterday's problems **Attention**

Learn To Fail
Or You Will **FAIL** MAKE NEW
Mistakes Faster
Fail To Learn CAPTURE
ACCIDENTS

Accept the Outcome + MOVE ON

BEGIN AGAIN

Every beginning comes from some other beginning's end

ENTREFESTO williambgartner.com © 2015
Designed in conjunction with UniqueDesignMaker (uniquedesignmaker@gmail.com)

Figure 1   ENTREFESTO

Conclusion: An 'ENTREFESTO'

William B. Gartner

So
Three years ago
I came up with the idea of ENTREFESTO.

Aphorisms and clichés you see
That were similar to what I saw in the manifesto 'Holstee'.[1]
Scholarship in elaborate form
Had become so much my norm.
I wanted some other way
To make sense of what I have to say.
While a complex idea in a few words
Might seem absurd,
A simple phrase
Might cut through the haze.
One might better mind it
And, see the thoughts behind it
At least, that is the hope
That clichés can be insightful in scope.[2]

Rather than elaborate explanation
Of each phrase in this concatenation
A few footnotes offered
For background on what is proffered.
And even these explanations
Cannot be a thorough elaboration.[3]

The primary struggle I see
Is between 'the given' and possibility
'Begin Anywhere' is about Machiavelli.[4]
Where we are is where we begin
And, what is 'now' began in the past, and that was a win.
So, 'traditions are solutions to yesterday's problems'
Says that if nothing has changed, then there really isn't a new stratagem,
Because people are happy with what already works.
Something new is just something that irks.

Or maybe 'Begin Anywhere' is really about Murray.[5]
That a beginning is the future's de jure.

And, you start where you are, not where you want to be.
So from my favorite uhde: the buddha
The big part is the start.[6]
And the entrepreneurial way
Begins in play.[7]

And, a longer way to say,
Where my thoughts hold sway,
You can bet
That it will be in Eliot's *Four Quartets*.
So, we start with our heart.
The risk is enchantment,[8] not money or time.
It is the calculus of love, not reason or rhyme.
We tend to frame entrepreneurship in terms of utility
Or ability,
But the future is the path of ambiguity.
And to walk through this path requires humility.

And to see.[9]
Again, it is not in the 'be'.[10]
So do me a favor and always link my work to behavior.
'Pay attention' is more about the cost
I have played this idea out before in what Willie Loman lost.[11]
I take it as a fact
That the future becomes when we act.[12]
The philosophy here
Stems from Vaihinger[13]
Act to increase the number of choices
Is not about real options reasoning voices
I point to sensibilities in constructivist realities[14]

The word FAIL is the biggest word so that it cannot be missed.
The focus on success
Has just been a big mess.
It is not a quirk that most entrepreneurships don't work.
Using baseball as an analogy,
We focus on hits but strikeouts are the reality.[15]
The words about failure are just platitudes about certain attitudes[16]
Is it luck or pluck?
I think it is indicative that entrepreneurship is non-predictive.
Things don't work: It is just a fact.
But, we still need to act.
I would focus more on the 'try' rather than the 'why'.

And the critical precept becomes that of 'accept'.

Isn't the point of creative destruction:
Today's winners will eventually be losers in the economic function?
So, we live (we hope) to play another day.
Becoming winners or losers, it doesn't matter
Accept the outcome and move on, there is no need to flatter
Ourselves with delusions that failure is just another way to learn
Sometimes failures teach us, most of the time, there is not much to discern.
Can one see through ambiguity?

And, we come back to Eliot's view
That every moment is new
And a 'shocking valuation of all we have been'.[17]
Experience is something we are always 'in'.
It carries us only so far along the path
Then, well, you do the math:
What is the real cost of being lost?[18]

'Begin Again' is not a Sisyphian situation
One does not go back to the same location[19]
Every day we are in the 'middle way'.
The will to believe
Struggles, always, with that which deceives.
Wisdom and humility go hand in hand
Because the future never goes as we have planned.

So, try as we might
To 'get it right'.
Getting the answers is not the task.
The insights come from the questions that we ask.

Notes

1. The 'Holstee Manifesto': https://www.holstee.com/pages/manifesto (last accessed 25 November 2015). You have probably seen it in some form, somewhere. The genesis for a poster of clichés and aphorisms came during a walk in Aarhus, Denmark on April 16, 2012. Once I saw the Holstee Manifesto poster, I found it ubiquitous in my travels. My first reaction was both a sense of hokum and a sense of appreciation for the optimism inherent in this effort to convey a set of beliefs. So, I found that I both hated the poster and loved it. The poster espouses the sensibility found in Karl Weick's riff (1979) on Thorngate's (1976: 406) idea that 'It is impossible for a theory of social behavior to be simultaneously general, simple or parsimonious, and accurate'. The Holstee Manifesto: general and simple. So, the problem becomes that such general and simple insights tend to fall apart in the specifics of a particular situation. These clichés: sort of true (broadly, in some vague sense of things), and sort of not (in that it will not cover every particular situation that one probably finds oneself in): As clichés are. Be that as it may, seeing the 'Holstee Manifesto' piqued my mind to consider what a poster of my beliefs about the phenomenon of entrepreneurship might entail. It was from that moment that I began to collect and create aphorisms and clichés that seemed to capture some sense of what I thought entrepreneurship is and how it might be brought forth (as manifestos tend to be exhortations to challenge people to act and think in certain ways, e.g. Danchev, 2011).
2. When I was invited by Richard Tunstall to speak at the 'Advancing European Traditions of Entrepreneurship Studies Conference' at Leeds in March 2013, I began efforts to design a poster, present it, and provide a logic for why such an effort might have some scholarly legitimacy (Gartner, 2013). My attempt at finding some basis for the value of a manifesto was limited to suggesting that aphorisms were an aspect of Benjamin Franklin's

'Poor Richards Almanac' (Franklin and Lemay, 1997), and, therefore, had a long history of practical usefulness, and that from an artistic perspective, the poster had a similar sensibility to Jenny Holzer's (1995) 'Truisms'. And, it was at this point, after making my presentation, that Simon Down introduced me to scholarship on the value of aphorisms and clichés (Davis, 1999; Down and Warren, 2008).

3. This problem of conveying one's insights to others is problematic. I keep thinking of a poem by Han-shan (which means 'Cold Mountain') translated by Gary Snyder (1958/2013), that ends with:

> How did I make it?
> My heart's not the same as yours.
> If your heart was like mine
> You'd get it and be right here.

4. If you go to my website (williambgartner.com) you will see an evolution of the ENTREFESTO poster. The core issue in ENTREFESTO stems from the dialectic between the idea of Machiavelli (below) and Murray (below) about whether doing something new has any value, and, if so, whether it will be perceived as being beneficial, or not. There is a 'truth' in both these perspectives. Discerning when, and under what conditions each perspective plays a role is, I think, a matter of both wisdom and luck.

> It must be considered that there is nothing more difficult to carry out, nor more doubtful of success, nor more dangerous to handle, than to initiate a new order of things. For the reformer has enemies in all those who profit by the old order, and only lukewarm defenders in all those who would profit by the new order, this luke-warmness arising partly from fear of their adversaries, who have the laws in their favor; and partly from the incredulity of mankind, who do not truly believe in anything new until they have had the actual experience of it. (Machiavelli, 1532/2012: 15)

5. 'But when I said that nothing had been done I erred in one important matter. We had definitely committed ourselves and were halfway out of our ruts. We had put down our passage money – booked a sailing to Bombay. This may sound too simple, but is great in consequence. Until one is committed, there is hesitancy, the chance to draw back, always ineffectiveness. Concerning all acts of initiative (and creation), there is one elementary truth the ignorance of which kills countless ideas and splendid plans: that the moment one definitely commits oneself, the providence moves too. A whole stream of events issues from the decision, raising in one's favor all manner of unforeseen incidents, meetings and material assistance, which no man could have dreamt would have come his way. I learned a deep respect for one of Goethe's couplets: Whatever you can do or dream you can, begin it. Boldness has genius, power and magic in it!' (Murray, 1951).

6. There are two mistakes one can make along the road to truth: Not going all the way and not starting.

7. 'Come on! Play! Invent the world! Invent reality!' comes from Nabokov (1990), but it refers to Daniel Hjorth's article (2005).

8. I am referring to the section of the *Four Quartets* that begins: 'Had they deceived us' and ends with '... humility is endless' (Eliot, 1943: 26–27).

9. 'The voyage of discovery lies not in finding new landscapes but in having new eyes' is a paraphrase of Proust (1934): 'The only true voyage of discovery, the only fountain of Eternal Youth, would be not to visit strange lands but to possess other eyes, to behold the universe through the eyes of another, of a hundred others, to behold the hundred universes that each of them beholds.'

10. Chapter 4, this volume.

11. Gartner (2008).

12. Act 'as if' and it will become.

13. Vaihinger (1924/2014).

14. Act always so as to increase the number of choices (Foerster, 1973/2003: 227).

15. I love this quote from Reggie Jackson: 'When you play this game ten years, go to bat 7,000 times and get 2,000 hits, you know what that means? That you've gone 0 for 5,000.'

16. 'Learn to fail or you will fail to learn', 'Make new mistakes faster', 'Capture accidents'.

17. Again, I am referring to the section of the *Four Quartets* that begins: 'Had they deceived us' and ends with '... humility is endless' (Eliot, 1943: 26–27).

18. I am referring to the poem 'Lost' (Wagoner, 1978).

19. 'Every new beginning comes from some other beginning's end' is from Seneca. But, I am aiming to capture the sensibility that can be found in the poem 'Love at First Sight' (Szymborska, 2000).

References

Danchev, A. (2011), *100 Artist's Manifestos: From the Futurists to the Stuckists*, London: Penguin Books.
Davis, M.S. (1999), 'Aphorisms and clichés: The generation and dissipation of conceptual charisma', *Annual Review*

of Sociology, **25**, 245–69.

Down, S. and L. Warren (2008), 'Constructing narratives of enterprise: clichés and entrepreneurial self-identity', *International Journal of Entrepreneurial Behavior & Research*, **14** (1), 4–23.

Eliot, T.S. (1943), *Four Quartets*, New York: Harcourt Brace & Company.

Franklin, B. and J.A.L. Lemay (1997), *Autobiography, Poor Richard, and Later Writings: Letters from London, 1757–1775, Paris, 1776–1785, Philadelphia, 1785–1790, Poor Richard's Almanack, 1733–1758, the Autobiography*, New York: Library of America.

Foerster, H. von (1973), 'On constructing a reality', in F.E. Preiser (ed.), *Environmental Design Research*, Vol. 2, Stroudsburg, PA: Dowden, Hutchinson & Ross, pp. 35–46. Reprinted in H. von Foerster (2003), *Understanding Understanding*, New York: Springer, pp. 211–28. (Page numbers in the text refer to the reprint.)

Gartner, W.B. (2008), 'Variations in entrepreneurship', *Small Business Economics*, **31**, 351–61.

Gartner, W.B. (2013), 'Entre-Festo', Advancing European Traditions of Entrepreneurship Studies Conference, Leeds, UK, 17–18 March 2013.

Hjorth, D. (2005), 'Organizational entrepreneurship with de Certeau on creating heterotopias (or spaces for play)', *Journal of Management Inquiry*, **14** (4), 386–98.

Holzer, J. (1995), *Jenny Holzer: Truisms and Essays*, New York: Barbara Gladstone Gallery.

Machiavelli, N. (1532/2012), *The Prince*, trans. L. Ricci and J.S. Byerley, New York: Digireads.

Murray, W.H. (1951), *The Scottish Himalayan Expedition*, London: J.M. Dent & Sons.

Nabokov, V. (1990), *Look at the Harlequins!*, New York: Vintage.

Proust, M. (1934), *Remembrance of Things Past*, trans. C.K. Scott-Moncrieff, New York: Random House.

Snyder, G. (1958/2013), *Cold Mountain Poems: Twenty-Four Poems by Han-shan*, trans. G. Snyder, Poem 6, Berkeley, CA: Counterpoint.

Szymborska, W. (2000), *Poems: New and Collected*, trans. S. Barańczak and C. Cavanagh, New York: Harcourt Professional.

Thorngate, W. (1976), '"In general" vs. "it depends": Some comments on the Gergen-Schlenker debate', *Personality and Social Psychology Bulletin*, **2** (4), 404–10.

Vaihinger, H. (1924/2014), *The Philosophy of 'As If'*, trans. C.K. Ogden, London: Routledge.

Wagoner, D. (1978), *Collected Poems: 1956–1976*, Bloomington, IN: University of Indiana Press.

Weick, K.E. (1979), *The Social Psychology of Organizing: 2nd Edition*, New York: Random House.